Richard Tedor

Prussia at War

1740–1813

ISBN 978-0-09883682-5-5

Kindle Edition: 978-0-9883682-6-2.

Front Cover: Friedrich the Great tries to stop his grenadiers
from retreating before the Austrians during the battle of
Torgau on November 03, 1760.

Back Cover: Johanna Stegen hands cartridges to *Jäger* of the
1st Pomeranian Infantry Regiment battling the French in
Lüneville on April 02, 1813, during the war of liberation.

Chapter Index

Chapter Footnotes and Name Index
are not included in the print edition.

They may be accessed on line at **prussiaatwar.com**

Prussia at War
1740 to 1813

Introduction

The philosopher Oswald Spengler wrote that the history of mankind is a chronicle of war. Armed conflicts are indeed milestones in the life of civilizations, contributing to their rise and precipitating their fall. No matter what excuse belligerents make for embarking on such a destructive enterprise, the ulterior purpose is usually to rob or destroy a neighboring lineage, clan or country to enrich themselves. In the Ancient World, the Roman statesman Marcus Tullius Cicero sanctioned Julius Caesar's campaigns in Gaul and Britannia as defensive wars. Throughout centuries of conquest, the justification was always that subjugated peoples are supposedly better off under Roman law. In modern times, the British waged wars to build an overseas empire and called the military domination of "hostile nations" the peace of Britain (Pax Britannica). William Sherman, a general in the American Civil War, conducted a scorched-earth policy in the South and later commanded the U.S. Army against the Plains Indians during the period of western expansion. He stated, "We must act with vindictive earnestness against the Sioux even to their extermination, men, women and children." He referred to his army as "God's instrument of justice."

Prussia's warrior-king of the 18th Century, Friedrich II (the Great), advocated preemptive wars against large European states that become too powerful. He thought it better to strike first than wait until "circumstances become so desperate that a declaration of war means nothing more than a brief postponement of complete enslavement." This may be an understandable reason for attacking, at least dispensing with the pious rhetoric governments employ to legitimize aggression, but the land of Friedrich's origin nonetheless acquired a reputation as one of the continent's most militant states. He once remarked that "the world does not rest as securely on the shoulders of Atlas as does Prussia on her army." When his country evolved from maintaining a professional standing army at the king's disposal to arming the population for total war, the renowned General August Neidhardt von Gneisenau proclaimed that Prussia must "nationalize the army and militarize the people." Upon seeing the country's militia in battle, an Austrian general asked if Prussian children become soldiers while still in the cradle.

Without her soldiers, Prussia would not have asserted herself as an independent nation and certainly not as one of consequence. A vassal of Poland in the 17th Century, she was surrounded by Russia, Austria, France, Denmark and Sweden. These countries frowned on her expansion and collectively dwarfed her in size. Wars sporadically waged over 175 years firmly established the country's Great Power status and created prerequisites for Prussia to eventually consolidate Germany under one flag. Usually outnumbered, Prussian soldiers proved unyielding in privation, stalwart in combat and resilient in defeat. Napoleon Bonaparte called them "the finest troops in the world." Prussia was, as Adolf Hitler once said, a "ridiculously small state" to take on such odds and astonish the world with her victories. During the period from the battle of Leuthen in 1757 to Leipzig in 1813, the influence of the Enlightenment, fruitless coalition wars against France and a shattering defeat inflicted by Napoleon led to the collapse of resistance and virtually destroyed the army upon which Prussia, as Friedrich the Great had boasted, rests so securely.

The magnitude of the disaster of 1806-07 required more than just restaffing the officer corps and replenishing regimental rosters to fight another round. An entirely novel approach to national defense became necessary. It was one that could not be implemented without a political, social and military metamorphosis. The transition would retain what was considered worth preserving from the old system and integrate revolutionary concepts unheard of for an absolute monarchy. This was achieved after a prolonged and bitter internal struggle in a nation already divided by social and economic castes that had little contact with one another. The war on the home front had to be settled before restoring Prussia's fortunes on the battlefield. Gneisenau wrote his daughter Ottilie that generations to come would be astonished to learn of the war behind the scenes, the unpublicized conflict of ideas that ultimately determined the resurrection of the state and had a significant impact on the development of warfare. When the battle of Leuthen was fought, the king waged war without the participation of the population. At Leipzig over 50 years later, the people took up arms without the wholehearted support of their king.

Prussia at War provides a detailed study of the significant battles and sieges in this pivotal period of the country's growth. It analyzes examples of both sound judgment and mistakes of generals involved, the condition and morale of opposing armies, influences of terrain, weather, logistics, reconnaissance and so forth; but these in themselves do not present a complete picture of why battles were won or lost. Events must be interpreted in the larger context of the struggle between rival ideological viewpoints captivating Prussia's martial hierarchy, the controversy over tactical deployment in combat, diverse attitudes toward the monarchy and the social discrepancy between officers and rankers. Never before had public mass participation in the war effort been considered necessary or even contemplated by more than a small minority of officers and suddenly it became paramount. This required restructuring the army's methods of induction, its disciplinary system, criteria for promotion, recruit training and battlefield strategy.

For the first time, civilian involvement became *the* issue for raising a new Prussian army to successfully defend the country. Making military service palatable to an educated, independent and self-assured stratum of the population, the middle-class burghers, demanded changing popular perception of armed service to regard it as an honorable occupation. This could only be done by transforming the army and reeducating an officer corps accustomed for generations to inherent class privileges and a fixed code of conduct. As in the rest of Europe, the ideals of the Enlightenment found fertile ground among civil servant, soldier and civilian alike. These ideas evoked sympathy for the French Revolution, Freemasonry and liberalism. They assailed the bastion of Prussian absolutism and undermined the tradition of unconditional obedience fostered in the military. As will be seen, Prussian reformers who affected the changes succeeded only after years of persistent, patient and wearying struggle against narrow-mindedness, vanity, jealousy and pigheadedness among old school commanders and the sovereign himself. This was the "secret history of this war" identified by Gneisenau. Nationalist patriots fought two parallel wars during the Napoleonic era; one against France's *Grande Armée* and the other against the legacy of Friedrich the Great.

Chapter 1

The House of Hohenzollern

Restricted Warfare

Wars can be evolutionary leaps in our history, tearing down what is moribund to clear a path for novel trends that revitalize civilizations. All too often the clash of arms also causes the ruin of much that is worth preserving. It impedes or overwhelms superior cultures that promote wholesome values and make a worthwhile contribution to humanity. War can therefore result in regression as well. Whatever the outcome, after every such struggle the deck is reshuffled, creating new political constellations and fresh challenges for nations and states. One of history's most destructive wars accompanied Europe's gradual transition into the modern age, which is fixed by many scholars as having begun in the 16th Century. The era was marked by intensifying antagonism between the Catholic and Lutheran churches. The Thirty Years' War, known in its time as the Great War, brought the rivalry to a head. Waged from 1618 to 1648, it would be nearly 300 years before the continent experienced an armed conflict of comparable loss of life and property damage. It exercised a profound influence on the evolution of European armies.

At the beginning of this protracted carnage, German lands were affiliated with the Holy Roman Empire, an informally declared Christian successor to the sphere of ancient Rome. The federation consisted of hundreds of duchies, principalities, free cities and minor kingdoms, collectively represented by the impotent *Immerwährender* Reichstag (Perpetual Parliament). Each state was permitted by treaty to choose its form of worship. Austria was the most powerful and its ruler, Ferdinand II of the House of Hapsburg, the elected emperor. He began a crusade to impose the Catholic faith throughout the empire by oppressing evangelical Christians in Bohemia. The province repudiated Ferdinand's sovereignty and staged an armed insurrection that the Hapsburgs crushed at the battle of White Mountain near Prague in November 1620. Protestant churches in Bohemia were demolished and many confessing to this faith executed or banished. Supported by contingents from Spain and Italy, the Austrians subsequently invaded western and northern Germany.

This brought England and Denmark into the fray out of concern over Austrian expansion toward the Atlantic coast. Danish King Christian also hoped to gain control of German strongpoints on the North Sea. Since Ferdinand II and his ally, the Bavarian Elector Maximilian I, were short of cash, their mercenary army often took payment by looting the indigenous population. Its leader Albrecht von Wallenstein defeated the Protestants in several battles and drove the Danes from Schleswig, Holstein and Jutland. The other Austrian commander, Johann Tserclaes Count of Tilly, captured Protestant Magdeburg in May 1631. He had hoped to preserve the fortress from destruction, but fires ignited during the siege spread out of control and burned almost the entire city to the ground. Tilly's soldiers massacred four fifths of the original 25,000 inhabitants. Among the victims were most of the children, who went to their deaths holding hands and singing church hymns. Tilly wrote the emperor in Vienna, "I am sorry that you and the ladies of the court were not present to enjoy the spectacle," and celebrated the bloodletting with a mass in Magdeburg's intact cathedral.[1]

German princes who had remained neutral became indignant over the excesses of Hapsburg's marauding hordes and the demand that confiscated church property be returned to the Vatican. They welcomed Sweden, a Protestant kingdom, into the struggle. How little the war actually had to do with religion is demonstrated by the fact that France, which was Catholic, eventually sided with the Dutch and northern German princes against the Holy Roman Empire; the French foreign secretary, the Duke of Richelieu, wanted to limit Austrian influence on the continent. Possessing a mobile, well drilled army that he personally led, Swedish monarch Gustav Adolf, the "snow king," defeated Tilly at Breitenfeld near Leipzig in September 1631. His forces then pushed south to directly threaten Bavaria and Austria. The merciless Tilly was killed defending the Lech River, gateway to Bavaria. Wallenstein was beaten by the Swedish army at the battle of Lützen in November 1632. The clash cost Gustav Adolf his life. In August 1634 the emperor's son turned the tide. He led an Austro-Spanish army to a decisive victory against Protestant forces at Nördlingen in Bavaria.

The German princes concluded peace with Ferdinand III, successor to the emperor who had provoked the conflict, but the most devasting phase was yet to come. A war that began as a religious dispute of Catholic versus Lutheran evolved into a typical power struggle between European rulers. They conducted diplomatic intrigues and military campaigns to augment their kingdoms and weaken their neighbors. German Protestants spent thirteen years after the battle of Nördlingen fighting to free their country of French and Swedish armies that recruited additional mercenaries to replace losses. Clear political objectives diminished as the war degenerated into looting expeditions by these murderous troops. Hireling soldiers ravaged the countryside and laid waste to countless villages and towns. In many areas state authority disappeared; Germany, the primary battleground, eventually experienced chaos. Nearly half the rural population dwelling in combat zones or in the path of mercenary armies perished. In Thuringia, out of 1,717 houses in a single district only 627 remained standing. Out of 35,000 Bohemian villages just 6,000 were inhabitable at the end.[2]

Further, the apocalypse inflamed superstitions and incited witch hunts. In 1625 and 1628 Philipp Adolf von Ehrenberg, the Bishop of Würzburg, condemned 900 people for witchcraft, establishing the place of execution in front of a house of worship. A thousand suffered the same fate in Neisse, Silesia, in 1640 and 1641. The inquisitors may have taken lessons from *Der Hexenhammer* (*Hammer of the Witches*), a literary debasement of womanhood first printed in Speyer in 1486. Eventually 24 editions were in circulation. The book contained passages reading, "Woman is by nature evil, since she is hastier to doubt the faith and faster to deny the faith. This is the basis for witchcraft... Her aspect is beautiful but dread her touch, her companionship is deadly."[3] Such trash fed public hysteria over the perceived influence of Satanism and provided a scapegoat for the universal misery of the times. Burning or hanging women for sorcery added to the war's body count while indulging the perverse fantasies of clergymen who tortured confessions from the accused.

The Fourth-Century Roman army officer Ammianus Marcellinus remarked, "No animal displays such unbridled hostility toward humans as do Christians when attacking fellow Christians."[4] This could well have described the Thirty Years' War. An estimated eight million people perished from pestilence, starvation and abuse, or in the 80 battles fought during its three decades. The belligerents became financially and spiritually exhausted. Austria was threatened by military incursions from the Ottoman Empire and could no longer devote full attention to oppressing evangelical Christians. The Treaty of Westphalia concluded hostilities in October 1648. It granted autonomy to Germany's over 500 separate states and allowed each Reich's city to conduct its own foreign affairs. The House of Hapsburg abandoned further attempts to impose the Holy Roman Empire's central authority over Europe. Weakening Austria satisfied the primary objective of her enemies. For years after the war's end, the Germans contended with gangs of discharged mercenaries and deserters who robbed and raped their way across the country.

The unparalleled suffering of the period left a horrendous impression on the people of Europe. Resorting to force of arms remained an alternative for settling differences, but belligerents introduced rules of conduct to prevent a recurrence of such widespread destruction. The absolute state, based on the supreme authority of provincial dukes and kings in their respective lands, became the modern administrative form. Although rulers still governed with the support of the church, the clergy's influence on politics diminished. Religious issues among various populations were dealt with as internal matters; no more were battles fought for the preeminence of a particular faith. The center of power shifted from clerics to the sovereignty of the princes. European diplomacy was neutral in religious disputes.

A latent awareness became manifest among rulers that in the event of war, civilian populations must be spared as much as possible. The Dutch philosopher Hugo Grotius, who lived in Hamburg during part of the Thirty Years' War and was involved in peace negotiations, published *De Jure Belli ac Pacis* (*On the Law of War and Peace*) in 1625, recommending guidelines to temper the conduct of armies during campaigns. Thomas Hobbes, renowned for his English translations of writings of antiquity and also a contemporary of the Great War, presented similar arguments in his *Leviathan.* Their treatises did not censure warfare, but acknowledged its expediency when diplomacy fails to resolve international disputes. Combatants however, have the responsibility to confine violence to the battlefield where it belongs, to reduce the enemy's military potential rather than smash his nation itself. This became known as restricted warfare.

The proposal to hold leaders accountable for the actions of their troops would not have taken root but for the Reformation, which had effectively defied the supreme authority of the Vatican in the 16th Century. Under the old Papal system, the church ordained monarchs as "God's vice-regents," ruling by divine right, therefore infallible in secular matters governing the kingdom and answerable to no one. After the Thirty Years' War, princes in Catholic countries, with the notable exception of Louis XIV of France, regarded coronation by a bishop as a ceremonial blessing and not as symbolic of unlimited power. In place of theologically based struggles the cabinet war evolved, whereby nations took up arms based on the resolution of the sovereign and his counselors. Henceforth, despite conflicting ambitions rulers observed a certain harmony; roughly equal in size and military potential to one another, maintaining order in Europe depended on preserving the absolute states as an oligarchy of Great Powers. Louis XIV's attempt to dominate the continent and destroy the balance through wars of dynastic succession proved unfeasible and this established the comparatively moderate cabinet war as the alternative.

Restricted warfare was supposed to minimize civilian losses and hold destruction of economic resources to tolerable parameters. It was therefore an essential component of the oligarchic system, which required that the integrity of individual Great Powers not be sorely compromised by the clash of arms. The problem facing this arrangement was how to address the customary employment of mercenaries. Soldiers for hire were usually foreigners recruited from the dregs of society, unskilled laborers who fought for pay or loot. They felt no particular loyalty to the sovereign they served and had no respect for the lands they conquered. Frequently unpaid, they claimed the right to seek compensation for services by extorting and stealing from the local population. This custom, accepted by various princes who had no other way to finance their armies, was responsible for the worst excesses of the Thirty Years' War. When troops were disbanded after hostilities concluded, some became highwaymen or formed gangs of thieves in lands where they had fought, remaining a public menace.

Aligning the military with the political and social structure of the absolute state and transition into a European oligarchy required abolishing the mercenary army. Proposals to institute national fighting forces, with able-bodied males from the general population eligible for induction, made no headway. The solution adopted by the Great Powers was to institute standing armies. This concept still allowed for foreign recruitment, but the troops remained on a war footing year around. Quartering the soldiers in barracks and providing uniforms, nourishment and regular pay eliminated the possibility of derelict bodies of hirelings roving the country during or after hostilities to steal food, money and livestock. Officers were able to keep a closer watch on their troops. The standing army's sustained readiness for action gave its sovereign immediate striking power. It therefore represented a formidable instrument of diplomacy in international negotiations. Another advantage was that unlike the old system, in which mercenary formations were leased en masse, soldiers of a standing army received steady military training in peacetime to maintain discipline, become familiar with new weaponry and tactics and to fight as a cohesive unit when deployed in combat.

The standing army came into being as a segregated class of society that was the sole bearer of arms, therefore sparing other strata this duty. It conformed to the strictly defined social structure of the absolute state and became a standard for 18th-Century warfare. Princes solicited recruits from abroad for military service. This allowed planters, merchants, educated persons and skilled craftsmen to remain in their civilian occupations and promising young adults to pursue their studies, therefore fostering a vibrant national economy. Drawing on domestic human resources to fill the rosters would have reduced the number of taxpayers and deprived administrations of sufficient revenue to meet expenses. Recruiting foreigners was in a sense competitive, since by hiring them, a state prevented a potentially hostile neighbor from enlisting the same men. In 1670 for example, France had an army of 138,000 soldiers of whom only a third were Frenchmen.[5] Louis-Charles Le Tellier restructured the French military as a standing army and the administrative apparatus he created to maintain it and pay the troops eventually became a model for Europe.

Transitioning to the standing army was a slow process for the Great Powers. They learned from one another and universally adopted the more feasible innovations. Spain was compelled to maintain a garrison in the Netherlands and became the first to incorporate her mercenaries into a standing army with regular pay. The Dutch followed suit. They gave the soldiers an internal organization that included systematic drills and enforcement of discipline. This welded them into a firmly unified fighting force. Seafaring nations with a favorable trade balance, Spain and Holland financed their armies with profits from overseas commerce. The progress made by France, Spain and especially the Netherlands in the realm of military reform was instructive to the leaders of Brandenburg-Prussia. Their state was relatively poor and lacked the fiscal resources of its neighbors. Prussians had to rely on taxation to revamp the military establishment. This brought the ruling Hohenzollern Dynasty into conflict with the classes that had to shoulder the tax liability. After the Thirty Years' War, people did not want to hear about establishing an armed force in peacetime, let alone pay for it.

The Grand Elector

Sometimes likened to the ancient Spartans, the people of Brandenburg-Prussia were by nature taciturn. They were anchored by a rugged agrarian stratum but had a progressive middle class, the *Bürger* (burghers), that was active in mercantile affairs and industry. The small domain lacked natural barriers on the frontiers such as mountains and woodlands. Here again it could be compared to Sparta where, it had been said, her walls were her warriors. The Hohenzollerns displayed an attention to the welfare of their subjects that surpassed that of most monarchs of the time. The royal court did not emulate the pomp and embellishments in vogue at Versailles. The aristocracy, as in most of Europe, embodied virtues associated with medieval knighthood such as loyalty to the sovereign, refined deportment, chivalry and valor. Its function in society was managing the large estates and serving as officers in the military. The farming community, burghers and nobility would eventually be joined by the standing army as a fourth pillar of society. Members of these strata felt little connection to one another socially or politically.

Prussia owes its odyssey to Great Power status to three rulers who proved to be exceptionally decisive and judicious. Friedrich Wilhelm, who came to power in 1640, was the first of these. His title was the elector. He inherited Brandenburg-Prussia at age 20, incorporating the Margraviate of Brandenburg, the duchies of Cleves and Prussia, and Mark County into a single state. The elector found himself governing a distressed land in the final throes of the Thirty Years' War. Half the population had perished or migrated abroad; Berlin had but 6,000 residents. He devoted attention to rebuilding the country's infrastructure by promoting conservation, planting orchards and constructing a system of canals to facilitate travel and trade. Friedrich Wilhelm also introduced a rudimentary form of centralized government. He established provincial administrations that were semi-autonomous but under his overall jurisdiction. He provided land to farmers' sons who had no inheritance tax-free for six years and gave them free construction materials to build houses and barns.

A policy of religious tolerance helped repopulate the duchy and became a model for subsequent Prussian rulers. The elector welcomed Swiss Calvinists, Dutch refugees and French Calvinists, the Huguenots, who wanted to escape spiritual persecution in their mother countries. He provided farmland for the Dutch and settled the Huguenots in cities. Himself a Calvinist, a Protestant denomination that had broken with the Lutheran faith, Friedrich Wilhelm extended the same hospitality to Catholics and Jews who were persona non grata in their own lands. There were many educated individuals among the new arrivals including artists and teachers, but most were merchants and business owners. Their integration into society energized the economy. They joined a community marked by lawful protection for every confession. The elector forbade quarrels and friction between various denominations. The country gradually developed a thriving textile industry producing cotton, silk, linen and wool, and also manufactured paper, glass and iron. The Peace of Westphalia awarded Minden, Cammin, Further Pomerania, Magdeburg and Halberstadt to Brandenburg and this strengthened the state.

Friedrich Wilhelm's endeavor to restore prosperity to the duchy was a continuous process over many years. In international diplomacy and conducting military campaigns, he picked his battles carefully to augment and solidify Brandenburg-Prussia. When he began his tenure in office, the army was in shambles like everything else; it consisted of just 5,000 soldiers of dubious reliability. He initially supported Sweden in her war against the Polish-Lithuanian Commonwealth, which was waged from 1655 to 1660, with 8,500 troops. He then changed sides to aid the Poles. By the end of the conflict the army had gradually increased to 16,000 men. At the peace treaties of Wehlau in 1657 and Oliva in 1660, he freed his land from Polish vassalage. He gained control of East Prussia and official recognition as an independent prince of the Holy Roman Empire. After the war the elector reduced the number of troops in active service as was the custom, but established a standing army capable of guarding the state without having to conclude alliances.

Internal opposition would not deter the elector. When eleven years old, he had personally witnessed the humiliation suffered by his father, Elector of Brandenburg Georg Wilhelm, because of insufficient defense capabilities. In May 1631, King Gustav Adolf summoned Georg Wilhelm to a parley in the Köpenick forest. The Swedish monarch arrived with an "escort" of a thousand soldiers and four cannons. He demanded that Georg Wilhelm hand over the fortresses of Spandau and Küstrin. The elector asked for half an hour to discuss the terms with his state ministers. Gustav Adolf engaged in courtly conversation with the princess and her entourage while Georg Wilhelm and his ministers debated. They invited the king to come to Berlin. He brought along his "escort," and assigned 200 men to assume watch at the city palace. The next morning, the entire Swedish army bivouacked outside the Berlin gate. Georg Wilhelm meekly acquiesced to Gustav Adolf's demands.

The Swedes then marched off to raise Tilly's siege of Magdeburg but were unsuccessful. Gustav Adolf returned to Berlin, blaming the failure on his Brandenburg and Saxon allies. The elector sent the duchess and princesses to the encampment of the king to mollify his anger and then came himself. He agreed to further demands that Gustav Adolf imposed on the duchy. When he returned to Berlin, Georg Wilhelm was greeted by the Swedish garrison with a cannon salute of three salvoes. The gunners had fully charged the guns and deliberately aimed them toward the city, so that the rounds damaged several buildings when fired; an example of the contempt they had for a ruler who was not master of his own house.[6] One can only imagine the mortification and rancor the young Friedrich Wilhelm must have felt at seeing his father forced to endure such insults. Georg Wilhelm apologized to an unsympathetic emperor in Vienna, pleading that his army was simply too weak to resist Swedish demands.

At the conclusion of the Polish-Swedish war in 1660, Friedrich Wilhelm systematically discharged mercenary units and replaced them with smaller contingents comprised of artisans and farm lads from Brandenburg. Foreigners were also enrolled, including rabble. At least now, however, the army possessed a cadre of reliable, indigenous volunteers with six-year enlistment. The elector invited nobles to serve as officers by offering tax exemptions. Brandenburg-Prussia had a burgeoning armaments industry with factories sited near sources of raw materials. Arms production facilities in Suhl, for example, manufactured 23,000 muskets and 10,000 pistols in 1658.[7] Berlin also became a major producer of military wares, as did Essen, Dresden and Solingen in other parts of Germany. Friedrich Wilhelm abolished the motley dress worn by mercenaries and issued uniforms to Brandenburg troops. He selected Prussian blue for the color of the tunic. He established a functional administration to pay soldiers on time and contract merchants to supply foodstuffs, uniforms, accoutrements and weapons. These became known as *Kommiss* (commission) wares, ordered or commissioned by the army. Even during World War II, bread rations were still called *Kommissbrot*, and a person serving in the military was jokingly referred to as being *im Kommiss.*

The creation of a peacetime standing army for Brandenburg-Prussia was unpopular with the public. Thanks to the rampage of Swedish mercenaries during the Thirty Years' War, people harbored a widespread odium toward the military. Soldiering was not considered an honorable occupation. Europe stood on the threshold of the enlightened age, and the *Stände* (classes), organized groups of affluent, educated individuals in clergy and commerce, considered martial discipline repugnant to freethinking peoples. Councilmen of Brandenburg-Prussian cities feared that placing so formidable an instrument bound to the elector's person in his hands would enable him to infringe on their semiautonomous status and bend them to his will. Under the old arrangement, provincial and city councils authorized temporary defense expenditures and a sovereign could not muster troops without their approval. The standing army would result in permanent taxation to finance it and deprive the councils of political leverage. This in fact became the case years later, when the *Stände* rebelled in Königsberg and Friedrich Wilhelm dispatched troops to suppress the uprising.

Members of the landed aristocracy also resisted establishment of the standing army. Since the age of feudalism, they had sworn fealty to the king but enjoyed considerable latitude governing their estates and principalities. The absolute state was an infringement of their ancestral authority. To pay additional taxes to empower a centralized government by giving its ruler a peacetime army would diminish the landowners' influence and contradicted their interests. When Friedrich Wilhelm appointed nobles to become officers in the army, he selected those from less affluent families who did not have such a vested interest in preserving the feudal system. He founded a military academy to train their sons with mandatory enrollment at age twelve. Bound to their regiment and the elector, these young men gradually shifted their allegiance from their stratum to Friedrich Wilhelm. As for the *Stände*, the elector ultimately lost patience with their perpetual obstruction to his programs and reacted with draconian measures, including executions.

Friedrich Wilhelm demanded that officers swear fealty to his person instead of to the Holy Roman Emperor. This nearly provoked a rebellion among senior members of the caste. Colonel Rochow, the commandant of Spandau, threatened to blow up the fortress rather than take the oath. The reaction of Dietrich von Kracht, the military commandant of Berlin, was similar. The commander of Peitz, Hartmann von Goldacker, surreptitiously marched his entire regiment out at night to join the emperor's service. Finally, the commandant of Küstrin and no friend of the Hapsburgs, together with his troops swore loyalty to the elector.[8] His example persuaded the other regimental commanders to follow suit. The result was that Friedrich Wilhelm now possessed a leadership cadre that could be relied on for loyalty and obedience. He nevertheless remained on good terms with Hapsburg emperor Leopold I. In 1673 and 1674 Brandenburg sent a thousand infantry, 600 cavalry and 700 dragoons to help Austria repel a Turkish invasion. The campaign left no doubt about the men's fighting capability.[9]

In the west, Louis XIV took advantage of German disunity and invaded the Republic of Holland. This caused Leopold I to declare war on France. Siding with Austria, Friedrich Wilhelm undertook two inconclusive military expeditions against the French. During a third in the spring of 1675, the elector was engaged in Alsace with his troops when Sweden invaded Brandenburg-Prussia; the French had negotiated an alliance with Stockhom. Friedrich Wilhelm learned of the invasion while in Schweinfurt. To check the Swedish offensive, he left for Brandenburg with 6,000 cavalry, two regiments of dragoons and 1,200 musketeers on May 26. He conducted a punishing 14-day forced march, allowing his men but one day of rest at Magdeburg along the way. He left most of his infantry behind to increase the tempo. The musketeers travelled on horse-drawn wagons. His subordinate, Field Marshal Georg von Derfflinger, reached the first objective, Rathenow, on the night of June 14. The Swedish garrison consisted of 600 troops. With visibility reduced by rain, he told the sentry in fluent Swedish that his troops are survivors of the Wangelin Regiment and therefore an ally. When the guard lowered the drawbridge, the 69-year-old Derfflinger personally struck him with his fist and knocked him to the pavement. His dragoons stampeded into the town and the coup succeeded.

Four days later Friedrich Wilhelm and Derfflinger faced an 11,000-man Swedish army at Fehrbellin. Though outnumbered in infantry and artillery, the Brandenburg army, with the elector fighting in the front line, soundly defeated its adversary. It had some 500 casualties and the Swedes around 3,500.[10] Estimates vary, since many Swedish soldiers lost their lives during the retreat. Hundreds were massacred by vengeful locals who were bitter over excesses committed by the Swedes against civilians. The Prussian troops showed captured

The Grand Elector leads his troops against Swedish forces at
Fehrbellin in June 1675. During the battle he became surrounded
until his dragoons chopped through the encirclement to free him.
The anniversary of Fehrbellin became a German national holiday.

Swedes no quarter. Friedrich Wilhelm's victory stunned Europe. Brandenburg
was a small duchy and Sweden a formidable military power at the time. Never
before had a Swedish army suffered such a defeat on German soil.[11] Friedrich
Wilhelm henceforth became known as the *Grosser Kurfürst* (grand elector).
Two years later, in December 1677, his soldiers wrested Stettin from a Swedish
garrison. The Prussians ferried 200 siege guns from Berlin by barge up the Oder
River to bombard the fortress. The following month his compact, spirited army,
gliding to the combat zone on skis, drove a Swedish contingent under Count
Benedict von Horn from Königsberg.

In 1686, A corps from Brandenburg under General Hans Adam von
Schöning, who had commanded troops during the investment of Stettin, joined
Austria and other European powers in another campaign against the Ottoman
Empire. This was the first military operation during which Friedrich Wilhelm
did not personally accompany the soldiers. They participated in the siege of
Buda which began in mid-June. Opposing forces were deadlocked until July
22. On this day a round fired by a Bavarian mortar struck a tower containing
the fortress's main powder magazine. This caused an explosion that blew a huge
breach in the wall. Five days later, a thousand of Schöning's men were among
the mixed force that fought its way through the rubble and into the streets. The

battle raged for weeks until defending troops abandoned the bastion early in September.

The Europeans slaughtered Buda's Muslim population. The city had been under Ottoman control for 143 years and many Turks were settled there. Hundreds of adults and children were massacred and countless Islamic women raped. Those who survived were auctioned off as slaves. As allies of the Turks, the metropolis's comparatively small Jewish colony suffered the same fate. An eyewitness, Major Christoph Friedrich von Bismarck, recorded this in his diary: "All praise to our Brandenburgers! They were the only ones to still obey their officers. We did not restrict them from taking booty they were entitled to. But we prevented them from staining with atrocities the long-standing glory of Brandenburg arms. Most berserk were the men from the (Holy Roman) empire. They were the last during the assault, but first to rape and murder the women. Truly, a Brandenburg musketeer of our Kurprinz foot regiment seemed to me during those days more noble and dignified than many a lieutenant from the empire."[12]

Friedrich Wilhelm closed his eyes forever in May 1688 after a lifetime of service to his country. As a very young man he had taken charge of a war-torn, depopulated domain with a ruined infrastructure, without defensible borders and surrounded by powerful neighbors. Through diligence and the patient labor

During the Great Turkish War, the Prussian Dönhoff Regiment storms Fort Osen at Buda in 1686. Unlike Prussia and Austria, France allied with the Ottoman Empire in continental wars for centuries. French collaboration with Moslem Turks against European Christians did not prevent the church from supporting France's monarchy and later Napoleon.

of decades he reformed Brandenburg-Prussia, uniting the provinces and consolidating administration. He overcame the self-serving interests of the landed
gentry and the *Stände*. This made it possible to conduct affairs of state without
significant internal opposition. The grand elector opened the door to spiritual
refugees and augmented the population with an influx of talented, vigorous
human resources.

Louis XIV and the Hapsburgs watched the little state's economic and indus-
trial growth with apprehension. Despite their mutual antagonism, in 1679 they
joined to compel Friedrich Wilhelm by treaty to relinquish Pomerania including
Stettin. This caused him to exclaim, "May an avenger rise from my bones!"[13]
The grand elector established friendly relations with France nonetheless, which
did not cool again until 1685 when he settled French protestant refugees in
Brandenburg. Friedrich Wilhelm provided the foundation for Brandenburg-
Prussia's increasing prosperity and independent foreign policy, tripled the size
of the country and left his successor a standing army of 30,000 men. The people
now lived in a state that was secure in its defenses. This was the legacy of the
grand elector.

The "Soldier King"

The reins of government passed into the hands of the grand elector's son
Friedrich, who would rule for 25 years. Lacking the Spartan constitution of
his father, Friedrich devoted public resources to foster learning and the arts,
construction of palaces and maintenance of a lavish court. He did not neglect
military matters. Hostile toward France, he joined the League of Augsburg, a
coalition consisting of England, Austria and the Dutch Republic, to combat
Louis XIV's pillaging expeditions into Germany. The Brandenburg-Prussian
army successfully invested French-held Bonn in 1689. Despite General
Schöning's previous service against the Turks, Friedrich relieved him of command for drawing his saber on another general during a quarrel. Friedrich then
personally directed the siege. According to the chronicle of the First Guard Foot
Regiment, Friedrich "was busy well into the night but already up again each
morning before dawn. At court he was a prince who loved pomp, in the field the
premier general. With genuine disdain of death, he placed himself in the greatest
danger every day. This was not just because countless cannonballs flew past him
or struck the ground beside him; he repeatedly came so close to the fortress that
he and his entourage were exposed to salvos of musket fire."[14]

Friedrich has been historically criticized for not aggressively promoting
Prussia's development as a martial power. His grandson would later write that
he was great in small matters and small in great ones. This judgment does not
seem justified; Friedrich had a military upbringing and at age 20, accompanied
the army during the siege of Stettin in the war against Sweden. Arguing that
Brandenburg-Prussia is not part of the Holy Roman Empire, Friedrich secured
her independence from the Hapsburgs. In recognition of the military services

Brandenburg rendered in wars against the Ottoman Empire and France and the duchy's value as an ally, the emperor granted Friedrich permission to be crowned king of Prussia in 1701. He therefore became Friedrich I and Prussia an independent country. The new monarch dispatched twelve infantry battalions commanded by Prince Leopold von Anhalt-Dessau to support the Habsburg Dynasty against the French in the prolonged War of Spanish Succession that began the same year.

Dessau's contingent aided the Austrians at the battle of Höchstädt in August 1704. Prussian troops fought side by side with Austria's Prince Eugen of Savoy and the English Duke of Marlborough against the Bavarians and the French in 1706 at Turin and at Toulon in the following year. Friedrich refused offers by the emperor to replace losses from campaigns with levies from throughout the Holy Roman Empire. He wanted to enlist Prussians to preserve the national character of the army. During his reign, the infantry received improved rifles and was equipped with the bayonet for the first time. Within his own country, Friedrich increasingly involved the public in programs to bolster national defense. The king instituted a rural militia for Prussia, organized into companies of 200 men each and allowing a stipend for every member's uniform and arms. When on duty, militiamen were subject to martial law. Since Prussians were expected to defend the country in time of war, possession of a rifle, saber and uniform became a requirement for citizenship.

It was unavoidable that at a time when the concept of compulsory military service was not firmly anchored in the population, it regarded such provisions as an assault on personal freedom. Rural recruitment proceeded slowly. It was initially limited to cities with public offices and the surrounding villages. Even though they were required to train for just two hours per week, little more than 20,000 men enrolled during the first two years. In March 1704, Friedrich issued a decree establishing a *national* militia as well. Members of the rural militia were not required to serve outside of their home districts, but one purpose of the national force was to replace losses sustained by the army during the War of Spanish Succession. Upon completion of a two-year contract, volunteers were exempt from having to serve in the rural militia after returning home. By establishing the basis for compulsory military service, Friedrich therefore introduced an important prerequisite for the country's future armed forces.

The replacement program for the standing army actually began in 1688. It called for "a specified number of men from our lands" to be enrolled.[15] Each district and municipality was assigned a quota and required to supply recruits for a particular regiment. The drawback was that town elders usually selected slothful individuals and misfits who wouldn't be missed. Friedrich initially approved the tendency because he preferred not to draw energetic elements from the work force. He acknowledged that "there is unsuitable rabble everywhere, so better to use these people in the armed service."[16] Drill instructors, however, made little headway with such types. This induced the king to abandon the practice in 1708

and order regiments to return to previous methods, especially soliciting voluntary enlistment. Recruiting officers often resorted to trickery to attract viable
prospects for the standing army. For example, they would buy them drinks at
a tavern until they didn't understand the contract they were signing. In some
cases, officers resorted to kidnapping.

In many ways Prussia was the worse for wear under Friedrich I. This was
due to expenditures for maintaining an extravagant court that prioritized
entertainment. It contributed to permissiveness and consequently to graft and
mismanagement in civil service. There was little trace of the austerity previously
fostered by the grand elector. Corruption spread to the administration of the
army. When officers purchased supplies for their regiment, they often sold them
on the civilian market instead. To make matters worse, pestilence broke out in
East Prussia in 1709. It claimed thousands of lives and unsettled the population.
Russian and Polish troops encroached upon territories ravaged by the plague.
They helped themselves to whatever booty could be found. Friedrich was with
the army in Holland at the time. He was therefore fighting for Hapsburg's
interests while his kingdom was at the mercy of foreign raiders. When Friedrich
I died in February 1713, the country was in a distressed state. It was he never-
theless, who won Brandenburg-Prussia's independence from the Holy Roman
Empire, established it as an autonomous kingdom and modernized the army by
introducing a functional reserve and replacement system.

The king's son, Friedrich Wilhelm I, resembled his grandfather the grand
elector in many ways. He was disgusted by the luxury and self-indulgence of the
royal court, incompetence and fraud in civil service and violations of Prussian
sovereignty in the east. He was determined to restore the stoic, martial atmosphere that had prevailed prior to his father's reign and make Prussia master of
her borders. The pomp and elegance of the court and its retinue disappeared;
Friedrich Wilhelm slashed the budget for maintaining the palace by 80 percent.
He disbanded the ballet and inducted the male dancers into the army. Formal
gardens were converted to parade grounds for drilling soldiers. The palace's
ornate silver service was melted down and replaced with plain tableware. The
king declared its elegant baroque furniture "blasphemous" and sold it off.[17] The
dandies who had basked in the society of the previous monarch were either dismissed or found themselves exchanging silk fineries for the basic uniform of an
army officer. No longer was the Prussian court a "cheap imitation of Versailles."
The king became his own finance minister. He created an accounting office, the
Oberrechnungskammer, to scrupulously audit state revenues and spending. This
curtailed pilferage by public officials. He slashed the salary of civil servants by
half but instituted pensions for their retirement.

In one of his first speeches as head of state, Friedrich Wilhelm advised his
ministers, "You should be aware that I don't need advice but obedience. My
father took pleasure in splendid buildings, lots of jewelry, silver, gold, furnishings and superficial magnificence. Permit me to say that I too have my pleasure

and it consists of a measure of good troops."[18] The army bequeathed by his father tallied 34,324 men including fortress garrisons and volunteer militia companies. During his first year in office, Friedrich Wilhelm augmented the size of the armed services by 10,000 men. In 1722 he founded the *Generaldirektorium*, a commissariat for procurement of military wares. This eliminated the practice of individual regiments conducting transactions with unreliable and corrupt civilian contractors. The office also regulated the defense budget and levied taxes for it. The king recruited trained physicians for army hospitals. In this way he replaced unqualified, self-proclaimed doctors and quacks earning easy money treating rankers. The Potsdam military orphanage opened its doors in 1722 as well, taking in street urchins to rear as future soldiers.

The army became the cornerstone of the Prussian state. The administration and the economy were subordinate to its interests. Companies manufacturing uniforms and equipment under military contract received tax incentives. The frugality and efficiency of government enabled Friedrich Wilhelm to devote fiscal resources to the armed forces. He eventually earned the epithet *Soldatenkönig* (soldier-king). Despite his fondness for martial affairs, the king waged only one war during his reign. In 1715 his army invested Stralsund and Stettin. These are strategic Baltic ports in Pomerania that the king of Sweden Charles XII garrisoned with troops. Friedrich Wilhelm led a force of 40,000 Prussians, reinforced by some 8,000 Saxons under Count August von Wackerbarth, to besiege the fortresses. The king visited camp daily, conversed with the ranks and offered words of encouragement. During the investment of Stralsund, according to an eyewitness, "while on one of the tours, he saw a soldier who looked somewhat haggard. He called over a woman on rounds distributing brandy, and personally extended a full glass to him to help him recuperate."[19]

Armies customarily experience a reduction in force after a war, but this was not the case in Prussia. After liberating Stralsund and Stettin, Friedrich Wilhelm restructured the fighting forces. He would have preferred every able-bodied Prussian be schooled in the standing army, reviving the ancient Germanic custom that every man should bear arms. When he was crowned, the army consisted almost entirely of Prussians. The king however, understood the negative consequences of drawing too much manpower from the agrarian economy, housing construction and textile manufacture, all vital to trade. He granted deferments to students and much of the domestic work force. He brought regiments to full roster by soliciting men from neighboring duchies. According to one personnel list, during a five-month period, 244 inlanders were mustered for the infantry and 699 foreigners. This was in accordance with his intention to have Prussians comprise no more than one-quarter of the military roster.[20] Most "foreign" troops were German, but Russians, Hungarians, Poles and Englishmen also joined the ranks.

As a prince of the Holy Roman Empire, Friedrich Wilhelm was authorized under the *Werbegerechtigkeit* (right to recruit) law to send recruiters to affiliated

German states. They received a bounty for each signed contract. Over a thousand such individuals, including "questionable officers and Jews," practiced this lucrative trade.[21] In order to satisfy the sovereign's preference for tall soldiers, they travelled the countryside seeking lads who fit the criterion. Parents often hid their loftier offspring in the hayloft or a nearby wood when recruiters came to town. In their zeal to snare the biggest and the best, officers on occasion resorted to shanghaiing prospective recruits. In Mecklenburg for example, a Corporal Behring and two dragoons attempted to kidnap a local man from the town of Gnoyen. They were rewarded for their labors with a thrashing from enraged townspeople. The magistrate rescued the trio from a fatal beating.[22] In general, recruiters preferred hanging out in taverns and buying rounds, flattering patrons and exciting them with tales of soldierly deeds until they were drunk enough to sign away their future. The king responded to complaints about young men being forced or tricked into enrolling by issuing edicts in 1714, 1717 and 1721 banning the practice. The law only applied to recruitment within Prussia.[23]

The entire system of providing manpower for the armed forces needed an overhaul. Coercive recruitment continued despite royal edicts. This did little to enhance Prussia's popularity in the rest of Germany. Inside Prussia, regiments competed with one another for viable recruits. Rural Prussians became so unsettled by the activity of recruiters that young men not wishing to serve sought their fortune in neighboring states. Friedrich Wilhelm published an edict in 1722 forbidding them to migrate. He warned that those who clandestinely leave Prussia will have their property confiscated and if apprehended, be punished as deserters. He eventually offered pardons for those who return home and join the army. Right after taking power the king disbanded the militias. He wanted the standing army to be the sole bearer of arms. In so doing he deprived it of another source for replacements.

Assisted by the counsel of Prince Leopold von Anhalt-Dessau, the able soldier who had served his father and led troops against the Swedes in 1715, Friedrich Wilhelm instituted the *Enrollierungssystem* (Enrollment System) of recruitment in 1733. Officers registered all boys of 14 or 15 years and older for potential military service. They were not inducted into the army, but classified as eligible for active duty when of age and as circumstances require. The same year, Prussia was divided into military districts called cantons. Each represented an area where a particular regiment was based. The king forbade regiments to recruit outside of their respective cantons. There were exemptions galore for landowners, farmers, artisans, merchants, students and civil servants, therefore elements deemed indispensable to economic growth. Since recruitment was localized, the arrangement at least allowed officers to personally solicit men for their regiments and hence seek better quality personnel. The canton system was regarded as a burden on the poorer classes and not well received. It nevertheless provided the army with a reliable replacement system that remained in force for the next 80 years and became a guide for universal conscription in modern times.

His contemporaries derided Friedrich Wilhelm's penchant for stocking his Potsdam bodyguard regiment with *Lange Kerls* (tall fellows). He subjected his "dear blue children" to arduous training and often drilled them personally. At its zenith the regimental roster numbered 4,000 men.[24] Given the military technology of the times, height was an advantage: A taller man could handle the cumbersome, long-barreled flintlock, which the user stood upright to load, more deftly than an average sized soldier and reload more quickly. In an age prior to mechanization, skirmishes were frequently decided by the bayonet or hand-to-hand combat. The individual's size and strength were significant factors. Enemy troops, especially those with limited combat experience, regarded a line of charging Prussian grenadiers with dread. It could unsettle their own marksmanship and steadfastness. As the name indicates, the grenadier was also tasked with throwing grenades. When closing on the foe, an individual displaying exceptional physical prowess could hurl a two or three-pound bomb further than a smaller man. This reduced the chance of one's own comrades in the battle line being injured in the blast. Superior stature became a hallmark of the Prussian grenadier.

Friedrich Wilhelm may have been a source of amusement to foreign statesmen for "playing soldier" and personally drilling his Potsdam guards, but on his watch the Prussian army became an armed force that would soon take Europe by surprise. The king's chief military advisor, Prince Leopold, designed a revolutionary training regimen that significantly elevated the infantry's striking power. He introduced the iron ramrod to his regiment. It replaced the wooden type that often cracked from barrel heat in combat. The innovation was universally adopted by the army. A stringent drillmaster, he emphasized repetition to train the infantry to fire by *Peloton* (half-company) with precise salvos. The front row of men dropped to one knee and the second stood behind it. The rows fired only on command. The men learned to execute battlefield maneuvers rapidly and with mechanical precision. Maintaining a uniform interval from man to man was indispensable for evenly wheeling the *Peloton* into firing position. To this end, the infantry marched in *Gleichschritt* (unison step), also called *Paradeschritt*. Later mocked by the British as the "goose step," the rhythmic stride accustomed the soldiers to observe proper spacing during practice so that the *Peloton* would deploy smoothly in action. The physically rigorous *Gleichschritt* also enhanced strength, balance and endurance during exercises.

The training program did not encourage individual initiative from the troops or for that matter, even cognizance. Its purpose was to merge them into a well-honed fighting machine that mechanically responds to orders. In theory, war should be no different for the soldier than peacetime; performing the same maneuvers in combat that he does during field exercise. Drill did not focus on cultivating the qualities of a fighting man or on animating a killer instinct, but on conditioning him to function in mortal danger exactly as he does on the firing range. In principle he was an object. He was to feel no sense of personal involvement in the war he is waging and do nothing unless by command. It is inevitable that when soldiers are in action, passions can prompt them to act independently. Some will exhibit qualities of courage and leadership that can turn the tide of battles. In the Prussian system such occurrences were considered anomalies. Soldiers "expressing themselves" could well reverse the day's fortunes instead. "The scenario was for the battle to develop like a maneuver… like clockwork."[25]

Under the tutelage of Leopold, the Prussian army became the best-drilled on the continent. According to one German source, "Service for officers and men was equally hard. Prince Leopold of Dessau, the king's friend, drilled the troops in the barracks and in the field. They continuously practiced marching in formation, loading muskets with the new iron ramrods and combat exercises. In this way Prussian soldiers learned to shoot and reload faster than those in other countries and had an advantage over every foe."[26] Consistent with democracy's historical antagonism toward Germany, there is a lingering perception that discipline in the 18th-Century Prussian army was inordinately harsh. The king's 1726 handbook for recruit training reads, "The new lad should not stand guard duty during the first 14 days or be given other assignments… From the start, a new lad must not be made sulky and fearful, but instead have enthusiasm and love for duty. All instruction should be presented benevolently, that is without scolding and belittling. The new lad should also not be driven too hard during initial drill, let alone be subject to beatings and such chicanery; especially if he is simpleminded or a non-German."[27]

The king further ordered that "a noncommissioned officer should not strike a soldier in the barracks whether he is drunk or not, but should arrest him or report it to the company."[28] France's Count Honoré Gabriel Mirabeau stated, "Anyone who imagines that discipline in the Prussian military is demeaning is thoroughly mistaken… Only those who deserve it are punished. The others are treated well, even honorably… the Prussian soldier therefore feels proud and truly worthy."[29] The death penalty for offenses was rarely imposed. Deserters from the French army were shot if caught, but the Prussian soldier going over the hill received twelve lashes with the *Prügelstock* (cudgel). England employed the cat-o' nine tails which inflicted serious lacerations. The United States surpassed all in barbarism by branding soldiers with a white-hot iron, "T" for thief and "C" for coward, a practice not abolished until 1861.[30]

Like the grand elector, Friedrich Wilhelm recruited officers from among the noblesse. The king believed the aristocracy's cultivated sense of honor to be unblemished by the burgeoning materialism and egoism of the enlightened age. He did however, encounter stubborn resistance from landowners. Nobles were accustomed to do as they please in their own fiefdoms. They took exception to the sovereign's contention that they, no less than an ordinary peasant, must bear arms in defense of the country. It required the full weight of the king's authority to compel them to enroll their sons in the cadet corps established to train future officers. While little could be done to improve the inveterate attitude of the older generation, Friedrich Wilhelm gradually won the younger nobility for his purpose. He elevated the army officer to the loftiest standing in society. A lieutenant wore the same uniform as the king. A bond of chivalry and camaraderie developed between ruler and the new military hierarchy: "Not for money or fortune did the officer enter service of the king, but for the honor of wearing the same uniform and for being looked upon by him as a comrade in arms."[31]

In addition to awarding commissions to sons of indigenous aristocratic families, the king appointed them to important civic posts. They served on state councils and tenanted teaching positions. Members of the military leadership caste were prominent at court. Though forbidding the nobility from serving in foreign armies, Friedrich Wilhelm encouraged their enlistment in his own. Once a year he personally visited every regiment in the army. Compelled by a sense of duty and no less by the honors bestowed on them, the young officers were loyal to their sovereign. They remained so even when the landed aristocracy from which they hailed opposed the king's infringement of their provincial autonomy. Foreign officers entered Prussian service during the period as well. This circumstance was not unusual for the times. Many Europeans of noble birth left their native lands to escape religious persecution and the families often enrolled their sons in the royal cadet corps to seek a military career.

An anecdote from the time relates how the king, known to be short-tempered, once struck a major and his servant with a cane. The major challenged Friedrich Wilhelm to a duel, noble to noble. As the aggrieved, the officer was entitled to fire first. He deliberately missed his mark by aiming in front of the monarch's feet. The major then took the remaining pistol from the king's second to dutifully fight the duel for his sovereign and shot himself in the head.[32] The incident must have impressed Friedrich Wilhelm with the uncompromising sense of honor among officers, indeed a caliber of men worthy to lead the Prussian army. At the same time, it illustrates the tact required of the king to demand obedience from members of the nobility without offending their pride. Ultimately, the "soldier-king" won the respect of the younger generation and became the father of the German officer corps.

Friedrich Wilhelm's parallel endeavor to draw young nobles from their ancestral country estates into public administration brought them into contact with the population. Occupying posts in local government and education meant dealing directly with and serving the people. A generation of noblemen witnessed the fruits of the king's efforts to unify his domain. Prussia became a refuge for 20,000 Protestants who migrated from Salzburg. The sovereign gave them free land, seeds and farming equipment with reduced taxation. He proved less sympathetic toward Prussia's Jews, not banishing them but restricting the number allowed to reside in Berlin.[33] He established schools and mandatory education for the population. This development was not instituted in England for another 150 years. In 1740 Prussia abolished torture; over 50 years would pass before America followed suit.[34] The Hohenzollern monarch founded *Charité* hospital in Berlin and an orphanage for children of deceased soldiers. Cities and commerce flourished and society experienced a growing sense of national identity. Historically, social and political restructure of an existing order to raise the lower classes to better status often requires a revolution. The Hohenzollerns used their rank not just to buttress their authority, but to improve the lot of their unprivileged subjects. They therefore brought about transformation peacefully and from above.

The Great King

In May 1740, the "soldier king" lay on his death bed. He said, "I die at peace, because I have so worthy a son for a successor."[35] Crown Prince Friedrich would come to be known as "the Great" during his reign. He had suffered poor relations with his stern father when growing up. He even attempted to flee to England when he was 18 years old. As an officer of the army this was desertion. Prince Leopold of Desssau helped persuade the king to reinstate Friedrich to rank. The crown prince eventually learned to respect and emulate his father's achievements. After touring Prussia and personally witnessing his progressive reform, Friedrich wrote a friend, "Everything I describe to you we have the king alone to thank for. He made the plans and he alone carried them out. He was wanting neither in caring nor in exertions, nor in important expenditures, nor was he lacking in fulfilling promises and bestowing awards."[36] When Friedrich II came to the throne at age 28, the population hoped for a reduction in armaments. The army numbered 83,500 men including 26,000 non-Prussians.[37] This was a disproportionately large force for a small state and a substantial burden on the treasury.

Critics of the monolithic military establishment became hopeful when the new sovereign announced that the Potsdam bodyguard regiment will be disbanded. They assumed that a general reduction in force will follow. Friedrich initially reaped praise from the French philosopher Voltaire, who composed a verse celebrating the impending disappearance of Prussia's "war colossus." Contrary to expectations however, the young monarch enlarged the country's armed forces. Less than a month after taking office, he wrote his friend Voltaire, "First of all, I am increasing the power of the state by 16 battalions, five squadrons of hussars and one squadron of *Garde du corps*."[38] Striving for world peace as a blessing to mankind may have fit Voltaire's dream for the enlightened age, but Friedrich perceived the harsh realities of statecraft more realistically. Dissolving Potsdam's premier regiment was not done to minimize defense spending. He took the step on the advice of his father, who shortly before his death had rescinded payouts to recruiters for enlisting *Lange Kerls*. The purpose was the opposite of what Voltaire and critics of Prussian militarism had anticipated.

Most of the king's personal guardsmen had been forcibly recruited and were non-Prussians. There were few desertions however, since the men enjoyed elite status, higher pay and greater privileges than soldiers in other regiments. They slept in feather beds. The salaries and cost of the elegant uniforms and equipment of their one reserve and three active battalions, at that time 99 officers and 3,000 grenadiers, would suffice to raise and equip two standard rifle regiments. Friedrich also felt life too comfortable for the parade troop and this could negatively influence its prowess in combat. Since the Potsdam guards had been drilled harder and were better trained than members of other regiments, many were disbursed to new formations to serve as instructors as the army expanded. In order to maintain the tradition of this renowned formation, the king incorporated its tallest, most handsome men into the new *Grenadier Garde Bataillon* Number 6 in July 1740. He offered to discharge those who no longer wish to serve, but only 32 men opted out.[39] This is an impressive statistic when one considers that most rankers had not joined voluntarily. The prestigious bodyguard was therefore not disbanded but renamed.

In addition to the Potsdam guard battalion, the Prussian army had 67 rifle regiments and eleven mounted squadrons, plus fortress garrisons and independent battalions. The infantry comprised 59,000 men. This represented 75 percent

Friedrich II had an informal rapport with the troops on military campaigns. In peacetime, he discouraged fraternization between aristocratic officers and enlisted personnel. The soldiers were increasingly demeaned and abused as consequence.

of the personnel roster. It was the fourth largest army in Europe and the best drilled. During peacetime, only half of the standing army remained on active duty except during April, May and June when it was at full strength for field maneuvers. Reservists were at home for the rest of the year, on leave without pay at their peacetime occupations. The state of nonbelligerency would be short lived. Friedrich II went to war in December 1740, just months after taking power. He disputed the House of Hapsburg's claim to the prosperous Silesian duchies of Jägerndorf, Liegnitz, Brieg and Wehlau bordering Prussia, upon the death of Holy Roman Empress Maria Theresia's father Charles VI. The War of Austrian Succession opened with Friedrich invading Lower Silesia with 30,000 Prussians. Leading the troops into the field confronted the king and his generals with a chronic issue in campaigns to come; that of desertion.

Several factors contributed to men going over the hill. The population still regarded the soldierly craft with disdain due to misdeeds of mercenaries during the Thirty Years' War. In a prosperous society, men in uniform were generally regarded as losers. Consequently, the army did not attract the best elements. Recruits who had signed contracts in taverns resented having been tricked and those with families were often homesick. The incessant, repetitious drill was tedious and discouraging. Non-Prussians represented a substantial portion of the roster. They saw little to gain by risking their lives fighting Austria. As the struggle against the Hapsburgs escalated so did the size of the army and this, together with mounting casualties, required continuous impressment to satisfy manpower requirements. This included forcibly inducting men from provinces invaded by Friedrich such as Bohemia, Saxony and Silesia. As can be imagined, their populations scarcely felt affinity for Prussia. The king himself reluctantly acknowledged that half the regiments consist of soldiers who "do not feel bound to the state," and will "try to run away at the first opportunity."[40]

In order to combat desertion, Friedrich upheld his father's ban on unnecessarily harsh treatment of soldiers. He forbade instructors to strike, shove or berate a recruit during training. He was to be disciplined with the *Rohrstock*, the corporal's redoubtable wicker rod, only when "quarrelsome, won't do as he's ordered or is malicious, and then in moderation."[41] The fact that the king issued this decree is itself an indication that it was necessary; officers and the cadre of noncommissioned officers (NCOs) still believed that fear of punishment is the only way to keep men inducted from the newly conquered territories in line. Friedrich drafted a 14-point guideline for preventing desertion. It instructed generals to bivouac in non-wooded areas, to patrol the camp's periphery with hussars and sentries at night, to have officers accompany details to fetch straw and water, to only march after dark when dictated by "compelling reasons," to hold the men in formation during daytime movements, to keep troops supplied with "meat, straw, brandy and so forth," and when retreat becomes necessary, to "conceal the fact from the troops and invent an excuse that the soldier wants to hear."[42]

On walls surrounding villages where troops were billeted stood *Schildwachen.*

These were military police identified by a crescent-shaped shield on a lightweight chain around their collars. A ranker standing post during the night who was a flight risk was paired with a reliable soldier with the latter's rifle loaded. When someone went missing, three cannon shots were fired. This alerted locals, who were required by a 1723 edict to proceed to prearranged posts to watch for the deserter. Officers checked these posts and if they found one unoccupied, the farmer assigned to it was fined. Hunters or farmers who caught deserters received a bounty from the captain. The deserter was usually sentenced to a few months' fortress arrest. The problem of desertion was so rife that one staff officer lamented that "half the garrison watches the other half."[43] Lieutenant Colonel Hans von Fleming wrote of the conscripts, "Only poor service can be expected from such compelled soldiers. Many don't have their heart in it. They're always thinking about their wives and children back home. On the march they seize the best opportunity to desert in full uniform and with their rifle."[44] During the Seven Years' War, 1,650 men deserted from the Prussian 39th Infantry Regiment alone. Friedrich lost the fortress of Glatz in 1760 because the entire garrison, the Quadt Regiment, switched sides and joined the attacking Austrians.[45]

Even though Friedrich Wilhelm I had published a decree in 1726 that deserters are to be hanged if caught, the sentence was usually commuted to a beating. Men returning voluntarily were not punished. Offenders in Friedrich II's army generally received a royal pardon after each war. This made threats of severe punishment ineffective. The 18th-Century German economist Johann Gottlieb von Justi remarked that clemency "gave young men of the country the opportunity to be disloyal. They learned, so to speak, how to safely shirk their duty."[46] Instead of accepting the obvious, that men forced into service to risk their lives in a cabinet war don't feel they should have to fight it, Friedrich II attributed the tendency to desert to their peasant origins; runners were supposedly men lacking noble virtues. Gerhard Günther wrote that the king "wanted only aristocratic officers in the infantry, because this was the main weapon and bore the brunt of the fighting. It had the highest rate of desertion and was therefore the most difficult to manage. The king placed value on an officer corps that possesses an especially lofty sense of soldierly duty... The officer corps was drawn almost exclusively from the nobility and had a loftier concept of honor than the common man."[47]

For Friedrich II, the sharp division between officer and enlisted personnel, the latter including noncommissioned officers, was no different than the contrast between noble and common. He was a disciple of absolutism to the core; superior standing in Prussian society was bestowed by birth, not earned. The officer belonged to the same caste as the sovereign he served. The king and all officers of the Potsdam guard regiment still wore the same uniform. The officer owed his commission to lineage and his allegiance to the royal family safeguarded his station in Prussia's social milieu. He could only preserve this status by discharging his soldierly duties with loyalty, courage and distinction. His ambition was to achieve honor. The Hohenzollerns prized the ambition of their company, battalion and regimental commanders to earn honors in wartime and recognized them by awarding promotions and medals. For a nobleman of rank to desert the colors would be unthinkable. Friedrich himself wrote that the true officer "will be guided by ambition."[48]

The perception that officers are trustworthy and enlisted personnel are not, Friedrich may have inherited from his father, who in 1713 rewrote the articles of war governing military conduct. They listed the table of offenses and corresponding punishments for dereliction of duty, insubordination, theft, desertion and so on. Swearing the oath of allegiance bound the soldier to these laws. They were not binding to officers. The new oath composed by Friedrich Wilhelm for them was worded differently than the one for rankers. There was no mention of the articles of war. Instead, officers pledged to "understand what regulations for wartime service and the king's edicts mean, and what the application of military justice entails."[49] The exclusive status afforded aristocrats in the Prussian army further diminished the rank and file's desire to serve. This is ironic considering that one objective of the policy was to minimize desertion.

During the reign of Friedrich II, this class-conscious attitude had other negative consequences for the army. Europe was in the modern age and the science of war evolved with it. Strides in technology and manufacture led to ongoing design, development and more efficient production of improved small arms, artillery and bridge building equipment. Adapting new weapons systems to field application, as for example when besieging fortresses, required commanders of superior intellect and learning. According to historian Günther, "Friedrich the Great did not want officers from the non-titled, educated class because he did not believe they have the sense of honor he demanded of his officers. Cadets from that stratum who were introduced to him he would chase off with his cane."[50] For those from the less affluent nobility, Friedrich's preference, "the level of education of the officer was minimal and his manners rather provincial."[51] Elder aristocrats apparently placed little value on enrolling their sons in public schools to study with children of the middle class.

Poor schooling and narrow-mindedness were the bane of the Prussian officer corps and would remain so for decades to come. In the age of the Enlightenment this was almost laughable. Colonel Johann von Scholten bemoaned that "officers are rarely capable of writing a letter without grammatical mistakes."[52] The cuirassier Georg Dietrich von der Groeben established a war library for his young colleagues to enhance their knowledge of military science. "He found practically no helpers and very few readers."[53] Instructors at the Berlin officers' academy were shocked that not a single one among a group of Pomeranian Junkers (young gentlemen) reporting for training could read or write.[54] The landed aristocracy considered this well and good. They believed that their birth and ancestral privilege of command suffice to lead.

The army's spokesman for this archaic viewpoint, Major Leopold Schönberg von Brenkenhoff, argued that education makes one effeminate and leads him astray from a martial disposition. Whoever delves in the sciences becomes mentally a civilian; better for him to "resign his commission and make studying his primary activity," else he is just half a soldier and the soldier's craft should not be a half-commitment. Brenkenhoff cited the alleged "deep recalcitrance of students in the army" as proof that the Enlightenment and war don't mix.[55] The "soldier king" Friedrich Wilhelm had thoroughly disdained the "whimsical erudition" of young adults, but Friedrich II, himself well educated, acknowledged the value of academics. He gradually demanded more of his aristocratic officers in this sphere. The king found it initially expedient to also promote burghers to command service arms requiring technical expertise and greater intelligence such as the artillery, combat engineers and logistics.

Friedrich retained certain demeaning discrepancies. These included promoting officers belonging to the nobility after three years' service in a regiment, while the burgher officer was not eligible before twelve years' active duty and then only if he "possesses very great merit and a sincere disposition and also a handsome external appearance."[56] Some who proved their worth the king knighted. These included David Kraul, an ordinary soldier of the Brunswick-Bevern Regiment who was first to force his way into Ziskaberg's fortifications during the attack on Prague in September 1744. After the Seven Years' War, the king discharged from the army many burghers who had been commissioned during the fighting or banished them to garrisons considered second-class formations. By the close of Friedrich II's reign in 1786, just ten percent of army officers were burghers. From major to field marshal there were 22 non-titled officers compared to 689 from the nobility.[57]

Blocking the advancement of motivated, educated individuals of the middle class, whose contribution to the country's military fortunes would have surpassed that of complacent officers of the nobility, would eventually lead to dire consequences for Prussia. They would not become manifest until years after Friedrich's reign. In his own time, the king's dominant personality and control over operations offset the disadvantage of depriving the army of fresh talent. In any case, whatever shortcomings existed in the officer corps, lack of courage was not one of them. Field commanders shared the rigors of combat and suffered casualties proportionate to those of the rank and file. During the two Silesian campaigns and the Seven Years' War, 48 Prussian generals were killed in action or died from wounds.[58] The trump card of Friedrich's war machine was superior training. Aware that his country was dwarfed by neighboring Great Powers, his father the "soldier king" compensated for by subjecting troops to repetitious drill. Friedrich II understood its value and fostered it during his own career.

After he fought his first major engagement in April 1741, Friedrich turned his attention to the cavalry. In his opinion, the horsemen were "colossi on elephants who know neither how to ride nor to fight."[59] He intensified the training to enhance their combat-readiness. Freiherrn von der Trenk, an ensign in the elite

Garde du corps training squadron, recorded his experience: "There is probably no soldier on earth more plagued than a *Garde du corps*. Often during peacetime I had in an eight-day period no more than eight hours of free time. Training began at four o'clock in the morning. Everything the king wanted to try with the cavalry took place here: We jumped trenches of three, then four, then five and six feet wide, until some men broke their necks during the exercise. We went over fences, charged in battle square formation for half a mile, and often returned from the exercise with some people dead or crippled, losing horses too.

"Back in Potsdam, the alarm would sound twice sometime in one night. The horses were in the king's stables and whoever did not appear before the castle saddled up and armed within eight minutes received fourteen days' arrest. We were scarcely back in bed at the barracks when the alarm sounded again. This was to drill alertness into the lads. In one year of peacetime, I lost three horses from broken legs or from being trampled during maneuvers and jumping ditches. Back then, the *Garde du corps* actually lost more men and horses during the years of peace than from enemy action later in two successive battles. We had three barracks in those days. In the winter it was at court near the opera in Berlin. In the spring during maneuvers, it was in Charlottenburg and in the summer in Potsdam or wherever the king was. All six officers sat at the king's table, on gala days beside the queen. There was probably no better school for soldiers on earth than this one."[60]

The Prussian and Saxon infantry relied on the linear tactic, also called the echelon attack. It was introduced to Prussia during the reign of Friedrich I. Troops formed a line across an open field, usually three men deep, and advanced in step to the beat of drums accompanied by fifes. Officers led the phalanx up to the enemy, ordered the men to halt and then volley fire by *Peloton* on command. Sometimes after a single salvo they bayonet charged. When carried out by a disciplined formation, this often sufficed to scatter the defenders. To repel cavalry attacks battalions rapidly formed into battle squares. These were boxes of three to four men deep per side with an open space in the center for officers, musicians and the flag. The troops faced outwardly with fixed bayonets. Battalion cannons were sited at the corners. The battle square was vulnerable to artillery fire but successful against charging horsemen. To execute these maneuvers in the confusion of combat without losing cohesion naturally required great precision. Infantry training focused on repetitive formation drill. Soldiers practiced reloading and firing quickly without emphasis on proficiency in marksmanship.

Historian Colmar von der Goltz explained, "The crux of King Friedrich's infantry tactic was rapid volley fire and speed in the movement of large bodies of troops. He valued training the individual only insofar as it made him a viable component of the grand mobile machine. He placed little worth on character development, even though pleased when occasionally encountering strong and decisive personalities. He did the thinking and decision-making for all; the mass had only to obey. His low opinion of the multitude worsened as the years passed and made him harder and more bitter. In this way he shared the fate of many great field commanders."[61] Friedrich may have gradually succumbed to deepening contempt for the common soldier, but this was certainly not apparent during military expeditions. Despite the absolutist mindset, the king felt confident enough in his authority to cultivate an unconstrained rapport with the troops in the field. He never projected the aloofness toward them that was characteristic for royals and aristocrats in some monarchial states.

When on campaigns Friedrich usually rode with the cavalrymen. They hailed him with "Good day Fritz". Guardsmen teased him about the scruffy, worn condition of his plain field tunic. He knew every corporal in his thousand-man First Battalion Guard by name.[62] He saw himself as a soldier first, setting the standard for officers. French Marshal Charles Belle-Isle described how "the king personally commands his army, not just in the main sense like an ordinary general, but also understands many other important duties. Beyond the fact that he pitches his tent in the middle of the camp, he issues all the orders and covers details that we would leave to the quartermaster. He also concerns himself with matters of

Soldiers of the Bernburg Regiment surround Friedrich II in gratitude as he praises them after the battle of Liegnitz in August 1760. The king shook hands with a member of the honor company and said, "All is forgiven and forgotten, but I will never forget what you did today!"

supply, the artillery and the engineers. The king rises at 4:00 a.m., mounts his horse and rides to each sentry post and then around the camp. He personally issues instructions to every high-ranking and junior officer assigned to this or that operation…. From getting up in the morning until retiring to bed, the king is fully dressed in a blue uniform distinguishable from that of his adjutant only by one military decoration and a slightly more elaborate shoulder board."[63]

In 1760, Friedrich disciplined the Anhalt-Bernburg Regiment because he felt it had performed poorly at Dresden during an Austrian counterattack. The regiment had already taken many casualties in combat during the Seven Years' War. The king ordered the men to cut the decorative tress from their uniforms. He forbade the bandsmen to play the Grenadier March. In a subsequent engagement, Bernburg's three battalions attacked without orders and dislodged Austrian troops defending the Katzbach River. Friedrich paraded the regiment and announced, "The stain on the honor of the Bernburg regiment has today been removed. Your majesty will himself purchase the tress for the uniforms, the men get their sabers back and all the officers of the army will know about this." Amid the rejoicing, a grenadier stepped forward and replied, "I thank your majesty in the name of my comrades for giving us back our *rights.*"[64] The soldiers surrounded Friedrich and some blamed the regiment's bad leadership at Dresden for their retreat. Friedrich disagreed and a fiery debate followed. Such an episode occurring in the 18th-Century French, Austrian or British armies would have been unthinkable. "Old Fritz" promoted the outspoken private who had so brashly thanked him to corporal.

Chapter 2

Leuthen

The Silesian Tug of War

When Friedrich went to war in December 1740, he had a dutiful officer corps, an infantry with a large percentage of foreigners and a superior cavalry. He faced enemies whose combined forces seriously outnumbered his own. In the course of three wars, he won dazzling victories that expanded the kingdom and elevated Prussia to Great Power status. Much of his generalship was unorthodox. This contributed to the renown of this solitary figure who became one of history's greatest military commanders. During the third struggle, the Seven Years' War, the Prussian army fought 16 major battles. Some of them were directed by subordinates such as the king's highly capable brother Prince Heinrich. Though at times displaying tactical brilliance, Friedrich II owed his ultimate triumph more to persevering after disastrous setbacks and in the face of seemingly hopeless odds. Beyond his iron will and talent as a field commander, other factors contributed to the success of his endeavors. The infantry kept its edge through perpetual field and shooting exercises pursuant to Dessau's regimen.

Holy Roman Empress Maria Theresia of Hapsburg was the primary antagonist in the three wars. Hostilities opened with the War of Austrian Succession in 1740. The Prussian army fought its first major engagement the following April at Mollwitz. The fire discipline of the infantry carried the day. In the age of smooth bore muskets, lines of riflemen substituted volume of fire for accuracy; those who could discharge the most rounds enjoyed the advantage. Friedrich's well-trained soldiers overwhelmed the enemy with superior firepower. An Austrian eyewitness recalled, "I can honestly say that I've never seen anything so superb in all my days. They marched with magnificent bearing and with the same precision as on the parade ground. The brightly polished rifles gleaming in the sun produced a fine effect. Their fire was no different than a continuous thunderstorm."[1] The Prussians practiced not only rapid reloading and firing, but how to reload muskets while advancing. Even when attacking, they could inflict casualties on opposing troops.

Simultaneously threatened by a Franco-Bavarian coalition, Maria Theresia arranged a cease-fire with Friedrich. The treaty concluded the following summer ceded Silesia to Prussia. The empress sought to regain the lost territory in the second Silesian war of 1744-1745. Friedrich defeated the Austro-Saxon army at Hohenfriedberg in June 1745, the Austrians alone at Soor in September and the Saxons at Kesseldorf in December. The Peace of Dresden on December 25 affirmed Prussian dominion over Silesia. The third Silesian conflict, the Seven Years War, was another attempt by the empress to recover the valuable province. Austria's state chancellor, Wenzel von Kaunitz, negotiated an alliance with the France to coordinate mutual ambitions against Prussia. Although simultaneously fighting England in the New World, French sovereign Louis XV proved receptive to the arrangement. Sensing the danger posed by this unexpected union, Friedrich attacked preemptively and invaded Saxony in August 1756. He incorporated the Saxon army into his own and seized the treasury. He soon faced a coalition of Austria, France, Russia, some Reich duchies and eventually Poland and Sweden.

Receiving financial aid from England, Friedrich marched into Bohemia the following April. He won a victory at Prague by driving the Austrians from a defensive position in a six-hour battle. It was a Pyrrhic victory for Friedrich, who reported his own casualties at 18,000 men. He wrote James Keith, a Scottish field marshal in his service, "After the losses we had, the only consolation for us will be to take the people in Prague prisoner... then I believe the war will be over."[2] The army was too weak however, to invest the city and simultaneously combat an Austrian relief corps under Count Leopold von Daun. The king abandoned the siege. He crossed lances with Daun's numerically superior force at Kolin in June 1757. This was the only battle where Friedrich was known to have ridden forward with his saber drawn. The precision and élan of his troops during the engagement impressed an Austrian regimental commander, who wrote, "Forming up with their rifles and starting the advance against us were the matters of an instant. Never was there a finer day, a more fascinating spectacle."[3]

The Austrians repulsed the Prussian assault but were themselves battered. The overly cautious Daun ordered a retreat to Suchdol. They won the battle because a Saxon cavalry officer under Daun's command, Lieutenant Colonel von Benkendorf, counterattacked with his riders against orders and smashed the Prussian left flank. The Austrian army was already retiring when most of the cavalry spontaneously followed Benkendorf, so Daun had to about face. After Benkendorf's successful charge, Daun stopped advancing and resumed the general retreat. One of his officers grumbled, "We beat back the attack but didn't win the battle." Another wrote, "Full of respect for the men who had made the victory so costly for us, we stood there on the battlefield we had conquered, before row upon row of equally unbeaten foes still before our front. A spectator who did not know what had actually taken place would at this moment have been uncertain as to who, we or the Prussians, were defeated."[4]

After Kolin, Maria Theresia created a new medal that she conferred on Daun, the field marshal who had withdrawn his army instead of exploiting the victory. For their part, the Prussians retired from Bohemia. The king however, was not one for defensive strategy. Beset from all sides, he relied on his maxim that he who tries to defend everything will defend nothing and resolved to strike at his enemies separately. Friedrich II left contingents in the east to guard Silesia. He then moved against a combined force of French and *Reichsarmée* troops of the Holy Roman Empire on November 05 near the Saxon village of Rossbach. The king could muster just 21,600 men; 16,200 infantry and 5,400 horse. Most had endured the defeat at Kolin, the demoralizing retreat from Bohemia and subsequent forced marches to Berlin and then over the Saale River into Saxony.

In solid defensive positions opposite them stood 30,200 Frenchmen and 10,900 Reich's troops. Despite being outnumbered, the Prussians enjoyed significant advantages. Soldiers of the *Reichsarmée*, Swabians from Württemberg and Bavarians, had simply been sold into Austrian service as a commodity by their princes who needed money to support an opulent court. Those from Württemberg mutinied when mustered. As Protestants, they resented having to fight against Prussia, whose population was of the same denomination, for Catholic Austria. The people of Saxony and Württemberg feared that the Austro-French alliance would lead to suppression of their evangelist faith. Pastors in these lands prayed for Friedrich during services.[5]

The conduct of French troops contributed to tension between the allies. Among their comparatively inexperienced officers were unrestrained and licentious types characteristic of a coming generation of Frenchmen influenced by the cosmopolitan, liberal sentiments of the Enlightenment. The elder French General Count Claude-Louis de Saint Germain asked rhetorically, "How can such young men with their debauched morals, dissipated by the companionship of whores, animate in their soldiers the sense of honor and decency that defines the spirit of an army? Ignorance, frivolity, negligence and cowardice have taken the place of manly virtues and valor."[6] While traversing Germany, some officers vented their disdain for the Protestant inhabitants. In the Saxon village of Weichschütz, a French colonel forced Pastor Schren, attired in his robes of office, to bow down with hands on the ground so that he could step onto his back to mount a horse. The rankers of the French army pillaged the countryside. They robbed houses where they were quartered, harassed local women and looted parsonages and churches. They broke into tombs of the nobility, flinging the corpses aside in search of valuables.[7]

The excesses fueled friction not just between the French and the indigenous population, but antagonized the leadership of the *Reichsarmée* as well. The commander of the imperial contingent at Rossbach, Prince Joseph von Sachsen-Hildburghausen, protested to his French counterpart, Prince Charles de Rohan-Soubise, about the desecration of Protestant churches. An ineffectual leader, Soubise could do little to curb his undisciplined soldiers. Hildburghausen complained in a letter to the emperor that Soubise "doesn't know how to assert the remotest authority over his army." He predicted that "God can't possibly give his blessing to the combat operations of such unchristian and wicked people."[8] Hildburghausen had joined the Austrian army at age 16. He converted to Catholicism to advance his career, but had been reared in the evangelical milieu and respected its traditions. Friedrich II described him as a "fool," but

Hildburghausen's fellow officers respected him. He did however, owe his present rank largely to the favor of Maria Theresia.

The decisive leadership known to the Prussian army was not apparent in the allied camp. In a report to Vienna, Hildburghausen denigrated Soubise's military advisors as a *Judenschule* (school of Jews). This is old Austrian slang for the chaotic babble that results when everyone at a meeting, qualified or not, contributes an opinion: "I myself have recently come with the Prince of Hesse from one of these war councils or better said, synagogues. There weren't just generals there, but the tiny general staff, secretaries and God knows who the other people are. Some wore hats in the presence of their commanding general. Each one chimed in as though he was the commander in chief, except for the one who should be making the decisions. In a word it was a genuine *Judenschule*, and that's how it is every day."[9] Hildburghausen advocated taking the offensive, while Soubise preferred a war of maneuver that eschews confrontation. The Frenchman's proposal conformed to the strategy of the age, to "make war more like foxes than lions" by attacking enemy supply lines and fortress depots to avoid pitched battles and destruction of life. The allies' disagreement was especially disadvantageous when confronted with an enemy like Friedrich, who commanded a disciplined army that he held firmly in hand.

The king of Prussia was not only decisive, but flexible. After aggressive use of cavalry and the superior firepower of the infantry won the battle of Mollwitz in 1741, he placed less emphasis on artillery. The cannons were subsequently underused at Prague and at Kolin. This was despite the fact that the artillery commander, Lieutenant Colonel Karl von Moller, demonstrated their potential during the battle of Lobositz a year before. Friedrich learned from the mistake and adapted accordingly. At Rossbach, he personally supervised placement of the batteries. He devoted as much attention to their deployment as to that of the infantry and mounted troops.[10] Moller had served in the Prussian artillery since 1720 and was an excellent gunnery officer. He trained crews to operate like dragoons, who rode into combat on horseback but dismounted to fight on foot. His gunners could rapidly shift their horse-drawn gun carriages from one position to another, unhitch the cannons and go into action right in the front line to provide close support for the infantry. The king marveled at Moller's innovative tactics and the devastating effect his concentrated fire had on enemy troops. One analysis of Rossbach maintained, "It is fully justifiable to attribute the glory for the decisive victory to the artillery."[11]

Although the allied armies occupied favorable ground for defense, Hildburghausen pressed Soubise to advance. He quarreled with his reluctant French colleague, exclaiming, "Now we see how you French are! When the enemy advances you pull back. When it's a matter of attacking him, you call a halt!"[12] Once Soubise was persuaded to move forward, he and Hildburghausen attempted a large-scale operation that their troops lacked the field training and experience to successfully carry out. Friedrich's fighting force promptly respond-

Rossbach was one of Friedrich's most brilliant tactical achievements. The Prussians won largely thanks to skillful direction of the cavalry by Friedrich von Seydlitz. The king put him in charge of all mounted troops at Rossbach over two senior generals.

ed to precise orders, executed mass movements without forfeiting cohesion and displayed a coordination of service arms in combat that left its adversaries in awe. One eyewitness recalled, "In less than two minutes all the tents were on the ground as though pulled back by a curtain line in a theater and his army was fully ready to march."[13] The complexity of the maneuvers the king directed reveals the confidence he had in the army to perform as an entity. He enticed the enemy forward by feigning a retreat, parried Soubise's attempt to outflank him and dispersed the French and imperial regiments with cavalry charges and artillery barrages.

Historian Goltz summarized, "The king's rapid comprehension and his skill and confidence at directing troops made it possible to flawlessly carry out the battle plan. But also important was the soldiers' unconditional obedience. This was the result of conscientious training to cultivate a bond between officers and men, and their firm trust in the king and in his imposing genius as warlord. In this way, hesitation and indecisiveness had been banished from the ranks. Various service branches smoothly functioned as a unit."[14] Friedrich's cavalry and artillery performed with such precision and élan during the 90-minute battle that the Prussian infantry was in action for just 15 minutes. Only seven battalions even fired their rifles.[15] During an artillery duel, both sides watched a number of rabbits cowering between the battle lines. They had huddled together to escape the converging infantry columns. When the guns opened fire, the rabbits stampeded in all directions. One was atomized by a French cannonball right in front of the Prussians. A grenadier exclaimed, "This is going well! The French are killing each other!"[16]

In what became known as Soubise's *bataille amusante* (battlefield farce), the French lost 6,000 men and 600 officers including eleven generals. The *Reichsarmée* lost 42 offices and 3,510 men.[17] Prussian casualties were initially fixed at 518 combatants including 30 officers. Of these, seven officers and 162 rankers were fatalities.[18] According to a modern "assessment of surviving original records," however, the Prussian army had three officers killed and just 67 other ranks.[19] Friedrich's soldiers captured 72 cannons. With commendable frankness, Hildburghausen wrote the emperor after the battle, "Everything went topsy-turvy with no more possibility of reforming the troops, and when someone thought to have a squadron or a battalion back together, if a single cannonball flew past everyone scattered like sheep. It was our good fortune that night came. Otherwise, by God, no one would have gotten away. I've never in my life seen such chaos and such panic."[20] Writing the war ministry in Paris, Soubise displayed less concern for truthful reporting: "We must hasten to rescue the honor of the nation and dump all the blame on the *Reichsarmée*."[21]

"Our Hearts Trembled"

After the battle of Rossbach, Friedrich the Great wrote on November 12, "I had good luck at the start, but will always need it. Now I have to go across to the other side to seek new dangers in Silesia."[22] Though still confronted with a formidable enemy in the coveted province, the victory over Hildburghausen and Soubise granted Prussia strategic advantages. Most surviving Reich's troops leased to Austria and France went home after the battle. A captain in the Bayreuth cuirassier regiment had six officers and 33 men left under his command. England increased subsidies to finance Friedrich's war effort. Prussia was diverting French resources that would otherwise be used to combat the British in North America. In France, news of the defeat sharpened public opposition to the war. King Louis XV suffered criticism for the military expedition's slipshod preparations. Hildburghausen had the impression that Soubise's troops were from France's worst regiments. They lacked tents, provisions, proper footwear and sufficient ammunition.

In the opinion of Count Saint-Germain, the general who covered the retreat from Rossbach, "had the enemy pursued us after he threw me back, he would have destroyed our entire army. I led a band of thieves and murderers who took flight at the first cannon shot and were always ready to revolt. There have never been soldiers like these. The king has the worst, most unruly infantry under the stars. Never has an army behaved so badly. Our defeat and our shame were decided as soon as the first cannon was fired."[23] French aristocrats sympathized with Prussia and disapproved of the alliance with Austria. Some were outspoken in their dislike of the sovereign's policy. In Versailles, a courier read aloud a letter that Soubise had composed the morning of the battle of Rossbach, stating that the Prussians are about to retire and confidently predicting the capture of Friedrich. In Louis XV's presence, the Duchess of Orleans exclaimed, "That's wonderful! I'll finally get to see a king!"[24]

Friedrich's aide-de-camp, Captain Friedrich Wilhelm von Gaudi, wrote in his journal after the victory at Rossbach, "On the day of this battle, one could see his true greatness."[25] Yet no less deserving of renown was the resolve Friedrich displayed when confronted with setbacks. During the expedition to the Saale to fight Soubise and Hildburghausen, the king received dispatches reporting defeats suffered by his army in Silesia. The corps of General Hans von Winterfeldt, who had served at Mollwitz and Prague, was overwhelmed by a larger Austrian force at Moys in September 1757. Winterfeldt was mortally wounded. On November 17, Friedrich learned that Schweidnitz, the city he considered the key to holding Silesia, had fallen to the Austrians five days before. He had presumed it to be too late in the campaign season for the enemy to besiege the fortress.[26] Prince Augustus von Bevern, the other Prussian general defending Silesia, had 28,000

The king parts with General Winterfeldt, charged with defending Silesia. Previously a lieutenant in the Potsdam grenadiers, Winterfeldt reorganized Prussia's military Intelligence system. After he was mortally wounded Friedrich lamented, "I'll never find another Winterfeldt. He was my friend."

men under his command. He waged an adroit defensive campaign, but was beaten, heavily outnumbered, outside the provincial capital of Breslau on November 22. Bevern was taken prisoner two days later by Croatian pickets while he was conducting a predawn tour of sentry posts.

Maria Theresia wanted Silesia conquered before year's end. She personally fixed the investment of "this detestable Breslau" as the campaign's next objective.[27] Franz Leopold von Nádasdy, who had captured Schweidnitz in a 16-day siege, moved cannons to Breslau to bombard the fortress. The empress had already published a decree in September calling on the population of Silesia to acknowledge her sovereignty. She promised freedom of worship for all denominations, moderate taxation and compensation for war damage. She admonished her officers to maintain the strictest discipline among the troops and prevent looting. Friedrich countered by warning the Silesians in the harshest tone to remain loyal to Prussia. Austrian sympathizers and residents fearing a siege urged members of Breslau's garrison, many of whom were less reliable Saxons and native Silesians, to abandon their post. They generously supplied the soldiers with wine to undermine discipline. Citizens' delegations pressed the governor, the elderly General Hans von Lestwitz, to surrender.

After Bevern's capture, General Freiherr von Kyau retreated with the Silesian army's remaining 18,000 troops first to Breslau but then to Glogau. During the march, a courier brought Kyau belated instructions from the king: He was to hold Breslau until the main army arrives from Saxony to raise the siege. The message came too late. Lestwitz was alone to defend the city. Faced with public opposition and a diminutive garrison of dubious loyalty, the governor was not up to the task. Austrian officers infiltrated the town and encouraged soldiers to desert. Nádasdy guaranteed them safe passage to Glogau upon surrender and promised the men may keep their weapons. Lestwitz complied and handed over the fortress together with its substantial supply depot. In the town square, the Austrian commander in Silesia, Prince Karl of Lorraine (Lothringen), addressed members of the Lestwitz Regiment as it formed up for the march to Glogau: "Lads, whoever no longer wishes to serve the king of Prussia should report to the sentry post at the Schweidnitz gate to receive a pass and traveling money."[28] Despite the efforts of regimental officers to keep the men in line, most scattered before their eyes and took advantage of the offer.

By granting safe passage home for soldiers who desert, Prince Karl implied that those who *do not* may face difficulties; most men of the Lestwitz Regiment were native Silesians. They feared that were Friedrich to lose the war, the Austrians will forbid them to return to their families. The Saxons in the garrison harbored the same concern. The governor had accepted the terms of surrender that stipulated his troops are allowed to rejoin the main army. For Lorraine to make an offer contradicting the spirit of the agreement after Lestwitz capitulated was an unchivalrous stratagem. Out of a thousand men in the Lestwitz Regiment, all but 150 deserted. The Saxon Jung-Bevern Regiment, which had fought the Austrians only days before, had entered the town with 726 men. Only four did not go over the hill. Children played with rifles stacked in pyramids in the town square and pounded on abandoned drums. Out of 4,288 men holding Breslau, just 471 marched out as a unit on November 25. Of these, 121 were officers. The townspeople welcomed the Austrians as liberators. The churches celebrated with a thanksgiving service.

News of Breslau's fate angered Friedrich. He left part of his army in Saxony and marched 14,000 men east to combine forces with Kyau's troops to retake the city. The accelerated tempo on bad roads and with provisions in short supply caused nearly 300 men to drop out from exhaustion along the way.[29] He ordered Kyau arrested for failure to defend Breslau, the fortress he complained to his brother Prince Heinrich had "surrendered to the enemy without a shot being fired," and replaced him with General Hans von Zieten on the 27th.[30] Friedrich himself arrived with his army at Parchwitz, a village along the Berlin to Breslau causeway, one day later. His troops surprised and routed the 800-man Austrian garrison. They inflicted heavy losses and seized the Katzbach bridge. The enemy had not expected the Prussians so soon. Dismayed that after having just driven the Prussians from Schweidnitz and Breslau they were suddenly at his doorstep, Prince Karl wrote the emperor, "This king of Prussia is like a hydra; when we cut off one of his heads, another grows immediately in its place."[31]

The approach of winter aroused a sense of urgency in Friedrich: "We had to attack the Austrians immediately and at all costs, and either throw them out of Silesia or accept losing the province for good."[32] Zieten reached Parchwitz with the Bevern army on December 02. Even though they had fought valiantly against superior forces, the late arrivals were dispirited after losing Breslau. Captain Jakob von Logan-Logejus, a hussar in the Silesian corps, described the retreat to Parchwitz: "We approached our monarch deeply ashamed. The anxiety we noticed in our army commanders, that not even Zieten was free from, dashed from our hearts the joy we had always felt at the prospect of serving directly under the king. But now this was all changed. Somber and silent, as though at a particularly solemn funeral procession, we rode on toward the fearful hour."[33] In the recollection of another cavalry officer, Captain von Bodgursky, "We dreaded the first sight of our monarch the way a criminal would fear seeing a judge. It's being said that the Duke of Bevern let himself be captured voluntarily, to escape the initial moment of the king's displeasure."[34] The sovereign however, was aware of how tenaciously the men had fought; 28,400 of Bevern's Prussians had held their ground against 83,606 Austrians, inflicted 5,000 enemy casualties to 6,000 of their own and only fell back the next day.[35]

Friedrich's treatment of these troops demonstrates a quality of leadership that measures far beyond that of a pure military tactician: "Scarcely had the king reached our regiment when he cheered us up at a glance. Completely contrary to custom, he took off his hat to us white hussars with the words, 'Good day lads! You've suffered a lot, but everything will be fine.' Officers and our mounted companies witnessed the nicest spectacle. Not 50 feet in front of us the king's victorious army marched past in review. Many formations loudly sang church hymns, others cheerful soldier's songs… Our commander, Colonel (Hans) von Krockow, rode up to us greatly excited. With tears in his eyes, he told everyone how the monarch has not only uttered not a word of reproach to the company commanders and senior officers, but expressly acknowledges and praises their courage, sense of duty and prudence."[36]

Writing in the second person, Friedrich described the rendezvous with Bevern's corps: "This army was disheartened and humbled by the defeat it had just suffered. The king appealed to the officers' sense of honor, reminded them of their previous victories and sought to wipe away the impression of the dismal circumstances that were novel to them. Even wine was provided to help lift their depressed spirits. The king spoke with the soldiers and had food distributed to them without charge. Every means imaginable was exhausted to revive the troops' confidence, without which any hope of victory is in vain."[37] One officer wrote that the sovereign camped "in the outdoors like a common soldier, warmed himself at the bonfire and made room for the soldiers standing nearby, so that they could warm themselves at the fire as well. He moved among the soldiers as one of them. He talked with the men about their tribulations and encouraged them in a most affectionate way. Their expressions soon became more cheerful and those who had beaten the French at Rossbach urged their comrades to take heart. The time of rest revitalized the soldiers. The army was ready to wipe away the disgrace it had suffered on November 22."[38]

The rest and encouragement rejuvenated the men for the battle ahead. Friedrich needed to attack his enemies in succession to prevent their armies from linking up. The Austrians had invaded Silesia with a force of 90,000 men. Some 60,000 infantry and 14,000 mounted troops stood just west of Breslau to block him from reentering the province. Their artillery consisted of 170 battalion field guns and 65 heavy cannons.[39] Reforms implemented by Count Wenzel von Liechtenstein had significantly improved the quality of Austrian training and equipment. The combined Prussian army tallied 22,000 infantry and 13,000 cavalrymen. It had 167 cannons. These included seven mortars and a battery of ten super-heavy *Brummer* (growler) siege guns. Friedrich had ordered Zieten to remove the *Brummer*s from the Glogau fortress and bring them along to bombard Breslau. Each fired a twelve-pound projectile and was drawn by a team of ten to twelve horses. Practically all of the remaining soldiers were native Prussians. Most of those recruited from German duchies had deserted during the campaign. The king decided to meet the enemy head-on. This was a larger, better-disciplined force than that the one he had conquered at Rossbach.

At the camp in Parchwitz, the king assembled his senior officers. They knew from experience that in major engagements an army can suffer a third of its soldiers and a higher proportion of officers as casualties. "Gentlemen," Friedrich began, "Prince Karl of Lorraine has succeeded in capturing Schweidnitz, defeating the Duke of Bevern and taking Breslau while I was forced to stop the advance of the French and Reich's nations. Part of Silesia, my capital and all of my military stores have been lost… If I were to do nothing, I would leave the Austrians with possession of Silesia… Relying on your courage and experience, I have prepared a battle plan that I must execute tomorrow. Against every rule of warfare, I will attack a foe who is not only twice as strong as we are but entrenched on high ground… If there are those among you who fear sharing these hazards with me, you may be excused today without experiencing the least reproach from me." The officers knew their sovereign was indirectly referring to Prince Moritz von Dessau. He had recently predicted, "Our circumstances are desperate and unfortunately will become even more desperate in a few days."[40]

Major Konstantin von Billerbeck interjected, "Right, such a man would have to be a real skunk; now, at such a time!" The king responded with a wry smile and resumed, "Before speaking, I was already certain that none of you will abandon me… Now go, and repeat to your regiments what you have heard from me. Tell them also that I will have my eye on every one of them. The cavalry regiment that does not fall upon the enemy immediately when ordered to do so will be relieved right after the battle and reassigned garrison duty. The infantry battalion that begins to falter, no matter what confronts it, will lose flag and saber and I will have the tress cut from its uniforms."[41] After the speech, an eyewitness recalled, "the old warriors who had won many a battle under Friedrich shook hands with one another and promised to stand together faithfully. They pledged to their young troops not to shy from the enemy, but instead to look him in the eye no matter what the resistance. A certain inner sense of steadiness and confidence became apparent in everyone and all anticipated victory ahead."[42]

That night Friedrich rode into camp to visit the common soldiers. "What brings you to us so late?" asked an older veteran. "Good news lads!" replied the king. "Tomorrow you slaughter the Austrians." An eyewitness recorded, "Riding all around the camp, he conversed with every regiment… Listeners spread the words of the king with great vim and it worked wonders. Everywhere in the Prussian camp that evening, from privileged to commoner, young to old, there was enthusiasm and rejoicing!" An artilleryman wrote how "all sense of danger disappeared and a certain confidence that victory is assured took its place. Were anyone to observe the state of the Prussian army, it wouldn't be hard to see the conviction that the king will strike down the enemy wherever encountered. Except for very few, the army consisted of nothing but indigenous lads. The foreigners had almost all deserted and those left assumed the character of our nation… If any people could be compared to the Spartans and Romans, it was surely the Prussians of this time."[43]

The Austrians had remained passive after capturing Breslau. Their priority was to find comfortable winter quarters. They considered the campaign season over. Postponing an offensive against the king of Prussia until spring was not an unsound strategy. The Austrians held almost all of Silesia, especially Breslau and

Schweidnitz, and through their posts in Liegnitz and Neumarkt even much of Lower Silesia. They could take up winter quarters in enemy territory and open the next campaign in favorable conditions. A courier rode to Vienna to deliver Prince Karl's proposal for winter encampment. "The entire army appeared to have settled into a peaceful, secure slumber."[44] Despite reliable scouting reports from General Philipp von Beck about the movements of the Prussian army, Prince Karl presumed that Friedrich will seek refuge for his troops for the cold season and not advance. This enabled Friedrich to combine his corps with that of Bevern's and reenter Silesia without interference.

News that the king has taken Parchwitz shook the Austrians from their "secure slumber" and Prince Karl of Lorraine convened a war council. He and his second-in-command, Field Marshal Daun, were at loggerheads over strategy. Daun advocated a defensive posture as usual. He urged that they await Friedrich's onslaught at the fortifications at Breslau. Count Giovan Serbelloni supported this strategy as "necessary and to good purpose."[45] Arguing for the aggressive alternative was the cavalry general Count Joseph Lucchesi. He claimed it would be unworthy of Austria's victorious arms to remain rooted to the spot and fail to exploit the advantage of having "five matadors and one bull." A pitched battle under such circumstances would supposedly decide not just the campaign but the war itself and assure "undying glory" for the empire.[46] Prince Karl considered it unbecoming to cower in a secure position expecting an attack by the "Potsdam guards on parade," as the Austrians derisively referred to Prussian grenadiers.

Lorraine proposed deploying the army just beyond the marshy countryside cut by narrow rivers and underbrush west of Breslau. During late autumn, the terrain could only be negotiated via bridges and by controlling them the Austrians could bar Friedrich's access to Silesia. The Prussian army would be unable to bivouac in tents during a late season campaign as the weather deteriorates. Beyond this argument, there was a less apparent but equally compelling motive to advance. The prince was under pressure from Vienna to get results. His brother the emperor had written him in late September, "I shudder for your honor. You yourself can judge the effect it will have on the whole world if this little Prussian army keeps finding the means to slip away from you, especially after it has so frequently and for such extended periods of time stood nearby without you being able to beat it."[47] He advised Prince Karl that some of Austria's allies are not comfortable with the idea of a total defeat of Prussia. It would therefore be prudent to take the field with forces on hand and vanquish the Prussians soon.

It seems surprising that the prince, already bested in battle by Friedrich several times, was anxious to seek a confrontation. Daun and Serbelloni remained vocal in their opposition to the plan. Napoleon said that an army is better off led by one bad general than by two good ones who quarrel. Daun and Prince Karl were not particularly good generals to begin with. The chronic discord and personality clash infecting them over the last few months had escalated to mutual hatred. Daun was subordinate to Lorraine even though he had beaten Friedrich

at Kolin and Lorraine had lost every battle against the Prussian king. The reputation of their adversary unsettled the Austrian soldiers. A survivor later wrote a
friend that shortly before the battle, the troops were ready to turn away "because
they had heard that the king is coming, whose name was much more fearsome
than a small army… The army of the Prince of Bevern had gone and joined him
and although we were 80,000 men strong, our hearts trembled before the enemy
purely because the king was there. The fear was not of the king's army, but of the
king alone."[48]

The Grand Maneuver

The Prussian army struck camp early on December 04. The first objective was
Neumarkt, two-and-a-half miles east of Parchwitz. Friedrich rode with the
hussars at the head of the *avant garde* (advance guard). The guard consisted
of 60 squadrons of dragoons and hussars, two *Jäger* (rifle) companies and the
Le Noble, Kalben and Angelelli *Freibataillone* (independent battalions). These
battalions were light troops not attached to a regiment. There were 14 of them in
the Prussian army. They had special tasks such as surprise assaults and reconnaissance missions. They could fight as either infantry, dragoons or hussars and
were equipped with field guns. Friedrich instituted them during the first Silesian
war. The army followed the *avant garde* in parallel columns. Friedrich received
a report along the way that Neumarkt is occupied by Croation troops awaiting
the arrival of the entire Austrian army. He decided to take the town because
the higher ground there was an advantageous defensive position. The Austrian
command expected the Prussians to move against either Neumarkt or Liegnitz,
but underestimated the swiftness of their advance.

　　Defenses at Neumarkt were inadequate. The king's hussars forced the gate that
evening and stampeded into town at full gallop. The 25-year-old Friedrich Eugen
von Württemberg, one of the Prussian army's most talented cavalry officers, led
the charge. The surprised garrison lost over a hundred men killed and nearly 600
taken prisoner plus forfeited a cannon. The Prussians had 22 casualties. The prize
was capture of an Austrian field bakery yielding 80,000 portions of freshly baked
bread. The presence of the large bakery forewarned Friedrich that the enemy's
destination is Neumarkt. At eight o'clock in the evening, confirmation came
that Prince Karl has struck camp at Breslau and shifted his army west. This was
welcome news to Friedrich. He boasted to the young Prince Franz of Brunswick,
"the fox has crawled from his hole, now I'll punish his bravado!"[49] The king sent
the advance guard under Württemberg half a mile east to watch the approach.
Friedrich Eugen's elder brother, Karl Eugen von Württemberg, served in the
Austrian army and would fight on the opposite side at Leuthen.

　　The Prussian army bivouacked in and around Neumarkt. The men were
satiated thanks to the captured bakery's supplement to their rations. After
spending the night on snow-covered ground, the soldiers broke camp at 4:00
a.m. It was December 05, 1757. Before dawn, an officer's patrol spotted enemy

horsemen north of Lampersdorf and heard what sounded like a large body of troops approaching. In the early morning light, the officers made out a line of cavalry, vaguely discernable in the mist, on elevated ground west of Borna. They assumed it to be the flank of the Austrian army. Closer reconnaissance revealed that it was an advance guard of Saxon *Chevaux-legers* consisting of the Prinz Albrecht, Graf Brühl and Prinz Karl Regiments and two of imperial hussars. Its commander, Count Georg Ludwig von Nostitz, had orders to reinforce the dangerously exposed garrison at Neumarkt, protect the bakery and observe the enemy. The instructions were of course no longer relevant. Prussian scouts reported to the king that Croatian foot soldiers are in the woods at Borna hill and around Lampersdorf.

Friedrich moved six infantry battalions forward and the Croatians withdrew. At the same time, he ordered a full-scale cavalry attack against Nostitz. The Austrian high command had sent his corps three quarters of a mile too forward without infantry support. Prussian hussars struck at around 9:00 a.m. They captured eleven officers and 540 rankers and drove the rest back to the Austrian front. Prussian officers managed with considerable effort to restrain their own riders, who had galloped to within artillery range of the main enemy position,

Friedrich directs his army during the battle of Leuthen from atop a knoll. The hills around Leuthen are not nearly as high as depicted in this period illustration.

from charging right into it. Still with the advance guard, Friedrich gathered 50 hussars as an escort. He told their officer, "Don't leave my side and make sure I don't fall into the hands of these rascals. If I die, cover the body with your coat and fetch a wagon. Lay my body in the cart and say not a word about it. The battle must go on and the enemy will be beaten."[50] The king then rode on to the slightly higher plain at Gross-Heidau, a hamlet east of Borna. He mounted the Schönberg rise together with his generals and adjutants. From here he surveyed the Austrian battle line. The Prussian army followed in four parallel columns in order to mass quickly upon reaching the combat zone.

At Gross-Heidau, Friedrich decided how to deploy his regiments. He followed a formula battle plan conceived after the second Silesian war. At that time, he prepared his *General Principles of Warfare* for field engagements and had copies printed and distributed to his generals. Recipients were under orders not to take the manual on campaigns (in 1760, two copies would nevertheless fall into Austrian hands). Friedrich's maxim was, "If you strike the enemy in his flank and proceed to totally smash that wing, the battle is already won." Explaining a sketch that he rendered for the manual, "You can see how I reinforce my right wing, from where I want to carry out my main attack. My left wing is only there to hold the foe in check while all my forces fight on the right. I place the infantry in front. It must outflank the enemy and open fire obliquely on his cavalry. Then my own cavalry will attack. Victory will be assured before the infantry comes to grips with the enemy. The general who sees this successfully develop can then boldly bring forward the entire infantry of the right wing to strike the enemy infantry in the flank and if possible, circumvent it… The whole system depends on the swiftness of the maneuver and on attacking no matter what. It cannot be stressed enough that the flank is the weak link of an army."[51]

Prince Karl's troops encamped two-and-a-quarter miles east of Neumarkt. The prince had expected a surprise attack and kept his men under arms all night. He moved the army from its encampment to a position 1,500 paces closer to the foe and from there witnessed the rout of Nostitz's cavalry. Anticipating that the Prussians will assail the right wing of his army near Nypern, he placed five cavalry regiments there with eight infantry battalions in reserve. Grouped into four batteries, some of his artillery—understrength given the size of the army— guarded the northern flank as well. Daun arrayed the troops along a defensive front he kept gradually extending until it became too long to shift reserves to threatened sectors in a timely and orderly manner. According to Prussian artillery officer Carl von Decker, "The enemy position… was highly unusual and dispensed with practically all tactical symmetry. A jumble of infantry and cavalry, some in the first and some in the second battle line, a few individual squadrons interspersed between both infantry lines, all in all appearing to have no tactical cohesion as though joined together by accident."[52]

The Austrian cavalry captain Jacob de Cogniazo maintained, "The eye of the casual observer would have been in awe to see a line of well-armed warriors drawn up from Nypern down to the Weistritz River, a stretch more than a German mile long. To Friedrich's experienced eye however, this disproportionately elongated body made a completely different impression: He saw immediately how easy it will be to topple this colossus if he manages to undermine one of its flanks."[53] Commanding an army of 84 battalions and 144 cavalry squadrons, Prince Karl felt safe enough to leave a third of the 320 cannons available to the army behind in Breslau.[54] On the front at Leuthen, "there could be no objection to the distribution of the Austrian artillery; it conformed to conventional practice," maintained Decker. "But the cardinal mistake was that it was too weak for such an enormously extended position. This was no fault of the artillerymen, but that of the field marshal."[55]

From the panorama atop Schönberg knoll, little escaped Friedrich's scrutiny. The Zettelbusch woods mostly obscured the enemy's right wing from his view, but also revealed the difficulties such terrain present to an attacker. The king dispatched scouts to patrol the Striegauer Creek in front of the Austrian position to the north to gain more accurate intelligence. The rest of Prince Karl's battle line was visible. Its center was strong enough to resist an assault. Less reliable troops from Bavaria and Württemberg held the Austrian left wing and the topography presented few natural obstacles. The ground was hardened from frost, facilitating troop movement. Friedrich was familiar with the countryside. His army had conducted peacetime war games there. His principle was, "My first priority is choosing my ground and the second is the battle plan itself."[56] While the field retains fixed characteristics, operations are under the influence of such variables as enemy action, weather, delayed reinforcements, miscommunication and so forth. The 19th-Century Field Marshal Helmuth von Moltke stated, "Strategy is a system of improvisation."[57]

In his own chronicle of the Seven Years War, Friedrich described his initial impression of the enemy deployment: "The first look at this position revealed from its topography that the main thrust should be directed at the left wing of the enemy. The wing was poorly arranged for defense, crossing the Kiefenberg at the village of Sagschütz. Were this position taken by storm we would have the advantage of terrain for the rest of the battle, since from there it slopes downward more and more steeply toward Nypern. Were we to move against the center instead, the Austrian right wing could fall upon an attacker in the flank through the Zettelbusch. Our only option was therefore to launch an attack on the Kiefenberg, because it controls the entire plain. This would spare the troops the worst difficulties; otherwise, exhausted from the fighting, they would no longer have been capable of great exertions."[58] The king followed the recipe set forth in his *General Principles* which had led to victory at Rossbach.

Having quickly formulated the battle plan, Friedrich ordered the army forward. He had the Saxon prisoners taken during the skirmish east of Neumarkt led past the advancing infantry columns to encourage his men. This was scarcely necessary, as the 19-year-old Prussian infantryman Georg Tempelhoff attested:

"One could see in the eyes of our valiant and resolute troops that they impatient-ly awaited the moment to come to grips with the enemy."[59] Forty-three cavalry squdrons of the Prussian *avant garde* formed up a thousand paces east of Borna. Two following columns of the main army passed north of the village. They slowly advanced toward the Austrian position. The other two columns crossed through and to the south of Borna. The king therefore feigned a direct attack against the Austrian right north of Frobelwitz, a town in approximately the center of Prince Karl's battle line. He and Daun observed the Prussian movement from the *Windmühlenberg* (windmill hill). The elevation is beside Leuthen near the southern end of the Austrian perimeter. Friedrich's massive cavalry charge against Nostitz's Saxons east of Borna and the Prussian infantry's movement persuaded Karl that his right wing is the enemy objective. Count Lucchesi, who was in command there, requested reinforcements.

Daun contradicted the prince. This was characteristic of the habitual differ-ence of opinion between them. He contended that Friedrich will not strike the Austrian right. The French brigadier Count Antoine-Marie Montazet agreed. He bluntly told Prince Karl that "because of the swamps, lakes and ditches in that area, only an army of snipes could cross it."[60] Unconvinced, Karl sent the entire reserve corps to the right wing. It occupied Nypern with three battalions and deployed the remaining five southeast of the village. The prince ordered Count Serbelloni, another of his critics, to lead most of the cavalry at a canter to support Lucchesi as well. The Austrian supreme command weighed the option of using this concentration on its north wing to *attack* the Prussians, but dropped the idea. The Welsh officer and eyewitness Henry Lloyd remarked, "It seemed as though they lost all sense upon receiving news of the king's advance. They stood there stiffly and without a thought, with no idea of whether they should move forward or fall back."[61]

Heinrich von Berenhorst, who served on Friedrich's staff, confirmed that "every notion of launching a determined attack escaped the senior Austrian generals. They carefully arranged their army across an immeasurable expanse like a slender thread, no differently than as though it were a matter of guarding sprouts or a field against foraging animals. There was a nervous tugging from one end to the other that reacted to every feint, to every trick of the enemy. All these movements unsettled their own troops, who gave in to anxiety. In a word, never have commanding officers more tellingly prepared their own subordinates for defeat."[62] Friedrich contributed to his adversary's confusion when he ordered the army to halt just after the lead units passed Borna. At 10:30 a.m., the troops wheeled 90 degrees to the right and resumed the march, now heading due south and parallel to the Austrian front. The two columns that had crossed north of the town reformed into one as its regiments made the turn. The pair that had traversed through Borna and to its south combined into a second column.

Six infantry battalions of the advance guard took point on the right-hand column and three battalions under General Karl Henrich von Wedell led the

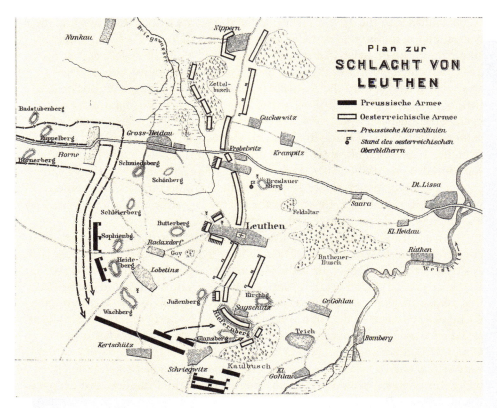

The map depicts the maneuver of the Prussian infantry to strike the left flank of the Austrian line. The small flag beside Breslauer Berg indicates where Prince Karl and Daun observed the battle.

left. The heavy artillery, grouped into five batteries, came behind Wedell and the ammunition wagons marched between the infantry columns. Forty cavalry squadrons under General Georg von Driesen brought up the rear. To partially screen the army from view, the king and Prince Moritz von Dessau rode south atop higher ground between the army and the Austrian line at the head of 25 squadrons of hussars. As rifleman Tempelhoff described, "The heads of the columns were always at the same height and kept the distance apart necessary to draw up for battle. The platoons maintained their intervals as precisely as though on review. In this way the army could deploy for action at the greatest speed."[63] While the main force marched south, Friedrich maintained the illusion of a planned assault against the Austrian right by stationing the three *Freibataillone* and two companies of *Fussjäger*, riflemen trained to fight in loose order, near Gross-Heidau.

The weather that dreary December morning was darkly overcast and hazy, perfect for concealing the Prussian maneuver from the enemy. The columns defiled south behind the Schmiedeberg, Schleierberg and Sophienberg hills. This made monitoring their movement even more difficult for the Austrians. The terrain around Leuthen is dotted with gentle rises just high enough to shift formations behind them without observation. It was apparent to the Austrian command however, that the advance had stopped. Prussian hussars screening the flank revealed the new march direction. Earlier, the king had withdrawn the squadrons that defeated Nostitz's *Chevaux-legers*. So far, he had undertaken nothing to test the Austrian defenses. These circumstances, together with the Prussian army's abrupt shift in direction and the fact that few hours of daylight remain, persuaded Lorraine and his staff that Friedrich is retiring. "The good people are leaving," opined Daun. "We should let them go in peace!"[64] The generals speculated that the king might try to circumvent their front to cut them off from Bohemia. The men in the front ranks saw things differently.

An Austrian officer recalled, "It was toward midday around twelve o'clock when General Count von Puebla, who had been in position with the first line of infantry on the left wing, rode up to the corps of officers gathered at the Leuthen windmill. He had been watching the enemy movement for a long time. 'What do you think gentlemen,' asked Puebla, 'where the main attack of the Prussians might take place, although I very much doubt that they want to take us on today?' The officers smiled at one another and said nothing. Only one among them, an older grenadier lieutenant who had almost as many scars as the number of battles he had fought in, an honorable but blunt man cut from the old cloth, ventured to answer his excellency: 'General sir, I much fear that we're letting our guard down. The Prussian attack against our left flank is no secret. Every lad you've positioned at this spot will tell you that those people there are going to outflank us.' 'Bah!' mocked Puebla angrily, 'You don't understand anything!' The officer replied, 'God hope that I don't understand. But if death leads the Prussians into our flank and rear, then we can cry out in amazement in the usual way, I never would have believed it!' Puebla gruffly turned away with his Neapolitans."[65]

Friedrich's troops marched at a brisk pace. The advance guard reached the initial destination, Lobetinz, at around noon. Here the army executed a second maneuver. The formations wheeled left and hastily advanced east toward the village of Schriegwitz at the southern tip of the Austrian deployment. As the columns bypassed the enemy position, the troops now formed an extended phalanx opposite the Achilles heel of Prince Karl's army. The Prussians turned north: Zieten's cavalry drew up on the right side of Schriegwitz, the infantry to the left. Wedell's three battalions stood in front of the village poised to lead the assault. The 25 squadrons of hussars that had screened the march south together with dragoons under Eugen von Württemberg deployed at the center of the second line in reserve. The turn east and forced march required half an hour, plus another 30 minutes to array the troops for action. By 1:00 p.m., the army was ready. Friedrich knew that it would not be possible to disguise his intention once the columns turn east. He relied on the speed of the operation to maintain an element of surprise.

"Changing direction makes staying in formation difficult," wrote a former German general. "This complicated maneuver was not planned or even discussed in advance. It therefore had to be guided by dozens of orders, all issued by the king in a timely manner, passed down the chain of command, understood correctly and properly carried out. The success of such a maneuver, close to enemy lines and in unfamiliar terrain, requires conscientious training, precise orders, mindfulness of everyone involved and discipline… Only in this way could the Prussians, after a complex cross-country march and sudden left turn, stand in battle order at the designated place."[66] Even after the Prussian army swung left toward Schriegwitz, Prince Karl did not react. "An absolutely remarkable indecisiveness and helplessness dominated the Austrian senior command," concluded a 1901 analysis.[67]

In charge of the left wing was General Franz von Nádasdy. He recognized Friedrich's purpose and sent pleas for reinforcements which Karl, who disbelieved Nádasdy's assessment, ignored. A farmer from Frobelwitz who tarried near Prince Karl and his staff testified that in the course of an hour, Nádasdy sent ten messengers requesting additional troops to no avail. When the prince and his staff finally believed Nádasdy and countermanded the orders that had shifted their reserves to Lucchesi on the right flank, it was too late. The new orders "naturally resulted in indescribable confusion, as the troops were frantically driven from one end to the other of a formation that was extended too far."[68]

The Onslaught

Four hours of daylight remained when the Prussian army assaulted Kiefernberg hill at Sagschütz. Both battalions of the elite Itzenplitz Infantry Regiment and the Meyerinck Infantry Regiment 26 formed the spearhead of Friedrich's attack. Generations later, the German army adopted the decorative tress adorning the Meyerinck uniform as collar insignia for generals. While the artillery was getting into position to support the advance, Friedrich appeared before Wedell's spearhead. Ernst von Barsewisch, a corporal in the Meyerinck Regiment, described what followed: "After his majesty the king carefully reconnoitered this enemy position from a slight hill out of range of the enemy, he gave orders before the army began moving forward to shift further to the right. We marched quickly against the enemy left wing and as soon as we in the *avant garde* saw it from higher ground, we received the order to advance. The army marched behind this hill in three echelons… When we went over this rise in the direction of the village of Leuthen, we could see the entire imperial position and its combat deployment from one wing to the other. His majesty the king paused at this rise and said to our commander, Lieutenant Colonel (Johann Friedrich) von Bock, 'March with your battalion straight toward that barricade where the white coats are dug in. The other battalions will follow your lead.'

"Here it should be mentioned that our regiment was on the right flank of the *avant garde* and the von Itzenplitz battalion was on the left flank of these three battalions. Then his majesty was so gracious and came to me and von Unruh, the *Frey Corporal* (independent corporal) marching with the standard, and said, 'You sir, of the honor company, are to march on those fortifications. But you must not advance too quickly, so that the army can follow.' Then the king turned to the soldiers of the battalion: 'Lads, see those white tunics over there? You're to chase them out of that bastion! You'll have to rush them to drive them out with the bayonet. I'll be supporting you with five grenadier battalions and the whole army. Here we conquer or die; before you is the enemy and behind you our whole army, so you cannot go backward and can only go forward as conquerors.'"[69] Prince Moritz rode up to the king to remind him to start the attack before the Austrians reinforce their vulnerable flank. Friedrich gave the order. He himself observed the operation from Wachberg knoll south of Lobetinz.

The Itzenplitz and Meyerinck infantry pushed forward toward Sagschütz with the grenadiers following 100 paces behind. *Brummer* siege guns supported the assault to the left of the battalions. The crews fired over the infantrymen's heads. The king had sent stragglers and survivors of Bevern's corps who had escaped Austrian captivity and returned to the army to the heavy artillery. These men together with cavalry recruits provided extra manpower to help position and operate the guns. "They were handled superbly," assessed the official Prussian army chronicle of the engagement, "even though unmounted cavalrymen pulled duty here, who had to be assigned out of a shortage of genuine artillerymen." Decker maintained that "schooled gunners are not absolutely necessary as long as the equipment and the team of horses is sound and the officers and NCOs are trained in tactics and in the function of the weapon."[70]

Friedrich ordered the infantry to keep shifting to the right toward Keifernberg as it advanced. This was to gradually circumvent the Austrians and provide a field of fire for the *Brummers*. Barsewisch wrote, "Scarcely anything more splendid in the world can be imagined than the view from this small hill: Before us the entire imperial army more in scope than the eye can measure, and behind us, front toward the enemy, the whole Prussian army in battle order. Our army advanced with bands playing as though on parade. The order was as superb as at an inspection in Berlin as the army moved under the gaze of its great monarch… As soon as the command to march was given I advanced directly toward the barricade. The left wing of our three battalions held back a little at this time, so that we could not be outflanked by the enemy cannons. The enemy stood calmly and did not seriously disrupt our military formation until we were some 200 paces from him. Here it should be mentioned that during the advance, his majesty sent an adjutant forward several times to tell us we should not advance so quickly, but very slowly. Our soldiers would have preferred attacking the enemy at a run. Our Lieutenant Commander von Bock and the other battalion commanders had their hands full holding the troops

The Prussian infantry takes fire advancing on Leuthen. Officers wore different uniforms than the rankers. This made them targets for enemy marksmen, but helped soldiers recognize their superiors amid clouds of smoke and the tumult of combat.

back from advancing too fast. They urged us with good words but also in part by force."[71]

To delay the Prussian advance, Nádasdy mustered 43 cavalry squadrons for a counterattack. He struck Zieten's horsemen on the right wing of the Prussian line while Wedell's three infantry battalions moved against the Austrian fortifications. Zieten's riders were in unfavorable terrain and had no time to fan out to meet the charge. The king however, had positioned the remaining six battalions of the Prussian advance guard to cover the cavalry's flank. These troops promptly greeted Nádasdy's sortie with a barrage of musket and case-shot fire. The Austrian squadrons fell back to regroup. The Itzenplitz and Meyerinck infantry crossed two ditches, volley fired once and stormed the defenses with the bayonet. Holding the line in a spruce grove were three regiments of Württemberg grenadiers with six light field guns. Six thousand of these Swabian troops had reached the combat zone toward midnight the night before. Their chief of staff had searched everywhere for Prince Karl and Daun without success. As a result, the regiments had no orders. The men had neither tents, straw nor wood for campfires. They had rested on the open ground throughout the frosty December night. The Austrians provided no food for them.

Lorraine did not consider the Swabians reliable. They were Protestants like the enemy and the brother of the Duke of Württemberg, Friedrich Eugen, was known to be in the Prussian army. Less than two weeks before, Prince Karl had received a letter from the emperor warning, "I've been told that practically all officers of the Württemberg corps are favorably disposed toward Prussia; I think that you should be careful with this corps and never place it in the line where it could create confusion. In addition, you must monitor the correspondence of the officers and also watch over their contact with captured Prussians."[72] The supply of ammunition the Austrians issued the Württemberg regiments was insufficient for a prolonged defense. Nádasdy nonetheless did not share have a negative opinion of these troops. He had seen the Württembergers fight at Rossbach and was impressed with their courage and prowess. Contrary to Prince Karl's recommendation, he positioned them in the front line to defend Kiefernberg against Wedell.

At a range of 700 paces, the defenders opened fire with their six cannons at Prussian Battery Number 1 as its gunners detached their weapons from their carriages and prepared for action. Not a single Prussian artilleryman was wounded during the barrage. The Württemberg infantry resisted but the Prussians, enjoying superiority in firepower, drove it from the grove. The Prussian infantry charged so swiftly that the defenders barely managed to fire two salvos before being overwhelmed. The Württemberg Roeder Fusilier Regiment lost eight officers and over 200 men.[73] To the right, Prince Moritz's six remaining battalions of the Prussian advance guard fired a few salvoes and forced back two Hungarian battalions beside the spruce grove. Prussian artillery continued to fire case-shot at the Württembergers as they retreated from Kiefernberg. The ten *Brummer* cannons brought from Glogau significantly contributed to the outcome. The battery disabled two Austrian guns right after opening fire. A Prussian artillery officer recalled, "The Austrians, who were exposed to *Brummer* projectiles for the first time this day, appeared inclined to consider their enemy barbarians who have violated international law. The prisoners bitterly reproached the Prussian gunners for making use of this cannon. To them it was a hell threatening to consume everything and fired on them before they could even see the Prussians."[74]

Screened by light infantry, the Austrians belatedly lugged a battery of 14 guns to the Kirchberg rise northeast of Sagschütz to bombard the attackers. This became a rallying point for Nádasdy's retreating units. Wedell prepared to assail the hastily improvised position, this time without support from the redoubtable *Brummers*. Crews attempting to move the heavy guns through a hollow in front of the elevation became bogged down in the sodden ground or in ditches. Since his advance guard had continuously shifted right during the advance, Wedell stood practically in the defenders' rear as they fell back. In tight formation, his battalions repulsed two more sorties by Austrian dragoons, whose riders again demonstrated their mettle against unfavorable odds. Survivors of the Württemberg battalions now atop Kiefernberg provided covering fire for the second line of defense. Wedell received reinforcements as well; led by Moritz, the Kremzow Battalion detached itself from the six battalions of the Prussian advance guard on the right and covered the attack. To strengthen the defense, Daun rushed brigade after brigade into battle. His operation was so hastily executed that three regiments left their artillery behind.

The 14 Austrian cannons atop Kirchberg were so close to the action that the gunners could not fire without hitting their retreating comrades of the infantry. The Prussians stormed the elevation and took it in less than 15 minutes. They captured the enemy battery. The advance was so rapid that Friedrich dispatched another adjutant to admonish Wedell not to proceed too far ahead of the main army. Nádasdy tenaciously established another line along the Gohlau ditch some thousand paces further back. Most of the troops occupying it had not yet been under fire; they had been forced to fall back to avoid being outflanked by the Prussians. All six battalions of the Prussian advance guard that had stood on the right now joined Wedell's three to converge on the freshly improvised enemy perimeter. Without artillery, the Austrians began to retire in disorder toward Leuthen shortly after the attack began. Coming from Nypern at *Doubliermarsch* (on the double), their reserves arrived mostly out of breath and had to form battle lines under concentrated Prussian fire.

Gaining momentum, the Prussian infantry marched toward them in parade formation, discharging volley after volley as it advanced. Steadily shifting right, the *avant garde* had bypassed the Austrian left and formed a hook that outflanked it. The *Brummer* battery was soon back in business. Its personnel had laboriously hauled the guns to higher ground. They raked the length of the enemy line. The bombardment disrupted deployment of Daun's new arrivals. The Austrian position was overcrowded and individual units, exposed to the merciless barrage, were unable to maneuver. The soldiers were more confused than frightened. They simply did not know where to form up and make a stand. The Prussians positioned a battery on Judenberg hill, some 800 paces from the Austrian line. It bombarded the retreating Palffy, Haller and Macquire Regiments. The southern wing of Prince Karl's army was smashed. Ten Prussian battalions and 43 cavalry squadrons, together with the artillery 8,000 men in all, had overwhelmed Nádasdy's corps of 26,000.[75] Austrian reserves continued to pour in.

Prince Karl Joseph von Ligne, a 22-year-old captain in an Austrian regiment commanded by his father, described the chaos: "They clamored for the reserve and that it should march up as quickly as possible. We ran forward as fast as we could. We lost my lieutenant colonel right at the beginning; I also lost my major and all officers but three, beyond eleven or twelve volunteers or cadets. We were soon across two ditches in an orchard to the left of Leuthen's houses and began to form up in front of the village. But we could not hold out. Beyond a scarcely imaginable cannonade, case-shot rained on the battalion that I now command-ed since a colonel was no longer on hand. At a distance of 80 paces the third battalion of the Prussian king's guard, which had already bypassed several of our regiments while they were mustering, began firing at us most vigorously. It stood as though at drill and waited for us without a stir.

"The Andlau Regiment on my right could not form up properly because of the houses. It stood 30 men deep behind me and from time to time fired and hit us in the back. The Mercy Regiment to my left took to its heels and this I found preferable. I could not get Bathiany's dragoons who stood 50 paces behind us to punch their way in and get me out of this dangerous spot. My soldiers were worn out from running forward and had no cannons; these had been left behind out of distress or intentionally. My men were scattered about. Their numbers were dwindling and they fought on out of pure frustration. Honor more than personal welfare motivated us so we did not run away. An ensign from Arberg helped me for a while to form a line from his and my remnants, then he was shot dead. Two grenadier officers led the troops to me that they still had.

"As soon as I had gathered their men and what was left of my valiant battal-ion along with some Hungarians who fortunately came back, all in all at most 200 men, I withdrew to the heights by the mill."[76] During the clash, Prince Karl attempted to shift the original battle line from front west to south incorporating Leuthen into the perimeter. Historian Martin Lezius stated, "This was an extraor-dinarily difficult movement given the troops' level of experience in maneuver, especially in great haste and in part carried out in the wrong formation. It was se-riously impeded by refugees from the battle streaming back. In addition, the sight of the irresistibly advancing Prussian army certain of victory and its artillery fire were not exactly suited to elevate the confidence of the imperial troops."[77]

After the unsuccessful sortie against Wedell's flank, only two of Nádasdy's cavalry regiments were at Leuthen. Most squadrons had withdrawn east to the wooded bank of the Westritz River. Here they fought seesaw skirmishes with Zieten's riders. The Austrians received support from infantry units sent by Daun and from cannons skillfully sited in terrain deeply etched with crevices and spotted with underbrush. Zieten was familiar with the area; he had participated in maneuvers there in 1754. His superior numbers determined the outcome. The Prussian cuirassier regiments *Gensd'armes* and *Garde du corps* routed the Jung-Modena Dragoon Regiment which lost half its men in the melee. The Austrians had five or six cuirassier and 16 to 18 dragoon squadrons left. They faced Zieten's 23 cuirassier and 20 dragoon squadrons. The Prussians put the enemy infantry to flight and took 2,000 prisoners. Although the Austrian horsemen were too few to reverse the day's fortunes, their tireless counterattacks prevented the Prussians from extending their hook against Nádasdy's left wing. Friedrich's troops could not advance far enough to block the retreat of the Austrian foot regiments. The official Prussian chronicle noted, "This cavalry held out as long as it could, until it was too sorely harassed by our heavy cannons and pulled back in confusion."[78]

Most of the haphazardly directed infantry units sent from the right wing by Daun gravitated toward the center of the combat zone. They intermingled with soldiers driven back by the Prussians. The Austrians jammed together behind Leuthen 30 to 100 men deep in some places, especially near the windmill hill. With such a concentration, superior numbers were of no advantage. Prussian infantry battalions advanced to within musket range of the town. Together with the artillery, their volleys thwarted the defenders' attempts to prepare breast-works and impromptu fortifications. The Austrians moved three batteries onto a gentle rise west of Leuthen beside the windmill. "The defenders could do nothing worse than concentrate more or less all of their artillery in one place… this left the entire remaining line without artillery," observed Decker.[79] The Prussian guns, by contrast, were evenly distributed. The Austrian command deployed grenadier companies that had originally stood on the northern flank behind Leuthen beside the windmill with the guns. Leuthen itself was weakly garrisoned. Stragglers from retreating formations sought refuge behind the wall surrounding the Catholic church in the center of town. Here the Austrians would make their next stand.

Friedrich remained close enough to the action to personally observe developments. He moved with his staff from Wachberg knoll to a small wood on high ground northeast of Radaxdorf. There he was exposed to fire from cannons on the right wing of the Austrian line bombarding the division commanded by his brother Prince Ferdinand. Unaware that the king was in the crossfire, the prince replied to the cannonade in kind until a messenger instructed him to stop firing while the king seeks a new observation point. An officer present wrote a comrade that night, "The king was constantly under heavy fire; it was not possible to hold him back, although I made every conscious effort to do so."[80] Friedrich's adjutant Franz von Wobersnow reported, "His Majesty the king exposed himself most extraordinarily in this battle, in that he was constantly riding between the lines and often risked being hit by his own cannons."[81] The Prussian artillery played a major role in the next phase of the battle, the assault on Leuthen itself. The village was not well fortified. The Austrian reserves were drawn up for the most part on its eastern side. Their attempts to form a cohesive firing line were incessantly disrupted by Prussian volley fire.

Trained to advance across open terrain in extended rows three to four men deep, the Prussian line infantry had little experience in street fighting. Villages represented a precarious obstacle to men accustomed to functioning as an entity marching, firing and bayonet-charging on command. Austrian grenadiers, together with Hungarian irregulars who had been stationed in Leuthen for days and were familiar with its layout, formed the backbone of the defense. The Austrian Roth-Würzburg Regiment held the church garden and cemetery. A massive brick wall with firing loopholes and turrets projecting from the corners surrounded the religious complex. The battalion had also fortified it with cannons. The garrison was not numerous however, and the Prussians again

Austrian troops man the wall of Leuthen's Catholic church to repel the assault by the third battalion of Infantry Regiment 15 as the battle approaches a crescendo. It was scarcely possible for Prussian line infantry to stay in formation when coming to grips with the enemy.

enjoyed superiority in artillery. The weight of the Prussian attack fell on the right with fire support from the opposite flank and following line. The second and third battalions of the guard regiment and the Retzow, Pannewitz and Münchow Battalions opened the assault at around 3:30 in the afternoon.

Greeted by murderous defensive fire, the attackers repeatedly stormed the walls without success. The commander of the third guard battalion of Infantry Regiment 15 froze in helplessness. The young Captain Wichard von Möllendorff impatiently brushed him aside and managed with a few grenadiers to chop through the western gate with axes and rifle butts. They fought their way through the breach and engaged the enemy holding the church cemetery. Among the Prussians who fell during the frantic charge was Premier Lieutenant Warkotsch, Leuthen's principal landowner. At almost the same time, battalion cannons blasted a hole in the south wall. This enabled the Prussians to pour into the complex from here as well. Bitter hand-to-hand combat followed. It ended with the defenders overwhelmed. The Austrian Roth-Würzburg Regiment was virtually annihilated; but 260 remained fit for action out of an original roster of 1,800 men.[82] After the church was taken, the Austrians still in Leuthen resisted for half an hour before abandoning the town.

During the battle, the left side of the Prussian line became engaged in a sustained artillery and musket duel with the enemy on *Windmühlenberg* hill, which was three to four hundred paces north of Leuthen. The initial barrage took the advancing Prussians by surprise. Six battalions fell back to seek cover despite the efforts of their officers to maintain formation. The son of General Wolf Friedrich von Retzow, a lieutenant and adjutant, led a single remaining reserve battalion—the rest were marching to support the assault on Leuthen—into the line to rally the troops and restore order. Austrian grenadiers conducted sorties from the windmill rise to try to keep the Prussians off balance. Friedrich observed the pressure on his soldiers. He ordered heavy batteries transferred to the southeastern slope of Butterberg, a hillock immediately west of Leuthen, with the *Brummer* battery to follow. The guns pounded the Austrian position and relieved the beleaguered troops below. Once again, the king's close proximity to the action gave him a decided advantage over his adversaries; Daun and Lorraine relied on messengers to report developments before formulating orders.

The Prussian battalions that captured Leuthen prepared for the next objective. Daun formed a sporadic defensive line north of the village. The Austrian troops were deeply echeloned and among them were fresh regiments including the grenadier corps. The massive host initially outnumbered Friedrich's fatigued formations in the front line, but the Prussians soon brought up sufficient reserves to balance the parity. The commander of the six advance guard battalions that had covered the Prussian right flank rode into Leuthen to survey the troops. Corporal Barsewisch recorded that since the men of his battalion had depleted their ammunition, "they had to hold up in the village in order to be safe from enemy cavalry nearby. As soon as Prince Moritz formed up his grenadiers he called to our soldiers, 'Boys, that's honor enough! Fall back to the second echelon.' But our lads answered, 'We'd be shirkers if we go into the second line. Get us more cartridges!'"[83] Casualties suffered from the fighting and gradual lengthening of the Prussian right wing left gaps in the line. These were plugged by fresh troops from the second echelon and by those transferred from the left wing who had been under fire from the windmill heights.

It required half an hour for the Prussians to regroup after taking Leuthen. The infantry received fresh ammunition and rested troops moved up to join the first wave. By now it was nearly four in the afternoon and daylight was waning. As they marched forward, the advance shifted from an outflanking maneuver to a frontal assault. Under heavy defensive fire, the Prussian infantry crossed a deep trench along the northern outskirts of the village. The entire advance guard took part and in many places the attackers outgunned the defenders. The Austrians resisted doggedly, but gave ground except for the Baden-Durlach and Wallis Regiments holding the *Windmühlenberg*. The king transferred a battery from the center of the line to support the assault there but the attack stalled. The proximity of nightfall, which would enhance Austrian chances of an orderly withdrawal, threatened to deprive Friedrich of the opportunity to exploit the victory. So far, the infantry had borne the brunt of the fighting on both sides.

Far from the action with his cavalry northeast of Gross-Heidau, Count Lucchesi observed the progress of Friedrich's infantry against the Austrian right north of Leuthen. It appeared that the Prussians had denuded their left wing of troops and were therefore vulnerable to a flank attack. Neglecting reconnaissance, Lucchesi mustered his squadrons under for a charge. Prussian scouts spotted his intention and immediately reported their observations to Friedrich. The king had ordered General Driesen to cover the army's left flank with the cavalry of the rearguard. Driesen was an energetic officer who had led a brigade during the defense of Breslau two weeks earlier. From the Sophienberg, he too saw the Austrian riders form up. His own 40 squadrons, yet to see action that day, stood behind Radaxdorf roughly due west of Nádasdy's original line. They were screened from Lucchesi's view by the Schleierberg and Butterberg hills. The king's own record of the day's events states that he ordered Driesen to strike Lucchesi's force as it advanced.[84] Whether this is true or not, Driesen knew his job and would have taken the initiative independently. Friedrich ordered that the long-range *Brummer* siege guns be turned toward the enemy cavalry and open fire while it was preparing to charge.

Exploiting the hills as cover, Driesen led his horsemen north to head off Lucchesi before he could attack the Prussian infantry. As the Austrians approached, Driesen's riders wheeled east, scaled the high ground at Schleierberg and formed up to attack. With the sudden appearance of Prussian cavalry on their flank, the Austrians became aware of the peril that faced them; a consequence of no preliminary scouting. Driesen sent ten squadrons of Bayreuth dragoons galloping against Lucchesi's force. Fifteen squadrons of cuirassiers followed. Ten squadrons of hussars attacked the Austrians from behind. Zieten's cavalry joined the charge. Only a few of Lucchesi's horsemen attempted to form a line to meet the onslaught. Most retreated to seek refuge behind Austrian regiments fighting north of Leuthen. The rider cannot control his mount when the herd instinct takes over; the Austrian horses stampeded en masse into the infantry, which was already reeling from the withering fire of the advancing Prussian battalions. Driesen's pursuing squadrons plummeted headlong into the tumult. The Prussian cuirassiers furiously hacked down enemy horseman and foot soldier alike. Count Lucchesi met his death in action.

The Austrian infantry of the right wing had already begun to waver as the kinetic whirlwind of Prussian and Austrian cavalrymen rapidly drew nearer. In the ensuing panic, entire formations turned to flee and many soldiers discarded their rifles. The center and left of the Austrian line followed suit and broke as the Prussian battalions surged forward. The charging Prussians repeatedly shouted "hurrah!" and thwarted attempts by the defenders to reform by thrashing into them with bayonet and rifle butt. Austrian officers tried to establish a new battle line between Frobelwitz and Lissa without success. The Baden-Durlach and Wallis Regiments holding the windmill heights resisted until overrun by cuirassiers, General Carl Friedrich von Meyer's Bayreuth dragoons and the three *Freibataillone* led by Ludwig d'Angelelli. As testimony to the valor of the Austrians, only one officer and eight rankers of the Baden-Durlach

The *Leib-Kürassier* Regiment *Grosser Kurfürst attacks* Lucchesi's cavalry at the climax of the battle. The Prussian cavalry underwent rigorous training, which paid dividends at Rossbach and Leuthen.

Regiment were still standing at the end of the battle.[85] Most surviving defenders were captured.

At dusk, the Schenckendorff Grenadier Battalion took the Austrian battery atop the *Windmühlenberg* in a bayonet charge. The indefatigable Nádasdy managed to restore order to the left wing and collected a few battalions and cavalry squadrons to cover the retreat of the army. His Croatians occupied the crossings at Lissa and Rathen, as well as a bridge of boats spanning the Weistritz River. They held them open long enough for remnants of the Austrian army to escape into the darkness toward Breslau. They established a collection point here to reorganize the retiring troops. The Austrians later thanked their Croatian auxiliaries by blaming them for the defeat.[86]

The Aftermath

Leuthen began with Friedrich's surprise flank attack throwing the Austrians into consternation and leading to the annihilation of Nádasdy's corps. Prussian artillery then pulverized the enemy's second line of defense and left wing. Effectively supported by the guns, Prussian infantry stormed Leuthen and subsequently rolled up the Austrian defenses. Karl of Lorraine and Daun possessed no battle plan; they initially persuaded themselves that Friedrich will not fight that day and did not dispatch patrols to monitor his army's movements. As the fighting escalated their tactical decisions were belated responses to Prussian maneuvers with no control over developments. Lorraine never even ordered a retreat; his men fell back out of instinct for self-preservation. Friedrich by contrast kept direction of his troops firmly in hand and held the initiative throughout the day. "It can therefore be said," summarized a German historian, "that were there ever a battle without a crisis, it was Leuthen... Friedrich alone was the architect of this masterful achievement."[87] The king himself wrote after it was over, "had the Prussians not lacked daylight at the end, this battle would have been the most decisive of the century."[88]

After dark, Friedrich rode into camp to solicit volunteers from among his weary regiments to march to Lissa. The Weistritz River, also known as the *Schweidnitzer Wasser*, was 200 feet wide at Lissa. Grenadiers of the Manteuffel, Wedell and Ramin Battalions took up their rifles. Together with the Seydlitz Cuirassiers, they followed the king at around six in the evening. Snow squalls tormented the Prussians as they trudged on. At Saara, they paused at a roadside tavern to ask for a lantern. Unwilling to part with it, the tavern keeper guided the column himself. The king called to him, "Come over here next to me and hold onto my stirrup!" As the man illuminated the way, Friedrich asked about his experience with the Austrians, whose officers had been in and out of his tavern before the battle. He complained about the "rabble" that had constantly demanded food and drink and that a fire be maintained in the hearth. The "swarm of officers" robbed him as well. During the retreat after the battle, "Nothing was orderly, riders and musketeers, everyone ran away in confusion." Friedrich replied, "I could never imagine this in my own army." The tavern keeper suddenly realized who he was speaking with: "My God, you are our merciful king! I beg your pardon for having in my simplemindedness spoken when I shouldn't have." Friedrich answered, "Not at all, you are an honorable man."[89]

By seven o'clock in the evening, the king and his men had approached to within 500 feet of Lissa. The glow of the lantern drew the attention of Austrian pickets. Positioned 60 paces ahead of the Prussians, they opened fire with their muskets and injured a few horses. Everyone jumped from the road to the left and right as officers shouted, "Lights out!" The small troop of hussars detailed to ride 30 paces ahead of the king had dropped back to listen to his conversation with the tavern keeper. The sudden fusillade therefore took the hussars by surprise. The Austrian pickets vanished into the night. The Prussians entered Lissa with the king riding ahead of the grenadiers with his entourage. At the Weistritz bridge, they spotted white-uniformed Austrian soldiers, 40 in all, emerging from buildings carrying bundles of straw. The grenadiers captured some and led them before the king. He asked what they are doing and received the reply, "Over there across the bridge is a captain with about 150 men. He has orders to pile straw on the bridge and as soon as the Prussians come and to burn it."[90]

A few Austrians escaped across the river and warned the captain that the Prussians are in Lissa. He commanded his men, some of whom were in surrounding houses, to open fire. Several of Friedrich's grenadiers were wounded. Crews of the cannons the Prussians had brought along shouted for their comrades to get off of the road. The men took shelter in buildings on each side. The cannons opened fire as grenadiers cleared the houses with the bayonet. The embittered Prussians showed the defenders who had been firing out of windows no mercy. During the nocturnal skirmish, with men running and shouting, the din of gunfire and commands ringing out, the king remained unperturbed. Upon hearing distant cannon fire from Lissa, Prussian troops bivouacked on the battlefield gathered arms without orders and marched off in that direction with the generals riding ahead. Friedrich instructed his infantry and gun crews along the river to continue firing "until the powder runs out." This was to maintain tension and prevent the enemy from establishing a perimeter on the eastern bank to delay pursuit the next morning.

The firefight died down and the king instructed his entourage, "Gentlemen, follow me, I know this place."[91] They crossed a drawbridge leading to the imposing manor house, the Lissa *Schloss* (palace) just north of town. The edifice was serving as refuge for wounded enemy soldiers and officers who had taken part in the battle. When Friedrich rode through the portal, the Austrians in the manor had just finished dining. Alerted by the sound of cannon and musket fire outside, some were already descending the staircase, lanterns in hand, to seek their horses. At the base of the steps, they found to their astonishment the day's nemesis, the king of Prussia, and his adjutants calmly dismounting. Friedrich, who had been in the saddle for 15 hours, opened, "Good evening, gentlemen, I'm sure you weren't expecting me. Are there any accommodations left?"[92] With lanterns raised to light the way, the Austrian officers obligingly conducted him up the stairs to the first bedroom. Some respectfully presented themselves to the king, who engaged them in friendly conversation. What food was still on hand provided sustenance for the unexpected guests. Such was the chivalry of the times.

Before retiring for the night, Friedrich unwound with his staff discussing the day's events. One officer wryly observed that Austrian generals probably won't mock the "Potsdam guards on parade" anymore after Leuthen. The king smiled and replied, "After the dumb things they did today, I can forgive the dumb things they *said*."[93] In a proclamation for the troops the next morning, Friedrich stated, "This day will bring glory to both your names and to the nation for all time."[94] He wrote in his own chronicle of the engagement, "It is unnecessary to be reminded that our whole army from officer to plain ranker performed miracles of valor during the battle. One only need let the deeds speak for themselves."[95] The Prussian army paid for its victory with the loss of 59 officers and 1,116 men killed or missing and 164 officers and 5,043 other ranks wounded. The Austrian army fixed casualties at 1,460 killed, 4,591 wounded and 13,343 captured or missing. The figures do not include the substantial losses auxiliaries from Württemberg and Bavaria suffered. The actual number of deaths is probably more than double the official tally published by Vienna. The Prussians captured 113 cannons during and after the battle.

Over the next few days thousands of Austrian soldiers deserted. Many did not attempt to cross the Weistritz River and surrendered instead. Prince Karl and Daun fixed a collection point for the army but had already lost control of the troops. Formations were dispersed everywhere. A wounded Austrian soldier recorded the next day, "The Prussians scattered us so completely that we didn't know where the army, even less where the regiments were."[96] The next morning two Austrian commanders, the Duke of Ahremberg and the Prince of Ligne, found a despondent Prince Karl and a reproachful Daun in the village of Gräbschen half a mile southwest of Breslau. "From here," recalled Ligne, "we went to Klettendorf, wanting to see if there is some way to find the army. One could say that the army has completely disappeared. If there still was an army then, it would truly have been very weak. By nearly eleven o'clock there was as yet no trace of it. Never again would I find myself in so dismal a situation as I was in back then. Every moment we received reports that Prussian hussars have crossed the Lohe River and we will be attacked anew. I came with the duke to Nádasdy, who had lost all presence of mind. No one knew what to do."[97]

After the battle, Friedrich devoted attention to the injured. Corporal Barsewisch, himself a casualty, wrote in his journal, "In and around Neumarkt there were some 20,000 wounded from both armies and there was great suffering everywhere. The imperial wounded were distributed in school buildings, churches and convents… in order to be sheltered from the bitter cold and falling snow. His majesty the king was compassionate, and in addition to the entire field hospital arranged to have surgeons and caregivers from every town taken to the wounded and the sick. There was no shortage of groceries and other necessities."[98] The king instructed Zieten to pursue the retreating Austrian army: "Don't let the enemy rest or grant him time to regroup. And even though I imagine that your people are tired, it can't be otherwise now and you must consider that the enemy must be far more exhausted than we are… One day of fatigue under these circumstances, my dear Zieten, will bring us a hundred days of rest as a result. So, stay in the saddle and keep on the enemy's heels!"[99] The pursuit continued until December 12. According to Friedrich, 20,500 enemy soldiers were taken prisoner by the time it was over and his troops captured 116 guns, 51 standards and 4,000 wagons laden with war materiel and ammunition.[100]

The king prioritized retaking Breslau over destroying what remained of the Austrian army. His strategy was to occupy as much territory as possible. This was to make waging war during the next campaign season more expensive for the Hapsburgs and less costly for Prussia. He hoped in so doing to gain concessions once peace talks opened. Friedrich invested Breslau on December 07. Surrender negotiations with its commandant, Baron Soloman Sprecher von Bernegg, followed. Most of the Austrians defending the fortress had seen action at Leuthen. Prince Karl left an unusually strong garrison to hold Breslau because the troops were exhausted anyway and bad weather had transformed the roads south into quagmires. Many of the army's sick and wounded were convalescing in Breslau as well. Sprecher capitulated on December 20 and 17,635 men including 740 officers became prisoners of war. Friedrich took Liegnitz on the 28th by granting its 3,748-man garrison safe passage out of Prussia.[101]

Gathering what was left of his force, Prince Karl passed through Schweidnitz and reached Bohemia shortly before Christmas. His army tallied at most 37,000 men, of whom 22,000 were sick. He wrote the emperor, "The fine Austrian army is in shambles, torn apart by a long campaign, without laundry, without uniforms, in a word in more miserable and pitiful condition than ever before. Due to the proximity of the enemy the men have to bivouac without tents."[102] Friedrich blockaded Schweidnitz and captured it the following April. About a thousand defenders died in combat or from illness during the siege and 4,912 men surrendered. Schweidnitz was the only city in Silesia not to fall to Friedrich in 1757. All told, the Austrian army lost 45,000 men in the battle of Leuthen, the subsequent retreat and at Breslau. Most of the officers necessary to train a new fighting force were in Prussian captivity; many were described by Friedrich as "officers of distinction."

In Vienna, the populace had become accustomed to reading about victories such as Kolin in June, General Andreas Hadik's brief occupation of Berlin in October and Lorraine's capture of Breslau and Schweidnitz. State Chancellor Kaunitz grandly publicized successes in order to demonstrate the alleged correctness of his diplomacy, especially the alliance negotiated with France. He now faced the problem of covering the reversal of fortunes precipitated by the defeat at Leuthen. The reports he released to the press understated losses. They represented the battle as a draw and boasted that Hadik has allegedly chased a Prussian army commanded by James Keith out of Bohemia.[103] More accurate news about the disaster in Silesia soon trickled into the capital via independent journalists, letters home from soldiers taken prisoner and the accounts of officers and men returning from the campaign. The Venetian ambassador Carlo Ruzzini wrote his government, "The anguish and panicky dismay can be read in every face, and the universal bewilderment is much greater now than it was last May after the battle of Prague."[104]

Prince Karl attempted to make Nádasdy, who had proven both circumspect and courageous at Leuthen, the scapegoat for the defeat. Right after the battle the two had a heated argument about who was to blame. An indignant Nádasdy, one of the imperial army's most gifted generals, resigned his commission and returned to Croatia. Upon the insistence of France and Russia, Maria Theresia reluctantly relieved her paladin Lorraine, who would not resign voluntarily, of his command. She threatened punitive action against citizens caught defaming the prince, yet graffiti and placards ridiculing him appeared on walls throughout Vienna. One popular cartoon depicted Prince Karl, known for his fondness for drink, Daun and Nádasdy at a war council discussing how to beat the Prussians: "Daun: With good sense and courage we could! Nádasdy: With sword and blood we should! Prince Karl: The wine here's really good!"[105]

Gerhard Johann David von Scharnhorst, one of German history's most eminent fighting men and future architect of the Prussian general staff, wrote this of Leuthen: "It will always be a monument to the genius of the great field commander and the skill at maneuver and valor of the army, as long as the coming world takes notice of our times." In the verdict of Napoleon, "This battle is a masterpiece of movement, maneuver and determination. It alone would suffice to immortalize Friedrich and rank him among the greatest of generals. It reveals in the loftiest measure both his moral and military capabilities."[106] The Seven Years' War would not end until 1763, with Prussia becoming firmly established as a European Great Power. Friedrich II won approximately two thirds of the battles he fought during the global conflict, but none earned him greater renown than Leuthen.

Chapter 3

The Infectious Revolution

Postwar Prussia

Victories at Rossbach, Leuthen and Breslau enabled Friedrich to recapture Silesia, but were not decisive against the hostile coalition. Preoccupied fighting his number one enemy, the Hapsburgs, the king could not prevent the Russians from conquering East Prussia in January 1758. During the following war years, he controlled the most important provinces of his kingdom largely thanks to subsidies from England and from the military achievements of the army of Hanover which kept the French at bay. With a vastly superior force, Daun ambushed the Prussian army at Hochkirch that October in a chaotic nocturnal engagement. In August 1759, a joint Austro-Russian force routed Friedrich's troops at Kunersdorf. The Russians could not exploit the victory due to overextended supply lines. The king defeated an Austrian army more than twice the size of his own at Liegnitz a year later. In November 1760, he fought the armies of Daun and another Austrian field marshal, Gideon Ernst von Laudon, to a standstill at Torgau. The Russians' logistical problems weakened their striking power, so Friedrich could again devote resources to combating the Hapsburgs.

Prussian fortunes declined toward the end of 1761. The Austrians took Schweidnitz and the Russians, after two failed attempts, captured the Baltic port of Kolberg. This allowed them to provision the army by sea. Their supply lines were no longer at the mercy of poor roads and raids by Prussian cavalry patrols. Constant attrition, particularly during the seesaw campaign for Saxony, gradually reduced Friedrich's army to 60,000 men. The king's situation was desperate and England threatened to withdraw subsidies. Circumstances abruptly changed upon the death of Russia's bibulous Czarina Elizabeth. Her son and heir, Peter III, withdrew from the coalition and helped mediate a cease-fire between Prussia and Sweden. He opened Russian army granaries and depots in Pomerania to distribute foodstuffs to the population. Russian officers and men in Maria Theresia's army left her service. While military resources available to the coalition therefore declined, those of Friedrich augmented. Prussian soldiers in Russian captivity were released to rejoin his army. Once the Russians evacuated Silesia, the king was free to induct men from the province into the military.[1] The Prussians also regained Kolberg.

Peter's reign as czar ended when the oversexed Queen Catherine deposed him in July 1762. She withdrew military aid to Prussia but maintained friendly relations and did not reenter the war on the side of the coalition. The strategic balance shifted in Friedrich's favor and the Seven Years' War became a stalemate. The king of France was under pressure to end hostilities. His people were weary of Britain's nautical blockade and of fighting in both Canada and Europe. The Hapsburg empress Maria Theresia had depleted the treasury conducting three campaigns to regain Silesia. Even though Britain ultimately suspended aid to Prussia, the war became too costly for Austria. The belligerents negotiated peace in February 1763. Prussia relinquished Saxony but kept Silesia. Count Alfred von Schlieffen, the future chief of the German general staff, wrote, "During his 74-year life he achieved greatness and might. But of all of Friedrich's deeds, the one that will remain eternally remembered as unique in the world is the Seven Years' War, the struggle of four or four-and-half million against 90 million."[2]

The prolonged conflict virtually ruined commerce for the nations involved. Some 530,000 enemy soldiers had died in the war including North America. Prussia lost nearly 180,000 men in combat, from illness or by desertion and 40,000 civilians.[3] During the war, Friedrich had made preparations for postwar reconstruction. Many fields were uncultivated and farms lacked seed, cattle and hands to work the soil. Once peace was restored, the king released to the

Friedrich visits Küstrin after it had been torched by the Russians. He pledged to the distressed population that the town will be rebuilt after the war.

agrarian population 42,000 bushels of grain and flour from army stockpiles and distributed 35,000 cavalry and pack horses as well. He discharged 40,000 native Prussians from active duty to return home. Prussia's sovereign practiced the utmost frugality in public administration. Revenue collected was devoted to helping the common people rather than landowners. Friedrich subsidized distressed provinces to restore commerce. Silesia received three million thaler (dollars), Pomerania and Neumarkt 1,400,000 thaler, Prussia 800,000, Brandenburg 800,000 and Cleves 100,000. Other districts also benefited from grants.[4]

Among the wartime measures the king had introduced to maintain fiscal solvency was gradually devaluing the thaler and paying civil servants with receipts instead of salaries. The receipts could not be redeemed in currency until the cessation of hostilities. These steps caused financial hardships for many middle class and affluent families, but enabled Friedrich to keep the oppressive national debt financing military expenditures within manageable proportions. The poorer classes were least impacted by these budgetary expedients and recovered more quickly after the war. The king founded the Berlin Bank in 1764 and funded it with eight million thaler. He established a credit system for the nobility to borrow from and also made provisions to provide public assistance for widows of fallen soldiers and their orphans. To expedite economic recovery, the king exempted Silesia from tax liability for six months and Neumark and Pomerania for two years.[5]

In 1766, with reconstruction in its third year, Friedrich described progress in a letter to Voltaire: "Fanaticism and the fury of ambition reduced flourishing regions of my country to wastelands. If you wish to learn the extent of the devastation that took place, then you should know that all told, I had to have 8,000 houses and buildings rebuilt in Silesia and Pomerania, and in Neumarkt 6,500… that makes 14,500 houses. Most of them had been burned down by the Russians. We did not wage war in such a loathsome manner; only a few buildings in the cities we besieged were destroyed by our side. The number is certainly not even a thousand. The wicked example did not corrupt us and my conscience is clear from any reproach."[6] Friedrich improved conditions for the civilian population. His domestic accomplishments include combating serfdom and modernizing the state bureaucracy and legal system. He welcomed 300,000 new settlers into the country.[7]

Reconstruction and social reform did not diminish attention to military matters. The king considered periods of nonbelligerency unnatural: "From the smallest to the largest state, count on the fact that augmenting itself is the fundamental principle of the government. This passion is as deeply rooted in every ministry as is universal despotism in the Vatican. The ardor of the princes has no bridle beyond the limitations of their power. Were a prince to preserve his interests less diligently than his neighbor, then the neighbor would only become stronger. The prince may be more virtuous, but would also remain the weaker."[8] Friedrich expanded the armed forces after the Seven Years' War to 240,000 men.

During the conflict, it had become increasingly difficult to recruit non-Prussians to replace losses. This made it necessary to induct more men from among the indigenous population. At the end of the war, the army comprised 103,000 Prussians and 37,000 foreigners.[9] To cover postwar manpower requirements, the military prioritized recruiting non-Prussians. During the final years of Friedrich's reign, nearly twice the number of foreigners would serve in the army as would Prussians.

Defense expenditures included repair and structural improvement of fortresses and construction of a new one in Silesia at Silberberg. Depots were restocked with cannons, generous stores of gunpowder, muskets, bridge building materials and field equipment. Reform was also on the agenda. Even though Friedrich won battles with conventional infantry tactics, he was impressed by the novel character of combat operations in the New World. The European practice of fighting in formation that required open, even terrain for optimum efficiency contrasted sharply with the decisive influence topography exercised on the battles in the French and Indian War and American Revolution. The king ordered the establishment of three light infantry regiments, called *Neue Regimenter* or *Frey Regimenter* (New Regiments or Independent Regiments) consisting of ten companies each. The men were trained to fight in loose order with emphasis on individual marksmanship and exploiting available cover. Friedrich's successor would add another 20 battalions of light troops. He renamed them fusilier battalions.[10]

The monarchy therefore implemented prerequisites to keep the army in step with the times as more modern tactics developed and better small arms and gunnery became available. In one realm, the military establishment regressed; with regard to the disrespectful attitude toward the common soldier. A contributing factor was the centralization of recruitment instituted in 1763. Prior to this, company commanders were responsible for enlistments in their own unit. As Friedrich's former aide-de-camp Gaudi related, every captain strove "to have a company consisting not only of fine-looking men, but also of those who were serviceable and well brought up. Each endeavored to outdo the other; whoever was slovenly or unsuitable was discharged and every officer thought about ways to make his company finer and to enhance it with good and reliable people."[11] Commanders were selective about non-Prussians they enrolled. Beginning in 1763 however, officers and NCOs no longer recruited for their own regiments, but for a general manpower pool into which "all recruits were tossed and then distributed." They lowered the bar with respect to the quality of personnel selected. In Gaudi's words, they paid no heed to "the morality of the recruits, but took in all sorts of dissolute rabble. These were types that the captains, when they had control of recruitment, would never have enlisted."[12]

The king himself dismissed many officers from the middle class and relegated those remaining in the army to insignificant posts. He reestablished the social gulf that had existed before the war. Friedrich published an order reading, "The officer must not be allowed to associate with commoners or with burghers, but must always fraternize with senior officers and their comrades who conduct themselves properly and are ambitious."[13] He reminded regimental commanders in 1763 that they "must first of all ensure that young officers have no more contact with the common man than what duty requires."[14] Thus the brotherhood of royal, aristocrat and plebian forged in blood on the battlefield, during which the ordinary soldier was acknowledged as an honorable person, was an artificial wartime expedient dispensed with when the danger had passed. The ranker again became a component of a martial monolith, absorbed into the absolutist system of forced compliance. "Men in the army were cudgeled and disciplined once more, just as though there had never been a battle of Zorndorf or of Liegnitz, when the king appealed to his soldiers' honor, devotion and loyalty and found resounding acclaim," summarized historian Reinhard Höhn.[15]

The king legitimized the supreme authority he exercised as ancestral right. He compelled subordinates to obey him as their lawful duty. He dispensed with nurturing the spirit of self-sacrifice and joyful allegiance he had animated in his troops during the war. It had been Friedrich's example to camaraderie and humility, warming himself at bonfires with the men, sharing hardships and providing for their welfare as best he could, that generated the voluntary nature of their wartime service. European monarchs regarded his unorthodox behavior as whimsical; kings customarily remained at court letting their field marshals conduct military operations. In his departure from this norm however, rested the very source of Friedrich's power. After the victory at Leuthen, a Prussian general found a blood-soaked grenadier lying on the battlefield with both legs shot off. The soldier was calmly smoking his pipe. "Comrade," asked the astonished superior, "How can you enjoy smoking tobacco in such dreadful condition, and so close to death?" The grenadier took the pipe from his mouth and shrugged, "It doesn't matter to me, I die for my king."[16] Such was the devotion the Prussian soldier felt for his sovereign, that hereditary fealty alone cannot inspire.

During the first year of the Seven Years' War, Prussian hussars entered the fortress of Gotha and surprised the enemy garrison. They discovered baggage abandoned by French officers that included dressing gowns, parasols, hair lotion, perfume and all the refinements a courtly gentleman of Versailles could scarcely be expected to dispense with during a campaign. Friedrich set a different standard for his troops, as an eyewitness described: "The condition of his apparel and laundry confirmed his reputation, that in the field he does not in the slightest measure allow himself more comforts than those of his humblest officer."[17] The king lived among his troops and esteemed them as worthwhile and virtuous comrades in arms. This, and not ancestral authority, was why before the battle of Leuthen, despite the overwhelming numerical superiority of the enemy, the Prussians stood by the colors to the man. "More than ever before," maintained one of Friedrich's biographers, "the soldier was elevated to the most privileged class in the state and promised the bounty most certain to arouse passion in a man; that of honor."[18]

Prussian soldiers at Gotha inspect officers' baggage taken from a captured French supply train. Indulging in such luxury during a military campaign would have been unthinkable for Friedrich the Great or his officers.

Field commanders who emulated their sovereign enjoyed the same loyalty and confidence from their men. One lieutenant reported that during all operations he participated in during the Seven Years' War, not a single soldier, Prussian or foreign, deserted when he personally led the mission. He understood it as his duty to "win the affection of his subordinates and care for them in every possible way, because the common soldier has such burdensome duty, often deprived of every comfort and convenience in life, with no recourse to remedy his needs and concerns but to appeal to his officer."[19] In light of his personal experience, it seems almost incomprehensible that after the conclusion of hostilities in 1763, Friedrich II would revert to a system that denigrated the men who had stood by him thick and thin throughout a prolonged and seemingly hopeless struggle. He himself wrote in 1768 that only fear of their officers will drive men into battle. When he subsequently took up arms against Austria in a tug of war over Bavaria in 1778, desertions in the Prussian army reached shocking proportions despite strict overwatch; a sorry comparison to Leuthen.

The considerable influence of Friedrich the Great notwithstanding, the army could not exist as a microcosm immune from social progress in Prussia or the

Enlightenment. A schism within the officer corps developed. Primarily the younger generation of military leaders was unwilling to accept the perpetual degradation of the ordinary fighting man who had fought the wars against Austria and France. The absolutist policy suffered biting criticism in *Bellona*, a military journal published in Dresden by Karl von Seidl, a lieutenant in a Württemberg dragoon regiment. An article described how old school officers "pay the soldier poorly, beat him half to death over trivia, make his life as miserable as possible, issue him sleazy clothing, don't properly care for his health when in the field or treat him when he gets sick. Thousands of the most valiant men are ruined as a result, yet things just go on in the same old way."[20] With peace restored, the Prussian army now had an internal battle to fight. It was one for the honor and welfare of the common soldier.

The Serpent's Egg

Advocates to reform the Prussian army faced an uphill battle. Friedrich II had won the Seven Years' War adhering to the accepted practices of 18th-Century warfare. The military hierarchy regarded his victory as proof of their correctness. Senior officers believed in maintaining strict discipline to control the troops and in the superiority of the linear tactic in combat. They saw no reason to overhaul an establishment that was a model for the continent. Moreover, reformers were not just taking on the conservative leadership of the armed forces; their proposals challenged the bastion of absolutism. A martial atmosphere pervaded public administration. It took a back seat to the interests of the military. The standing army was at the sole disposal of the sovereign and a manifestation of his authority. It could not be restructured without penetrating the core of the society it represented.

A major bone of contention was the parochial perception of the common soldier as a "shooting machine" performing mechanical functions within a bloc of insensate men shifting en masse as directed. Scharnhorst, a trailblazer of the reform movement, warned in an April 06, 1806 memo to the commander in chief of the army, "We've begun to prize the science of war more highly than military virtues… Valor, steadfastness and self-sacrifice are the cornerstones of a people's freedom. If our hearts no longer beat for these we're already lost, even if in the course of a great victory!"[21] The reform movement received impetus from an external source. Europe was evolving under the Enlightenment. The absolutist system was moribund and states clinging to it risked being overtaken by progressive ones embracing new ideas. The confrontation was unavoidable. Absolute monarchies could not coexist with states fostering public participation in government. Novel methods of waging war would emerge as well. In the military hierarchy's reluctance to adopt them, Prussian reformers saw the weakness of the army.

Prior to the industrial revolution, most Europeans lived by farming with little opportunity for education or advancement. The nobility and the clergy were sovereign over the peasant population, even though Europe was not without princes who sought to improve the common people's standard of living from time to time. It was inevitable that a system prioritizing the preeminence of exclusive, numerically insignificant and nominally talented strata would be overcome by undiscovered, superior human resources from among the multitude; men and women prepared to defy a stagnant political and social structure that stifles aptitude and initiative and resists progress. The transformation found expression through the Enlightenment. It began as an intellectual revolution. It represented a form of natural selection that recognizes that commoners displaying ability should have the right to self-development and if qualified, assume leadership. It was however, a "serpent's egg" of Shakespearian metaphor: By shifting focus from royal or communal obligation to freedom of the individual, the Enlightenment, when hatched, would "grow mischievous" and undermine concepts and established institutions that help ensure a cohesive, functional society.

The American Revolution in 1776 introduced a militant side to the philosophy. Colonists in the New World, primarily from Germany and the British Isles, waged a war of independence against England. The revolution succeeded largely thanks to Thomas Paine, an immigrant from Norfolk, England. His widely read pamphlet *Common Sense* and the *American Crisis* essays, the first of which began with the famous sentence, "These are the times that try men's souls," redefined the relationship of people to government. Paine subsequently wrote *The Rights of Man* in 1791 in defense of the French Revolution. He argued that it is a nation's right, indeed duty, to overthrow a government that fails to represent its interests. France was fertile ground for revolution. The impoverished peasantry and emerging middle class still suffered under the royals. The nobility and clergy owned nearly half the land of France with a disproportionately small tax liability; common people shouldered the burden via the unpopular *taille* land tax.[22] Peasants encountering aristocrats on walkways were required to remove their hats or bow submissively.

The King of France, Louis XVI, sought to alleviate economic and social discrepancies but was hampered by the country's aristocracy. Public resentment over the opulence of the court of Versailles and the king financing the American Revolution instead of addressing problems in his own country fueled resentment. What Paine did for the American colonists, giving their frustration and sentiments tangible political expression, the Swiss-born philosopher Jean-Jacques Rousseau did for the French. His essays, based on the premise that "man is born free and everywhere lives in chains," provoked the enmity of the beneficiaries of absolutism. Expelled from France, Geneva and Bern, Rousseau appealed to Friedrich the Great for sanctuary in 1762. The Prussian monarch settled him in Neuchâtel. He wrote its governor, "We must succor this poor unfortunate. His only offense is to have strange opinions which he thinks are good ones."[23] Rousseau's writings animated political awareness among the French.

An uprising began in July 1789 after a crop failure and resulting food shortage pushed the population of Paris over the edge. The Revolution stripped the royal house of absolute authority and eventually replaced it with an elective regime. While European wars of the 18th Century were waged to gain territory, the American and French Revolutions were fought by men and women seeking to control their destiny. England lost thirteen prosperous colonies overseas to self-rule and France's monarchy and aristocracy all political influence. The transformation shook the foundation of the European monarchial system. French revolutionaries, by the *very existence* of their new state form, created grounds for conflict with their neighbors. Kings feared that their own subjects will follow the French example; that dissatisfied with limited opportunities in life, the people will demand rights that an absolute state cannot grant without surrendering autonomy.

France did not seek alliances with other states, nor did she attempt to annex a strip of border territory from a neighbor. Instead, she demanded diplomatic recognition of her representative government. For the monarchies, this was not possible to grant without repudiating their own institutions. The only alternatives for relations with France were unconditional friendship or unconditional hostility. This polarization of Europe jeopardized the oligarchic balance of continental states. French leaders inspired their troops with the slogan, "war on the palaces, peace for the cottages," and pursued an aggressive foreign policy under the pretext of leading the peoples of Europe "out of the darkness of absolutism and tyranny and into the light" of liberty.[24] The princes mobilized military resources to invade France and forcibly restore the king. Conventional European armies earmarked for the task were about to face an unexpected metamorphosis in the complexion of warfare.

The nature of military campaigns had already experienced a significant transition after the religious wars and witch hunts of the 17th Century drastically depopulated central Europe. In the following century, armed conflicts caused less distress to noncombatants. Princes fought to conquer provinces and augment their kingdoms or to resolve disputes over royal succession. They limited war aims by a shared interest in maintaining the European state structure and interrelationship of nations. This mollified the devastation and "passions, bitterness, hatred and thirst for revenge" customarily accompanying the clash of arms, as the military analyst Carl von Clausewitz pointed out.[25] Peace treaties were compromises designed to prevent a resurgence of belligerency.

Rural populations were largely indifferent to whether they paid taxes to a Hapsburg, a Hohenzollern or to a provincial duke. Friedrich Wilhelm I, the "soldier-king," believed that since the common people do not participate in government, they should not be obligated to fight in wartime. He forbade the formation of militias or even mentioning them in his presence. His son Friedrich the Great was of like mind: When during the first Silesian war the Prussians in Frisia prepared an armed uprising against France, Friedrich ordered them to stand down. He, like the Hapsburgs, shielded civilians during the clash of arms as best he could. Only one villager died during the battle of Leuthen; an 86-year-old man named Stoos who was hit by a blast of case-shot.

A month before Leuthen, Friedrich had been scouting Thuringia to locate the French army of General Soubise and the *Reichsarmée* in the hope of drawing them into battle. He eventually succeeded in doing so at Rossbach. During the interim, the king expressed indignation that his elusive adversary was pillaging the countryside. He wrote his sister Wilhelmine, "I would doubt the very existence of the enemy army had I found any horses in this country; but there aren't any. Someone must have stolen them and that someone has to be this invisible army."[26] Prussian troops rarely had a stake in the monarch's war aims. They harbored no personal animosity toward the civilian populations affected. Requisition of privately owned foodstuffs, farm animals and timber were sometimes necessary, but princes established a supply system of well-stocked fortresses to satisfy most of the army's requirements. Campaigns were not looting expeditions. Civilians could demand and frequently receive compensation for what was taken from them.

Friedrich the Great had once stated, "the peaceful citizen should remain relaxed and undisturbed in his home and not even know that his country is at war, had he not learned of it from reports in the press."[27] In France, the liberation of the peasantry granted everyone the right to seek public office and share in government. This carried with it the obligation to defend the country in an emergency; to actively participate in politics and war. In February 1793 the National Convention, as the government was called, introduced the *levée en masse* (mass conscription). This made all able-bodied males eligible for military service. Armed conflict was no longer an affair of princes and their private armies but of the entire nation. In the words of Clausewitz, "the French Revolution had thrown the whole weight of the people and all its forces into the scale which had hitherto nothing but the weight of a limited army and of the limited revenues of the state."[28]

The French regarded coalition campaigns launched by absolute states against their country not as conventional cabinet wars between governments but as attacks on the people of France. On this basis a concept of warfare emerged that is foreign to the absolute state. The previously unpolitical mass of subjects took up arms and went into battle in the *levée en masse* as free citizens for a political goal that they regarded no differently than as a struggle for their very existence. This war was therefore unique in its own way for the times. The French government emphasized that "never has any nation been called to arms for a more important matter."[29] As a national war, it became a righteous one compared to the absolutist cabinet war that had the odium of a campaign of conquest and was downright loathsome.

For France it was a struggle to protect the fruits of the revolution, a revolution symbolized by the new constitution. Interim foreign minister Antoine de Lessart declared in January 1792 that the French constitution "has become a sort of

Patriotic volunteers and soldiers assemble at a recruiting station and pledge to defend France in 1792. Thanks to public support of the Revolution and *levée en masse*, the Republic had an inexhaustible manpower pool to fight the coalition wars.

religion" for the majority of the population, to be "emphatically defended."[30] The French conscription act of August 23, 1793, read, "From this moment until that in which our enemies shall have been driven from the territory of the Republic, all Frenchmen are permanently requisitioned for service in the armies. The young men shall fight; the married men shall forge weapons and transport supplies; the women will make tents and clothes and serve in hospitals; the children will make up old linen into lint… No one can hire a representative to replace him in the service he has been assigned to. The call-up is universal."[31] All France therefore prepared for war "against our princes, against our Roman Catholic priests and against the exalted children of the king's secretariat," in the words of the National Assembly delegate Pierre du Pont.[32]

Based on the history of religious wars, pundits in absolute states shunned ideological confrontations as the most baneful of all armed conflicts. Scharnhorst warned that involving the general population in warfare will revert to the butchery of 17th-Century campaigns: "If the ordinary citizen wages war, it will be fought with more bitterness. The nature of the affair demands cruelty, since this is how it achieves its purpose."[33] Sir Francis Bacon, an English statesman and pioneer of the Enlightenment, considered it "a thing monstrous to put the temporal sword into the hands of the common people."[34] The eminent Italian historian Guglielmo Ferrero would later maintain, "Restricted warfare was one of the loftiest achievements of the 18th Century. It belongs to a class of hot-house

plants which can only thrive in an aristocratic and qualitative civilization…
It is one of the fine things we have lost as a result of the French Revolution."[35]

What led these learned and perceptive men to draw such conclusions? Rousseau stated that the only legitimate government is that of majority rule, so one could not demand of a modern Frenchman aware of his natural rights that he take up arms for his country without purpose. The battle cry of the Revolution, "liberty, equality and brotherhood," applied to *all* mankind; the liberation of the people of France was supposedly the first step in the crusade against oppression beyond the frontier. It was a mission of faith in the ideals of the Revolution, for a better life together for all of humanity for the future. It was therefore a humanitarian duty to bring the accomplishments of the Revolution to other peoples and liberate them from the yoke of absolutism.

French leaders portrayed European monarchs as tyrants who enslave their populations and intend to restore the monarchy to France. Warfare took on an ideological dimension. As the theologian Augustine of Hippo wrote centuries before, those who are persuaded that their cause is righteous can easily conclude that the enemy is waging an unjust war; from here it is a short step to the conviction that he fights for an evil purpose because he himself is wicked.[36] In such a struggle, there was little place for the mutual respect customarily shared by opposing warriors in Europe's professional armies, protection of civilians, compassion for enemy wounded and moderation in victory. The uncompromising attitude of the French is demonstrated in a December 1792 letter to the United States Congress reading, "Either the torch of liberty will be extinguished or our principles will triumph over the league of despots in every way."[37]

The Convention introduced an insidious element to inflame emotions and motivate the population to wage war; that of propaganda. The law invoking conscription demanded that citizens who are elderly or otherwise unfit for duty betake themselves "into the public squares to rouse the courage of the fighting men, to preach the unity of the Republic and hatred against kings."[38] The French royalist Mallet du Pan saw propaganda as a "hellish tactic worthy of the monsters who invented it… Fifty thousand savage beasts, foaming at the mouth with rage and yelling like cannibals, hurl themselves at top speed upon soldiers whose courage has been excited by no passion."[39] The German-American journalist George Viereck wrote, "Without hate there can be no propaganda."[40] To persuade the people of the righteousness of the democratic cause, the Convention had to represent the opposition as unprincipled, depraved and a threat to freedom. Thus the "restricted warfare" as defined by Ferrero, and chivalry as well, gave way to the unrestricted warfare of the "enlightened" Republic. "The motive force of democracy," wrote British military historian John Frederick Fuller, "is not love for others, it is the hate of all outside the tribe, faction, party or nation."[41]

Despite the hysteria infecting much of the population, the policies of the Convention were by no means universally popular throughout France. In March 1793, the people of the Vendée, a coastal region at the estuary of the Loire River,

rebelled against the Republic. Locals were sympathetic to the provincial aristocracy, which dwelled among them instead of at Versailles. The Vendée's inhabitants were devoutly Catholic and appalled at the Convention's hostility toward
religion; particularly as the new government supposedly advocated freedom
of expression. Another catalyst was repugnance toward the unpopular *levée en
masse*. The Republic's response was not long in coming and inconsistent with
British historian Arnold Toynbee's assertion that democracy "breathes the spirit
of the Gospels" and its motivating force is love. Fuller ironically summarized,
"The Republic set out to march to liberty over the corpses of her subjects."[42]

The insurgents formed the Catholic and Royal Army that fought Republican
forces for several months in the region, where some 800,000 people resided.
After the revolt was quelled by General François Westermann, the National
Convention sent the *colonnes infernales* (infernal columns) to "pacify" the
Vendée. Some 170,000 prisoners and suspected sympathizers of the rebellion
were massacred. Many were forcibly drowned in the Loire. A Jacobin officer
brought a mobile oven with his unit on this punitive expedition, which he
periodically fired up to roast local women and children alive.[43] During France's
wars against European states around this time, the Convention forbade officers
to make prisoners of English or Hanoverian soldiers who fell into their hands.[44]
By contrast, during the three Silesian wars waged by Friedrich the Great, Saxony
and Silesia changed hands several times. The allegiance of the populations
had no influence on their treatment; the common people remained virtually
unaffected by war, with the exception of occasional requisitions or looting by
Soubise's ragtag invasion force that was beaten at Rossbach. Prisoners of war
received fair treatment. The Enlightenment was the beginning of the end for
Europe's absolute monarchies, but not all that followed was the blessing on
humanity promised by its visionaries.

Partisan warfare was another element soiling the coalition wars. This sinister
fighting method surfaced in the Vendée and later during the French occupation of Spain in 1808. A young Swiss officer serving in the French cavalry, John
Rocca, described an encounter with Spanish guerrillas in the mountainous
Malaga province: "Soon we heard shouts. The inhabitants had massacred six
hussars and two blacksmiths who had carelessly gone into the village to shoe
their horses. Then the musket fire began. We quickly mounted our horses and
the largest part of the detachment followed the commanding officer to the
designated assembly area… One of my comrades told me that the rearguard is
almost completely surrounded and the Spanish are pouring heavy fire onto our
detachment from the rocks above and out of windows… My horse was hit in
the neck by a bullet and fell. I forced it up again and reached my detachment…
After that we saw almost all the hussars who followed us go down. Women, or
better put unleashed furies, pounced on our wounded with dreadful cries and
competed to kill them in the most painful way. They stabbed them in the eyes
with knives and shears and reveled savagely at the sight of their blood. The

excessive, justifiable anger toward those who had invaded their country had completely dehumanized them."[45]

Witnessing such sadistic behavior served to harden the troops. They responded by mistreating captured enemy soldiers. Rocca recalled, "We encountered some Spanish prisoners who came from Ucles and were being taken to Madrid. Many of these unfortunate souls collapsed from exhaustion and others died from want of food. If they couldn't march anymore, they were mercilessly shot dead. This spiteful order was issued as retaliation because the Spanish were hanging captured Frenchmen. It was an inopportune time for such measures against a disarmed enemy and could in no sense be excused by the necessity of reprisals. They contradicted the overall purpose of conquest, continuous subordination of other peoples."[46] Similar unchivalrous episodes redefined the countenance of war as democratic governments employing both volunteers and conscripted manpower gradually replaced the professional soldier and henceforth interpreted the battle between nations as struggles of good versus evil.

Over a century after the coalition wars against France, the Austrian-born financier and essayist Felix Somary wrote, "An indirect result of democracy and universal conscription is the novel principle of making the entire nation liable for fighting wars… Paramount is that the civilian population that is called to arms be infused with hatred toward the enemy. A declaration of war therefore becomes the same as banishment did in the Middle Ages, except that it does not affect one individual but extends to the inhabitants of an entire country. They are deprived of the right to life, freedom, honor and property. The honor of the enemy is tarnished in a way that far surpasses in brutality the most furious excesses of Napoleon and even the orgies of abuse of the Reformation."[47]

Reluctantly to War

Whether suppressing Catholic dissenters of the Vendée, coercing French citizens into military service or fighting battles against continental armies, the Republic displayed a ruthlessness that initially proved advantageous against opponents who were psychologically and materially unprepared to wage war *aux allures déchaînées* (at unbridled tempo). In the long run however, it would prove its downfall. Beginning in 1792, France was almost always fighting various coalitions for the next 23 years. Her leadership's unshakable belief in the superiority of the French system of government and design for Europe obstructed compromise with monarchies perceived as outdated. As Fuller pointed out, "The peace treaties wrung from the vanquished were generally so unreasonable that they were no more than precarious armistices; the losers only signed them through duress, and with the full intention of repudiating them at the first opportunity." Ferrero cited "the psychological error" committed by both the Convention and its successor Napoleon, "of imagining that tremendous and crushing victories assist one to secure peace, whereas they really make it more difficult or even impossible to secure."[48]

Prussia was not ready for an armed clash with France in 1792. The two countries had been on different courses since the Seven Years' War. The French aristocracy impeded social reform and commercial expansion in order to maintain political autonomy. This unintentionally steered the population toward resentment and upheaval. Thanks to the vitality and enterprise of the Prussian middle class and the prudence of the king, Prussia recovered from the ravages of war more quickly. The country developed a flourishing economy, but the road to prosperity led to complacency as well. The spirit that had captivated the nation during the reign of Friedrich the Great began to erode as the hardships and sacrifices that had steeled the people during that era diminished. The Hohenzollerns provided the common people opportunities for economic advancement. Abridging serfdom and introducing mandatory public education helped guide Prussia into becoming a modern state. It shifted the people's focus from military concerns to social welfare.

Members of the educated class, the burghers, were steadily overtaking the nobility in fortune and influence. Reduced taxation improved the standard of living for the common people, especially farmers. Affluent burghers bought ancestral manors from impoverished aristocrats. This was a development that had irked Friedrich the Great toward the end of his reign. By 1800 for example, 250 of Silesia's roughly 1,600 estates had been acquired by non-nobles.[49] The public questioned the merit of a caste that owed its lofty station in society to royal patronage and heredity. An essay in the *Teutscher Merkur* (German Mercury) in 1774 stated, "In an enlightened era and in a refined nation, a citizen's rank and standing should be based on personality, not inherited; it should be earned, not accidental."[50]

The officer corps resisted modernization during the comparatively short reign of Friedrich the Great's hedonistic nephew Friedrich Wilhelm II, who took the throne in 1786. "Fat Wilhelm" was interested in military reform. He appointed state minister Friedrich von Heinitz to chair a committee that included General Möllendorff to identify problems and draft proposals. During this period of national security however, the army hierarchy lapsed into stagnation. When Karl Friedrich von dem Knesebeck entered service at age 15 in Kalckstein Regiment, he observed that "Most senior officers were over-aged, portly figures. They were finally to get a very generous income after long anticipation and having endured such poverty, and now wanted to enjoy a life that had thus far been nothing but hardship…. The staff officers were for the most part even older, and only rarely could one be found who could still ride without having to hang onto the saddle horn to stay on the horse."[51] British General John Burgoyne attributed the prowess of the Prussian army to the technical know-how and sense of duty of its cadre of younger lieutenants and noncommissioned officers. He opined that quality decreased "as the ranks ascend, and other qualifications than those of mere execution become requisite."[52]

The Prussian army was still a capable fighting force, but lacked the leadership required to take on a European Great Power. King Friedrich Wilhelm II failed to comprehend the political climate in revolutionary France. He believed that "troublemakers" and a "gang of bandits" had intrigued to usurp the government and were universally rejected by the people.[53] The king issued a joint declaration with the Hapsburg emperor Joseph II in August 1791. It threatened military intervention in France if the monarchy is overthrown. Prussia and Austria became allies not to defend their *countries*, but to rescue French absolutism. Historian Franz Uhle-Wettler maintained, "The war the princes were to wage against the Revolution was therefore already on shaky ground. The princes did realize that they have to combat the enemy with respect to propaganda as well. But with a program championing absolutism they could scarcely gain sympathy... They spoke as though addressing servants and did not realize that the French people, or better put those of the middle class, have long since become aware of their power... It only stiffened resistance."[54]

A war to restore France's Bourbon Dynasty would also be difficult for Friedrich Wilhelm II to sell at home. No one in Prussia owed anything to the king of France. Since the early 17th Century, French monarchs had invaded neighboring German provinces to try and extend their country's frontier to the Rhine River. Many German states, just like France had been, were governed by despots who enjoyed an opulent lifestyle. Most among Germany's intelligentsia therefore sympathized with the French Revolution. Prussians were scarcely interested in a military adventure. One historian summarized, "After over 70 years of the stringent authority of two exceptional kings during which everything served the state, the inclination under a comparatively mild regime was now to enjoy mounting prosperity brought about by the economic upswing of the times. Even though the common man still lived modestly, there were good prospects that overall social conditions and material circumstances for ordinary persons would noticeably improve... The burghers were content because their sons were pretty much shielded from military service. For those in charge to maintain peace on the border was prized as the zenith of statesmanship."[55]

The German intelligentsia regarded "the sport of kings," as cabinet wars were called, as repugnant to liberal principles of the modern age. They believed that rulers should settle their differences without force. As the concepts of mutual respect and worldwide cooperation gained influence, traditional political and economic boundaries between states became less defined, at least to the educated and mercantile strata. The Enlightenment fostered brotherhood among nations. It contributed to the growth of cosmopolitan sects and so-called reading clubs. Freemason guilds established in the Middle Ages formed the basis for 18th-Century secret orders whose members hailed from middle class and noblesse alike. They promoted fellowship with affiliated lodges abroad and cooperated to achieve common goals. Secrecy was necessary because adherents were watched by the police and those in public administration risked losing their jobs.

Around 1770, French revolutionaries founded a fringe order called *Les*

Illuminés (The Enlightened). Based at Château Erméneville, the sect advocated executing the royal family as the first step in an international campaign to exterminate tyranny, in other words the European aristocracy. The notorious 18th-Century occultist Alessandro Cagliostro-Balsamo is believed to have been affiliated with *Les Illuminés*. It became closely associated with plots against the monarchy and played a role in the early stages of the French Revolution. The order's existence soon became known to the authorities. They suspected that its purpose is to establish a democratic world republic by force. Among them was the advocate general of Paris, Antoine Séguier. In 1770 he warned, "A godless and audacious sect has risen among us. It presents its false teachings as philosophy. It has hoisted the banner of rebellion. Governments should tremble that they tolerate a sect of nonbelievers right in their lap. It is one that appears to have no other purpose than to stir nations up under the pretext of enlightening them."[56]

England's ambassador to Prussia, the Earl of Malmesbury, recorded in his diary a conversation on the subject with his sovereign King George III: The monarch "understood from what he had heard that these *illuminés* were a sect invented by the Jesuits to overthrow all governments and all order. That this scheme was only known to a very few at the head of the sect, and instructed in its mysteries, and that all the followers were kept in ignorance, and taught to consider it as innocent, and more moral than Freemasonry."[57] After the French Revolution unseated the royals, members of *Les Illuminés* would fall victim to the guillotine during the Reign of Terror in 1793-1794. The sect is often confused with another secret society, the Illuminati, founded by Dr. Adam Weishaupt in May 1776. Both orders propagated abolishing absolutism in favor of a democratic form of government.

Weishaupt hailed from Ingolstadt in Bavaria and earned a doctorate in law in 1768 at age 20. Captivated by the cosmopolitan, liberal ideals of the age, he visited a Freemason lodge for the first time in Nuremburg two years later. Dissatisfied with what he perceived as its members' insincerity toward the pre-scribed mystic rituals among other things, he established his own quasi-masonic order. First called the *Bund der Perfectibilisten* (League of Perfectibles), it was renamed *Orden der Illuminaten* in 1778. Weishaupt was a rationalist advocating brotherhood of all mankind and rejecting the absolute authority of kings and clergy. Unlike the revolutionary movement in France, he opposed the "illegal" use of force to achieve political objectives. The Illuminati excluded monks, Jews, members of other lodges and women from membership, which is paradoxical for an order advocating universal equality and freedom of beliefs. Weishaupt preached peaceful reform and there is no evidence that he became personally affiliated with the radical *Illuminés* in France or was actively involved in the French Revolution.

This was not always the case among Weishaupt's membership. The former Illuminati Siegmund von Rotenhan wrote this about the order in 1818: "The French Revolution broke out and attracted universal attention, naturally also that of the secret Illuminati. A greater field of opportunity than in Bavaria opened up to its adherents. They became cosmopolitan, joined together with the Frenchmen of the Revolution and adopted their principles. They advanced step by step with the Revolution. When the guillotine supplanted human rights in France, when an unsavory exultation of the filthy sans-culottes (poorer classes) replaced equality before the law, and when instead of legally protected liberties the most frightful anarchy prevailed, along with the dishonorable murder of the king, in short as the French Revolution degenerated, the Illuminati participated all the more zealously. This decline of morality corresponds completely with their methods and their beliefs. They therefore sided with the Jacobins. This close union of the Jacobins and the Bavarian Illuminati spread into Germany."[58]

In 1780 Johann von Wöllner, an officer in the Berlin Freemason lodge *Neuen Gold und Rosenkreuzerorden* (New Golden Order of the Rosicrucians), orchestrated a malicious smear campaign to destroy Weishaupt's sect. In addition to publicly denouncing the Illuminati in libelous tracts, Wöllner provided Bavarian authorities with fabricated evidence of its alleged subversion. The Illuminati indeed distributed democratic literature in Bavaria, as did other groups including *Les Illuminés*, but the pamphlets did not advocate overthrowing the government. Wöllner's endeavors were so successful that the sect was outlawed in Bavaria. Illuminati members employed in civil service were dismissed and others exiled or imprisoned. Weishaupt was stripped of his professorship in Ingolstadt. In 1787 the Duke of Saxe-Gotha-Altenburg granted him asylum and he lived out his days in Gotha writing books about illuminism.

In France, persons affiliated with *Les Illuminés* were not the only subversives seeking to overthrow the monarchy by unscrupulous means. The Duke of Orleans for example, was grand master of the Grand Orient Lodge of France. He provided financial assistance to revolutionary movements in the naive belief that were Bourbon kings deposed, it would create a path for himself to the throne. The radicals who flattered and patronized him of course had no intention of replacing one tyrant with another, but needed his money so said nothing to him to dispel the delusion. In the spring of 1789, the duke disrupted food deliveries to Paris by purchasing surplus grain in an attempt to corner the market. In the opinion of the English historian Nesta Webster, "There can be no doubt that the famine of 1789 was deliberately engineered by the agents of the duke, and that by this means the people were driven to the pitch of desperation necessary to produce the Revolution."[59]

Among English Freemasons politics and religion were not discussed. This was not the case in German states. Masonic lodges and prior to being proscribed the Illuminati as well, disseminated propaganda to advance the revolutionary agenda opposing absolutism, the royals' frequent war waging and the political influence of the church. "The educated classes became more and more captivated by them, especially academic youth in secret student orders", a German study observed.[60] Grand Duke Karl August of Weimar warned Friedrich Wilhelm II that "there is quite a stir in the Prussian ministry, because the order is believed to have a huge following in the Prussian army."[61] Prominent government officials urged the king to ban the student societies. These included state ministers Philipp Karl von Alvensleben and Count Christian August von Haugwitz. They submitted a memorandum to Friedrich Wilhelm urging that he recommend the same course of action to the Reichstag in Regensburg.

The Prussian ambassador in Vienna, Count August von Goltz, considered such an initiative "pointless… because in Berlin like everywhere else, there are people in the king's ministry who are still affiliated with the orders or had previously belonged to them, and they can easily… create obstacles."[62] Historian Hans Riegelmann stated that one result of the lodges' intrigues was "the unusually weak, inadequate Prussian war preparations before 1792, the frivolousness of the generals and so forth, all this was essentially the fault of those forces and their influence. The ideological propaganda had planted the ideas of Freemasonry and the Illuminati so deeply into the state's leadership class that no one really took the coming war seriously."[63] Prussian cavalry General Johann Bischoffwerder told his quartermaster Christian von Massenbach for example, "Don't buy too many horses. The comedy won't last long. The freedom swindle is already going up in smoke in Paris… We'll be home by autumn."[64]

By way of comparison, Napoleon wrote, "At the moment when war is declared, there are so many things to be done that it is wise to have looked a few years ahead… I am accustomed to think out three or four months in advance what I should do, and base my calculations on the worst (possible scenario). Nothing is gained in war except by calculation."[65] Friedrich Wilhelm II ignored the discord in his government and officer corps, disregarded his people's negative attitude toward war and underestimated the Revolution's domestic appeal. He believed that a marginal show of force will suffice to scatter the French army like at Rossbach. The French regarded the looming confrontation as a matter of national survival and mobilized the country's resources to resist. Their parliament, the Legislative Assembly, instructed farmers to destroy crops and granaries and to arm themselves. French women enlisted in the army, though rejected by some recruiters. Others accepted them and praised their patriotic example for enrolling "not out of love for their men, but out of love for freedom."[66] The first disguised themselves in men's clothing, but others soon joined dressed in their gender apparel.

At this time, the king of Prussia's mistress had a more realistic appraisal of the situation than her sovereign. She warned him in a letter, "I give up on you completely if you get mixed up in this undertaking with such a frivolous attitude. Either you march at the head of 200,000 Prussians and 250,000 Austrians or renounce any hope of victory. With this handful of people, you're just gambling with your life and offering up your honor for ridicule."[67] Beyond the ambition to preserve a waning political system, there was nothing for the king to gain by opening hostilities. France had no quarrel with his country. The Prussian agent in Paris, Benjamin Ephraim, reported in 1790 that the majority of rev-

olutionary leaders are "warm supporters of friendship with Prussia."[68] Once
the French Legislative Assembly concluded that war with Austria is inevitable,
it invited Duke Karl Wilhelm Ferdinand of Brunswick, a field marshal in the
Prussian army, to command its armed forces. During the Seven Years' War,
the Franco-Austrian alliance against Prussia had been unpopular in France.
General Charles François Dumouriez described it as "the source of all our woes."
Historian Jacques Bainville later wrote, "The Revolution and hatred of Austria
are inseparable."[69]

For Prussia, an alliance with France would be a tacit acceptance of her liber-
al-democratic regime. General Ernst von Rüchel grumbled that such a compact
can only be concluded after the French are "cured of their swindle about freedom and equality."[70] Anticipating invasion, the Legislative Assembly compelled
King Louis XVI to declare war on Austria and Prussia in April 1792. The French
army invaded and occupied the Austrian Netherlands that same month. More
than half of the army's personnel consisted of former royal troops including cavalry and a proficient artillery train. The balance was a motley assortment of enthusiastic but ill-trained volunteers with inexperienced officers. Reinforcing the
Prussian and Austrian regiments meanwhile, was the *Armeé de Condé* tallying
around 4,500 French royalists. Those who had taken refuge in Koblenz falsely
persuaded Friedrich Wilhelm's headquarters staff that the French populace will
welcome allied armies as liberators from the tyranny of Jacobin revolutionaries.[71]

For their part, propagandists of the Legislative Assembly prepared leaflets to
distribute to Prussian soldiers to encourage disobedience: "The free people of
France have reanimated the human rights of the citizen. Brothers, before you
take up arms, first demand an explanation for this campaign. When you reflect
on humanity in the political sense and on the citizen's rights, you will learn
that all mankind is born equal, that only virtue and talent distinguish one from
another. You will learn that a person is born free... that the power to make laws
rests with the people; law is but an expression of the universal will and the princes are here only to enforce it."[72] Regarding leadership, Napoleon once remarked
that the quality of the soldiers does not determine the outcome of a battle, but "it
is the one man who is everything."[73] The maxim is not universally valid but did
however, hold true for the futility of the first coalition war against France.

Friedrich Wilhelm appointed Karl Wilhelm Ferdinand, the Duke of
Brunswick who had declined the offer to lead France's army against Austria, to
be commander in chief. As a young officer, he had served with distinction in the
Hanoverian army during the Seven Years' War. In September 1787, he led an
army of 20,000 Prussians into the Netherlands to quell the Batavian Revolution.
He accomplished the task in less than a month and reaped accolade for conducting a classic 18th-Century campaign of maneuver that resulted in minimal
loss of life. He was however, seriously conflicted about the new commission. The
duke endorsed the principles of the French constitution and sympathized with
the Revolution. Regarding Freemasonry, he had been reared in a household that

Duke Karl Wilhelm Ferdinand of Brunswick served with distinction during the Seven Years' War. An advocate of the linear tactic, he became a Prussian field marshal in 1787. His military fortunes declined during the coalition wars against the French Republic.

embraced the international fellowship it stood for. His uncle Ferdinand had been grand master of all Scottish lodges in 1772 and his father protector of the lodge of Brunswick.[74]

Historian Adolf Rossberg summarized Brunswick's dilemma: "The duke was on one side a Prussian field marshal and on the other a friend of revolutionary France. He was therefore the least suitable commander in a war that was not just a purely military conflict, but more a titanic struggle over a new ideological doctrine. He believed that as a soldier he has to perform his duty to the king of Prussia, but as a philanthropist saw himself being forced onto the wrong side politically. This contradiction of military, political and philosophical principles in the heart of the field marshal completely paralyzed the conduct of the war in 1792… There are few examples in the history of war of such a disastrous blunder in choosing an army commander. The duke had shown himself to be a valiant soldier in the Seven Years' War and indeed possessed a range of outstanding qualities that captivated his entourage. He was however, fundamentally of a conflicted nature; the soldier's sense of duty and notions of the philosopher revolved discordantly in his mind."[75] Colmar von Goltz concluded, "Right from

the start, the entire operation suffered from the conflicted spirit of the commander in chief. He was obviously not in favor of the war and lacked all hope of
a favorable outcome."[76]

The Cannonade of Valmy

In February 1792, the Duke of Brunswick sent King Friedrich Wilhelm II a
memo warning him not to trust the promises that "the immigrants so carelessly spread around." He cautioned his sovereign, "Events are taking place with
unforeseen consequences, because the men who govern France possess an inertia
rendering them capable of making the most extraordinary decisions."[77] His advice
fell on deaf ears. The invasion of France began five months later. Under the duke's
vapid leadership, the Prussian army advanced at a sluggish pace. Setting off from
Koblenz on July 30, it halted in Trier less than a week later and tarried seven days,
allegedly due to insufficient rations. Dysentery already began to break out among
the troops. They did not cross the frontier into France until August 20: "A march
that should have taken at most ten days required three full weeks."[78]

Brunswick recommended a pause at the border to establish a central supply
base. The king, supposedly along as an observer, rejected the suggestion. The
slow advance of the coalition armies bought time for the French to address the
worst shortcomings of their military preparations and get the formations into
tolerable fighting shape. Brunswick's troops entering France found the indigenous population more hostile than anticipated. Armed civilians ambushed
couriers and staffs and raided depots. The invaders' ponderous supply train,
requiring 15,000 personnel to maintain, was repeatedly harassed by partisans
and delayed. They neither gave nor accepted quarter; officers of France's former
royal army were shocked at the raw brutality of their countrymen.[79]

Resistance stiffened due in part to a tactless ultimatum, the Brunswick
Manifesto, that the duke issued on July 25. Copies reached Paris a week later.
It was signed by Brunswick but written by the Prince de Condé, commander
of a French royalist contingent in the coalition army. The manifesto stated that
Austria and Prussia, "convinced that the sane portion of the French nation
abhors the excesses of the faction that dominates it," have entered a "defensive
alliance" to invade France. The objective "is to dispel anarchy" and restore monarchial authority. The declaration pledged that German troops entering France
will respect the lives and property of the population. Were the royal family
harmed by revolutionaries however, the coalition army "will inflict memorable
vengeance by delivering the city of Paris to military execution and complete
destruction."[80] The publication was intended to frighten the French people and
diminish support for the Revolution, but Parisians found the manifesto laughable. They also suspected from its tenor that Louis XVI was collaborating with
the coalition.

Propaganda prepared by French royalists in the coalition camp to subvert the
revolutionary army backfired as well. Quoting Reinhard Höhn, "All the passionate

appeals that the immigrated officers directed to their 'brothers in arms' in France to persuade them to desert, as well as the banishment declaration in case of non-compliance, had little success. It was the same with their appeals to the ordinary soldiers. In both the political and military aspects, the ideology of the immigrants collapsed… All their hopes from when the campaign began came to naught. The prophesied internal upheaval repeatedly declared imminent did not take place. The French populace, who according to the immigrants will happily welcome their liberators, exhibited not the least sympathy for them. The fortress commandants did not join them with flags flying. The French troops of the line, who based on immigrants' rumors were assumed to be royalist in disposition, stood firm."[81]

The invaders plodded into France and captured the border fortress Longwy on August 23. The French central army withdrew to Metz. It rained almost every day. This turned roads to mud and hampered troop movements. Artillery and heavy ammunition wagons struggled to advance. Camps where the soldiers bivouacked became quagmires. Despite the hostility of the elements and partisan activity, the invasion made progress. The army reached Verdun on August 30, brought forward artillery and opened fire on the fortress. The city surrendered three days later. An episode there reveals the fanaticism of some revolutionary commanders. As described by an eyewitness, "We then encountered a character trait of the Republicans. Commandant (Nicolas) Beaurepaire came under pressure from the distressed townspeople, who saw their whole city burned and destroyed by continuous bombardment. He could no longer refuse to surrender; but as soon as he gave his consent during a full session of the city council, he drew his pistol and shot himself."[82] Just before pulling the trigger Beaurepaire told the council, "Live on with your shame and your dishonor because you can. For me, faithful to my oath, these are my last words; I die a free man!"[83]

By September 14, Brunswick's main force stood between two smaller French armies under Generals Charles Dumouriez and François Kellermann that were attempting to link up. The duke was informed of the location and intention of the enemy. Had he taken the initiative, it would have been entirely possible to deal with each French army in turn and destroy both. He did little except to complain to royalist immigrants at headquarters about the hardships of the campaign. "Since entering France the army suffered from dysentery and continuous bad weather; difficulties in the rationing system mounted. The far more important circumstance, that the powers of resistance of French troops on the border as well as at Longwy and Verdun had proven negligible, was not weighed as a factor," observed Goltz. "The bearing of the Prussian troops was good, superior to that of the French despite the unfavorable influence of poor weather… insufficient rations, sickness, privations and toil."[84] The opposing French army was indeed wanting of the training and discipline of its adversary: A column of 10,000 men under Dumouriez advancing without scouts on flank security was charged in a surprise attack by 1,500 Prussian hussars and after brief resistance completely routed.[85]

The French armies joined at Valmy on September 20. Their 53,000 troops defended elevated ground. Kellermann and Dumouriez placed them with their backs to a wooded range of hills. The territory beyond the hills was controlled by coalition forces. With a reversed front facing west, it was impossible for the men to flee or desert in the event of an enemy assault. Duke Karl Wilhelm deployed 34,000 Prussians to attack. An Austrian and Hessian force was a day's march away and in the rear of the French. Despite inferior numbers, "with respect to its inner stability, the Prussian army was greatly superior" to its opponent.[86] The "battle" of Valmy was little more than a prolonged artillery duel that inflicted minimal casualties on both sides. By late afternoon, French and Prussian batteries had each discharged some 10,000 cannonballs. During a pause at around 1:00 p.m., the Prussians observed no change in the enemy lines. "No one knew where this was going," recalled Johann Wolfgang von Goethe, who took part in the battle.[87]

An explosion caused by a direct hit on a French ammunition wagon spread confusion among the defenders. Brunswick languidly ordered a few infantry regiments forward. He abruptly halted the advance when they had approached to within several hundred yards of the French line. Telling his staff, *hier schlagen wir nicht* ("We won't fight here"), he withdrew his formations from the field. After lingering for ten days the duke ordered a general withdrawal from France. The Swedish Count Axel von Fersen, in Paris during the Revolution, attributed this singular conduct to "cowardice and indecision".[88] Historians offer tenuous

The Prussian infantry deploys at Valmy. The Duke of Brunswick ordered a few battalions to march uphill toward the French position then recalled them before they reached enemy lines.

explanations for the sudden recall of the Prussian infantry at Valmy just as it was about to come to grips with the enemy. These include muddy conditions, the accuracy of French gunners, dysentery among Brunswick's soldiers, the élan of the defenders and even their shouts of *vive la nation* that supposedly "had a crushing effect on Prussian morale."[89] The genuine causes of the withdrawal and subsequent "unaccountable retreat from Paris" remain a mystery. The duke told the Comte de Jarnac, "Why I retreated will never be known to my death."[90]

There was no military justification for Brunswick's decision. In the words of Rossberg, "The French army of 1792 was torn apart by politics. Many of the troops were still loyal to the Bourbons. The new military units possessed no real confidence in their prowess at war and were not closely bound to their officers. Some of the most popular generals had turned against the Revolution's leaders after the arrest of the king in August 1792 and had fled to Germany, leaving behind a dismayed army."[91] French Field Marshal Armant de Biron had written of his soldiers on September 09, "I already have too many people who want to eat but far too few who want to do anything in return."[92] French Captain François Laurent wrote that Brunswick's retreat prevented a "major disaster… when I saw the condition of our troops back then, I could scarcely imagine how they could have even deployed in such unfavorable terrain."[93]

Eyewitness Goethe wrote of the Prussian infantry, "We all had the burning desire to fly at the French, at that moment officers and men alike were eager for our field marshal to launch the attack."[94] Georg von Valentini, a Prussian officer there, recounted "descriptions by those French eyewitnesses of the anxious, frightened manner of Kellermann's troops on the Valmy heights at the opening of the cannonade and when some powder wagons blew up," as well as the "calm, sober fighting resolve of the Prussians."[95] The explosion of the powder wagon demanded the utmost from French officers to keep their troops in line: At this moment, an energetic attack would have put the French in an embarrassing position. Valentini summarized that in months to follow, Brunswick "avoided every battle. It is difficult to comprehend his perception and intentions."[96] According to Höhn, all the battle of Valmy demonstrated is that the French will not run at the first sight of the enemy.[97]

An officer on Brunswick's staff later related how the duke told him that he called off the attack because French forces might be concealed behind the Valmy heights. Goltz contended, "This would have been easy to reconnoiter. The terrain was not an insurmountable obstacle. There was no shortage of horsemen. In any case the lack of knowledge was no greater than in countless similar situations."[98] Senior Prussian commanders had become susceptible to political ideas promulgated by the country they were at war with, enough to the disobey a direct order to advance on Paris. They conducted secret negotiations with the enemy to form an alliance, ultimately causing the defeat of the very armed force entrusted to their command. During 1792 a "party of discontented" in Prussia opposed war against France. Known in Berlin as "the clique", it included Freemasons,

Plagued by dysentery, the Prussian army retreats through the Champagne after Valmy. Rainstorms compounded their misery during the march, especially for the artillerymen whose guns became stuck in quagmires.

influential persons at court or in finance, diplomats, politicians and army officers. This party asked Prince Heinrich to persuade the king to break with Austria and side with France. Among other dissenters was Franz Leuschenring of the Neuwieder Illuminati lodge, whom Friedrich II had fired as his nephew's philosophy tutor in 1784, and Prussian finance minister Karl Struensee.[99]

After the cannonade of Valmy, the duke authorized Colonel Ernst Johann von Manstein, a Freemason on his staff, to conduct secret negotiations with French commander in chief Dumouriez to avoid further bloodshed.[100] Manstein, in the opinion of British ambassador Malmesbury "an empty good-for-nothing fellow,"[101] even invited the French general to dine at Prussian field headquarters. The talks were in direct defiance of Friedrich Wilhelm II's orders. The king considered French revolutionaries a "horde of barbarians, whose steps are to be traced by anarchy and cruelty wherever they came."[102] Brunswick must have reached a clandestine understanding with the French; the prominent state minister Georges Danton instructed Dumouriez to follow the retreating Prussians without engaging, since they "are not the natural enemies of France."[103] French journalist Camille Desmoulins wrote, "All the soldiers of the vanguard of our army will tell you that when the rearguard of the Prussians called a halt, we called a halt; when they went to the right, we marched to the left. In a word, Dumouriez led back the King of Prussia rather than pursued him, and there was not a soldier in the army who was not convinced that there had been an arrangement between the Prussians and the Convention by the medium of Dumouriez."[104]

The Rootless Tree

After the battle of Valmy, the French declared their country a republic and stripped the king of the last vestige of authority. The National Convention replaced the Legislative Assembly as governing body. The French army invaded the Pfalz (Rhineland-Palatinate) region with an 18,000-man army under General Philippe de Custine. It captured Worms and Speyer in late September, sacking and torching the latter. The army marched north toward the Rhine River fortress of Mainz. This was a haven for French aristocrats who had fled the revolution.[105] The Germans had been reinforcing Mainz since April. They stocked it with extra powder and artillery rounds, refilled the moat, shored up fortifications and imported enough corn to withstand a two-year siege. The military garrison initially consisted of 2,000 soldiers mostly from the province, a squadron of Austrian hussars and 900 men retuning from medical leave under Captain Andujar. The investment of Mainz would reveal the discord among Germans caused by the insidious influence of republican values and the military hierarchy's failure to provide a semblance of leadership.

Custine's approach induced some residents to leave Mainz. "No nobleman thought of offering resistance", the historian Karl Klein maintained in an 1861 chronicle of the siege, "None of those who just before had railed against the French possessed the courage to stay. They wanted only to rescue themselves and their property, unconcerned about the duty they had to the state, not worried about what would happen to it…. But the ordinary citizens did not leave. They remained in the city of their fathers and would not abandon house and hearth. On the contrary, they were resolved to offer the enemy the most resistance possible."[106] A herald directed those lacking serviceable weapons to report to the armory. "And they rushed there to arm themselves for their city; citizens and tradesmen, students and very young people, practically boys, all got weapons. On the first day alone over a thousand rifles were distributed."[107] On October 16, court chancellor Franz von Albini wrote the duke in Kaisenberg, "Yesterday we mustered 1,200 handworkers and the governor was amazed at how well these lads already do in training… there's a genuine spirit of nationalism among us."[108]

Albini had already written Kaisenberg on the 11th of the example the city has set for the Rhine territories: "The French have their intelligentsia here. They think to disarm us… and want to scare us into joining the revolution. But we've beaten them to it and have saved ourselves and the whole region. Frankfurt, Koblenz, every place except for Mainz had already decided to open the gates, but now they've pulled themselves together thanks to our example. The Rhine districts want to defend themselves with us to the last drop of blood."[109] The following day Albini notified Kaisenberg that public enthusiasm and the number of volunteers is so great that the administration can barely provide enough arms. Everyone wanted a weapon and anyone who spoke of surrender to the "French windbags" was arrested on the spot: "Without Mainz the French would have their revolution, but our preparations are commanding the respect of the entire region."[110]

While expressing confidence in the "unbelievably determined townsfolk", Albini complained in an October 18 dispatch that there are scarcely any recruits from wealthy families. He described the "wretched impression" upper class citizens make on fellow residents "whenever they timidly show themselves" on the street.[111] The French proclaimed a "war for the cottage and against the palace," yet their primary supporters in Germany came from among the affluent. Klein wrote, "The same men, worldly and spiritualistic, had been a part of the widely spread Illuminati order... When in 1784 the order was outlawed in Bavaria, its main branch, many came from there to us. They suffered the same fate here in 1786, but supporters remained true to their beliefs... When the French Revolution began, these men got a fresh start and were no longer afraid, as they had been before, to publicly confess their democratic principles, praising the blessings of French liberty."[112] The chief court solicitor of Mainz, Anton Hauterive, warned that wealthy residents previously affiliated with the Illuminati are spreading revolutionary propaganda and represent "a far more dangerous society for the state" than ever before.[113]

Tenanting a sensitive position was the former Illuminati and university professor Major Rudolph Eickemeyer. According to a 19th-Century biographer, he "had no liking for the patrician state and felt in his heart no patriotism for Germany."[114] An officer of engineers, he was assigned to fortify the city walls: "In his capacity as chief of fortress construction he bears a certain responsibility for the deficient state of Mainz's fortifications... In a frivolous manner, the fortress construction program of 1790/91 was only partially completed by Eickemeyer."[115] Among other things none of the arsenal's inventory of flares, essential for engaging the enemy at night, were distributed. Six-pounder cannonballs were delivered to twelve-pounder guns positioned on the parapet. "Even in the final days the greatest negligence prevailed, which can only be attributed to wicked and downright treasonous intentions."[116] From the university telescope set up in the bell tower of Mainz's Stephan Church, Eickemeyer observed the French camp. He reported to the military governor, General Freiherrn von Gymnich, that 30,000 infantry and cavalry and a large artillery train are investing the city.[117] The estimate of enemy strength was "ridiculously exaggerated."[118]

Eickemeyer supplied the French with vital intelligence about Mainz's defenses via his friend Georg Wedekind, a professor and physician who left the city for several days ostensibly to treat sick residents of Nackenheim. On October 18 he met General Custine instead and provided accurate information about the garrison and fortifications.[119] Wedekind participated in reading society discussions, "vocally expressing his enthusiasm for the new liberty, even as the French waged war against Germany and were literally at the gate."[120] He had previously proclaimed in his weekly newsletter that "patriotism is a convention that has been overcome," and denounced the "heathen princes" for preaching that there are "so-called racial differences in mankind."[121] Regarding Wedekind's visit, Custine wrote French General Armand Louis de Gontaut, "I know for certain the number of troops there and I have been informed of every detail of the defenses."[122] After the fortress capitulated, Wedekind told the French commissioner of Mainz on February 21, 1793, "Without me Custine would probably have had difficulty taking Mainz or at least would have had to sacrifice a great number of people… What I did consists of first winning over with considerable effort Colonel Eickemeyer, and second that while he was already attacking the city, I personally brought Custine the information he needed."[123]

Time was on the side of the Germans. A Prussian army would arrive to raise the siege in less than two weeks. Several hundred local farmers came to Mainz to upgrade fortifications and reinforce the combat troops. A mounted contingent of French royalists joined the garrison before Custine surrounded the town. The total armed force defending the fortress swelled to 5,780 men. The volunteers practiced daily to hone their marksmanship. "The citizens had little experience with firearms, but stood bravely and energetically beside the soldiers, especially the artillery."[124] As he marched on Mainz, Custine consistently detached troops to protect his army. He left 500 men in Worms, another 500 to guard Rhine bridges, sent 1,500 soldiers to Frankfurt and 2,000 toward Binger and Kreuznach to cover the flank against possible Austrian counterattacks. He had just 45 cannons. Most were eight-pounders and there were no heavy calibers.[125] The French possessed too few troops and guns to take Mainz.[126]

On October 18, Custine deployed six field guns before Mainz. The crews fired a few rounds that bounced off of the walls without causing a single casualty. Inconclusive artillery duels followed. The next day he issued three successive surrender demands. The wording was a paradoxical blend of exaggerated promises and threats, which the town council convened to discuss. Albini and the two other civilian members voted to fight on. Inclined to surrender, Generals Gymnich and Prince Franz von Hatzfeld deferred the decision to the war council. The elderly Gymnich told it that Mainz is low on ammunition and cannot resist a 25,000 to 30,000-man French army for long. The strength of the enemy host he based solely on Eickemeyer's estimate.[127] He also mentioned the large number of scaling ladders spotted in the French camp. Eickemeyer reported having observed from the Stephan tower 14 to 16 wagonloads of them.[128] Custine had in fact confiscated some "chicken ladders" from a large farm in Moosheim and from barns along the march, loaded them onto wagons and unpacked them at Mainz to bluff the defenders. None were tall enough to surmount the city walls.[129]

The military council, which included the Prussian ambassador, voted for the garrison to lay down its arms. The councilmen feared that a French army forcing its way into town in heavy fighting will take revenge on the civilian population. The officers signed the capitulation on October 21. When the decision was announced, "the public was dissatisfied to the utmost with the surrender."[130] Custine allowed the military garrison to leave the city unmolested. Hussar Captain Andujar, whose name was added to the cease-fire document without his knowledge, said of Gymnich, "He's a disgrace to beg for a retreat that he could have accomplished by force of arms."[131] Curious townspeople ventured beyond the walls to visit the French encampment. "They were more than a little amazed at the small and insignificant army, how a large number of empty tents had been pitched, how little ammunition and food supplies were on hand, how there were no heavy guns, nothing for a bombardment in the camp, how the dreaded ladders were only suitable for haylofts and so forth."[132]

On October 23, 5,000 French troops marched through the city gates led by a military band playing *La Marseillaise*. Residents watching the procession were askance at the unsoldierly bearing of the invaders. One observer wrote, "Now we could see with our own eyes how little cause for fear there was for the supposedly overwhelming French superiority. The 40,000 enemies Eickemeyer told us about shrunk to 11,000. Their scruffy and motley appearance scarcely evoked respect. If one went to the camp they left behind outside the city, one saw not only the swindle of the unoccupied tents set up for show, but also the obvious lack of cannon: There was not one large caliber gun so indispensable for a siege."[133] No less lame was Gymnich's excuse that Mainz, despite having over 200 guns, is indefensible due to lack of ammunition. Inventory taken by the French upon capturing the town included 20,983 bombs, 27,684 howitzer rounds, 7,757 grenades, 250,973 cannonballs and 468,000 pounds of gunpowder. The supply was more than adequate to hold the town.[134] The day after Mainz fell, Custine wrote the war ministry in Paris, "I could clearly see that I had no other way to capture this fortress than to frighten its defenders."[135]

"The reason for the retreat from Valmy and the closely connected, subsequent betrayal of Mainz," Riegelmann summarized, "can ultimately be found in the resistance of a peace party within the Prussian army against the will of the king."[136] Eickemeyer received a colonelcy in the French army and was promoted to brigadier general in May 1793. Explaining that he switched sides "to defend the rights of mankind," he served in General Jean Moreau's army of occupation along the Rhine. In this capacity Eickemeyer "was in no way humane in the treatment of his countrymen."[137] The people of Mainz did not fare well under the new master. "Not only did they have to hand over much property through various decrees, but provide labor to build more fortifications. Also, since the French frowned on arrangements some citizens had with the allies, they closely monitored every word, every transaction with sharp eyes and terrorized the city to the utmost."[138] Klein observed with understatement, "The citizens of Mainz were not disposed to democratic conviction."[139] A dismayed German wondered, "How is it possible that the Gaul's rootless tree of liberty could plant itself in our midst instead of the oak of Wotan?"[140]

Against King and Country

The betrayal of Mainz was a consequence of conflicting ideals and social barriers dividing Germans. When Friedrich Wilhelm I, the "soldier king," took steps to abolish medieval serfdom the landed aristocrats rebelled. They did not welcome compulsory education for peasants and regarded the burgeoning middle class with suspicion. Many German princes, especially in the Rhineland-Palatinate, owed their titles to having sided with the French against their own country-men.[141] Most did nothing to hinder Custine's 1792 invasion of the western Rhine territory. Prince Charles Theodore of the Palatinate professed strict neutrality. He delayed countermeasures of the allied royalist coalition by refusing to allow its armies to cross the Rhine anywhere in his domain.[142] The landgrave of Darmstadt led 3,000 troops to Giessen, withdrawing from threatened territory, and instructed remaining administrators "not to cause offense" to the French and to supply them with provisions. "He is completely on the side of the enemy," the Prussian ambassador wrote Berlin. "Palatine officials even want to create dif-ficulties for the Mainz patrols."[143] French spies received Palatine passes in order to move inconspicuously behind German lines.

The collusion angered Friedrich Wilhelm II, but he lacked the firm hand to direct his country in the turbulent political and social climate of the time. Without natural frontiers, Prussia was held by force of arms; she was in a sense an artificially created Great Power. Smaller than her European rivals, survival depended on resolute leadership especially in the realm of national defense. After Friedrich the Great died, Prussia gradually lost much of her martial char-acter.[144] Educated society and the aristocratic officer corps conducted aesthetic discussions about the merits of the Enlightenment. Visiting Paris in 1789, the journalist and educator Joachim Campe lauded the French "miracle" in the *Braunschweigische Journal* (*Brunswick Journal*). No longer, he wrote, did he and his travelling companion feel themselves to be Brandenburger and Brunswicker: "All national differences, all national prejudices vanished. Now all have their long withheld human rights and for our part we feel the same… that this transforma-tion in the French state is the greatest and most universal blessing for mankind since Luther's Reformation… Humanity all over the world, white, black, brown and yellow, we all praise God together."[145]

Historian Siegfried Fiedler analyzed attitudes among Prussian intellectuals: "Little was heard regarding a deeper comprehension of the unromantic side of the Enlightenment, the side made graphically clear by revolutionary Jacobinism and subsequent practical application via the saber by Napoleon Bonaparte. This led instead to all the more longing for a world of benevolence and beauty. Public interest focused on literature and the theater or on events in other countries rather than on policies at home. Philanthropic sentiments about civilization based on peace and liberal values increasingly obscured awareness of the exter-nal threat. More and more, recognition of the certainty of war and necessity of feverishly preparing for it receded to the background… No one wanted to hear

French troops invading the Palatinate help themselves to whatever they can steal. Their conduct turned the rural population against them while German intellectuals praised the Republic for promoting "brotherhood of mankind."

about an expanding the military and unavoidably increased taxation."[146]

In a dispatch to foreign secretary Lord Grenville in London, ambassador Malmesbury expressed dismay over "the progress of French opinions in Germany" and how certain state ministers have become "infected with the principles of the *Rose-croix* and *Illuminés*." These ideas, he added, "have long since been instilled into the minds of the rising generation here, most insidiously and plausibly, by the professors of different Universities, and which, if they once get head, would soon overthrow a fabric so tottering and so complicated, but at the same time so important to be preserved, as that of the German Constitution. The nobility, the gentry, and large capitalists in this town and neighborhood, the most populous and most independent in Germany, cannot be made to understand the danger with which they are threatened, and which is at their very gates. They are all clamorous for peace, and, by the most fatal error which ever perverted the human understanding, attribute the evils of war and its duration, not to the enemy, but to the very powers who are endeavoring to rescue them from destruction."[147]

The peace party in the Prussian army had wanted to conclude hostilities after Valmy. They considered France a better ally for their country than Austria.

Friedrich von Kalckreuth led the faction. He was partial to France and made no secret of his aversion of fighting her.[148] Malmesbury wrote London, "This sentiment, I am sure, prevails in the Prussian army. A spirit of party and perhaps corruption may influence the conduct of some of its principal commanders; but there is, besides this, a strong taint of democracy amongst the body of officers and men, and a dislike for the cause for which they ought to be fighting."[149] Thinking in the officer corps had fundamentally changed since the Seven Years' War. Officers had learned to debate in the lodges and preferred discussing philosophy and politics to the science of war.

Captain Gebhard von Blücher criticized the "sentimentality and lack of martial spirit" in his colleagues, whom he said are arousing a "dangerous abhorrence of war" among younger officers.[150] The statesman and diplomat Hans Freiherr von Gagern offered this perspective: "The national hatred between Austria and Prussia, despite their recent treaties, is too deeply rooted... We suffer from poor administration, the extravagance of Friedrich Wilhelm II, as well as overconfidence and an underestimate of the enemy and his potential. Revolutionary ideas and phantasies about the (French) constitution infect our minds from Prince Heinrich down to second lieutenant."[151]

Supported by England, coalition states launched a second campaign against France in 1793. The French army suffered several defeats due to insufficient training and untalented leadership. It did profit from disharmony among its adversaries and the cautious strategy of the Duke of Brunswick, who was again in command of the coalition army. After helping liberate Mainz in July, the Prussians advanced at a snail's pace. It took them two months to reach the French frontier. On September 14, French General René Moreaux broke camp at Hornbach and marched his Vosges Corps to Pirmasens. Under political pressure from Paris, he attacked the fortified Prussian position there and was repulsed losing 4,000 men. Since just three of Brunswick's eleven infantry battalions were heavily involved in the fighting and the cavalry was intact, he should have pursued the retreating Vosges Corps. According to a survivor, it was in "complete dissolution", plagued by desertion and had become "just a horde of refugees."[152] The French forcibly herded local farmers into columns to march along with the army. This was to give Prussian scouts the impression of a larger force.[153]

King Friedrich Wilhelm sent two letters to the duke at this time. One stated his intention to come to Pirmasens and the second ordered an offensive against Hornbach to exploit the victory. Brunswick instead detached unnecessarily large Prussian contingents to secure the flanks against a possible counterattack. This served to water down the main strike force. He postponed further advance to await reinforcements. In the verdict of the historian Goltz, "Like all other successes, the victory at Pirmasens was not exploited."[154] The duke sat with his army at Pirmasens till mid-November. The only significant operation was a risky night assault he personally planned against Bitsch, a French strongpoint with a large supply depot. The 1,800-man attack force, all volunteers, was repulsed with a loss of 500 men. The coalition established limited strategic objectives that did not pose a mortal threat to the Republic.

In October, Austrian Field Marshal Dagobert von Wurmser assaulted the 65,000-man French army entrenched between Weissenburg and Lauterburg. He inflicted heavy losses on it and forced it to retreat to Hagenau. The Duke of Brunswick at this time was concerned with finding winter quarters for the army. This gave the French time to replenish their field forces. Early in November the Moselle Army, commanded by the energetic General Lazare Hoche, tallied 40,000 men and the Republic's Rhine Army 60,000. Hoche pursued the withdrawing Brunswick with 20,000 of his troops but was rebuffed at Biesingen by the smaller Prussian rearguard. The French suffered 760 casualties and 42 men captured while only 16 Prussian soldiers were killed.[155] Undaunted, Hoche regrouped and attacked the duke's fortified encampment at Kaiserslautern on November 28. In a three-day battle, the Moselle Army was again repulsed by the outnumbered Prussian defenders and finally driven away in a counterattack.

Despite the weakened state of Hoche's force, Brunswick failed to capitalize on the victory. According to Lieutenant Georg von Valentini, "Hoche would not have brought a single cannon back with him across the Otterbach, had his steadfast foe not been content with simply parrying the assault."[156] Pursuing the French with his hussars, Captain Blücher sent a note to the duke stating, "The enemy isn't retiring, he's running!"[157] After winning a skirmish at Sambach, he aborted the chase because Brunswick sent no infantry to follow. The duke did however, write adjutant-general Manstein asking forgiveness for having allowed the successful counterattack. He apologized because it delayed settling into comfortable quarters for the winter.[158] Granted another respite, the Moselle Army rallied and struck Wurmser's forces entrenched around Reichshofen on December 08. The seesaw battle raged for 14 days. Austrian troops under General Friedrich von Hotze bore the brunt of the defense.

Brunswick dispatched eight infantry battalions and some dragoons to help. "Why not the whole force," Valentini ventured, "is hard to imagine. It should have been such a natural, almost mechanical step to press forward with both armies, just as the enemy had done."[159] In a letter to his sovereign, Brunswick attributed his meagre contribution at Reichshofen to "muddy, difficult terrain that prevents employment of guns"[160] (an obstacle that did not hinder the French). Prussian journalists blamed the valiant Hotze for the failure to hold the position. The Austrians fell back to the Rhine and crossed at Germersheim. Brunswick followed suit and nestled his army in the Palatinate for the cold season. The Prussian garrison abandoned Kaiserslautern on December 30. The War Commissariat, "in those days a regular corps of thieves," used the retreat as a welcome pretext to burn the military depot at Frankenthal. This was ostensibly to prevent it from falling into French hands. The actual purpose was to avoid inspection of inventory well below what was declared on the manifests and to inflate invoices to replace stores.[161]

"The only positive gain of the campaign was the recapture of Mainz," summarized Goltz, "but despite the (Prussian) army's material and moral superiority and repeated tactical victories, in the end it was all just a general retreat. The campaign cost the army losses as great as what a couple of decisive battles would have demanded. According to surviving and reasonably accurate casualty figures, we can reckon with 400 officers and 10,000 men all told… no proof that wavering, artificial war waging is more humane than one of freshness and vitality striking heavy blows."[162] General Louis Desaix wrote the French ambassador in Bern, François-Marie de Barthélemy, that during the fighting Prussian officers occasionally visited his headquarters at night to advise him "of movements which the Austrians propose to make the next day."[163] It does not matter whether the Duke of Brunswick knew of these intrigues, which cost Prussian as well as Austrian lives, or privately approved of them. A general is responsible for the conduct of his officers and here too, Brunswick bears a great measure of responsibility for the failure of the coalition forces during 1793. At the end of the campaign, he was relieved of command at his own request.

The belligerents prepared for another round the following spring. Prussia was again the weak link in the allied chain. In February 1794 Malmesbury wrote Lord Grenville from Berlin, "Your Lordship will undoubtedly have heard from different quarters that this Court has agents at work to negotiate either a truce or separate peace with the Convention."[164] He added that the rumors stood in "direct contradiction to the positive assurances I hear daily from the King of Prussia," and found it difficult to suspect duplicity "from so high a quarter." The peace party carried on its intrigues nonetheless. Kalckreuth and his accomplices sought to enlist the Duke of Brunswick to help end the war. The duke would later write Hanover's Field Marshal Johann Wallmoden, "By 1793 they already wanted to get Prussia out of the coalition and see me mediate this sordid business to dump the blame on me."[165] Visiting Malmesbury, Brunswick described himself as having been "a puppet on a wire, a puppet of people whom I despise."[166] Upon Malmesbury's proposal that he assume command of the Austrian army instead, the duke retorted that its "men are good, but the officers Jacobinically inclined." Summarizing the dialog in a dispatch to London, the ambassador related the duke's apprehension that "that nonsensical sect of *Illuminés*, which were laughed at and treated too lightly in the beginning, had now taken such a root, and had acquired so many followers, that they governed everywhere."[167]

Support of republican ideals was not the only factor influencing Berlin's peace party. The other coalition states pursued self-serving interests. Prussian chancellor Karl August von Hardenberg received intelligence that Vienna regards the alliance with England and Russia as an opportunity to reestablish Austria as an "independent and unassailable Great Power".[168] Austrian foreign minister Freiherrn von Thugut was "filled with an uncompromising hatred of Prussia, out of recognition of the irreconcilable conflict of interests" between the two countries.[169] He insisted that "Prussian troops participate in the third campaign in full force." His ulterior purpose was to weaken Prussia through war.[170] Friedrich Wilhelm demanded that neighboring German states contribute to the military effort "if not with man and horse, at least with money."[171] Thugut did not contribute Austria's share of subsidies for the Prussian army. In the east, Moscow and Berlin were at odds over the division of Poland. England considered a "French Belgium" a threat to national security and wanted Prussia to fight her battles for her on the continent. Kalckreuth and the peace party therefore perceived their country as becoming a stooge of the coalition partners. They advocated devoting military resources to combat the insurrection in Poland instead of to fighting France.

In February, Friedrich Wilhelm transferred Möllendorff from Poland to take charge of the Palatine army. Praised for "enlightened humanitarianism," and previously on the king's committee for military reform, he lobbied to mollify the severity of discipline, increase pay for the troops, and provide them with better quality uniforms and more serviceable equipment. He admired France for her progress in this realm. Like Kalckreuth, Möllendorff was hostile toward the Hapsburgs. "Together with his ideological perception," French historian Albert Sorel maintained, "Hatred (of Austria) animated in him a certain partiality toward France and made him indulgent toward the Revolution."[172] Prussian officers and men shared his resentment of Austria. During the previous winter, Prussian troops had repeatedly skirmished against French harassing attacks while the Austrians for the most part remained in winter quarters. England and Austria planned the 1794 campaign without soliciting input from Prussia. This was perceived as marginalizing the king and his generals.

Embittered over a dearth of financial support from Austria and the Rhine states, Friedrich Wilhelm ordered Möllendorff to prepare to withdraw the army from the Palatinate on March 11. This brought the coalition partners to the conference table. For this reason, foreign minister Count Haugwitz countermanded the king's order three weeks later. The Haag treaty signed on April 19, 1794, approved subsidies for the Prussian army so it remained on the Rhine. The compact obligated Prussia to mobilize 62,400 men for war. During the diplomatic haggling, Möllendorff kept the army sidelined due to the uncertain political climate, lack of funds and his skepticism regarding the Anglo-Austrian campaign strategy.[173] Now the deck was cleared for action, but major preparations had been delayed for months. Unlike 1793, the campaign "was not to be a defensive, but an offensive one."[174] The "strategy" that Möllendorff, who had served with valor at Leuthen during the Seven Years' War, now explained to his headquarters staff is rather singular for a military commander: "He said aloud at his table that at the slightest advance of the enemy, since our allies can't be relied on, he will move the army inside the walls of Magdeburg and that Prussia must not seriously contemplate continuing the war."[175]

Möllendorff kept his 55,000-man army, which included a Saxon corps, deployed in a half-circle around Mainz till mid-May. He was uncertain about direct support from 75,000 Austrian troops along the Rhine and a Dutch force of 9,000 under General Freiherr von Blankenstein at Trier. The field marshal opted for a limited offensive. He concentrated the bulk of the Prussian army against Kaiserslautern about 20 miles west of the Rhine. The French held it with a few thousand soldiers including unarmed recruits. Once captured, the fortress could serve as a supply base to advance on Saarlouis. This, he calculated, could draw France's North Army from Belgium and bring relief to allied forces operating there.[176] Möllendorff attacked on May 22. General Jean-Jacques Ambert withdrew the outnumbered garrison toward Neustadt. The French lost 1,000 men and 17 guns in the fighting. They killed or wounded just 110 Prussians and even fewer Saxons.[177] Blücher's cavalry pursued. It captured 17 officers, 2,000 men and 19 guns and repulsed a counterattack.[178] Instead of pressing further, Möllendorff halted his regiments and fortified a 15-mile-long defensive cordon. "The French army was beaten," historian Julius Sommermeyer wrote, "but the Prussian offensive petered out on its own."[179] Goltz concluded, "So once again, the initiative was left entirely to the French."[180]

Wichard von Möllendorff was sympathetic to the Poles when governor of their lands taken by Prussia. When the king transferred him to the west, a lady of the Polish aristocracy remarked, "When he came to us, we feared him. As soon as we learned to love him, he left us." "

While his army languished for weeks at Kaiserslautern, Möllendorff met with Malmesbury and British General Charles Cornwallis on June 20. The ambassador faulted Prussia for not honoring her obligation defined in the Anglo-Austrian plan to march the army into the Austrian Netherlands. Möllendorff retorted that his country is an equal partner in the coalition yet had no say in strategic planning. He cited the lack of supply depots and hospitals necessary for an advance, and pointed out that the operation will leave Mainz, Mannheim and Koblenz undefended. The opposing French force is 60,000 strong and could invade the central Rhine once the Prussians march off. Malmesbury brought Cornwallis to refute such arguments but the general remained silent. This implied that he concurred with Möllendorff. The next day Malmesbury wrote London about "all the idle difficulties the Prussians attempt to throw in the way of their march."[181] He protested to Haugwitz in Berlin and again blamed Freemasonry for Prussia's ambivalent attitude: "I have had several conversations with him on the present situation of his own Court… He averted to the principles of the *Illuminés*, whom, rather to my surprise, he spoke of with great abhorrence, said they want to destroy all good order and subordination, and were one of the great instruments of the Jacobins."[182]

The Prussian reformer Freiherr vom und zum Stein attributed a *financial* motive to the army's static defense. Möllendorff's staff controlled a company contracted to provision the troops. Field equipment, foodstuffs and other necessities were delivered at a fixed rate. The further the army advanced from the Rhine the more extended the supply lines became. This increased transportation costs and correspondingly diminished profits.[183] Malmesbury's observation supports the accusation. He saw Möllendorff as "led by the crowd of advisors who surround him. Besides his being totally unequal to combat with them on political grounds, he is influenced by the most paltry military considerations. His army is still in cantonments, and not a regiment encamped; by these means the tents are saved, provisions are spared, and the troops preserved, as if they were in one of their own garrisons; and, in fact, it is impossible to see men in finer order, or who have less the appearance of being harassed by war."[184] Möllendorff explained his reasons for not marching northwest into the Netherlands to the king in a June 27 letter and received permission to keep the army in the Palatinate.

The French were less passive. General Claude Michaud's reinforced Rhine Army assaulted the cordon on July 02 without success, but overpowered the German position at Edenkoben eleven days later and captured its guns. The allies thereupon judged the whole cordon untenable. They abandoned Kaiserslautern and fell back toward the Pfrim River on July 31. The defeat of a few battalions caused the withdrawal of an army of 70,000 men.[185] That same month Möllendorff sent Lieutenant Knesebeck to Frankfurt to secretly meet with captive French officers and discuss a possible cease-fire.[186] Considering that Knesebeck was under orders from his sovereign to wage war against France, this is pure insubordination, if not treason, by a Prussian officer. Möllendorff personally negotiated with the French as well. This was also done without the king's knowledge. The irony is that when rumors reached the army that summer that Austria is conducting separate peace talks with the "blood-stained Robespierre" in Paris, Prussian soldiers reacted with anger and resentment.[187]

The retreat from the cordon moved the Prussian line further from Trier, a bastion projecting beyond the coalition front and defended by Blankenstein. On August 03, a French staff officer deserted and warned the Prussians that 40,000 of Michaud's troops are preparing to besiege the town. Möllendorff sent 11,000 men under Kalckreuth in relief, but distance, difficulty of terrain and foul weather prevented his corps from intervening in time. Blankenstein pulled the garrison out on August 08. The loss of Trier not only demoralized the allies, but fragmented any surviving structure of unified, cohesive command. During the march on Trier, Möllendorff had ordered Prince Friedrich Hohenlohe-Ingelfingen to harass the French Rhine Army with feint assaults. Pursuant to what Lieutenant Valentini called the field marshal's "half-hearted, do-nothing policy"[188] of minimizing combat operations so as not to disrupt peace talks, he then entrusted Hohenlohe's corps to defend the Rhine valley.

An audacious commander, Hohenlohe "knew how to circumvent the politics of the grand headquarters through military craftiness,"[189] and initially disguised his advance on Kaiserslautern as a reconnaissance in force. The corps broke camp at Göllheim on September 17. The advance guard drove back French pickets as the operation progressed. Michaud counterattacked over the next two days and was repulsed. Hohenlohe's corps smashed its adversary in a pitched battle on the 20th. It captured 100 officers and 3,000 men, four guns and eight standards. Blücher's cavalry rode down retreating French units, so that according to Valentini "only shattered remnants of the enemy reached Pirmasens."[190] Hohenlohe then destroyed French fortifications guarding Kaiserslautern. "Under his leadership," Valentini maintained, "Prussians and Austrians, Palatine farmers and other troops belonging to the *Reichsbund* fought side by side as brothers, gaining mutual respect."[191] Coalition losses were negligible.

Friedrich Wilhelm II acknowledged Hohenlohe's deed in a personal letter: "I congratulate you my dear prince, for the glorious, brilliant victory you have just won over the enemy. This new laurel you have reaped augments the extraordinary respect, the friendship and the gratitude I harbor for you, which I cannot imagine how ever to adequately repay."[192] The success at Kaiserslautern boosted morale of the Prussian and Saxon troops, who for months had stood on the defensive against a foe they felt superior to. But Möllendorff "took no joy in this pointless victory."[193] He ordered Hohenlohe to withdraw his corps to the Pfrim River near the Rhine at Pfedersheim. He then reassured the French peace envoy that if the Austrians launch an offensive to retake Trier, the Prussian army will refuse to support them and limit activity to reconnaissance. In a gesture unparalleled in military history, Möllendorff actually *apologized* to the French for Hohenlohe's victory at Kaiserslautern. He pleaded that it was "not on the agenda."[194]

Since August, Malmesbury had all but abandoned hope of Prussia fighting for England's objectives. He told a diplomat, "The loss of Trier is to be attributed solely to willful negligence on the part of Kalckreuth. I have pressed Möllendorff strongly to make an attempt to retake it, but I am certain without effect, although there is little doubt but the measure would succeed... Möllendorff is a dotard; his parts and mind are gone, and nothing remains but vanity and malice. The army is in as high an order as possible, but we never shall derive any real benefit from it. All the leading officers are ill-disposed, and many of them with decided Jacobin leanings."[195] Historian Rossberg concluded, "Under Möllendorff's leadership, the army completely disconnected from the framework of Prussian foreign policy. The bearing of the generals had changed so much since the death of the great Friedrich that they could even stand against the king. Since (Friedrich Wilhelm) had left no doubt that that he is resolved to maintain the alliance with Austria and continue the war against the 'king murderers,' secret negotiations (with the French) were tantamount to a conspiracy against the crown."[196]

Möllendorff concentrated his force around Mainz. He kept the troops ready to resist a French attack rumored to be in preparation. On October 16, with subsidies from England suspended, Friedrich Wilhelm instructed the field marshal to take the army back across the Rhine. The letter blamed the *Austrians* for "having given up all further offensives" as justification.[197] The French capitalized on the command paralysis of the enemy and conquered Belgium and the Netherlands. Peace proponents in the Prussian government joined forces with Möllendorff, Kalckreuth and their supporters in the army to pressure Friedrich Wilhelm II. Finance chairman Struensee, according to Custine "as much a partisan of the Revolution as a Prussian minister can be,"[198] formed a commission to advise the king that the war can no longer be funded. In December 1794 Prince Heinrich, also sympathetic to France, persuaded the monarch to enter negotiations.

Chancellor Hardenberg and French envoy Barthélemy ratified the Treaty of Basel on April 5, 1795. Under its terms, German lands west of the Rhine River fell to France. Paris agreed not to treat Prussia as an enemy and to seek her mediation in disputes between German duchies and France. In the verdict of Gagern, "A German can scarcely mention the peace of Basel without disgust; Reich and alliance completely dissolved, making a mockery of loyalty and faith, refuting states and nations' rights and begging the question, do either exist at all?"[199] After Basel, Hardenberg told Freiherr vom Stein that the king "would like to chop Möllendorff's head off."[200] Prussia left the coalition. This caused the allies to conclude peace with France at Campo Formio in October 1797. Friedrich Wilhelm II died less than a month later.

Chapter 4

Prussia Unprepared

Prussia on the Fence

Marshal Ferdinand Foch, who commanded Allied forces during World War I, said of the cannonade of Valmy, "The wars of kings were at an end; the wars of peoples were beginning." Absolute regimes failed to realize that it is not practical to wage war against a new world ideology from the platform of an outdated state system and way of thinking. When France invaded the Rhine states resistance collapsed, "because the political and social structure there was inferior to the French revolutionary ideology in every way and unable to animate any moral vigor."[1] At the beginning of the 1792 campaign, Austrian officers joked that it would be embarrassing to bring cannons to fight the sans-culottes, since water hoses will be sufficient.[2] Scharnhorst wrote, "Perhaps never was such mutual contempt for troops as great as at the opening of the wars of the French Revolution. The coalition armies considered the French a horde of people scraped together lacking discipline, training and organization."[3] For their part, the French despised their adversaries for slavishly serving the royals. The National Assembly proclaimed to the French army in May 1792, "We swear never to enter negotiations with the haughty or the tyrannts.!"[4]

France fought the first coalition wars to prevent absolute states from restoring the monarchy to power in Paris. These states now faced an increasingly militant opponent inspired by an international mission to liberate European populations from royal oppression. Prussian and Austrian rulers had nothing to offer their own countries to counter French propaganda extolling liberty and equality, nor did they adapt their armies to the enemy's superior battlefield tactics. Moreover, revolutionary ideals infected a portion of their own command: "Prussian officers were in no sense conscious traitors, but saw the enemy army as the representative of a new age and novel ideology. They no longer felt themselves fully committed to what they have to defend," summarized a German historian.[5] In a taut diplomatic climate, Prussia opted for a peace at any price. This surrendered initiative in foreign affairs to a Great Power that conducted an outwardly aggressive policy while internally subverting its opponent's will to resist.

Foreign Minister Haugwitz interpreted the 1795 Basel treaty as a declaration of nonbelligerency and it became the foundation of his diplomacy. "There appeared to be good cause for satisfaction with the achievement of Prussian policy, as prosperity was on the rise in Prussia while neighboring countries had suffered a great deal because of war," wrote the military historian Eduard von Höpfner.[6] "But at the same time it should have been apparent that the growth the state experienced was in no sense matched by a proportionate elevation of its esteem abroad." Austria, England and Russia felt left in the lurch by the former comrade in arms. Haugwitz's contemporaries saw him as "a small, wishy-washy man with a sparkling smile and the pleasant manner of a diplomat, but wanting of any steadfastness of character."[7]

Prussian neutrality became tenuous with the meteoric rise of Napoleon Bonaparte, the young artillery colonel who captured the strategic naval base at Toulon in December 1793. In March of the following year, at age 27, he took charge of French artillery in Italy and defeated the Austrians. He subsequently took command of France's 38,000-man *Armée d' Italie* in March 1796. Promising to improve conditions for his miserably equipped, underpaid troops, he devoted himself to their welfare and gradually transformed them into a seasoned, spirited fighting force. Napoleon cultivated a personal relationship with his men not unlike that which Friedrich the Great had with his army. The rank and file knew him as "the little corporal" and as countless anecdotes testify, often volunteered tactical advice when he rode past in the heat of combat. He defeated the Piedmont and Austrian armies holding northwestern Italy and negotiated the peace treaty himself, which was signed on April 18, 1797.

Napoleon waged war in a way that radically departed from 18th-Century convention. Previously, to protect civilian property, states fighting cabinet wars established supply bases to equip and nourish their troops. This substantially reduced requisition and looting. It also limited the range that armies can advance beyond their own border. Generals sought to outmaneuver the enemy and cut his army off from its depots. Campaigns could in this way be decided without a single major battle. Field commanders who demonstrated a talent for this strategy, such as the Duke of Brunswick, gained renown because so few lives were lost. Napoleon by contrast, sought to destroy opposing armies by ruthlessly pursuing retreating formations after defeating them. He violated the territory of neutrals and supplied his troops with whatever could be taken from the indigenous population. These methods shocked his contemporaries, who likened him to a barbarian. Bonaparte cynically boasted to the Austrian diplomat Klemens Wenzel, the Prince of Metternich, that thanks to *levée en masse*, he can afford to lose 30,000 soldiers a month.[8]

France's augmenting power disquieted European leaders. This drew battle lines anew. Unwilling to accept French control of Italy, Russia sent Prince Nicolai Repnin to Berlin to try and enlist Prussia for another campaign against the Republic in 1798. Haugwitz sidestepped commitment and Prussia sat out the second coalition war. French victories at Marengo in June 1800 and at Hohenlinden that December forced Austria and England to make peace. Napoleon took the lead role in the Republic after the November 1799 coup and became first counsel of France. By freeing the common man from bondage ten years before, the country had cast down the gauntlet before the European monarchies. France rose to the occasion by ultimately bringing to the helm a dynamic leader adroit at waging war, crafty at diplomacy and fully capable of defying the hostile allied coalition.

With a population of six million souls facing a country numbering 25,300,000, Prussia needed a ruler the caliber of Friedrich the Great; authoritative, resolute and of sound judgment. Her new king, Friedrich Wilhelm III, was none of the above. He was shy, indecisive and lacked self-confidence. In the words of a German historian, "Friedrich Wilhelm III was guided by humanitarian concepts of the Enlightenment. These principles formed an unhealthy combination with his faltering character that did not risk defying the progressive democratic influence on the Prussian state and drove Prussia, out of fear of war, into fatal isolation."[9] The king himself wrote, "The greatest good fortune for a country surely rests in perpetual peace. The best policy is therefore that which keeps an eye on this principle, since our neighbors want to leave us alone. We should not interfere in foreign matters that don't concern us… and guard against alliances that sooner or later will entangle us in foreign affairs against our will."[10] His future nemesis Napoleon judged the Prussian monarch as "the dumbest blockhead in the world, without talent, without perception, incapable of carrying on a conversation for more than five minutes."[11]

Rarely did Friedrich Wilhelm determine policy without soliciting the opinion of advisors. Among the more influential was Karl von Köckritz, whom Stein described as a "limited, unrefined man of base character."[12] The king depended on Haugwitz's counsel regarding foreign policy. Haugwitz was under the spell of privy cabinet advisor Johann Wilhelm Lombard. The son of a wigmaker from Berlin's French colony, Lombard was a gambler, at home among decadent social circles and suspected of frequently leaking state secrets to the French ambassador.[13] It was impossible for Prussia to maintain a consistent, forceful foreign policy when issues were debated by a cabinet comprising individuals advocating a tough stand against France versus those who want to ally with her. Stein cautioned, "We'll gain no advantage from being untrue to our principles, since our conduct's absence of moral character will make us the object of universal contempt and disgust."[14] The cabinet's pro-French faction misread the devious character and real intentions of Bonaparte, who disguised them with flattery and insincere expressions of friendship.

Napoleon gradually maneuvered Prussia into an untenable position. After France and England went to war in May 1803, General Eduoard Mortier marched a French army from Holland into the duchy of Hanover. It had been under English jurisdiction since 1698. Mortier blockaded English merchant ships from entering the Elbe and Weser Rivers. In so doing he disrupted Prussian overseas trade. The operation violated northern Germany's neutral zone and was an indirect affront to Prussian regional autonomy. Friedrich Wilhelm's passive response betrayed the weakness of his administration. As a result, neighboring states lost confidence in him. Scharnhorst made this comparison: "A state is like a commercial enterprise: Once it loses credit it's on the verge of collapse."[15] Napoleon transferred a generous portion of French-controlled German territory to Prussia as a reward for not taking sides against him. He simultaneously instructed his Berlin ambassador, Antoine de Laforet, to negotiate an alliance with Friedrich Wilhelm III.

Unwilling to commit to a military compact, the king attempted to compromise. He agreed not to allow the Russian army the rite of passage through Prussia to attack France and pledged to endorse Napoleon's intention to proclaim himself emperor. Friedrich Wilhelm was unhappy about French encroachment in Baden, a Rhine duchy in southern Germany, in May 1804. He nonetheless asked Russia to withdraw a protest to the German parliament in Regensburg about the violation of Baden's sovereignty. Napoleon was unimpressed. He raised his troop strength in Hanover to 30,000 men in defiance of a convention concluded with Haugwitz in June 1804. Berlin limited itself to an official protest. At the same time Russia, Austria and England urged Prussia to rejoin the allied coalition. The British prepared to land troops in Hanover via the North Sea. A Russian army massed on the Polish-Prussian border to intimidate Friedrich Wilhelm. Bonaparte was dissatisfied with the king's counterproposals to avoid a direct alliance and considered the concessions a sign of weakness. Diplomatic haggling continued into 1805, while Napoleon consolidated gains in Italy and negotiated various treaties to augment French influence on the continent.

On August 30, 1805, the king received a letter from Czar Alexander Romanov of Russia advising of his decision to declare war on France over her annexation of Italy. Though cordial in tone, the czar insisted on permission to march an army across Prussia to engage the enemy. The following month Berlin rejected Napoleon's parallel offer of Hanover if Prussia does not side with Russia and England. Meanwhile Marshal Jean Bernadotte led a French army into Prussian Ansbach on October 03. This would gain France a springboard to invade Austria. French troops wrangled with Blücher's hussars who refused to leave. Haugwitz responded with a formal protest to Paris (without result) and ordered the hussars to withdraw. Napoleon had previously promised to respect Prussian sovereignty in the region. General Kellermann, who had served at Valmy in 1792, brazenly announced that the advance will continue even if fired upon. The provocation was sensed throughout Prussia. On the eighth, the king conferred with state ministers Hardenberg and Friedrich von der Schulenburg and military commanders Möllendorff and the Duke of Brunswick to discuss how to respond. Napoleon sent an imperious letter from Ludwigsburg warning that Prussian neutrality will no longer be respected.

The blatant contempt Napoleon exhibited infuriated many Prussians, including much of the officer corps. Friedrich Wilhelm had already received a petition on September 04 signed by Stein, General Rüchel, General Friedrich von Schmettau, Colonel Karl von Phull and four princes charging that "based

French troops under Kellermann force their way into Ansbach, which was under Prussian sovereignty, to gain a favorable position to invade Austria. The lack of an energetic response from Haugwitz and the king increased Bonaparte's contempt for Prussia.

on notorious facts… your majesty's cabinet is colluding with Bonaparte to either purchase peace with the most disgraceful submissiveness or go to war with weak half measures… Our concerns are no different than those of the army and the public." Haugwitz and his advisors had supposedly "long since lost everyone's confidence. All of the insolent advantage Napoleon has taken of your majesty's love of peace is their fault. Public opinion talks of bribery. We want this investigated."[16] The king was angry over the petitioners' "punishable arrogance," though he cannot have overlooked the factual justification for their complaints.

Blücher told a friend, "We're at full strength now and it would be cowardly to think we can't resist these braggarts. Our army is good and in the best of spirits. And even if there are those who aren't with us, it was the same for Friedrich the Great."[17] Blücher wrote the king, "The measure of hatred and contempt in the army toward the French is unbelievable, more than your imperial majesty can imagine, and there is but one wish among us: to wage a bloody war against this nation and right now! Just one victorious battle and we'll have allies, money and resources from every corner of Europe. And what glory for our valiant army, to humiliate this horde of thieves that so far has conquered more through deceit and the wretched conduct of its enemies than through valor! They will never beat a Prussian army and will never beat us!"[18] After demanding without success that France pay 66,000 gulden to Ansbach for damages, the king received the czar in Potsdam to approve a treaty with Austria and Russia on November 03. General Pyotr Tolstoy marched a corps of Russian and Swedish troops from Lauenburg to Hanover two weeks later. An English-Hanoverian corps landed at Ritzebüttel. Britain agreed to pay to equip and arm 100,000 Prussian troops to fight for the coalition.

Haugwitz and his cabinet, nicknamed the "French party," delayed war preparations. Hoping Bonaparte will back down, the king authorized Haugwitz to negotiate. The French themselves understood the ultimate consequences of this policy better than Berlin did, as revealed by an in-house analysis prepared in November by the Parisian diplomat Count Alexandre de Hauterive: "Prussia has abandoned the principle that she is founded on and that justifies her existence. She maintains at significant cost a grand military apparatus but has allowed it to rust out over the years. Its prestige is still maintained by recent memories and splendid maneuvers, but it cannot withstand the test of a war forced on it. On the day that all of the shameful excuses for Prussia's timid policy of wanting to avoid war are exhausted, she will be fighting for her honor and for her very existence at the same time."[19]

To undertake his diplomatic mission, Haugwitz received a French pass on November 13 to visit Napoleon. He stalled travel, first pleading illness and then the explanation that the Duke of Brunswick told him that the army will not be ready to fight before December 22. He finally met with the French leader on November 28. Count Haugwitz was condescending and did not firmly present Prussian demands. The four-hour session was inconclusive. Napoleon deferred further talks. He sent the count on a wild goose chase to Vienna supposedly to resume the dialog there. As a result, Prussia was inactive during the battle of Austerlitz on December 02, when France's new emperor decisively defeated the combined Austrian and Russian armies. This gave Napoleon a stronger hand in negotiations with Prussia.

Returning to Schönbrunn castle in Vienna, Napoleon summoned Haugwitz to discuss a Franco-Prussian alliance. At the meeting on December 15, the count congratulated the emperor on his military victory at Austerlitz. His host dismissed this as "a compliment that has only changed addresses"[20] and threatened the Prussian envoy with war. Haugwitz submissively signed the convention in Vienna, which shuffled some territory and more or less made his country a vassal of France, without advising the king of the details. No longer able to rely on promised support from Prussia, Holy Roman Emperor Franz II concluded the treaty of Pressburg with the French on the 26th. The compact forced his empire to relinquish sovereignty over an area comprising a thousand square miles and 3,000,000 inhabitants.[21] Friedrich Wilhelm did not learn of the terms Haugwitz accepted until he returned to Berlin on December 27th. The king was not happy with the foreign minister's arbitrary diplomacy.

Clausewitz, famous for his rambling book *Vom Kriege* (*On War*), described the foreign minister as "a little man of about 50 with a friendly face and engaging manner, but with the impression of superficiality, rashness and falsehood, yet all blended into such sophisticated and composed demeanor that nothing seems odd about him."[22] The cabinet sought to circumvent the compact's obligations to France. This angered Napoleon, who imposed a tougher treaty on Prussia in February 1806. Without allies, Berlin ratified it on March 03, 1806. Historian Höpfner summarized, "The treaty of Paris forced Prussia out of her long-professed neutrality and placed her in an extremely awkward situation. She had no foothold and was completely isolated, viewed by the allied powers with hostility or mistrust and treated by France without respect."[23] Had Prussia joined Napoleon's enemies in the second or third coalition war, the Prussian army could have tipped the scales at Marengo, Hohenlinden, Ulm or Austerlitz. Prussia would have enjoyed esteem and peace by the sword instead of fragile neutrality by the grace of a contentious neighboring state.

Haugwitz was dismissed after the Vienna fiasco, but recalled as foreign minister in April 1806 upon Napoleon's insistence. This was because his replacement Prince Hardenberg did not cower before the French. When Haugwitz returned to the ministry in Berlin, army officers demonstratively cheered Hardenberg as he left office.[24] In July Bonaparte formed the *Rheinbund* (Confederation of the Rhine), a supposedly defensive league of 16 German states with France as "protector." He did not consult Prussia in advance. *Rheinbund* states pledged to provide Napoleon 63,000 soldiers in wartime. On August 06, Emperor Franz dissolved the thousand-year-old Holy Roman Empire. News reached Berlin that Bonaparte has offered England Hanover in exchange for peace. He had previously promised the province to Prussia. On August 07, the king received a letter from his ambassador in Paris, Marquis Girolamo Lucchesini. He wrote, "The talk is of war against Prussia, they want to take Bayreuth from her. The whole world may be assured that Napoleon is just looking for an excuse for war. There are large troop movements along the Wesel."[25]

To defend against a potential French invasion, Friedrich Wilhelm mobilized 147,000 troops two days later. He kept diplomatic channels with France open to buy time for rearmament. Clausewitz wrote of the period, "Prussia's policy from the peace of Basel to her catastrophe (in 1806) was characterized by weakness, spinelessness, carelessness and at times an unbecoming readiness to comply, all traits deeply rooted in the nature of Count Haugwitz."[26] General Dumouriez, who had fled France and the guillotine in 1793, analyzed Napoleon's policy in a December 1805 memo. He predicted, "After Bonaparte defeats Austria, Prussia will be the first power he attacks. Based on his whole political system, on his very character, he cannot and will not tolerate a state in his proximity, no matter how moderate its principles may be, that can mobilize two to three hundred thousand men against him within two months."[27]

The Prussian Army of 1806

The Prussian state about to take on Napoleon in 1806 had not progressed in administration, military structure or the attitude of its leadership since the Seven Years' War. France's victories in the coalition wars and infiltration of her radical doctrines into Prussian society and the officer corps made little impression on the king. Few perceived that "the French Revolution of 1789, a reaction to excessive despotism, had torn a huge rift in the fabric of absolutism shrouding Europe," as the 19th-Century army journal *Deutsche Wehrzeitung* (*German Military Times*) maintained.[28] For Scharnhorst, the lost campaign of 1794 demonstrated "the superiority of the French." Circumstances now required "a completely different way of waging war than what has been employed up till now."[29] The high command of the army saw Friedrich the Great's victories as proof of the correctness of the old fighting methods. In his last testament and his *General Principles of Warfare*, he had endorsed these inflexible, well-tried tactics.

Scharnhorst warned that "The French war will seriously shake up the valid military system, even in Prussia. If other measures are not adopted, the most frightful destruction of many a good arrangement will result."[30] He observed that generals attribute France's success to "temporary bad luck tracing its origins to a military mistake, an accident, treason, a disagreement or some other insignificant circumstance which probably won't happen again."[31] He countered, "A battle can be lost by one small omission at a junior command level and a fortress can fall due to treachery; but when ten campaigns waged by five or six armies in five years practically always end badly… then this is not just accidental nor is it caused by bribery, discord, a clique or mistakes resulting from uncertainty; the source rests with some universal evil."[32] These were bold accusations in a martial state where authority was everything and ideas contrary to the prevailing mindset were an affront to the supreme command.

Scharnhorst was not alone; others realized that the French army outclassed Prussia's in organization, tactics and morale. Another veteran of the coalition war, Knesebeck, considered his countrymen equal in courage to the enemy, "but not so motivated body and soul as those enflamed with enthusiasm. This is the difference between an army in which every man from first to last is passionately committed to the cause and one whose men are driven on by the ambition of their superiors."[33] Clausewitz wrote on the subject, "The enormous external influence of the French Revolution is much less to be found in France's novel methods and views regarding waging of war as in the totally altered state and administrative form, the character of the regime, the attitude of the people and such. That other governments misread all of these things and wanted to hold their own against fresh and overwhelming forces by conventional means was a failure of policy. Could these mistakes be identified and corrected solely from the standpoint of a military perception? Impossible!"[34]

The Revolution had indeed galvanized the population of France and with universal conscription, the army as well. An estimated 6,000 out of 9,000 officers of aristocratic birth had migrated abroad.[35] Former NCOs of the royal army filled the void. Men of peasant or middle-class origins tenanted positions of authority. Unlike the German infantry, a company commander did not ride on horseback but marched with the soldiers. There were no pack horses carrying his personal belongings. Officers and men shared meals and hardships. The soldiers them-selves were "focused warrior-types with defined, political-revolutionary goals."[36]

Prussian officers explored ways to improve their fighting forces to meet the threat. Scharnhorst described how "The frightening situation facing the French, surrounded by many armies that in their mind want to enslave them and trans-form them into an eternally miserable people, inspires the soldiers with courage and motivates citizens to make voluntary sacrifices… They believe that the good fortune of all mankind will be extinguished if they fail to hold out against the coalition armies; that they fight not just for their own future and welfare but for all of humanity; that such telling motivation to make every sacrifice has never before existed in a nation and for a less energetic and proud people, never could."[37] The Prussians labeled the new spirit enthusiasm, the French called it exultation. According to Louis Antoine de Saint Just, a radical Jacobin politi-cian, "Exultation rests within the firm resolve to defend the rights of the people and the Convention. Exultation is based on contempt for riches and esteem for simplicity and manners. Exultation is a virtue and not frenzy."[38]

A generous supply of musicians augmented the roster of the French army. Composers wrote marching songs for the campaign they accompanied. This roused the men and generated the enthusiasm that "personified the active and militant will of the Revolution, to overcome at all costs the political, economic and military resistance of the times… It knew no peace between the Revolution and absolutism."[39] Desertions in the French army "vanished on their own," as the journal *Deutsche Wehrzeitung* pointed out, "because the conscripted soldier, if he deserts, turns his back on his country as well as the flag."[40] Characteristic of their lack of comprehension for revolutionary ardor, Prussian commanders wanted to undermine the enemy's cadre of noncommissioned officers, the backbone of the French army, by bribing its members with gold to desert.[41] Elder Prussian generals scorned French enthusiasm as an "impulse of the rabble," a "straw fire" that will burn out once the danger passes.[42]

The French army possessed leaders motivated by love of country and a sense of mission who led by example. The Prussian officer corps fell flat by compari-son. After the Polish insurrection was suppressed, the land of nobles who had taken part in the rebellion often passed into the hands of Prussian aristocrats serving in the military or at court in Berlin. A lively trade developed buying and selling the properties via mortgages. These commercial ventures included the ac-quisition of impoverished estates in Silesia. Fortunes were made, but the extrav-agance resembling the previous court of "Fat Wilhelm" and the orgy of spending also shook confidence in business circles as indebtedness mounted. Referring to his Order of the Black Eagle, a prestigious military decoration conferred by

Friedrich the Great, a general exclaimed to another officer, "I'd give my Black Eagle Order if I could be free of my red one!"[43]

Company commanders often regarded the unit inventory as personal property. The post "became a matter of making money… barracks were like factories where all kinds of civilian business enterprises were carried on and the captain appeared to have become a board member who supervised employees."[44] Subalterns performed clerical tasks for these activities. In some cases, officers tasked the wives of their subordinates to sew clothes to fill civilian contracts. There was no improvement in the quality of uniforms for the soldiers. Company commanders and squadron chiefs received a clothing allowance to buy fabric for the troops' field dress. Officers opted for inexpensive, sleazy material and pocketed leftover funds.[45] A royal commission calculated the sum required to increase each soldier's pay by 25 percent as the king wanted. It recommended imposing a land tax on the nobles to finance it. They protested that this violates the rights of knighthood and confronted their sovereign with ancient charters confirming the tax-free status of their estates.[46]

Deutsche Wehrzeitung summarized the attitude of the army leadership: "In the assumption that war will never come, none of the commanding officers wanted circumstances so beneficial to them to change."[47] There was no mandatory retirement age, so they tenanted positions of command long after capable of performing their duties. *Deutsche Wehrzeitung* published a description by Wilhelm Henkel von Donnersmarck of the leadership of his regiment: "All of the officers turned out for drill, but at the gate three or four company chiefs routinely reported sick. General Marwitz, the chief of the regiment, was 70 years old and suffered from gout, so the drills were torturous for him. A same-named Colonel Marwitz had hemorrhoids and his exercises were limited and clumsy. Colonel Wins had to be handed his broadsword because of poor eyesight. Colonel Quitzow had abdominal pains; Major Combles was truly original, after dismounting from his horse unable to climb back on; Major Brunsemann was a hedonist whose thick stomach had abrasions from rubbing against the saddle horn, and Captain Hildebrand was better on the viola than on a horse because he was too fat and felt abdominal pain."[48]

Prussia's middle-class burghers offered the nation a reservoir of fresh talent. The military hierarchy nevertheless continued to prioritize recruiting young noblemen for the officer corps. Many were foreigners, for example hailing from Poland's smaller aristocracy. National identity was not as important as belonging to the noblesse. Oscar von Lettow-Vorbeck wrote of the foreign elements, "There were many adventurers among them and the practice robbed the officer corps of a uniformly patriotic stamp. It certainly would have been better not to exclude the sons of indigenous middle-class families from officer positions in the infantry and heavy cavalry, as was the custom."[49] Even in 1806, there remained a conscious effort to block burghers from command in these service branches. There was not a single middle-class officer in the cuirassiers and there were just two in the dragoons.[50] Instead, they held higher rank in artillery, engineers and *FeldJäger* (field rifle) regiments, that demand technical know-how. Army regulations still required these regiments to maintain a fixed number of subaltern officers of noble birth on the roster.[51]

The widely circulated periodical *Bellona*, published from 1781-1787, had "expressly advocated the privileges of the nobility," according to an article in *Deutsche Wehrzeitung*. "The justification for the necessity of having aristocratic officers was supposedly because the nobility, by nature more gallant, loves armed service more than the money-hungry burghers, and the aristocracy in its poverty would otherwise starve."[52] This viewpoint is ironic considering that profiteering among regimental officers at that time was rife. *Deutsche Wehrzeitung* wrote of the period, "The universal demoralization is plain as day. The officers are no longer free men of strong will, longing for a challenge to do credit to their pride in awareness of their prowess, burning for love of country and their class. They are broken and slipshod. They possess no will and no hope for themselves. Sunken into a deep lethargy, they are resigned to accept whatever happens to them, come what may!"[53]

Such types could scarcely inspire the troops; fear and brutality were the means to enforce discipline. Friedrich Wilhelm II had forbidden officers to abuse the men, but his successor was lax in enforcing the decree. One general's recipe for maintaining "the right disposition" was to "accustom the soldiers to the toughest, most arduous work, deprive them of all will, bring them to a state of downright slavish obedience and transform even the most stubborn people into machines that only the voice of their officers can activate."[54] Captain Hermann von Boyen offered this impression: "Punishment in the army in 1806, floggings, beatings with a staff, thrashings with short rods wrapped in wire, stem from an earlier age and sharply contradict the subsequent evolution of customs and attitudes. In the civilian sector, the law has for the most part already abolished such measures and made them contingent on court judgment. In the military by contrast, with the exception of flogging, the manner of corporal punishment is left to the caprice, mood and discretion of the commander... A respectable number of officers abhor this brutality. Even though Field Marshal Möllendorff has made stopping this his primary objective, the majority of officers regard such arbitrary conduct as their inherent right."[55]

The king appointed Möllendorff chair of the Immediate Organization Commission in 1795 to address the army's shortcomings. A year before his coronation, Friedrich Wilhelm III had reviewed a memorandum prepared by Lieutenant Colonel Karl von Lecoq. Among other things it advocated a more compassionate attitude toward troops. Möllendorff endorsed the proposal, but also recommended limitations on the number of foreigners recruited and an increase in pay and rations for the soldiers. The king responded that "both matters appear to me of equal importance... the second is necessary out of human compassion alone."[56] In Berlin, Möllendorff ordered officers under his command

One of the worst kings in German history, Friedrich Wilhelm III began as a friend of the Enlightenment. When Prussia's reformers left to serve in the field during the war of liberation, aristocrats opposing representative government filled the void as royal advisors and turned the king against reform.

to exercise "humane treatment of subordinates and an even temperament." He demanded they respect men from the lower class and concern themselves for their health and well-being. Möllendorff required that his officers explain to the troops the purpose behind their orders. Beyond his immediate jurisdiction, such measures were rarely implemented.

The Potsdam chaplain Ruhlemann Ephraim offered this impression of conditions facing the ordinary soldier: "The internal disintegration had already begun. Outwardly, everything was just a shiny façade… The garrisons are like prisons, the barracks sites of poverty… The cane and cudgel rule the world, at least over the non-noblesse, the citizenry… No respectable person who otherwise had opportunities for advancement wanted to wear the blue coat, and… a man would rather secretly leave his fatherland and seek his fortune abroad."[57]

Historian Johannes Scherr described how "Regardless of a few feeble attempts by Friedrich Wilhelm to mollify the officers' brutality, the soldier was treated squarely in the manner of Prussia's good old days, that is like a wild animal that can only learn discipline through brutal beatings and floggings. The rations and clothing were miserable, training grounds echoed with the coarsest profanity and the raw savagery of the drill instructor made them genuine torture places for the recruits."[58] *Deutsche Wehrzeitung* wrote that at that time, the ranker was perceived "not as an individual, but as a piece of a larger whole. Weapons training was less calculated to prepare the soldier for war as it was to drill him into a dim-witted automaton."[59]

Officers remained attentive to their own comforts. "Every regiment took along a hundred servants and behind many battalions was a baggage train of 40 carts. The officers needed their camp stools, tables and beds and many let their wives and children follow. The youngest infantry lieutenant possessed a horse, the company commander had six."[60] Despite support from senior commanders including Scharnhorst, Blücher and Rüchel, the overhaul of the army did not take place. Friedrich Wilhelm lacked the backbone to overcome the opposition. As summarized by Goltz, "A prudent, strong-willed and resolute prince before Jena would have pushed the reforms through and probably broken the resistance of the privileged without significantly disrupting internal operations of the state. The international situation at that time, when the most precarious danger could surface at a moment, placed in the king's hands a formidable weapon, that of full justification for decisive reforms and sacrifices."[61] All that this vacuous monarch accomplished for his troops was a modest increase in bread ration.

The Enlightened versus the Cudgel

The Enlightenment exalted the individual in society and venerated technology and inventions as manifestations of progress. Improved weaponry and production techniques satisfied conservative army officers that the military establishment is moving forward with the times without having to revamp its inner structure or social hierarchy. "A Dream of Posterity," an article published in *Bellona*, attacked this illusory attitude: "Every state that wages war hastens today to promote the science of war by introducing new types of rifles or faster ways to load them, more functional clothing, reduced baggage or improvements in artillery and fortification construction. There has been correspondingly little attention devoted to the moral element of warfare, especially in proportion to its significance. One seems to forget that an army consists of beings who are not just vessels but have a conscious soul; one seems to regard an army only as a lifeless machine that runs by the will of its operator without worrying much about its moral mainspring."[62]

After Friedrich the Great died, officers openly criticized this attitude. Among them was General Guillaume René de Courbiére. He wrote Möllendorff in January 1798, "There's nothing sadder than to realize that no one in an army of

200,000 men is happy and no one has enough to eat because he has no outside resources."[63] In an 1802 article in *Neue Bellona*, a Leipzig periodical first published in 1801, the Hessian Major Friedrich von Porbeck wrote of the coalition forces, "The outward appearance of all of the troops was radiant and magnificent, the weapons formidable, the evolution of most of the German warrior states imposing, yet there was no cheerful common spirit, no moral understanding among them."[64] Discontentment among the rankers ran the risk that they would embrace French revolutionary ideals. As Porbeck pointed out, many coalition troops were morally opposed to a war "that the great majority considers unjust."[65] Massenbach wrote that French propaganda is "a far more dangerous weapon" than rifle and cannon fire, and a sound means "to indoctrinate our common soldiers with republican values."[66] He visited General Kellermann's headquarters to warn him that unarmed French soldiers from Alsace who speak German will be fired on if they approach Prussian sentries "as friends."

Massenbach belonged to a growing company of officers aware of the need to generate enthusiasm among the soldiers for the cause they are fighting for. An 1801 article in *Neue Bellona* warned that despite better weaponry, "the institution of our standing army will never achieve the lofty goals we strive for if we don't try to guide and nurture the overall moral character of the combatants and inflame their passions."[67] It would not be easy to inspire downtrodden men to campaign against a foreign country proclaiming the intent to set them free, but German officers explored options. Major Friedrich von Bülow saw the remedy in issuing a generous brandy ration right before going into action: "I will let my boys attack with enthusiasm, shouts and laughter, but will know how to guard against total drunkenness. In battle, just like in a shipwreck, being half-drunk warms the blood in a healthy way while clarity of thought remains."[68] More sober-thinking officers recognized the need to draw lessons from the French without letting the army fall for their revolutionary ideas; since their monarchy could offer no goal beyond maintaining the old system, their position was hopelessly defensive.

The reform movement gained national attention with the publication of Berenhorst's three-volume *Observations on the Science of War* toward the end of the 18th Century. The author asserted that renovation of the military establishment is also a political question; that no serious undertaking in this sense can be accomplished without revising the absolute state itself. This supposition, as can be imagined, shocked monarchist officers of the army. They acknowledged that his book "created a sensation" among the public. Previously, scarcely anyone outside of the army perused military science literature. Berenhorst by contrast, was widely read by burghers and enjoyed universal acclaim.[69] He argued that maintaining an officer corps owing its authority to noble birth instead of to ability and performance, an arrangement repugnant to the Enlightenment to begin with, not only makes ordinary men indifferent to who their leaders are but allows members of the exclusive caste to abuse the privilege with impunity.

Drawing a comparison between noble and common in the army, Berenhorst wrote this: "Just as in any state the poor are filled with ill will and envy toward the rich, such is in great measure the case of the ordinary soldier toward the officer. The apparel of the officer as to quality of fabric and tailoring, often with gold or silver braid, is completely different from that of the soldier; the former has a topcoat and overcoat. The latter, by the end of the campaign, goes along half naked and barefoot. While the common soldier struggles under the weight of his pack or is exhausted from hauling it through the mud, he sees all of his superiors on horseback… The officer is provided with better quarters and has his bed on a packhorse. He never does without, is never the soldier's comrade. Then this soldier, accustomed to such meager meals, is inclined to presume that his officer always eats his fill."[70] *Neue Bellona* endorsed Berenhorst's criticism: "What good does it do to work on the men's spirits when no thought is given to the body? All sense of honor, of love of country and of enthusiasm are hollow phrases to one living in poverty."[71]

The essay in *Neue Bellona* continued, "If the soldier knows that in the course of matters his stomach is provided for, he will endure anything born of accident or necessity; if it's no better for his officers, with unbelievable composure. But as soon as he notices that even in good days there are shortages and that it is the fault of the institution, then he will become surly and ultimately rebellious."[72] General Friedrich von Saldern, drillmaster of the Prussian army and proponent of the inflexible linear tactic, had nevertheless admonished his peers in a 1781 tract to "regard the soldier as a person… he will do more for the officer who treats him well and has his confidence than for one he trembles before."[73] Porbeck contrasted his country's military leadership with that of the French: "The (French) are the soul of contemporary duty; accustomed to making sacrifices, not reared in the school of effeminacy and luxury… All infantry officers march with their pack on their back up to battalion commander and his adjutants. Our battalions require 50 luxury horses. General Rüchel was my patron; I sent him a memorandum about this. He answered, 'My friend, a Prussian nobleman does not go on foot!'"[74]

Based on social welfare programs introduced after the death of "Fat Wilhelm," reformers proposed appealing to the troops on the notion that the absolute state is actually beneficial to them. Shortly after taking the throne, Friedrich Wilhelm III established an institution to care for war invalids. He contributed 100,000 thaler per annum to its maintenance and required officers to donate a portion of their monthly pay as well. The king also provided financial assistance to soldiers' widows and orphans. The crown took responsibility to educate and care for children of soldiers on active duty. These measures, together with the increase in bread ration for the troops, were supposed to persuade them that the cause is worth fighting for; an argument intended to generate artificial enthusiasm to parry the influence of French tenets. Officers were to be instructed in how to present these advantages to men under their command.

A cornerstone of the reform movement was elevating the common soldier's craft to "an honorable and respectable occupation" which is not a disgrace to belong to. This and love of country were "the only true cornerstones of military spirit, a spirit anchored in the moral and physical powers of the individual as well as in the whole, upon which rests the genuine strength of an army," according to a 1781 article published in *Bellona*.[75] A prerequisite required to achieve this was to abolish the system of corporal punishment prevalent in the standing army. In a treatise on military law, Boyen declared that "only through humane treatment, when he is universally esteemed and not regarded as an object of ridicule for being handled in a degrading manner, will the soldier evolve into a passionate defender of the fatherland."[76]

Berenhorst criticized "inhuman punishment… degrading the soldier to a drill machine with the help of beatings instead of appealing to his moral strengths." He contended that "without enthusiasm, every tactic goes on crutches… A fiery spirit, physically and morally combined, is the path to victory."[77] Möllendorff issued an order in 1785 for officers to cease "holding the common man to his duty through barbarism, tyrannical beatings, shoving and cursing."[78] The movement to esteem the ordinary soldier as an honorable warrior was unsuccessful despite the sympathy of many officers. To seriously attribute honor to the individual soldier transgressed against the absolutist mentality. Only officers had honor. Friedrich II wrote that men in the ranks must fear their superiors more than the enemy to perform their duty. The army was not held together by humanitarian principles or by patriotism, but by discipline and punishment. Answering Knesebeck's recommendation to outlaw the entire punitive system, the Immediate Organization Commission replied, "We must regard the proposed abolishment of established penalties as precarious. The soldier is already used to them as a part of his existence and eliminating them would be detrimental to discipline and the military constitution."[79]

Parallel to efforts to bring the army's perception of the individual soldier into conformity with enlightened principles, reformers combated Prussia's outmoded battlefield tactics. The Prussian and Saxon infantry still relied on the obsolete linear tactic, the echelon attack. Under Friedrich's command, the Prussian army had won the Seven Years' War using the linear maneuver. Many generals in 1806 had served as young officers back then and had personally witnessed its impetus. Subsequent developments made no impression on them. "At Kaiserslautern and Pirmasens, the armies of revolutionary France had been overcome using the traditional formation," summarized Lettow-Vorbeck. "This confirmed the infallibility of the Prussian echelon attack. No conclusions were drawn from the progressive measures that gave Napoleon his victories. Furthermore, he wrested these victories from Austrians and Russians, whose armies were regarded as greatly inferior."[80] The linear attack also fit the Prussian army's system of compulsion and mechanical drill that correspond to the absolutist mindset more closely than recognizing the soldier as a personality with honor and loyalty to his country.

An illustration by Carl Röchling of Prussian infantry advancing in echelon at Leuthen depicts this once formidable method of attack. Napoleon's emphasis on artillery, increased firepower of new cannons and novel light infantry tactics rendered the linear formation obsolete.

The military hierarchy's recipe for improving combat tactics consisted of honing the linear advance though application of precise mathematic calculations to determine the ratio of battalions to firepower, the maximum number of rounds a unit is capable of shooting per minute, increased cadence drill ad nauseam. In a February 1784 order for example, the Prussian drillmaster Saldern criticized "the great deal of swaying that one still sees here and there. I must expressly urge commanding officers to maintain complete uniformity on the march. To be sure, it is especially important for officers and noncommissioned officers, no less than for the lads, that they remain consistent in beat, number and spacing of steps. I am certain that every mistake is caused by everyone not marching forward in the same way and at proper interval."[81] Berenhorst, the man who achieved the "spiritual breakthrough" to arouse public awareness of problems within the army, made discrediting the linear attack a primary thrust of his *Observations*.

This controversial officer analyzed the maneuver. He quoted Saldern's directives to demonstrate how unrealistic it is to presume that precision can be maintained in combat. Berenhorst began by pointing out the obvious, that the parade ground where troops practice does not resemble a battlefield. No matter how well drilled the infantry is, it is impossible to hold formation in uneven terrain; ponds, fences, ditches or a single house in the path of the advance is sufficient to disrupt the line; not to mention smoke and the effect of enemy defensive fire. Exercising on a flat, open field does not prepare the men for action and is hence a waste of time and effort. Further, the monolithic linear phalanx is made up of human beings who, unfortunately for the army, have fears and passions. All too often in the excitement of battle, so Berenhorst, "the usual waves of fire follow, when everyone whose weapon is loaded discharges it, squads and ranks merge together, the men in the front row aren't able to fall to one knee even if they want to and the officers from lieutenant to general can't do anything with this mass. Instead, they have to wait to see when it will finally set itself in motion and move either forward or backward."[82]

Testifying before the Military Society in 1802, staff officer Captain Moritz von Schöler related his personal experience: "Whoever has taken part in an even moderately serious battle will not contradict us when we assert that even a tenth of the order that prevails on our training grounds is absolutely unthinkable when in action. The emphasis is on bringing sufficient masses of men close enough to the enemy, which then enables them to blindly plunge right into him."[83] The linear advance was not discontinued. A third of Prussian infantry personnel were foreign volunteers. The rest were conscripted via the canton system. They were mostly farm lads with a percentage of understandably reluctant Poles. Foreign and especially Polish troops going over the hill remained a chronic problem. Deserters marauded the countryside doing no credit to the army's reputation. Between October 1805 and February 1806, 9,558 soldiers deserted.[84] Grouping the men into linear formation allowed officers to oversee the troops in combat. This made it difficult for them to flee the colors undetected. "In the Prussian army, practicing maneuvers on the parade ground became widely disconnected from the reality of the times," concluded Lettow-Vorbeck. Nevertheless, "the might of the echelon maneuver remained in highest esteem."[85]

Despite the drawbacks of the linear advance, most reformers agreed that the primary cause of coalition defeats by republican France are traced more to German leadership's failure to recognize the importance of enthusiasm and to incorporate certain French fighting methods. How else, asked Scharnhorst, could a "hodgepodge of revolutionaries" beat soldiers "who have drilled in continental armies for years?"[86] French combat techniques were initially improvisation. There was no time to school the French soldier in echelon attack, so methods for his level of training were adopted. These were in part based on lessons learned in America. France fielded Tirailleurs, swarms of sharpshooters in loose formation who use natural cover to approach the enemy and inflict losses with harassing fire. Their job was also to launch feint attacks and disguise the movements of massed infantry battalions. Tirailleurs were individual fighters who did not fire on command as the Prussians did. When confronted by superior numbers, they spontaneously withdrew to take up positions further to the rear, again exploiting terrain to their advantage. Scharnhorst contended, "It's a proven fact that the dispersed masses of riflemen of the French decided almost every battle of this war."[87]

Berenhorst described Tirailleur tactics as a natural method of fighting. It conforms to the individual's instincts to take cover under fire, react independently to the ebb and flow of combat and aim and shoot at recognized targets. The linear attack by contrast, requires incessant drill to perfect because it is repugnant to human reason and emotion; standing exposed when being shot at, trying to hold formation marching across broken ground and reacting only to an officer's commands instead of what one's impulses dictate. Soldiers confronting French skirmishers soon developed a healthy respect for their prowess in battle. An eyewitness called them "as sharp-sighted as ferrets and as active as squirrels."[88] One Prussian officer stated, "In the woods, when the soldiers break rank and have no drill movements to carry out, but only to fire under the cover of the trees, they are not only equal but superior to us. Our men, accustomed to fight shoulder to shoulder in the open field, find it more difficult to adopt that seeming disorder which is yet necessary if they are not to be targets for the enemy."[89]

An article published in *Neue Bellona* on sharpshooting recounted an officer's firsthand experience dueling Tirailleurs: "The enemy did not confront us when he didn't want to. We found no parade ground, but a thousand obstacles of terrain that make a mockery of our tactics. Behind every tree, out of every window lurked death. No river current was too fast, no morass impassable, no defile too narrow, no mound of snow or icy peak too imposing for the daring and highly mobile infantrymen to negotiate and attack us at the very place where our helpless tactics don't work. The force of our lungs and our cudgels have transformed our soldiers into rigid machines; they stumble through the wilderness, jump ditches and become dispersed behind trees, with no other weapon than a rifle that they only know how to fire blindly on command. We of course succumbed to the rawest of lads. They were confident in their unrestrained vitality, unburdened by cumbersome apparel, armed with flintlocks they know how to aim from practical training and accustomed to taking advantage of every cover that nature has to offer."[90]

Progressive German officers urged that the army be instructed to emulate the tactics of the French light infantry, including retraining line regiments. The critical military journalist Dietrich von Bülow, who had served in America, saw the enemy's unorthodox fighting method as giving the individual soldier back "his courage, his effectiveness, his common sense and use of physical capabilities."[91] Tirailleurs not only cast doubt on the viability of the linear maneuver, but cast down the gauntlet before the absolutist state itself. Just as the linear tactic was inseparably bound to the standing army, the French alternative became symbolic of more than a novel fighting method. The Tirailleur was the product of a revolutionary ideal liberating mankind from the yoke of absolutism. He exercised judgment in combat, brought individual talent to full expression and displayed personal initiative. His mechanically drilled adversary, trained by the cudgel to suppress both natural inclinations and his very personality, did not fight for a cause.

Tirailleurs carried the political struggle into the military sphere. It was not uncommon for soldiers of the standing army to desert when opportunity presented itself. The Tirailleur was entirely on his own yet stood and fought. When he fell back it was only to strike again at the next moment to confound and defeat his enemy. His existence threatened not only the coalition armies but the system they defended. Berenhorst was correct when he contended that to revise Prussian battlefield strategy, the state must also be restructured. *Levée en masse* and the Tirailleurs, as pillars of France's military system, could only be successfully countered by corresponding political adjustments in Prussia; drafting a constitution to involve the people in government and creating an army of freethinking individuals comprising all strata of society, motivated by enthusiasm for liberty and their Christian faith.[92] Defenders of the linear tactic presented a variety of arguments to discredit proposals to convert line infantry tactics to French techniques.

One objection was that Tirailleur warfare is foreign to German nature. French skirmishers fight from concealment, set ambushes, climb trees, run before a superior force and shun no means to gain the advantage; it is a system of cowardice and deceit; artful, unchivalrous and contrary to the rules of warfare. Stemming from a "lack of both training and fundamental tactical know-how," the ruses of this "horde without discipline" supposedly nourish the latent "natural baseness" of humanity.[93] "Tirailleurs simply run away when confronted with a solid body of troops with bayonets," and are "driven from their position." Sarcastically criticizing this mindset, Goltz pointed out, "No one considered that retreating hordes of riflemen can take up resistance again behind the next hedge, trench or edge of a forest, or that Tirailleurs attacking in large numbers can achieve a mightier and more dangerous penetration than battalions marching in parade step."[94]

Conservative generals contrasted the supposedly devious nature of Tirailleur operations with the linear attack's manly, chivalrous and "German" character which conforms to the natural disposition of the Prussian. He suppresses the impulse to duck or escape danger. He stands his ground in the face of hostile fire and shuns any action that might dishonor himself or his regiment. Every nation develops a type of warfare that corresponds to its intrinsic spirit. This cannot be assumed by other peoples without debauching their collective personality as a homogenous ethnic community. This, so argued the defenders of absolutism, is an element overlooked by their colleagues in the officer corps advocating adoption of the Tirailleur system. Höhn summarized the perspective of the old school generals, who frowned on France's "democratic mass-army" that flees without reservation when a battle appears hopeless. Holding one's ground in the face of unfavorable odds, the generals contended, is the honorable way to fight:

"How, they asked rhetorically, will it affect the esprit de corps of a proud regiment that has till then never shown its back to the enemy and has trained generations of soldiers in this spirit, were it suddenly told that it must flee and scatter as soon as it is no longer considered possible to hold out in battle against a superior enemy force?"[95] These were tenuous arguments, easily lanced by army reformers. Where is pride and honor, they parried, in an army whose men are whipped until they learn to hold a battleline because fear of their own officers overshadows that of a foe trying to kill them? Also, is victory not the priority? Are the Prussians to go down fighting in observance of pedantic rules of engagement that the enemy disregards just to preserve the Prussian army's reputation and tradition?

Another protest to adopting Tirailleur tactics was that soldiers schooled to fight shoulder to shoulder and respond only to officers' commands will have difficulty adjusting to a looser form of combat requiring cognizance of terrain and independent action, hence contrary to their training. This contention is equally lame, since formations practically always dissolve during the fluctuations of battle as men give way to their natural instincts and commanders have to continually reform the units. In any case, "cudgel officers," as the absolutist faction was called, confronted the "enlightened officers" of the reform movement with the reply that the Prussian army already has fusilier and *Jäger* light infantry battalions that fulfill the function of skirmishers like the French. Each line regiment was required to provide a fixed number of smaller men for the light infantry. Officers customarily selected *Knechte*, former stable hands and servants, the poorest of the poor, from the roster. This contributed to the unflattering reputation of the light infantry, which "public opinion considered of little worth."[96]

Prussia's previous monarch Friedrich Wilhelm II had valued this type of formation because it had been effective in the American Revolution. The 20 fusilier battalions he added to the army in 1787 each had a full-strength roster of 680 men trained to fight in loose battle order, use cover and develop superior marksmanship. Revised regulations in 1788 assigned every infantry company ten sharpshooters armed with weapons equipped with rifled barrels instead of with less accurate smoothbore muskets. Fusilier battalions received 20 sharpshooters per company. These men were to fight alongside their comrades but not in formation. Dietrich von Bülow predicted, "Future battles will be decided by Tirailleurs," and advocated retraining every linear-schooled battalion to become light infantry. He proposed that "shooting on the rifle range should be practiced lying down, standing, crawling and even running, in every possible position of the human body except kneeling."[97]

None of the major changes urged by reformers were implemented before the Prussian army went to war against Napoleon. Cudgel discipline remained in force, the linear advance the primary battlefield maneuver and the infantry was not retrained according to the French example. The echelon attack as the perfection of combat operations had become so ingrained in the thinking of the supreme command that talent in field commanders was neither sought after nor prized. Directing troops in battle according to mathematical equations for maximizing the effectiveness of this tactic was considered all that is necessary to achieve victory. The army hierarchy attributed the greatest victories of the Seven Years' War to the practice of generals conducting campaigns according to this dogma. The army stagnated while that of France progressed. "Prussian officers, mostly aristocrats, clung to a sort of self-indulgent lethargy... The Prussian officer corps was seriously overaged and mentally no longer flexible enough" to accept new concepts.[98]

Prussian fusilier and *Jäger* light infantry proved equal or superior to French Tirailleurs whenever they crossed lances in action. They were however of little value to generals who did not understand how to properly use these formations. Instead of deploying Tirailleurs and infantry columns to work in conjunction, Prussian fusilier battalions fought separately. Sometimes they were assigned to guard bridges, cover flanks and conduct reconnaissance in force along with the cavalry. These were missions that other troops could have performed. In Goltz's opinion, "Without dispute the echelon tactic would not have suffered such a fiasco in 1806 if instead of useless affectations such as keeping the grenadiers separate, the far simpler and more natural means had been chosen; that is, to closely coordinate the old linear fighting method with the novel role of the light infantry and not just employ the latter for special purposes."[99]

By 1806 Prussian grenadiers and musketeers practiced *zerstreutes Gefecht* (dispersed battle order) no longer, fusiliers rarely and then at the discretion of the individual battalion commander. Only Colonel Johann Ludwig Yorck's *Feldjäger*, an independent, 2,000-man rifle regiment comprised of sons of forestry officials and led by respectful, energetic younger officers, consistently conducted target practice and loose formation drill. Marksmanship training in the rest of the army remained sorely neglected. Joint maneuvers among various service arms did not take place. Garrisons were small. They were divided according to cavalry, artillery, the infantry and engineers and scattered throughout Prussia. Officers seldom had contact with colleagues in other branches of service.

Everything military reformers targeted for change was bound to the absolutist system. Some among the highborn suspected that Prussians who laud France's military innovations privately sympathize with the French cause: "There was an unexpressed presumption that the dispersed fighting tactic and revolutionary sympathies are connected... both were blood relatives of the Revolution and had many enemies in the monarchist camp."[100] A Hessian officer was therefore treading on thin ice when he wrote in *Neue Bellona* that the French army, "with respect to rations, armament and smoother movements on the march and in battle, thanks to its leadership and to its fanatical belief in freedom, is at great advantage over the allied armies."[101] Scharnhorst himself bemoaned, "Those who do not speak with the greatest contempt for the French, who do not belittle their resources, their power, their measures and their armies as much as possible, who do not say that their generals are cobblers and tailors or that their troops are cowardly, the fortresses are poorly provisioned and so on, those are the ones suspected of being supporters of the French Revolution."[102]

The Fight for a Militia

Berenhorst was the trailblazer of Prussian military reform, but Scharnhorst became its most influential and productive apostle. While Berenhorst called for dissolution of absolutism to clear the path for modernizing the armed forces, Scharnhorst worked within the framework of the existing state form and standing army. He could not alter the political structure of Prussia. His goal was to improve the military by incorporating lessons learned from the wars against France as much as possible. Scharnhorst served in the Hanoverian army during coalition campaigns of 1793 and 1794. He distinguished himself in combat and attained prominence through publication of his military handbooks. He entered Prussian service in 1801. Friedrich Wilhelm promoted him to lieutenant colonel, doubled his pay and entrusted him with a role in army reform. Like many officers, Scharnhorst was impressed by the novel tactics employed by colonists in America. The French had already adjusted their method of waging war to emulate that of the New World. To effectively fight back, Scharnhorst believed that the Prussian army must follow suit.

Scharnhorst was among German officers who demanded an explanation as to why the best armies in Europe have accomplished nothing against the French since the Revolution. Publishing his reflections in the *Neues militärisches Journal* (*New Military Journal*), he attributed France's success to the advantage of defensible terrain and to the political dissonance between Prussia and Austria that precluded forming a united front against her. In a series of essays, he also called attention to the unprecedented élan that has galvanized the foe: "The Jacobins fight for a fresh new ideal. They believe their cause is the salvation of humanity. They have torn down all class barriers and enable the most talented people to advance to the loftiest stations. They have transformed the whole country into a gigantic war industry where gunpowder is produced faster than it is fired, where even civilians do their share for victory, where there are no slackers."[103]

Since joining the Prussian army, Scharnhorst had been a proponent of reform. He presented his ideas in a series of essays for the officer corps. He advocated a militia by arguing, "In France and in England as well, formation of a national militia has aroused the military spirit of the nation and generates an enthusiasm for the country's independence not seen in other lands."[104] Scharnhorst believed that it would be easy for his country to do the same: "In every class of citizens, Prussia has a good measure of patriotic men who are aware of the situation the state is in and for whom the concept of national honor is bound to that of military honor. They not only have a comprehension of the military, but are also distinguished by the spirit of their superior culture. The country also has many former soldiers who know the duties required and are accustomed to discipline."[105]

Warning of Prussia's dilatory preparations, he recommended that the state expand troop strength by 25,000 men. Regrouping the army into 18 divisions, each combining infantry, the artillery and cavalry, and establishing six mounted reserves was another of his proposals. The divisions were formed in September 1806. Scharnhorst found himself swimming upstream urging an overhaul of the officer corps. He contended that promotion "should not be a reward for length of service. The selection should be determined not by what one has earned but by how one leads."[106] In an enlightened age with as successful a middle class as Prussia's, the public regarded the practice of selecting and promoting officers based on merit instead of on bloodlines as long overdue. The aristocracy naturally regarded Scharnhorst's proposal as an affront. *Bellona* claimed that "the Prussian officer corps possesses a certain radiance compared to those of other armies because it consists almost exclusively of nobles. Are the officers of this army not universally respected because of this, and is this not a superb basis for a point of honor?"[107]

Scorned by senior officers, Colonel Scharnhorst found his niche training their replacements. Berlin's *Académie militaire* enjoyed the patronage of Queen Luise, who often visited the institution with an entourage of princesses and duchesses. In 1804, the king appointed Scharnhorst to serve as deputy director to the elder General Levin von Geusau in revamping the Academy of Military Science for Young Infantry and Cavalry Officers in Potsdam. The colonel introduced an enterprising three-year curriculum which Friedrich Wilhelm approved. Scharnhorst lectured cadets on battlefield tactics and strategy by drawing lessons learned from continental and colonial warfare. In his faculty guidebook he wrote, "It would be a great mistake when explaining these campaigns (those of Friedrich the Great and the Duke of Brunswick) for the instructor to encourage the inclination to criticize them, as we so often like to do. He should focus on what is worth adopting and not emphasize mistakes. In describing the operations of the above-mentioned campaigns, he should conform to the principle of pointing out what is useful in this or that situation."[108]

One of Scharnhorst's most successful initiatives was founding the Military Society in Berlin on January 24, 1802, the birthday of Friedrich II. Four instructors of cadets and two civilian professors, one of them the celebrated historian Christian August Stützer, belonged to the committee that helped Scharnhorst establish the Military Society. Scharnhorst defined its purpose as to explore every avenue of the science of war to achieve a balance between theory and practical application. Participants met weekly to discuss and analyze a selected topic. In the four-year duration of his Military Society in Berlin there were 188 members including the king, various German princes and a considerable number of generals and senior officers. Before mobilization it conducted 160 sessions involving lectures, debates and the reading and evaluation of essays on martial matters. Scharnhorst wrote, "The industriousness and activity it manifests offers a positive impression of the spirit that prevails in our army."[109] The society disbanded when war preparations required the officers to return to their units.

It was customary in the army for field commanders to be assigned an adjutant to counsel them and assist with administrative tasks. Men tenanting this prestigious post were politically connected. They were often young and inexperienced officers whose influential relatives had secured the appointment for them. As academy director of Potsdam's cadet school, Scharnhorst sought to replace the conventional patronage system by supplying more qualified candidates. Cadets received comprehensive training in planning and executing combat operations incorporating lessons from France. They took classes in logistics, technical aspects of the artillery and engineers, reconnaissance and terrain. Students were also instructed in the personal qualities demanded of a leader. In this way, "a network of schooled military men capable of expediting every important decision will be distributed throughout the army."[110] Thus was born the general staff, which would profoundly influence German military fortunes for the next 140 years.

In March 1804, the quartermaster general staff consisted of three departments called brigades, each responsible for a region. Phull from the Württemberg Military Academy was assigned East Prussia and Russia. Massenbach, from the same academy, had the area from Pomerania and Silesia to Saxony and Bavaria. The third was Scharnhorst himself. He was in charge of the western frontier including Hanover, Westphalia and the northwest German mountains. Making him responsible for the area where Prussia was most threatened demonstrates the confidence that the king placed in him. There were 75 general staff officers in all. The three quartermasters, officially called quartermaster lieutenants, acknowledged the importance of a well-schooled general staff, but only Scharnhorst realistically assessed the shortcomings of the army and endorsed the reforms necessary for the military to fulfill its mission. Geusau was chief of staff. He saw no merit in proposals to restructure the armed forces by adopting techniques of the French army. Scharnhorst made headway nonetheless.

As defined by one historian, the Quartermaster General Staff "recruited the most talented of the young officer candidates to prepare them for taking part in future battles and place them in very influential positions in wartime. They would be assigned to army commanders and generals commanding divisions and brigades as chiefs of staff. The right hand of the generals, they would work out battle plans and regulate the administrative mechanism, but always as a subordinate, as an advisor. The final responsibility, the last yes or no always rested with the general in command. Scharnhorst forged that miraculous fusion of intellect and will that gives the contemporary armed force its character... With this organization he crowned the modern tactics borrowed from the French. He gave a disconnected army back what it needed to become an entity and an organic form again; a brain and central nervous system."[111]

Leading the charge against Scharnhorst's unprecedented ideas were the king's personal adjutants. They endeavored to protect unqualified officers serving as advisors and resented the favor that Scharnhorst enjoyed with Friedrich

Wilhelm. He was a Saxon, hence foreign, not particularly military in his bearing and his parents were farmers. Senior commanders were comfortable with
their current adjutants and regarded the academy director as a "theorist and
know-it-all."[112] He had already aroused Möllendorff's disapproval for fostering
a national militia, disparaged by the field marshal as a "ruinous project." In the
opinion of his peers, Goltz wrote, Scharnhorst "was considered a school master,
an egghead, and stood in low esteem in Prussia."[113] Soliciting others' opinions as
usual, the king forwarded his suggestions to the Duke of Brunswick for review.
The duke nominally approved Scharnhorst's ideas in evaluations submitted to his
sovereign. At the same time, he adroitly expressed misgivings in such a way as to
make it appear that the concepts look good on paper but are unworkable.[114] He
insidiously sabotaged every reform except for grouping the army into divisions.
The king thanked Scharnhorst for his efforts, conferred knighthood and did
nothing to implement the other proposals.

Arguing for a national militia drew Scharnhorst into one of the most controversial debates of the period. France was much larger than Prussia and possessed
an enormous reservoir of manpower thanks to *levée en masse*. The most secure
path for Prussia, he reasoned, was to follow the French example: "Only by
arming the entire mass of the population," he maintained, "will a smaller nation
achieve a sort of parity of strength in a defensive war against a larger one that
wages offensive wars to enslave others. Due to logistical difficulties, the leader of
the aggressor state cannot bring up as many combatants as the one it threatens
can. Moreover, he will lack any justification for such a commitment of national
resources and arming the entire nation. He therefore cannot demand of his
subordinates what the monarch of the threatened country can whose people are
forced to fight for their very existence."[115] Scharnhorst calculated that an efficient
recruitment program can expand the size of Prussia's fighting forces by 300,000
militiamen. Further, if the newly acquired Polish territory is gleaned, together
with the standing army the country could field 520,000 soldiers.

Selling the militia to the public was a delicate task. It "is not just physical
force that decides a war," Scharnhorst wrote, "but morality just as much… If the
masses of passionate people are not skillfully directed, enthusiasm will be lost
and discontent take its place."[116] The middle class disdained the military because
the troops were badly treated. "For burghers, the soldier's occupation was a
sort of 'penal institution' filled with drifters and rabble at best."[117] Supporting
the militia concept, *Bellona* published an excerpt from a 1782 address by army
pastor Dr. Merkel: "If I and my property are forcibly attacked, I am bound as a
person to defend myself and my belongings. And when the security, freedom,
and life of a hundred or a thousand people are violated, then this hundred or this
thousand people have the right to defend themselves against any use of force.
Wars are started against entire nations and waged against their very existence.
The obligation to wartime service and to defend the fatherland is absolutely the
affair of every member of the community."[118]

The reformers pointed out that armed service for every able-bodied man has been a Germanic custom since the Ancient World. Berenhorst contended that "every citizen should in principle also be a defender of the state."[119] His number one literary antagonist was Johann von der Decken. His articles in *Neues militairisches Journal* argued in favor of keeping the standing army as Prussia's sole bearer of arms. Decken wrote that the concept of an "army of citizens" is only valid for tribal cultures; as civilizations mature, those who prosper become reluctant to take risks because there is too much to lose: "The decline of martial virtues is an unavoidable consequence. Even raising cattle, if it makes significant progress, has a detrimental influence on the warlike spirit; it leads to the concept of property. The person nurtures some animals and provides them with food. In this way he develops feelings of moderation for the first time. Cultivating the soil completes the process. The person gains partiality for the land that nourishes and clothes him. One could say that he develops roots."[120]

Decken pointed out that militiamen are only on active duty for a few days per year for training. During this period, they practice unconditional obedience to an officer. They then return to peacetime occupations without further contact with military life. Such types, so Decken, can scarcely be expected to maintain discipline required of troops in wartime. They won't fight as hard as those in the standing army anyway. This is because the professional soldier "loses more from the demise of the state than other citizens, since his source of livelihood is cut off and the prospect of being cared for by the state in old age is lost as well."[121] By comparison, military defeat will not necessarily impact the militia recruit; when a civilian again afterward, life will scarcely be different under a new master. Decken cited the case of Silesia, which changed hands several times during the Seven Years' War: "Did Silesia experience a noticeable change under different regents between previous and present circumstances?"[122]

France's victories during the coalition wars, Decken asserted, are misinterpreted. He described them as having little to do with the idealism that allegedly motivates the French citizen-soldier: "What could a hastily scraped together mob that knows nothing of all the incidents of war have achieved against the armies of the coalition, had France not previously maintained a standing army that was practiced under arms and possessed so much training and experience, which merged with the conscripted mass? This army conveyed to the mass the martial spirit of unconditional obedience. And what could it have achieved were not well-schooled artillery and engineer corps on hand?"[123] Other officers contributed articles to the controversy. They were published in the military periodicals *Bellona*, *Minerva*, *Neue Bellona* and *Neues militairisches Journal*. Despite diametrical viewpoints, Scharnhorst and Decken were close friends. Ultimately it was not their arguments that decided the militia question, but self-interests of the king and ultraconservative aristocracy.

The standing army was integrally bound to the absolute state; to compromise its prerogative as sole bearer of arms would weaken the authority of the

A veteran of Valmy and advocate of a Prussian militia, Knesebeck aided the Russians in 1807 and later proposed the strategy used by the czar's army to lure the *Grande Armée* deeply into Russia in 1812 and annihilate it.

monarchy. The Enlightenment had animated in common people an awareness of the rights of man; to arm them to defend a regime that bars citizens from government to fight against a nation that gives the population a voice in public affairs was a dubious undertaking. Knesebeck drafted a memorandum for the Immediate Organization Commission recommending a Fatherland Reserve of 130,000 men trained to fight differently than the standing army. He confessed in his report, "Arming the people is the premier means to a revolution, dangerous in any state. It is even more risky on the frontier of a realm that has a constitution growing more fragile from day to day and has a neighbor that sets the example of anarchy and rage as an ideal."[124] Army leaders had previously reacted sharply when the Duke of Saxony-Teschen prepared to arm the people of the Lower Rhine region and Westphalia to resist French invasion in 1794; Möllendorff thought the plan "politically dangerous."[125]

Knesebeck criticized the commission's aversion of a militia. He mocked that the standing army's discipline and way of fighting are less suited for war than for peacetime. In its evaluation of his proposal for a Fatherland Reserve issued in December 1803, the commission warned that Knesebeck's ideas could provoke "a complete upheaval in the army and its relationship to the state" and compromise military establishments in other countries as well.[126] Möllendorff proclaimed it his duty to oppose proposals that can cause "extremely unhealthy" consequences for the royal house. Equally unwelcome was Knesebeck's call for universal patriotism to arouse the fighting spirit of the kingdom. The populations of Pomerania, Prussia, Magdeburg and Brandenburg felt a provincial pride in their respective lands that is not the same as love of country in a national sense. In the eyes of the commission, cultivating a sentiment to weld the various tribes together will itself threaten the monarchy, if this unified mass rises as one as had been the case in France. Preserving the local patriotism of the provinces kept them disunified.

The commission defined the incompatibility of the absolute state with national-patriotic sentiments: "The means proposed by Major von Knesebeck to awaken patriotism in the indigenous population appear to us not only superfluous but in a measure dangerous. The peoples of Mark County, Magdeburg, Pomerania and Prussia in no sense lack patriotism and national pride. Each race is peculiar to its own province and we consider it highly questionable to revise this. The inveterate patriotism would be destroyed without something better taking its place. The independent national spirit would be lost, and this could easily shake the foundation of the army and the state as a result."[127] The Immediate Organization Commission endorsed the merit of arming civilians to guard the coast line and garrison fortresses, since otherwise thousands of soldiers would be drawn from the standing army to fill these stationary posts. Further, a *Landmiliz* (rural militia) was necessary to protect East Prussia from looting expeditions by Cossacks, because without Poland Prussia and Russia shared a common frontier. The commission recommended substituting a "pension militia" to fulfill the role of Knesebeck's Fatherland Reserve.

Möllendorff's commission proposed forming battalions comprised of "soldiers with 20 years of active service" and "dispensable men with conditional exemptions" recruited from the canton system. Battalion commanders were to be "already pensioned majors or majors and captains in the army close to retirement."[128] Such a composition of manpower would not be politically dangerous to the regime. It was in fact, nothing more than an expansion of the army with second-rate personnel and not a militia. The king rejected the commission's suggestion to call the members "National Grenadiers" and substituted "Land Reserve Troop" for this watered-down compromise of Knesebeck's blueprint. The commission did not regard Knesebeck's militia concept as support for the army but as competition. It sent him the haughty reply, "It seems totally incomprehensible to the commission that any member of a victorious army, one that has long represented an unrivalled standard for all of Europe and will remain so, could presume to recommend a total alteration of its structure and in a way that would reduce it to a mere peasant militia."[129]

Efforts to stifle a national militia found public approval. At a time when commerce flourished, the middle class continued to expand and the Prussian standard of living improved, burghers resisted an institutional reorganization of the military that would obligate citizenry to perform armed service. The canton system, designed to provide replacements for the army from the general population, failed to mobilize national resources. Only sons of farmers, tradesmen and unskilled labor were conscripted. Regional authorities, many of them estate holders, feared that expanding the eligible manpower pool will reduce the work force and impact commercial growth. "Even extending the term of enlistment would have robbed landowners of a portion of their subservient labor force," wrote Lettow-Vorbeck.[130] Beyond economic considerations, maintaining Prussia as a martial state by drafting private citizens contradicted the popular "individual freedom" concept fostered by the Enlightenment. East Frisia's president of the chamber of deputies, Ludwig Freiherr von Vincke, denounced conscription as "the grave of science and business, civil liberty and every human blessing."[131]

General Rüchel, a personal friend of the king, tried to persuade him to revoke the table of deferments that excuse tens of thousands from armed service. The influential cabinet advisor Anastasius Luden blocked the initiative. In so doing he reaped accolade from liberal and financial circles for his "determination and courage."[132] Those categorically freed from compulsory duty included the entire aristocracy, affluent landowners, councilmen's sons, civil servants, students and university professors, immigrants and their offspring, clerics, physicians, economists, miners, factory workers, seafarers, Mennonites, Jews and members of the pacifistic Moravian church.[133] Not a single man from the cities of Berlin, Potsdam, old Magdeburg, Breslau, Stettin and Königsberg, the Silesian mountains or the duchies of Cleves and East Frisia was conscripted.[134] As Höpfner summarized, "The burden of military service was essentially born by the poorer segment of the population."[135]

A forceful memorandum by Blücher advocating a national army to replace the standing army called attention to the uncertain diplomatic climate; preserving the present structure of the military won't mean much were the country overrun by Napoleon. The king approved the formation of 78 Land Reserve Battalions of 600 rifles each, with a roster combining pensioned soldiers and young recruits from the canton system. Lists of candidates were in preparation but civilian authorities managed all sorts of obstructions to delay the process. By the time Prussia began the campaign against France in the fall of 1806, not one battalion had been mustered. Though the burghers resisted participation in national defense, the blame for this failure belongs at the feet of Möllendorff, Geusau and Colonel Ludwig August von Guionneau, typical representatives of an obsolete system who sat on the Immediate Organization Commission. As Höhn summarized, "The commission was stuck in the thinking of the old maneuver strategy and seeing a battle as a line formation in Friedrich's style that decides the outcome by rapid maneuvers in an open field. A militia trained differently than the standing army would only disrupt and weaken that army."[136]

As for the army itself, the men spent their time training or confined to barracks, closely watched to prevent desertion. They were isolated from the population. They fulfilled their duty to protect and obey the monarchy without belonging to the nation they supposedly defend. The king and his military advisors wanted as little contact between the troops and the populace as possible.[137] Summarizing the climate of the times, *Deutsche Wehrzeitung* offered this perspective: "The people had only obligations; no rights, no opinions, no will. The caprice of the prince was law. Only a disarmed, effeminate nation bends silently and patiently to such a yoke. The weapons had been taken from the people's hands. To wage its wars, absolutism forged a class of soldiers sorted out from its own nation. These men alone reserved the right to bear arms and the privilege of using them. But fighting a foreign enemy was not their only purpose. They were also there to increase the splendor of the throne and to serve the head of state as a scourge of the nation if it becomes inclined to turn against the patriarch's whims. Such was the origin of the standing army!"[138]

Mobilization

In September 1806, Scharnhorst became the Duke of Brunswick's quartermaster general, the chief of staff. He was denied permission to bring along the newly formed general staff. Scharnhorst wrote his daughter, "Since my arrival at the headquarters of the duke or king—I don't really know which to call it—I haven't slept one night more than three hours. It's no trifle to direct an army of nearly a hundred mounted squadrons and so many battalions, batteries, reserves, hospitals and so forth, without communications, without a general staff, and instead having to deal with people who hate the duke and never miss an opportunity to complain. With all these concerns, all the griping and the disputes, I marvel at my good health. Without bragging I can fairly claim that not many persons in my situation would be able to hold it together."[139] Clausewitz later said of Scharnhorst, "It's almost unbelievable under what difficult circumstances this man worked. Never in my life have I encountered someone who was better suited to master difficulties of this sort than the man I'm speaking of here."[140] Brunswick's lack of appreciation for his tireless subordinate's endeavors is revealed in a letter he sent the king reading, "It seems to me that the plans my general staff chief has for the Prussian army are not adaptable."[141]

With a command structure like this, Prussia's king and his generals expected to defeat Napoleon. For years, Friedrich Wilhelm III's naive efforts to preserve peace had delayed war preparations. Frugality in government slashed defense spending. Queen Luise repeatedly warned the king of France's belligerent intentions. At Napoleon's direction she was libeled in *Rheinbund* newspapers as a "war-monger." This offended the population of Prussia. Her public appearances were marked by spectacular ovations of admiration and approval.[142] The king's passivity garnered only disdain from the French warlord. Napoleon wrote the diplomat Charles-Maurice de Talleyrand on September 12, "The notion that Prussia would risk standing alone against me is too ridiculous to be worth mentioning. My alliance with Prussia is based on fear. The cabinet is contemptible, the sovereign without character."[143] Prussian General Duke Karl August, a veteran of the Rhine campaigns against France, was even less delicate: "The king should crawl into the deepest hole in the earth so no one will see him anymore. I hope to never have to look at him again."[144]

Friedrich Wilhelm sent Napoleon a 20-page ultimatum on September 25. Expressing his "good faith in the unblemished friendship with France," he demanded the withdrawal of French troops east of the Rhine, no interference with Prussia forming a league of northern German states and return of territories that French Marshal Joachim Murat annexed to augment his Grand Duchy of Berg. The document was Haugwitz's idea. The October 08 deadline warned Napoleon that Prussia is about to declare war. This gave him justification for military measures. He had already issued marching orders to his troops on September 19 and left to join them on the 25th. He arrived in Mainz three days later. Napoleon never read the ultimatum. It did not even reach his headquarters, by then in Bamberg, until October 07. Prussia declared war two days later. The French army in Germany numbered 140,000 infantry, 32,000 horse and 20,000 artillerymen plus logistical personnel. It could also rely on the support of *Rheinbund* troops, though fewer than pledged.

Many officers welcomed war. They had tired of their sovereign's conde-

Anxious to take on France, officers of Prussia's elite *Garde du corps* sharpen their swords on the steps of the French embassy in September 1806. Napoleon remembered this taunt and humiliated the regiment after conquering Prussia.

scending demeanor toward a French upstart who treats their king with disdain. Scharnhorst wrote his daughter, "I lack the casual attitude that others have, the calmness and confidence with which they look toward the future."[145] The underestimate of French military capabilities resulted in taking the offensive before sufficient forces were available, and in half-measures in preparation. Negotiations with Austria and Russia began too late for them to send troops or aid. There was almost no attempt to conclude military compacts with northern German states. A better plan would have been for the Prussian army to strategically withdraw, fighting rearguard actions along the way if necessary, and take up defensive positions behind the Elbe and then the Oder Rivers. This would have allowed a link-up with a Russian force of 60,000 men preparing to deploy. Although the withdrawal would probably have cost Friedrich Wilhelm the direct support of some 20,000 Saxon troops, the Prussian reserve army in the east would have reinforced him instead.

As he advanced, Napoleon would have had to detach contingents to garrison fortresses and protect lines of communication and deplete his main force by nearly 50,000 men.[146] The longer Bonaparte's troops campaigned on foreign soil, the weaker they became. Already in 1805, "Things are not well with his army," Goltz maintained. "Privations and disease decimate it. The death rate is so high that he has to abandon Brünn to advance on the Donau. He has lost the flower of his soldiers in combat and must inadequately replace them with troops mustered in Swabia and Bavaria. Italy can offer little assistance and he can be cut off from replacements from France. A vigorous 'diversion' on the lower Rhine would weaken his resources even further and weary the French nation of a war that is consuming its vitality to serve one man's ambition."[147] By opting for an offensive, Friedrich Wilhelm may have hoped to restore prestige by defeating Napoleon without help from the coalition. Prussia forfeited the opportunity to draw the enemy deeper into hostile territory, extend his supply lines and expose his troops to prolonged psychological, physical and material hardships.

In the summer of 1806, Napoleon had ordered the conscription of another 80,000 Frenchmen to bring regimental rosters to full strength. The army transferred hundreds of officers and NCOs to depots in France to train recruits. He wrote Marshal Nicolas Soult on August 06, "it's better to settle the matter with a single blow than to lay down the sword only to keep taking it up anew."[148] Regarding *Prussia*'s war preparations, as pointed out by Höpfner, "It is remarkable to see from the measures taken that despite the crushing superiority of France in every respect, it was still not considered necessary to bring the entire army onto war footing."[149] Remaining in garrisons in Silesia, East Prussia and Warsaw were 33 infantry battalions, 55 cavalry squadrons including horse artillery, in all nearly 34,000 men, plus 198 cannons. Economic considerations did not influence their non-deployment since these soldiers were already on active duty. There was no need to designate them as a strategic reserve. One could have been created by calling reservists to the colors.

Leaving a garrison in Warsaw may have seemed prudent, since it would guard against a possible Polish insurrection in annexed territory that was proving more trouble than its worth. This reasoning is also flawed, because a French victory on German soil would require Prussia to transfer these troops to the western theater of operations anyway. On the other hand, were Napoleon defeated by a superior Prussian force, this in itself would discourage the Poles from rebellion. Many soldiers in the Prussian army in the east were of Polish nationality. They had been forcibly conscripted and could scarcely be relied on to suppress an uprising in Poland. The king and his military pundits left one field artillery and six infantry battalions to hold fortresses in Silesia, hence another 5,000 men, in case the French army stationed in southern Germany crosses Bohemia to invade. Napoleon kept this force there to hold Austria in check, not to invade Prussia. Had the government formed the militia as Blücher, Knesebeck, Rüchel and Scharnhorst advocated, its battalions could have garrisoned the strongpoints and released thousands of combat troops for frontline service.

In addition to the 34,000 troops not deployed, other forces that Prussia more or less voluntarily relinquished for the campaign include 26 infantry battalions and 20 mounted squadrons of Hessians. These were particularly militant fighters who had better training than the Prussian army. The Prussians also made no use of 8,000 Saxons and 10,000 soldiers from smaller German duchies who were available. The king's military planners detailed 5,600 men to guard the frontiers of Westphalia and East Frisia and left six mobile battalions comprising 4,000 troops in Magdeburg, Hanover, Hameln and Nienburg. In his analysis of the campaign, Major Gerhard Gieren concluded that "since Prussia had left substantial portions of her army behind in Upper Silesia, East Frisia, Westphalia and Hanover, she could scarcely demand of Oldenburg, Mecklenburg and Brunswick that these states denude their territories of troops" to send to war.[150] The combined Prussian-Saxon army that engaged Napoleon's invasion force in October tallied some 128,000 men. An energetic effort to recruit allies and marshal domestic military resources could have increased this force by over 100,000 soldiers on the day of battle.

Regarding the leadership of the army about to cross lances with France, Boyen divided the officer corps into three categories. Senior commanders like the Duke of Brunswick, Möllendorff and Kalckreuth had served under Friedrich the Great and retained confidence in the fighting methods he employed. They had not kept pace with the subsequent evolution of warfare and were detached from the younger generation of progressively thinking officers. Kalckreuth for example, mocked the new general staff as "a tyranny as hated as it is ridiculous."[151] Boyen was harsh in his criticism of company commanders and squadron chiefs commissioned after the Seven Years' War. Possessing little combat experience and accustomed to the monotony and comfort of garrison routine, they prioritized frugality of administration to ensure a secure retirement. Not up to the rigors of a campaign, these men more or less opposed war. The younger generation of officers, many of whom had attended Scharnhorst's lectures, Boyen judged favorably. Fueled by the ambition to prove themselves in battle, they possessed personal valor and embraced modern concepts of strategy and tactics.

The active officer corps was overaged. Of 244 men in senior positions of command, 166 exceeded 60 years of age and more than half of these were over 65. Only 13 were younger than 50. Of the Prussian army's 54 chiefs of infantry regiments, all were aged past 60 and twelve were 70 or older.[152] These elder gentlemen resisted reform, for example thwarting initiatives to economize the enormous supply train that slows troop movements. Since soldiers were not issued overcoats, columns included large, cumbersome tents for bivouacs. The Prussian army required 3,134 supply wagons, 33,440 pack horses and 11,995 transport personnel to move baggage.[153] Officers brought beds, bedroom furnishings, sofas and pet parrots with them to war. A lieutenant in the Möllendorff Infantry Regiment brought a piano.[154] A proposal to eliminate surplus supplies to increase the army's mobility was formally rejected by the Immediate Organization Commission with the justification, "To take tents away from the regiments or riding and pack-horses from the officers appears repugnant to the spirit of the Prussian army and could have negative consequences."[155]

Officers conducted pedantic rituals every morning during field operations, as Captain Johann von Borcke recalled: "First the senior commanders inspected the uniforms and their neatness, punishments were carried out, the daily password announced, interminably long orders were dictated and much time was wasted in superfluous trifles. This ponderous formalism would consume a couple of hours before the regiment set off. During the march itself, the troops were fatigued by halts and delays. Sometimes it was due to some insignificant obstacle of terrain, sometimes to having to drag a stuck cannon or broken wagon. It was torturous how no town, no miserable hamlet could be traversed without stopping first, even in the worst weather, for the men to change into parade dress. When the exhausted and chilled troops finally reached their quarters, there were a hundred obligations and duties to carry out, so that the officers and NCOs could not think of rest until late in the evening. The vitality of the troops was pointlessly squandered and officers and men became surly.

"The result of this corrosive routine and remorseless severity of senior commanders toward the common man soon became apparent" in the alarming rate of desertion. "After the first marches, these observations already dampened my good spirits and longing for war... There were clear signs that boded nothing good for the future."[156] Even marching to battle, members of the old officer corps still regarded the "spirit of the Prussian army" as a carte blanche to sustain their status, lifestyle and archaic convention. This catch phrase, summarized by Goltz, "had to be preserved without sound reason for doing so. The 'spirit of the army,' this incomprehensible something to which all great deeds, victories and glory are attributed... prevented the formation of Knesebeck's national reserve and honorary legions and blocked abolishing officers' riding horses, field beds and countless pack-horses. It was also the spirit that would not permit universal adoption of the dispersed battle order... This spirit was on stage every time, spreading disorder and confusion."[157]

The French army was anything but outmoded; nor was there doubt about its centralization of command and the authority of the man in charge. The French Revolution had initially introduced a regime that was rife with brutality and corruption. The quarrels of rival political factions were customarily settled by the guillotine. Public administration was in shambles. In this atmosphere of chaos, the door opened for the "child of the Revolution," the charismatic Napoleon. General Fuller wrote of the period, "However fervently the people may support the revolutionary ideals, anarchy is the one thing they will not for long tolerate, and when it prevails, they readily look for the man who will deliver them from it. When he appears, the normal sequel is for the energy generated by the anarchy to be directed outwardly in the form of a foreign war. This, in its turn, consolidates the people and normally leads to the establishment of a coercive regime which, with full military backing, takes the place of the original government."[158] Napoleon eliminated political graft and mismanagement. This greatly enhanced his popularity. He had the advantage of controlling both the civilian government and the military.

Bonaparte gradually transferred the enthusiasm and loyalty of the army from its commitment to the Revolution to his person. He possessed a dedicated and formidable instrument of power and no warlord knew better how to wield it. Some admirers of Napoleon have historically credited him with a downright supernatural ability to anticipate events. A good measure of his success as a warlord, however, was the result of attention to fundamentals. Having stabilized public administration, he mobilized human and material resources for war without debate as was the case in Prussia. Providing good personal equipment and adequate nourishment for his troops was an absolute priority. They were issued overcoats for operations in cold weather. The Prussians received only blankets. French infantry carried the upgraded Model 1801 rifle that was more durable, accurate, and lighter than the Prussian M1780/87. Napoleon authorized the army to requisition foodstuffs from the locals during campaigns. This reduced the risk of shortages caused by extended supply lines.

Prior to entering enemy territory, Napoleon instructed agents to procure maps and reconnoiter the terrain ahead. This provided intelligence about rivers, hills and forests in advance. When towns were captured, he ordered officers to interrogate residents and seize postal correspondence. He therefore gained information about opposing forces in proximity and their intentions. Napoleon maintained liaison with his corps commanders. "It's urgent that your reports arrive quickly and frequently," he wrote Marshal Jean Lannes on October 07, "so that I can compare them with other news about the intentions of the enemy... Write me very often."[159] The next day he advised Marshal Soult, "Send me news constantly. In a combined war like this one, only through very frequent reports

A French officer turns a deaf ear to pleas from a farmer and his wife not to requisition their cattle and hay for the *Grande Armée*. Prolonged occupation by Napoleon's forces left the people of Germany practically destitute.

from all sides can a good result be achieved. Make this your first priority."[160] Since France's *Grande Armée* moved faster and its officers had more combat experience than their Prussian opponents, Napoleon entered battle on a solid foundation; well-equipped, robust troops, a system in place to nourish them and close communication with his commanders to rapidly respond to enemy maneuvers and shift formations accordingly.

Scharnhorst criticized the Prussian army for keeping officers of advanced age on active duty. He wrote that "men should be promoted to divisional, brigade and regimental commanders who have distinguished themselves through their actions, talent and courage," and that promotion "should not be a reward for long service."[161] By comparison, French field marshals were in their thirties and forties and most generals were not from the nobility. These men possessed the ambition and vitality of youth. This enabled the emperor to rely on them to carry out his orders energetically. Napoleon developed a four-phase blueprint for attack. First, he sent in Tirailleurs; their purpose was to wear the enemy down and help disguise the movements of the main army. Next came the artillery, which Napoleon massed to bombard a single sector instead of distributing cannons across the battlefield to support individual units. The major attack followed.

Deep columns of infantry struck against the defenders who had been targeted by the barrage. Cavalry came last. It pursued the retreating foe and took prisoners. Bonaparte kept a strong reserve on hand to reinforce the line where needed.

Tirailleurs fought in collaboration with infantry columns. These columns consisted of blocs ten to 20 men deep. They maintained cohesion as they punched through the thin enemy firing line while skirmishers kept the defenders occupied or pinned down. The column attack corresponded to Napoleon's preference for converging his forces on a designated point to achieve a breakthrough. The conservative Prussian infantry generals rejected this form of assault. In their perception, summarized by Goltz, "In battle the side has the advantage that knows how to concentrate all its firepower against one place... The bullet decides, and the thin line alone can bring all its rifles into action at once. The men in a (French) column's third, fourth or eighth row follow along unable to do anything against the enemy... Only in thickly wooded areas, at night or in great confusion among combatants can a closely compacted column be effective; in that case it's just a matter of pushing forward instead of actually fighting."[162]

A historical confrontation between an 18th-Century standing army and one embracing the political and military innovations of the modern age was about to unfold. France had been fighting wars for her national survival for over a decade; the Prussians had committed only a third of their troops to the coalition wars.[163] Civilians were unaffected and pursued their peacetime occupations throughout the conflict. Oswald Spengler wrote that few nations can survive a long war, but none can survive a long peace. It was in some ways unfortunate for Prussia that her greatest king created through conquest the preconditions for a prolonged era of security and prosperity. They gradually devitalized the armed forces and the merit of personal honor they personified; and this at the dawn of an age that would assail the country and its values politically, socially and militarily.

Ironically, Friedrich the Great and his army in a sense did too good a job. The Seven Years' War left Europe with a respect for Prussia's martial capabilities that discouraged diplomatic rivals from provoking a serious confrontation. During the first coalition wars, the French had been reluctant to fight Prussia. She prospered during the period of national security while the army survived on its reputation and its established traditions. The towering personality that gave life and purpose to this arrangement, however, was no longer present. The military hierarchy became complacent and resisted modernization. Had the government conducted an adroit foreign policy and the continental balance of power remained stable, this would not necessarily have become a serious impediment. All began to change as the Enlightenment gained influence. It provoked an unprecedented political and social upheaval destined to transform the world and the fundamental principles of warfare.

Chapter 5

Prelude to Disaster

The Prussian Debate Club

In the campaign of 1806 and 1807, Napoleon conquered Prussia and approached the zenith of his power. The peace treaty he imposed at Tilsit was so unworkable that it provoked an uprising a few years later. Prussian and Saxon troops and their frontline officers fought bravely in the war. They suffered from a senior command lethargy that made the sacrifices in vain. Count Schlieffen marveled at Napoleon's "especially great accomplishment" at Jena. He praised his alleged tactical genius for smashing Prussian battalions "one after another." Yet as will be revealed below, the Emperor of the French made blunders before the battle that a capable adversary such as Friedrich the Great would have punished severely. The Prussian command did not capitalize on these mistakes. Historian Gieren wrote that over a hundred years later, "We still wonder how the entire direction of Prussian operations in 1806 could have been so unrealistic, and to such a strikingly vast degree that a young recruit could have demonstrated more tactical intuition than the general so rich in experience and length of service" in charge.[1]

Despite Duke Karl Wilhelm Ferdinand of Brunswick's dismal performance at Valmy in 1792 and the inconclusive Rhine campaign the following year, the king assigned him to lead the army. Möllendorff was too old and Friedrich Wilhelm III had confidence in the duke. Karl Wilhelm had denied the foreign ministry's request the previous July to draft a plan to wage war against France. He even asked Haugwitz for permission to send an emissary to negotiate with Napoleon. This arbitrary step embarrassed and annoyed the king. The duke was hesitant to accept the king's commission. He feared that Bonaparte might annex the Duchy of Brunswick in retaliation. Given his rank however, the duke could scarcely refuse and ultimately assumed command. The king entrusted the leadership of his armed forces in a war against France to a field marshal who was reluctant to offend Napoleon. The Duchy of Brunswick itself remained neutral, hence the duke's own troops did not enter the war. Clausewitz would later write of him, "Deliberation without end crippled his resolve, dissension disrupted his thinking and disobedience made what was left completely ineffective."[2]

The duke was a vacillating, indecisive commander in chief unwilling to accept accountability for a course of action. He relied on the consensus of his staff. Rüchel later opined, "It was not a field marshal, but an assortment of advisors that in truth determined the operations of the Prussian army. Of all the military shortcomings that became apparent during the ill-fated war, this was certainly the most calamitous."[3] To make matters worse, the king was habitually prone to micromanage the army and it was customary for a Hohenzollern monarch to accompany it during wartime. Since a military campaign unavoidably influences the country's political fortunes, the commanding general will under such a circumstance feel obliged to explain operational plans to the sovereign. Responsibility for the decisions then becomes shared. Friedrich Wilhelm was himself inclined to "ask all the world for advice."[4] This contributed to the jumble of ideas and opinions to be aired and debated before taking action. The drawn-out conferences delayed operations, and this against a foe who assessed situations quickly and issued corresponding orders without hesitation.

On September 08, the king approved the plan drafted by the *Oberkriegskollegium* (Supreme War Council), his military advisory staff. Since reports from southern Germany presumed Bonaparte's army to be billeted in dispersed locations throughout the region, it proposed an offensive strategy to engage French contingents in succession. Friedrich Wilhelm forwarded it to the Duke of Brunswick for evaluation. He replied on the 11th, "The rules of war ordinarily dictate attacking the enemy before he marshals his forces. If the army's rations are sufficient to lead it across the Thuringian Forest, then this plan should be carried out without delay. If food stores are inadequate for an offensive operation, then all available resources should be mustered to address this important matter."[5] The duke endorsed an immediate advance instead of opting for the more practical alternative, retiring to the Elbe to await reinforcements from Russia and draw Napoleon deeper into German territory. He recommended concentrating the entire army except for Blücher's troops at Naumburg. The town is on the Saale River about 20 miles southwest of Leipzig. He wrote Rüchel on September 22, "I will set before the king, as is my duty, two offensive projects."[6] The plans were very likely drafted by Scharnhorst, who reached the duke's headquarters the same day.

Colonel Scharnhorst was swamped serving as Karl Wilhelm's chief of staff. The field marshal surrounded himself with a personal "staff" as well. Hardenberg wrote, "The duke of Brunswick, who regardless of his more than seventy years of age cannot do without female companionship, has brought with him the French actress Mademoiselle Duquesnoi. Also in his entourage is a certain secret advisor named Hallatin from Geneva whom he needs as his minister of foreign affairs and is considered pro-French—I don't know if justifiably—and Monsieur de la fort, a French immigrant whom the duke likewise retains in his diplomatic service."[7] The king's adjutant, Wilhelm Henckel von Donnersmark, later testified that officers suspected the duke's French mistress of relaying military intelligence to the enemy as they did his personal adjutant, a Frenchman named Montjoie. The latter's brother was an officer in Napoleon's army. On the 23rd the king arrived in Naumburg with Queen Luise in tow. The royal couple added to the accumulation of militarily-useless baggage confounding the nerve center of the Prussian army.

Prussian infantrymen greet Queen Luise in her carriage on the road from Kösen to Weimar. Repeatedly warning the king about the threat Napoleon poses, she accompanied her husband to the theater of operations in Thuringia.

One advantage the Prussians *did* have was location. The decision to bivouac the troops on the Saale River's western bank was sound. Winding north from Bavaria, the Saale snakes its way through Thuringia's broken, heavily wooded countryside and flows into the Elbe near Magdeburg. Its course has the character of a steep mountain valley. About 20 miles south of Naumburg is Jena, eleven miles west of Jena is Weimar, and another 13 miles beyond that Erfurt, where the king moved with his staff. Only one road followed the river's eastern bank. A network of roads facilitated movement in the region on the opposite side. Bluffs, elevated plateaus, thick underbrush and deep ravines sculpt the western bank into a nearly impregnable natural bastion. Clausewitz maintained, "Scarcely in history can an example be found of a more advantageous position for a defending army. From a central disposition at Erfurt, it could move against anything coming from Eisenach (further west) or through the Thuringian Forest (in the south) and fall upon the enemy's divided columns with a superior force. Were the enemy to approach from Bayreuth, we could advance to Weimar and occupy the Saale crossings. If he tried to completely bypass us, which would be unthinkable, we could move in concealment through the Saale valley and… cross the Saale behind him and attack in the flank and rear."[8]

While the Prussians made camp, Napoleon prepared to marshal his forces to deal with them before the Russians intervene. He told Soult, "The enemy can do what he wants. If he attacks me, I'll be delighted. If he lets me attack him, I won't fail to do my part. I very much want a battle."[9] The Prussian army could ambush the French as they negotiate the narrow passes of the Thuringian Forest, stand firm on the Saale should they wheel to attack, or strike their flank should they attempt to bypass it. According to Höpfner, "Detachments of combined arms could hold the Saale crossings while the army occupies a central position on the plateau of the left bank… ready to move in any direction. These detachments would be capable of defending against a greatly superior force until the army arrives and falls upon the enemy's separate columns. With their backs to the steep Saale valley and line of retreat in their furthermost eastern flank, they would be hit hard and scarcely able to escape defeat."[10]

On September 24, the Duke of Brunswick convened the war council. In attendance were quartermasters Colonel Scharnhorst and General Phull, adjutant Friedrich von Kleist, Major Gustav von Rauch, Captain Karl von Müffling and assorted staff officers. Instead of pressing his plan for an offensive, the duke deferred it to discussion. Nothing was resolved. Two sessions took place the following day. Friedrich Wilhelm attended both and old Möllendorff the latter. At a time when prompt action was crucial, the king weighed pros and cons with this "military debate club." It included, historian Gerd Fesser stated, "not only senior commanders and general staff officers, but all sorts of conspiring armchair generals who didn't even command troops."[11] One officer present wrote Hohenlohe's chief of staff Massenbach, "No one really knows what to do. Today threatened by invasion, they want to go on the defensive, tomorrow it's let's take the offensive, the next day probably negotiate, in short confusion beyond compare."[12]

As is often the case, it is not necessarily the best idea that prevails but the one most eloquently expressed. In the first three talks Major Rauch, who opposed the duke's plan to keep the army together, persuaded his colleagues to revert to the one previously drafted by the Supreme War Council. This envisioned dividing the Prussian-Saxon force into large components. The formations were too far apart for mutual support and each too small to fight Napoleon on its own. As Goltz summarized, "The massing of all available forces at the decisive point was necessary for victory."[13] Brunswick considered dislocation of the army important to confuse mounted French officers who were allegedly traversing the countryside disguised as merchants to gather intelligence. This apprehension was completely unfounded. The war council did not consider it risky to disperse the army. The duke believed that Napoleon will leave 90,000 men behind to watch Austria. In fact, the emperor detailed just 20,000 Bavarian auxiliaries for the purpose and marched against Prussia with almost the whole French army in southern Germany.

During the conferences, the war council reaffirmed the plan for an offensive. Deploying Hohenlohe's corps in Saxony and Rüchel's in Hesse was supposed to entice Napoleon to split his own force to protect his flanks. Karl Wilhelm and the main army would then strike out of Erfurt in the center. The Prussians deferred the operation until the king's ultimatum expires on October 08. They apparently assumed that Bonaparte will sit idle for the next two weeks. He was in fact drafting orders to deploy the troops for invasion. Scharnhorst wanted to ambush the French in the Thuringian Forest and strategically withdraw through Saxony until the Russians arrive. Fellow officers considered the plan incompatible with the honor of the Prussian army.[14] Scharnhorst lacked the charisma to successfully promote his ideas. Only one of his reforms was implemented. This was forming the army into divisions, each encompassing all three branches of combat arms. The order came while the army was moving forward. A less opportune time for carrying this out could not have been chosen, since infantry battalions, artillery batteries and cavalry squadrons had to find their assigned divisions and join them right in transit.

On October 03, the staff at Naumburg received a report from Bavaria that Napoleon is coming to Würzburg and gathering a force of 60 to 70,000 men to move north. The emperor was marching the *Grande Armée* into Saxony in three separate columns to follow the Saale River toward Leipzig. He fixed a city as the preliminary objective since he did not know where the Prussian army is. Somewhere along the way, he reasoned, the Prussians will make a stand and deliver the battle he seeks. The final destination was Berlin. The capital was about ten-days' march from the French army's assembly points at Bamberg, Bayreuth and Würzburg. Despite Bonaparte's superior numbers, the Prussian and Saxon army occupied defensible terrain and had good prospects for success. History attributes the one-sided outcome to Napoleon's "tactical genius," Clausewitz lauding him as the "god of war," but he conducted a hazardous and flawed campaign. The emperor's routine doctoring of his *Bulletin de l'armée* (army bulletins), editing articles for Paris newspapers and penchant for exaggeration contribute to the image of his infallibility but understate his enemy's mistakes.

Overestimating Friedrich Wilhelm's cognitive function, Napoleon initially presumed that the Prussians will occupy a defensive position behind the Elbe to await reinforcements from the czar. He soon revised his opinion. He wrote Soult on October 05, "According to what has reached me up till today, it appears that if the enemy is in fact on the move, it will be directed against my left flank, since he is reported to be in Erfurt with his main force."[15] The report was unconfirmed when the French entered the mountainous Thuringian Forest on October 08. Soult's IV Corps out of Bayreuth covered the right flank. The VI Corps of Michel Ney followed a day behind it. Murat with the cavalry and Jean Bernadotte's I Corps were in the center, trailed by Louis Davout's III Corps and the Imperial Guard. To the left was Lannes's V Corps and then Pierre Augereau with the VII Corps. There were 50,000 men on the right, 70,000 in the center and 40,000 on the left. Napoleon still had no accurate knowledge of the Prussian disposition and was groping in the dark. The columns were to converge on Saalfeld, a Saale

River town in the forest 20 miles south of Jena. Until then, the *Grande Armée* was dispersed traversing narrow defiles in uneven country and uncertain about the movement and intentions of the Prussians.

Poor reconnaissance was just one problem facing the invader. Having drained Bavaria's resources for months, the French were unable to requisition the antic- ipated quantity of additional provisions from the population for the campaign. On the precarious left flank, Lannes's men were overextended and on their own. Lannes himself wrote Napoleon on October 09 that he has no maps and cannot find a local to serve as a guide. "Today was horrible for the troops and the artil- lery," he reported. "The roads are awful and the land provides absolutely nothing useful."[16] Lannes informed the emperor that the enemy appears to be deployed along a line from Weimar to Gotha. Napoleon himself now decided that the Prussian-Saxon army is in Gera nearly 20 miles *east* of Jena; in the opposite direction from where it actually stood. Gera seemed a logical choice; from there the Prussians could protect Saxony and secure their retreat to the Elbe. He duly informed Soult in a letter on October 10, "I no longer have any doubt that Gera is the assembly point of the Prussian army."[17]

To continue toward Berlin, the French would have to cross to the right side of the Saale into Saxony and proceed northeast following the river. To accom- plish this, they had to eliminate the opposing army defending the left bank. The narrow valley they were about to traverse stood between the Saale and the Bohemian border. At one point the valley is just nine miles wide. To enter neutral Bohemia would invite a diplomatic headache while France was trying to isolate Prussia. The French line of communication was too vulnerable not to address the threat posed by Brunswick. Lettow-Vorbeck stated, "The disad- vantages facing the French army as it passed would be so great that the difficult attack across the Saale valley was the better option."[18] If properly deployed, the Prussians could hold a practically unassailable position or fall upon enemy formations strung out on postal roads marching in the wrong direction. In addi- tion, Prussian reconnaissance would soon monitor the disposition and progress of the *Grande Armée* and supply the duke's headquarters with better intelligence than what was available to the French. Facing an army enjoying a well-deserved reputation for prowess, Napoleon had embarked on a risky enterprise indeed.

Death of a Prince

Once French troops set foot on Thuringian soil their country would be at war. The October 08 deadline for the king's ultimatum lost relevance. The Prussian and Saxon army deployed where it could intercept the French if its field marshal chose to do so. Instead, Karl Wilhelm presented the option to his staff for debate. Since the duke had in a sense demoted himself from commander in chief to committee chairman, deliberation preceded every decision of the war council. On the docket was whether or not to cancel the planned offensive through the forest now that the enemy is moving. The duke invited officers for consultation at his new headquarters in Erfurt on the evening of October 04. This was to exchange ideas prior to a major conference scheduled for the next day with the king and Möllendorff. Present were the army's three quartermaster generals Scharnhorst, Phull and Massenbach, plus Major Rauch, Captain Müffling, adjutant Kleist and another colonel with the same surname. Brunswick considered it "probable" that Napoleon will occupy the Thuringian Forest ahead of the Prussians, but did not seem too concerned about it.[19]

The duke asked Massenbach for his opinion. A compulsive talker, Prince Hohenlohe's quartermaster had a flair for expressing views that lack supporting evidence. He presented them with such conviction that his weary audience was often too baffled to propose an alternative. Lettow-Vorbeck found it "incomprehensible that this man with his confusing ideas could repeatedly make a stronger impression than the precise, sober Scharnhorst."[20] Massenbach opposed the operation. He contended that without knowing the enemy's disposition the expedition force might be destroyed. He predicted that Napoleon will invade Saxony and proposed transferring Hohenlohe's corps to the right bank of the Saale River to stop him. At this time the *Grande Armée* was still in its assembly areas and the Prussians could only speculate on the emperor's plans.

Napoleon could march north then turn east at Eisenach to invade Saxony or cross to the right side of the Saale to proceed northeast toward Leipzig. Massenbach wanted Hohenlohe to transfer his corps to the right bank of the river based on a hunch. The idea was to enable the army to respond more quickly if the French invade Saxony. The valley along the eastern bank, where Massenbach proposed sending Hohenlohe's corps, had no fresh water and only one road. The fact is that were Bonaparte to enter Saxony, Hohenlohe did not need to be on the right side of the river; he could simply cross it to attack. Massenbach "pushed ceaselessly for an immediate return to the right Saale bank as the only way that the army can be rescued from annihilation. But there was so little clarity in all of his fanciful scenarios that just a few were convinced and it only served to increase the inconclusiveness" among the staff.[21]

The war council convened the following morning with Friedrich Wilhelm, Möllendorff, Haugwitz and a few generals in attendance. The duke suggested deferring the offensive until after a reconnaissance mission. The majority agreed. The king then asked *Massenbach*—out of all the officers in the room—for his thoughts on the subject. The colonel emphasized the hazards of an attack south but soon returned to his fantasy about moving Prince Hohenlohe's corps across the Saale. Chronically mesmerized by his chief of staff's rhetoric, the prince supported the proposal. This opened the debate. Scharnhorst interrupted that it is better for the staff to agree on a course of action than to continue unproductive discussions that delay taking action. Most of the participants were skeptical of Massenbach's recommendation. They did work out a plan for the reconnaissance mission. It called for a disproportionately large contingent of combined arms to push into Thuringia while sending similar units in other directions, to return on

October 14. When the draft was submitted to the king for review that evening, he decided that the detachments would be scouting too far from camp and disapproved the plan.

Captain Müffling was familiar with Thuringia's terrain and volunteered to scout the mountains. The duke approved the mission after the king rejected the war council's over-engineered reconnaissance project. Müffling departed with a small escort at noon on October 06. The council spent the day in debate. It called off the offensive for good. The fluent Massenbach achieved some of his objectives and the council adopted his proposal for Hohenlohe's corps to defend the Saale from Jena down to Rudolstadt with 42,000 Prussian and Saxon troops. The Duke of Brunswick would take the central army of 57,300 men to Erfurt. General Rüchel's corps comprising 22,000 soldiers would march to Eisenach, some 30 miles west of Erfurt. General Kalckreuth was given a reserve corps of two divisions. The king wrote Rüchel the following day explaining his orders "to concentrate the army between Gotha, Erfurt and Weimar so that it can be assembled in a single day."[22] If attacked in the west, the general was to hold until the central army arrives in relief.

The order for new deployment contradicted one issued for some units the previous day. In the resulting confusion, troops assigned to receive their bread ration and fodder for the horses at Gotha were instructed to proceed to

Prussian hussars on a scouting mission. In the Seven Years' War, the campaign of 1806 and the war of liberation in 1813, Prussian reconnaissance was generally superior to that of the enemy.

Erfurt instead, where stores were insufficient. October 08 was a rest day for the Prussian and Saxon army. During the morning, Erfurt received intelligence from Duke Karl August of Weimar's advance guard that 75,000 French troops are in Bamberg preparing to march north. Shortly thereafter, Lieutenant Friedrich von Eisenhart arrived at headquarters bearing a letter from Müffling about the scouting mission: Napoleon's troops, the letter stated, are moving in three columns to attack General Bogislav Tauentzien's division, which belongs to Hohenlohe's corps, as soon as they emerge from the Thuringian Forest. Tauentzien's troops were leaving Hof, a Saale River town 45 miles south of Jena, but maintained hussar rearguards at Lobenstein and at Saalburg.

Müffling was astonished by the enemy's carelessness. He wrote in his dispatch, "Emperor Napoleon is so totally indifferent to his rear and flanks that I believe we could pull off a real coup. The marching order of the troops of his army is in no way militarily disposed. The weapons are not properly distributed and every security measure is neglected. The marching troops… have posted no lookouts in our direction. I think that if ten to 15 squadrons of hussars with a mounted battery from here hurl themselves against their line of march, not only will it be broken up, but from what I can see there will be far-reaching consequences."[23] The crown prince of Koburg, an officer in Russian service who volunteered to help in the war against Napoleon, conducted his own reconnaissance of the French advance. He came to Erfurt and confirmed Müffling's observations. Count Tauentzien's scouts corroborated them as well.

"Only rarely in warfare," Lettow-Vorbeck summarized, "were there better reports, especially in such harmony, as these. The situation was completely clear. Based on the personal observations of a general staff officer, it was now certain that the enemy is not expecting to be attacked in a position behind the Franconian Saale (a separate river southwest of the Thuringian Forest) as the Duke of Brunswick had thought. All reports left no doubt that Napoleon will proceed along the right bank of the Saale. This was one of his options discussed in the conferences."[24] Goltz added, "One could scarcely hope for a better basis on which to formulate a plan of action in wartime" than the information provided by Müffling, the Duke of Koburg and Tauentzien.[25] A cavalry raid against the French columns will enjoy the advantage of surprise, Müffling wrote the duke, since Napoleon "has absolutely no knowledge of our position."[26]

Duke Karl Wilhelm categorically rejected Müffling's recommendation because he felt that the hussars detailed for the operation will be "too exposed unless a strongpoint can be established behind them."[27] Gieren pointed out, "Why then did the Prussian cavalry have horse artillery? It was there to guarantee the cavalry the necessary firepower" in such situations.[28] At 1:00 p.m. on the 8th, Brunswick issued orders that took no advantage of the valuable intelligence: "The Duke of Weimar shall advance with the Rudorf Hussars Regiment and one half of a mounted battery plus whatever light infantry is considered necessary toward the Franconian Saale, and patrol to Schweinfurt to see what the enemy still has stationed in the region there, try to take prisoners and disrupt his rear as much as possible."[29] Karl August, the Duke of Weimar, had urged that the entire army attack Lannes's corps on the left flank of Napoleon's columns before the emperor can send reinforcements. Instead, Weimar's mixed force was instructed to camp at Meiningen. The town is in the western half of Thuringia in the opposite direction from where the two armies were about to butt heads. Brunswick sent part of Rüchel's corps across the mountains even further west, toward the Hessian city of Fulda. "While in the southeast across the Saale the storm clouds were brewing, 12,500 of the best troops were sent southwest on this adventure," wrote Goltz.[30]

These formations dispatched on October 08 were supposed to return to the central army by the 14th. Not only was the progress of Weimar's force slowed by bringing light infantry at the duke's insistence, but the objective was four day's march from Erfurt. The recall order came on October 11. This was too late for the Rudorf Hussars and their support elements to return in time for the battle. Karl Wilhelm also sent instructions to Duke Eugen of Württemberg, whose reserve corps was up in Magdeburg. Brunswick did not order it to join the main army. It marched instead to Halle which is over 40 miles north of Jena. The Saxon corps was 20 miles east of the Saale at Mittel-Pöllnitz. Opting for a defensive strategy compelled the Duke of Brunswick to shift formations around to try and cover both Hesse and Saxony. By October 09, the outnumbered Prussian and Saxon army was spread out over 75 miles. This was more than twice the distance separating Napoleon's two outer columns. Captain Boyen wrote at this time that indecision was "becoming more apparent, especially with respect to the duke."[31]

French and Prussian troops first clashed on October 08. Napoleon's spearheads were southeast of Brunswick's central army and about to cross to the right bank of the Saale. A contingent of Hohenlohe's hussars withdrew from Lobenstein just west of the river when French cavalry appeared at around 11:00 a.m. It was Bernadotte's I Corps, vanguard of the French center column. The horsemen passed through Lobenstein, reached the river town of Saalburg and searched for a suitable ford. Supported by light infantry, they crossed and continued northeast. Prussian riflemen of General Rudolf von Bila's light brigade stopped them at the woods south of Oschitz. This is a village on the road to Schleiz, which was the destination of Count Tauentzien's retreating division. Bila's infantry held until ordered to withdraw by Tauentzien. He based the order on an inaccurate scouting report by Lieutenant Lanzac-Chaunac warning that French cavalry is threatening the flank.

The prolonged but insignificant engagement cost the defenders a few wounded, yet Tauentzien wrote to Hohenlohe at 2:00 p.m. that "the bravery and will of the troops is unbelievable. The French appear to have noticed the difference from the previous year and shunned trying anything brazen."[32] Tauentzien boasted, "the French were beaten back wherever they showed themselves."[33] Such a mendacious claim could only give the addressee an unrealistic impression of the parity of arms. Further southeast, Soult's IV Corps reached Hof the following morning. Its troops discovered 45,000 bushels of oats in storage that the Prussians had left behind. The Duke of Brunswick urged his generals to "exercise caution" against the invaders and Tauentzien gave up his intention to defend Schleiz. He withdrew when the French approached in force. He moved his corps north to Auma instead of following roads leading northwest that would bring it closer to the central army. It was a poorly organized retreat.

Tauentzien detached a battalion to guard Krispendorf on his right flank. The battalion was too far from the main force to help when attacked. Infantry and hussars formed the rearguard. The rearguard would have had an easier task had Tauentzien included horse artillery in the formation. Bila's cavalry successfully counterattacked Murat's pursuing horsemen three times, but in turn received little support from the Prussian infantry; the troops were not deployed to cover their comrades' retreat after an unsuccessful charge. Under relentless French pressure, the Prussian and Saxon battalions gradually lost cohesion. Tauentzien finally sent the Saxon Maximilian Infantry Regiment to stop the route. Its artillery fired indiscriminately into a melee of French chasseurs and Prussian cavalry. The barrage caused the confused Frenchmen to break off the engagement. The battle of Schleiz, which cost the defenders twelve officers and 554 men, was characteristic of the poor coordination of service arms that plagued the Prussians. Neither Duke Karl Wilhelm or any of his generals had thought of reconnoitering the Saale River crossings to determine where the enemy was most likely to cross, let alone of defending them.[34]

Lannes' V Corps advanced toward Hohenlohe with its left flank exposed. Still uncertain of his enemy's disposition, Napoleon was concerned that Lannes could be overwhelmed by a determined attack. The capture of Saalfeld, where he planned to unite the *Grande Armée*, was therefore a priority. The significance of the town was recognized by Prince Louis Ferdinand, the king's nephew and commander of Hohenlohe's advance guard division. Having led a brigade at age 20 against France in the first coalition war, this audacious officer was an advocate of modern military tactics, the idol of the younger officer corps and believed destined to become one of Prussia's great military leaders. The prince presumed that Hohenlohe will move his corps into the Saale valley to support Tauentzien. Defending Saalfeld, Prince Louis reasoned, will protect Hohenlohe's right flank as his columns cross the river. This would also buy time to transfer Saalfeld's supply stores by oxcart to Neustadt. He positioned General Karl von Pelet's fusiliers, *Jäger* companies and foot artillery at Blankenburg on the Schwarza River, a tributary of the Saale between Rudolstadt and Saalfeld, to guard his own right. To his left stood General Christian von Schimmelpfennig's hussars at Pösneck.

Prince Louis felt it crucial to hold the Schwarza River bridges as a springboard for the central army, which he thought is marching south to attack Lannes. Höpfner confirmed that "the prince was anticipating the arrival of elements of the main army."[35] On the evening of October 09, he sent dispatches to Friedrich Wilhelm III and to Hohenlohe explaining his purpose to "contest the most important Saale crossings until the whole army of the Duke of Brunswick is gathered in the camp at Blankenhayn" just north of Rudolstadt.[36] Days before, Brunswick had rejected Müffling's proposal to ambush Lannes in Thuringia's mountain passes on the grounds that the mission is too dangerous. Yet neither he nor the king recalled Prince Louis's 8,300-man advance guard as it moved south to defend Saalfeld against a French column reported by scouts to number 16,000 to 20,000 troops.[37] Having deployed his infantry, cavalry and artillery before Saalfeld on the morning of October 10, the prince dictated letters to Brunswick and Hohenlohe at 9:00 a.m. This was an hour before the battle began. They had already been informed of Prince Louis's initiative the evening before, but delayed issuing a countermanding order.

Lannes had 12,800 men and the advantage of terrain. His troops were concealed in woods along high ground that overlooks the valley where the Prussians and Saxons formed up. He could clearly observe the movement of his enemy. Even though outnumbered in artillery, Lannes continually committed fresh troops as they arrived on the battlefield. By contrast, Prince Louis would have no direct support from Generals Pelet and Schimmelpfennig because their flanking positions were too far from Saalfeld. Leaving Pelet with a reinforced battalion, three cavalry squadrons and a half-battery in Blankenburg "can only be regarded as a mistake," wrote Lettow-Vorbeck.[38] Further, the prince attempted to control too long a front line with the units under his command. He initially repulsed an assault by Tirailleurs and two cavalry regiments. Despite shifting formations and conducting repeated counterattacks to keep the French off balance, Louis was unable to prevent his soldiers from gradually succumbing to Lannes's augmenting force. Most decisive was that no reinforcements were on the way.

The battle was raging when Count Caraman, carrying the letter Prince Louis had dictated for Duke Karl Wilhelm at 9:00 a.m., reached Brunswick as he was leading a column of troops to an encampment at Blankenhayn. The count recalled that the sound of cannon fire from Saalfeld was clearly audible. "The duke became very worried about the steadily loudening fire" as his battalions marched south.[39] After some delay, Brunswick dictated a weak reply for Caraman to take to the prince. It advised that "for the moment there is nothing more to do, your imperial highness would do well not to cross the Saale but to take a position behind the Schwarza, at best at Rudolstadt, for the night."[40] An hour into the battle Lieutenant Heinrich von Egidy, who had carried the prince's second letter, returned from Hohenlohe's headquarters to Saalfeld. Edigy delivered Hohenlohe's response to adjutant August von Nostitz. It ordered that "the prince should remain in the position (at Rudolstadt) he had occupied on October 09 and not attack."[41] The letter stated that the Duke of Brunswick with the central army has been instructed by the king to defend the Saale basin instead of moving forward to support the advance guard.

When Louis decided to retreat, he told Captain Valentini, "I don't like leaving Saalfeld. If only we could hold long enough till I receive word from Prince von

Prince Louis Ferdinand fighting at Saalfeld. Napoleon claimed letters found on his body reveal that the "war party" of the young prince and the queen feared that the king's love of peace "might spoil their cruel hopes" for war.

Hohenlohe or until the *avant garde* of main army gets here and takes over this position, I could cross the Saale and join up with Count Tauentzien."[42] Prince Louis led a charge to scatter advancing Tirailleurs to prevent them from harassing the Prussian withdrawal. His troop became embroiled in a skirmish with enemy hussars. According to the French he died in a sword duel with Sergeant Jean-Baptiste Guindet. In the sergeant's own words, "I saw Prince Louis, decorated with a shiny medal, energetically issuing orders left and right and thought him the general in charge. At this moment I imagined what an honor it would be for me, were I fortunate enough to capture him… I galloped up with saber in hand and shouted, 'Give up general, or I'll kill you!' He answered in a firm voice, 'No, you rascal!' and struck me in the face with his blade. He defended himself valiantly and did not want to surrender. I attacked, determined to not let him get away, and dealt him several blows that he smoothly parried. But he was unable to ward off a stab to the chest and a blow to the back of his head."[43]

The narrative of an eyewitness, the Prussian adjutant Lieutenant Nostitz, is worth reproducing at length because it is the only surviving account that flatly contradicts Guindet's. It was discovered among Nostitz's papers after his death: "The Saxons stampeded in retreat and dragged squadrons still fighting along with them. A terrible melee ensued. Prussians, Saxons and Frenchmen merged into a disorderly mass that collided with artillery withdrawing to Wöhlsdorf. Prince Louis saw the danger at a glance, and followed by me, rushed to the fore of the men in flight. He managed to stop some and form them into a pocket of resistance. He risked his life with the coolness of a warrior accustomed to all the terrors of battle. A premonition of disaster caused me to try to protect him and I had the good fortune to parry more than one blow aimed at him. In the meantime, this fearful chaos intensified to a struggle of man against man. Suddenly I saw with horror the prince reeling, the bridle about to slip from his weakening grip. He had received a wound to the neck, followed almost immediately by a saber thrust to the center of his chest. In a rapid maneuver I lifted him from his horse and swung him onto my saddle; then I turned about to disengage from the melee…

"I held onto the prince with that strength of stimulation that the soul energizes in a desperate situation. Weakened by blood loss and suffering pain from the double wound, the prince became faint. He could no longer cling to me and slumped hard across the saddle. I struggled to lift him back up and pressed him against my chest. His head swayed and fell against my left side while his feet dangled and bounced against the chest of my horse. I held the prince firmly with my left hand and gripped the reins with the right, spurring my mount on. Meanwhile, an enemy rider gained ground and a glance backward revealed to me the savage expression of his countenance. I dropped the bridle and not without difficulty, drew a pistol which I fired at the rider who wanted to take my life. At the same time there was a second shot; of the shots we exchanged, neither missed its mark. Mine struck the hussar's horse, causing it to fall forward and take him down with it. The round aimed at me tore away my hat and wounded my head…

"Then I noticed not far away a hussar who had dismounted to tighten the billet strap. His shako was shredded, the dolman covered with dust. It was impossible to identify the original shape of the shako, and in the brownish color of his dolman I thought to recognize one of our hussars. I slowed the pace of my horse and turned to him. 'The prince is wounded,' I called to him, 'come to his aid, I'm losing the strength to hold him.' Without stirring from the spot, the hussar looked at me in surprise and gave no answer. Angered over his indifference, I spurred my horse toward him to punish him for his cowardice. But at that moment he jumped right onto the saddle, drew his saber and charged. He shouted in an Alsatian accent, 'Just wait, I'll give you and your prince some help!' I realized my mistake; deceived by the color of his jacket, I had mistaken the French hussar for one of ours. Except for a few details the uniform is almost the same. Thereupon began one of those desperate struggles that can only end in the death of one combatant or the other. With a wild gaze, his eyes narrowed and lusting after the booty before him, the Alsatian doubled his tempo. My horse was weakening and galloped on with difficulty. Every second I saw the distance separating me from my foe diminish.

"Fortunately, we approached the bank of the Saale and the terrain became more and more uneven. Accustomed to steeple chases, my steed jumped the obstacles with an alacrity that amazed me. The hussar's undersized horse began to fall behind. I thought I had made it when two shots rang out. It was the hussar, who desperate to catch up had fired his pistols at me. One bullet missed, the other shattered my arm. My whole frame shuddered, and I involuntarily let the reins slip. My horse, responding to my slightest motion, slowed its pace. Then I saw the hussar approach, furiously spurring the bleeding flank of his mount, which reared in pain. With mouth foaming and widely flared nostrils, the animal carried its rider forward. As he passed, I saw his saber about to strike at the head of the prince. The prince slid from my arm to the left side of the saddle. Heedless of my wounds, I made a superhuman effort, such as one is capable of in moments of extreme anxiety when risking his life to rescue another who is dear to him. I summoned all my strength to press the prince to my chest and shield him with my body. The saber blow struck me in the face and sliced it from forehead to chin, but the prince was at least spared; I had been able to protect his head.

"Blood covered my face, but nevertheless I could see that the hussar had lost control of his mount. A curse from heaven fell upon him; the animal plunged into the Saale, disappearing with its rider. Maimed, fatigued and broken by all the exertions I had endured, especially from loss of blood, unable to steer my horse, I felt faint, clung to the saddle and awaited my final moments. My horse continued to pace in circles. Exhausted by the double burden, it slumped to the ground and the prince and I fell with it. From this moment on, I remember nothing more… Riding past the place where I lay on the ground, the victors probably recognized the prince by his medals. I was presumed dead and left lying there. One of these men was not above taking the prince's watch and inventing the story that he had slain him because he had refused to hand over his sword… There is not a word of truth in his report. If it was Guindet who took the prince's body, then the prince was no longer alive, and this sergeant under no circumstances had to duel a live enemy. All he did was collect a stone-cold corpse."[44]

Guindet unchivalrously stripped the prince of sword, medals and dispatch case and presented the trophies to Napoleon, who personally decorated and promoted him. Thanks to publicity accorded Guindet by the emperor, his version is historically accepted as true. As for the engagement, Prince Louis's advance guard suffered 29 officers wounded, five mortally, over 1,700 rankers killed, wounded or taken prisoner, and lost 33 guns and four standards at Saalfeld. The retiring units became so widely dispersed that even after three days, the average strength of a Saxon infantry regiment that had fought there numbered just 400 to 450 men. The defeat at Saalfeld and death of Prince Louis Ferdinand, whose example to courage and élan had gone far to revitalize the Prussian officer corps, was an ominous prelude to the battle of Jena.

"Exaggerated rumors over losses, the spectacle of fleeing soldiers without rifles… and of troops scattering in all directions," demoralized the army and were regarded as bad omens for the upcoming battle, wrote Höpfner.[45] Brunswick was transitioning from bad decisions, for example sending the Rudorf Hussars to western Thuringia, to non-decisions, such as allowing Prince Louis Ferdinand to determine on his own when and where to engage the enemy. Duke Karl Wilhelm formulated his letter to the prince more like a polite suggestion than a definitive order. The day before the battle at Saalfeld General Julius Grawert, in command of Hohenlohe's first division comprising 9,600 men and 22 cannons, asked for orders and received no reply.[46] Transferring away the Duke of Weimar's contingent and squandering the advance guard at Saalfeld had cost the Prussian army 20,000 men before Napoleon was even ready for battle. The Prussian and Saxon army was losing confidence in its leadership and some officers discussed the possibility that their supreme commander is a traitor.[47]

On October 11 Friedrich von Gentz, a Prussian publicist in the employ of Metternich, visited Brunswick's headquarters. He recorded his impression of the duke's reaction to the defeat at Saalfeld: "I knew, and this was the opinion of everyone else, that the Duke of Brunswick was seized by panic and fear when first hearing the bad news. His withdrawal to the rear and the unfortunate idea to establish camp here had no other purpose than to gain for himself a little time to recover from his initial anxiety and seek advice… I encountered General Phull and he told me, 'This can only turn out as badly as possible, since they've all lost their heads.' Most bleak of all was uncertainty about the enemy's movements. Here in Weimar, we knew just as little as those in Berlin or in Vienna did at the same time."[48] With the emperor's columns emerging from Thuringia, Brunswick did not even order out patrols to scout the right side of the Saale River.

Front Southwest

On October 10, Bonaparte received information that Prince Louis Ferdinand's advance guard is proceeding south from Rudolstadt toward Thuringia. The emperor was not in communication with Lanne's corps and anxious about its status. He also received reports that Hohenlohe is at Jena. Soult wrote his commander in chief that after the engagement at Schleiz, Tauentzien's troops recoiled due east to Plauen and "this morning the enemy cleared out of the city and has withdrawn toward Gera. It was a thousand horse, an artillery train and some infantry. I've been assured that there are no troops between Plauen and Zwickau. According to the same reports, the army guarding Dresden, 50,000-men strong of whom 17,000 are Saxons, hasn't passed Freiburg yet and the advance troops have only reached Chemnitz."[49] Soult's dispatch satisfied Napoleon that the Prussian and Saxon army is at Gera and he fixed Gera as the objective of the *Grande Armée*. Murat sent reconnaissance patrols in various directions but not far enough to learn anything useful. The leader of the cavalry failed to make an accurate assessment of the Prussian disposition.

Despite the defeat of the advance guard at Saalfeld, the Prussians could still batter Lannes. Brunswick's central army was intact and its location undetected by French scouts. Scharnhorst pressed him to take the offensive. The quarter-master proposed that instead of ordering the Duke of Weimar's 12,500-man force at Meiningen to rejoin the army, it should march east along a shorter route south of the Thuringian Forest and assault the enemy from behind. He also wanted the central army to move forward and simultaneously strike his flank. The field marshal showed no interest in the operation. Scharnhorst wrote his sister, "The French are bypassing us on our left. We have to fall upon them in the flank, but we're simply too slow. Only a few realize or even have an inkling of where we stand."[50] The leadership of the Prussian-Saxon army had no compre-hension of the overall situation. Instead of taking action, Brunswick convened the war council. Boyen described how "almost everyone there felt compelled to put forth an opinion in this atmosphere of blatant helplessness. It was unbe-lievable how quickly at that moment the normally structured military hierarchy vacillated. The situation was truly hopeless."[51]

With the exception of Scharnhorst's appeal that Brunswick rejected out of hand, the option of attacking the French was never broached by the command-er in chief and his staff.[52] The war council decided to group the entire army at Weimar and Jena, to either await an attack or march north and bypass the French should Napoleon attempt to cut the route to Berlin. The duke drafted the order on the night of October 10. Hohenlohe and Massenbach responded with hastily-formulated orders that demanded the impossible of the soldiers with respect to distances they were expected to march within fixed time frames. General Grawert received instructions to leave a garrison at Orlamünder on the Saale, proceed to Rudolstadt to absorb retreating remnants of the advance guard, link up with General Friedrich von Holtzendorff's cavalry and then withdraw at night to Kahla, a river town between Jena and Rudolstadt. The Saxon division faced a forced march from Mittel-Pöllnitz through Roda to Jena with orders to cross the Saale and find quarters.

Goltz described how "among Hohenlohe's troops the confusion had reached such measure as to say that headquarters had completely lost its grip on the reins of command. At that moment nobody there even knew where individual units of the army are. The Saxon troops and Tauentzien's division were so exhausted from night marches, useless exertions and hunger that for the moment they could not be regarded as fit for combat."[53] A Saxon officer taking part in the nocturnal trek to Roda recalled, "A single enemy cavalry regiment would have sufficed to scatter the entire column. General (Hans) von Zezschwitz was physically and mentally in a state that made him momentarily incapable of exercising judgment. When I rose at midnight to go back to Jena and ask him for orders, he didn't recognize me even though I had scarcely left his side for the past twelve hours. He finally said to me, 'Tell the prince I am in such horrible straits that I don't know which way to turn.'"[54]

Duke Karl Wilhelm had always harbored misgivings about stationing Hohenlohe's army on the right bank of the Saale while the balance of the army stands to the left of this natural barrier. Persuaded by Massenbach of the necessity of protecting Saxony, Hohenlohe, whose formations included Zezschwitz's Saxon division, disregarded the field marshal's wishes. Hohenlohe kept his force on the right bank. He simply capitalized on the duke's indecisiveness. Fearing the ultimate responsibility of command, Brunswick issued ambiguously worded orders that offered subordinates latitude in interpretation. Massenbach himself wrote, "I knew the duke and knew that he just wanted to be carried along" by events.[55] Brunswick's reluctance to take charge and Hohenlohe's bad judgment led to the defeats at Schleiz and Saalfeld.

Luckily for Hohenlohe, Napoleon was headed in the opposite direction. He hastened to Gera to take personal command of the troops in anticipation of battle. Arriving on October 11, he found no one to fight; unaware of recent movements of the Prussian and Saxon army, he now presumed that it must be at Erfurt instead. The emperor wheeled his columns from north to west with new marching orders. To preserve France and posterity from the revelation that he too makes mistakes, Napoleon presented the errant trek to Gera supposedly as a skillful maneuver to cut off the Prussians, whose location he of course knew all along, and draw them into battle. He wrote Talleyrand, "Events are running their course here exactly as I had foreseen two months ago in Paris, blow for blow, nothing has deceived me."[56]

Beyond this fantastic explanation, the French enjoyed one advantage taking Gera. They captured stores of bread, fodder and straw that Brunswick's staff had arranged to be stockpiled there and inexplicably not transferred to Jena. "The measures of the allies," Lettow-Vorbeck opined, "were in part totally incomprehensible."[57] Allowing provisions to fall into French hands at Hof and at Gera, abandoning Prince Louis at Saalfeld and the obvious reluctance to confront Napoleon increased speculation among the troops about the loyalty of those in command. Jena university professor Heinrich Luden encountered a group of 40 Prussian soldiers retreating from the battle of Saalfeld and was told by their corporal, "Prussia has been betrayed, sold out!"[58] The worst shortcoming facing the rank and file was the dearth of provisions. The three quartermaster generals, Massenbach, Phull and Scharnhorst, competed to promote their views about strategy before the war council, yet none tackled a quartermaster's parallel responsibility of nourishing the army.

There was poor coordination between combat arms and logistics throughout the campaign. Bakeries and supply trains were often delayed. They travelled to the wrong destinations or sat in idleness without orders. On October 10, for example, a field bakery at Lobeda, a village on the outskirts of Jena, received news of the defeat of Saalfeld 20 miles away. It immediately broke camp. In their haste to retreat to Weimar, personnel tossed 20,000 loaves of freshly baked bread into a pond. Two days later, the unit was still sitting in Weimar without orders to resume baking.[59] Men of General Tauentzien's division who had fought at Schleiz had nothing to eat throughout the following day. They marched to the Saale after dark on empty stomachs. Saxon troops stationed at Mittel-Pöllnitz had been under arms for hours when Hohenlohe's orders to transfer west to the river arrived at 2:00 p.m. They too were without sustenance. No provisions were delivered in advance to Jena to provide them meals when they reached the city.

The following afternoon, Prince Hohenlohe reviewed the haggard Saxon troops coming from Schleiz as they paraded through Jena. Cries that the French are at the outskirts suddenly went up, transforming the orderly march into pandemonium. Soldiers took up defensive positions and units that had already traversed Jena turned around and stampeded back through its gates, intermingling with outbound columns. Wagons and cannons overturned as drivers cut the teams loose to escape on horseback. Troops looted army baggage trains. Hohenlohe's adjutant Captain Ludwig von der Marwitz provided this account: "The terror and disorder in the city was indescribable, a genuine scandal and bad omen for the army!... Soon no one could get through because all the gates out of town were jammed. Residents were screaming in the streets or locked up their houses, so that officers who wanted to retrieve their horses could not get back in."[60]

After Hohenlohe rode out personally and discovered no evidence of the French, it took an hour to restore order. "Now the extent of the chaos could be seen," wrote Lettow-Vorbeck. "Outside of the city, the roads and fields were covered with discarded rifles and packs. In the ditches were inverted cannons that had been abandoned by the crews. What an extraordinary effect recent events had exercised on the minds of the exhausted, famished soldiers! A similar occurrence could scarcely be found in the history of warfare."[61] A military supply train ferrying rations to Jena for the Saxons was a mile away from entering the city when the false alarm sounded. Its commanding officer, Major Wiersbitzsky, abruptly about faced and took his wagons to another village.

At dawn that morning, Brunswick's central army broke camp at Umpferstedt three miles east of Weimar and took till nightfall to march twelve miles. The men found no bread, wood or straw at the new camp. There was a large stockpile of lumber nearby. Since it was civilian property, officers forbade the soldiers to use it to build fires to keep warm that night. The men raided the locals in search of food, fodder for the horses and timber. A civilian, Johann Wackernagel, recorded this: "In the villages they broke open the barns and carried bundles of wheat and straw off to their camp. They forcibly took sheep and cows and butchered them... They took all of the pigs and left only a few of the hens. In part they had to. They also did it to leave nothing for the enemy."[62] Lettow-Vorbeck described how "the mood in the army became even less positive as details of the battle of Saalfeld became known, as a result of the withdrawal to Weimar and the lack of orderly food rationing. Confidence in the leadership diminished... the men sought a scapegoat and found him in the king's chief advisor, the Duke of Brunswick."[63]

The ration problem became so acute that on October 13, two of General

Zezschwitz's majors, Karl von Funck and Karl von Watzdorf, presented Hohenlohe with an ultimatum: The Saxon division will withdraw from the army unless fed. Hohenlohe ordered the Prussians to divide all provisions with their ally, billeted Saxon soldiers in the more prosperous villages and sent the cavalry on a massive forage. Hohenlohe had already complained to the king during a conference on the 12th about the inadequate food supply. Friedrich Wilhelm promised to arrange a delivery from the depot at Weissenfels. Before the measure could be implemented, Davout's troops captured the town. No further steps were taken by the king. So far only a small part of the Prussian-Saxon force had engaged Napoleon, yet most troops were already fatigued, anxious and demoralized. Massenbach in particular was far too involved in operational planning to carry out his duty as quartermaster to provision the men. The ultimate responsibility rested with the duke for his laissez-faire policy to run an army.

Napoleon now presumed the Prussians to be west of the Saale as Lannes had reported on October 09. The emperor deduced that their commander in chief wishes to avoid battle. The French strategy was therefore to occupy the region east of the river and block their retreat to Dresden or Berlin. Bonaparte regrouped his forces for the advance west on the 12th. The former center column consisting of Bernadotte's I and Davout's III Corps now covered the right flank. Soult's IV Corps and Ney's VI Corps, previously in that position, took center. The V and VII Corps of Lannes and Augereau were at Kahla and Jena. This was also the destination of the Imperial Guard. The French again marched in separate columns. Napoleon's plan was for them to merge and attack with full force at Erfurt. He was again in error, since Brunswick's main army was at Weimar and Jena. Hohenlohe's divisions at Jena were two days' march closer than Bonaparte surmised. The corps of Lannes and Augereau were outnumbered and dangerously exposed. By sending Davout to Naumburg further to the north, Napoleon split his force.

At the duke's headquarters, as Goltz pointed out, "no one thought anymore about carrying out bold surprise attacks or about exploiting every promising opportunity as is so crucial in warfare. They were concerned about personal safety instead."[64] Brunswick issued morning orders on October 10 for troop movements but none for reconnaissance. At midday on the 11th, Hohenlohe finally received word to send hussars to scout the eastern bank of the Saale. That night engineer-Major Ludwig von Engelbrecht reported to Duke Karl Wilhelm that the French are in Gera and will probably reach Naumburg, 20 miles north of Jena, the next day. The duke replied impatiently, "They can't fly too!"[65] Davout's cavalry did in fact arrive at Naumburg at 3:30 p.m. on the 12th. It captured 24 pontoons belonging to Hohenlohe's bridge construction train. When Davout entered the town with the advance guard in the evening, the Prussians' huge military depot fell into his hands. It included a supply of enough copper-reinforced components to construct 18 bridges.[66]

That same night Brunswick received news that Naumburg has fallen.

Scharnhorst described it as an "unheard-of blunder, that the enemy got behind the army before we knew it."[67] The news was so bad that at first no one wished to believe the officer who had brought these tidings. Instead, the staff wanted to court-martial him because he based the information on the assurance of a merchant he had encountered on the road.[68] Since the outbreak of hostilities, the Prussians had done nothing to defend the Saale River crossings or to destroy its bridges. The question of whether Napoleon will follow the Saale north toward Leipzig and Berlin or cross the river and assault the Prussian army now preoccupied Brunswick and the war council. At headquarters, Scharnhorst and the duke again disagreed. The colonel predicted that Napoleon will attack and the field marshal that the emperor will bypass the defenders. Anyone familiar with Bonaparte's previous campaigns should have known that he customarily seeks battle.

The fact that Napoleon's invasion force about faced at Gera and was marching directly toward the Prussian and Saxon army should have made it obvious that he wants a confrontation. Davout's capture of Naumburg gave the French the option of turning the Prussians' left flank and trapping them. Eschewing an engagement, the duke opted to march the central army north across the Unstrut River, a tributary of the Saale winding northwest from Naumburg, between Freyburg and Laucha. This would allow the troops to escape before Davout closes the snare. In this case, the duke's caution was not entirely unjustified. Scharnhorst's plan to have the army cross the Saale and attack the French in their rear would require the utmost boldness and vitality. This was scarcely possible for a fighting force weakened by hunger and pointless marches for days and whose officers and men have no confidence in their commander in chief. Instead of taking action, the duke devoted October 12 to discussions with the staff.

In his analysis of the battle of Jena and Auerstedt submitted on January 08, 1808, Scharnhorst recalled the field marshal's ponderous way of addressing pressing military matters that overshadowed headquarters on that fateful October 12: "How the duke commanded the army was not commensurate with the prompt initiative that the situation here demanded. For every issue to be dealt with, he gathered Major General von Phull, Colonel von Kleist, the king's adjutant and me and discussed his ideas at length; then he conferred with many generals about his plan, and only after that advocated before the king what course he considers best. In this way an unavoidable delay resulted."[69] Had the army prepared to march as soon as the fall of Naumburg became known, it could have been on the road well before dawn on the 13th. Advance elements would have reached the Unstrut by early afternoon and secured the crossings. As it was, twelve hours passed before the troops began to move.

General Kalckreuth caustically told the visiting Gentz that the duke "knows neither what he is doing, what he wants to do, where he is going nor where he is."[70] Napoleon wrote Lannes, "All the letters we've intercepted show that the enemy has lost his head. They trade advice day and night and don't know what they should do."[71] The emperor had Davout's corps in Naumburg and Bernadotte's further south in Dornburg. Jena was the objective of the balance of his army. By now it was becoming clear to Brunswick's staff that the French will cross to the left bank of the Saale and attack. As to *where* precisely, the Prussians were uncertain. When King Friedrich Wilhelm and the duke visited Prince Hohenlohe's camp on the 12th, the monarch expressed anger that nothing has been done to reconnoiter the right side of the river as ordered. Two small cavalry patrols conducted a scouting mission as a result but learned nothing useful.

In the absence of precise intelligence, Duke Karl Wilhelm surmised that the French will cross the river at Rudolstadt, some 18 miles *south* of Jena, and hit the Prussian army from the southwest. "It is impossible to discover the basis as to why this idea carried weight," Goltz stated.[72] Hohenlohe's argument that Davout will attack the left flank of the Prussian army in the north and block its withdrawal to Leipzig made little impression on the duke. He ordered Hohenlohe's entire force to maintain a defensive position to repel an enemy operation that would supposedly come from the southwest. The central army's three divisions deployed with their backs to the road from Weimar to Jena, also with front facing southwest. Lettow-Vorbeck was another historian dumbfounded by the duke's decision: "How was it even possible that an attack out of Rudolstadt could be expected when there was nothing to support the assumption?"[73]

During the October 12 situation conference at noon, Massenbach aired his theories and proposals in the same old way and ventured the opinion, without corroborating evidence as usual, that the French will commit only a small force to launch an assault from Naumburg. Capitalizing on their earlier victory well to the south at Saalfeld, he argued, they will use Rudolstadt as the springboard for an offensive. While Hohenlohe asked the king to release stores from the Weimar depot to feed his undernourished troops, gunfire was heard from the direction of Magdala some three miles south of the road connecting Weimar to Jena. Conference participants accepted this as confirmation that the French are indeed advancing northeast from Rudolstadt. No one thought of dispatching a patrol from among the cavalry stationed in camp to ascertain whether this is actually the case. The king rode back to Weimar before the cause of the shooting was determined. Duke Karl Wilhelm was in a bad mood because General Grawert's division, which had sat out the battle of Saalfeld on October 10 without orders, had not yet rejoined the main army. It was still encamped at Coppanz; officers of the general staff forgot to send a dispatch rider to Grawert to deliver his marching orders.[74]

It seems remarkable that given its historical reputation for efficiency, the Prussian military could have performed so dismally in 1806. Clausewitz mentioned that a number of officers, generals among them, suspected Duke Karl Wilhelm of treason. Dividing the army when confronted with a numerically superior adversary, perpetually subjecting the troops to pointless, fatiguing movements, chronic failure to properly equip and nourish them, and the total lack of boldness, initiative and resolve he displayed weakened and discouraged the army. Brunswick was an experienced commander with a long and distinguished service record. This makes his conduct during the campaign all the more questionable. Arranging the army with its front to the southwest, literally with its back to the enemy, was an unforgivable error. Erich Ludendorff, a prominent German general in World War I, offered this perspective: "When I first studied the campaign of 1806/07, it seemed to me militarily incomprehensible. An army does not deploy on the left bank of the Saale and turn its back on its homeland as in the battles of Jena and Auerstedt on that disastrous October 14. Battles are not fought to hand a proficient army to the enemy to be slaughtered."[75]

The Impossible Order

The Prussians could at least fight Napoleon to a standstill had there existed the will to do so. The French had marched for days without respite. The emperor still believed that his enemy is at Erfurt, so planned to use the 14th and 15th to assemble his forces for an attack. Without ruling out the possibility of an assault on Lannes, he surmised that the Prussian army will retreat to Magdeburg, 60 miles north of Jena.[76] Napoleon's keen perception was still struggling without success to penetrate the veil of uncertainty regarding his adversary's whereabouts. "He repeatedly drew the wrong conclusion."[77] He was also surprised by the difficult terrain along the Saale. When he arrived at Jena and saw the valley, town and heights beyond, he realized how seriously he had underestimated the topographical obstacle his army faced.

"It is the rim of a high plateau from Jena to Dornburg, descending into the Saale valley," one historian related. "The steepness varies, significant at Jena, less so behind the villages of Löbstädt and Zwätzen, then again at Dornburg there is a nearly vertical massif 80 meters high that is almost impossible to climb. The entire range is a natural fortress and stronghold for an army. From the projecting peaks the movement of the enemy in the valley can be closely observed, while one's own maneuvers along the plateau cannot be seen from below. Were this formidable position occupied and even only haphazardly defended, the enemy would have to conduct a time-consuming detour since direct assault would demand a huge cost in blood and lives."[78] However advantageous, making a stand at Jena would have meant fighting and this sufficed to deter the king and his staff; hence the October 12 decision to march the troops north along the Saale, cross the Unstrut River west of Naumburg, absorb Württemberg's reserve corps at Halle and proceed to the Elbe.

Brunswick wrote his orders at 4:15 a.m. on the 13th: "The army will execute a retrograde movement, in part to link up with Duke Eugen of Württemberg and in part to be free in the rear again… The Prince of Hohenlohe will remain in position so that the enemy learns nothing of our movement."[79] Duke Karl Wilhelm therefore designated Hohenlohe's entire command, 38,000 men, as the rearguard. This is a mission that a few cavalry squadrons with horse artillery and some fusilier battalions, if properly deployed in defensible terrain, would ordinarily carry out. The measure kept the army divided. Receiving instructions that same morning to move his corps to Webicht, a wooded area just northeast of Weimar, it took Rüchel hours to form it into marching order. Brunswick had told him to assemble the corps at a single location the day before, but the order was not carried out. Rüchel left a regiment in Erfurt and his troops did not set off until afternoon. He detached various continents for random security duties along the route. This pointlessly weakened his force.

Captain Borcke described how the march began: "What happened was remarkable and scarcely believable. General von Rüchel rode ahead before the troops had finished forming up to march off, but none of the generals present knew *where*! Not one from among the many general staff officers stayed behind to lead the column. All had followed the commanding general and none of the remaining generals knew what direction we were to march in nor had any of them received specific orders. Dismay and confusion resulted. Our regiment was at the front and the platoons had already turned to march when the matter came up for debate. One asked the other and all fine and good, no one wanted to take charge and march the column off. Unfortunately, General von Larisch had ridden after General von Rüchel without leaving orders for the regimental commander... Regardless of who was responsible for this hopeless confusion, this start was a bad omen and caused every one of us anxiety about the near future...

"I was ordered to lead the *avant garde* without being given a specific destination. In this pleasant situation, as a young and inexperienced officer I was worried to death about a bad outcome to the affair but could do nothing about it. I rode ahead toward a high point while the advance guard followed me into the unknown. I finally reached high ground and discovered a mass of troops in the distance... Upon approaching I recognized my general with his adjutant. They came riding toward us. While still far away, the general began cursing frightfully and carping about where we had been for so long. I didn't mind this torrent of rage dumped on me by the man who was most probably responsible for the problem, because I was so relieved that the affair is over."[80] Larisch's troops joined Rüchel's corps and the entire force resumed the march toward five o'clock in the afternoon.

Meanwhile the Duke of Weimar's troops, who had been on a wild goose chase toward Schweinfurt since October 08, about faced and were on their way back. Advancing northeast from distant Ilmenau as ordered, they managed just eight miles on the 13th when they should have covered 20 to 25. As for the central army, Brunswick fixed the first objective as Kösen. This is a Saale River town a few miles west of Naumburg. Despite the proximity of the enemy, the Prussians did not occupy the Kösen pass. Davout took it on the night of October 13. He left some infantry and cannons to guard the pass and the Unstrut River bridge. Duke Karl Wilhelm did not send patrols to reconnoiter the bridges at Freyburg and Laucha, where he intended to cross the Unstrut with the army the next day.

This was up river from Davout's corps in Naumburg, but apparently no one thought it important to ascertain whether the French have destroyed the spans to block the retreat.[81] Brunswick ordered Hohenlohe to detach a corps to guard the strategic crossings at Dornburg and Camburg from where the French could strike the retreating Prussian army in its flank, but did not call for recapturing either these towns or Naumburg.

The army set off for the Unstrut that day in a column of 50,000 men plus baggage on a single road. There were in fact three suitable routes available; one following the Ilm River through Apolda and Sulza then continuing past Kösen, a main highway through Auerstedt to Freyburg that the central army of three divisions could have used, and a postal route leading to Laucha for the reserve divisions trailed by the baggage column. Had the central army marched in three columns, it would have reached the strategic Kösen pass ahead of Davout.[82] "The leadership in senior and supreme positions of authority failed utterly, almost without exception."[83] The day before, Scharnhorst had sent Captain Boyen to clear a section of road choked with supply wagons. Having efficiently redirected traffic to open the route for a waiting infantry column, Boyen saluted when the king unexpectedly rode past with his entourage. Friedrich Wilhelm's adjutant suddenly wheeled about to bring the captain a personal message from his sovereign: The ribbon binding Boyen's wig was loose and he is to get his uniform back in order at once.[84]

It would have been prudent for the king to pay more attention to the *condition* of his soldiers than to their appearance. Borcke described in his memoirs, "It was a cold night. Privation and hunger had already reached such great measure that even the most frugal no longer possessed a crumb of bread… Even harder to comprehend is that nothing was done for the most elemental needs, not even to provide wood and straw… The night passed with hunger, chill and exhaustion. Everyone longed for morning in anticipation that circumstances will improve."[85] Forbidding the troops to take necessities from the population was a dogma in the Prussian army. The king, Möllendorff and Kalckreuth were popular with the public for enforcing it but the troops suffered. Officers punished transgressions. "Protection of private property was so over-emphasized," wrote Borcke, "that hungry soldiers weren't even allowed to dig for potatoes in a field that had already been harvested. Several were beaten half to death for trying… (Officers) preferred to let the soldiers starve rather than impose upon the farmers of this prosperous region. Bechstädt alone could probably have supplied enough food to sustain the regiment for 24 hours."[86] At this time a colonel boasted to Boyen in Weimar, 'You see that my people are encamped in a cabbage patch, but not one head of cabbage is missing.'"[87]

One officer wrote his comrade Captain Grollmann on October 12, "The common soldier, weary from inordinate marching, now grapples with hunger. Many are apathetic; some have become averse of waging war. There is courage among them but no enthusiasm. We have sought to beat subordination into our soldiers; in consequence their sense of honor and their spirit are gone."[88] Ample provisions for the troops were on hand in Weimar and in Jena, the small yet affluent university town in the path of Napoleon's army. "In and around our little city was an army of over 100,000 Prussians and Saxons," Weimar resident Johanna Schopenhauer wrote her son. "The soldiers were in ill spirits over the unnecessary, fatiguing marches, the local farmers over having to quarter them and the resulting cost."[89] Before stores of grain and fodder could be purchased from the populace for the army, officers had to request authorization from the king. Permission had still not been granted when the troops had to evacuate Jena and relinquish it to the French.

Napoleon had no scruples about disregarding private ownership. It was the custom of the *Grande Armée* to seize whatever foodstuffs and fodder it needs in foreign countries without compensation. This enabled the emperor to move large bodies of troops more quickly than the Prussians, whose armed forces were encumbered with significant baggage and supply trains. However burdensome the citizens of Jena and its surroundings may have considered their countrymen in uniform, the arrival of Tirailleurs on the morning of October 13 soon dispelled speculation about which intrusion was preferable. Napoleon's troops defiled into town throughout the day. Most bivouacked on the outskirts, but many camped in Jena's market square. Thousands marauded the streets that night. The first military objective was household wine cellars. Having transferred the contents into pails, rucksacks and their mouths, intoxicated soldiers turned on the locals.

Most townspeople approached them in a friendly manner, reported eyewitness Johann Danz: "They offered the French food and beverage, even money; but only a few of them were satisfied with that. They became unruly, demanding more than what has been given them. They pressed bayonets against people's chests and threatened to shoot them, subjected persons to the basest treatment and forced their way into houses. Doors not opened quickly enough were smashed in. We heard the door of our neighbor's house broken down, heard the brutal demands of the intruders, the screaming and sobbing, the whimpering and pleading, the begging for mercy of the beleaguered… Loaded with booty, the monsters stumbled from the house, loaves of bread stuck on bayonets, wine in buckets, beds on their backs, off they went."[90]

The enlightened soldiers of the *Grande Nation* hauled furniture from homes to break up for firewood. Hundreds of books from Jena's personal libraries landed in campfires. Entire collections comprising countless volumes that belonged to university professors and local scholars fed the flames. A conflagration broke out after 2:00 a.m. during the looting and 19 houses burned down. Many citizens fled the town. They preferred to spend the night shivering in nearby woods. Jena's rabble took advantage of the chaos and robbed shops and houses. Families were caring for Prussian wounded from the battle of Saalfeld. They billeted them in the courthouse, the university chapel and in private homes. The pandemonium distressed these convalescents as well. In outlying areas, the French raided farms and occasionally inflicted savage beatings on the owners. This was Napoleon's so-called requisition system. By refusing to confiscate civilian property to maintain the army, Prussian generals indirectly provided more for the enemy to subsist on. The "little corporal" and his marshals bridled their men's pillaging only when it impaired their combat-effectiveness, but some French officers still intervened to try and protect homeowners.

On the afternoon of the 13th, amid the autumn splendor of Thuringia's picturesque countryside, Napoleon arrived in Jena. He tarried briefly and then scaled Landgrafenberg mountain west of town at 4:00 p.m. From its summit, the Windknollen, he and Lannes saw the panorama of Hohenlohe's camp; endless rows of tents across the plateau. Napoleon conducted a personal reconnaissance, close enough to Prussian lines for sentries to fire at him. He was perplexed that his foes relinquished the mountain; controlling it gained him possession of practically every trail leading from the Saale valley to the left flank and rear of Hohenlohe's army. It enabled Bonaparte to arrange his formations in concealment to deploy them centrifugally onto the plateau. He ordered Lannes' V Corps to occupy Landgrafenberg. After requisitioning Jena's wine, the guard infantry also began the climb with bottle and musket in hand. Some 25,000 increasingly intoxicated soldiers collected atop the formidable massif overnight. Under Napoleon's personal supervision, gunners and engineers hauled the corps artillery under strenuous conditions to the summit. Bonaparte pitched his tent in the middle of this boisterous company.

The failure of the Prussians to exploit the military value of Landgrafenberg remains an enigma. After Captain Müffling's successful scouting mission into the Thuringian Forest, subsequent reconnaissance had become woefully inadequate. From Landgrafenberg, the disposition of the French could have been easily monitored. Abandoning a key position immediately before the decisive engagement was the result of an absolutely senseless order from the Duke of Brunswick on October 13. The night before it was issued, General Tauentzien evacuated the Saale valley to transfer his sorely tried, outnumbered troops to the river's left bank. The French pursued cautiously. This enabled him to complete the nocturnal maneuver with only Captain Haxthausen and 30 men detailed to guard the Jena bridge—which was left intact for the enemy—being taken prisoner. The Prussians crossed at Jena. Tauentzien left only the first battalion of the Saxons' Rechten Grenadier Regiment to occupy Landgrafenberg, despite ardent appeals from his officers to station a strong garrison atop it instead.[91]

Lannes's men began their assault at 10:30 a.m. on the 13th: Tirailleurs scaled the heights with agility. They jumped over ditches, climbed or bypassed cliffs and boulders and allowed no obstacle to deter them. Even the light cavalry struggled upward and rode trails considered impassable for horses. The Saxon grenadiers were too few in number to defend the crest and its flanks, all in all a line extending over a mile from the small Rau valley just north of Landgrafenberg west to Flohberg. The French circumvented them on the left and penetrated the Isserstädt woods beyond Flohberg. The defenders had to retire at 2:00 p.m. Casualties on both sides were comparatively light. The Tirailleurs impetuously advanced beyond Landgrafenberg into the villages of Cospeda and Lützeroda. At midday, as the sound of battle echoed across the countryside, Prince Hohenlohe mustered his forces for a counterattack. He recalled cavalry regiments conducting foraging expeditions and summoned the Grossmann Horse Battery and the five battalions of the Cerrini Brigade.

Supported by the Rosen Fusilier Battalion and Werner *Jäger* Company, the Saxons drove the Tirailleurs back by midafternoon. More of the prince's formations arrived including cuirassiers, hussars, artillery and infantry. The Saxons and Prussians cheered as he told them, "Finally a serious battle is at hand, one that will release you from all the distress and privations so far, avenge the shame of Saalfeld and revive hope in us all."[92] Though Lannes held Landgrafenberg, it was weakly defended on the 13th and his soldiers had been in action for hours. The marshal believed he was facing a vastly superior Prussian force of 50,000 men. Hohenlohe had more than sufficient fresh troops at his disposal to drive the French from the mountain.[93] He duly formed up the army for attack. Yet control of this pivotal elevation was decided not by Lannes or by Hohenlohe, nor by the brave and determined officers and men under their respective commands, but by Colonel Massenbach.

Prince Hohenlohe had just delivered the fiery address to his soldiers when his chief of staff returned from Weimar. He had sent Massenbach there to get food, fodder and ammunition but he came back empty-handed. His quartermaster returned instead with Brunswick's written orders and the king's hollow promise to send provisions. Massenbach asked to speak with the prince aside. The instructions were for his army to "remain in position at Jena, but during the 13th to detach a sufficiently strong corps to send to Dornburg and Camburg, to secure the right flank of the main army from an unexpected ambush during its march."[94] Massenbach added verbally, "that the prince may under no circumstances attack (Landgrafenberg) and will be held accountable in the harshest way should he transgress against this order."[95] The colonel told Hohenlohe, "There is strong reason for me to believe that the cause (of the order) was the reckless operation of Prince Louis at Saalfeld, since all he had in mind was taking the offensive; it will therefore cost you your head if you either attack the enemy or find any sort of pretext to engage in battle."[96]

While listening, Hohenlohe repeatedly struck himself on the thigh with a riding crop, his custom when angry. He reluctantly called off the attack. Schlieffen concluded that "the enemy was not just handed Landgrafenberg, but the Saale valley south of Jena… and allowed to do here whatever he pleased."[97] Goltz opined that Hohenlohe's recapture of Landgrafenberg "would have completely changed the situation the army was in. The presence of Lannes's entire corps and advance of other French columns could not have remained unnoticed. It would then have become clear to the prince the danger he and his army are in."[98]

Hohenlohe's orders were to hold at Jena, guard the withdrawal of the central army and not engage the enemy. "Any military layman would see at first glance that this bastard of an order was a complex of contradictions impossible to carry out," Gieren observed. "The prince was to remain at Jena even if he was attacked. If that happened, he would have to engage in battle since he couldn't just stand down while struck dead or taken prisoner. The second part of the order demanded that the prince cover the retreat of the army. To do so he would have to fight! How someone is not supposed to give battle when trapped in a situation like this is rather hard to imagine."[99]

Captain Müffling wrote, "During the conversation with Prince Hohenlohe on October 12, the Duke of Brunswick had seen how anxiously the prince awaited the opportunity to dispel the bad impression the battles of Schleiz and Saalfeld have made on the troops and on the world and how he hopes to achieve this by attacking… and so he assigned Colonel von Massenbach to say to the prince that he is absolutely not to attack and will be severely reprimanded if he oversteps his orders."[100] Given Massenbach's penchant for drama, it seems likely that he embellished the duke's order when verbally relaying it to Hohenlohe. There would be no purpose for Brunswick to threaten a general of the prince's stature with repercussions for disobedience. His orders were seldom so specific and offered field commanders a measure of interpretation. Also, both men belonged to a cultivated aristocracy that prides itself on etiquette. For the duke to address a prince and fellow officer in such disrespectful language would have been inconsistent with the custom of the times.

Hohenlohe himself recalled, "After all this was ordered (the attack on Landgrafenberg), I spoke with General Count Tauentzien and he assured me that all necessary instructions pursuant to my wishes have already been implemented. All pressure from the enemy had ceased and from both sides there were at present only random cannon shots being fired. It therefore seemed as though the enemy will be satisfied with just occupying Jena for now… My intention was to let General Tauentzien push forward as far as possible as soon as the reserves arrive to support him, in order to block the enemy from advancing beyond the (Saale) valley and to throw him back down into it. When Colonel von Massenbach returned from the king's headquarters, I was busy arranging the reserve columns under General von Holtzendorff that had just come up in the order I believed they could be best used for the purpose. I could clearly see (Massenbach's) embarrassment when he saw me thusly engaged. My own embarrassment and distress were even greater when he announced the king's orders for me, that I may not attack the enemy and must avoid any serious engagement with the enemy this day. Almost at this very moment, the report arrived that the enemy has occupied Dornburg with 1,800 men. Since the orders from the king's headquarters also included instructions for me to deploy artillery along the passage at Dornburg and Camburg, I quickly decided to march to Dornburg and throw the enemy out at all costs."[101]

Boyen related later that perhaps for emphasis, Brunswick sent him to Hohenlohe that day with the same orders that Massenbach carried: The prince was "to protect the march of the main army and not let himself be drawn into battle."[102] Hohenlohe's account suggests that he did not interpret the instructions literally, because he decided to drive the French out of Dornburg and Camburg. He set off at the head of the Sanitz Brigade's three infantry battalions and two batteries together with 400 volunteers, ten cavalry squadrons and half a horse battery. "It's unbelievable how much the thought that we're moving forward rouses morale among the soldiers," wrote Marwitz. "Our little corps cheered and sang the entire way, as though going to a festival."[103] The Kollin Grenadier Half-Battalion and more mounted troops joined him along the march and the soldiers reached Dornburg by 5:00 p.m. The enemy was nowhere to be seen; only meals for 12,000 men that French scouts had ordered the townspeople to prepare in advance of their army's arrival. Hohenlohe's troops indulged themselves in the feast instead. French quartermasters were more efficient at sustaining their army in a foreign country than the Prussians were at providing for their men under arms inside of Germany. Beyond dinner, the trek to Dornburg was a wasted enterprise caused by typically insufficient reconnaissance.

Prince Hohenlohe returned to his headquarters at Wasserburg castle in Capellendorf at around 10:00 p.m. He received a letter from Duke Karl Wilhelm relaying a prisoner's testimony that Marshal Augereau's corps has arrived at Jena while Davout's corps at Naumburg controls the Kösen bridges. The information was accurate, except that the duke initially presumed that Napoleon is also at Naumburg. Hohenlohe believed the emperor to be still in Gera. The prince's force covering the central army's withdrawal north extended in echelon from the village of Capellendorf in the east along the road to Weimar, which was nicknamed *Die Schnecke* (the snail) by locals. The road wound its way to Landgrafenberg and the plateau. The Saxon Niesemeuschel Division and some of Tauentzien's troops were encamped along the roadside. Prussian cavalry was at Hohlstedt and behind this force stood the Prussian-Saxon reserve.

Grawert's division guarded the right flank north of Capellendorf. It was the only division in Hohenlohe's army that was an entity and not dispersed about the combat zone. To its left was Ludwig von Dyherrn's brigade comprised of both Prussian and Saxon contingents and cavalry. All of these formations were positioned with their front turned toward the southwest. Their sentries stood post facing southwest as well, because the Prussians still expected the enemy to attack from Rudolstadt.[104] Not one to mince words, Major Gieren summarized, "During the night of the 13/14th we see the following unbelievable picture: The enemy stands atop Landgrafenberg and at Jena practically in the rear of the Prussian forces, who as though on a bivouac maneuver sit in their camps with their front in the wrong direction. That must have taken nerves of iron."[105]

On the plateau opposite Landgrafenberg was Tauentzien's motley force. It comprised twelve-and-a-half infantry battalions, two *Jäger* companies, seven cavalry squadrons and one-and-a-half artillery batteries, a hodgepodge of units tossed together from five different corps. Riflemen exchanged shots with French pickets during the night. Tauentzien scouted the front personally and observed the arrival of enemy reinforcements. To guard against a possible surprise attack, he retired his foremost battalions 600 to 700 paces in silence. Men stayed behind to maintain campfires. The count himself recalled that the day before, Brunswick had "inspected the position and after I assured him that I can hold against an enemy attack with the troops under my command, he marched off with the reserve without issuing further orders… and left me the Saxon Cerrini Brigade… I never would have imagined that at this position (Lützeroda and Closewitz) an enemy attack is to be expected. Otherwise, it would have been prudent under the circumstances to dislodge the enemy from the dominating heights and defend the passes. This without the slightest doubt could have been accomplished on the 13th."[106]

The light infantry that had been skirmishing with the French for days had exhausted its ammunition but little was done to replenish it. Four infantry battalions belonging to Tauentzien's corps were left behind in a base camp because no one sent orders for them to move forward to the plateau.[107] On the eve of battle, the Prussians were not the only ones in the dark—figuratively as well as literally—about the disposition of their adversary. Napoleon at Jena believed himself to be opposite the enemy's entire force. This was because "he could never entertain the notion that the Prussians will march away with part of their army and leave the rest standing here. He would never expect them to do anything so unreasonable" right before a battle.[108] The emperor slept little that night. He was apprehensive over the possibility of a surprise attack. Younger Prussian and Saxon officers had in fact urged such a raid, but senior commanders rejected the idea.[109]

French patrols reported to Davout in Naumburg that Prussian troops are approaching from Auerstedt. With the fall of darkness, he left only weak units forward. Davout had no idea that the main Prussian army was before him. Brunswick's central army seriously outnumbered Davout's corps. This was an advantage that would prove of no avail. There were many factors causing one of the worst defeats in German military history on October 14, 1806. None could better attest to the incompetence of the Prussian supreme command than positioning Hohenlohe's army with its back to the enemy. Five days after the battle a wounded Prussian officer wrote a comrade, "Friedrich lost battles too; who has ever remained unbeaten? But to lose such a battle like we lost this one, under such circumstances and at the beginning of the war, in a reversed position with our face turned around from the capital, that's dreadful, it's unheard-of."[110]

Chapter 6

The Botched Battle

Aimless Attacks

Though occurring on the same day and but a few miles apart, Jena and Auerstedt were entirely separate engagements. The clash at Jena had no influence on Auerstedt and vice versa. There were notable similarities in how the fighting progressed. The primary cause of Prussia's lopsided defeats was the lack of central command. Attacks and retreats by particular formations were seldom supported by neighboring units; cooperation among generals and communication were poor. The army's action could best be described as haphazard. "The valiant Prussian troops were pointlessly led to catastrophe by incapable leadership," summarized Lezius.[1] The Prussian army had lost faith in its commander before the first shot was fired. On October 11, a delegation of officers tried to persuade Kalckreuth to replace Duke Karl Wilhelm as commander in chief. Two days later, General Zezschwitz's aids threatened Hohenlohe with desertion of the entire Saxon corps. The Duke of Brunswick said of his subordinates, "Prince Hohenlohe is a weak, vain man who lets Massenbach control him, General von Rüchel a braggart, Field Marshal von Möllendorf a dimwitted old man, General Kalckreuth a cunning schemer and the rest of the generals are run-of-the-mill types without talent."[2]

The duke could have disparaged himself as well, since forbidding Hohenlohe from retaking Landgrafenberg on October 13 robbed the rearguard of its best opportunity to delay Napoleon while the central army withdrew toward the Unstrut. Brunswick's obvious reluctance to issue definitive orders—and to fight—invited disobedience from officers. For instance, Hohenlohe did not sufficiently arrange to guard the Saale bridges, contrary to the duke's instructions, and they were taken by the French. Those at Dornburg and Camburg were wooden and could have easily been destroyed before capture. As a result, Hohenlohe's line of communication with the central army was compromised before the battle began. "The actions of the prince can only be described as baffling," was Lettow-Vorbeck's verdict. "Bernadotte found the crossings undefended the next day, and expressed his amazement over this to the officers of his staff and later to Scharnhorst in Lübeck."[3]

It was irresponsible of Hohenlohe to personally lead the expedition to Dornburg on the afternoon of the 13th. He left most of his army behind without anyone in charge. General Tauentzien, commander of the third division of the prince's combined force, received no direction from Hohenlohe and had to decide on his own what to do about Landgrafenberg.[4] The prince himself was not particularly concerned, since "he was under the delusion that the following day will be uneventful."[5] After the expeditionary force returned from Dornburg, Hohenlohe went back to his headquarters in Capellendorf. The village is on the western side of the plateau opposite Landgrafenberg. There he read a dispatch Rüchel had written earlier that night, advising that he and his corps are encamped at Weimar. Rüchel also reported that Duke Karl August of Weimar's force has arrived at Ilmenau and should reach Erfurt some time on the 14th. Why three large bodies of troops-- the Duke of Weimar's corps at Ilmenau, the Duke of Württemburg's at Halle and Rüchel's at Weimar—were stationed so far from the combat zone remains another mystery of Prussia's singular campaign strategy.

Since receiving orders three days earlier to return to the main army, Karl August had marched his troops just 22 miles. He halted at Ilmenau, ostensibly because there were no orders for him to continue the advance.[6] With Brunswick and the main army encamped at Auerstedt, an obscure village ten miles southwest of Naumburg, Hohenlohe was on his own to face the main French invasion force led by Napoleon himself. Although Bonaparte was initially outnumbered, reinforcements continued to arrive throughout the morning of October 14 and would give him a significant numerical advantage before noon. Some 40,000 of his men had marched all night. Prince Hohenlohe's army comprised 38,000 men and Rüchel's corps at Weimar tallied 15,000.

Hohenlohe was unaware of what was in store for his army, but the men on the frontline on the night of October 13/14 were not. Huddled around campfires, they could see and hear French reinforcements steadily coming in. A Prussian soldier recalled, "The watch fires of the enemy opposite us became more numerous and extended during the night. In the light of the flames, we could see the units as they arrived, clearly enough to count them. The sound of artillery arriving and being hauled up was unmistakable. At around three in the morning, the freshly arrived troops must have been formed into two groups and the emperor rode past them, surrounded by lit torches. As he approached each formation, we could clearly hear shouts of *vive l'empereur!*"[7] Tauentzien sent Captain Derschau to report this to Hohenlohe. The prince did nothing to arrange his divisions for battle during the final hours before dawn.

General Holtzendorff's four infantry battalions, 16 cavalry squadrons and two batteries—in all 4,700 men—were billeted overnight in a dozen villages. Hohenlohe had instructed the general that upon hearing a signal of three cannon shots, he was to assemble his foot troops at Rödigen and the cavalry at Stiebritz. Firing three rounds was customary to send a message, the problem being that artillery duels often open battles and can therefore drown the signal. Napoleon opted for a limited attack with the forces on hand. He issued written orders instructing his marshals where to deploy their divisions, then spoke with Lannes at 4:00 a.m. Two hours later, 20 minutes before sunrise, he gave the order to advance. The V Corps would cross the plateau toward Closewitz and Cospoda, the first objectives. Louis Suchet's division couldn't find Closewitz in the mist and followed the natural hillside too far to the left.

The emperor did not work out a detailed operational plan. In the path of the French was Tauentzien. He had marshalled his troops at dawn to retake Landgrafenberg. They included the first battalion of the Rechten Regiment that had unsuccessfully defended it the day before, the Zweiffel Regiment, the Herwarth Grenadier Half-Battalion, the Studnitz Horse Half-Battery and the Pelet Fusilier Battalion. Fusillier and *Jäger* companies took the lead. Behind the first wave and in the flanks marched additional infantry battalions, some cavalry squadrons and an artillery battery formed from separate units. Tauentzien ordered the men to reoccupy the forward position that they had silently withdrawn from the night before. The light infantry made contact with the enemy and opened fire. Tauentzien's troops deployed over too wide a front in proportion to their manpower. His 8,000 men formed a line almost two miles across in front of the high ground at Dornberg (not to be confused with Dornburg on the Saale River). Dense fog shrouded the early morning landscape. This compounded the problem of maintaining cohesion.

Given the limited visibility, a compact formation would have been easier for officers to direct in combat. At the same time, the impenetrable haze reduced the effectiveness of the Tirailleurs' marksmanship. Conditions were ideal for the traditional, much-feared tactic of the Prussian army; a determined bayonet charge. Here again, the necessary boldness was lacking and the general soon halted the advance. The men stood their ground, volley firing into the mist at vaguely discernible muzzle flashes of enemy musketry. The Prussian fusillade was not effective, since Tirailleurs' take cover under fire. The Prussians and Saxons stood in echelon. They were an exposed wall of human targets, unavoidably suffering greater casualties than the dispersed French. Moreover, Tauentzien was woefully outgunned in artillery. Lannes had brought his guns over Landgrafenberg, the place that Hohenlohe had assured his generals is too steep, hence "impracticable" for hauling cannons, and they poured round after round onto the plateau. Lannes was reluctant to move his corps forward against what he presumed to be the main Prussian army; his 17th Infantry Regiment on the flank had already taken heavy losses.

The stationary exchange of fire raged for one-and-a-half hours before Tauentzien pulled the badly mauled Zweiffel Regiment out of the line and moved the Friedrich August Battalion forward to replace it. Survivors of Zweiffel's formation had the bad luck to be mistaken for Frenchmen as they withdrew in the dense fog and were fired on by fusiliers of the second echelon. The rising sun began to disperse the mist. This made it apparent to Lannes how numerically inferior the force he faced actually was. He thereupon pressed the attack with vigor. At this moment a division of Soult's corps reached the plateau to reinforce him. The uneven parity became equally clear to the Prussians and Saxons. The ranks began to waver, "since even the best formations become unsettled when serving as practice targets for hours against an enemy they can scarcely make out," as one historian concluded.[8] The Rechten Battalion, mainstay of Tauentzien's first echelon, slowly fell back. Tirailleurs supported by artillery pursued it, followed by three columns of French infantry. Grenadiers of the Thiollaz, Lichtenhayn and Lecoq Battalions, Werner's *Jägers* and Erichsen's fusiliers bore the brunt of the French counterattack.

Tauentzien sent the Thiollaz Battalion to check an enemy thrust across the Ziskau valley. It repulsed two French assaults but retired in disorder when outflanked. The general was able to regroup his men thanks to effective fire support from Captain Tüllmann's mortar battery. It had taken position on high ground and gone into action while the defense was crumbling. Tauentzien rode up to its commander and ordered him to move the guns forward, therefore *downhill*, to close the range on Lannes' infantry. According to an eyewitness whose narrative was published in the *Leipziger Zeitung* (*Leipzig Times*) supplement No. 45, 1858, "Captain Tüllmann explained to the general that loss of the battery will inevitably result from such a risky undertaking, since the horses, weakened by fatigue

Napoleon directs his legions at Jena. The Imperial Guard waits in reserve at right. Brunswick marched his army into a region cut by hills, forests and waterways generally unsuitable for the compact-formation fighting technique of the Prussia army.

and some of them wounded, will be unable to pull the guns back up the slope. Enraged, General Tauentzien pressed his pistol against the head of the captain and threatened to shoot him dead if he doesn't carry out the order immediately."[9] Such was the lack of composure of a Prussian general in combat when contradicted by a subordinate who dutifully reported the condition of his unit.

The battery advanced some 100 paces. Since Tauentzien sent no infantry to protect its eight mortars, Tüllmann was soon outflanked by Tirailleurs. The horses, assisted by gunners pushing, accomplished the laborious climb back to the original position after only a few rounds had been fired. Decimated by superior firepower and running low on ammunition, the Prussian-Saxon troops retired for the most part in order. Lannes felt his right wing vulnerable to possible counterattack and did not vigorously pursue. Harassed by Tirailleurs, Tauentzien's men withdrew to the heights at Dornberg. Here they about faced to form a defensive line. Throughout the engagement, Tauentzien had repeatedly dispatched riders to Hohenlohe pleading for orders without receiving an answer. Only after the retreat was in motion did the coveted response arrive. It advised him to withdraw to Kleinromstädt to receive fresh ammunition. The battered formations were absorbed into the prince's army at 10:00 a.m. Tauentzien left half his soldiers dead or wounded on the battlefield. He lost Closewitz, Lützeroda, the Ziskau valley and the Zwätzen wood to the enemy. Also lost were Tüllmann's mortars. They had continued to blast case shot and cannonballs into the advancing French and only when deserted by hussars assigned to protect them did the gallant captain retreat. The guns became stuck in a ditch and were abandoned.

Grawert mobilized his first division for action. It was not formed up in time to support his colleague's attack against Lannes. Grawert therefore sent an adjutant to Massenbach at 7:30 a.m. to recommend he order Tauentzien to break off the engagement and retreat via Dornberg to Vierzehnheiligen. Massenbach rejected the idea. He replied that "the gap at Jena must not be lost," since the French could then jeopardize the route for withdrawing the army's baggage.[10] His explanation for leaving Tauentzien's force hopelessly exposed to murderous enemy fire for another hour-and-a-half is beyond absurd; relinquishing Dornberg would have no tactical influence on control of a so-called "gap"—whatever that was—at Jena. The city was already in French hands anyway. The infantry stood against a larger enemy force for nearly three hours. The men took heavy losses with absolutely no support from the rest of Hohenlohe's army and with haphazard direction from their own general. They only abandoned Dornberg when belated orders came from Capellendorf to do so.

Hohenlohe's conduct during the early hours of October 14 reveals how detached from the reality of the situation he actually was. Just before 5:00 a.m., Major Christoph d'Egidy, chief of staff for Zezschwitz's Saxon division, arrived at Capellendorf. Hohenlohe sat in bed as d'Egidy told him that the French have reinforced their front at the Schwabhäuser basin with infantry and artillery during the night. Strong contingents (Augereau's corps), the major continued, have occupied Cospeda. He protested that no one notified General Zezschwitz that the Saxon Cerrini Grenadier Brigade was transferred to Tauentzien's command. Hohenlohe replied that the troops should be prepared to move out if called upon, but otherwise nothing must be done to "unnecessarily fatigue" them since a serious engagement is not expected. He arranged to distribute seven casks of brandy to the Saxons at his own expense.[11] The prince then wrote Tauentzien to inform him of d'Egidy's intelligence.

As for Zezschwitz, he became anxious over the cannon fire in the east heralding Lannes's attack, mobilized Niesenmeuschel's division and moved it forward. Joined by Colonel Karl von Boguslawski's Prussian fusilier battalion and the Marsars *Jäger* Company, the troops occupied the *Schnecke* where they had stood the day before and the front of the Schwabhäuser basin. Zezschwitz did not share Hohenlohe's casual attitude regarding the day ahead. The ominous clamor of battle from the plateau west of Landgrafenberg was heard in Capellendorf as well, but all remained tranquil in camp. Apparently undisturbed by the distant gunfire, Hohenlohe dressed and composed long letters to the Duke of Brunswick and to the king. He described to the latter the events of the previous day: "The affair of General Tauentzien, during which the cannonade was rather lively, has ended well. The French went back to Jena."[12]

Hohenlohe relayed d'Egidy's report and added that "every possible security measure for my left wing" has been taken and there is little to fear thanks to support from Rüchel's reserve corps. Regarding the pointless expedition up the Saale and back, Hohenlohe wrote, "Yesterday I wanted to attack the French holding Dornburg but they were already gone." After completing the letters, with the din of artillery fire from the plateau steadily augmenting, he arranged for fusilier Captain Neidhardt von Gneisenau to escort a suspected French spy to Auerstedt, ate breakfast and then read some dispatches.[13] Without an attempt to acquaint himself with details of the battle Tauentzien's division was embroiled in, the prince sent an adjutant to find Massenbach and convey to him the *request* that he tell Tauentzien to retreat.[14] By the time the order to retire reached Tauentzien his troops were beaten.

Had Hohenlohe taken action at first light, there were sufficient forces at his disposal to have driven back Lannes before enemy reinforcements came up. The prince could have formed an infantry reserve from the four Saxon battalions encamped at Kötschan and the five of the Dyherrn Brigade. Niesemeuschel's Saxon cavalry, supplemented by Grawert's mounted brigade of 19 squadrons and one-and-a-half horse batteries, could have joined Tauentzien's eight squadrons along with three more stationed at Hohlstedt to achieve an overwhelming superiority in horsemen to charge Lannes. The full-strength Rabenau and Rühle Fusilier Battalions sat in Capellendorf without orders. Hohenlohe did nothing with these units to support the beleaguered general. He issued almost no orders during Tauentzien's attack.[15]

At 7:45 a.m., the prince mounted his horse to ride to the base camp outside of Capellendorf. He saw the men of Grawert's division preparing for action. The commander of an infantry regiment, Colonel Hans von Kalckreuth, described the scene: "By daybreak gunfire up by the sentries could be heard; at first just occasional shots with small rifles, but soon the shooting became more intense and interspersed cannon fire could be heard. In camp everyone was dressed. As the shooting became livelier, General von Grawert ordered the tents broken; this occurred between seven and eight o'clock. Toward eight o'clock, Prince Hohenlohe came into camp with his staff and seemed shocked to find the tents taken down."[16] The prince was aghast that Grawert had mobilized the division without orders and presumably caused the soldiers "unnecessary fatigue" as he put it. Hohenlohe rode along a column of troops marching out of camp, angrily shouting "stop, stop!" His aids attempted to halt the formations as well. The nearest battalions obeyed while others did not. This caused confusion and widened the interval between units.

Grawert himself was soon on the scene and expressed to the prince his apprehension about what the cannon and musket fire portend. After announcing he will "bet his head" on the need for his preparations, he persuaded Hohenlohe

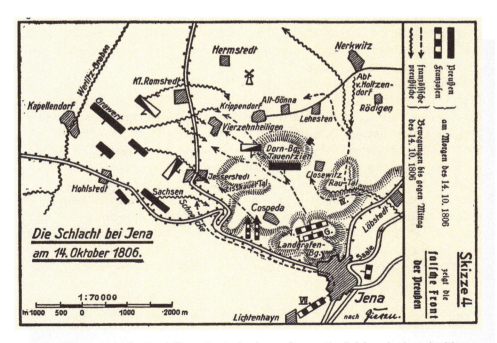

This map in Gerhard Gieren's study shows Grawert's division deployed with its front facing southwest, hence in the wrong direction, on the morning of the battle. At upper left is the Werlitz ditch, where the Prussians regrouped to stop the enemy pursuit in late afternoon.

to allow the division to change position so that that Lannes will not be able to strike in its flank and rear. Grawert had already sent his cavalry, including horse artillery, to Kleinromstädt as a precaution to guard the flank. Even at this stage, Hohenlohe's army was still deployed with front southwest.[17] The time required for Grawert to turn his division prevented him from marching to support Tauentzien. While the latter's troops bled, the prince and Grawert argued for a long time about what to do next. Hohenlohe finally decided to deploy the main part of his force for a counterattack, despite reports that the French have reinforced their position during the night and there was no current assessment of enemy strength and disposition.

Encamped on the northeastern flank of Hohenlohe's army, General Holtzendorff's mixed force was still dispersed in villages around Rödigen at dawn on October 14. The French had driven his pickets from Dornburg and Camburg overnight. Even though he was entrusted with the defense of these towns, Holtzendorff did not marshal his forces until hearing the sound of cannon fire heralding Tauentzien's clash with Lannes in the morning. The general dispatched Captain Alvensleben to Hohenlohe to request orders but never received a response.[18] The units formed up in their host villages to march to the assembly area at Rödigen. Those quartered at Pfuhlsborn lost their way in the fog. The Kollin Half-Grenadier Battalion and the Gause Half-Horse Battery went to Grawert's division by mistake. It took hours to gather the men. Holtzendorff himself rode out to personally reconnoiter the front. The haze prevented him from learning anything useful.

When the mist lifted at around nine, Holtzendorff discovered that the French occupy the town of Closewitz and have cut his line of communication to Hohenlohe. Prince Hohenlohe himself had waited too long to send an adjutant, Lieutenant Diederich, with orders for Holtzendorff to support Tauentzien by attacking the enemy in the flank. Diederich failed in his mission. He opted for a wide detour to avoid the French and joined a group of Saxon grenadiers headed for Stobra. He remained with them and never reached his destination. Without instructions from the prince in Capellendorf, Holtzendorff weighed the options of either driving right through the enemy to Hohenlohe or retreating to Nerkwitz, a village north of Rödigen, to circumvent the *Grande Armée* in a wide arc and reestablish contact.

The occupation of Closewitz by Soult's IV Corps was possible due to treason on the German side. Before dawn on October 14, Soult sought a guide for the Rau valley to reach the plateau north of Landgrafenberg. The village pastor of Wenigenjena, C. W. Putsche, conducted the troops through the treacherous defile. Testifying in November 1806 before a panel in Weimar, Putsche claimed that a French colonel led him to Lannes and found him "in the company of several generals at a campfire, lying asleep on straw. The colonel woke him and introduced me." The pastor asked two villagers to serve as guides, "but neither were willing to do so." He tried again, this time escorted by French soldiers, and led

Philipp Granert, Balthasar Möbius and Adolph Eicke before the marshal. Granert pleaded ignorance and the other two said they are "domestic servants who arrived in town only a short time ago and know nothing of the trails." Lannes spread a map before the pastor and questioned him about the area. Putsche provided detailed answers. According to Putsche, Lannes said, "You'll have to guide me. You've studied in Jena and must therefore be familiar with the region."[19]

Like everyone in Wenigenjena, Putsche had suffered property damage and loss at the hands of the French. He valued it at 2,000 guilden. Lannes supposedly told him, "I will not only compensate you for everything you've lost, but this will also bring you into high regard with the emperor Napoleon." Putsche claimed to have initially refused to cooperate, but acquiesced when a French captain threatened to shoot him. The pastor was therefore "forced to serve the French army as a guide to the battlefield behind Closewitz." Public accusations that he is a traitor, Putsche protested, are "an assault on my honor." The allegation of treason, he claimed, caused him greater distress than when the French threatened to shoot him.[20] Certain details of Putsche's narrative are doubtful, since Lannes was not in Wenigenjena the night before the battle. Also, other residents who refused to help the French were neither shot nor threatened. In any case, since Weimar was incorporated into Napoleon's *Rheinbund* just weeks after the battle, Putsche escaped punishment. His endeavors to salvage his reputation did not prevent him from accepting 8,000 francs from the French government to replace stolen property.

On the battlefield, General Holtzendorff's troops paid the price for the pastor's collaboration with the enemy. Holtzendorff's detachment consisted of 2,500 infantrymen, nearly 2,000 cavalry and a disproportionately large artillery park of 22 guns. Driving a wedge between his force and Hohenlohe was the IV Corps' first division commanded by General Louis de Saint-Hilaire. Saint-Hilaire had eight infantry battalions tallying 7,700 men, six cannons and nine mounted squadrons totaling 1,400 riders. For the Prussians to withdraw in the face of such odds seemed to Holtzendorff the better option. Retreat was in itself dangerous, since the hilly terrain offers only a few narrow passes to serve as escape routes for the detachment. The troops could be vulnerable to concentrated French fire while crowding into the defiles.

Holtzendorff therefore first launched a linear attack to drive the enemy back far enough to gain space for his formations to retire in order. A single battalion, he reasoned, can then hold the forward position while the balance of the infantry pulls back. Had Holtzendorff capitalized on his superiority in artillery and advantageous parity in cavalry to strike Saint-Hilaire head-on, his infantry in support, then the unexpected thrust might well have punched straight through the enemy line. He was unfamiliar with the uneven terrain before him and this may have contributed to his reluctance to risk such a bold maneuver. The Prussian infantry formed echelons shortly before 10:00 a.m. Drums beating, the men began the measured, awesome procession into battle so strongly identified with this legendary fighting force. The troops had to cross a deep ravine and then negotiate a steep, overgrown slope.

Concealed among trees and shrubs, Tirailleurs waited for them at Heiligholz directly ahead. Taking advantage of natural cover as usual, French sharpshooters tested their marksmanship against the volley fire of the attackers. Once again, the French tactics proved superior; the Prussians slowly advanced as though on parade, exposed and in formation. Their musketry was ineffective against the rapidly mobile defenders. Not even the case shot of the Hahn Horse Battery on the left flank, firing in support of the advance, could disrupt the French aim. As the echelons approached, the Tirailleurs fell back to Lobholz to make a stand at the edge of the wood. Unable to pursue them into the underbrush, the Prussian line halted and discharged volley after volley. The ranks thinned as French reinforcements arrived and the defensive fire intensified. Unlike Tauentzien, Holtzendorff was not paralyzed by indecision. He ordered the withdrawal before losses seriously mounted. The Losthin Grenadier Battalion of the first wave covered the retreat.

As the detachment retired toward Nerkwitz, the Losthin grenadiers began to give ground. The Guyot Cavalry Brigade charged the battalion. The Prussians rebuffed the horsemen with musket fire and bayonet. The Borcke Battalion was also attacked but formed a square and retreated in order. Two regiments of Saxon light cavalry, the Prince Clement and Prince Johann *Chevaux-legers*, rode to support Losthin. In the ensuing melee, they were scattered by the enemy's superior numbers and stampeded to the rear. The victorious French again turned on Losthin's men, who broke another charge. "Only the iron composure of the grenadiers prevented a complete rout," wrote Lettow-Vorbeck. "They ejected the enemy from their ranks wherever he broke through and repulsed with their firepower the ones who followed."[21] The Schulenburg Foot Artillery with its eight guns covered the battalion's withdrawal until it entered the 150-foot deep Nerkwitz ravine where French cavalry could not follow. The Hahn Horse Battery galloped through the French line and avoided capture. Captain Hahn had kept the *Chevaux-legers* assigned to support him in the fight by threatening to fire canister shot into their ranks if they try to leave the field before the grenadiers and cannons are safely away.[22]

Narrowly escaping capture, Holtzendorff had successfully disengaged his detachment from a superior force; despite casualties, his infantry and mounted troops were still fit for duty. The general marched to Stobra, a village northwest of Nerkwitz, shortly before 11:00 a.m. He regrouped the formations and tarried for well over an hour. He was safely north of the enemy, followed only by French patrols. Nothing blocked the route southwest via Hermstedt to Hohenlohe's army. Holtzendorff proceeded a further two-and-a-half miles *northwest* to Apolda instead and arrived there at around two in the afternoon. Joined by a battalion of the Schimmelpfennig hussars, there were now 21 cavalry squadrons at his disposal. He had lost some cannons in the clash with Saint-Hilaire, but could still have joined Hohenlohe's army in its battle against Lannes after Tauentzien's defeat. The horse troops were especially missed. Even without orders, Holtzendorff should have led his force back into action. His decision to move to Apolda and remain there defies military logic and was tantamount to desertion. "The only explanation for what Holtzendorff did is that he completely lost his head," ventured historian Paul Schreckenbach.[23] In the opinion of Gieren, "This general should have been stood before a court-martial the next day and summarily shot. It was a monstrous case of dereliction of duty!"[24]

Prince Hohenlohe's Death March

After the campaign, Prince Hohenlohe offered no explanation for what prompted him to order the army to attack after he had just reprimanded Grawert for mobilizing the first division. The day before, Hohenlohe made no attempt to retake Landgrafenberg in compliance with Brunswick's instructions not to engage the French. The prince no longer felt bound by this order. Had he made up his mind to advance at dawn on the 14th to support Tauentzien's division, when the fog was so dense it reduced visibility to 20 paces favoring the attacker, the outcome might well have been different. Now the survivors of Tauentzien's decimated formation were low on ammunition and Holtzendorff's contingent was fighting on his own half a mile away. Even at this time, a properly conducted operation had a chance of success. When the prince moved forward, the Prussians enjoyed parity in infantry and superior cavalry. Lannes's soldiers, many hung over from the previous night's debauch, were fatigued from combat. Hohenlohe managed to lose the battle anyway. He repeated the mistakes of Tauentzien and Holtzendorff. Just as when he had personally led the insignificant expedition to Dornburg the day before and left no one behind in charge, he failed on the 14th to provide the army with the central leadership an engagement demands.

Toward nine o'clock, Hohenlohe's men formed up with their front toward Vierzehnheiligen, a 400-year-old village two-and-a-half miles due east of Capellendorf and in the center of the plateau. Poised to advance were eleven Prussian and nine Saxon infantry battalions as well as 19 Prussian and 20 Saxon cavalry squadrons. Napoleon could muster 19 of Lannes's wearied foot battalions, six of Ney's, the 5,000-man guard infantry in reserve and 15 cavalry squadrons. Grawert's ten Prussian battalions formed the vanguard of the assault. Saxons made up the second echelon. At 9:30 a.m. they began moving up the gentle slope toward Vierzehnheiligen. The men marched with fixed bayonets, the officers with sabers drawn, "in quick step with the band playing, in formation as orderly as on the parade ground," as Höpfner described.[25] The Glasenapp and Wolframsdorf Batteries covered the flanks. In a line extending nearly three-quarters of a mile marched the Sack and Hahn Grenadier Battalions, the Hohenlohe, Sanitz and Zastrow Regiments and the first and second battalions of the Grawert Regiment on the left protecting a twelve-pound battery. The artillery on the right was reinforced by the mortar battery of the Dyherrn Brigade stationed at

Kleinromstädt. The first battalion of the Müffling Regiment followed directly behind Sanitz and Zastrow. Each grenadier battalion numbered 650 men, the musketeer battalions 700. The first wave of infantry counted some 7,000 soldiers.[26]

After driving back Tauentzien, Lannes's corps had fanned out on either side
of Dornberg between Krippendorf and Lützeroda. Behind it stood the Imperial
Guard. Advancing on the left was the Desjardin Division of Augereau's corps.
It pursued Tauentzien's right wing through the Isserstädt woods. To Lannes's
right was Saint-Hilaire, who turned to engage Holtzendorff's detachment, and
Dominique Vedel's brigade supporting Saint-Hilaire. The French prepared to
meet Hohenlohe's attack. The prince positioned his cavalry at the vanguard
of the Prussian and Saxon infantry. He arranged the squadrons in chessboard
formation and personally led them to the small patch of woods just south of
Vierzehnheiligen. Supported by the fire of the Studnitz and Steinwehr Horse
Batteries, they slowly moved forward, increasingly harassed by Tirailleurs. Major
Loucey proposed leading part of the cavalry to roll up the French sharpshooters
and send the balance of the horsemen to assail the weakly protected enemy artillery. "Nothing would have been more suitable to gain for us the poise, opportunity to plan the next move, time and overview of the disposition of the enemy
than this suggestion," wrote Marwitz. "And since we had 50 squadrons detached
from General Holtzendorff with us, the operation would have been easy to carry
out."[27] Hohenlohe disregarded the suggestion. A massive mounted force was at
his disposal which he made almost no use of.

Hohenlohe rode back to rejoin Grawert. He left his adjutant Major Röder to
stay with the cavalry and charge in case attacked. The mounted troops could
have exploited the gap in the French line between Lannes's V Corps near
Vierzehnheiligen and Augereau's VII Corps further south at Isserstädt, but once
again left the initiative to the enemy. At this time, the remnants of Tauentzien's
division passed through the Prussian line toward Kleinromstädt to regroup and
replenish ammunition. Marshal Ney's advance guard consisting of five infantry
battalions, six mounted squadrons and six guns went into action as soon as it arrived. Ney observed the devastation the Steinwehr Battery's fire was wreaking on
the French infantry and decided to fill the breach between Lannes and Augereau.
He sent the 10th Chasseurs Regiment against the Prussian gunners' left flank. It
was opposed by 250 riders of the Holtzendorff Cuirassiers guarding the battery. A
typically chaotic, see-saw cavalry melee ensued, with additional units joining in.

During the skirmish, two squadrons of cuirassiers lost heart and fled before
a smaller French troop. They stampeded into a Prussian infantry battalion.
Hohenlohe rode up to the battalion and told its soldiers to volley fire into the
retreating horsemen. Not one man obeyed the order. One of the battalion's
officers shouted to the prince's adjutant, "Those are our own people! Are we
supposed to shoot at our own people now?"[28] The French overran the Steinwehr
Battery and made off with its carriages. The Henckel Horse Regiment recovered
the guns and ultimately repulsed the foray, capturing 73 chasseurs and driving

the rest back to Ney's infantry squares. The battery had lost mobility however, rendering it ineffective. Napoleon increased the artillery supporting Ney to 25 guns. In the face of such overwhelming firepower, Hohenlohe withdrew his mounted units and stationed them behind and on the flanks of the line infantry. The prince was displeased with the cavalry and from then on designated no one to lead it. The Prussians did not conduct another major mounted attack for the duration of the engagement.

Ney capitalized on the lull and dispatched the advance guard's *Voltigeur* battalion to capture Vierzehnheiligen with the support of Lannes's 40th Infantry Regiment. The French took the town while Hohenlohe fumbled with positioning his cavalry behind the foot regiments. For the past hour, Prussian grenadiers had been formed up five minutes' march from Vierzehnheiligen and Hohenlohe sent not a single man forward to hold it.[29] At half-past ten, as the sun dissipated the last of the morning mist, he had to commit thousands more to accomplish the same task. Lannes's men, in action since six in the morning, braced themselves for another round. The marshal sent the 21st Light Infantry Regiment to help the garrison. "This was the only moment," Höpfner maintained, "when by committing the entire force and making vigorous use of numerically superior cavalry, the recapture of Vierzehnheiligen could have achieved a temporary success; a lasting one was no longer possible since pushing on now meant dealing with 40,000 Frenchmen who could receive reinforcements at any time."[30]

Ney advanced a battle square of grenadiers south of the village and a battalion commanded by his chief of staff to Isserstädt. There were as yet few French reserves. Half of Ney's and Soult's corps had still not reached Jena. One of Augereau's divisions was stuck in the woods and the other was at Mühltal. Part of Lannes' corps was grappling with Holtzendorff. Retaking Vierzehnheiligen, which Hohenlohe could have achieved had he used cavalry to support the linear attack, would hold Napoleon until Rüchel's reserve corps arrived on the battlefield. Relying on his foot soldiers, the prince left the horse troops to guard the flanks. Thin lines of Tirailleurs came into view. They received support from meager infantry columns and some cavalry squadrons. Hohenlohe rode across his wall of men and exhorted them to prove worthy of "the old Prussian renown and the deeds of their fathers," and was greeted everywhere with hurrahs and clamor to attack.[31]

Neither Tirailleur musketry nor artillery case-shot slowed the procession. As they marched onward, Grawert's grenadiers loomed inexorably larger in the eyes of the taut defenders. The Tirailleurs fell back. Intact infantry formations also gave ground. Ney later described the anxiety he had felt at this juncture. He believed that the *Grande Armée* had ventured too far ahead of its delayed reinforcements and at no time was in a more vulnerable, precarious position than at this moment.[32] For all his fiery oratory however, it was *Hohenlohe* who wavered. Uncertain of enemy strength and anxious about the belated arrival of his own reserve, the prince called a halt once the troops came to within effective musket range of Vierzehnheiligen. He declawed the linear attack by depriving it of its deadliest element, indeed its very purpose; the bayonet charge. The Prussian left wing arced slightly forward to partially envelop the village. In smartly aligned rows, the troops volley fired on an enemy concealed behind fences, bushes, walls and houses. The Prussian fusillade was practically ineffective, but the return fire of the defenders was not. Standing in blocs in the open, Grawert's men had disproportionately high casualties.

French cannons on a hill next to Krippendorf inflicted such heavy losses on a battalion of the Sanitz Regiment that it retreated, only to be led back into the line by Hohenlohe. A Prussian battery opened fire on the French gunners. It silenced several guns and detonated some munition carts. Major d'Egidy described the scene: "There was now firing all along the line. Violent canister fire on both sides also began. That of the enemy was more effective, since we faced nothing but a thin Tirailleur line with a few cannons while we stood in a compact infantry line formed by battalions. The infantry lines and columns of the enemy remained out of effective range of our fire."[33] Captain Marwitz saw the carnage in this way: "Our horse artillery was of outstanding service to us. It could clearly be seen that the gunners fired two rounds before the French could fire one and that they hit their targets just as well. Nonetheless we were already losing a noticeable amount of our people but could scarcely see the enemy. Much to our disadvantage, he fought as though from behind a curtain. His Tirailleurs used every aspect of the uneven terrain, lying behind cover and firing into our ranks. His batteries were positioned behind high ground or dug in so that little more than the barrel muzzles could be seen. The Tirailleurs retired under covering fire from these batteries and then protected the batteries when they too had to fall back."[34]

Lannes and Ney drew from troops massed behind Vierzehnheiligen to replace losses at the front. To relieve pressure on the strategic town, Napoleon ordered the V Corps' 40th and Jacques Desjardin's 105th Infantry Regiments forward. Lannes sent two fresh cavalry regiments, the 9th Hussars and the 21st Chasseurs, to charge the right wing of the Prussian line. They rode headlong into the Saxon Polenz Regiment and two squadrons of Henckel Cuirassiers guarding the flank. A pair of *Chevaux-leger* squadrons supported the Saxon counterattack. They practically annihilated the two French regiments in a rapid, violent skirmish. The Saxons captured eight officers, 50 men and 70 horses. The French suffered another setback when the Erichsen and Rosen Fusilier Battalions together with a company of *Jägers* emerged from the forest east of Isserstädt and wrested the village from Desjardin's men. The fusiliers were separated from the rest of Tauentzien's division earlier that morning and had sought refuge in the woods. Their reappearance surprised the French preoccupied holding Vierzehnheiligen. Not one to surrender the initiative, Napoleon ordered another assault. Lannes personally led his last reserve of six battalions against the Prussian left wing.

The Kollin Grenadier Battalion and Gause Battery, supported by a squadron of Saxon cavalry, about faced to meet the attack head on. Dispatching five more

Saxon cavalry squadrons in support, the prince outmaneuvered and repulsed Lannes's attack. The concentrated fire of the eight-pound batteries of Captain Ernst and the Saxon Johann Haussmann forced Lannes to abandon the enterprise. Captain Haussmann recalled, "From our position the French cavalry that deployed next to Vierzehnheiligen was effectively bombarded in the flank from long range. The enemy infantry columns advancing from Krippendorf to Isserstädt were forced to turn back and the enemy cavalry regiments approaching Vierzehnheiligen from Lützeroda were driven from their position. Twelve-pound enemy guns being brought onto the plateau were also forced to quickly retire thanks to our flank fire."[35]

Grawert had extended his line further to the right toward Isserstädt and moved the Cerrini Brigade to bolster the center. The Dyherrn Brigade and Kotsch Battery reinforced a mounted battery on the right wing. The punishment the French were taking, even under Bonaparte's personal direction, reveals what a mistake it was for Hohenlohe to have halted the linear attack a thousand paces short of Vierzehnheiligen. Now hundreds of Prussian soldiers lay dead and wounded before the town. They had been leveled by cannon balls or by marksmen they could neither see nor effectively engage. Napoleon held out with Ney's weak force and Lannes's exhausted corps, both low on ammunition, without having to commit the guard. Hohenlohe reconsidered a bayonet charge, but the troops were seriously depleted by attrition and psychologically strained to the utmost.

True to form, Hohenlohe opted not for an attack but for advice. Grawert opposed the plan. He argued that losses are too high, hand-to-hand combat will disrupt formation and there is no reserve. He told the prince, "We can hold this position and we must, until General Rüchel arrives with his corps. Then we can take the village and have a complete victory. But if just one or two of our attacks now are repulsed, we'll have a gap in our line and nothing to fill it with. The enemy will certainly make use of this and snatch victory away from us!"[36] Massenbach wrote, "At this moment our courage soared. The prince shook my hand and I said to him, 'your highness should take a trumpeter and place yourself at the head of the cavalry, leave General Grawert to lead the infantry and have us attack. Do what you had decided earlier to do. We can't wait for Holtzendorff. God knows what's become of him.' But Hohenlohe wavered and did not pursue the attack."[37]

Massenbach's proposal to launch a massive mounted assault was not a bad suggestion; having the prince at its head was. One must marvel at the logic of a chief of staff who urges the general responsible for overall direction of a battle to personally lead a horse charge. In any case, as historian Schreckenbach observed, "The responsibility was Hohenlohe's alone. Grawert was an outranked general and the prince could have ordered him to hold his tongue. In such a situation the commander in chief should know what to do and not listen to the babble of subordinates."[38] During the debate, a lieutenant delivered a dispatch from General Zezschwitz, whose Saxon division was on the *Schnecke*. It warned of "several strong columns" of French reinforcements sighted marching to Vierzehnheiligen.[39] Based on this intelligence and on the condition of his men, Hohenlohe postponed a direct assault on the village without Rüchel's reserve corps on hand.

After the battle, Lieutenant Heinrich von Förster of the Prittwitz Dragoons testified that he had left camp at 6:30 a.m. for Weimar to deliver the prince's first message to Rüchel requesting support. It read, "I am just now being vigorously attacked and have marched the Prussian division to the left. I ask your excellency to send me whatever Prussian troops you can spare."[40] Förster handed the message to Rüchel shortly before nine o'clock. The general replied, "I'm coming at this moment to your highness with most of the force on the road from here to Capellendorf. Send me orders quickly where you need us the most. I'm glad to help and will do whatever is in my power as a friend."[41] The message reached Hohenlohe just as the cavalry was returning from routing Lannes's chasseurs. Hohenlohe dispatched Förster with a second appeal at ten o'clock. He wrote Rüchel, "Up till now it's all been going well, I'm beating the enemy at every place. The cavalry has taken cannons; I'll be pleased with whatever you bring me against Vierzehnheiligen."[42]

This correspondence scarcely conveyed to Rüchel the seriousness of the situation. Moreover, the cannons "the cavalry has taken" were not French, but those from the Steinwehr Battery recovered in a counterattack. The reserve corps broke camp and set off for the battlefield at around 10:00 a.m. Rüchel marched with 12,000 men. He senselessly left 3,000 soldiers behind to guard the base camp at Webicht. His situation was not enviable. He was not directly under Hohenlohe's command but under the Duke of Brunswick's. Karl Wilhelm had instructed Rüchel to provide a strongpoint to guard the flank of Duke Karl August of Weimar's corps sitting in Ilmenau. The general disobeyed orders and marched to Capellendorf instead. His troops were passing through Umpferstädt when Lieutenant Förster returned with Hohenlohe's second plea for help. Rüchel replied simply, "Fine, I'm on my way."[43] As the troops reached Frankendorf, the last village before Capellendorf, a courier arrived with a letter from the king commanding the reserve corps to immediately march north to join the main army at Auerstedt. Rüchel reasoned correctly that he is too far away from Auerstedt to intervene there in time, but can still aid Hohenlohe. He therefore disregarded the sovereign's order.

Back at the front, pursuant to Grawert's advice that the present position be held until the reserve arrives, Hohenlohe kept his infantry in formation across an open field—hardly a tactically advantageous position—exposed to continuous French fire for well over two hours. Adjutant Marwitz offered this impression: "We stood just a few hundred paces from the French batteries and the case-shot wreaked unbelievable havoc on our battalions. We had nothing left to replace our losses. Our artillery practically pounded the village to rubble and the oldest soldier, Prince Hohenlohe himself, assured us that he could never have imagined such a bombardment. Along the whole line one battalion salvo followed another, in many places without result. The area in front of the village was nevertheless a scene of horrific bloodletting. The Hohenlohe Regiment and Hahn Grenadier Battalion, standing directly opposite the village, came away from this killing ground with far less than half their people. Officers were continuously the preferred targets of enemy riflemen. But our heroic troops did not fall back until they were ordered to retreat."[44]

Prussian cannons pulverized Vierzehnheiligen, but there remained among the rubble ample cover for the Tirailleurs. Upon advice from the artillerymen, Hohenlohe switched from cannonballs to incendiary rounds. They set the village ablaze. The flames drove the enemy back and this encouraged the Prussians. Without a direct assault however, the stubborn defenders could not be dislodged. The prince disregarded the maxim of the echelon maneuver, that battalion volley fire is but a prelude and the infantry charge paramount. "Only the bayonet could have helped here."[45] As Grawert and Hohenlohe awaited Rüchel's 12,000 men, far greater numbers became available to Napoleon. Saint-Hilaire was free to menace the Prussian left wing after Holtzendorff retired to Apolda. Ney's corps beefed up the center of the French line and the rest of Soult's force scaled the plateau on the right flank. Etienne Heudelet's division belonging to Augereau's corps moved against the *Schnecke* while its sister formation, that of Desjardin, turned to Isserstädt. The reserve cavalry arrived. This gave the emperor 51 squadrons with more on the way. It was at last possible for Bonaparte to advance.

Prince Hohenlohe still held out waiting for Rüchel. As Colonel Kalckreuth recalled, "Now the enemy brought more artillery into the position from where he completely dominated us. He continued to bombard us most vigorously and sent reinforcements to his light troops. I could only counter this enemy artillery fire with three of my regimental cannons, which I had arranged as a battery as favorably as the ground allows. The fourth cannon had been sent back to Weimar with a broken axle for repair. Spurred on by the officers who command them, the riflemen of the regiment prevented the enemy's light troops from further penetration, although they were concealed everywhere in terrain that was very advantageous to them. It was unavoidable that during the fighting, which we had to endure for hours, we suffered a great loss of men from both the enemy artillery that was vastly superior to ours and to Tirailleur fire."[46]

Napoleon ordered the *Grande Armée* to attack along the entire front. Ney's corps pushed forward in the center to the blare of military bands. Hohenlohe's troops caved in. "The inability to do anything against the destructive fire of the enemy Tirailleurs caused the men to lose their composure," stated the after-action report of the Saxon Lecoq Grenadier Battalion.[47] "What a test of courage for the ordinary man," one historian marveled, "when all around his comrades are convulsing in their own blood and there was nothing, absolutely nothing one could do but stand fast and keep firing at an enemy no one can see!"[48]

Isserstädt fell to Desjardin. This tore the first gap in Hohenlohe's overextended line. Boguslawski's fusiliers defending the Schwabhäuser basin and the Saxon Niesemeuschel Division were cut off from the main force, but Niesemeuschel repulsed Heudelet's assault on the *Schnecke*. The cavalry on the right fell back. Under intensifying enemy fire, the Prussian left lost cohesion. The Sanitz Regiment was first to break; neither pleas, threats nor the example of the officers could persuade the men to hold. The Zastrow and Grawert Regiments wavered, but a wounded adjutant succeeded in leading the latter back into the line. Its commander, Major Eberhardt, was killed.

The withdrawal of Prussians was not without individual acts of valor. The slain Major Eberhardt's 15-year-old son, serving as ordnance officer in a battalion at Vierzehnheiligen, saw the men turning to flee. He shouted to the standard bearer, "What kind of skunk are you, running away with the colors? For shame!" Young Eberhardt planted the flag pole in the ground beside his horse and admonished the soldiers, "Here comrades, is your standard. Don't run off like scoundrels, come here, gather around me and show that you're Prussians!"[49] Motivated by the ensign's example, the battalion turned to face the enemy once more. Another who braved shot and shell to keep the men fighting was the even younger Prince Bernhard of Weimar. He became so heedlessly exposed to hostile fire while exhorting wavering troops that an aid forcibly pulled him from danger. Battalions that stopped retiring were only able to hold briefly and soon had to rejoin the general retreat. The Xavier and Klemens Regiments, whose men were out of ammunition, abandoned their positions. Battalions of the Müffling and Kurfürst Regiments formed a bloc around the colors but soon fell back.

Tauentzien's troops who had regrouped after the morning's carnage buttressed the defense at Kleinromstädt. This temporarily stabilized the Prussian left wing. Infantry out of formation is especially vulnerable to cavalry attacks, so Napoleon unleashed Murat's riders to charge the disorganized, fleeing mass of soldiers. Much of the variously distributed Prussian and Saxon cavalry was ineffective amid the chaos. In places where groups of French horsemen, many of whom were intoxicated, became overextended and separated from their units, the Prussians failed to capitalize on the opportunity. Marwitz recalled, "Wherever individual squadrons gained the advantage, which happened several times, it could not be exploited because our people were without self-control and too drastic. When a Frenchman fell into their hands, ten men or more pounced on him and hacked him to pieces till nothing was left. And with each of these blows just as many enemies could have been put out of action, who instead reformed and then took back from the Prussians the advantage they had gained."[50]

Colonel Kalckreuth recalled, "These enemy troops cut down the men fleeing in scattered groups. They hacked many with sabers and took a considerable number of prisoners back with them. It probably wouldn't have been nearly so bad had our own cavalry ridden up and not allowed that of the enemy so much time. Soon afterward, some squadrons of Count Henckel's regiment attacked

Lieutenant Colonel Julius aus dem Winkel's grenadiers conduct a fighting withdrawal in battle square formation as the Prussian and Saxon army falls back at Jena. The cannons are positioned in corners as prescribed. (*Staatliche Kunstsammlung Dresden*)

these enemy cavalrymen, threw them back and chopped them down. Colonel von Oelfen, whom I had ordered out of action because of a bullet wound to his left foot and shrapnel in his right hand caused by a cannonball that landed beside me, then rallied some of the fleeing soldiers and formed them into combat groups."[51] Henckel's cuirassiers inflicted losses on Murat's squadrons and freed many prisoners. But by now most of the Prussian mounted artillery was lost and the retreat of Hohenlohe's troops gradually degenerated into a rout.

The breakwater in this human flood of a defeated army was a battalion that left the field with composure and military precision. Marwitz witnessed the spectacle: "Only one unit remained unshaken, the Saxon aus dem Winkel Grenadier Battalion… Surrounded by men put to flight who in desperation were running away without weapons, in the midst of the frenzied disorder of so many thousands who would no longer obey an officer, ceaselessly attacked by the enemy and at no time wavering, this battalion retired in full marching order, in measured step and with the band playing. It formed an open battle square and as the enemy came on, always turned to face him. Neither the cavalry (Ney's cuirassiers) that many times wanted to hack its way into the square, nor the incessant, accurate fire of the Tirailleurs could disrupt the formation. As soon as the battalion had a breather, the troops reformed and resumed the retreat, again with their music as though on the parade ground. Whenever the enemy came at them, all about faced and in an instant stood ready to fight."[52] In the center of the impenetrable wandering phalanx was the vanquished general who had so frivolously underestimated his adversary on this somber day; the wounded Prince Hohenlohe.

Captain Borcke related how after the failed attack there was much grumbling among the troops. The infantry blamed the cavalry for letting it down and vice versa. Like all surviving accounts however, Borcke praised the valor exhibited by troops who stood steadfastly under fire for hours until overtaken by the sheer hopelessness of the situation: "As much as we tried to downplay the bad impressions and negative remarks of the men, this did not entirely succeed, since they couldn't exactly be blindfolded. Nonetheless, the majority demonstrated an undiminished spirit and the best of will. Indeed, most expressed the ardent desire to share a victory with their comrades or perish. To do honor to this dismal day it may be said that the spirit of the common soldier remained outstanding to the last moment and in view of his recent privations downright amazing."[53] Massenbach himself described how before Vierzehnheiligen, the Hahn Grenadier Battalion and Hohenlohe Regiment lost half their men, yet "many stood unshaken like a wall," still defying the French barrage.[54]

After Hohenlohe ordered a linear attack that morning, he had remained throughout much of the battle in the Prussian center. The limitation the prince imposed on his own authority seems to have impressed Marwitz, who wrote, "In this highly critical situation Prince Hohenlohe performed miracles of personal valor. Right from the beginning of the advance he was always with the furthermost battalion. He turned to wherever the fire on the right or left became most intense and would ride along the front of the line there to maintain order. (During retreat) he tarried among the last to fall back and tried by example, encouragement and threats to seize hold once more of the ebbing fortunes of war."[55] Is such praise justified for a general charged with leading a 38,000-man army, whose scope of the operation and conduct differed little from that of a battalion commander?

Lettow-Vorbeck criticized Hohenlohe's bravado as follows: "The limited circle of people that such a personal example of course positively influences scarcely compares to the disadvantage that results if the supreme commander in this way forsakes his more important duties as leader. The commander must choose a place where he remains preserved from the immediate effects of the fighting as much as possible."[56] Tauentzien and Holtzendorff fought separate, abortive actions without direction. Hohenlohe underused the cavalry, which had initially outnumbered that of Napoleon. He apparently forgot about some units, including the Rühle and Rabenau Fusilier Battalions languishing in Capellendorf. Boguslawski's fusilier battalion, trained to employ the modern tactics of the Tirailleurs, sat in the Schwabhäuser basin throughout the day without taking part in operations. One historian summarized that Hohenlohe was "in reality not the supreme commander, but concerned himself throughout the entire duration of the battle exclusively with Grawert's division."[57]

The Final Fiasco

History offers many examples of beaten armies that fall back but regroup to achieve victory another day. The Prussians were defeated at Ligny on June 16, 1815, but remained an intact fighting force to decisively contribute to the allied victory over Napoleon at Waterloo two days later. Once retreat at Jena became unavoidable, it was the duty of the commander in chief to mollify the loss by organizing the withdrawal. Hohenlohe's first task should have been to designate exit routes for various formations and their stragglers. Assembling a rearguard from among units still fit for action was of equal importance. A rearguard's job is to maintain collection points for fleeing soldiers and conduct limited counterattacks to delay enemy pursuit. Tauentzien's infantry, having replenished its ammunition and somewhat rested, was available for the purpose, as were the two fresh battalions at Capellendorf and elements of the Dyherrn Brigade.

The Prussian and Saxon cavalry, thanks to its limited use by the prince, was still formidable. Once on the scene, Rüchel's reserve corps could have joined the rearguard to effectively check the French who had themselves been in combat for hours. This would have enabled the army to retire in order and reform for further operations. As Höpfner pointed out, "The Marchand Division of Ney's corps and elements of the light cavalry of the cavalry reserve arrived on the battlefield. The Imperial Guard was moving against Vierzehnheiligen. It would take some time for all of these forces to deploy. This was therefore a favorable moment to retreat together with the Saxons to Rüchel's corps and establish a new assembly area behind the Werlitz ditch."[58] Assigning retreat routes and forming a rearguard are naturally more difficult once an army is already falling back. Hohenlohe gave the order to retire too late, since he did so after regiments were losing cohesion and withdrawing without their officers' permission. Under such circumstances, only the personal intervention of the supreme commander could have restored discipline.

Since Saint-Hilaire's division blocked the road to Apolda, the better option for the Prussians and Saxons was to head west to Weimar. To ensure an orderly flow of traffic on the main road to Weimar should have been a priority. Fleeing soldiers jammed the thoroughfare. The terrain around Capellendorf is defensible. Troops occupying the ridge north of Frankendorf could hold the flank against Napoleon's forces until nightfall. Hohenlohe did not take advantage of the natural barrier to shield his army, nor did he designate lines of retreat before the battle as a contingency in case of an unfavorable outcome. Since according to various eyewitnesses, the prince's main endeavor was to admonish troops closest to the enemy to continue resistance, here again, as before, he was deficient as a leader. While the army disintegrated, Hohenlohe remained with Julius aus dem

Winkel's grenadier battalion and personally conducted its withdrawal. When the reserve corps reached the combat zone, the prince was not immediately available to confer with Rüchel about where to deploy. It is ironic that Hohenlohe's battle plan hinged on when the reserve will arrive and yet by galloping all over the field made it difficult for Rüchel to find him.

General Rüchel must share the blame for the defeat. The sound of gunfire heralding Tauentzien's clash with Lannes echoed across the countryside at around six in the morning. Rüchel did not march out of camp at Webicht for another four hours. He did not go into action until 2:30 p.m., therefore eight-and-a-half hours after the battle began. The corps should have covered the distance from Webicht to Capellendorf in less than two hours. "There is no explanation as to what could have caused such a significant delay."[59] In Scharnhorst's verdict, "It has been established that Prince Hohenlohe called upon General Rüchel several times to rush to his aid. This occurred early enough for (Rüchel) to have taken an active part in the battle. He must therefore bear a great measure of responsibility for the misfortune Hohenlohe's corps suffered."[60] One historian speculated, "Is the reason the natural slowness of this man, or that pedantic preparations for the march squandered valuable, irreplaceable time, or something different, something worse? Did he march off too late on purpose?... Voices were not lacking that accused him of treason."[61] Massenbach bluntly suggested that he came too late intentionally, because during a minor engagement at Frankenthal in 1794, Hohenlohe had failed to support Rüchel's right flank.[52]

In a study published on the 100th anniversary of the battle of Jena, Shreckenbach scorned that Rüchel was "either a man without honor or a total blockhead."[63] The general's conduct was dubious at best. While his famished troops shivered overnight on October 13/14 at their outdoor encampment, Rüchel slept comfortably in a house in Weimar. Napoleon camped among his soldiers atop Landgrafenberg. Prior to leaving Webicht the next morning, Rüchel reformed his infantry regiments by combining battalions from separate units. As a result, they served under unfamiliar commanding officers. He left behind seven battalions, six cavalry squadrons and two-and-a-half batteries around Weimar and marched to Capellendorf with eleven infantry battalions, twelve horse squadrons and one battery. During the trek two battalions in Capellendorf and one from Tauentzien's division joined his force. Despite the delayed departure, his column should have reached Vierzehnheiligen in time to support Hohenlohe.

Eyewitness Captain Borcke recalled, "The march went on for several hours in the direction of Jena, on terrain to the right of the causeway, moving very slowly like on the training field. The further we advanced, the more the road filled with wounded heading to the rear and scattered troops of every service arm. Everything we saw displayed unmistakable signs of dissolution and panicky flight. To divert the attention of our soldiers from this unpleasant spectacle, generals and officers endeavored to observe even stricter march discipline. The battalions had to march in step with eyes front, platoons at the prescribed interval. Woe to the corporal who strayed from the correct distance between platoons, woe to the soldier who fell out of step or looked in another direction! Rod and club governed in the usual way, just like in training."[64]

Capellendorf rests in the center of a valley divided by the Werlitz ditch, gently sloping upward to the east and west. Once Rüchel observed Hohenlohe's army falling back in disarray, he should have realized that the battle is lost. The correct course would have been to form a collection point for the fleeing soldiers along the western ridge of the valley. This could have facilitated an orderly withdrawal to allow combat formations to reorganize beyond the reach of French cavalry. Had Rüchel taken advantage of terrain and defended the ridge, incorporating the intact battalions of Tauentzien's division that were in proximity, he could have held the position while Napoleon awaited reinforcements. As the reserve corps came into view of Capellendorf at around 1:00 p.m., Colonel Massenbach rode up to Rüchel. According to Rüchel, he asked where he could help the most. "Only through Capellendorf now," was supposedly Massenbach's reply, which he himself later denied having said.[65]

Rüchel resumed the advance. He left the twelve-pound Schäfer Battery, a squadron of Köhler Hussars and two battalions of the Schenk Infantry Regiment behind on the left wing concealed in the brush. He placed the Borstell and Hallmann Grenadier Battalions in the center behind Capellendorf, and on high ground to the right an understrength infantry battalion, 30 cuirassiers and the Kirchfeld twelve-pound battery. The Sobbe Fusilier Battalion occupied the Werlitz ditch. All of these units were too far back to support the main assault. Their deployment negated the purpose of a reserve. At Rüchel's request, Tauentzien sent his last four and three-quarter foot battalions north to Wiegendorf. Just like a third of the remaining intact force, they sat out the battle with no influence on the outcome. Historian Eduard Leidolph summarized, "The fresh troops arriving at Capellendorf could have been brought into position somewhere along the range of hills rising west of town, where they could reorganize the defeated army and await an enemy attack. The most disadvantageous step imaginable was taken instead, in that Rüchel's corps was sent forward to assault Sperlingsberg east of Capellendorf."[66]

Lettow-Vorbeck observed, "The available 23 and two-thirds for the most part fresh battalions with their artillery could have stopped the battle-weary French of the first wave. The French would then have been forced to await the arrival of their divisions further back and their deployment would have required even more time."[67] The causeway into Capellendorf was so narrow that the Prussians had to traverse it four abreast, so that battalions reformed before entering. Compounding the resulting delay, as Borcke recalled, "The march through the village was even more difficult because the street was completely packed with cannons, wagons, wounded soldiers and dead horses. These obstacles had to be cleared out of the way first."[68] Only part of Rüchel's reserve corps traversed Capellendorf while the rest passed to the left and right of the town. The general marched his corps into the valley and divided it into three columns. The advance guard consisted of five squadrons of Bailliodz Cuirassiers, three of Katte Dragoons and four of Köhler Hussars—600 riders in all—and the Neander Horse Battery. The main force comprised the Strachwitz, Tschepe, Alt-Larisch, Winning and Wedell Infantry Regiments. The Rühle, Rabenau and Pelet Fusilier Battalions supported the right wing of the assault.

Hohenlohe at last appeared on the scene and Rüchel offered him command of the operation. The prince said that he has lost the battle and does not wish to rob his subordinate of the glory of reversing their fortunes and carrying the day.[69] By approving this gamble, Hohenlohe again neglected the interests of the whole army, which was at this time dispersed and desperately in need of decisive leadership to restore cohesion. He even suggested taking personal command of the Saxon cavalry covering the right flank, therefore assuming a secondary role to that of Rüchel. The attack began *en échellon* at 2:30 p.m. The Prussian cavalry soon came under heavy fire from French cannons deployed on the high ground at Sperlingsberg directly ahead. It was not possible for Prussian artillery to bombard the enemy guns in return, which could have significantly reduced their effectiveness. This is because Rüchel had positioned most of his batteries 2,000 meters from Sperlingsberg, hence out of range.[70] The cavalry swung to the side to allow the infantry room to advance. In the first echelon were battalions of the Alt-Larisch and Strachwitz Regiments. They bore the brunt of French musketry and case-shot as they briskly assailed the slope.

Defending Sperlingsberg were Tirailleurs, Desjardin's division, Lannes's cannons and another brigade. Borcke's description mirrors the experience of Grawert's division against Vierzehnheiligen: "The attack began and the line advanced a few hundred paces in exemplary order... Enemy artillery and Tirailleur fire intensified and already many of our people were falling. We had nothing to set against them but a pair of regimental guns that came apart or broke down after a few rounds, fell silent and were left behind. On toward the enemy we went with battalions faltering, clumsily deployed in double rows and without artillery. Favored by terrain and scarcely visible, the enemy used only his artillery and Tirailleurs against us."[71] Troops of Lannes, Soult and Ney stood further to the left of the Prussian line in the direction of Apolda. To avoid fire from these formations, Rüchel shifted his line to the right. Losses mounted from the withering defensive fire. Massenbach was present and criticized the maneuver: "In this way Rüchel exposed the left flank, indeed practically the rear, to the enemy. The enemy battery of Soult raked the Prussian line with cannister-shot along the entire length."[72]

In Borcke's recollection, "To give the attack another direction, further to the right, the command, 'left shoulder forward!' came after a while." The order did not reach all units simultaneously, "with the result that the commanding general and the other officers kept repeating it. Battalions on the left flank gradually lost cohesion, unavoidably causing vacillation and confusion. We were already

Saxon cavalry skirmishes with chasseurs and dragoons of the French mounted reserve while General Rüchel's corps advances on Sperlingsberg. Napoleon is at far right giving orders.

taking enemy case-shot fire and the French exploited our ponderous movement superbly. More and more guns and Tirailleurs fanned out and served us with a murderous hail of shot and shell. The more we shifted to the right and gained ground, the greater the rifts in our battalions."[73] The disproportionately high loss of officers made it increasingly difficult to keep the troops in formation. Borcke, whose battalion commander was wounded and the adjutant killed, struggled with surviving sergeants and subalterns to direct the men. "Without normal leadership and commands, at this time our people started firing at will. This quickly spread along the entire line and the unit began to dissolve."[74] The grenadiers broke ranks and charged forward into the devastating fire of case-shot. They took the summit of Sperlingsberg with the bayonet. The Tschepe Regiment on the left wing wrested Grossromstädt from the defenders as well.

Adjutant Marwitz gave this account: "The Alt-Larisch Regiment from Berlin took the lead and rushed with genuine impatience, certain of victory, toward the enemy batteries. Its commander Colonel Walther was shot dead on the spot, right in front, and many officers were badly wounded. The ranks of the soldiers were torn apart as well. Since there was now no one left to lead, the regiment first became hesitant, then wavered and finally turned back as fast as it had advanced."[75] Troops fled to the second echelon. This caused confusion yet some battalions continued uphill. Among these was the Müffling Regiment; it had suffered such heavy casualties at Saalfeld that the survivors were reformed into a single battalion. "Many troops of the second line followed its example, but this was just the last faint, impotent attempt to salvage an already lost cause. The second echelon was beaten just like the first, wiped out, the ultimate calamity," summarized Borcke.[76]

The Prussians had charged to within 200 paces of the French line when Lannes's gunners hitched their cannons and abandoned the position. The Tirailleurs melted away to regroup, eluding hand-to-hand combat. Rüchel's vainglorious assault had cost half of his command, inflicted minimal losses on the enemy and temporarily gained a hilltop that could not be held. In an engagement that lasted half an hour, the Winning Regiment alone lost 17 officers and 674 men killed or wounded.[77] It left the field with Premier Lieutenant Zglinicki in command. "The standard attack of the Prussian infantry had once again provided a brilliant spectacle, one that Europe would perhaps have marveled at on the parade ground," opined Goltz, "but here was without any real value and the doom of these brave troops."[78]

During the attack, Saxon squadrons advancing on Kötschau furiously assailed cuirassiers and dragoons of the French cavalry reserve and hurled them back to the refuge of Ney's corps. Napoleon however, sent reinforcements to retake Sperlingsberg. They enveloped the Prussian infantry and after a fierce exchange of musket fire forced it back. Borcke described the retreat: "Some officers managed to bring remnants of their troops to a halt for the time being, combating the spreading panic with words and by example. One detachment moved forward again and offered resistance against the cavalry. Together with fear, cowardice and dereliction of duty there were many lessons in valor from among the multitude, from those who could not bear the disgrace of running away. My eyes saw such men, brimming with rage and desperation, in one hand a rifle and the other a saber, who held up those who were fleeing until they themselves were overrun and cut down."[79]

Swept along with the maelstrom, Captain Borcke seized a standard from an ensign and together with other officers made a stand in front of Capellendorf. Supported by Saxon dragoons, they collected 400 to 500 stragglers and formed a combat group to block the road. French artillery opened fire and dispersed it. This compelled Borcke to take flight toward Weimar with the men. Rüchel, himself wounded, ordered the Borstell and Hallmann Grenadier Battalions to cover the retreat. Supported by cavalry and a twelve-pound battery, these formations occupied the heights west of Capellendorf and halted the French pursuit; precisely where Rüchel should have positioned his corps to rescue the army instead of attacking in the first place. The objective of the Hohenlohe's retreat was the Ilm River, a tributary of the Saale that joins it at Bad Kösen. Once on the opposite bank of the Ilm, it would be possible to march northeast to the main army at Auerstedt. Some of Zezschwitz's cavalry crossed at Denstedt. The remnants of Grawert's division, with General Johann von Zweiffel now in charge, together with Tauentzien's battalions negotiated the waterway at Ulrichshalben further northeast.

Most of the army continued on the road to Weimar. At Webicht, the patch of wood outside of the city and previous encampment of Rüchel's corps, General Karl von Wobeser established a collection point for the retreating soldiers. Hohenlohe, back with the aus dem Winkel Battalion and some Saxon horsemen, received news at Umpferstedt along the way that Rüchel is wounded. He left the column to find his friend, who was receiving first aid at Leutenthal. Before galloping away on his personal errand, Hohenlohe told Massenbach to ride ahead to Webicht and reform stragglers into combat formations. This was ill-advised; by reorganizing the troops on the *right* river bank, they had the steep Ilm valley at their backs. It would have been prudent to first cross the river at Weimar or at nearby Oberweimar. This would have placed the deep ravine, a natural barrier, between them and the French. Marwitz recalled, "The Treuenfels Battalion was positioned forward, the left wing in the woods and the front toward the enemy and Jena. The fusilier battalion guarded the right flank facing Oberweimar. Behind these as yet intact fighters we began to collect and bring order to all who were coming back and to reform the dispersed battalions. It all went well and no enemy showed himself who could have disrupted us."[80]

Up till this moment, organizing the retreat was going well. Some cannons and ammunition wagons arrived and officers grouped the mass of soldiers into ten infantry battalions. It was possible for the army to cross the Ilm bridges, proceed through Weimar and maintain an undisturbed, orderly withdrawal up river to rejoin the main army. Hohenlohe returned, but did not give the command to march. Instead, bread and brandy from military stores in Weimar were distributed. "It never occurred to anyone that this could be done just as well on the opposite side of town, where we would be shielded by the narrow defile," wrote Marwitz. "It was as though we imagined that a guardian angel is here, spreading her protective wings over us."[81] Hohenlohe calmly debated with Massenbach, initially the only man he would speak with,[82] and then a few other officers for more than an hour over what direction to continue retreating; Brunswick had never designated a location for the army to reassemble in case of defeat. The prince decided on Liebstedt, a small village a few miles north, as the objective. This was Massenbach's suggestion.

Around 5:00 p.m. the column began to move when the familiar clamor of musket and cannon fire shattered the tranquility. French cavalry arrived, including horse artillery that opened fire. The Prussian and Saxon infantry battalions lined up on the road in close formation were unable to deploy. Marwitz continued, "The prince had just ridden up to the furthermost Treuenfels Battalion and the fusiliers when they about faced and ran off. Not surprising that when fresh troops do this, those who have just come from battle are also seized by panic and fright. The entire body of at least ten battalions turned away, threw down their rifles and cartridge cases and stampeded downhill in wild disorder toward Weimar. They darted between retreating gun carriages and overturned cannons, ammunition wagons and baggage carts… On the bridge, at the gate and in the narrow streets of Weimar the last semblance of order dissolved. We wanted to try to halt this unhinged throng on the far side of town, but weapons had been discarded and the routed infantry ran mechanically along the large causeway leading to Erfurt."[83]

Borcke was also present at the spectacle: "The wave of stragglers hastening back drove all before it, all who did not want to be trampled by our own cavalry, guns or carts. A large number of wounded and exhausted troops who could no longer be swept along with the tide fell victim to the chaos. Those who sought refuge riding on gun carriages and wagons were pitched into the ditch along the side of the causeway when these went off the road in the surge. When the carriages overturned, they were crushed in the most gruesome manner. Blood marked every step; with every step the scene of misery intensified, the air filled with the clamor of the fleeing and the dying, with savage cries of terror from this tormented multitude."[84] The chaotic episode was not without examples of valor by Prussian officers and men. Major Adolf von Oppen wrested permission from a reluctant General Wobeser to counterattack with his riders. Oppen led a charge, cut down the French cavalry commander right in the front line and followed by his adjutant, a few officers and half a squadron of dragoons, hacked his way into the enemy mass. The French suffered the worst of the melee, which continued until both sides sounded recall.[85]

The Prussians gained some respite from Holtzendorff. After languishing in Apolda with his detachment throughout much of the battle, he sent his cavalry to guard the retreat. Hohenlohe opted not to continue due west to Erfurt. Fearing that the troops will be overtaken by French riders on the road, he resumed the march in a northwesterly direction instead. His tattered army reached the village of Vippach at ten o'clock at night. The men were granted but short respite. They set off again at midnight because of a false rumor that the enemy is at hand. At seven in the morning, they reached Tennstedt. After a one-and-a-half-hour pause they were on the road once more, destination Sondershausen. During the procession, many soldiers simply discarded their weapons and began the trek home as though the war is over. The French had almost completely suspended pursuit upon reaching the Ilm River. Thanks to typical neglect of reconnaissance, the Prussians at first had no notion of this.

When they realized that the French are off their backs, the troops organized a proper bivouac to regain composure. Marwitz recalled, "After they found quarters, most of the officers thought of nothing else but eating and relaxing, scarcely concerned about the common soldier. While he often had to spend the night outdoors, the officers were usually billeted in a house instead of staying by the campfire to set an example and speak encouragement to him, so that it would be easier and more comfortable for him to fulfill his duty. As a result, the ordinary man in many regiments grumbled and said aloud that the officers only care about themselves. The men may have often been wrong, since the officer in many cases possesses as little as the soldier. But ultimately the inveterate separation provides a catalyst to believe the worst. The soldier must know his commanding officer and trust in him like a father if he is to follow him and accept privations and difficulties without resentment."[86] Another problem of command had been a frivolous attitude toward the enemy. In the words of Borcke, "Generals and senior officers never described the French other than as ragtag rabble that can never under any circumstances stand up to troops led by our valiant king and our men of repute, and that they will run for their lives like at Rossbach."[87]

Various Saxon contingents were distributed among Hohenlohe's units. Their main force, General Zezschwitz's first division, spent the day on the right wing of the prince's army to protect its flank. Many troops had received no rations since October 09. Regarding the march to the front days before, Lieutenant-Colonel Metzsch reported, "The men were so fatigued from the previous day's exertions and because of the shortage of bread, scarcely half of them could be kept on their feet every time the column stopped." Metzsch stated that a normally seven-hour march the night of October 10/11 required 16 hours.[88] Another officer, Lieutenant Gottfried Leonhardi, added, "Straw, firewood, water, bread, we had absolutely none. But my men still didn't grumble."[89] The Saxon force consisted of the Niesemeuschel Division comprising the Burgsdorf and Nehrhof Brigades, with Boguslawski's Prussian fusilier battalion and the Marsars and Kronhelm *Jäger* Companies in support.

Zezschwitz sent a messenger to Hohenlohe before dawn to request orders. He defended the heavily-wooded ridge along the causeway leading to Weimar, the *Schnecke*, from the Schwabhäuser basin leading west by northwest to Kötschau. The Mühlthal ravine separated the division's area of operations from the plateau where Hohenlohe's other formations grappled with the French at Isserstädt and Vierzehnheiligen. Fighting on the plateau had raged for hours before Zezschwitz received instructions from the prince to hold his ground.[90] The Saxons faced not only Frenchmen but Germans as well; troops sent by the landgrave of Hesse-Darmstadt, the only *Rheinbund* state to aid Napoleon at Jena. The elevated position allowed Zezschwitz's men to monitor the movements of the *Grand Armée* as it deployed to attack. Three batteries assigned to the Burgsdorf Brigade together with riflemen bombarded Desjardin's division as it menaced Grawert's right flank. The guns also delayed the enemy's advance on Isserstädt. French cavalrymen attempted to overrun the Bonniot Foot Artillery's eight twelve-pound guns to neutralize the effective supporting fire, but infantry protecting it repelled three consecutive charges.

The right wing of Grawert's line was falling back when Heudelet's division moved against the *Schnecke* in three columns. One crossed the Isserstädt forest to strike the Nehrhof Brigade in its left flank. A battalion of the Bevilaqua Infantry Regiment plus the Niesemeuschel and Low Regiments, each consisting of two battalions, defended the flank. The other two French columns conducted a frontal assault from Flohberg and the Mühlthal. Under fire from Saxon heavy artillery, Tirailleurs nimbly descended the steep slope at Flohberg into the valley and scrambled up the *Schnecke* ridge. They took cover along its rim and in the undergrowth and unleashed a fusillade against the Saxons that wounded 60 to 70 men in a short time. Zezschwitz's troops withdrew to the next line of defense. They thereby exposed the rear of the two *Jäger* companies and Boguslawski's fusiliers. This compelled them to abandon the Schwabhäuser basin. The French occupied the position, but the *Jägers* massed along the high ground beyond and halted them with their accurate marksmanship.[91]

Staff officers realized that their position is untenable given the enemy's superior numbers. They recommended falling back to rejoin the main force. Their general took no heed of this sound advice. He felt it his duty instead to obey the prince's instructions to protect the army's right flank. Leidolph is among historians who pointed out that at this juncture, "There came no further orders from Hohenlohe because in the excitement of battle he had completely forgotten about the Saxons."[92] Zezschwitz's men fought steadily to stave off Heudelet's attack, even as the assaults against Vierzehnheiligen and Sperlingsberg on the central front collapsed and dissolved into routs.

Prussian generals had exercised bad judgment all day, and by stubbornly holding his position their Saxon colleague was right in step. In Höpfner's words, "From the moment the fog lifted, General Zezschwitz could clearly observe from his position the course of the battle and arrival of ever more reinforcements on the enemy side. He should have been aware from this that no adjutant of Prince Hohenlohe could have made it through to him. It appears that his attention was completely focused on the *Schnecke*."[93] Only when French cavalry reached Kötschau, a village situated behind his lines, did Zezschwitz order Nehrhof's brigade to retreat. Saxon adjutant Lieutenant Johann Erdtel received a belated message "from above" (probably from Grawert) that French cavalry is outflanking the *Schnecke*. Erdtel was told to find Zezschwitz with orders to retreat to Weimar. As he recalled, "although this mission was dangerous because of the proximity of the enemy, I had to try because everything depended on it."[94]

The Nehrhof Brigade formed a square with the battery in front. The Low Regiment was on the left flank and the Bevilaqua Battalion to the right. The Niesemeuschel Regiment took position in the rear. Masar *Jägers* followed to the left of the square along the *Schnecke* ditch with fusiliers and the Kronhelm Company acting as rearguard. Fighting in loose order, the riflemen kept the French at a respectable distance. The pursuit halted when the Burgsdorf Brigade appeared on the heights between Isserstädt and Kötschau. The Saxons opened their battle square and formed columns. They resumed the march toward Kötschau with the band playing. The failure of Rüchel's attack released more French formations to block Zezschwitz's withdrawal. Despite spirited resistance, the Burgsdorf Brigade was simply overwhelmed by enemy cavalry and compelled to surrender. General Burgsdorf was wounded and taken prisoner. The Bonniot, Haussmann and Ernst Batteries were captured as well.

The eyewitness account of artillery Lieutanant Leonhardi offers an impression of the tumult: "We received the order to retire. I hooked up the prolong ropes and brought the cannons onto the causeway to cover the retreat, hoping that the Low and Niesemeuschel Regiments will remain on the field to the left. But they too moved onto the road. At the same time some batteries drove right between my cannons and munition carts. Just after that French cavalry was fighting hand-to-hand against the Niesemeuschel and Low Regiments that were coming up behind me… The retiring column was bombarded with cannon fire. Cavalry came from Schwabhäuser and I was fired on from Kötschau and Hohlstädt. We were surrounded on all sides and in the present confusion as good as captured. Trapped in the middle of a number of wagons, my cannons became separated from one another and could no longer be deployed. All moved on as quickly as possible, but some of my crewmen were not fast enough and were captured. A few of them were wounded."[95]

Persuaded by his adjutant not to enter captivity with his men, a despondent Zezschwitz rallied. He gathered some 400 riders belonging to a mounted rifle regiment together with a squadron of Albrecht *Chevaux-legers* and led two charges against French dragoons and chasseurs blocking the retreat. The Saxons punched their way through to Hohlstedt. This allowed Zezschwitz to join his younger brother, also a general, whose horsemen had supported Rüchel's abortive advance shortly before. Two days earlier, Zezschwitz junior had been instructed to detail sentries to guard the base camp. Amid the sound of distant gunfire this officer—a general, no less—asked if the sentries also have to stand post at night.[96] Six squadrons of Bila and Gettkandt Hussars also fought their way out of encirclement and escaped to Weimar. No such good fortune accompanied the Nehrhof Brigade. It was assailed by Augereau's chasseurs during the march along the causeway. The Masar and Kronhelm *Jägers* inflicted heavy losses on the attackers, but together with the Saxons ultimately succumbed to the vastly superior force.

When likewise assaulted by French cavalry, Colonel Boguslawski's fusiliers attempted to form a square without success; they too fell victim to a horse charge. General Heinrich von Cerrini organized Saxon stragglers at Webicht into a combat group and helped cover the retreat of Hohenlohe's army. The Niesemeuschel Division lost 1,176 men killed, wounded and missing during the fighting on October 14.[97] Total Saxon losses at Schleiz, Saalfeld and Jena were officially listed as 23 officers and 603 rankers killed or missing and 199 officers and 7,110 men captured,[98] though statistics vary from source to source. The Saxons forfeited all but eleven of the 106 cannons they deployed. Many could not be rescued simply because the horses had been without sufficient fodder for 24 hours and were too weak to haul the guns away, as artillery Lieutenant Heinrich von Roth pointed out.[99]

Regarding the wounded, many subsequently died from their injuries. Some were billeted in Vierzehnheiligen. The townspeople returned home after the battle and aided the injured soldiers as best they could. Well over 100 perished before they could be transferred to the hospital at Jena. Before the battle, Hohenlohe had not established field dressing stations or a military hospital to care for his wounded soldiers.[100] Prussian casualty figures at Jena are acknowledged to be estimates. Höpfner and Klopfleisch fix them at 30 officers killed and 168 wounded, but neither offer a statistic for the number of rankers,[101] many of whom deserted. "Losses on the Prussian side cannot be established because of the continuous pursuit (by the French) and rapid dissolution of entire troop contingents," explained Lettow-Vorbeck.[102] Modern sources place the tally of Saxon and Prussian dead and wounded at Jena at around 10,000 men.[103]

As is often the case in battle, an army can lose more soldiers and equipment retreating than from fighting in the front line. A Saxon battalion commander, Major Heinrich von Klengel, reported, "Thanks to the grip of panic spreading everywhere and the disgraceful flight that resulted, artillery, ammunition, rifles and baggage were abandoned and left for the enemy along the causeway, not captured by him on the battlefield. This alone proves that a better organized retreat could have allowed the establishment of a formidable army in front of or behind Weimar."[104] Leidolph maintained, "Had Hohenlohe decided to retire in time, it would have been possible for him to arrange in a natural way to link up with the main army at Auerstedt. But there could be no thought of this after the army had been so utterly pulverized."[105]

Individual battles from Tauentzien at Vierzehnheiligen to Rüchel at Sperlingsberg were completely haphazard, as Goltz scorned: "First 8,000, then 5,000, then 25,000, then 12,000 to 15,000 men each fought a superficial, isolated engagement without any connection. Every one of them was accompanied by glorious but pointless deeds of daring."[106] Lettow-Vorbeck summarized, "Tauentzien's troops fight for three long hours without any support. Only after they are routed does Holtzendorff's operation make itself felt. To be sure, his attack coincides with the advance of Grawert's division, but when this division halts it becomes possible for Napoleon to deal with Holtzendorff first and then turn against the other foe. Only after this one is also driven to flight does Rüchel appear on the battlefield. Thanks to his senseless form of attack, he rushes headlong to the same fate. The entire time, the Saxon division is involved in minor skirmishes with elements of the VII French Corps without essential influence on the course of the battle… Truly, had the purpose been to intentionally ruin an army, it could not have been accomplished more skillfully."[107]

Chapter 7

Encore at Auerstedt

The Fate of the Innocent

When the Prussian and Saxon army crossed the Ilm River and continued on the road from Weimar toward Vippach castle, Hohenlohe was no longer fit to command. He was nearly captured in the skirmish with French cavalry at the bridge and there were but 60 horsemen left in his entourage. Just beyond Weimar he learned that Brunswick lost at Auerstedt and was wounded. The prince suffered a mental breakdown. "Decisively defeated for the first time, a half-bewildered Prince Hohenlohe let himself be borne along in flight by his retinue. His grief over the day's misfortunes so obsessed him that those attending him scarcely recognized this normally so energetic man," wrote Goltz.[1] Despite the magnitude of the disaster, thousands of troops assembled overnight a few miles north of Erfurt near Sömmerda. "An unheard-of despondency gripped the spirit of senior Prussian commanders," Lettow-Vorbeck stated.[2]

As for the Saxons, Zezschwitz led his surviving troops away in a wide arc, initially north to Sangerhausen. This was to avoid the chaos surrounding the scattered Prussian contingents. Some 1,800 infantry and 1.300 cavalry were all that remained of his command.[3] There were rumors that King Friedrich Wilhelm fixed Magdeburg as the destination for intact units and that the army is to regroup there. This did not sit well with the Saxons. They objected to marching further from their homeland. They anticipated being condemned to monotonous garrison duty guarding fortresses for the Prussians, whose prince had left them in the lurch at Jena while he withdrew with Grawert and Rüchel. Cut off from Dresden, their own capital, Zezschwitz's soldiers could not be made to march further and desertions mounted.

Napoleon capitalized on the resentment of the Saxons to divide his foes. The day after the battle of Jena, he met with captured Saxon officers. With the aid of a bad interpreter, he assured them that he has not come to conquer their country but to liberate it from Prussian yoke. Bonaparte pledged to release them as soon as they promise not to take up arms again and their duke agrees to withdraw his army from Friedrich Wilhelm's service. The common soldiers he freed without stipulation and issued them passes to return to their peacetime garrisons. The emperor instructed his envoy bound for Dresden to warn the duke that in case of noncompliance, "I will destroy the Saxon Dynasty down to its very name."[4]

The Saxon war counsel in Dresden voted on October 17 to request a cease-fire and dissolve the Prussian alliance.

Friedrich Wilhelm III accepted the resolution graciously. He told General Dyherrn in Magdeburg that his government must do what is best for its own land and people. After some hesitation, Hohenlohe discharged Saxon soldiers still in his army. Napoleon made their cavalry hand over its sabers, horses and field equipment to restock his own dragoons as a condition of surrender. The Saxons were out of the war. The emperor's magnanimity however, did not extend to the populations of Jena and Weimar. American historian Owen Connelly related how Napoleon boasted that his "only desire for Europe was to give the nationalities the benefits of the French Revolution."[5] Just how German civilians experienced the benefits of the Revolution tells a different story. Even as the last Prussians escaped west from Weimar on the afternoon of the 14th, French troops entered the city. Bonaparte authorized 36 hours of looting. This ultimately cost the townspeople over 3,000 head of cattle, 7,000 bushels of grain, practically all of their food and left them 1,400,000 *Reichstaler* (Reich's dollars) poorer.[6]

An eyewitness account reveals that the *Grande Armée*'s previous rampage in Jena was not an isolated occurrence: "Doors, windows and cupboards were broken into by these barbarous soldiers who robbed us of everything of value they found. On the street, they tore articles of clothing from men and abused the women. They saw the residents of Weimar sobbing and wringing their hands, but the French soldiers hauled away cattle and wares they had stolen. Wherever one looked, doors, shops and windows were smashed in. Many houses were emptied and desolate. The wild, savage shouts of the plunderers and the crash of doors and shops being broken into echoed continuously... Even the church's silver candelabra were stolen by the French."[7]

Johanna Schopenhauer described the invaders as follows: "Officers and cavalry abstained from this dreadful conduct and did what they could to protect and help us. But what could they manage against 50,000 unruly men who could do as they please because their supreme commander allows it! Many buildings were simply picked clean; first of course all of the shops: clothing, silver wares and money were taken, furniture, and what could not be transported was destroyed... Many people were driven from their homes at bayonet point... The officers were beside themselves over this but not permitted to stop it... The gulf between cavalry and infantry in the French army is enormous. The former bear all the attributes of a civilized nation right down to the rank-and-file hussar, the latter are a savage lot insensitive to everything."[8]

During the ordeal, German women demonstrated defiance and courage in the face of their tormentors. Weimar's most renowned citizen, Goethe, served wine to impatient Tirailleurs who had demanded entry into his house. He placated them as best he could and then returned to his bedchamber. Soon the intoxicated intruders clambered up the staircase, forced the door to his room and threatened the poet with their sabers. Goethe's girlfriend Christiane Vulpius

1813

R. Knötel

Flüchtende Landleute

The clash of armies forced villagers to flee with their belongings. They returned after the battle to find their homes often destroyed and livestock stolen, facing winter with neither shelter nor sustenance.

thrust herself between him and the French. She clamored loudly for help, pushed the surprised soldiers from the chamber and bolted the door. This likely rescued her man from death.[9]

Under less boisterous circumstances the Duchess of Weimar saved the city. She confronted Napoleon with grace and composure. Her husband was with the army and the servants had fled. Duchess Luise Augusta remained in the palace with her mother. Flames from nearby houses torched by marauding Frenchmen provided illumination through the windows. Napoleon had selected the edifice for his residence. "Who are you?", he brusquely demanded when the unassuming Luise Augusta appeared atop the staircase. "I am the Duchess of Weimar," she replied calmly. The emperor retorted, "Too bad for you. I'm going to destroy your husband."[10] He left her standing there as he returned to his room to dine. Unperturbed, the duchess sought an audience with the intruder. Acceding to her request, Napoleon assumed his customarily pretentious manner toward European nobles, trying to mimic their refinement and impress them with his importance at the same time.

True to his nickname among cultivated circles, the "crowned plebian,"

Napoleon made the duchess stand during the meeting. He demanded to know, "How could your husband be so crazy as to wage war against me?" In a controlled voice, she explained that the duke has been in the service of the king of Prussia for 30 years. How then, could he abandon his obligation as soon as a war started? Would this not be dishonorable? She asked how Napoleon himself would judge a relative who deserts him at the opening of a campaign. Mollified by the logic of her argument and dignity of her demeanor, the emperor relented and listened patiently to her account of Weimar's distress. He ordered measures implemented to protect the town and reassured Luise Augusta that no action will be taken against the duke. After the audience Napoleon told his aide-de-camp, General Jean Rapp, "There's a woman our 200 cannons couldn't frighten."[11]

Johanna Schopenhauer wrote her son Arthur, "The duchess demonstrated amazing courage and rescued us all. The emperor spoke with her for two hours, something no other duchess could have managed. She stayed here by herself while all those around her ran away. Had she left too, Weimar would no longer be standing."[12] During the time that Napoleon was in Weimar, Jena was again delivered to the caprice of the invaders. "The agitated soldiers, intoxicated by their victory, were in an even more wild and enraged state than yesterday."[13] French soldiers with axes entered the church and chopped the wooden pews loose to make room for the wounded. They hauled the pews into the square in front of the edifice to fuel a massive campfire. Within the church, there was no distinction made between Prussian and French wounded. Gabriel Henry, a French immigrant residing there, estimated the number of patients in Jena at 3,800.[14] Houses that had been emptied of furnishings also served to shelter them.

Looting and abuse of townspeople resumed after sunset. "Neither pleas nor tears helped; brute force everywhere. Once again, many sought to save themselves by flight."[15] Having reveled or robbed much of the night, the next day some of the French soldiers at least helped extinguish the flames that had been unintentionally ignited by their campfires. Returning to Jena that morning, Heinrich Luden offered this impression: "I scarcely recognized the town, and the people not at all… Here and there some were already out repairing damage… The persons I saw all appeared to belong to the lower classes. Their faces were long, the expressions despondent; no rosy cheeks, indeed not one bearing an ounce of color. They stared nervously straight ahead and nowhere was a joyful word heard, nowhere a trace of cheer. Even the children were reserved and glanced fearfully at individual Frenchmen as they passed."[16]

A delegation from the university visited Napoleon at the Jena palace to complain about the soldiers. Town elders also requested an audience. Bonaparte agreed to preserve Jena from further abuse. The French army departed the city on October 16. The provisional hospital remained in operation. Napoleon appointed the sympathetic Colonel Bouchard garrison commander. Imposing the death penalty for looting, Bouchard put an abrupt end to the wanton mistreatment of civilians. The people of Jena owed much of their salvation to Gabriel

Henry, the French royalist and pastor who taught at the university. Belonging to the delegation of professors, he had helped persuade Bonaparte to alleviate the population's distress. In 1813, during a political witch hunt after Germany's liberation, a junior clerk named August Kotzebue falsely accused Monsieur Henry of having led Soult's troops through the Rauthal on the night of October 13/14, 1806. As a result, Henry spent over a year in jail in the fortress of Silberberg. In 1815 he returned to Jena. It had been his home for many years, but he was forced to leave.[17] The real culprit, Wenigenjena's Pastor Putsche, remained unscathed. A fellow clergyman paid the price for his treachery.

Prelude to Battle

When he entered Weimar on October 15, Napoleon was unaware that Davout had beaten the Prussians at Auerstedt. The emperor presumed that he had defeated Brunswick's main force at Jena. Both he and his marshal had profited from the ill-advised campaign strategy of their adversary: Before his Russian ally was mobilized, Duke Karl Wilhelm had taken his army well beyond Berlin, generally anticipated to be Bonaparte's objective, and encamped west of the Saale River where he was easily bypassed by the French. He then improvised a hasty retreat to circumvent the *Grande Armée*. He hoped to consolidate the contingents he himself had dispersed and outrace the French to the Elbe where he should have positioned his troops in the first place. The fighting at Auerstedt began for the Prussians with poor leadership and ended with none at all. Clausewitz later ventured that it should have been impossible for them to lose the battle.[18] Their army consisted of five divisions and a light brigade, all told 49,800 soldiers, though some sources fix the number at 53,000. Davout's III Corps opposed it with 27,300 men grouped into three divisions and one cavalry brigade. Brunswick had 230 guns and 8,800 cavalrymen. Davout had 44 cannons and just 1,300 horsemen.[19]

One of the most brutal commanders of the age, the "iron marshal" Davout was a bold and gifted tactician. He received orders to follow the Ilm River to Apolda and surprise the enemy from behind. Davout wasted no time getting troops across the Saale. After occupying the stone bridge late on October 13 with two batteries of the 25th Infantry Regiment and 800 riflemen, he sent the balance of the regiment and a squadron of chasseurs over early the next morning. The entire operation hinged on beating the Prussians to the plateau beyond Kösen. The narrow road crossing the river valley climbed the Saale's steep western bank through defensible terrain; had Brunswick's soldiers arrived first, "the smallest infantry and artillery contingents would have made it impossible (for the French) to surmount the left rim of the valley… With possession of the pass, the battle of Auerstedt would never have been possible," Höpfner maintained.[20]

Davout personally led the first of his three divisions available, that of his friend Charles-Etienne Gudin, onto the plateau toward Hassenhausen. Reaching the village by 7:30 a.m., the marshal deployed most of Gudin's division to the right of the town and a single regiment to its left. He stationed a weak garrison inside Hassenhausen. He ordered adjutant Colonel Bourke to scout ahead with a detachment of chasseurs. The stage was set for the battle of Auerstedt. Like Jena, it would be fought on a wide plateau with a single village assuming pivotal significance. The road leading west from Kösen continues through Hassenhausen and Taugwitz, turns south at Poppel and proceeds in that direction through the villages of Gernstedt and Auerstedt. Several roads converge at Auerstedt because of its postal station. Poppel, Gernstedt and Rehhausen form a triangle between Auerstedt and Hassenhausen. The Saale and its tributary, the Ilm, are on the southwestern boundary of the 1806 combat zone from Kösen down to Auerstedt.

The Kösen pass became the "Landgrafenberg" of the battle of Auerstedt. It could have been the key defensive position for the Prussians. In French hands, it enabled the *Grande Armée*'s III Corps to deploy across the wide plateau beyond. Without control of Hassenhausen, Davout could not hold the position. The village therefore played the role that Vierzehnheiligen did at Jena. Davout went into action at Auerstedt with a third of his corps. He sent orders directing the rest of it to Kösen, but Louis Friant's division did not arrive before nine o'clock in the morning and that of Charles Morand at half-past ten.

While his army already marched north toward the Unstrut River, Friedrich Wilhelm left Weimar for Auerstedt, the new headquarters, at noon on October 13. Along the way he and his entourage encountered Queen Luise in her carriage. She had followed her regiment *Königin Dragoner* (Queen's Dragoons) into the field. The Duke of Brunswick urged her to turn around, telling her that a battle will take place the next day. The queen returned to Weimar. She narrowly avoided capture by a French patrol along the way. From there she penned a letter to her husband encouraging him to have more confidence in himself. Luise then resumed her odyssey to the Berlin suburb of Potsdam. Upon reaching his own destination, the king took up quarters at the Auerstedt postal station. Brunswick and the general staff resided in the castle of district commandant von Zedtwitz. A mid-size village of 435 inhabitants, Auerstedt was a prosperous community thanks to a strong agrarian economy and supplemental income from transients using the postal routes.

Inhabitants of Thuringia and the Saale River region expected the fighting to take place on the Elbe and closer to Berlin. When troops were billeted in the locality in September, this was an ominous sign to the contrary. A battalion of the Prussian Burg Regiment, over a thousand soldiers, camped in Auerstedt for thirteen days. The village became so crowded that postmaster Junge sheltered 120 men in his house and the innkeeper Weise found accommodations for another 96. "Yet even here the residents remained unperturbed," recalled the butcher Johann Krippendorf, "because during this time the Prussian military men conducted themselves well. During the quartering of troops there was not the slightest discord or quarrel between townspeople and the military. After this battalion moved out, Auerstedt was occupied by combat troops practically every day. On Sunday, October 12, a Prussian battery took up quarters here."[21]

When the Prussian and Saxon main army marched to the Unstrut, General Schmettau's third division led the way. Brunswick instructed him to occupy the Kösen pass on the 13th. Schmettau sent patrols no further than Gernstedt, even though occupation of the Kösen pass would have guaranteed the safe retreat of the army.[22] "Just like at Jena," wrote Höpfner, "the importance of the pass was completely overlooked by the Prussian side."[23] Delayed in setting off, the Prussian army plodded toward Auerstedt throughout the night of October 13/14. Staff officers had proposed marching the army north in separate columns utilizing three serviceable routes, but Brunswick rejected the idea. Funneling 50,000 troops onto a single road, "artillery and infantry advanced at a snail's pace."[24] General Leopold von Wartensleben's division did not arrive at Auerstedt until two o'clock in the morning of October 14. The men were hungry and exhausted after a nine-hour march. They bivouacked to the left of the village that cold, damp night and were compelled to rise and prepare for action just a few hours later.

Even though the king and Brunswick were also at Auerstedt, discipline lapsed and the famished soldiers began looting. Eyewitness Krippendorf described how "the army rested here without bread and fodder. Everything needed was taken from the village. In this way Auerstedt suffered like no other town. Many barns were completely emptied on this night. There was no bread, beer, or brandy left in the village. Practically all of the timber was hauled out, gates and barn doors burned for campfires. Some cows were led away and slaughtered along with many geese and hens. This night the district commandant alone lost 600 sheep."[25] Krippendorf added that at his own shop, the first soldiers asked politely for some meat from a cow that he had butchered two days before. Those who followed were unruly, forcing him into a corner while they helped themselves to the remaining flesh. An officer appeared and stopped them. The frustration of these troops can only be imagined, as they soldiered for leaders who failed to provide them with the most elemental necessities.

Reconnaissance was neglected, since "the cavalry carried out its scouting missions rather languidly," as Gustav Höcker observed.[26] A Prussian patrol spotted a French one northeast of Gernstedt. Auerstedt's magistrate dispatched a civilian rider to warn the army that Davout has already crossed the Kösen pass. The news was relayed to General Kalckreuth. He retorted, "You're mistaken, the French couldn't possibly be that far."[27] The general nevertheless sent a major to report the messenger's intelligence to the Duke of Brunswick. That evening the duke told Kalckreuth, "A few hundred riders may have crossed the Saale, but nothing significant."[28] On the night of October 13, a general staff conference took place in Auerstedt. Several senior officers including Blücher were absent. This would have negative consequences, since it further impeded coordinated operations.

During the session, Brunswick regurgitated his plan to cross the Unstrut at Freyburg and Laucha so that the troops can link up with the Duke of Württemberg's reserve army. He admonished the staff to keep a tight interval

Blücher was Prussia's premier field commander and an advocate of social reform. At a victory ball in 1813, he blocked an attempt to separate aristo-crats and burghers and insisted on a joint celebration, arguing, "In wartime, all classes risk their lives and give their possessions without distinction."

between formations on the march. The 81-year-old Möllendorff was in atten-dance. He does not seem to have understood the topic of discussion and vented opinions on the best way to attack the French.[29] At the time of the conference, General Blücher was with his troops on the road to Auerstedt. Lieutenant Job von Witzleben of the Wartensleben Regiment brought instructions from the king for Blücher to ride ahead and report to headquarters. Blücher therefore left his formation. It was supposed to be the advance guard of the army and consist-ed of the Blücher Hussar and Irwing Dragoon Regiments, General Friedrich von Oswald's fusilier brigade and the Weimar Sharpshooters Battalion. Blücher told Oswald to follow with the men as quickly as possible and galloped off.

The situation conference was over by the time Blücher reached Auerstedt. "The place was so crowded with artillery and baggage that not a single man on horseback could get through," he recalled.[30] The king had already retired to bed. Blücher spent the night in a barn. He received a visit from Lieutenant Ludwig Wilhelm Adolf von Lützow between two and three o'clock in the morning. The young officer together with a handful of Reitzenstein Cuirassiers were just back from scouting Hassenhausen. They had encountered a patrol of French riders there and in the ensuing saber duel killed all but one. Returning with some captured horses, Lützow related the experience to Blücher.

The general went to headquarters at dawn. The staff informed him that the king has already left on horseback. Blücher rode toward Hassenhausen and found Friedrich Wilhelm forward with Schmettau's division. According to an eyewitness, "The king greeted him joyfully and told him that several regiments of cavalry have crossed the ravine at Kösen and that he is to throw them back. He will receive more precise orders from the Duke of Brunswick. When Blücher reported to the commander in chief that hours may pass before his advance guard arrives, the duke told him to get cavalry wherever he can find it."[31] As for the king and the duke, they had already devoted a portion of the morning not to prepare for battle, but to discuss a letter from Napoleon that an envoy delivered to Hohenlohe's camp. Brunswick did not alter his previous night's orders for disposition of the troops.

Schmettau provided 600 mounted personnel, a horse battery and the second battalion of the Alvensleben Grenadier Regiment for the advance guard. The rest of the division was to follow 15 minutes behind with the cavalry in the rear. "The desire to meet the foe head-on and the hope of capturing or wiping out the enemy cavalry that had crossed the pass is probably the main reason that customary caution was dispensed with, scouting the enemy and the terrain were neglected and they did not wait for the fog to lift," Höpfner opined.[32] The Wartensleben and Oranien (Orange) Divisions were still on the road to Auerstedt along with the pack train and bridging equipment. The order to march came just before dawn. It found Schmettau occupied bringing the *Königin Dragoner* Regiment and horse artillery to the front of the column. The soldiers were entering terrain that had not been reconnoitered and with visibility reduced by fog to 50 paces. The only patrol sent out was conducted by Major Rauch. He led a squadron of Queen's Dragoons to check out a false rumor that French riders were on Schmettau's left flank. All he found was the Graumann Horse Battery that had become disoriented in the mist.

The fog caused Brunswick to halt the advance of Schmettau's infantry. He told his quartermaster Scharnhorst, "It's still a rather risky matter to move forward like this. We don't know what's ahead of us."[33] Brunswick had however, received intelligence about enemy strength the night before. Auerstedt's judge had assigned the butcher Krippendorf to report to Duke Karl Wilhelm as a guide. The duke's adjutant, Colonel Kleist, introduced Krippendorf in the manor house. Brunswick asked him about the Saale bridge at Kösen. Krippendorf replied, "At Kösen it should hold anything heavy, since yesterday evening I saw that the Kösen heights are already occupied by the French and a battery has gone across the Kösen bridge." His host replied, "The garrison won't be strong. When we move forward with as much as we have, they'll pull back. The whole army against us here is also not all that strong. It can't be more than 30,000 men. I know this for certain from a spy."[34] Despite Brunswick's numerical advantage, the French corps defended higher ground and French reinforcements could reach the combat zone more quickly because the Prussians were using a single road.[35]

Blücher Forward

General Blücher scrounged for units to drive the French cavalry from the Kösen pass as ordered. He was unaware that Gudin's infantry was also west of the pass deployed around Hassenhausen. Blücher sought to take command of the Heising and Bünting Cuirassiers attached to Schmettau. He refused to release his cavalry for the enterprise. Schmettau protested that both regiments are a necessary component of his division. Blücher reported to Brunswick and expressed his embarrassment over demanding troops from a general who is his senior. The duke disregared Schmettau's objections and gave the cuirassiers to Blücher. A hundred riders of the *Königin Dragoner* formed up under Major Forestier to lead the charge. The Schmude Squadron together with elements of the Malschitzky Infantry Regiment were detached to patrol the Ilm valley on the right wing. The Malsburg Squadron was to cover the left.

The first battalion of *Königin Dragoner* set off at 7:30 a.m. Less than half an hour later, they reached Poppel and clashed with some 400 chasseurs. This opened the battle of Auerstedt. The Prussians drove them away, then stormed slightly higher ground at Taugwitz. The Queen's Dragoons turned onto the causeway and rode east toward Kösen. The second battalion under Colonel Zieten together with the Graumann Horse Battery followed at a prescribed interval. Blücher's cavalry rode through Hassenhausen. The town was weakly defended by Tirailleurs. Just north of the village was Ranzen hill. The general fanned out his horsemen at the base of this gentle upward slope to press the flank attack. He forced another French cavalry unit from the high ground and it escaped in the fog.

Blücher then rode ahead, escorted by 20 riders, to determine the enemy's disposition. He assigned two squadrons of dragoons from the first battalion to remain in reserve at Poppel. Others were diverted for reconnaissance missions including two from the Bünting Cuirassiers. Their mission was to search the underbrush covering the elevation on the left flank. Two more squadrons scouted the Saale. Another remained on the causeway to link up with the right wing of the infantry. Two additional squadrons detached for flank security and three more remained at Hassenhausen. This left two understrength squadrons of dragoons and the Heising Cuirassiers, eight squadrons in all, to press on.[36] Blücher had begun the operation with 20 squadrons. The number diminished thanks to the Prussians' chronic dispersal of forces.

The dragoons crossed the ravine just east of Hassenhausen and came under case-shot fire from a battery that Davout placed on higher ground 600 to 700 paces beyond the village. The dragoons took refuge in the ravine to escape the sudden barrage. Despite the mist, muzzle flashes from the cannons illuminated riflemen of the 25th and 12th Line Regiments deployed in battle squares beside the guns. Blücher rode forward with a small escort, heedless of enemy cannon fire. He spotted on his right a column of French infantry about 50 paces ahead. Thanks to the haze, he had initially mistaken the column for a row of hedges. In his own words, "I sent my adjutant, Captain Count von Goltz, with a message to the duke that the enemy has formed up in battle order and consists not just of cavalry and that I have outflanked him. I asked to be sent more cavalry and especially more troops in support, so that I will be able to carry out a decisive blow. In the meantime, I pushed closer toward the right flank of the enemy.

"Count von Goltz didn't come back, so I sent Captain (Franz) von Blücher to the duke as well and told him to implore the duke to send me more troops as quickly as possible… My intention was to bypass the left of the enemy battery that was causing me so much trouble and capture it as soon as I receive reinforcements. This couldn't fail because the battery was no longer protected by cavalry. After that I planned to attack the enemy infantry in the rear and in the flank with the bulk of my cavalry. The operation could not go amiss. Captain von Blücher came back but brought no answer. He had asked the duke twice but could not get a decision from him. When he finally asked Colonel von Kleist, the duke's adjutant general, what he should tell me, Kleist referred him back to the duke. And so back he came to me without having obtained a definitive answer."[37]

Reinforcements arrived when Colonel Zieten galloped through Hassenhausen with three squadrons from the second battalion of *Königin Dragoner* and the Graumann Horse Battery. They advanced along the causeway to engage the French cannons bombarding the cavalry. Blücher considered their assistance useless. The Prussian guns deployed too close to Hassenhausen and in an exposed position. "I have subsequently learned," Blücher later testified to a board of inquiry, "Captain Graumann commanded the battery. This officer should tell who ordered this ill-advised maneuver; had he joined my cavalry, he would have been of great value and other troops would perhaps have followed his example. With the loss of this battery began the misfortune that never ceased to torment us throughout the rest of the day."[38]

Graumann's six cannons deployed for action despite the fog. While bombarding the enemy, Graumann received an order to withdraw. He judged it a mistake and hitched his field pieces back to the teams to move forward instead. French chasseurs and infantry suddenly emerged from the mist and fell upon the position. They captured most of the guns and forced their crews back. "Why the squadrons that were with them did not wrest the guns free has never been explained," wrote Goltz.[39] Wounded by a saber thrust in the clash, Graumann fell back toward Hassenhausen with his men and the dragoons. Friedrich Wilhelm witnessed the engagement and tried to regroup the cavalry and lead it forward again. His horse was shot from under him. Supported by the Meerkatz Horse Battery and three squadrons of Reitzenstein Cuirassiers assigned to protect it, Blücher arrayed the cavalry once more to outflank the enemy north of Hassenhausen. The battery commander positioned his guns atop a small hill a few hundred paces to the left of Hassenhausen. They bombarded the French artillery and battle squares, in so far as these could be discerned in the haze, as the signal to attack sounded once more. Davout's chasseurs skirmished with Prussian cuirassiers and then withdrew behind the squares.

Deploying three fresh foot regiments and ten cannons on an elevation, Davout personally conducted the defense. Thanks largely to his example, moving among the men shouting orders and encouragement, the French repulsed three assaults that Blücher led. During the final charge, the squadrons were almost on top of the enemy when those on the right rode directly into the fire of the Meerkatz Battery. Believing themselves assailed on all sides, the Prussians hesitated. General Reitzenstein had been wounded in close combat against the chasseurs. His riders, faced with a steady fusillade from the enemy, did not press the advance without him. The horn signal to advance was misunderstood by the Heising Cuirassiers in the din and they abruptly withdrew.[40] The cavalry also spotted the French 108th Infantry Regiment in the distance. It was moving up to reinforce the defense.

Around 8:30 a.m., the Prussians "broke into a wild and confused flight" toward the forest north of Spielberg.[41] Blücher was so angry over taking fire from the Meerkatz Horse Battery that he galloped to its position and swung his saber at some of the crewmen.[42] He turned to overtake his horsemen and stop the rout but his mount was hit. In his official report he recalled, "My horse was shot and I would have been captured, since I had no more cavalry with me. The trumpeter Feige saw me fall. He came over, jumped from his horse and helped me onto it. Thanks to this noble act of Feige's I escaped captivity. I thought that he would be recommended for a reward by his regiment. But since the trumpeter Feige assured me that this didn't happen, I consider it my duty to testify to his outstanding conduct."[43] Blücher rode to Spielberg and waved the standard before the fleeing horsemen. He was only able to halt a couple of squadrons. Blücher told his sovereign, "With my heart bleeding, I must report to your majesty that the cavalry has not done its duty."[44] Captain Meerkatz later apologized to Blücher. He explained that a general staff officer mistook the riders for fleeing French cavalrymen in the fog and ordered the battery to open fire.[45]

Slow and Unsteady

The Duke of Brunswick held back Schmettau's advance because of the fog. He had halted his division before Hassenhausen to await reinforcements and clearer weather. The elderly Möllendorff impetuously persuaded the king to overrule Brunswick. Friedrich Wilhelm thought that the troops face weak French elements and ordered the infantry to move forward again. Swayed by others as usual, Duke Karl Wilhelm gave in to Möllendorff's enthusiasm and abandoned his reluctance to attack without proper reconnaissance. Möllendorff arbitrarily directed Schmettau's infantry to follow right behind the advance guard. He considered the 15-minute interval ordered by Brunswick pointless.[46] The duke arranged Schmettau's division with the right wing leaning toward Taugwitz, the center fanning out northeast of Poppel and the left wing toward the Mertsch ravine. In front was the Alvensleben Regiment marching directly on Hassenhausen to dislodge Tirailleurs who had reoccupied the village.

Riding forward with his staff, Brunswick crossed to the right side of the causeway leading to Hassenhausen and surveyed the high ground south of the plateau. He could observe little of the enemy through the haze. Some dragoons informed him that the French are in position where Graumann's battery had been deployed. He exclaimed theatrically to his staff, "That's the key to victory. If we occupy these heights with our infantry and guns, victory will be ours."[47] He ordered Captain Boyen to ride back with orders for the Wartensleben Division to move in this direction once it reaches the battlefield. Even with both formations on hand however, the Prussians would be at a disadvantage. Davout had Friant's fresh division at his disposal by nine o'clock. After Blücher's abortive sallies much of the cavalry was scattered. Now Schmettau's regiments were advancing without the full weight of the cuirassiers and dragoons in support; once again, poor coordination of service arms.

The interval between Blücher's and Schmettau's movements granted enough respite for Gudin's troops to replenish ammunition and reform. The Orange Division was still stuck on the road to Auerstedt. Kalckreuth's reserve corps consisting of the Arnim Division and half of General Johann Ernst von Kunheim's sat on the Eckartsberg heights northwest of Auerstedt awaiting orders. The other half of the Kunheim Division and the Oswald Brigade marched to Sulza south of the combat zone. Gieren called this a "useless squandering of the fighting potential instead of concentrating at one place in full strength."[48] A better strategy would have been what Brunswick himself had intended, that being to seize the high ground south of Hassenhausen with Schmettau's formation and hold it until reinforcements become available. As at Jena, having an irresolute personality in charge led to the Prussian army's piecemeal commitment at Auerstedt. After appointing Brunswick commander in chief, the king undermined his authority by countermanding his orders.

Möllendorff, the catalyst behind Schmettau's ill-advised assault, was a *Schlachtenbummler* (camp follower); a marshal without troops, along for the ride more or less as a spectator. That the Duke of Brunswick would surrender the initiative against his better judgment under such circumstances attests to his weak character; a true leader would have asserted his command, even in defiance of the sovereign. Blücher's attacks were repulsed due to insufficient artillery and infantry support. He speculated that had he received from the duke "just three battalions of infantry and a horse battery with some more cavalry, I would have been in a position to completely roll up the right wing of Davout's corps, that I had by a stroke of luck outflanked in the fog."[49] The king had ordered Blücher forward at the onset of the engagement while the foot troops were still arraying for battle and therefore unready to go into action.

To be sure, instructions formulated by the duke on the evening of October 13 state, "The army will follow the road to Kösen with the Schmettau Division at its head. The cavalry and the division's advance guard will quickly hurl themselves against the enemy cavalry."[50] The order was composed without precise knowledge of the disposition of Davout's infantry and of course without awareness that the battlefield will be enveloped in morning mist. Once confronted with these variables, Brunswick did not revise his strategy. In Höpfner's analysis, it was a serious mistake that "part of the cavalry right at the beginning of the battle and in such fog, charged the completely unshaken enemy infantry instead of leaving the cavalry in battle order behind the (Prussian) infantry. It would then stand ready to cut down enemy Tirailleurs whenever they risked pushing forward against the Prussian infantry line... As soon as the advance guard cavalry came up against the mass of enemy infantry in the haze, it was unwise to allow General Blücher to attack this infantry... New infantry tactics render cavalry incapable of overpowering steadfast, resolute and poised infantry."[51]

When Schmettau's division resumed the advance on Friedrich Wilhelm's orders, the duke again voiced no objection. The Prussian infantry marched at a slow, measured pace to allow time for Wartensleben's troops to arrive.[52] The first line encountered Blücher's fleeing horsemen at Taugwitz. The broken terrain favored the defenders, though fluctuating fog caused problems for both sides. With visibility impaired, French chasseurs rode headlong into Schmettau's grenadiers, turned to flee and galloped between the first and second lines of Prussian infantry. The latter opened fire at once. Some rounds struck men of the Alvensleben Regiment ahead of it. Under fire from the grenadiers and pursued by Prussian cuirassiers, scarcely half the chasseurs escaped to Hassenhausen. Davout had just eleven battalions to defend the village. He had shifted Friant's 33rd and 48th Regiments, momentarily his only reserve, to support the 108th Regiment in a vain attempt to outflank the Prussian left wing at Spielberg. The 48th lost its direction in the fog and only returned to the battlefield at around three in the afternoon.

Schmettau's northernmost battalion went onto the defensive to hold off the French at Spielberg. "What was especially missed here was cavalry," wrote Goltz. "There was not one horseman available, while the (French) chasseur brigade controlled the right wing of the enemy position at Hassenhausen."[53] The Alvensleben Regiment suffered increasingly heavy casualties from French artillery further up the slope; without reinforcements the French defenses were too strong to breach. As stated, Boyen had returned to Auerstedt with new marching orders for Wartensleben's fatigued troops. He found the division in disarray. The rankers were "no longer in the hands of their officers, practically scattered all over the field."[54] The street through town was choked with army supply wagons and handcarts filled with baggage of the headquarters staff. There was a worse traffic jam at the bridge spanning the Emsbach creek. The overpass was structurally weakened by the passage of artillery and cavalry. This required the following mounted troops to ford the shallow but muddy waterway 50 paces upstream. The foot troops preferred not to follow this path, where the soft ground was soon churned by hooves and littered with horse dung. Thousands of infantrymen defiled across the narrow bridge instead. They shared it with the supply train. The army had bridge building equipment on hand but no one thought of constructing a second crossing.[55] As more units traversed the Emsbach, it became increasingly difficult for officers to reform them once they were across; particularly when consistently harassed by adjutants the duke kept sending back to urge haste. The horsemen of Blücher's belated advance guard finally arrived as well. They claimed rite of passage and galloped through the infantry column. It became divided and this compounded the confusion. Another problem was that the artillery and cavalry, initially marching at the rear of the army, was ordered to move to the front ahead of the infantry; all of this on a single road that the duke insisted be used.

It is difficult to imagine that anything further could be done to delay progress of the army, but Brunswick managed to do so. Having negotiated the Emsbach, the army could now proceed on high ground north by northeast via the road through Gernstedt to Poppel. At Poppel, the road turns east and continues directly to Hassenhausen. The duke sent orders to Wartensleben to leave the road at Gernstedt and march his division east into the marshy countryside bordered by the Liesbach creek. The decision was "incomprehensible, probably the result of insufficient knowledge of the terrain," suggested one historian.[56] It required great exertions of teams and gun crews to drive the heavy artillery carriages through the mud and undergrowth. All the while, the men were impatiently listening to the distant echo of battle as Blücher and Schmettau fought the French. A battery of twelve-pounders became stuck in the bog and its gunners were only able to bring the guns forward one at a time. The unit consequently could not provide concentrated fire support during the engagement.[57] After passing Gernstedt, Karl Alexander von Wedell's first brigade negotiated the Merrettig ravine south of Taugwitz. Johann von Renouard's brigade wheeled to the right before Gernstedt and crossed the natural obstacle immediately north of Rehhausen.

As Wartensleben's two brigades plodded on, Schmettau's grenadiers exchanged fire with Tirailleurs defending Hassenhausen. Duke Karl Wilhelm ordered Colonel Scharnhorst forward "to find out what the rifle fire is about."[58] He told him, "Ride to that place over there and see what's going on. I'm making you responsible for everything that happens there."[59] Scharnhorst dutifully rode off, never to see Brunswick again. The two had quarreled for days over strategic options. "The clear-thinking and aggressive general quartermaster was vastly superior to his vacillating commanding officer. More and more he had become aware of the 'miserable state of the army's leadership.' There had consequently been a serious rupture between the two men," wrote Schreckenbach.[60] The colonel interpreted the duke's order as a form of banishment; as a way for Brunswick to rid himself of a troublesome critic. Since Saalfeld, he had excluded Scharnhorst from military conferences. Karl Wilhelm dispensed with his chief of staff and top military advisor right in the middle of a pitched battle.

Schmettau's troops were already advancing when Scharnhorst arrived in the front line. Schmettau, who had been concealing a wound to remain with his troops, was hit a second time while reforming a wavering battalion. This injury warranted his evacuation. Despite the presence of two brigadier generals, Scharnhorst took command of the division and remained with it for the rest of the day. He quickly restored order to its ten battalions. Davout transferred Gudin's 21st Regiment to shore up the garrison holding Hassenhausen. He placed the 12th behind the 85th Line Regiment to the left of the village as Wartensleben's formation approached the French left flank. The shift substantially denuded the French front on the right. Scharnhorst left a single battalion facing Spielberg. He sent several requests to the duke for cavalry, but received only 120 Queen's Dragoons as reinforcement. Led by Colonel Seelhorst, they drove back Tirailleurs harassing the Prussian line, recovered the abandoned Meerkatz battery, captured some enemy guns "and demonstrated what a stalwart mass of riders, if properly committed, could have achieved."[61]

The French infantry formed squares behind Hassenhausen in anticipation of a renewed charge. Scharnhorst could do little with a single squadron of dragoons that had 50 men still fit for duty. "The Prussian army had 80 cavalry squadrons," summarized Schreckenbach, "but only a few were available where they were most needed."[62] Schmettau's infantry took the ground north of the village, but the division had suffered such heavy losses that Scharnhorst put off a direct assault. Wartensleben's regiments were at last on the scene. This enabled both divisions to advance together on Hassenhausen. The French on either side of the town gave ground. Led into the line by Boyen, the Kraft Grenadier Battalion drove the enemy before it until stopped by a barrage of case-shot and musketry. The formation fell back upon the Prince Louis Regiment of Wedell's brigade and attempted to reform for another assault. The devastating fusillade put a third of Kraft's grenadiers out of action.[63] The survivors remained steadfast and shot volley after volley into the ranks of the defenders.

The Irwing Dragoon Regiment, the first of Blücher's troops to reach the combat zone, deployed on the French left. Its aged commanding officer was reluctant to lead a charge as ordered. His subordinates asked an adjutant of the general staff who was present, Major Friedrich von Jagow, to assume command; a phenomenal development by Prussian military standards. The dragoons surged forward. They scattered Gudin's sorely tried 85th Line Regiment. In Jagow's own words, "Their whole left flank consisting of four battalions ran back to Hassenhausen, breaking their formation. Regiment Irwing cut into the fleeing and scattering enemy, some of whom threw away their muskets. The entire plain between Rehhausen and Hassenhausen was filled with enemy infantry and our dragoons… The consternation of the enemy was so great that during this fight many Frenchmen who had thrown down their arms ran toward our infantry to save themselves."[64] According to the French, the 85th Regiment took 600 casualties in this single skirmish.

While some soldiers of the 85th escaped to Hassenhausen, others began to form a battle square. Jagow regrouped his squadrons for a second charge to

disperse them before the square became fixed. His riders came to within 50 paces of the enemy when they were held up by a narrow depression in the terrain.
At this moment the French volley fired into their ranks. The horses were out of
breath, so Jagow withdrew to reform. A column of Karl von Beeren's cuirassiers
arrived. They did not launch an immediate assault which Jagow's dragoons could
have taken part in. The commanding officer first aligned his horsemen into
rows for a formal line attack. Survivors of the 85th Regiment exploited the delay
to firmly establish their square. As a result, they smoothly repulsed the charge.
Their case-shot and musket fire cost the Irwing Dragoons alone one officer
and 77 rankers killed, plus seven officers and 105 wounded from among the
initial complement of 480 men.[65] Even though squadrons of Bünting Cuirassiers
arrived, the Prussians did not launch another attack without artillery support.

With the exception of the Braun Grenadier Battalion and the Heuser twelve-
pound battery, all of Wartensleben's troops were on the firing line. Thanks to the
punishment the cavalry had inflicted on the 85th Line Regiment, Wartensleben's
right wing pushed forward south of Hassenhausen. The left wavered. It was held
in check by Tirailleurs deployed in the ravine in front of the village. Exposed
to case-shot bombardment and rifle fire, the Prussians involuntarily halted as
casualties mounted. They fired individually at their adversaries instead of by
volley; the clamor of battle drowned the officers' shouts to shoot on command.
Their fire was ineffective, since the French were behind garden walls and hedges
and in the ravine. In the diminishing fog, it became apparent to Brunswick and
his generals how little cavalry Davout had; it would therefore be impossible
for him to defend the plains west of Kösen if dislodged from the pivotal position at Hassenhausen. Schmettau's infantry was deadlocked before the town;
Scharnhorst brought men from the second echelon forward to replace losses in
the first line.

Exhorted by its officers, the Kleist Infantry Regiment rallied and drove the
Tirailleurs from the ravine before Hassenhausen. Brunswick rode along the
causeway almost to the front line. He wanted to find out why the regiment is not
advancing beyond the ravine and also order the Hanstein Grenadier Battalion
to take the town in a bayonet charge.[66] This was the critical juncture for Davout.
He later wrote that his left wing was on the point of collapse, had not General
Morand's 13th Regiment and two cannons arrived in the nick of time.[67] Too close
to the action, Brunswick did not share Davout's luck; the duke was struck by
a bullet that entered near his left ear and exited through the nose and left eye.
His guide Krippendorf described his impression: "The armies stood for a while
facing one another, without either gaining the advantage. Many men were falling
on both sides. Here the duke rode along the causeway at Taugwitz by the linden
trees along the rim. He made a brief stop about 100 paces across the meadow
and looked to the right over the Rehhausen heights. As he tarried there, his hat
spun on his head. I thought to myself, had only the hat been hit, it would have
flown into the air. Then the duke turned around and there was blood running

down his face. At the same time someone cried, 'The duke is wounded!' This happened at midday."[68]

Two officers escorted Brunswick from the battlefield on horseback. His head was swathed in a makeshift bandage. Krippendorf arranged for six-man relay teams of locals to carry the duke from the combat zone. He received medical care at the village of Colleda, where the wound was examined by a physician. "Everyone had thought that he had suffered injury to both eyes," Krippendorf continued, "but when the original bandage was removed and his face exposed, the duke said, 'children, my right eye is fine, I can see with it.' After receiving a fresh dressing, he asked to rest for a couple of hours."[69] The duke was too seriously injured to resume command. Some historians describe this as the turning point in the day's fortunes, Lettow-Vorbeck for example: "Given the superior numbers available on the Prussian side, the battle would probably have been won had the duke maintained its overall direction."[70]

Do the facts support this statement? By detaching Hohenlohe's army and Kalckreuth's reserve corps, Brunswick went into action at Auerstedt with half his force. After Scharnhorst had reorganized the army to give divisional commanders their own artillery and cavalry, the duke deployed these service branches independently in combat. Generals had to send messengers to request fire support or mounted troops when the infantry was held up. This was Brunswick's "overall direction" of operations. Further, he sent Scharnhorst, his chief advisor and most astute student of Napoleon's tactics, to the front line where Schmettau and two brigade commanders were already on hand to lead. The duke marginalized Blücher as well, as this capable, charismatic officer himself later complained: "For some years I had already been in command of larger army corps, while during the battle (Auerstedt) I was limited to leading a few cavalry squadrons. I left the battlefield feeling sad that I was unable to make an important contribution to the day's outcome."[71]

By designating a single causeway for the movement of the entire army, Duke Karl Wilhelm virtually guaranteed that individual formations would be committed piecemeal against Davout's corps as they arrive. Even before Brunswick was injured, the infantry, artillery and cavalry did not fight as a mutually supportive entity, but in separate skirmishes against an enemy who concentrated his available resources. What a disaster for Scharnhorst, wrote Lettow-Vorbeck: "The man who after the labor of decades had ultimately accomplished the organization of combined divisions at the last minute, found himself at the decisive moment without the very weapon with which he hoped to achieve victory."[72] Brunswick allowed the king and Möllendorff to make his decisions for him. There was practically no "overall direction" on the Prussian side *before* the duke was injured.

Gieren argued that "It's nothing but an empty phrase to suggest that the lack of leadership can be excused by the sudden loss of the supreme commander. It is simply a military matter of course that after losing the commander in chief the next ranking general takes his place on his own volition; and that the general staff chief, assuming he has not been deliberately excluded, must run things until then… The general staff chief belongs at the side of the supreme commander, to advise him and see to rapid and precise carrying out of his orders… It is rather remarkable for a commander in chief at the beginning of a battle, with the fate of the state and nation in the balance, to dispense with the counsel of a very capable general staff chief and scoot him off like some common ordnance officer."[73] Scharnhorst would have probably mastered the situation had he not been preoccupied with Schmettau's division on the left flank instead of at the duke's side.[74] No one even notified him that Brunswick was injured. In addition to losing Schmettau, General Wedell was seriously wounded and Wartensleben's horse was shot from under him, restricting his mobility.

In this leadership crisis, responsibility for either appointing a new supreme commander or personally taking charge fell to the king. Friedrich Wilhelm did not designate Kalckreuth to replace the injured Brunswick for hours. The king issued orders to individual formations in response to the ebb and flow of combat, but central direction of the battle ceased. Möllendorff, divisional commanders, adjutants and staff officers maneuvered troop contingents according to their limited personal perspective. Numerous Prussian horse squadrons remained hopelessly dispersed across the field instead of being deployed en masse. Between Rehhausen and the river stood four squadrons of the *Garde du corps*, elements of the Beeren, Heising, Bünting and Quitzow Cuirassiers and several squadrons of the Queen's Dragoons; "All without a common commander, some formed into lines, some into columns according to what each officer considered appropriate, in part hemmed in between Rehhausen and the Saale valley," as Höpfner described. "Majors Knesebeck, Rauch, Kamptz and other general staff officers were present and attempted to achieve a collective deployment, but without success."[75]

Rauch found an elderly cavalry general behind the lines and implored him to assemble and lead the mounted troops. Indignant that he had not been given a combat command at the beginning of the campaign, the general refused. He replied that since he wasn't needed then, he isn't needed now.[76] Brunswick and the king had imprudently denuded Schmettau's division of cavalry for Blücher's abortive sorties, then robbed Wartensleben of his squadrons and horse artillery for the same purpose. When his division went into action, Schmettau had just two squadrons of Quitzow Cuirassiers at his disposal. Wartensleben sent adjutants back begging for more cavalry. Now his division, together with Schmettau's, stood against Gudin and Friant before Hassenhausen. Scharnhorst later wrote, "The Prussian infantry not only resisted the French, but threw them back on both flanks. The only reason that the battle was not decided on the left wing is that there was no cavalry on hand. Ten squadrons would have probably sufficed to settle the battle then and there."[77]

The Prussians could do little against the French entrenched in Hassenhausen. They inflicted heavy losses on Davout's regiments defending the plain to left and

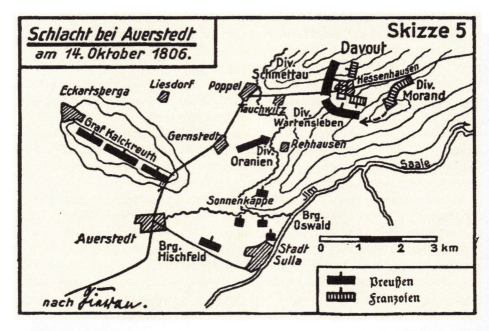

The map shows the advance of the Schmettau, Wartensleben and Prince Orange Divisions against Hassenhausen. The Oswald Brigade and Kalckreuth's reserve corps are deployed too far from the frontline to support Prussian troops on the plateau.

right of the village, but could not take the town. Earlier, Möllendorff had ordered the Prince Louis Regiment of Wartensleben's division forward, but its bayonet attack failed. The troops halted before Hassenhausen and exchanged fire with the Tirailleurs. "The number of wounded increased in unbelievable measure," observed Höpfner.[78] Healthy soldiers helped their injured comrades to the rear for first aid. This further depleted the number of combatants.[79] Schmettau's infantrymen fought their way into the village but the French forced them out again. Prince Wilhelm Friedrich of Orange's troops at last arrived but did not mass for a central thrust. The prince received orders to reinforce the left wing of the Prussian line. The directive was soon followed by a second, conflicting order to support *both* flanks.

Prince Wilhelm of Prussia's mounted carbines regiment and the Willmann Horse Battery moved south across Rehhausen beyond Wartensleben's right wing. The *Leib-Kürassier* (elite cuirassier) Regiment accidentally rode too far south to Sulza where it could not take part in the attack. The king ordered the Rheinbaben Grenadier Battalion of Prince Heinrich's brigade to Poppel. The brigade's two infantry regiments went to reinforce Schmettau. Orange's second infantry brigade, that of Colonel Johann von Lützow, supported Wartensleben at Rehhausen. This brigade was not at full strength, since its Knebel Grenadier Battalion was still west of Auerstedt; again, what Goltz called "the incurable dispersal of forces that we see on the Prussian side, like an epidemic disease."[80] As for Scharnhorst, the lack of cavalry caused by the duke transferring Schmettau's horsemen away prevented him from inflicting a decisive blow to Davout's troops defending Hassenhausen.

Davout's last division to arrive was that of Morand. It filled gaps in his line. Major Knesebeck asked Prince Wilhelm to lead 300 Blücher Hussars against these fresh troops, who themselves had no cavalry, before they discover the proximity of the Prussian squadrons. Morand's infantry quickly formed battle squares and repulsed two charges. Almost all of the Prussian officers taking part in the charge were either wounded by rifle and cannister fire or hurt in falls when their mounts were hit; half of the hussars' horses were killed or injured in the action.[81] The prince then galloped to the *Leib-Kürassier* Regiment to renew the assault. He had suffered a serious wound in the previous charge and toppled from his horse. Corporal Johann Pickert offered this perspective: "Many from our regiment were already wounded or killed. The horses of both men in front of me had their feet shot off. We attacked, during which our commander Prince Wilhelm was wounded. We took losses and had to fall back, then everyone began to withdraw. We tried to surge forward one more time, but were driven back in great disorder. Then there was no stopping, everyone retreated."[82]

Supported by fire from the Willmann Battery, the *Garde du corps, Königin Dragoner*, two squadrons of Beeren Cuirassiers and some surviving hussars attacked several more times. These charges were also unsuccessful. The cavalry retired from the field, making a bad impression on the infantry. The Wartensleben and Möllendorff Infantry Regiments, together with the twelve-pound Lehmann Foot Battery, drove the Tirailleurs from Rehhausen and continued to advance toward the high ground defended by Morand. The French held the ridge. They had concealed two batteries in shallow ravines and greeted the attackers with a hail of shot and shell. Count Vollrath zu Löwenstein-Wertheim, a captain in the Wartensleben Regiment, offered a firsthand account of the fighting beyond Rehhausen: "As luck would have it, my brother was ordered to the commanding officer and my ensign, Count von Keller, to the Prince of Orange. My rogue of a sergeant reported sick as soon as we broke camp at Weimar, so that I had no one obedient to support me… As soon as we were ordered to halt, I formed a flank with my first platoon to at least have some protection from cavalry until the Möllendorff Regiment moves up.

"Since the Möllendorff Regiment was further back and took up a position at an interval of several hundred paces behind us, I maintained my flank security. The Tirailleur and canister fire from the French side had just begun, while two columns of French infantry formed up against our right wing. Some rounds landed in the company. The first soldier who was hit was grazed by a case-shot round that ripped the cartridge-case harness across his chest. He cried, 'I'm wounded' and wanted to step out of the line. I saw that it is just a mild contusion and so said to him, he may wish to get back in the line since such a wound is nothing to be concerned about. A second canister round struck a ranker on his ankle and he wanted to leave the formation as well. Since the shot had fallen without injuring the ankle, I wouldn't let him step from the line either. I told him, 'pick up this round as a souvenir, you don't get a keepsake like this every day!'… I noticed that a few of my people who had been placed in the front rank by me wormed their way into the second row. I pressed them back into the first rank with the pommel of my sword. I threatened that I will cut them down if they try this again, since I will have to regard it as a sign of cowardice."[83]

The divisions of Schmettau and Wartensleben were so decimated that instead of taking the offensive, most of the Prince of Orange's men were deployed plugging gaps in the line. Four battalions of Prince Heinrich's brigade advanced on Hassenhausen but could not retake the town. Due to the heavy defensive fire, the Prince of Orange was unable to rouse the men to attempt another bayonet charge. Prince Heinrich's Rheinbaben Grenadiers initially drove Tirailleurs of the 108th Regiment and two squadrons of French chasseurs from nearby Poppel, but then came under intense fire once beyond the village. Without artillery, the Prussians retired to an isolated position just behind the town. They held out here against several charges by the chasseurs. The second battalion of the Puttkammer Infantry Regiment took part in the fighting and pushed the French back to Zäckwar.

To the south, Morand's division surged forward against the Prussian right flank. His 13th Regiment had been first to arrive and was deployed at Hassenhausen. Its infantry suffered frightful losses. Half of the men were wounded in a short time.[84] The four fresh regiments that followed drove back the depleted remnants of the Schmettau and Wartensleben Divisions. Orange's troops could not hold the French for more than an hour. Four squadrons of the *Leib-Kürassier* Regiment moved up to cover Orange's left flank. The squadrons received "all sorts of countermanding orders," were dispersed and "could not carry out their actual assignment."[85] Morand's eleven battalions spread across the terrain toward the Saale that Prussian cavalry had vacated. They overran a battery and circumvented the Prussian infantry's flanks. Lacking artillery or mounted support and low on ammunition, the Prussians began to buckle at around 2:30 in the afternoon. Among the troops reeling from the assault were those of Löwenstein-Wertheim. In his report, he described the effort to keep his company in line:

"Despite all of the exertions, as other officers of the battalion also found out, it was impossible to hold the men in formation during the retreat. Neither good treatment nor severity helped here. All that could be done was to try to keep the fire of my people from injuring their own companions by constantly directing them where they should shoot. I struck down the rifles of several men taking aim. They either carelessly risked harming their comrades with their fire or wanted to shoot into the air. I tried as much as possible to stop the retreat of my people or to make it more difficult for them to fall back. I even took a carbine and held it at one end while Corporal Bader gripped the other end to forcibly block the men who were retiring. Commander (Major Ludwig) von Ebra then said to me, 'We want to try once more to attack the French with bayonets. Try to get your people to advance again, Count Löwenstein!' I thereupon took a rifle from one of the dead and shouted to my men, 'Whoever is a brave lad, follow me, we want to attack the French with the bayonet!'

"Some of the people followed me, among them Corporal Rohde and Private Tasch, who conducted themselves valiantly. Beyond them only a few. Commander von Ebra thereupon told me, 'I can see there's nothing more that can be done, so just go with the others who are retiring.' So back we went toward Auerstedt. I felt totally drained of energy."[86] Fourteen Prussian infantry battalions had stood exposed and under fire before Hassenhausen for hours. Since the Prussian cavalry had been sporadically employed, not decisively influencing the engagement, the antagonists experienced almost equal parity. The divisions of Schmettau and Gudin were the first to square off. Then Friant joined the fray for Davout and Wartensleben for Brunswick. While the Prince of Orange's troops replaced casualties all along the line, those of Morand concentrated for a final thrust.

Despite the tactical superiority the French enjoyed, the Prussians had a trump card that could have restored their fortunes. This was the reserve corps of Count Kalckreuth. It included General Alexander von Arnim's division with ten infantry battalions and two batteries, 8,800 men in all, and Kunheim's eight battalions, three batteries and 15 squadrons comprising 7,400 men. General Oswald's light brigade consisting of four fusilier battalions, 25 cavalry squadrons and an artillery battery were still at Sulza with a brigade of Kunheim's division. Oswald's job was to guard the Ilm crossing and the area between the river and Emsen basin. In all, the Prussians had eight battalions covering the right flank. One fusilier battalion and a few cannons to occupy the crossing over the Emsbach and a squadron of hussars to patrol the Ilm bank would have sufficed.[87]

Beyond two battalions of the 48th Regiment on the right wing, Davout had no reserve left. Napoleon assigned Bernadotte to reinforce him with the I Corps. Bernadotte marched from Dornburg to Apolda instead and missed the battle. He later claimed to have contributed to the victory at Auerstedt by "threatening" the rear of the Prussian army.[88] Davout's III Corps was deployed along a battle line over a mile long and seriously depleted from attrition. Gudin's division lost 41 percent of its men in combat and those of Friant and Morand also took heavy losses.[89] The French were vulnerable to a determined counterattack from Kalckreuth's intact corps. In Lettow-Vorbeck's view, "Thanks to the valiant resistance of the frontline divisions, there was easily enough time to bring reinforcements up from among the numerous reserves… Placing the reserves too far back, on the wrong flank and not committing them caused the disaster at Auerstedt."[90] The only troops to move forward were ten squadrons of Irwing Dragoons and Blücher Hussars, and ten more of Beeren and *Garde du corps* Cuirassiers. The infantry of the reserve stood *Gewehr bei Fuss*—under arms awaiting orders—while their comrades bled.

In the verdict of Blücher, "Never has a reserve been less ambitious than ours was on the day of Auerstedt. Had it marched to the left during the engagement, it could have circumvented Davout's corps with minimal effort. This corps was not strong and already embroiled in a murderous battle. Davout would then have been lost beyond salvation."[91] Kalckreuth was offended that Brunswick assigned him to lead the reserve instead of a frontline formation. In his report to the general staff of February 1808, Kalckreuth wrote, "I did not have the determining influence of a commanding general over the reserve divisions under Lieutenant-Generals Count von Kunheim and Count von Arnim, since his highness the duke sent his orders directly to the lieutenant generals themselves." Kalckreuth expressed dissatisfaction with Scharnhorst as well: "The eleventh was a day of rest, just not for the queen's regiment. Without my knowledge, it was hauled from its quarters toward evening by two gentlemen from the general staff. On a very cold night, it had to march all over the place for nothing… At roll call, I expressed my complaint to the honorable General von Köckritz. He was of the opinion that I should make my disapproval known to the staff; I did so but got nowhere."[92]

As the army reserve, Kalckreuth's two divisions were at the rear of the column moving through Auerstedt on the night of October 13. He detached the second battalion of the Arnim Regiment to about face and escort the king's baggage to Frankenhausen.[93] Kalckreuth described how early on the 14th he was summoned to headquarters. The king told him where to march his corps that day, "based on the notion that none of the French army will be across the Saale… not one syllable about attacking."[94] He continued, "The fog was so heavy that that we had to search for the troops as though in the darkest night. The bridge in Auerstedt was jammed with artillery of the foremost division so there was little hope of getting my divisions Arnim and Kunheim over any time soon. My adjutant had to lead my cavalry, comprised now of the Beeren, Gensdarmes and *Garde du corps* Regiments, one at a time through a farmstead and across the water. All was still tranquil and I assembled 15 squadrons, one behind another, with the advance guard under Captain von Göckingk in front, at about where the head of von Wartensleben's infantry was; therefore, ahead of both my divisions. So, when the pamphlet writers preach in their ignorance that the reserve came too late, this criticism is not valid for the cavalry… If the infantry arrived late, which I had no control over, I have already demonstrated that the cause was the clogged Auerstedt bridge."[95]

Oswald's fusiliers belonged to Blücher's advance guard, but had been unable to work their way through the traffic jam to reach their general; they therefore fell in with the reserve. Kalckreuth sent his adjutant Major Ziethen to ask the king where his corps could be of the most use. While awaiting a response, he learned that the duke was wounded. Then, so Kalckreuth, "His majesty replied that for the moment he doesn't need me, so I should remain in readiness."[96] Kalckreuth established Arnim's infantry and artillery and Colonel August von Plötz's brigade, which was part of the Kunheim Division, on the Eckartsberg heights. As Goltz stated, "So this very formidable force which probably could have won the battle, was placed 4,000 paces behind the area where the action will be decided in a covering position that was of no use whatsoever. Unimaginative, ineffectual measures were the hallmark of this ominous day."[97] Kalckreuth kept his troops west of Gernstedt and observed the fighting from afar. With Kalckreuth present, Captain Carl von Tiedemann of the general staff urged General Arnim to lead his division forward to bypass the enemy's right flank. He was unwilling to take the step without orders.[98]

From the panorama of their elevated position, the Prussians observed an enemy column advancing on the reserve corps' left flank. A mounted patrol from the Gendarmes Regiment rode forward to confirm that the French are moving toward the village of Lisdorf in front of them. Major Jagow recommended detaching a portion of the reserve force to occupy Lisdorf, push from there to meet the threat head-on and then proceed toward Hassenhausen. Kalckreuth left the proposal unanswered and rode off to the right wing of his corps. On his own initiative, Jagow mustered the Zenge Regiment and marched it toward Lisdorf. No other units followed to support him. This forced Jagow to return with the troops to the rest of the corps. The French were free to continue their maneuver.

Regarding Tiedemann and Jagow, historian Gieren maintained that "these were totally correct proposals demonstrating decisive thinking that absolutely refute the false image of the alleged ineptness of the Prussian officer corps. This important fact should be vigorously emphasized to finally drive from the hearts of the German people the delusion that their officers were all incompetent."[99] Many company and battalion commanders were wounded two or three times but stayed with their troops.[100] As Scharnhorst summarized, "The lack of resolve of our leaders, the uncertainty of our generals and senior commanders and the poor organization of our army plunged us into a disaster."[101]

The Respectable Retreat

Having underestimated Davout's force when he ordered Blücher to gather the cavalry and push it back to Kösen early in the morning, Friedrich Wilhelm now presumed the French to be stronger than they actually were.[102] He was unwilling to renew the offensive with Kalckreuth's well-rested corps, fully equipped and practically the only foot soldiers in his army who had received a hot meal the night before. Instead, he randomly dispatched its individual units to danger spots to ensure an orderly general retreat. The Prussian right wing gave ground before the left side where Scharnhorst was in command. The King's Infantry Regiment was duly detached from the reserve and led by Plötz to Rehhausen. It occupied the western slope to hold the French and buy time for Wartensleben to fall back. The Rabiel Grenadier Battalion dug in at Gernstedt nearby.

The holding action was successful because Morand diverted three battalions and his artillery to assail Sonnendorf, an obscure hamlet just south of Rehhausen. Davout had observed the Oswald Fusiliers and General Karl von Hirschfeld's Grenadier Guards Regiment take control of the high ground northwest of the town. The marshal suspected that the Prussians plan to advance from there up the Ilm and Saale Rivers to cut his III Corps off from Kösen.[103] As French troops scaled Sonnenberg hill, their cannons bombarded the fusiliers above. After a furious firefight, Oswald's men withdrew to join the grenadiers further back. They suffered 53 casualties and 235 men captured, but had sufficiently delayed the enemy to facilitate Wartensleben's retreat. The French continued the advance but were soon stopped by stiffening resistance. The four guard battalions, supported by artillery and cavalry, checked their progress. They were reinforced by the Weimar Sharpshooters and Oswald Fusiliers, who proved a match for the Tirailleurs in marksmanship and tactics.

Prussian batteries fired more rapidly and with greater accuracy than their adversaries, whose wearied gunners had been in action all morning without respite.[104] The French bombardment was ineffective. Tirailleurs pressed toward the Emsbach basin. They became deadlocked in a prolonged firefight and could not force the defenders back. As Morand's infantry extended its line toward the Ilm to outflank the position, the fusiliers blocked the maneuver. The Prussians held the line until ordered to retreat. The withdrawal proceeded almost without disruption. Both French chasseurs and Tirailleurs were kept at a respectable distance by the fire of the *Jäger* and even forced back out of the woods near Sulza right after they had taken them. During the seesaw engagement, some Prussian troops became embroiled in a disadvantageous skirmish while others stood by and watched. Coordination of efforts and unity of command was lacking everywhere.

On the left wing of the Prussian line, elements of the reserve corps also came forward to facilitate the army's orderly withdrawal. Prince Heinrich's adjutant Captain Hacke regrouped a few battalions of the Schmettau Division and temporarily pushed the enemy back. With flanks exposed, the troops soon had to withdraw. They were pursued by Friant's column. Some of the men retired south to Rehhausen, the rest to Taugwitz and Poppel along the road to Auerstedt. A French brigade under General Georges Kister drove the Rheinbaben Grenadier Battalion from Poppel in heavy fighting. It then took control of the swampy terrain surrounding the town. The brigade therefore cut the line of retreat for Schmettau's division. Hacke rode to the king to request reinforcements. Friedrich Wilhelm released the Knebel and Gaudy Grenadier Battalions. He assigned Prince August, the brother of Prince Louis Ferdinand who had died at Saalfeld, to bring his battalion forward and assume command of the relief force.

As was the custom of the times, Prince August detached Gaudy's battalion to

Scharnhorst, who was wounded at Auerstedt and subsequently taken prisoner at Lübeck. Exasperated with generals who surrender to the French, Scharnhorst wrote his daughter, "It's a shame that one has to deal with so many miserable, stupid and cowardly people and undeservedly share their fate."

remain in reserve at Gernstedt. The Rheinbaben Grenadiers had retreated there, so he regrouped them to spearhead the attack. A bayonet charge forced Kister's Tirailleurs from Poppel. This succeeded in part due to a simultaneous thrust in the French rear by the last of Schmettau's infantry trying to avoid encirclement. With the escape route for the Schmettau Division reopened, Prince August returned with his men to join the reserve battalion in Gernstedt. His own battalion captured a French battery in position at Benndorf, a hamlet just north of Poppel, that had been bombarding the causeway. During the assault on Poppel, Prince Heinrich was injured in a fall when his horse was wounded. Scharnhorst, who had directed part of the operation to retake the town,[105] helped him onto his own mount. This enabled the prince to ride to safety. Himself wounded, the chief of staff picked up a rifle and continued fighting at Poppel on foot, "like an ordinary soldier" and was among the last to leave the field. Bleeding and overwrought, Scharnhorst made his way back to Eckartsberg. He did not put down the rifle until the king ordered him to Auerstedt to receive first aid.

When Scharnhorst saw his sovereign, historian Max Lehmann recorded, "The normally so composed and taciturn man was scarcely recognizable this day. He was seething with anger. When he encountered the king, he showered him with accusations and blamed him for losing the battle."[106] After receiving first aid, the colonel procured a horse and rode back to report for further duty. Two days later, he wrote his daughter Julie, "The battle has ended badly. On the left wing where I was, we were victorious; and may I say, due alone to skill and bravery. Only when the enemy occupied a village (Poppel) behind us that we had to move through did I decide to retreat. The enemy was thrown out of the village again by a single battalion… The entire front, twelve battalions across and with a depth of 300 paces, was saturated with dead bodies, cannons, horse cadavers, rifles and so forth, all tangled together. After the battle there were still 22 battalions that had seen minimal action. But we could not strike back again because the rest of the army had suffered too heavily. We have many that were left behind or were wounded."[107]

After the last of Schmettau's troops traversed Poppel, the French brigade of General Claude Petit moved through the town toward Eckartsberg. The Scholten Horse and Bychelberg Foot Batteries shelled his brigade as it debouched from Poppel. French artillery bombarded Scholten's position but his gunners remained steady and continued to direct their fire on Petit's infantry. Under pressure from Tirailleurs, the Zenge Regiment abandoned its position at the Pluck woods and retired in order toward Reisdorf. It was soon followed by the Schlieffen and Hülsen Grenadier Battalions as the French stormed Eckartsberg. The *Leib-Kürassier* Regiment was in a position to strike the exposed left flank of the Tirailleurs as they fanned out but let the opportunity slip away.

As the troops collected around Reisdorf, the Gensdarmes Regiment turned again to face the enemy. Captain Tiedemann of the general staff held off pursuing chasseurs with four cannons and a company of grenadiers. These units had not received an order to retreat even though the king had already decided to do so. He considered it better to march to Hohenlohe and Rüchel to combine forces and resume the fight another day. Friedrich Wilhelm still had no information about the fiasco at Jena. His plan was apparently based on the assumption that after defeating Prince Louis at Saalfeld on the 10th, Napoleon will remain passive. The Prussian monarch made up his mind that the battle of Auerstedt was lost before the reserve corps and guard battalions had fired a single round.[108] Blücher learned of this while the frontline troops were falling back and rode to Eckartsberg to protest. Disregarding the convention of the times, he voiced his displeasure with the king's decision to the sovereign himself. He insisted that there is still hope and recommended a massive counterattack.

In Blücher's recollection, "In the meantime French cavalry moved up and took position beneath the high ground where our reserve was. It was within range of our artillery, which didn't open fire. I therefore gave the order to fire and this was done with the best effect. The enemy cavalrymen bravely maintained their composure. They rode from one place to another, leaving men and horses lying dead wherever they had stood, but would not abandon the field. I then decided to attack with the Gendarmes Regiment. I addressed the staff officers and said that I hope they will prove worthy of their traditional glory and that I will lead them. Everyone showed great eagerness. It is shameful libel for some journalists to claim that the Gendarmes Regiment did not do its duty during the battle. But the regiment did not see action, just as our reserve failed to play its part. The moment I wanted to begin the attack… Lieutenant von Unruh brought me his majesty's order to undertake nothing more. The reserve also began to withdraw and I covered the retreat with the above-named regiment."[109]

It could be argued that responsibility for the ultimate defeat wrests more with Kalckreuth than with the king. Friedrich Wilhelm placed him in charge of the army at approximately 2:45 p.m.[110] Though wavering, Wartensleben's division had not yet begun the retreat to Rehhausen. As one historian summarized, "On the Prussian side still stood two divisions and a brigade of fresh troops! Had their commander in chief Kalckreuth led them into battle as a solid formation, nothing could have rescued Davout's burned out and decimated regiments."[111] Though moving forward, the French were seriously understrength; the badly mauled 12th and 21st Regiments under Petit had an aggregate of just 400 men under arms left.[112] Kalckreuth did not capitalize on this. He stated in his report to the general staff that he received no orders from the king to commit the reserve.[113] Lettow-Vorbeck justified the general's passivity with the explanation that "the radius of action for the commander of the reserve must be considerably limited, since the troops being held back remain the only means for the leadership to respond to fluctuations of combat to win the battle. Reserves are exclusively at the disposal of the designated commander in chief. Independent initiative on the part of the chief of the reserve is therefore unwarranted."[114]

This argument overlooks the fact that in midafternoon, Kalckreuth was appointed commander in chief of the entire army. He had the discretion to deploy the reserve as he saw fit. He summarized his tenure as supreme commander in these words: "The Wartensleben and Prince of Orange Divisions, one after the other just like the Schmettau Division, gradually came back from Hassenhausen after suffering the worst of the encounter. The enemy advanced against our position on the Eckartsberg mountain but was held at bay by fire from our batteries. The troops demonstrated the old Prussian steadfastness, but were not in the better position when Lieutenant von Schöning of the *Garde du corps* brought his majesty the king's order after four o'clock that I may want to retreat, as though I alone am in command. From then on there could be no more maneuver, but only determining how to rescue what could still be salvaged. I therefore marched off in sections. The men were so weak and exhausted that they could scarcely keep their platoons in formation."[115] Historian Gieren summarized developments more bluntly: "The reserve under Count Kalckreuth could easily have become the heroes of the day, but knew of nothing better to do than begin a retreat."[116]

Sharing Friedrich Wilhelm's pessimism, Kalckreuth saw no hope of reversing the day's fortunes. He could have covered the retreat more effectively had he at least committed the reserve as an intact fighting force. Lettow-Vorbeck analyzed its flawed deployment: "The best service that Count Kalckreuth could have done the army under these circumstances would have been to gain as much time as possible for a smooth withdrawal. The advance of Davout's battalions, worn down by continuous fighting, against an elevated position held by rested infantry and 58 guns was not easy. The French themselves could muster just 30 cannons. A resolute counterattack by the Prussians could have bought enough time for an orderly withdrawal; especially if their cavalry, which still enjoyed superior numbers, supported it with the horse artillery. This however, depended on keeping the forces together. The opposite took place. Of the four battalions of the Malschitzky Brigade, one was detailed to Eckartsberg and the projecting heights far away, the Zenge Regiment sent riflemen to the periphery of the Pluck woods and the main body to the slope opposite Lisdorf, while the Hülsen Grenadier Battalion stood behind it on the right.

"Further to the right, the other nine battalions formed a line with considerable distance between each formation. The force was therefore extended across an area spanning 3,000 meters. Had Count Kalckreuth concentrated the reserve in a position on both sides of the Gernstedt-Eckartsberg road where it turns south toward Auerstedt and echeloned reserve units behind the left wing to prevent being outflanked at Lisdorf, then I don't know how the retreat could have been seriously endangered by the enemy who was himself dispersed. The view from the elevated position at Eckartsberg is superb. It allows one to spot the enemy's movements well in advance."[117] After the campaign, Kalckreuth told the Prussian general staff, "Marshal Davout personally said to me that the retreat was conducted in such respectable order that he didn't risk pursuing such valiant men, but was content just with occupying the Eckartsberg."[118] Much of the French III Corps was in fact so fatigued and numerically weakened from constant fighting that it lacked the strength to take advantage of the circumstances.

The "respectable order" of the retreat under Kalckreuth's leadership was poorly coordinated. The Prussian right wing was too strong for the enemy to punch through its line yet was first to give ground. On the weaker left wing at Eckartsberg, the Malschitzky Brigade was more or less on its own to face the French outflanking maneuver. Its ordeal was described by Lieutenant Reichenbach of the Hülsen Grenadier Battalion: "In the battle of Auerstedt, the battalion was almost at the far end of the left wing. Like the whole reserve corps, we never conducted an actual attack, assuming I disregard the skirmish of the sentries who soon shot off their ammunition. The battalion had the twelve-pound battery von Bychelberg on the right wing and an enemy battery moved up opposite it. Some of its rounds landed in front of the battalion, some flew over it without injuring a single man. The firing had lasted perhaps an hour when Colonel (Ernst) von Magusch warned us that he is going to retire with his regiment. Major von Hülsen asked whether the colonel has orders to do so and was told no, but everyone on the right flank is doing so and he is going to follow.

"Scarcely had the colonel ridden away when French infantry advanced from the underbrush on our right flank and fired on us. The woods on our left flank were occupied by the French at the same time. The battalion was therefore under fire from three sides. As I remember, Major von Hülsen gave the order to withdraw. Then General (Johann) von Malschitzki commanded us to halt and open fire! These conflicting orders caused great confusion; no one knew where to aim. Instead of three rows of men there were four or more in many places, and we killed or wounded some of our own people in the crossfire."[119] Major Hülsen's battalion, which stood at the summit of Eckartsberg with the downward slope at its back, wavered when the Zenge Regiment on its left wing began to fall back. Three times during its withdrawal, Hülsen's troops turned and volley fired into the pursuing enemy.

The men broke formation as they rushed down the hill. The major and some officers including Reichenbach were able to bring order to the grenadiers upon reaching the plain below. Joining with neighboring units, they formed them into a huge battle square just beyond a village. At this moment, one of the king's adjutants galloped up with the order to retire![120] The soldiers resumed the march to Auerstedt. What rescued the army from total destruction was Bernadotte's passive conduct at Apolda. Davout's adjutant urged him to attack with his corps. Having lost much of their artillery and with columns widely scattered, the Prussians were vulnerable to an assault by cavalry. Bernadotte replied, "Go back to your marshal and tell him that I am here and he need not be afraid. Ride off!"[121] At 4:30 in the afternoon, he allowed retiring Prussian regiments to pass under his nose without taking action. After sunset, he dispatched mounted patrols across the Ilm River that bagged five cannons and a few hundred prisoners.

Chapter 8

The Command Crisis

The Aftermath

As the din of battle waned, Friedrich Wilhelm III led the Prussian cavalry through Auerstedt out of the combat zone. Artillery followed, then the infantry. Weimar *Jäger* formed the rearguard. When initially ordering the army to retire, the king did not fix a destination. The general staff could not formulate proper orders and sent Captain Tiedemann to ask. The monarch had no answer. Tiedemann suggested Artern. Friedrich Wilhelm surmised that the enemy will be there and decided on Weimar instead. French batteries shelled the road leading from Gernstedt to Auerstedt, the main line of retreat for the army. The Prussian right wing remained too strong for Morand's Tirailleurs to disrupt the withdrawal through Auerstedt. Many homeowners helped care for the wounded including those of the enemy. This did not prevent Davout from bombarding the town with heavy mortars as the Prussian infantry defiled through. Fires broke and compounded the chaos as troops made their way along a causeway choked with marching columns and horse-drawn carts. Kalckreuth could have steered the army off the road and around the town, but the idea did not occur to him during the "respectable order" of his retreat.[1]

Scharnhorst believed that Auerstedt could be defended to allow the troops a rest period. They could resume the withdrawal somewhat regenerated at dawn: "Since the enemy was not pressuring us," he opined, "we could have stayed here well into the night without having to fight a significant engagement."[2] A third of the infantry was still intact and fit for action, but units dissolved or became disoriented during the toilsome nocturnal trek. Most of the main army initially retired in good order. It ultimately lost cohesion as it intermingled with stragglers from Hohenlohe's force. The king and Kalckreuth changed the march route several times. Some troops headed for Erfurt and others for Magdeburg. The majority moved toward Sömmerda. The king was nearly snared by one of Bernadotte's patrols. Arriving in Sömmerda, he said to Blücher, "We should congratulate one another for getting through this."[3] It was then that Friedrich Wilhelm learned of the defeat at Jena.

Desertions from the main army assumed catastrophic proportions. Captain Löwenstein-Wertheim described his own experience: "Toward ten o'clock at night we stopped in a village, whose name I don't recall, to rest for a few hours.

Separated from their units during the fighting, Prussian stragglers together with soldiers who escaped French captivity collect on a road. Many sought to rejoin the main army, others simply went home.

After scarcely half an hour a rumor spread that the French are nearby, so we marched off again. We had to leave behind poor Colonel von Tholzig, commander of the Schimonsky Regiment, because he was seriously wounded. The retreat resumed nonetheless and at 3:00 a.m. we landed in a village where we called a halt. Four generals, Captain Count (Gustav von) Wartensleben, Lieutenant von Müffling from the Renouard Regiment and I all camped on straw in a room in a farmhouse. At five in the morning, General von Wartensleben wanted the column to move off again. Imagine how surprised we were to find that there was not a single soldier left in the village and we seven officers were all alone."[4]

According to Höpfner, one field marshal, three generals, seven staff officers and 36 other officers lost their lives in the battle or succumbed to their injuries. One marshal, five generals, 34 staff officers and 181 other officers were wounded. The army lost 57 cannons. This figure does not include those allotted to infantry battalions that normally have two guns each. Nearly half the infantrymen deployed at Hassenhausen were casualties.[5] The town erected a monument to commemorate the battle. It lists Prussian losses as 46 officers including four generals and five staff officers killed together with 7,000 rankers. A further 239 officers including six generals and 35 staff officers are recorded as wounded, as well as 1,300 from the ranks.[6] Davout placed his own losses at 258 officers and 6,794 men. This is over a fourth of his corps.[7] His claim of taking 115 cannons and inflicting 15,000 Prussian casualties is overstated.

One difficulty in determining the exact number of officers injured in combat at Jena and Auerstedt is that some who reported to dressing stations or field hospitals were still fit for duty. The journal *Deutsche Wehrzeitung* published an excerpt from the diary of an army *Feuerwerker* (fire worker) that provides evidence. A *Feuerwerker* was a corporal responsible for arranging manufacture and procurement of ammunition for his regiment. He was usually recruited from private industry and the position required an advanced education. "In Magdeburg," he wrote in November 1806, "officers of every age and rank were gathered who were not wounded (at Jena or Auerstedt). Instead, they were classified as 'detached' from their regiments as it was called. Some wore bandages on their uninjured heads and arms or limped even though their legs were fine. No one heard them ask, 'Why did Magdeburg surrender?' Instead, they asked, 'how much money do I get now?'"[8]

The statistics do not remotely convey an impression of the gruesome tragedy that took place that day in and around Hassenhausen. A student who surveyed the battlefield after the fighting graphically described the scene: "It was the most frightening moment that could be imagined, since thousands of fighting men were victims of this devastating battle. We found ourselves in the middle of the battlefield where row upon row of infantry and cavalrymen lay spread across the terrain. We heard nothing but moaning and cries of pain. Here lay one whose arm was shot away, there one stretched over him missing a leg. Some were trying to crawl forward among the dead scattered about the ground. Even though it was not possible for them to do so, others who were seriously wounded and could barely stand still tried to move away from the place. The confusion was great. Horses stampeded everywhere. Some of them dragged wounded riders who had a foot snagged in the stirrup."[9]

Residents of Hassenhausen, together with local farmers, helped bury bodies littering the battlefield. While clearing them away, a farmer discovered a French officer presumed dead to be still breathing. He loaded the man onto his wheelbarrow, rolled him to his house and placed him in a bed. The injured officer survived the night, so the farmer delivered him to the hospital at Naumburg in the morning. Before departing the farmhouse, the Frenchman gave his rescuer his watch and money purse for safe keeping. A few days later, the farmer visited the convalescing officer. His condition had greatly improved. The patient wished to give him a gift to express his gratitude for having saved his life and went into an adjoining room to fetch it. When he returned, he discovered that the farmer was gone. The officer found his watch and purse on the table beside his bed.[10]

Napoleon's accounts of the battle reflect his penchant for self-aggrandizement and mendacity. Despite the exertions of the past several days, he was at his desk by three o'clock in the morning on October 15 composing a letter to his wife about the "grand victory." He claimed among other things, "It was 150,000 men" that he had defeated at Jena.[11] This was before there was any information about events at Auerstedt. While his troops bivouacked on the night of October 14, the equally fatigued Davout burned the candle before retiring. He drafted a detailed after-action report for the emperor describing the battle. An adjutant delivered it to Napoleon the next morning. The more he read, the more annoyed Bonaparte became. With an insensitive reference to Davout's poor eyesight, he blustered, "Is your marshal seeing double?"[12] To be sure, there was no reason to doubt the veracity of Davout's account; since their first acquaintance at the military academy in Brienne, Napoleon had known him to be a correct officer.

Davout had defeated a Prussian army twice as large as his own without having expected serious opposition. This meant that Napoleon had achieved his "grand victory" over a rearguard that his army outnumbered two to one. To salvage the day's glory for himself, he arranged for the marshal's account to disappear into the Paris military archive. It would not be discovered for decades. Bonaparte published a lengthy bulletin describing the battle of *Jena*, offering Parisians the opportunity to read of his brilliant exploits. Davout received mention as having commanded the "right wing" of the French army "at Jena." The 213-page bulletin devoted just eight pages to Davout's contribution to victory.[13] Not wishing to offend this valuable asset too much, Bonaparte promised Davout that his corps will have the honor of being first to enter Berlin. When Davout's troops paraded into the capital on October 25, they found Lannes's cavalry already there. In any case, Napoleon's fondness for exaggerating his victories was nothing new; the English diplomat Lord Malmesbury had cited this about him as far back as 1796.[14]

Napoleon did not pursue the Prussian army after nightfall. He pulled his tired formations out of the line and left the task to Soult and Ney. Uncertainty over the disposition and remaining combat effectiveness of the enemy persuaded the emperor to break off the action. This granted the Prussians a respite. A few days later Napoleon bragged in his bulletin, "Of this handsome, splendid army there is nothing left but wreckage, a formless chaos that deserves to be called a hodgepodge rather than an army."[15] He still admonished his marshals to exercise caution. Despite the outcome at Jena and Auerstedt, the Prussians had substantial reserves yet to be committed. From this point on, Bonaparte's rapid conquest of Prussia was less the result of his strategic genius than of the chronically poor judgment, cowardice and treason of over-aged Prussian generals. The French warlord himself remarked in a letter on October 20, "The Prussian troops fought fairly well. Their generals understand nothing of war."[16]

Lettow-Vorbeck maintained that all of Napoleon's efforts after October 14 "would have yielded comparatively minimal results, had Prussian leadership at practically every level of command not piled more mistakes onto the ones they had already made."[17] Friedrich Wilhelm wanted to escape with as many men as possible either to Magdeburg or back across the Oder River and elude a confrontation with enemy forces. "A tolerable retreat over the Unstrut to resume the battle would have been possible, had a man been found who could take charge with a strong hand, galvanize the multitude and reanimate the waning courage of officers and men," concluded Goltz.[18] Beyond Prince August of Prussia, General Blücher and Yorck, scarcely any senior commanders had the heart to fight on. Little was done to coordinate the retreat or maintain communication among various contingents.

The Duke of Weimar, having absorbed Winning's detachment from Rüchel's corps, led his troops to Mühlhausen, hence away from the army. When he learned the king was in Sömmerda with 10,000 soldiers, it was too late to alter the route of his infantry. He still he made no attempt to contact his sovereign for further instructions.[19] Duke Eugen of Württemberg arrived at Halle with his reserve corps on the 14th. Despite audible cannon fire from the direction of Auerstedt, the duke sat out the battle because he had no orders to advance. Even after receiving news three days later of the disaster that befell the main army, the only step he took was to convene his generals for a war council. The French I Corps under Marshal Bernadotte advanced up the Saale River toward Halle. Württemberg and his staff presumed that the enemy will move against them, but lacked precise knowledge since no patrols were sent out.

Duke Eugen should have marched to the Elbe River to block the road to Berlin. He stayed in Halle and waited to be attacked. When Bernadotte arrived, General Johann von Hinrichs' brigade was in position on the left bank of the Saale. He did not withdraw across the river to rejoin Württemberg's main force because there were no orders to do so; the French overwhelmed and captured his brigade. The duke's troops fought a pitched, seesaw battle in the streets of Halle. As French reinforcements arrived, the corps was cut in two by Bernadotte and dispersed. The Tresckow Regiment had also been ordered to march to Halle. No messengers warned it of the proximity of Bernadotte. It blundered straight into the French and almost all personnel were taken prisoner. Some escaped by swimming the river. The company guarding the baggage train escorted it safely to Magdeburg. The fiasco cost the Prussian army 87 officers, eleven guns and some 5,000 men. The French had 800 casualties. In his report to the emperor, Bernadotte doubled the number of officers actually captured.[20] Had Friedrich Wilhelm sent new orders to Duke Eugen in a timely manner or had the latter withdrawn from Halle on his own, his corps would have been saved.

The king rode from Sömmerda to Sondershausen on the morning of October 16. Stragglers from various regiments collected at Sondershausen. The only intact units were two infantry battalions and six squadrons of cavalry. Friedrich Wilhelm left for Magdeburg with a mounted escort. His departure had a demoralizing influence on the soldiers; many gained the impression that their monarch considers further resistance pointless.[21] Many troops prioritized personal welfare over duty. Discipline often gave way to panic. Lieutenant Carl Rehfeld described the conduct of his retreating artillery battery in an official report: "At the approach of the French cavalry, Captain Haussmann had to abandon the rest of his battery. The disorder escalated to such a degree that no one was able to form a clear picture of what is going on. Men and horses, guns and wagons of all sorts pressed forward and drove over or under one another in a chaotic tumult.

"Whoever was lucky enough to escape capture came in danger of either being ridden down, knocked aside or impaled on tent stakes strapped to the pack horses. It took my full attention to get through this uninjured. After all of these immense exertions succeeded, when I came to the fork in the road, I lost sight of the captain as well as of the other officers."[22] By comparison, battery commander Haussmann reported on the bearing of the same men as they fought to repulse an assault by Lannes' corps at Jena on the 14th: "It is my duty and my honor to testify that all crews assigned to the battery fulfilled their duty in the strictest sense of the word. During the battle, they demonstrated the greatest determination as well as all other characteristics expected of valiant soldiers."[23] Such is the contrast in the actions of men when there is something to fight for and when they are abandoned by their king. During the retreat, Clausewitz witnessed how the personnel manning a battery of six to eight guns ran away upon the approach of two enemy chasseurs.[24]

A case could be made that the haphazard withdrawals cost the Prussian army more men and ordnance than it lost in combat. The absence of a functional supply system made the troops carry out forced marches without sufficient nourishment. No staff officer or quartermaster thought of organizing the distribution of grain from well-stocked depots the Prussian army maintained in the region.[25] The foodstuffs fell to the French instead. Prince August reported that even intact units retiring in order plunder villages and farms in search of food. A narrative describing Count Yorck's retreat illuminates the hardships the soldiers faced: "What the enemy did not do was accomplished by hunger, fatigue and distress. Dead and exhausted men were left lying on the road and the regimental rosters thinned out without the destructive effects of battle... At a very early hour the troops broke camp at their outlying quarters and formed into columns. Then followed needless waiting over apprehension about a potential enemy attack. Only after this concern had dispelled and a hearty march were the men dismissed and sent for a brief rest, usually to remote villages that are difficult to find.

"The pauses were occasionally interrupted by alarms from the sentries. Pointless nocturnal mustering and stand to under arms followed. Then the dead-tired troops would set off on the march again. I regarded these ceaseless withdrawals ever more angrily and could not understand why the army is being ruined in this way instead of risking a battle."[26] The count ultimately turned his *Jäger* companies to fight a rearguard action against Bernadotte's three pursuing divisions. The *Jäger* inflicted casualties and stalled the French advance. Having suffered minimal losses, Yorck's light infantry then retired in good order. They had fought an engagement that a British historian described as "certainly one of the best contested of the war."[27]

On October 16, Kalckreuth set off with over 10,000 men to follow the king.

Fighting in loose order, six companies of Yorck's *Feldjäger* and three fusilier battalions prove their worth after the defeat at Auerstedt. Here they cover the retreat of Blücher's corps at Altenzaun as it crosses the Elbe by ferry at Sandau.

After a few miles the Prussians encountered a weak French cavalry division comprised of some 2,000 riders blocking the way. The French occupied low ground and were at a disadvantage. "What a stroke of luck," recounted Goltz, "to offer the opportunity to achieve a brilliant success with a rapid thrust. News of the first Prussian victory would have breathed life back into the whole army."[28] Instead of attacking, Kalckreuth negotiated a truce and marched the army *around* the enemy division without bloodshed. The same afternoon, the Prussian column came face to face with more French cavalry, also inferior in number, at Greussen. The contingent was led by Soult. He parlayed with Kalckreuth. During negotiations the Prussian provided Soult with a detailed description of the condition of the army. He also revealed its destination as Magdeburg. He told Soult that the Duke of Weimar's corps, which Napoleon had no information about, is still far behind. He described what he knew about this force as well, for example that its men lack provisions. Soult prolonged this amicable dialog until enough of his troops arrived to attack the Prussian rearguard and inflicted heavy losses.[29]

From Erfurt to Berlin

The defeat of the Prussian and Saxon army on October 14 and its failure to regroup in no sense sealed the country's fate. Together with *Rheinbund* contingents, Napoleon had 192,000 men to control Prussia and northern Germany. The force was not large enough to fulfill its mission if confronted with determined resistance. German cities and many towns were surrounded by massive brick walls and moats. Fortifications included parapets for cannons. There were bombproof bunkers to store ammunition and other supplies. Population centers were a network of well-provisioned fortresses capable of defying siege for weeks, in some cases for months. The garrisons could deadlock French divisions that were investing them and harass their supply convoys. Reinforced by intact field units under Hohenlohe, Blücher, Kalckreuth and others, the bastions were in a position to delay the enemy until Friedrich Wilhelm could muster the reserve army in the east and join with the Russians to strike back.

Officers and men staffing fortress garrisons were committed to continue the war against France. They were nevertheless subordinate to generals who simply had no stomach for a fight. The dearth of leadership surpassed even what had been experienced at Jena and Auerstedt. It is arguably the worst example in the history of warfare of a nation giving up before it is beaten. The first fortress would fall just one day after the French victory at Jena. This was Erfurt, a bulwark guarding the route from Jena and Weimar to Sömmerda. Erfurt could block Napoleon's pursuit of the Prussians and buy time for them to conduct an orderly withdrawal: "Every day that the corps of Murat and Ney were tied down would benefit the retreat of the army."[30] Despite Erfurt's strategic location, Rüchel did not include the city in the regional defense plan until October 13.

Its two citadels, Petersberg and Cyriaksburg, were upgraded when mobilization was declared in August. Petersberg, an imposing brick structure, was stocked with provisions and gunpowder. It had 65 cannons, some transferred there from Magdeburg. Palisades were constructed and convicts employed to dig trenches. It would have taken Napoleon's forces weeks to capture the fort. They had no siege equipment on hand. In 1813/14, French General Alexandre Dalton would successfully defend Petersberg against the allies for six months.[31] Fort Cyriaksburg's defenses were also formidable. Rüchel reinforced the garrison's two battalions of infantry with the Kurfürst Regiment. Men of the Larisch Regiment arrived from Jena. They formed up on an elevation immediately north of Erfurt with the town and the Gera River at their back. Choosing unfavorable ground for a defensive position showed once again that Prussian leadership neglected elemental requirements of tactical deployment.

On the afternoon of October 15, Murat approached Erfurt with the vanguard of his cavalry. Larisch withdrew his infantry into Erfurt. The French horsemen drove his riders across the river. Thousands of soldiers, among them wounded, were in the city. There were many stragglers who refused to obey officers. Larisch's artillery and cavalry deployed north of the fortress. A few cannon salvoes from artillery brought forward by the Duke of Weimar halted Murat's squadrons. Weimar's corps tarried three miles west of town. It consisted of 12,000 infantry, 30 cavalry squadrons, 24 battalion cannons and three batteries. The duke lingered to support the anticipated retreat of the Larisch Regiment. He expected it to exit Erfurt and join his corps to march together toward Langensalza. Several messages he sent into the fortress urging the troops to evacuate produced no result. The duke could have committed his battalions to rescue them but took no action. Möllendorff was in Erfurt and ordered Larisch to leave with his command.

Larisch prepared to march his regiment out of Erfurt, but Prince Wilhelm of Orange stopped him at the gate. He expressed concern that the men will be overwhelmed by French cavalry and taken prisoner on the road. (Murat did not have enough horsemen to prevent the regiment's withdrawal.) The irony of this is that keeping it in Erfurt virtually assured its capture. Orange, among the generals taking refuge in the fortress, told Larisch to have his troops man the walls instead. Prussian generals in Erfurt assumed that the city is surrounded, which was not the case.[32] During midafternoon, Colonel Claude Préval approached to demand its surrender. This was a colossal bluff; Murat had no infantry and not a single cannon.[33] While Préval was negotiating with the Prussians, Murat wrote the emperor, "With cavalry alone I cannot take the city, which is occupied by four regiments of infantry and three regiments of cavalry. They will probably try to escape in the night. Since the (French) infantry has not come, I threatened the place that if it refuses to surrender, I will reduce it to ashes."[34] A couple of Murat's batteries eventually arrived and exchanged shots with cannons at Petersberg.

Préval offered Prussian officers safe passage home upon their word of honor not to resume active service until formally exchanged. This was customary for the times. The rankers were to surrender their weapons and become prisoners of war. The commandant of Petersberg, the 63-year-old pensioned Major von Prüschenk, initially refused. Entrusted with defense of the fortress by the king, he had authority over refugee generals in Erfurt. He nevertheless caved into pressure from the Prince of Orange to surrender that night. Orange drafted the article of capitulation personally. Not wishing to sign it himself, he made subordinate officers do so instead.[35] He wrote the king, citing "the huge supply of gunpowder that is not secure in bombproof shelters, the disorganized garrison, lack of food, exhaustion of the troops, preserving the city, care for the wounded and no prospect of being relieved" to justify surrender.[36] Friedrich Wilhelm relieved Prüschenk of his post and wrote on December 01 that regardless of whether Erfurt surrenders or not, the commandant has the duty to defend Petersberg and Cyriakburg with their generous stores of powder and ammunition.

Some troops escaped from Erfurt in the dark, but 14,000 Prussians, 8,000 of whom were sick or wounded, fell into French hands. The generals were content to surrender without a fight, but the ranks reacted differently. Some fired at Préval when he arrived to demand surrender. According to eyewitness Lützow,

"With steady gaze and bitter anger, the Prussian troops watched the victors file past them. The suppressed rage of many among them gave way to outbursts of cursing the French. Many more stood by silently as though in a daze, sunken in deep thought. Others were visibly tortured by anguish. One could read in their faces the desire to just get the torment over with quickly. A loud 'halt!' had scarcely sounded from the French ranks when a muffled command could be heard before the Prussian front. It was the faint order, 'rifles down!' This was the moment that everyone felt most keenly; all faces turned pale. This was when the limbs of the men who were no longer allowed to fight convulsively locked. With bitterness and painful restraint, the old warriors directed their gaze skyward to the eternal Friedrich. Thousands of tears of frustration rolled down their emaciated cheeks and greying beards."[37]

Two days before the fortress fell, Haugwitz wrote Berlin of the danger facing the capital. The letter arrived from Erfurt on the 16th. Count Friedrich Wilhelm von der Schulenberg, whom the king had left in charge, convened the city council. He ordered the treasury, state archives, the royal couple's children and naturally the palace's silver tableware evacuated to Stettin. The next day, cavalry Captain Dorville rode into Berlin with news of the debacle at Jena and Auerstedt. Queen Luise arrived the same evening and followed her children to Stettin. When news came of the defeat of Württemberg's corps at Halle, Schulenberg lost what composure he had left and wrote the king that the enemy is expected to arrive "daily, indeed hourly." He wrote ambiguously, "in any case we, as soldiers and Prussians, will resist and not accept capitulation, as long as an incalculable misfortune for the city is not to be feared as a result. We therefore consider it better to march out with the six battalions stationed here."[38]

The last obstacle barring the French march to Berlin was Spandau, a fortress dating to 1560. Nothing had been done before the war to repair the dilapidated fortifications. A hurried attempt to shore them up was made after Jena. An engineer officer who was partially blind and deaf was assigned to the project.[39] The citadel was nonetheless formidable. On October 23, the commandant, Major Benekendorff, reassured Friedrich Wilhelm that he will defend the fortress until there is nothing left but rubble.[40] He refused a surrender demand from General Henri-Gatien Bertrand, who did not consider it possible to take the fortress by assault. He wrote Napoleon, "If the place is not handed over after the cannons thunder, it can defy a siege. Beyond the ponds, it has its own trenches filled with water, which can clearly be seen from the rooftops of the houses."[41] Before the French began the bombardment, the commandant called a war council. The insufficient store of ammunition, inadequate size of the garrison and whatever other negative factors that came to mind were discussed, with the result that all present except for engineer Captain Meinert voted to capitulate.

After the French sent another surrender demand, Benekendorff agreed to negotiations. Lannes, who arrived with Suchet's division, crossed the drawbridge into Spandau to take part in the talks. During the meeting, French troops rushed across the lowered drawbridge and forced the defenders from the walls. Count Henckel von Donnersmarck recalled that Benekendorff "understood not a word of French. The French general who parlayed with him knew not a word of German. The conditions of surrender were quickly settled anyway, since the general had them written down and the commandant signed without even understanding what the terms are."[42] As at Erfurt, the compact concluded on October 25 allowed Prussian officers to leave with their weapons and personal property. The common soldiers went into captivity. Spandau was taken without a shot being fired. The road to Berlin was open.

Historian Fesser remarked that "in the following weeks, one could gain the impression that among the Prussian fortress commandants there was competition to see who could accomplish the most disgraceful surrender... But the civilian authorities of Prussia still managed to trump the generals."[43] In Berlin, the government laid the groundwork for collaboration with the French before they even reached the city. Schulenberg and a few state ministers left for Stettin on the 19th with five battalions of the city garrison, a battery, some cavalry depots and the staff of the Supreme War Council. Another battalion, the depots of the *Garde du Corps* and the *Jäger* regiments transferred to Küstrin. Schulenberg's son-in-law, Prince Hatzfeld, became civil governor of the capital. On October 21, Berlin newspapers published an edict from the mayor and city council ordering the population to "remain calm and offer no resistance upon the eventual entry of French troops." The edict threatened violators with incarceration or the death penalty.[44]

Two days later, Berliners received instructions to provide shelter to the invaders: "Everyone must prepare a decent room facing the street and it is assumed with confidence that every resident will accept the quartering of troops in a friendly and trustworthy manner."[45] The council demanded that Berlin merchants donate 100,000 thaler for "contributions" to the French garrison. On October 22, the council of Mittelmark, a district southwest of Berlin, issued an edict that surpassed in slavishness those of the capital's politicians. Upon the arrival of the enemy, "Commoners are instructed to provide foodstuffs and fodder and are admonished to take in the troops they are assigned to quarter in a friendly way. Not only are they to offer no resistance, but they must prove accommodating in all matters. They must not only attempt on their part to facilitate the march of these troops, but to ensure that they do not lack nourishment."[46] Hatzfeld blocked the evacuation of 10,000 brand-new rifles and 50 cannons stored in the *Berliner Zeughaus* (armory), which the army wanted to prevent falling into enemy hands. He explained that "the French, who are expected in a few days, may take offense."[47]

The prince also stopped Lieutenant Braun, sent by Hohenlohe to destroy four bridges linking Spandau to Oranienburg, a suburb north of Berlin, from carrying out the mission on the grounds that it will jeopardize food deliveries. General Pierre-Augustin Hulin, designated by Napoleon to take charge of the city, arrived on October 24. He entered an enemy capital with a population of

Johann Palm, a native of Württemberg, is led to the firing squad in Braunau following a sham sedition trial. He had distributed a tract criticizing Napoleon and refused to tell French authorities the name of the author. Suppressing free speech was one of Bonaparte's "blessings" for Europe.

157,000 with a 100-man escort. He demanded that all weapons in the city be turned in. The *Bürgergarde* (civic guard), two battalions each consisting of 800 volunteers formed to police the streets, Hatzfeld placed at Hulin's disposal. These were the only inhabitants permitted to bear arms. When the emperor entered Berlin on the afternoon of October 27, Hatzfeld arranged for the church bells to ring in celebration. Seven state ministers and various senior members of the civil service, dressed in gala uniform, stood dutifully at the Brandenburg Gate to welcome their new master. The magistrate presented Napoleon with the keys to the city. Public officials swore an oath of "eternal fealty" to him. Berliners who out of curiosity turned out to witness the degrading spectacle watched in silence. Few citizens observed the order to illuminate their windows that evening to pay homage to the conqueror.[48]

News coverage of these events bore little resemblance to the facts. The French seized city newspaper offices and manipulated the content of the press. The *Vossische Zeitung* and the *Spenersche Zeitung*, two leading publications, printed the utter falsehood that when Napoleon entered Berlin, "An immeasurable throng of people welcomed his majesty with the liveliest outcries of joy" and "everywhere the shout, 'long live the emperor!' rang out."[49] Only French soldiers and a few hirelings sprinkled among the onlookers cheered. Editors refusing to cover the news according to French dictates lost their livelihood. The periodical,

Berlin oder der preussische Hausfreund (Berlin or the Prussian Household Friend)
was suppressed in January 1807 for "outspoken" criticism of the occupation.[50]

Napoleon had already revealed his attitude toward the press in August. At
that time, the Augsburg bookseller Johann Palm was arrested by French authorities for distributing the anonymous pamphlet, *Deutschland in seiner tiefen
Erniedrigung* (*Germany in her Deep Humiliation*). The tract criticized Bonaparte
and the bad conduct of his troops garrisoning Bavaria. After a sham trial in
Braunau am Inn in which Palm was forbidden to testify in his own defense, a
French military court sentenced him to death on the emperor's personal order.
The draconian sentence was not without consequences, as a French historian maintained: "Although most German intellectuals had shown themselves
favorable to Napoleon when he was first consul, they now saw him as nothing
but a despot."[51] Bonaparte expressed the ambition to spread the "blessings of
the Revolution" to Europe, but these did not include the eleventh tenet of the
Declaration of the Rights of Man of 1789. It reads, "The free communication of
ideas and opinions is one of the most precious rights of man."

Despite the cooperation of public administration and orderly conduct of
Berlin's residents, Napoleon rubbed in his victory to mortify the population. In
the famous *Lustgarten* park, he staged a parade of the Imperial Guard carrying
captured standards of Prussian regiments. He forbade members of the Prussian
army to wear their uniform anywhere in the city. There was one exception,
however: On October 30, he required the Prussian Gendarmes Regiment to
march past him in review. Professor Lange's *Telegraph*, a newspaper in French
service, reminded readers that just before the war, brash young officers of this
regiment had sharpened their swords on the steps of the French embassy to
taunt the occupants. Bonaparte visited the tomb of Friedrich II in Potsdam.
He took the great king's sword, tunic and medals for "remembrance" and sent
them to Paris for public display.[52] He summoned Vivant Denon, curator of the
Louvre Museum (which was immodestly renamed the *Musée Napoléon* during
those times) to Berlin. The emperor instructed him to confiscate art treasures
from Prussian palaces for shipment to France. Among the objects taken was the
chariot atop the Brandenburg Gate.

Visiting the field at Rossbach, the emperor ordered the monument com-
memorating Friedrich the Great's victory over Soubise in 1757 dismantled
and shipped to Paris, "a notable instance of Napoleon's pettiness" as historian
Loraine Petre observed.[53] Returning from the Erfurt Congress in 1808, Bonaparte
invited German princes to a rabbit hunt he staged on the former battlefield at
Auerstedt.[54] Beyond taking Friedrich II's relics from Potsdam, none of his igno-
ble gestures aroused Prussian ire as much as the persistent libel of Queen Luise.
Like French and *Rheinbund* publications, Berlin newspapers were forced to
print Napoleon's frequent bulletins. These became the main outlet to express his
vehemence toward Prussia's dignified, patriotic queen. The *Telegraph* dutifully
mirrored his words. It speculated on "how well things would stand with the king

of Prussia, had he not lent his ear to the misleading words of a reckless princess."[55] When introduced to the queen, General Bertrand told her that the emperor is "enraged" over attacks on her published in the French press, even though Bertrand knew that Bonaparte was the architect of the libel.[56]

On November 09, Prussian civil servants swore an oath pledging "to devote all their energy to implementing arrangements in the service of the French army, and neither through exchange of letters nor any other type of connection to communicate with enemies of the same."[57] Since Friedrich Wilhelm III had not accepted the emperor's crippling peace terms, Prussia was still at war with France. Public officials were therefore forbidden to correspond with their sovereign. No state minister objected to this, nor even to Napoleon's practice of belittling the queen. The citizens of Berlin offered a gesture of defiance by illuminating their windows on the evening of Luise's birthday in March. As events during the months following Jena and Auerstedt would demonstrate, Prussian generals did more to dishonor their country than anything Napoleon could achieve in this sphere.

"I Saw No Heroes"

While Napoleon basked in Berlin's royal palace, intact formations of the Prussian army defeated on October 14 marched northeast toward the Elbe River to bypass Berlin. The harsh peace terms demanded by the emperor could not be enforced without destroying Prussia's defense capabilities. Bonaparte lacked adequate resources to trail retreating enemy columns and invest the fortresses simultaneously. As long as these bulwarks resisted, the invaders could not access their stores of food and fodder. Foraging and finding shelter in rural areas would become increasingly difficult for French troops with the approach of winter. Prussian divisions west of the Elbe and fortresses capable of provisioning them therefore depended on one another for survival. This mutual resistance could overstrain France's armies and compel the emperor to mollify his armistice proposals.

Hohenlohe led a large body of troops seeking to escape capture after Jena. In addition to fully equipped regiments, thousands of stragglers joined the column. Many had no rifles. Their presence obstructed an orderly withdrawal and undermined discipline. Early on October 18, the entire force broke camp at Stollberg and marched to Quedlinburg. Having prepared for its arrival, the townspeople generously nourished the infantry while the cavalry found sustenance in villages. At this juncture, Major Knesebeck presented his report on the state of the corps to the prince and his staff. He advised against continuing toward Magdeburg, where the Elbe was to be crossed. Harassment by pursuing French units would prevent reorganizing the troops and once past Magdeburg, the column would be cut off from a base of operations and more vulnerable to attack. Continuous forced marches would steadily weaken fighting potential as men desert or drop out from exhaustion. Knesebeck advocated moving in the opposite direction to a fortress *west* of Magdeburg.

Captain Marwitz summarized Knesebeck's plan: "He proposed tricking the enemy by sending all of the unarmed soldiers to Magdeburg. We would then elude the enemy by marching sideways with the armed and organized troops and head for Hameln… We could in this way link up with the unscathed corps of the Duke of Weimar, the large artillery train that General Blücher is bringing across the Harz and the troops of General Lecoq. From Hameln we could incite Hesse and Westphalia to revolt, fall upon Holland, and draw the enemy away from Berlin and from pursuing our dispersed army by threatening his own border… to buy the king time to form a new army and bring it forward to join the rest of us… Practically all who were present shared the opinion of Major Knesebeck and it appeared as though the prince will give his approval."[58] Hohenlohe turned to quartermaster Massenbach to solicit his opinion. Habitually inclined to take a solitary path, Massenbach replied, "Strategically speaking, I have to recognize the plan of Major Knesebeck as the more expedient, but under present circumstances I believe we still have to march to the Oder" (a river east of Berlin).[59]

Hohenlohe followed the bad advice of his quartermaster and the column resumed the trek to Magdeburg. The troops reached the fortress on October 20. Hohenlohe rode ahead to make arrangements and found the city in disarray. Little had been done to prepare a proper defense. Within the walls were thousands of stragglers. The garrison had nourished and rearmed them as best it could. None of them were reorganized into battalions. Marwitz wrote that when the column entered, "one could get neither bread, nor fodder, nor ammunition… Magdeburg was all in all a totally messed-up sieve that anyone who wants to can squeeze through."[60] On the heels of the Prussians, Murat sent his chief of staff Augustin Belliard to demand the city's surrender. The Prussians conducted the envoy to the prince without a blindfold. Belliard reported to Murat that Hohenlohe's army is inside the walls and disorganized.[61]

Preparations to continue the march made slow progress. The prince instructed adjutants to clear the details with Massenbach first. They experienced difficulties dealing with him, recalled Marwitz, since "most of them either had to wait for hours or were brusquely turned away. There were countless complaints… that contributed more than a little to augmenting the spirit of vacillation, willfulness and ill temper in the army… Major Fagel, adjutant of the Prince of Orange, was assigned by Prince Hohenlohe to ride up the Elbe and confiscate all of the wagons and transfer them to the right bank. He had to draw up notices for this on the night of October 20 /21 and bring them to Colonel Massenbach, but could get no further. The attendant said, 'the colonel has expressly forbidden being disturbed before six o'clock in the morning, when he is to be brought his coffee.' Major Fagel had to wait until then."[62]

Hohenlohe per the king's orders detached around 9,000 men to reinforce the garrison and set off with the rest the next morning. As Knesebeck had forewarned, the country east of Magdeburg left the column exposed to attack. The mountainous terrain along the Elbe gave way to an expansive plain marked by gently rolling hills, creeks and marshlands. There was little by way of sustenance: "The Prussians, driven from their magazines, had lost most of their provision trains, and were reduced to living as best they could on what the country would yield," noted Petre.[63] They reached Genthin on the evening of October 22 and Rathenow late the next day. The men faced the omnipresent threat of attack by Murat's cavalry; the marshal hoped to overtake the Prussians and block their retreat to Stettin. Hohenlohe sent three brigades of cavalry and some infantry to the left flank. This contingent marched parallel to the main column at a distance. The right flank was guarded by General Schimmelpfennig's 1,300-man brigade. Since pursuing French forces were on the right, the Prussian cavalry could not support Schimmelpfennig if he was attacked.

At Rathenow, Hohenlohe received intelligence that the enemy has crossed Treuenbrietzen southwest of Berlin marching toward the capital. The prince quickened the tempo to try and pass through Friesack and Fehrbellin to reach Neuruppin northwest of Berlin by October 24, Gransee due north of the city on the 25th and Templin the next day.[64] As chief of staff, Massenbach was involved in the planning. He exclaimed to the prince that the plan is a "strategic monstrosity."[65] He argued that it is too risky in such proximity to the enemy (exaggerating the immediate threat posed by Murat) to forge straight ahead with such a large column. The colonel proposed an indirect path to Neustadt first and then an arc to Neuruppin for the "security of the march."[66] Hohenlohe retorted that there is no danger of being attacked at Friesack because a Prussian corps holds the ground to the south. He had a report that Brandenburg is free of the enemy as well. Sensing the hostile mood of the officers, the undaunted Massenbach led the prince into a separate room and privately pressed him again. They emerged after 15 minutes. Hohenlohe announced that the army will proceed to Neustadt as the quartermaster recommends.

Knesebeck had ridden ahead to ask villagers along the originally designated route to bake bread to distribute to the troops when they arrive. "Colonel Massenbach," wrote Marwitz, "managed to arrange it so that after Rathenow we did not come to any of these places… We marched to Neustadt and therefore lost an entire day and missed the midday rations in Friesack and the evening rations in Fehrbellin that Major Knesebeck had arranged for us."[67] The troops belatedly reached Neuruppin on October 25. Here Massenbach handed the prince a memorandum recommending a halt of several days to rest, "discipline" and reform the army. Without advance preparations, there was little in the town for the soldiers to eat. The nights were cold, so the stopover would weaken rather than rejuvenate them. As for reforming the army, there had been an opportunity for Massenbach to do so at Magdeburg. He spent most of his time there in bed with a bandaged hand. A frustrated Marwitz later informed the general staff, "We soon learned that this man has little talent at drawing up plans and none at carrying them out. His plans were habitually unworkable."[68] Hohenlohe considered it dangerous to tarry at Neuruppin and pushed on.

The army broke camp and resumed the trek east toward Zehdenick. Captain Bülow recalled, "There were complaints from all sides about the excessive fatigue of the troops that has resulted from the forced marches."[69] The circuitous detours avenged themselves on the 26th when the French caught up. General Antoine Lasalle's light cavalry brigade mauled Schimmelpfennig's hussars at Zehdenick. Hohenlohe had positioned them too far out on the right for the army to support them. After a seesaw battle in which more units became involved on both sides, the Prussians were dispersed. They lost about 250 men. Survivors escaped to Stettin. Hohenlohe sat with the main army at Gransee just west of Zehdenick and awaited news of the outcome. The first reports of Schimmelpfennig's defeat were superficial. They proved sufficiently disquieting for Hohenlohe, as usual, to seek advice.

Massenbach persuaded the prince how dangerous it would be "to continue the march to Zehdenick and without cavalry head into a potential battle against this same service arm."[70] He proposed that the column turn left and proceed due north to Fürstenburg to elude the French and close with Prussian cavalry on the left flank; "therefore another useless and time-robbing detour," as Gieren observed.[71] Once at Fürstenburg, the army would turn right and march east to Prenzlau. Massenbach rode ahead to Fürstenburg to personally arrange for food distribution to the troops once they arrive. "Herr von Massenbach could not even expedite this simple task," Marwitz recalled. "He was so helpless on horseback it was ridiculous. He left with a small escort some time before the column set off, but soon the head of the column overtook him and marched past. It arrived in Fürstenburg before he did. The inhabitants of this small Mecklenburg town were well disposed toward us and gave the soldiers what they had to offer. But the number of soldiers was too great for the little village, so not everyone received something to eat."[72]

That evening Hohenlohe ordered Marwitz to ride five miles east to Boitzenburg, the next destination, to collect foodstuffs and fodder for the column. This village lacked resources to bake enough bread for the army. Marwitz therefore sent a rider to Templin to instruct the magistrate to gather the food already stocked by Knesebeck and transfer it to Boitzenburg. He sent word to Prenzlau, just a few miles east of Boitzenburg, to deliver brandy there as well. The time lost in rerouting the army to Fürstenburg enabled General Edouard Milhaud to reach Boitzenburg with his cavalry brigade ahead of Hohenlohe; the French helped themselves to the food and brandy that Count von Arnim had stockpiled per Marwitz's instructions. The Prussian advance guard reached the place at around two in the afternoon of October 27. They drove off Milhaud after a three-hour battle.

On the Prussian right, three regiments of French dragoons belonging to General Emmanuel Grouchy's division captured the Gensdarmes Cuirassier Regiment following a pitched battle. Its riders had blundered into a swamp after offering fierce resistance. Despite tactical victories, Murat lacked the infantry necessary to block the progress of the Prussian column toward Prenzlau. With Boitzenburg secure, Hohenlohe planned to allow the men to consume what was left of foodstuffs and brandy and resume the march at night. "Then for the fourth time," as Marwitz reported, "Colonel Massenbach stood up and again worked it so that the foodstuffs were left behind. With nothing to suggest that the danger was anything but imaginary, we marched in a wide arc to the great fatigue of the soldiers."[73]

"It was scarcely possible to get the exhausted column moving again," wrote Bülow, "and some soldiers would have preferred to die at that moment rather than endure more such exertions and privations."[74] Petre pointed out, "(Anton von) Bila and Quitzow, with three cavalry brigades and Hagen with his brigade of infantry, were approaching Pasewalk and must soon appear on Murat's flank as he pursued Hohenlohe toward Stettin. That Murat would have dared to follow, in the face of this threatening superior force, is more than doubtful."[75] Marwitz continued, "In the meantime, the three dragoon regiments of Prittwitz, Kraft and Wobeser arrived. This therefore removed any alleged reason not to advance on the straight road. God knows what Colonel Massenbach must have said to the prince to cause him to authorize another peripheral march... We encountered not the remotest sign of the enemy."[76] Massenbach led the advance guard together with the *Leib-Kürassiere* Regiment to Schönemark and arrived around midnight. The main army reached the town two hours later. The officers presumed that halting six miles west of Prenzlau was to reform the column.

When Hohenlohe entered Schönemark, he was surprised to find Massenbach still there with the advance guard. The colonel told him that the French may already be in Prenzlau, so patrols should be dispatched first.[77] In Marwitz's words, "Or one could also say, to give the enemy time to get there ahead of us!"[78] Hohenlohe convened a war council. The soldiers relaxed in Schönemark while the generals debated; rather senseless considering how close the army was to its objective. Lettow-Vorbeck maintained, "Prenzlau was the decisive point, this almost everyone instinctively felt. Once it was reached it would place the protective barrier of the Ucker River with its large lake between the army and the enemy. One could then hope to reach the defile at Löcknitz practically unmolested. This would be almost the same as getting to Stettin and tantamount to rescue of the army... Why then, did the prince not immediately send the *avant garde* and the *Leib-Kürassiere*, whose men had in the meantime recuperated, forward?"[79] The prince followed Massenbach's suggestion instead and ordered Captain von Alvensleben and Lieutenant Nostitz to reconnoiter Prenzlau with an escort of 50 riders.

Scarcely an hour later, at about half past six in the morning, Nostitz returned with the news that Prenzlau is free of the enemy and that the patrol has secured the town. During the mission Nostitz had spotted Lasalle's hussars. The French could not ascertain the strength of the Prussian patrol and kept their distance. Hohenlohe's column set off once more, but not before the prince had wasted three hours at Schönemark discussing options and waiting for Nostitz. Part of the honor regiment and the Dohna Grenadier Battalion preceded the main column to Prenzlau to prepare distribution of provisions stockpiled by Knesebeck. The King's Regiment, the Prinz August Grenadier Battalion and Quitzow Cuirassiers formed the rearguard. The Prittwitz, Kraft and Wobeser Regiments covered the right flank. The rest of the *Leib-Kürassiere* and Neander Horse Battery made up the vanguard. What Lasalle could not accomplish by force of arms, he now attempted to achieve through deception. Count Schwerin was crossing the Ucker with the cuirassiers when a French officer, Captain Hughes, rode up and presented himself as an envoy of Murat. Schwerin sent him to Hohenlohe.

The prince dismounted and conversed with Hughes. The Frenchman, "untrammeled by scruples on the subject of truth," asserted that Murat is already there with 30,000 men. Lannes, he continued, stands with 60,000 troops between Prenzlau and Stettin, therefore barring further progress of the Prussian army.[80] Peace negotiations were supposedly under way. Hughes urged Hohenlohe to surrender. Lieutenant Ernst von Tippelskirch had just returned from scouting the right side of the Ucker River and reported that there are no enemy troops ahead, but the prince believed Hughes instead. He told General Hirschfeld, "We're surrounded." He ordered Tippelskirch out once more, this time to reconnoiter the road all the way to Löcknitz. Instead of preparing the troops to repulse an attack by Murat, Hohenlohe spent his time parleying with Hughes. The Prussian infantry defiled along the Berliner dam into Prenzlau. Enemy cavalry appeared on the flank. General Kraft could not attack the French to keep them at safe distance without intersecting the column on the dam. Hohenlohe forbade him to do so.

"The circumstances were completely different now," Marwitz later stated in a deposition. "To enable the infantry to get into the town safely, the cavalry had to move against the enemy on the plain as far from here as possible and hold him there. There was no way it could do this unless it crossed the bridge. In this there was no time to lose since the infantry was already jammed up on the bridge. I tried to persuade General (August Friedrich von) Kraft to execute this maneuver but he didn't feel right doing it because the prince had forbidden it."[81] Marwitz rode to Hohenlohe and found him in a meadow with Massenbach and Hughes. Unable to draw the prince aside to explain the urgency of the situation, the impatient officer returned to Kraft and ordered the attack. He gave Kraft the impression that the prince has authorized the operation. Kraft welcomed the news and moved his cavalry forward. Hohenlohe told his quartermaster to accompany Hughes to the enemy camp to see if the Prussians are outnumbered as claimed. The French brought up six small cannons and bombarded the Prittwitz Regiment. Hohenlohe led a mounted battery into position to return fire. The battle for Prenzlau was on.

Murat committed one regiment after another to prevent the Prussians from escaping into Prenzlau. As Bülow described, "The fire became lively and the

Formed in a battle square, famished men of the Prince August Grenadier Battalion repel charges of three enemy cavalry regiments whose personnel outnumber them six to one. The Prussians surrendered when they could no longer maneuver in the mud.

mounted battery von Studnitz acquitted itself superbly. But since the enemy brought up more guns, our cavalry was so fiercely bombarded that it soon had nearly 200 dead and wounded and also lost many horses. This shook the confidence of the cavalry. Without heeding the example of the prince, it retired in disorder and pressed through wherever it could… The enemy cavalry followed, took the battery, cut off the rearguard and slashed its way into the King's Regiment."[82] In the confusion, many laid down their arms. "Only a boy of 14, the *Fahnenjunker* (officer candidate) von Petersdorff, defended himself in a manly way. When they tried to tear the flag from him, he would not let go until it was slashed to pieces and he himself repeatedly wounded."[83] The French forced Prince August with his battalion into a marsh where it had to surrender. The last Prussians to pass through the gate shut it behind them. This halted the pursuit. When the Dohna Grenadier Battalion continued east through Prenzlau, two companies assigned to guard the gate abandoned their post and followed.

On the east side of town, the column passed through the exit onto the road leading due north to Pasewalk instead of using the exit for the east road to

Stettin. Caught in the maelstrom of dragoons retreating through Prenzlau, Hohenlohe finally appeared on the causeway beyond as well. "He was in a visibly rattled state and busied himself with trivial details."[84] This Goltz regarded as "a sad token of the distress confounding a field marshal in a critical situation."[85] The Prussians, still some 10,000 strong, formed blocs on high ground east of town. The French broke down the gate and flooded into Prenzlau. Murat sent Belliard with another surrender demand which Hohenlohe refused. His troops were famished and fatigued but so were Murat's; they had ridden all night to reach Prenzlau. The road to Stettin was wide open for the Prussians. Except for a single battalion of Lannes's *Voltigeur* light infantry, all Murat had was cavalry. The French were greatly outnumbered.[86] The rest of Lannes's corps was in Templin. "The withdrawal was no longer possible without fighting," wrote Goltz. "But those being pursued had no reason to shun this fight, since it was just a matter of repulsing cavalry."[87]

While French envoys played for time until reinforcements reach Prenzlau, the Prussian infantry stood in squares and the cavalry deployed beside it. Hohelohe negotiated with Belliard right among the troops. This allowed the envoy to assess the strength of the Prussian corps. At this point Massenbach returned. Murat himself arrived with an escort to personally take part in the negotiations. Resplendent in plumes, furs, and gaudy uniform suiting his vanity, he endorsed on his "word of honor" the fantastic claims of Hughes and Belliard. Massenbach told Hohenlohe that the French outnumber the Prussians in cavalry, the column may be surrounded "at any moment," and he has already seen enemy infantry on the eastern bank of the Ucker River blocking the way. The quartermaster predicted, "We would have a continuous rearguard battle during the entire retreat. We can rely on our artillery alone. It is our best weapon and it alone can rescue us."[88]

As though on cue, Colonel Heinrich Christian von Hüser approached the prince without having been asked and reported that there are only five rounds left per cannon and most of the infantry is low on ammunition. "Then we're lost!" exclaimed Massenbach theatrically.[89] Marwitz saw Murat gesticulate in various directions to demonstrate the alleged proximity of the corps of Lannes, Bernadotte and Soult. All anyone could see were about 800 horsemen Murat had on hand. Hohenlohe placed his palm on Marwitz's shoulder and motioned toward a hillock obscuring the view ahead. He said, "My friend, over there is Marshal Soult."[90] Marwitz retorted, "Everything the French have told us is a lie!" To which the prince replied, "I still have to believe what my quartermaster general has seen for himself."[91] After the campaign, both Bülow and Marwitz contended that in the time Massenbach was away with Hughes, at most an hour, he could not have covered as much ground on horseback as he claimed to have done to observe so many French formations supposedly surrounding the army.[92]

While Hohenlohe parleyed with Murat and Belliard, there was a dull explosion in the distance. A French officer interjected that this is the signal that Soult has arrived. The reverberation was actually caused by a Prussian powder wagon that accidentally blew up. The patrol conducted by Captain Tippelskirch did not return in time to report to the prince that the pass at Löckenitz, which Massenbach believed to be held by the French, is occupied by Prussian troops. Massenbach later tried to justify persuading his prince of the hopelessness of their position: "Should I have been a part of thousands sacrificing their lives for nothing? Or should I rescue these people and accept the damning judgment of the multitude? I preferred to describe the truth as I saw it in that moment and then await the decision."[93]

In a study conducted decades later, Count Schlieffen regarded Massenbach as having merely "endorsed the monstrous lies" of the enemy.[94] As for Hohenlohe, historian Goltz scorned, "Some field marshal, who so slavishly depends on the opinion of a subordinate!"[95] Regarding Colonel Hüser, the commander of the 2nd Artillery Regiment, his report that there is almost no ammunition left for the guns is as false as Massenbach's claims. Captain Neander stated after the campaign that his battery alone had more than a thousand rounds on hand.[96] Most of the infantrymen had not fired their weapons so there was no shortage of ammunition for them either.

Before acceding to Murat's terms, Hohenlohe convened his officers to solicit opinions. By referring the question to a majority, he sought to escape responsibility for the decision that he as commander was obligated to make. Based on the testimony of Massenbach and Hüsen, he painted the situation in the blackest way imaginable. The assembly remained silent and one general shrugged his shoulders. Marwitz later described his impression: "The generals and staff officers were… so blinded by the false reports of Colonel Massenbach and Hüser that none of them raised a voice to propose what is most natural. They were so convinced by Colonel Massenbach's false information about our inability to offer resistance, our weakness and the lack of courage in our troops that not once did anyone risk an honorable response. Among the chiefs of cavalry regiments who were present were men who had demonstrated the greatest valor on the 14th and none of them had abandoned their regiments. The horses were not nearly so tired, since the French exchanged ours with their own afterward.

"Had just one man, even from among the lowest ranking officers, stepped forward at this moment and shown them the everlasting shame that they are resigning themselves to, how this timid act will infect the spirit of the nation and the army, and what our duty as soldiers in an unfavorable situation in the face of the enemy is… a sudden surge of spirit would have punched through the gloom and cast aside the disgrace!"[97] According to one account, "The soldiers often demonstrated more courage and readiness to fight than their commanders."[98] When officers announced to their troops that Hohenlohe will surrender, universal outbursts of disapproval and anger were the responses from men who wanted to go into action rather than into captivity. Marwitz concluded in his own testimony that every officer who demurred during Hohenlohe's pathetic speech deserves to be put to death including himself. Massenbach wrote after the battle, "I saw no heroes at Prenzlau!"[99] He later falsely blamed Scharnhorst for the surrender at Prenzlau; in an article published in 1807 in the Leipzig periodical *Lichtstrahlen* (*Beams of Light*), he purported that Scharnhorst persuaded Blücher not to join Hohenlohe, so the column was consequently too weak to resist. [100]

The Retreat to the Oder

Hohenlohe's actions at Prenzlau had worse consequences for Prussia than did the defeat of October 14th. Had the prince defended the fortress and amalgamated Blücher's cavalry, there would have been 24,000 soldiers to defy a siege. The corps of Murat and Lannes had long forced marches behind them and depended on overextended supply lines to replenish ammunition. Blücher was ready to march to Prenzlau, but upon learning of its capitulation moved his troops to Strelitz instead. The French sent 60,000 men in pursuit. Had Hohenlohe and the fortress commandants demonstrated the resolve of Blücher, Napoleon would have been unable to subdue them. No less detrimental was the *psychological* impact of Prenzlau: An intact corps comprising 10,000 men, 1,800 horses, 30 guns and as many regimental cannons had surrendered in open field to less than a thousand French horsemen. Napoleon's *Bulletin de l'armée* Number 22 inflated

Shadowed by French cavalry, Hohenlohe's army defiles through Prenzlau to form blocs on an elevated plateau. Murat assured Hohenlohe on his honor that the Prussians are surrounded. This was a lie. Historian Gieren commented, "A word of honor assumes that a man of honor is giving it," which Murat was not.

the number of prisoners taken to 16,000 infantry and six regiments of cavalry.[101] Lettow-Vorbeck concluded that "Prince Hohenlohe not only disgraced himself but the Prussian name and its valiant army."[102]

In his report of September 1808 to the board of inquiry, Marwitz described the influence of the affair on morale: "It gave the signal for all others to surrender. 'Prince Hohenlohe has capitulated with the entire army!' said every single commander, 'so what am I supposed to do?' They handed the fortresses over to the enemies of the Reich! 'The king no longer has an army, so what help to him are the fortresses?' asked every derelict commandant. All of this would still have been bearable, but it undermined and destroyed the spirit of the nation. It planted the seed of cowardice and self-interest in all hearts, spread notions of treason among the people and pervaded the viewpoint that kills everything great, noble and manly, namely that 'it was all for nothing!' A stalwart defense, even had it ended in the defenders being destroyed, would have filled every Prussian who heard about it with defiance and awe and inflamed his courage against the enemy! Just as a great deed tends to generate greater ones and turns men into heroes, committing a shameful or weak and powerless act is also not without consequences… An insidious poison is at work, degrading an entire generation!"[103]

Repercussions were not long in coming. Among the formations that escaped Magdeburg were two battalions of the Treuenfels Regiment led by Colonel Hagen. On October 22, a single battalion each from the from the Prince Ferdinand, Pirch and Zenge Regiments joined his command. He received orders from General Schwerin, whose column marched parallel to Hohenhohe's, to meet him at Hasselförde. Hagen's infantry brigade arrived on the morning of October 27 and found Schwerin's cavalry already there. Hagen continued separately to Fürstenwerder. He picked up what was left of the Bailliodz and Katte Regiments along the way and proceeded toward Pasewalk as ordered. Hearing cannon fire in the distance, the force reached the town the following afternoon. Receiving reports that the enemy is near, Hagen assembled his officers to propose resuming the trek that evening to head for Stettin via the pass at Löcknitz. As he testified later, "The commanders and all the other officers assured me that an immediate march is not possible because the soldier from lack of energy is dead tired and can't be roused from his quarters today."[104]

Colonel Poser followed Hagen to Pasewalk with his own brigade. It was comprised of the *Leib-Karabinier*, Heising, Holtzendorff, Bünting and Count Henkel Cavalry Regiments. Their combined force tallied 75 officers and 1,957 infantry and 110 officers and 2,086 cavalrymen with 2,087 horses. There were eight cannons and a powder wagon as well. Shortly after Hagen's brigade arrived in Pasewalk, Lieutenant Meyer of the *Leib-Kürassier* Regiment brought news of Hohenlohe's surrender. The colonel summoned his staff for a second conference. Poser told his officers the news about Hohenlohe, adding that "the pass at Löcknitz is occupied and we'll have to fight our way through."[105] Two subordinates he assigned to assess the condition of the troops, Major Thielau and

Lieutenant Moritz von Prittwitz, reported that the horses are too fatigued to expect a good outcome. Prittwitz added however, "It is dishonorable to surrender
without being attacked."[106] Colonel Winning solicited the opinion of a sergeant,
a corporal and two cavalrymen from each squadron. He related to them Poser's
assertion that Löcknitz is held by the enemy. The consensus, according to what
Poser claimed, was that "we can't punch through but have to capitulate."[107]

Officers of Poser's horse brigade participated in an evening conference with
Hagen's staff. Hagen told them that he does not have enough information to
decide whether or not to march on. Also present was Landgrave Podewills of
the Demmin district northwest of Pasewalk. He had just come from Stettin
and told the assembly that the road to the fortress is free of the enemy. Hagen
told Podewills that this contradicts other reports he has received and he cannot
accept it. The conference ended at nine in the evening. Poser arranged to surround the cavalry camp with *Vedetten-Chaine*, teams of three riders each posted
as sentries. He instructed the watch commander not to engage the enemy if
approached. Poser dispatched a messenger to recall the Bünting Regiment which
had resumed the march to Stettin. He ordered it to return to the cavalry bivouac.
He sent out Lieutenant Königsdorff with two horsemen with instructions to find
the French and inquire about surrender terms. After they came back without
having made contact, three more officers left with escorts toward morning on
the same mission.

Hagen and Poser did not assign scouts to reconnoiter the road to Löcknitz
to determine if it is blocked by the enemy, let alone order squadrons forward to
hold the pass open if not. Major von Stülpnagel of the Bailliotz Regiment later
testified that he reported to Hagen that riders coming from Löcknitz say it is
clear and recommend occupying it with an advance guard. Hagen did not act
on the suggestion. Patrols could have also explored alternate routes to Stettin or
simply asked townspeople in Pasewalk to guide them. The fact that Lieutenant
Königsdorff could not find the French suggests that the enemy was neither
nearby nor even knew that Prussians were in the area. The two commanding
officers disregarded the pleas of Major Neder of the Holtzendorff Regiment,
Major Lossau of the Henckel Regiment and Count Sparr of the *Leib-Karabiniers*
that their formations are capable of marching to Stettin and fit for combat.[108] It is
perhaps singular in military history that officers commanding an intact fighting
force that had eluded the enemy would seek him far and wide to surrender.

Toward dawn on the 29th, one of the lieutenants Poser had sent out located General Lasalle and told him that five Prussian cavalry regiments wish to
capitulate. Lasalle diverted a squadron from his march on Löcknitz to take the
five regiments into custody. "He considered a single squadron sufficient," concluded Lettow-Vorbeck. "What a low opinion he must have had of the Prussian
cavalry!"[109] Another envoy found a French officer named Brassart of the 13th
Chasseur Regiment. Brassart rode to Pasewalk and asked Hagen to assign an
officer to accompany him to General Milhaud. The designated officer, Lieutenant

Hohendorff, left with the chasseur carrying a surrender document that Poser and Hagen had drafted and *signed*, therefore before negotiations had even begun.[110] Milhaud sent back Lieutenant Guillaume to conclude the convention with Hagen and Poser. The Prussian soldiers had just broken camp and were prepared to push on to Stettin when informed that they will be marching into captivity instead.

Reviewing the vanquished formations, General Lasalle observed the remaining 400 men of the *Leib-Karabinier* Regiment weeping in frustration as they defiled past. He wrote in his official report, "This despair is the surest sign of the downfall of the Prussian monarchy. It is painted on the faces of all of the Prussian officers. They blame their generals and the leaders of the cabinet... Witnessing this reinforces our conviction that there are still many valiant officers and men in the regiments so shamefully handed over to the enemy by their commanders. These men would have preferred an honorable soldier's death to the disgrace of surrender."[111] Lasalle cautioned his officers to tread carefully when confiscating horses from the Prussian cavalrymen. He intuitively sensed that the submissiveness of these soldiers is not to be taken for granted.

Lasalle turned his attention to Stettin. The fortress was the mecca for Prussian units attempting to cross the Oder River. These included elements of three battalions of Württemberg and Köhler Hussars under Colonel Wiersbitzki who had eluded the enemy and reinforced Stettin. Other hussars holding Löcknitz, which contrary to Hagen's insistence was not in French hands, withdrew to Stettin upon Lasalle's approach. Despite Murat's assumption that the fortress is poorly provisioned and held by stragglers, it was a formidable obstacle. Characteristic of poor planning by Friedrich Wilhelm's staff, no effort to shore up its defenses was under way until October 20. Repairs concentrated on Fort Preussen (Prussia) and the main wall. The French had no siege guns. Without them they were powerless to breach the wall. The garrison comprised 100 officers and 5,184 men including a fortress artillery company. There were 187 modern cannons in Stettin. More than half of them were strategically placed to defend against the enemy's most likely avenues of approach and inflict serious casualties. Another 94 older guns complemented the ordnance.[112]

Stettin had 11,420 artillery rounds and a corresponding stockpile of gunpowder. Foodstuffs for the garrison included 8,000 bushels of rye, 700 of flour, 4,000 of hay and 1,200 oxen.[113] These supplies had been earmarked for Hohenlohe's army but never got past Stettin. The fortress was capable of sustaining an energetic defense. The Achilles heel was the governor, General Friedrich Gisbert von Romberg who was 81 years old. Shortly before the war began, he had written the king requesting that he send a replacement. Romberg explained that he regards the comparatively tranquil post "as a sort of subsistence," but feels himself "too old and infirm to preside over it at such a serious time."[114] Friedrich Wilhelm refused to relieve him of command. Except for Romberg, "the garrison was motivated and in the best of spirits."[115] What an affront to the Prussians, that

General Lasalle sent a single hussar officer with a bugler to the gates to demand the fortress surrender! Romberg sent him away with an evasive answer and alarmed the garrison.

The envoy employed the same lie that had deflated Hohenlohe. He told Romberg that the French army at hand is 100,000 men strong.[116] This was sufficient to rattle the old general. He never considered sending out a patrol to scout the enemy disposition. Before the French arrived in strength, the Württemberg Hussar Regiment appeared at the gate. It had separated from Hohenlohe's corps to avoid capture. An officer asked to lead the regiment through Stettin across the Oder. The governor refused to open the gate. He explained that since Hohenlohe has surrendered and the Württemberg Regiment is under his command, it must share the fate of the rest of the corps![117] Only after the hussars threatened to remain in front of the wall and be slaughtered rather than submit to the enemy did Romberg allow them through. Lasalle brought his brigade to within four miles of Stettin. An artillery officer at Fort Preussen opened fire on the French advance guard, a regiment of light cavalry, that ventured too close to the wall and drove it off. Romberg ordered him arrested for firing without permission.[118]

Lasalle dispatched a second envoy at 4:00 p.m. and the governor agreed to hand over the fortress. He summoned General Bonaventura von Rauch, General Gottfried von Knobelsdorff, the engineer Major Harenberg and a few other officers to discuss what terms to request. The envoy presented Lasalle's demands and left the fortress the next morning. The men of the garrison had no idea of what their commanders were up to. Those on the walls shot at enemy cavalrymen who occasionally ventured too close until Romberg ordered them to hold their fire. During negotiations a Prussian cavalry officer rode up to the gate. He requested that Romberg allow General Bila's eighteen-and-a-half squadrons of cavalry that has eluded French pursuit to pass through Stettin and escape across the Oder. The governor denied the request with the explanation that surrender negotiations are under way. General Bila led his men several miles north along the river bank seeking a ford. Unable to find one, he reluctantly turned back and on November 01 surrendered his command to the invaders. Romberg bears responsibility for the capture of Bila's 2,173 soldiers.[119]

That night the French negotiator returned to Stettin with Lasalle's counterproposals. He imposed harsher terms and the governor acquiesced. At dawn on October 30, a fully equipped fortress with 5,000 men surrendered to less than 800 French hussars with two cannons.[120] The soldiers had been kept in the dark about the negotiations. When they learned of the surrender, they angrily surrounded Romberg and pulled him from his horse. He barely escaped a beating from his own men.[121] Lasalle's horsemen entered to supervise the Prussians as they stacked their rifles. The defenders attempted to reclaim the weapons and offer spontaneous resistance. Lannes's infantry were entering the fortress and without bloodshed, prevented the Prussians from rearming. There was no reason for Romberg to deliver the garrison into captivity. It could have abandoned

Stettin and escaped to the eastern bank of the Oder River to reinforce Prussian units in the process of forming a new army. The bridge at Stettin was the only one for miles and Lasalle lacked the resources to block it. Many soldiers, including officers, disobeyed orders and crossed the Oder anyway to join other Prussian formations.

The surrender of the fortresses dramatized the gulf between the overaged, reactionary leadership of the army and the ardent spirit of the younger officer corps and steadfastness of the ranks. It also revealed the downside of martial discipline. Only through subordination of individual will can an army function as an entity under the direction of a single warlord. To move thousands of men on command, compel them to endure privations, respond without hesitation to orders, execute complex maneuvers under strenuous circumstances and hazard their lives in battle requires training and unconditional compliance. Only through obedience to his superiors was it also possible for a Prussian soldier to accept the odium of surrender. Carrying out orders issued by officers whom he had no confidence in superseded his personal sense of honor and purpose. Too many officers, especially those on the staff, followed this code. It resulted in them complying with orders that they knew are wrong to obey.

A military establishment that molds the younger generation into a dutiful fighting machine must provide leaders who nurture and emulate the spirit of this army. No matter how well-honed the blade of an axe, an aged or weak person cannot wield it. When a commander falters his troops must also, regardless of their fighting potential. The relics on the Immediate Organization Commission and the king's staff posted officers in their seventies, several of whom were already pensioned, to fortress commands. The younger officer corps embraced the Enlightenment, regarded by older veterans as a liability for the traditional system that had promoted their own careers. Having succeeded in the absolutist milieu, they sought to maintain it by granting authority to men of the old generation. In their youth they had possessed ambition and courage. Ancestral deeds gradually elevated their stratum to power and influence in society, but it subsequently regressed from advancement to consolidation; preserving the fruits of its labors became the priority. Such an attitude clings to a static value system that stifles the progressive thinking and fresh perspective without which a nation cannot flourish.

Chapter 9

From Küstrin to Danzig

The Dominos Fall

Two days after Stettin changed hands, the Prussians lost Küstrin. This was a fortress on the Oder River east of Berlin. On October 31, Davout ordered the vanguard of Gudin's division to proceed there from Müncheberg. He planned to cross with his corps at Frankfurt am Oder further south and then invest Küstrin, which rests on the eastern side of the river. The main access from the western bank of the Oder was the Küstrin bridge. The entrance to the span was protected by a bridgehead fortified with an abatis and ditch. A moat surrounded the entire city. General Mathias von Laurens had inspected the defenses and expressed satisfaction with the preparations.[1] The outer works were equipped with palisades and there were 80 cannons sited on the main wall with twelve more in reserve. Each gun had 200 rounds of ammunition. Despite lackluster cooperation from civil authorities to deliver additional foodstuffs, the supply of provisions within the fortress was capable of sustaining a 5,000-man garrison for six months.[2] Consistent with the Prussian army's talent for posting the wrong officers to positions of command, the military governor of Küstrin, Colonel Friedrich von Ingersleben, was an opportunist of the worst sort.

During the 1792 campaign in France's Champagne region, Ingersleben was decorated by the king. The sovereign attached particular significance to never abandoning a cannon, which was an issue in the limestone soil peculiar to the Champagne. On one occasion artillerymen were struggling to free a gun mired in soft ground when Ingersleben's regiment passed on the road. He himself was astride an immense steed that suited his bulk. Leaving the ornately wrought saddle and decorative blanket on the horse, he climbed down and hitched his mount to a harness. Apparently taking no notice of Friedrich Wilhelm II, who was observing, Ingersleben stepped into the mud and helped gunners push while the horse pulled the weapon free. Noticing from the steed's accoutrements that it belongs to an officer, the king asked about its owner. He awarded Ingersleben the *Pour le Mérite* on the spot. As soon as his majesty moved on, Ingersleben unhitched his horse, remounted and rode off. He left the cannon at roadside.[3] In the course of the campaign Ingersleben was discharged for bad conduct in the face of the enemy. Acquaintances at court arranged his transfer to Küstrin.

Returning to 1806, Friedrich Wilhelm III and Luise arrived at Küstrin on October 19 and stayed at the *Goldener Hirsch* (Golden Stag) inn. During a tour of the walls, the king asked Ingersleben if he can be trusted to fulfill his duty. Ingersleben replied, "I will defend the fortress until my handkerchief is ablaze in my pocket."[4] The royal couple left Küstrin on October 24. The fortress was regarded as impregnable. It was held by depot battalions of the Prince Heinrich, Prince of Orange and Zenge Regiments plus 500 artillerymen. Ingersleben's second in command was Colonel Weyher, an arrogant man who treated soldiers and townspeople with equal contempt. A week after the king's departure, 250 French Tirailleurs appeared and exchanged fire with Prussian sentries. The officer in charge of the men screening the outer walls requested reinforcements. Ingersleben responded, "I cannot allow any of my people out of the fortress because they will all run away."[5] The pickets set the bridge piers ablaze and retreated through the gate. Fire from cannons on the walls drove off the French marksmen. The Prussians burned the remaining Gorin bridge and disabled the König bridge. "The fortress was completely secure against an attack by force," maintained Lettow-Vorbeck.[6]

Colonel Ingersleben contemplated surrender as soon as the French appeared. Public officials, merchants and ordinary citizens visited his office or implored him on the street to spare the city. Either moved by their pleas or bribed (as was suspected), Ingersleben instructed the fortress engineer, Lieutenant Thynkel, to take a bugler outside the walls and contact the French to open negotiations. The lieutenant replied that it would be better to show the enemy Küstrin's teeth than display signs of weakness. The colonel dispatched an artillery officer instead. During the day, the main enemy column arrived outside of the fortress. At midnight, Ingersleben met surreptitiously with the French in a house beyond the walls and agreed to surrender. The next morning, November 01, he assembled his staff behind closed doors and informed it that he has "reliable information" that the French will arrive the same day with 100,000 men; the magic number Napoleon's envoys routinely cited to bluff the Prussians.[7]

During the session, the colonel disclosed that he has agreed with the enemy to suspend hostilities and there is no hope of being relieved. Colonel Weyher chimed in that many soldiers in his battalion are untrained recruits. Both he and Colonel Manteuffel recommended capitulation. The commander of the Prince of Orange Battalion, Major Hitzacker, retorted, "We have enough food, cannons and ammunition. The enemy has no cannons, so why should we give up?"[8] Lieutenant Thynkel told the officers, "With its 1,600-man garrison and the guns of the batteries so well placed, the fortress can be defended very well. It should be defended at all costs and the enemy won't be able to take it... Even if he penetrates into the outer defenses, the enemy will not be able to hold them because of the defensive capabilities of the main wall."[9] Ingersleben asked Thynkel whether bombardment of the civilian part of Küstrin can be prevented. The engineer said this is irrelevant and the fortifications have casemates that can withstand a barrage. The colonel answered that he cannot allow Küstrin to be "reduced to ashes."[10]

The commandant ordered Thynkel to ride out with a bugler to ask the French for an eight to 14-day cease-fire. Enemy pickets took him to meet with General Petit. He bluntly told Thynkel that unless Ingersleben comes personally, he will begin the bombardment in two hours. After objecting to the dishonorable nature of the threat, the Prussian officer duly rode back to the governor and relayed Petit's demand. Ingersleben exclaimed, "There's no time to lose!" and ordered the reluctant envoy to accompany him to the enemy camp. At the gate Ingersleben was confronted by his wife. She implored him not to relinquish the fortress to the enemy and disgrace the family. As Thynkel testified later, she was on the point of persuading her husband to fight on when the president of Küstrin's chamber of deputies, Ernst von Schierstädt, interrupted and told her, "Dear lady, for heaven's sake do not prevent your lord husband from doing this good deed that will bless us all. We must erect a statue in his honor."[11]

Schierstädt then turned to the vacillating colonel and prevailed upon him to finalize the negotiations. During the following session with the French, General Nicolas Gautier informed his visitor that Hohenlohe has surrendered and Stettin is lost. He then repeated the empty threat about shelling Küstrin until every house is destroyed. He demanded that French troops be admitted into the town by noon. Ingersleben acquiesced to Gautier, even though Prussian artillery officers Captain Schreiber and Lieutenant Wille advised the commandant that the French have at most three battalions on hand with no cannons. Ingersleben forgot to bring his official seal of office to the meeting with Gautier and sent subordinates scurrying to locate a substitute. An officer returned with the borrowed seal of the local textile dyers' guild. Ingersleben affixed this seal to the document next to his signature, therefore adding a burlesque quality to the sordid transaction.[12] Thynkel refused to sign.

When the garrison learned of the capitulation, soldiers angrily smashed their rifles, sabers and cartridge cases against the pavement to render them unserviceable. Ingersleben was surrounded and threatened by officers and men of the Prince of Orange Battalion. After that he feared showing himself in public. To ensure his personal safety, he sent barges to ferry the French advance guard over the Oder to occupy the fortress and protect him; the enemy had no other way of getting across.[13] On the walls, an alert gunner spotted the barges conveying French soldiers. He took aim with his cannon and prepared to light the fuse. An officer belonging to Ingersleben's surrender clique abruptly struck the artillerymen's hand with the flat of his saber and prevented him from opening fire. Many officers and men escaped captivity. They made their way to Kolberg to reinforce its garrison. A few days later, Napoleon reviewed the surrender document signed by Ingersleben and scratched out the paragraph guaranteeing him a commission in the French army. He remarked, "I can't use a man who betrays his sovereign."[14]

Ingersleben later blamed Küstrin's surrender on Thynkel. He claimed that he had neglected to properly shore up the defenses. In its 1808 inquiry, the Immediate Investigation Commission offered this verdict: "If von Ingersleben and the staff officers who approved his capitulation cite prevention of burning down the town and suburbs as a reason for signing… they do not realize that by sparing a small part the greater part suffers endlessly more as a result. The state itself is dealt an incurable wound as well, in that the loss of fortified places repeatedly portends the loss of entire provinces. On the other hand, provinces are not regarded as lost as long as their fortresses defy capture."[15] Stripped of his *Pour le Mérite*, Ingersleben fled Prussia. The investigation commission ordered him court-marshaled in absentia. He was among seven officers condemned to death and the only one to whom the king did not grant clemency by commuting the sentence to fortress arrest. Ingersleben spent the rest of his life living outside of Prussia in obscurity.

The Immediate Investigation Commission was founded after the king issued an edict on December 01, 1806, the *Ortelsburger Publicandum*, to "put an end to various abuses in the army." The purpose was to examine the "unfortunate circumstances" of the military defeat and identify officers "whose conduct remains dubious." The edict stated that the officer corps, "because of the war occurrences of 1806 has forfeited an alarming measure of prestige. If the army is to be reconciled with the public and the soldierly occupation given a new sense of moral worth… no officer can be burdened with a blemish on his career of any sort."[16] The "Commission to Investigate the Surrender and Related Events of the Last War" first convened on November 27, 1807. The king's two brothers, Princes Wilhelm and Heinrich, were the chairs. Gneisenau, *Generalauditeur* (Chief of Military Justice) Johann Friedrich von Koenen and Major Karl von Grolman also sat on the commission. Its task was to determine to what extent the capitulation of the Prussian fortresses was justifiable or whether commandants had "shirked their duty," and recommend punishments for those found negligent.

At this time Magdeburg was still holding out. When Hohenlohe arrived, he was told that so much bread from the stockpile of 60,000 loaves has been distributed to refugees that there isn't enough to nourish his corps. The military governor, Franz Kasimir von Kleist, was 73 years old. He was an autocratic, obstinate general woefully lacking interpersonal skills. He gruffly rejected Knesebeck's suggestion that cavalry be sent out to collect foodstuffs and cattle from the villages to supplement Magdeburg's food supply and remarked that hungry troops are welcome to leave if they choose.[17] Kleist displayed greater attention to civilian interests. He denied the fortress engineer's request to burn down suburban houses in front of the walls to deprive the enemy of cover. Such demolitions were standard procedure to prepare a fortress for siege. He issued passes to merchants wishing to leave the city for Tangermünde. Some felt no qualms about describing the fortifications to the French.[18]

Despite these drawbacks, the town was capable of resisting for at least two months. The investigation conducted by the commission in 1808 concluded, "The condition of the fortress of Magdeburg, with respect to its fortifications and endowment of guns, ammunition and provisions, the strength of the garrison and the talent of the engineer and artillery personnel, offers no military justification for its surrender."[19] After Hohenlohe detached men from his command to reinforce it, the troop strength available to Kleist tallied 24,118 men. There were 6,563 horses and the bastion had 577 cannons. The supply of food and munitions was such that "there was never the slightest cause for anxiety," as Petre wrote.[20] The French commander, Marshal Ney, estimated the size of the garrison at 8,000 men and invested Magdeburg with a much smaller force. Napoleon detached two dragoon regiments from Ney's already inadequate corps to employ elsewhere. Blockading the city on October 23, Ney limited operations to insignificant raids against Magdeburg's outposts and sending Kleist surrender demands.

With the manpower the Prussians had on hand, they could have counterattacked: "Sorties and attacks against the enemy camp, had they succeeded, would have served to gain accurate information regarding the strength of the enemy and animate the courage of the troops," the Immediate Investigation Commission later opined. "The weakness of the cavalry would of course be a hinderance to the sorties, but the enemy was proportionately no stronger in this category and had to maintain an extended chain of mounted pickets."[21] Instead of harassing Ney's troops and gathering intelligence about their disposition, Kleist allowed two French envoys into the city without blindfolds. "Marshal Ney could find no surer way to get news about the morale of the garrison and the confusion that initially prevailed among its personnel than this."[22] In a militarily incomprehensible gesture, Kleist promised an enemy officer not to disrupt movements of the French army as long as they take place beyond the range of Magdeburg's artillery.[23]

General Wartensleben, whose division had fought at Auerstedt and had initially bivouacked outside of Magdeburg during retreat, was also within the walls. In 1802, Gneisenau had served with him at Erfurt. He wrote home at that time, "Wartensleben is really hated here. He is unpopular, proud, domineering and uncivil, and contradictory and vacillating in his poorly contemplated orders. His manners are terrible and he has lost everyone's respect."[24] At Magdeburg, Wartensleben became cozy with the enemy. A French envoy complained to him of Kleist's refusal to surrender. Wartensleben privately confided to him, "Hurl a few good bombs and shells into the city and this stubborn governor will think differently."[25] On November 05, Napoleon granted Ney permission to bombard the fortress and sent four mortars from Erfurt. Ney informed the garrison of his intent to open fire. The mortars were not heavy siege guns and incapable of seriously compromising the defenses. They sufficed to unsettle Kleist, or perhaps provide him with an excuse to surrender.

Persuaded by Wartensleben that the troops are unreliable, Kleist assembled his staff the next day and announced his intention to capitulate. He did not convene a war council according to protocol, during which officers discuss a situation and strive for consensus. Kleist described it as "dubious glory… to devastate a tract of such fine and prosperous country" just to prolong resistance of a fortress that "dire necessity" will compel to surrender soon anyway.[26] The artillery and engineer officers objected. Generals protested that morale of the troops is good. None of the 19 generals present wrested authority from the faltering governor to comply with the king's order to defend Magdeburg. Murat sent a captured Prussian officer into the fortress to report that Hohenlohe's army has capitulated at Prenzlau. Kleist signed the surrender with the French on November 08 and his troops entered captivity three days later. Thus Magdeburg, as Petre summarized, "fell ingloriously into the hands of a besieging force much inferior to the garrison in numbers. The defense, if such it can be called, was a disgrace to the governor."[27] The soldiers grumbled that they "would like to massacre that old hound of a general."[28]

A Prussian officer present later wrote his brother, "As much as my mind struggles to find a sufficient reason for this singular occurrence, it hasn't succeeded. There is no way I can comprehend the conduct of the 80-year-old Kleist who already has one foot in the grave… The strong fortress lacked neither the troops, the guns nor the food necessary to manage prolonged and energetic resistance. The little nuisance attacks of the enemy in no sense deserve to be called a siege. Without positioning any batteries of importance and without digging trenches, the enemy shelled the town for two or three evenings and it surrendered to the amazement of the citizens and the soldiers. The people of Magdeburg were firmly convinced that General von Kleist, as he had boldly announced, would resist with the utmost obstinacy as an elder, seasoned officer from the glorious era of the Seven Years' War, and would seize this fine opportunity to defend the fortress entrusted to him like the valiant heathens in Kolberg."[29]

Kleist wrote the general staff that he had learned from *French* bulletins that there is no hope of a relief column coming to his aid and that the impending arrival of "heavy guns the enemy is bringing from Spandau… will transform Magdeburg into a heap of rubble." He allegedly surrendered "to preserve royal interests," reasoning that the peaceful transfer of the fortress will be a bargaining chip in peace negotiations.[30] The Immediate Investigation Commission retorted that Kleist's opinion that delaying surrender will only bring misfortune to the city is not based on the "military perspective" expected of a general. Further, "giving up a fortress like Magdeburg with such a strong garrison substantially increased the fighting forces available to the enemy. This circumstance was therefore not suited to mollify peace terms connected to negotiations, but was instead more disadvantageous for the state… A prolonged and energetic defense of the fortress at such a late time of year would have tied down significant enemy forces and prevented them from taking part in other operations. It is therefore probable that without the fall of Magdeburg, enemy operations would have taken a different course."[31]

Beyond strategic factors cited by the commission, the capitulation shook the troops' confidence in the leadership of the army. One officer expressed the sentiment in this way: "The spirit that had once spurned our fathers to valor

appears to have left us, at least our generals. We hear only about disgraceful surrenders. Wherever we look, we see Prussian officers who, like at Prenzlau, Stettin,
Magdeburg, Küstrin, Lübeck and many other places, were taken prisoner and
released on their word of honor. They all curse their generals. Only the courageous Blücher is praised and everyone speaks of the will to fight on that possesses
their subordinates and the vehement opposition to surrendering. Such shameful
capitulations weigh heavily on the heart of every soldier. Even the common
soldier acutely senses the mortification of laying down his arms in such a way.

"With the most vocal expressions of disapproval, our units marched with military pomp past Marshal Ney. The French formed a wide square in front of the
bastion and turned to face us like on the parade ground. The rifles and cartridge
belts were stacked. The officers were ordered back into the city to receive their
passes while our poor rankers were driven away like a herd of sheep. Of all the
many misfortunes that fell upon us in so short a time, my soul was never so sor-
rowful as it was during this separation of my valiant countrymen, who handed
over their weapons in suppressed rage and cursed the governor to the utmost.
Our contented conquerors won our universal respect through their decent
conduct. They showed sympathy for our dismal situation instead of taunting
us. Some of my comrades remarked that our troops, were the circumstances
reversed, would probably not have acted in so humane a manner."[32]

In addition to the potential to embroil the French in protracted sieges and
limit Napoleon's strategic options, the fortresses provided a refuge where dispersed contingents of the Prussian army could rest and regroup. Their diverse
locations, if defended, would require the emperor to dispatch divisions in all
directions to neutralize them. Prussian fortress garrisons combined with refugees from the main army represented a perpetual threat to understrength French
forces in Germany. Hameln for example, was well west of Prussia and in a position to siphon troops from Napoleon's army needed for the campaigns in Poland,
Silesia and Pomerania. Hameln is on the Weser River just south of Hanover.
Napoleon considered it one of the strongest fortresses in Germany. A brick wall
30 feet high interspersed with 22 turrets and eight bastions surrounded the city.
The Weser River fed a deep moat that covered the circumference of the outer
wall. The water barrier was 200 feet wide in places.[33]

Prussian engineers began upgrading the fortress when the French relinquished it by treaty on March 31, 1806. The river and mountainous terrain made
Hameln a natural barrier in itself. On the adjacent Klüt massif, with an elevation
of over 2,000 feet, three forts were incorporated into the defenses. The garrison
had 3,058 soldiers. It was supplemented by over a thousand stragglers from
Jena and Auerstedt. Provisions were on hand to nourish a 6,000-man garrison
for three to four months.[34] There were 93 cannons on the walls and a generous
supply of powder and ammunition.[35] A fortified island on the Weser directly opposite the fortress enabled the defenders to trap besieging troops in a crossfire.
The mobile corps of General Lecoq, numbering 3,000 men, joined the garrison

Fortified since the 13th Century, Hameln was virtually impregnable. The *Osterthor* blockhouse is on the opposite bank. On the slope at right are three stone forts on the Klüt mountain. The Prussian army stored its ordnance in fortresses, which was lost to the enemy when strongpoints capitulated.

on November 13. This helped to eventually raise the roster to 8,855 combatants. There were 1,050 horses and a corresponding number of stable hands within the walls as well. Hameln was among the best-equipped, well-maintained fortresses available to the Prussian army. The French investing the town were outnumbered and their artillery consisted of twelve six-pounder cannons and three obsolete 30-pounder mortars towed by oxen.

Marshal Mortier received orders to invest Hameln with his French and Dutch divisions. Prussian artillerymen on the walls reported their approach on November 07. A regiment of mounted rifles and one of Dutch dragoons advanced from Ärzen. They reconnoitered the fortress and skirmished with sentries outside of the gate. The defenders were forced back suffering two dead and a pair of wounded, while a French sergeant and a colonel were mortally wounded from cannon fire. An attack on the modern *Osterthor* (East Gate) blockhouse was repulsed two days later. Hameln's commandant inexplicably ordered the *Osterthor* evacuated and it fell to the French. Just three months before, it had been constructed at a cost of 25,000 thalers. The blockhouse possessed the greatest tactical value, cited to prevent the enemy from redirecting the channel used to flood the terrain. By abandoning the fort, the commandant deprived Hameln of the ability to control a potentially insurmountable water barrier. He justified the decision by stating that the *Osterthor* is indefensible. This is a dubious explanation after its gunners had beaten off an attack.[36]

The fortress commandant was General Johann Friedrich von Schöler, who was 75 years old. His adversary Mortier proceeded to Hanover with 5,000 troops. The remaining 11,000 men, most of them Dutch soldiers initially led by Jean-Baptiste Dumonceau, established camp at Vischbeck and Oldendorf over an hour's march from Hameln. King Louis I of Holland, a brother of Napoleon whom the emperor had placed on the throne, took command of the Dutch troops. He sent an envoy to Hameln demanding surrender on November 10. Louis offered free passage for the entire garrison. Schöler presented the terms to his officers and they agreed to enter negotiations. They made little headway due to quarreling between Napoleon and his younger sibling. Faulted by the emperor for not supplying enough troops for the campaign, Louis soon marched off with most of his army. He left behind just four battalions, a cavalry regiment and ten guns, 2,560 soldiers in all, to watch the two Weser fortresses Hameln and Nienburg. Prussian patrols observed Louis withdrawing. A sortie from the garrison destroyed a bridge built by the besiegers to flank the city.

Lecoq estimated remaining enemy troop strength at 6,000 men. He could have attacked with superior numbers and dispersed the invaders, but limited operations to a few insignificant skirmishes. Napoleon sent General Jean Savary to Lecoq on November 19. Savary explained the alleged "hopelessness of their position" and falsely informed the Prussians that Napoleon and the king of Prussia are about to conclude a peace treaty (which Friedrich Wilhelm refused to sign). Lecoq, who usurped command from the infirm Schöler, met with Savary at the gate to Hameln the next day to conclude the capitulation. Reentering the city, Lecoq assembled the staff officers to announce the decision. Almost all objected. Younger officers pushed their way into the room and demanded the agreement be rescinded. Engineer Lieutenant Rhade drew his sword and swore "to defend Hameln to the last drop of blood. Practically all officers present, young and old, followed his example."[37]

Adalbert von Chamisso experienced the betrayal of the garrison as a young officer. In a letter to a friend, he described the reaction of the troops: "They shot bullets through the windows of the cowardly commandant's rooms… They smashed their rifles on the pavement so that they would never be born valiantly by foreigners. The old Brandenburgers wept as they bid farewell to their officers. In the company of Captain von Britzke of the von Haack Regiment were the two Warnawa brothers. They were sons of a soldier. Each pointed his rifle against his brother's chest and they fired simultaneously, falling into each other's arms. They could not endure the disgrace to their armed service. Only one thought preoccupied officers and men; to preserve the traditional glory, though assailed by both the enemy without and the enemy among their own. Not one recruit, not one drummer boy would have dropped out. We were indeed a united, loyal, splendid and stalwart band of warriors. If only such men had stood at our head!"[38]

The rankers wanted to kill Lecoq and Schöler. Some planned to raid the store of gunpowder and blow up the fortress. Two colonels, Orthel and Hamelberg, the latter chief of the Hagken Infantry Regiment, dissuaded the men from pursuing such a violent course. Soldiers on the ramparts attempted to turn the cannons inward to bombard their own fortifications but were prevented by two artillery officers. The troops smashed down the drawbridge, surged from the fortress and threw their rifles and ammunition into the Weser. Almost all of the men escaped captivity. They scattered to the winds before the French entered Hameln. Schöler asked Savary to occupy the fortress ahead of schedule to curb unrest and protect himself and Lecoq from the enraged garrison.[39] Dutch troops entered on November 21 without resistance.

When the conquerors occupied the fortress, they found almost no one left but officers.[40] Prussian *Peleton* and company commanders had distributed money out of their own pocket to the troops for them to make their way home. Lecoq snuck out with the treasury's gold reserve worth 45,000 taler concealed in a fodder wagon.[41] After taking possession of Hameln, Savary sent Dumenceau to the nearby fortress of Nienburg on November 24. Two days later the elderly commandant, General Ludwig von Strachwitz, surrendered the nearly impenetrable fortress with its 4,000-man garrison without resistance. In 1808, Napoleon ordered the fortifications at Hameln and Nienburg dismantled; the city walls, outer forts, ammunition bunkers, moats and towers were taken down. It took thousands of laborers, 26,000 horses and 6,000 wagons six months to remove the military installations from Hameln alone.[42] This offers insight into how formidable its defenses had been. Bonaparte had the walls and bastions dismantled to avoid having to leave troops to garrison them.

In 1808, The Immediate Investigation Commission reported its findings regarding Hameln: "There is not another example in the history of warfare where an impregnable fortress equipped with every necessity, and which had a corps available for deployment to defend it from the outside as well, could surrender in such a disgraceful manner without attempting to offer any resistance at all to a handful of enemy troops without guns. According to enemy records there were one French and two Dutch regiments with just six cannons. The responsibility rests less with the commandant Major General von Schöler, a fainthearted, 76-year-old with dulled senses, than the one standing at his side General Le Coq. He had been honored by the confidence the king placed in him and the commandant had trustingly depended on him as well… For surrendering Hameln, Generals von Schöler and von Le Coq are condemned to fortress arrest for life. Colonels von Heyn and von Caprivi are condemned to four years' fortress arrest. The king has approved the sentence for the generals but reduced that for both colonels by two years."[43] Schöler soon died and Lecoq was allowed to reside in the city of Spandau instead of languishing in prison.

The Battle on the Baltic

A major problem facing Napoleon was Prussian control of the Baltic Sea ports Danzig and Kolberg. Their garrisons could be reinforced at almost any time, weather permitting, by ships from Russia, England and Sweden. Danzig was a potential staging area for the allies to operate against the *Grande Armée*'s left flank and rear. Without a secure base on the Vistula River near the Baltic, the emperor would have to abandon his move against the Russian army.[44] With over 50,000 inhabitants, Danzig was a massive fortress with 19 bastions. Fourteen of them formed an arc facing the Vistula to the north and west. There are marshy lowlands east of the fortress. The defenses had been neglected since a siege in 1734 and they were in disrepair. In 1793, the Duke of Brunswick blocked an initiative to restore them and advocated that they be dismantled instead.[45] Not until 1805, when war clouds cast their ominous shadow over Prussia once more, did restoration begin. Progress was slow until November 01, 1806, when the king ordered Danzig's fortifications quickly upgraded and equipped with artillery.

Preparations were completed on schedule due to Lieutenant Samuel Pullet, an industrious, circumspect engineer who was 37 years old. His tactful, unassuming manner won the cooperation of senior officers who might have resented a younger subordinate entrusted by the king with full authority. Pullet enlisted Danzig's 500 carpenters to rebuild the palisades on the walls and hired 400 laborers to assist in various projects together with the unemployed. Ultimately nearly 5,000 men were performing repairs.[46] In the raw December weather, Pullet's workers demolished homes in the prosperous Neugarten hamlet to clear a field of fire for the artillery. "The people had to be forcibly driven out and only left when the beams splintered and the walls caved in… The order not to resettle the residents in the city, but for them to seek accommodations in the countryside, increased the misery of these people who at a single stroke lost their means of livelihood and their homes."[47]

There was a good supply of food in Danzig, rationed to avoid price gouging and hoarding. The apothecary was well stocked with medicines and medical supplies. A sufficient number of qualified physicians were available to treat the sick and wounded. Schools and convents were converted to inpatient wards. Citizens including the merchants contributed money to ensure better care for the injured.[48] The governor of Danzig was General Kalckreuth, who had been away since 1805 and served with the main army at Auerstedt. In his absence the vice-governor, General Ernst Johann von Manstein, conducted expeditions against Polish insurgents in the neighboring Stargard and Schöneck regions. The operations contributed nothing to the defense of Danzig, wasted ammunition and offered unreliable soldiers the opportunity to desert.

Manstein neglected to transfer the large store of gunpowder at the Krakau powder mill a mile from Danzig into the fortress. Much of the supply fell into enemy hands. Carl Friedrich von Hamberger became commandant in December 1806. Unnecessarily strict toward the townspeople, he was an infirm, crotchety

While Danzig prepared for siege, survivors of the main army made their way to Memel. Here Queen Luise watches in awe as Prussian guardsmen who had fought at Jena and Auerstedt defile past her and the king. It took the troops weeks to reach Memel after a demoralizing retreat.

general and extremely disliked, yet fiercely defended Fort Hagelsberg during the investment. "Father Kalckreuth" had previously been popular as governor and the residents of Danzig rejoiced when he arrived from Memel on March 12, 1807. His leadership inspired the public to greater sacrifices. Merchants donated 9,000 thaler to support widows of soldiers killed in action and affluent families volunteered their sons to dig defensive trenches.[49]

By the end of December 1806, the garrisons of Danzig and Fort Weichselmünde at the Vistula estuary comprised 9,000 troops. There was insufficient funding to provide uniforms and weapons for a larger force. Since cavalry was essential for reconnaissance, the defenders were reinforced by the second battalion of the Queen's Dragoon Regiment consisting of 300 men. The Count of Krochow raised a corps of 650 riflemen and 100 of cavalry, partially comprised of volunteers from Danzig, that participated in combat operations. The count himself later became so passionately involved in the Prussian reform movement that he joined a conspiracy to overthrow the king. Thanks to Friedrich Wilhelm's mercy, he was pardoned after spending a year in jail for high treason. Count Kalckreuth attempted to form another volunteer corps bearing his own name.

Many townspeople who owned hunting rifles were willing to enlist. Senior Prussian officers objected, concerned that armed citizenry may demand a say in how to defend the fortress.[50]

On March 16, 17 and 18, three Cossack cavalry regiments disembarked at Neufahrwasser on the Baltic coast west of Danzig. The townspeople marveled at the weaponry, songs and ethnic dances of these singular troops with their rugged, shaggy ponies. Three Russian infantry battalions came ashore a few days later, so that Kalckreuth had 4,799 of the czar's fighting men at his disposal. More Prussian contingents gradually joined the garrison. It eventually swelled to 21,706 men, though some sources fix the number at around 16,000.[51]The governor had 12,000 combatants for sorties beyond the walls. Such operations are indispensable for a successful defense; they include sending out scouts and conducting raids. Their mission is to destroy redoubts and parallels to prevent the enemy from digging artillery positions close to the fortress. Due to the broken terrain around Danzig, crisscrossed with ravines and streambeds, the Prussian sallies out of Danzig often forfeited the essential speed and surprise.[52]

Before the king's order to upgrade the fortress, Danzig had 50 serviceable cannons. Barrels were salvaged from storage and new carriages built for them. Soldiers drew from regional depots to augment the ordnance. By the beginning of December there were 249 guns on the walls, 32 more at Weichselmünde and 19 at Neufahrwasser. Others were restored or imported until the tally rose to 349. This included cannons on four cutters that Kalckreuth ordered fitted with six guns. The garrison had 1,275 men assigned to the artillery of whom 386 were trained gunners.[53] The fortifications represented an expansive complex and the artillery was still not adequate to cover all of the bastions and full length of the walls. The weakness of the fortress gunnery, as would soon become apparent, was the insufficient supply of gunpowder caused by Manstein's failure to transfer stores from the Krakau powder mill into Danzig.

The new French X Corps under Marshal François Lefebvre began operations against Danzig on March 10. This was just as Lieutenant Pullet had completed restoring the main wall. The besiegers included two Italian divisions, 5,000 Poles under General Jan Dombrowski, 4,133 *Rheinbund* soldiers from Baden, 6,000 from Saxony and 2,148 soldiers of the *Légion du Nord* (North Legion) consisting largely of Prussian prisoners persuaded to switch sides. The French formations were the 2nd Light Infantry Regiment and the 19th Mounted Rifle Regiment.[54] Napoleon hoped for Danzig to capitulate without resistance and delayed supplying the X Corps with enough artillery for an investment. Lefebvre's troops were inadequately provisioned and suffered from malnourishment. This, together with exposure to the cold, damp weather, caused widespread sickness. Many Poles and soldiers of the *Légion du Nord* deserted. By late March the siege corps had become so weakened by sickness and desertion that for a brief period there were less than 8,000 men fit for duty. Napoleon eventually sent Lannes's and Mortier's corps to reinforce Lefebvre.

The French besieged Danzig from the west. The defenders repulsed the first attack on Neufahrwasser on March 13. Three days later, the Prussians successfully held the village of Zigankenberg bordering Danzig against a determined assault. Lefebvre ordered General Jean Adam Schramm to assault the Frische Nehrung with 2,000 men before dawn on March 20. This is a narrow, sandy peninsula 43 miles in length that separates Danzig Bay from a long coastal lagoon, the Frisches Haff. Since the defense of the city depended on controlling the coast, Kalckreuth was negligent in not sufficiently garrisoning the Frische Nehrung. The Prussian general charged with its defense, Hans von Rouquette, had too few troops to hold the Nehrung. The French approached it on barges under the cover of darkness. The sound of ice floes colliding in the current of the Vistula prevented the sentries from hearing the barges. In the battle that followed, some Prussian soldiers deserted; a sergeant led 40 men in full order over to the attackers and opened fire on his former comrades.[55]

After losing 320 soldiers in combat and from desertion, Rouquette gathered his remaining 600 men and conducted an orderly withdrawal to Danzig in two columns along the beach and dunes. The French mendaciously reported that the Prussians "fell back in panicky flight."[56] The king's investigation commission summarized in December 1808, "Because there were too few troops, the Nehrung could not be more strongly held. General Rouquette should therefore have been all the more vigilant. He was not so and allowed himself to be ambushed. He couldn't even rally his men and under these circumstances arrived in Danzig. In every respect, the loss of the Nehrung was a great disadvantage for the defense of Danzig."[57] The commission cited Manstein's failure to properly fortify it during late autumn and winter. It also faulted Kalckreuth for sending a small formation of Cossacks to support Rouquette instead of a Prussian infantry battalion and cavalry.

The Prussians still held Fort Weichselmünde at the mouth of the Vistula, but control of the Frische Nehrung enabled the French to tighten the ring around Danzig. A few hours after the battle, Kalckreuth sent a message to Rouquette reading, "The general is to attack the enemy immediately, eject him from the Nehrung and reestablish communication with Pillau. For the purpose you will be reinforced by a detachment of Cossacks."[58] Rouquette had regrouped and there were 700 men under his command. Some hailed from recently annexed East Prussian territories and were of dubious loyalty. Together with a few hundred Cossacks, he was expected to counterattack and retake a position held by over 3,000 seasoned soldiers. He replied to Kalckreuth, "I will use all my energy to carry out the assignment I have been given, but will need more reinforcements than Cossacks."[59] Schramm meanwhile, received additional troops from Lefebvre and sent Tirailleurs forward to skirmish with the Prussians.

The Cossacks arrived at 4:00 p.m. Rouquette led an assault against 60 French horsemen without success. Persuaded by his officers that the East Prussian infantry is unreliable, he withdrew into Danzig. Roquette was blamed for the loss

French mortars hurl explosive charges over the walls of Danzig during the siege of 1807. Like most fortresses, it was practically impossible to take by direct assault. The siege corps resorted to prolonged bombardments to wear down resistance and force the defenders to surrender.

of the Frische Nehrung but acquitted by the investigation commission. The next day, March 21, the French attempted once more to take Neufahrwasser. This time Kalckreuth reacted quickly. He sent 1,400 Cossacks and 800 men of the Krockowsch Volunteer Corps against them and committed additional reserves as the battle developed. They drove the French back to the villages of Oliva and Wonneberg and burned their camp. Despite forfeiting control of the Nehrung, Danzig could be supplied by sea via the Vistula River as long as Neufahrwasser and the Holm, a fortified island on the river immediately north of the fortress, remained in Prussian hands. The governor ordered a sortie of 3,000 men against Wonneberg on March 26 to disrupt enemy siege preparations. His troops thwarted an attempt by the French to cross the Vistula at Heubude on March 28. They also beat back an assault against the Rückfort floodgate on April 01. Kalckreuth organized a small, armed corps of Danzig volunteers, the *Bürgerwacht* (Civic Watch), to police the city.

Attacks and counterattacks outside of the walls continued during April. Lefebvre received 17 *Würfgeschutze* (launchers for hurling explosive mines) and 55 siege cannons from Schweidnitz. He incorporated them into the forward battery positions on the 22nd. In the course of the investment the number increased to 100 guns.[60] They began bombarding Danzig at one o'clock in the morning on April 24. A resident recorded the experience: "The starry sky was clear and bright, still faintly illuminated by the half moon, when a frightening hissing sound penetrated the air. Fiery projectiles with long trails of smoke, shrilly whistling, came hurtling toward the city. The sight of this unexpected, horrifying spectacle provoked fear and amazement. All were roused from their sleep. Flash after flash followed, one detonation after another! Every bomb that hit the city wrought destruction! The collapse of buildings, the cries of the injured and dying presented a pitiful, hair-raising scene."[61]

The French hurled 1,200 projectiles into the city over the next twelve hours. Lefebvre's cannons shot 600 rounds at Danzig's fortifications and at Fort Hagelsberg guarding the western side of the fortress. Danzig emergency personnel extinguished fires caused by the barrage by seven o'clock in the evening. Three days later the besiegers poured another 1,930 rounds onto the defenders. Prussian artillery bombarded sites where the French were extending their trenches. The devastation inflicted on the fortifications by French gunnery was substantial. The garrison at Hagelsberg took an average of 40 casualties daily.[62] At night, work crews repaired damaged walls and palisades. Fatigue and stress compounded the plight of the defenders; the number of sick augmented. Each day there was a four-hour cease-fire for both sides to retrieve and bury the dead.

Lefebvre concentrated artillery fire on the fortifications, but many rounds landed in commercial and residential areas. The primary military targets were Fort Hagelsberg and the Holm. The French repeatedly shelled these positions. Their capture would give them control of the Vistula and cut Danzig's lifeline to the harbor. After a few weeks the Holm, an eyewitness recalled, looked like a sieve. Owners of houses wrecked by bombs were forced to seek accommodations elsewhere. The home of a member of the war council sheltered 122 displaced persons and the *Eugenia* Freemason lodge 80. Others sought refuge in schools and church buildings. Kalckreuth shifted many sick and wounded from the hospital to less vulnerable structures. On April 30, Lefebvre received more cannons and ammunition from Warsaw. The superior manpower enjoyed by the besiegers and their great supply of ammunition enabled them to maintain constant pressure on Danzig. The fortress artillery began running low on gunpowder.

Early in May, the French marshal learned that the allies are preparing a relief operation in Pillau, a port near the eastern end of the Frische Nehrung. He arranged for 800 French and *Rheinbund* troops from Baden to stealthily cross from Schellmühle to the Holm in small boats to assault the island. Prussian lookouts spotted the preparations and sent warnings up the chain of command. Kalckreuth reinforced the fort with another 400 men. Around midnight on May 06/07, a lively exchange of gunfire could be heard from the direction of the Holm and the Kalkschanze, the adjacent entrenchment. At sunrise, both positions were in French hands. The first 300 French soldiers had disarmed the

Holm's sentries and then overwhelmed the 1,400-man Russian garrison while the men were sleeping off hangovers. The Baden Germans followed to consolidate the position. Without support from Prussian artillery on the Holm, the 150 troops defending the small Kalksschanze surrendered. "There has never been a satisfactory explanation as to how exactly the Holm was lost," a surviving member of Danzig's garrison recalled.[63]

A civilian wrote a friend about the island's capture: "In spite of everything that has been said about the loss of this position, the actual cause remains a mystery. According to reports in general that reached the public, plain carelessness and the deep slumber of the garrison was at fault. It's also believed that the major in command wasn't even at his post, nor were several subalterns. Moreover, some Baden officers say that the major was caught by surprise in the arms of a girlfriend he was sleeping with but escaped… Some who claim to know more assert that Prussian artillerymen on the Holm were indignant over their treatment by Russian officers and formed a conspiracy to show the enemy the way in. Whatever the case may be, the enemy or rather the victor came in small numbers across the Vistula in boats and took the Holm without losing a single man. Everything on the island is gone! This loss aroused universal consternation; since by occupying the Holm, the enemy has inexorably severed the city from navigable waters and the sea."[64]

Kalckreuth telegraphed Colonel Schüler, commandant of Neufahrwasser, and ordered him to assemble 1,000 men from his position and from Fort Weichselmünde, board British ships moored there and counterattack. Schüler replied that French guns along the river bank and at the Holm will blast the ships at close range. The governor abandoned the idea. Taking the Holm enabled the French to outflank Fort Hagelsberg, which so far had borne the brunt of the attacks. Enemy control of the island curtailed nautical traffic on the Vistula and deliveries of foodstuffs and powder to Danzig. Both Friedrich Wilhelm and Czar Alexander agreed that an expedition to relieve Danzig is essential. General Levin von Bennigsen, commander of the Russian army operating against Napoleon, allotted 5,300 Russians under General Nicolai Kamenskoi and 1,300 Prussians with twelve cannons for the task. Bülow's corps, consisting of 2,500 infantrymen and 280 riders, retained a foothold on the Nehrung and was to support Kamenskoi during the operation. Its objective was to retake the Frische Nehrung. Bennigsen was aware of the strength of Lefebvre's siege corps and pessimistic about the prospects of success.[65]

Kamenskoi, the son of a field marshal and a valiant officer, departed with his men in transport vessels from Pillau. Calm winds delayed part of the fleet. Protected by British and Swedish warships under the command of Royal Navy Captain George Saunders, Kamenskoi's troops landed at Neufahrwasser in transport vessels on the night of May 10/11. Reinforced by Lannes, Lefebvre stationed his reserves to strengthen the French position near the coastline. Within the fortress, Kalckreuth had two battalions of Russians, the Schmeling

Grenadier Battalion, the Holtzendorff Horse Battery and all the cavalry poised to simultaneously attack the French in the flank and rear during Kamenskoi's operation. The relief force from Pillau assembled at Weichselmünde and launched the attack in three columns at four o'clock in the morning on May 15. Lieutenant Schenk led the advance guard of 60 Prussian riflemen in direct assault against the coastal wooded area on the eastern side of the Vistula, behind which the French had established a redoubt. The attackers were unable to remain in formation negotiating the difficult terrain and a murderous infantry duel developed.

Schenk allowed his men to become embroiled in a firefight instead of employing a bayonet charge to rapidly clear the woods. This bought the French time to bring up more troops. Schramm defended the French position opposite Weichselmünde with the 2nd Light Infantry Regiment, a Saxon brigade, a Polish contingent and a regiment from Paris in reserve. He counterattacked upon receiving another light regiment and 200 more Saxons as reinforcements. Schenk's skirmishers, a Russian battalion and two reserve companies of Prussians repulsed the assault and put Schramm's men to flight; they took the first enemy trench with the bayonet but were unable to capture the redoubt. Three British warships designated to provide artillery support were unable to sail down the Vistula due to calm winds. General Nicolas Oudinot's grenadier division moved forward to bolster the redoubt and the French rallied. The allied attack floundered after several hours of combat and Kamenskoi withdrew.

The Russians lost 14 officers and 422 men killed in action and 41 officers and 895 rankers wounded. The Prussians forfeited 44 dead and 114 wounded. Four of them were officers. The French suffered nearly 2,000 casualties but claimed only 225.[66] Throughout the battle, Kamenskoi had anticipated a powerful sortie from Danzig in his support. Kalckreuth sat on his hands and did nothing. In his official report he stated, "I observed only that the attack by General Kamenskoi in the forest failed as it was doomed to fail. Without hope of being relieved, nothing from the garrison's side could be undertaken."[67] In his own account of the battle, artillery Captain Braun cited the omission of a timely sortie from Danzig as a primary reason for the defeat.[68] It is possible that Kalckreuth allowed his personal dislike of Kamenskoi to influence his lack of initiative. The downright insulting messages they exchanged reveal a genuine antagonism between the two generals.[69]

Even had the relief operation succeeded in retaking the Nehrung, it is unlikely that this would have raised the siege. With the arrival of Mortier's corps, the French force at Danzig numbered nearly 60,000 men. The British 22-gun corvette *Dauntless* navigated the Vistula in an attempt to deliver 150 barrels of gunpowder to the fortress. It ran aground under heavy fire from French batteries at the Holm and along the river. It attests to the courage and discipline of the English seamen that they sailed a ship laden with explosives through an enemy barrage to carry out a mission. Danzig's infantry garrison had lost a third of its men. Those on duty were exhausted and stores of ammunition and food ran low. Fortifications at Hagelsberg, the key defensive position, sustained irreparable damage. The 7,000 soldiers occupying it were likewise strained to the breaking point. Just 622 out of the 1,500 troops considered necessary to hold Weichselmünde remained. In nearly eleven weeks the French hurled 20,000 bombs into Danzig. An eyewitness wrote, "The outermost fronts under attack present a picture of complete devastation."[70]

Lefebvre was aware of these dire circumstances thanks to Lieutenant Braun's dispatches recovered aboard the grounded *Dauntless*. He sent his adjutant to Kalckreuth to propose a cease-fire to open negotiations on May 21. The governor agreed and the guns fell silent the next day. Lefebvre's insistence that the garrison enter captivity angered the staff of Fort Hagelsberg. The officers persuaded their commander, Major Heinrich von Horn, to compose a letter for Kalckreuth in protest. Horn, highly respected for his exploits during the siege, delivered it while the governor was dining with the French envoy. It read, "The disgraceful terms the enemy demands of us have moved me and the entire officer corps having the honor to defend Hagelsberg to respectfully entreat your excellency to allow us to swear an oath on the flag that we prefer to be buried beneath the rubble of Hagelsberg than submit to a capitulation that is dishonorable for a Prussian officer."[71] The envoy remained obstinate. Kalckreuth broke off negotiations.

Napoleon was anxious to capture Danzig so he authorized Lefebvre to negotiate the terms. The marshal approved the governor's proposal to grant the garrison safe passage home if its members do not take up arms against France again for a year. Kalckreuth signed the treaty. Many soldiers did not trust the French to honor the compact; during negotiations nearly a thousand men deserted over several nights. On May 27, the Prussians paraded out of the gates, 12,448 defiant troops under arms with the musicians in front, flags flying and gunners bearing lit torches for setting cannon fuses. The investigation commission summarized, "The garrison deserves the most notable praise for its spirited defense. It achieved everything that could be expected of human endurance, especially at the forward Hagelsberg fort against which the strongest attacks were directed. The garrison, its commander Major Horn and the artillery under Major Holtzendorff have earned everlasting renown… The officer corps and the entire garrison can share the fine sentiment that they have performed a useful service to their fatherland and have fulfilled their duty as soldiers in every sense."[72]

Kalckreuth deserves praise for negotiating good terms for his men. This resolve was woefully lacking in many fortress commanders. Karl Friccius, a lieutenant in the garrison, provides posterity with this view: "The garrison consisted in part of unreliable troops who were born in Polish provinces rebelling against the Prussian government and they preferred desertion to avoid Prussian military service. The greater part of the garrison however, was made up of good, loyal and valiant soldiers. Together with their officers, their wartime handiwork and fortress duty improved with each passing day. The difficult, prolonged defense of Hagelsberg can be called genuinely heroic. The garrison demonstrated that all in all, an outstanding esprit de corps prevails in the army… All of the residents had a positive attitude and were willingly prepared to make the necessary sacrifices. Everything the garrison authorities demanded was given to them without complaint and the merchants voluntarily donated substantial sums for the benefit of the garrison. Such harmony with the population is a great advantage for the commander of a beleaguered fortress. It mollifies his concerns and toils and lifts the spirits and confidence of the garrison, which regards the residential community as part of its brotherhood and as its advocate."[73]

Chapter 10

The Defense of Silesia

Glogau and Breslau

Prussia's Baltic strongpoints were not the only obstacles to Napoleon's plan to neutralize Russia. On the French right flank was Silesia, with a mountain range and eight Prussian fortresses, some guarding strategic passes. Four forts were along the Oder River and four stood further south. The population was loyal to Friedrich Wilhelm III and a source of additional manpower for the Prussian army. Silesian strongholds also protected Austria; were the Hapsburg empire to reenter the war against France, its army had a safe staging area. Bonaparte had to conquer Silesia, which meant capturing the fortresses, to protect his rearward communications, hold Austria in check and deprive his enemy of a province rich in material and human resources. He assigned the task to his brother Jérôme. His corps consisted of 23,945 men from Württemberg and Bavaria.[1] They crossed into Silesia during the first week of November 1806. The mounted vanguard skirmished with a Prussian patrol on the seventh.

When Friedrich Wilhelm declared war on France, few imagined that the fighting would spread well east of the Saale. The cabinet order to arm and prepare Silesian fortresses for defense was not issued until October 24. The fortifications were broken down. The onset of cold weather made shoring them up, restoring moats and stocking provisions especially difficult. The king instructed Reinhardt von Lindener, a general of engineers, to help mobilize the province and arm the fortresses. Lindener had already ordered defense preparations on the 19th when he received news of Jena. Prussian troop strength in Silesia amounted to 18,500 men. The number grew as soldiers who had escaped French captivity returned to report for duty. Leaves were cancelled and regiments transferred from their peacetime barracks to the fortresses. In an October 28 decree, Lindener notified their commandants of the king's orders and concluded with the words, "We should and will hold, that is will only give up the fortresses when we see that it is unwise to hold any longer."[2]

Though implementing measures to strengthen fortifications, Lindener privately told commandants that the purpose is "only to be secure against a coup de main so that we can get better terms for surrender… Everything is lost and it's all over." He bluntly wrote the king, "as an honorable man I cannot express to your majesty the remotest hope that the fortresses can resist a formal siege because the time is too short."[3] He cited the advanced age of the commandants and most

Some disguised in civilian apparel, Prussians soldiers who escaped from the French trek east to rejoin the army, avoiding towns and roads to elude patrols.

battalion and company chiefs. The king left him in charge. Another problem confronting the army was an insurrection, encouraged by Napoleon, of the Polish population in their lands annexed by Prussia. Many Poles who had been drafted into Friedrich Wilhelm's service wanted to join the insurgents.

Bonaparte assigned first priority to capturing Glogau, the northernmost Silesian fortress. Together with Stettin and Küstrin, this would provide a solid foundation along the Oder River to support the expedition east. Control of Glogau, a town of some 10,000 inhabitants, would also open a direct line of communication between the *Grande Armée* and Dresden. He sent Lefebvre's brigade and a light artillery battery to Glogau in the hope of persuading the commandant to surrender without a fight. The vice-governor, General Franz Joachim von Reinhart, and his adjutant Captain Brockhausen reached Glogau on October 24. The fortress had a roster of 73 officers and 3,545 men plus thirteen surgeons. There were 124 cannons on the walls of mostly heavier caliber. The commandant, General Otto von der Marwitz, arranged for 600 foresters to fell trees to provide lumber to rebuild the palisades. Neighboring villages donated the necessary money and manpower to complete essential repairs and continue reconstruction during the siege.

The French sighted Glogau on November 07. The commandant rejected a surrender demand and they began bombarding the town the next morning.

Napoleon ordered Lefebvre to keep up the barrage day and night to unsettle the population.[4] Most French guns were howitzers which fired rounds at high trajectory. They cleared the fortress wall and exploded inside the city. On the night of November 16 alone, incendiary bombs shot from seven enemy batteries caused 30 fires to break out. Supported by the townspeople, fire brigades extinguished all but two before serious damage resulted. One eyewitness recorded, "Most of the residents of Glogau spent half their time during the last ten days in the cellars and in arched chambers considered safe. This subterranean life which we became accustomed to was a world in itself. The arches were seen as the best roof, the most secure shield... The cellars shut us in with people of the most varied classes, people who had never seen each other before, never noticed or never spoken with one another. You couldn't find a more colorful hodgepodge at a Leipzig fair or at an annual Dutch market as here in these arched chambers."[5]

Bombarding houses was standard practice for the French. Danzig was the only fortress where reducing military defenses was prioritized. Waging war against civilians "was to make the commandants more receptive (to surrender) out of concern for the residents," Höpfner summarized.[6] A citizen of Glogau recalled, "It was naturally dreadful for the townspeople to have to hold out from day to day and from night to night without hope of escape... There was a good measure of resignation over forfeiting everything one calls his own, of losing all joys of life and indeed life itself, secretly harboring the wish that it will all be over soon... But there was nothing that could fault Glogau's residents for lack of spirit... The hope that the city will be handed over was nowhere heard aloud, and people encouraged one another not to let their courage wane."[7]

According to one account, "Despite considerable damage to the houses that primarily the explosive rounds caused, morale among the inhabitants was not seriously shaken. They were especially devoted to the members of the garrison manning the walls, delivering them breakfast and sometimes even bread for lunch."[8] Heavy caliber guns enabled Prussian artillerymen to inflict serious losses on the besieger and delay his trench digging to establish enfilades close to the walls. The French were often outgunned during cannon duels and forced to temporarily withdraw their crews. Fortresses with larger garrisons conducted sorties to ambush pickets, demolish enemy parallels and spike howitzers. This made prolonged investments as nerve-racking for Napoleon's troops as they were for the defenders. After the Prussians shot up an enemy battery on November 15, "The good results that the artillerymen achieved with their fire this day resulted in a special collection the city took up for them, during which the Jewish community immediately provided 100 warm overcoats for sentries and artillerymen on the walls."[9]

J. J. Gaupp wrote in his account of the siege, "although the artillerymen had already been on the walls for eleven days, day and night in cold and rainy weather, they still demonstrated much obstinate courage and industriousness.

They did not complain about their difficult duty and men stayed in position even when sick."[10] Gaupp also described his impressions as a civilian: "In our imagination the lovely, tranquil past appears with twice the enchantment and the difficulties of those times in a much milder light. The present is filled with anxiety and fear and offers a sobering glimpse into a future harboring much that has never happened before, fraught with uncertainty and the ominous threat of frightful occurrences. We struggle under the heavy burden of conflicting emotions. Yet all of this is not without significant advantages. Being forced out of the mundane routine of our daily existence, suddenly aroused from its day-to-day banality and thoroughly shaking our entire personal essence, is certainly not without consequences. The insensitive begin to feel, the lazy give up their rest, various strange thoughts penetrate the soul, the egoist is compelled to pitch in and there is love for one another. What a broad field opens to attain self-satisfaction and be of service to others!"[11]

On November 24, Prince Jérôme sent two local politicians into the fortress to try and persuade Reinhart to surrender. The governor turned them away. Jérôme was preparing to attack the next day when he received orders from Napoleon to transfer two divisions and the cavalry brigade to Kalisch in South Prussia and leave one division at Glogau. The prince assigned the Württemberg division, comprising 8,000 men, to continue the siege and marched off with the Bavarian Wrede and Deroy Divisions to support the investment of Breslau. This was an example of how Prussian fortresses could indirectly support one another simply by holding out. All of the troops who besieged Glogau, with the exception of their commander in chief, were *Rheinbund* Germans. Napoleon understood how to make good use of these auxiliaries. He once cynically remarked, "I don't need to create discord among the Germans, since any sense of unity has long gone from their midst. I need only to cast my net and they dive into it like frightened animals. They've always displayed more bitterness toward one another than against their true enemy."[12]

Dominique Vandamme replaced Jérôme in command on November 28. He was an excessively brutal general who prior to Napoleon's coup had been suspended from the royal army for looting but was reinstated under his reign. The next day Vandamme received four heavy howitzers, four heavy mortars and six light mortars to bombard Glogau. In the icy conditions, unloading and emplacing the guns was an almost insurmountable task; the four heavy mortars had to be left behind. The first bombardment took place on the morning of December 01 and lasted nearly three hours. It killed a woman and a young girl, injured six laborers and demolished some houses. Prussian cannons were not shy in response. Vandamme sent an envoy into the fortress. He served up the usual lies to weaken Reinhart's resolve; the king has supposedly fled to Russia, there are no Prussian or Russian armies left to fight, a peace treaty will be concluded soon and so on. The French general put the claims in writing and signed the document, pledging his word of honor as to their veracity.[13]

The defenders had observed the departure of Jérôme's Bavarian divisions and knew that the siege corps is too weak to take Glogau. There were ample supplies in the fortress. Reinhart wavered nonetheless. The French heavy guns could not destroy the fortifications but were capable of damaging the town. Concerned for the welfare of the population, the governor was also unsettled by the conduct of Polish members of the garrison. They represented a substantial portion of his troop strength and although many did their duty, those who deserted kept Vandamme updated on conditions within the walls. On the night of November 28, a corporal incited 96 members of the Zastrow Musketeer Battalion to mutiny. They seized the Zerbauer redoubt. The mutineers sabotaged its cannons, blew the barrier to the drawbridge and escaped to the enemy leaving the drawbridge down. The same night, officers discovered a similar plot hatched by men of the Tschepe Battalion and shot the ringleaders.[14]

At one meeting of the war council, Reinhart had proposed meeting with the enemy even before Jérôme left. Major Puttlitz of the Grevenitz Regiment passionately opposed the notion and wrested the governor's consent to fight on. Reinhart's adjutant, Captain Brockhausen, delivered a written rejection of Jérôme's demand to French headquarters. Vandamme's first envoy had been turned away by Reinhart on December 01 because the French guns were still firing. Vandamme halted the barrage and sent his man back into the fortress at 11:00 a.m. that same morning. Even though he had previously assured Puttlitz that he will be "buried under the rubble" of Glogau before surrendering, Reinhart told the French envoy he is willing to surrender the fortress.[15] The cease-fire revealed to the garrison what was afoot. Insubordination spread and the men looted the supply depots. Vandamme's troops entered the town before negotiations were concluded to restore order. Reinhart reached an agreement with his adversary and the fortress was formally handed over on December 03. Many soldiers smashed their rifles before relinquishing them.

The terms of surrender were similar to those imposed on other garrisons. Officers were granted safe passage upon condition not to take up arms against France. NCOs and enlisted personnel who were married were allowed to go home. The rest of the garrison was to enter captivity in France, though many among them were released anyway. Only one percent of Reinhart's men had been killed in action and less than five percent were unfit for duty due to wounds or illness.[16] The governor surrendered a fortress that could have tied down the Württemberg division for months. "Glogau fell," Höpfner concluded, "without the enemy initiating the labors of a siege or risking an assault. The walls had not suffered at all; damage to the citizen's homes was minimal; the fortress guns were all in good condition despite the resident artillery officer claiming the opposite. Ammunition and provisions were in abundance. Losses to the garrison amounted to 30 to 40 dead, about as many wounded and nearly 200 deserters… there was not the remotest justification for the capitulation."[17]

Reinhart's conduct at Glogau was a classic example of a leader acting diametrically to the interests of his country and spirit of the population. The king's declaration of war had ended the anxiety of not knowing what lay ahead, and "ignited a blaze of patriotism that rose from souls long starved of deeds, in which bold words that have not been heard for years arouse passions… Even intellectuals with completely different convictions at least found solace in observing that our race still harbors enough traces of vitality to deserve to truly become a nation, that universal participation in public affairs has given rise to a more noble interest than just idle curiosity," as a contemporary of the times declared.[18] The invaders, moreover, were making themselves unwelcome in Silesia. They pillaged the countryside "with unparalleled barbarism," as Höpfner recorded: "Within a few days ten persons died from beatings and eight or nine (French) prisoners who were brought to Schweidnitz, in addition to carrying many valuables, were found to have 4,000 thaler on them."[19]

France's *Rheinbund* corps marched southeast down the Oder River toward Breslau, the provincial capital and next fortress in line after Glogau. Napoleon believed its capture will significantly demoralize the population of Silesia and provide the *Grande Armée* with siege guns, ammunition and ordnance to turn against fortresses still holding out.[20] The fortifications surrounding Breslau, a city of over 50,000 inhabitants, were imposing. Like most fortresses there was a main wall and an outer wall equipped with protruding bastions and moats guarding both. The main wall was unusually tall and wide, with a 120-feet wide ditch that could be flooded to a depth of ten feet. The outer moat was 60 to 70 feet wide in places and nearly seven feet deep. Fortifications however, were in need of repair. The drawbridge no longer functioned and the Breslau Gate had actually collapsed. There was a dearth of artillery and gunners.

Lindener's defeatism negatively influenced preparations to fortify Breslau. A resident recalled that "the accepted principle was to welcome the enemy in a friendly manner. Nevertheless, measures to prepare the defense of Breslau began on October 23; but at best, these arrangements were considered necessary just to obtain an advantageous capitulation… Several thousand hastily mustered recruits were sent to Graudenz. They came back along with a field artillery train because the road leading there was cut off. Had there been any initiative to do more, which would have been the honorable course, this valuable source of manpower would have been armed and put to good use. True to the prevailing attitude, the men were transferred from one Silesian fortress to another and then sent home because of an alleged lack of weapons… The first military authorities on the scene reassured worried property owners in the suburbs that their houses are not in danger because there can be no thought of serious resistance."[21]

On November 21, the king instructed Prince August von Anhalt-Pletz "to provision fortresses not yet surrounded by the enemy with all necessities, strengthen their garrisons and arm the recruits who can me mustered and the many stragglers roaming the countryside as well as possible. When this is accomplished, a special corps to take control of the province is to be formed."[22] The

Schanzenbau.

Employing civilian labor, French soldiers construct fortifications. This made areas more defensible and in the case of sieges, digging trenches called parallels allowed cannons to be emplaced close enough to bombard a fortress.

king ordered Pletz's adjutant Count Friedrich Wilhelm von Götzen to employ "exceptional measures to revive sunken spirits and harness all the powers of the state by any means, no matter how unusual, to dam the rising tide of French arms."[23] The king's directive to hold the fortresses stifled Breslau public officials' intent to surrender. They formed a militia comprising 650 foresters and hunters. These were experienced marksmen whose pay, weaponry and maintenance were financed by the crown. Several hundred pensioned soldiers and cavalrymen joined the garrison. Götzen augmented the original force, 1,500 men drawn from two battalions of the Thile Regiment, with land reserve recruits and some from depot battalions of the Treuenfels and Hohenlohe Regiments. There were 800 artillerymen to service the fortress guns. The final roster, 5,550 soldiers, included 2,000 ethnic Poles.[24]

Count Götzen, himself a major, purchased 200 horses from officers who had surrendered to the French and were on their way home. He elevated Breslau's cavalry contingent to 240 riders. He instructed Lieutenant Fiebig to establish a mounted battery consisting of volunteers from the field artillery and cannoneers from the captured Hahn Horse Battery who had escaped from the French. There was not sufficient time for Breslau's two resident engineers to fully restore the fortress, but 208 cannons of various caliber were distributed along the walls with 46 in reserve. The supply of powder and ammunition was substantial. Before Götzen left for the city, government officials had expressed mistrust of its residents. Upon his arrival on December 03, he therefore summoned community elders to courthouse. He appealed to their loyalty and sense of duty. "Almost in unison and without prompting, they swore with tears in their eyes to sacrifice their possessions and their blood for the king. This satisfied the count that the people of Breslau have been done an injustice."[25] The citizens contributed money to provide overcoats for the men and donated ample beer and brandy to distribute to them.

The governor of the fortress was General Alexander von Thile. The commandant was General August von Krafft. They were not cut from the same cloth as Götzen, who left the city on December 05. Nor was Lindener. Contrary to the count's orders to leave Breslau he stayed. On the 7th, the Bavarian Wrede Division and the Württemberg Division commanded by the redoubtable Vandamme appeared and came under fire from Prussian artillery on the walls. The next day, Thile ordered suburban houses outside the city gate burned down to offer his gunners a clear field of fire and deny the enemy shelter during the autumn nights. The order was given too late to destroy all of the buildings, since Thile had hesitated to issue it to avoid upsetting the townspeople. The fires impressed the enemy to anticipate determined, prolonged resistance. Vandamme brought large caliber cannons from Glogau. His gunners opened fire on the morning of December 10, despite the fact that the fortress artillery had maintained steady shelling during the previous night to disrupt French efforts to emplace the guns.

The besiegers ceased fire after a few hours to dispatch an envoy with a surrender demand. Negotiators were admitted because the temporary respite from the shelling afforded people the opportunity to emerge from the cellars, survey damage and take the fresh air. An eyewitness recalled, "As clearly as the danger threatening the city now was before their eyes, the spirit of the inhabitants did not appear to have been weakened by this first serious test, but strengthened instead. Rejoicing over rejection of the demand was universal. Since nothing about the negotiations was made public, we listened with longing for the cannonade to resume. The first rounds fired were received with a certain sense of relief since they confirmed that there is no capitulation."[26] The daily bombardments reached a crescendo on the 14th. The townspeople counted hundreds of rounds fired. Prussian fortress artillery always returned fire but was unable to silence the besiegers' guns. Town pastors opened the churches for services that Sunday. Attendance was negligible.

The barrage continued on Monday. On the 16th, two French envoys arrived and were led to the governor without blindfolds. When the surrender demand was refused the bombardment resumed, but without particular intensity. After several more days of shelling, Vandamme arranged another cease-fire to send in a negotiator. It was the afternoon of December 25. During the talks, General

Thile received a petition signed by the magistrate and some town merchants. It described the town's distress and asked the governor to turn the fortress over to the French. A delegation of six citizens bearing the same request was admitted at almost the same time. Its members declared that they speak "in the name of all corporations and enterprises" of Breslau.[27] Thile assembled his staff to solicit opinions about the petition and whether or not to continue negotiations with the French. With the exception of Major Löpel, all the officers present were inclined to take the misery of the population into account. Thile disagreed and notified the magistrate that this alone is not sufficient motive to surrender.

A separate deputation of citizens visited the governor at 8:30 a.m. the next morning. They reaffirmed their commitment to sacrifice whatever is necessary for king and country and pledged to support the military in every way possible. Crowds gathered and expressed the wish not to be delivered to the capriciousness of the invaders. Most officers opposed capitulation. They cited the intact condition of the fortifications, minimal casualties and adequate stores of food and ammunition. Thile voided the cease-fire at ten o'clock in the morning. On the 27th, a third delegation of townspeople appeared at the governor's headquarters. It protested the surrender appeal delivered by the mercantile class and the magistrate, expressed its loyalty to the king and urged the general to fight on. Two days later Thile received a report that city merchants are price gouging and creating artificial shortages of food and currency so that the government will become receptive to the resulting hardships and capitulate.[28]

Around this time, Prince Anhalt-Pletz deployed the 10,000-man army corps he had mustered to relieve Breslau. On Götzen's suggestion, the expedition approached from the southeast between Ohlau and the Oder River. The French chief engineer considered the terrain too difficult for a mass of troops to cross and it was virtually undefended. Plans for the relief operation were betrayed to Vandamme on December 23.[29] He learned that Anhalt-Pletz was assembling his corps in Strehlen to the south of Breslau. Vandamme shifted troops to meet the threat. Instead of holding Strehlen until reinforcements arrived, the Prussians attacked in open field with inferior numbers. They failed in part due to the passivity of Thile. He could have launched a sortie from the fortress timed to coincide with the relief action but did nothing. During the officers' conference on December 26, Thile then disclosed rumors that Anhalt-Pletz has been taken prisoner, the fortress of Brieg has fallen and Schweidnitz is about to, the Russian army in Poland has been defeated and the king has fled Prussia. None of this was true.

A second operation conducted by Anhalt-Pletz to raise the siege began on the morning of December 30. The Prussian cavalry reached Oltaschin, a village on the outskirts of Breslau, without incident. Vandamme was again forewarned and transferred available units there to defend Oltaschin. The Prussian infantry joined the fighting. Artillery on both sides opened fire and the battle was on. The prince was depending on a simultaneous sortie from Breslau's garrison to take the enemy from behind. Götzen had previously arranged with Lindener that the relief force will signal him when to attack by torching the windmill at Dürjentsch. In addition to this, the sound of musketry and cannon fire coming from Oltaschin was audible to the soldiers on the walls. At nine o'clock that morning, Lieutenant Schorlemmer reported to Thile that the French are hastily pulling troops and light artillery from the trenches in front of the fortress and rushing them to the battle. The governor dismissed him with the words, "The enemy is maneuvering to entice the garrison out of the city."[30]

A short time later, Schorlemmer returned and reported, "The enemy is not maneuvering, the relief troops can clearly be seen." The lieutenant then tried to convince Krafft, who retorted, "Don't tell me what's happening. I can judge things for myself."[31] Höpfner noted, "Others had seen how enemy infantry were running from the trenches in the direction of the battle and it was apparent that most of the trenches were abandoned by the enemy. A sortie was not only justifiable, but absolutely necessary. Others claimed to have seen the Prussian cavalry near the Jewish cemetery between Huben and the Schweidnitz suburb. The correctness of this observation was later confirmed by the suburb's residents… Even though there was a shroud of mist, troops could be spotted between Oltaschin and Dürjentsch, as well as rising smoke and muzzle flashes from large cannons. The firing also seemed to be getting closer to the city. One could only conclude that a (relief) attack was under way."[32] Thile took no action. Without support from the garrison, Anhalt-Pletz was unable to push through to the city and withdrew in the afternoon.

The governor's apathy toward the relief attack invited speculation as to his motive. Some assumed that Thile didn't trust the Polish members of the garrison enough to send them outside the walls. Others suspected that he wished to deprive Prince Anhalt-Pletz, a much younger officer, of the glory of rescuing the provincial capital.[33] The sentiment that soldier and citizen alike shared was ill feeling toward the governor. Everyone understood the necessity of a sortie and attributed ulterior motives to him. The unprecedented surrender of so many fortresses had evoked universal mistrust of the governors. This was particularly the case at Breslau; nowhere had the population of a city contributed more to the well-being of its garrison. Out of gratitude for its sacrifice, both the wealthy and those of modest means there were in a genuine competition to outdo one another to provide for the soldiers. The men of every bastion and rampart received ample and varied supplies of foodstuffs as well as beer and brandy.

On January 03, a man who had circulated a petition signed by citizens wishing to surrender delivered it to the courthouse along with a letter from the magistrate with the same appeal. There were but 160 signatures on the petition in a city of over 50,000 people. Others expressed the desire to continue fighting. The governor summoned Generals Krafft and Lindener to his office and showed them the petition and a report from the logistics office that there isn't enough firewood left for baking bread. All agreed to capitulate and began negotiations with the enemy the next day. After the usual haggling, an agreement was reached on January 05. The citizens clamored to be armed rather than surrender. The soldiers angrily looted military depots. The garrison, comprising 116 officers and 5,270 men, relinquished the fortress on the 7th. Unmarried rankers began the long trek to camps in France. The Prussians left the French 240 serviceable cannons and a huge store of powder.[36]

The governor later offered the investigation commission his excuses for surrendering one of Silesia's most formidable strongholds after one month's siege. He cited the alleged insubordination of the garrison. There was in fact no unruliness until it became known that he had capitulated. Thile also claimed that the fortifications were too dilapidated to conduct a proper defense. In fact, satisfactory repairs had continued even after the investment began. His assertion that there was too little timber left for baking is exaggerated. Thile's contention that the frost was about to freeze the moats, therefore making it nearly impossible to keep the enemy at bay, is untrue; Lindener's personal journal recorded milder temperatures on January 03. The result was that moats and the Oder River were free of ice. It would be another ten days before the onset of severe cold.[37] Further, there is absolutely no justification for allowing the garrison to enter captivity; the men could have been ordered to leave the city before the capitulation was ratified to either join the main army or proceed to another fortress.

Thile also expressed his concern about protecting the city from being "reduced to ashes" by bombardment. As already established, this is not a valid military reason to cease resistance. The besiegers fired some 10,000 rounds into Breslau. Bombardments killed 35 citizens and injured 88. Nearly 1,500 houses were damaged but very few totally destroyed.[38] After surrendering, the governor expressed surprise that citizens had not taken refuge from the shelling in the subterranean bombproof bunkers. Even though they were vacant, people did not enter them because they were military property and presumed off limits. One word from Thile granting public access could have saved lives and spared hundreds from anxiety, illness and injury. It never occurred to him to give the order.[39] The fall of Breslau brought most of Silesia under Napoleon's control. It allowed him to concentrate his forces on remaining strongholds and pursue his campaign in Poland.

Kosel and Neisse

The next Prussian position on the Oder was Brieg. The town was weakly fortified and Napoleon's Bavarian auxiliaries captured it in a week. There were minimal casualties on both sides. The booty that fell to the enemy included 153 cannons, a corresponding inventory of gunpowder, over a quarter of a million rifle rounds and a generous supply of foodstuffs. The last river fortress remaining in Prussian hands was Kosel. General Bernhard Deroy, a *Rheinbund* ally of Bonaparte who had fought against France during the first two coalition wars, led 5,000 Bavarians and four field batteries straight from Brieg to invest the stronghold. The expedition reached Kosel on January 23, 1807. Polish insurgents were active in the area east of the Oder until Götzen sent cavalry to disperse them. Although renovation of the old fortress had begun in 1797, repairs were not scheduled for completion before the summer of 1807. Five brick bastions protruded from the main wall. Fort Friedrich Wilhelm on the small river island across from the fortress had an earthen roof.

Kosel's garrison of 67 officers and 4,249 men was poorly equipped. Soldiers of recently established National Battalions were armed with lances or scythes. Others belonged to so-called *Dritte Bataillonen* (Third-Class Battalions) unfit for campaign service. Some 800 farmers were shanghaied to keep the Oder River clear of ice floes and prevent the moat from freezing over. The frost had reduced its width to 15 feet in places. The farmers sought opportunities to desert. Conscripted Polish recruits were almost as unreliable. The commandant of Kosel, Colonel David von Neumann, therefore faced a difficult task. He had served as a lieutenant during the Seven Years' War as one of Friedrich the Great's burgher officers. His achievements in the Prussian army earned him a knight-hood in 1779. As commandant of Kosel, he dealt with slackers with the utmost severity. Neumann also rewarded men demonstrating superior performance with military decorations or financial incentive. He ensured that the troops were properly clothed and nourished; "The commandant spared no effort to improve the spirit of the garrison."[40]

Inhospitable terrain and the harsh climate made digging trenches and re-doubts for the cannons difficult for the besiegers. Neumann dispatched an assault party to burn down a few houses outside of the walls. Deroy's sappers dug up the water line at Reinschdorf to cut off delivery of pure water to Kosel. The towns-people and garrison drank what they drew from wells within the city or from the brackish water of the Oder. The enemy opened the bombardment on February 04. During the eight-hour barrage, Bavarian artillerymen fired 1,250 rounds into the fortress. Their siege guns were emplaced so far from their target that they had to be loaded with an extra charge of powder. The blast often extinguished the fuse of the bombs when discharged, so that they landed as duds without starting fires. Mortars were aimed at such high trajectory that many rounds detonated in flight. This negated their effectiveness. Those that found their mark caused considerable damage thanks to the poor construction of houses in the city and its small confines. Residents cowered in cellars while Neumann detailed 240 men from the garrison to combat the flames.

Deroy knew that Kosel cannot be taken by assault. He sent a French and a Bavarian captain to demand the city's surrender on February 11. They an-nounced that Schweidnitz has capitulated, Napoleon has beaten the Russian army at Allenstein and that further resistance at Kosel is therefore pointless. Neumann replied, "I don't care in the least about things that happen outside the fortress," and curtly sent the envoys away.[41] The bluff about the hopelessness of Prussia's situation discouraged some commandants but not Neumann. Though boxed in, he had 229 cannons at his disposal and totally outgunned the opposition.

General Deroy and his staff oversee the investment of Kosel, a small fortress that held out until the end of the war. The king had assigned Its commander, the elderly Colonel Neumann, to the tranquil post before hostilities began to spare him "the rigors of field service."

His artillery inflicted serious casualties on Bavarian gun crews. They became utterly demoralized by the superior firepower of the defenders and by having to consistently repair redoubts destroyed by Kosel's counter-barrages. Deroy's chief engineer, Colonel Blein, sent a report to Breslau describing the impossibility of continuing the siege without significant reinforcements.

An early thaw flooded the Bavarian position. By February 14, the Oder River swelled to a depth of thirteen feet and emersed the besiegers' trenches. Crews abandoned the redoubts and left heavy guns submerged. It was not possible to resume shelling Kosel until February 24. The French sent another envoy on the 28th but he was turned away at the gate. Shelling continued on and off until March 04. By then the fortress had been under fire for a total of over a hundred hours.[42] The French high command denied Blein's request for more men and cannons. It ordered the artillery transferred to Glogau on March 04. Neumann sent out a patrol on March 07. Two lieutenants leading a platoon of *Jäger* and 30 volunteers from the Sanitz Battalion drove off Bavarian pickets and returned to the fortress with a captured 24-pound cannon. On March 17, the invaders' 4th and 14th Line Infantry Regiments, the 4th Light Battalion Braun and the Vandouve Battery left Kosel and went to Warsaw, Danzig and Graudenz. Residents of Leischnitz brought brandy and tobacco for the Prussian artillerymen inside Kosel, even though the enemy had looted their village of most of these commodities.[43]

Neumann arguably had more problems inside of Kosel than beyond the walls. Desertion and mutiny plagued the garrison. On the night of March 04/05, officers discovered a conspiracy involving over 200 men. At midnight, 95 deserters had already passed through the Oder River gate when checked by Captain Josef von Brixen, who was in command of Fort Wilhelm. Sentries opened fire on them but 55 escaped to French lines. The crew of the Kobelwitz redoubt plotted to murder their company commander, Captain Wostrowsky. They intended to bind the other officers and throw some into the river, sabotage the cannons and shoot fellow soldiers who refuse to mutiny. Supported by loyal NCOs and his *Jäger*, the captain locked all doors and windows to the barracks, gathered over a hundred men from other strongpoints and arrested his entire company. He spent the night interrogating suspects and reported the findings to the commandant. Twenty ringleaders were arrested; Neumann ordered every fifth one shot.[44] Wostrowsky pardoned the rest of the mutineers, who fell to their knees in gratitude.

Kosel had a respite from siege for 21 days until the Bavarians returned in early April. A formation under Major Wreden took up positions on the right bank of the Oder to blockade the fortress from both sides. It was not possible to completely surround Kosel. Local peasants continued delivering foodstuffs to the city. On April 06, Prussian *Jäger* conducted a reconnaissance sortie. A force of hussars and horse artillery sallied from the fortress four days later to cover the retreat of the *Jäger*. They kept the Bavarians off balance and disrupted their preparations. On April 16 Kosel lost the gallant Colonel Neumann. He died from an infection caused by a leg injury. Several times during the siege arthritis and a neurological disorder had forced him to temporarily place adjutant Ludwig von Puttkammer in charge. Neumann had always resumed as commandant when symptoms abated. When bedridden, he discharged administrative tasks such as drafting reports and official correspondence. Deeply mourned by loyal members of the garrison and the population, he was laid to rest in the Rheinsdorfer bastion as he had requested. Colonel Puttkammer took over as commandant.

Enemy shellfire compelled soldier and civilian alike to seek refuge in subterranean chambers. Jammed together in dank, overcrowded conditions, tormented by anxiety, drinking impure water, those within the walls contended with disease as well. On February 21, 309 members of the garrison languished in the hospital. By May 01, there were 781 soldiers under treatment.[45] A month later, typhus claimed an average of 14 lives a day. On June 01, Puttkammer opened negotiations with the enemy. He appointed a war council and its officers agreed that he should inquire about conditions to hand over the fortress. The capture of Danzig on May 24 improved France's strategic position. This allowed the besiegers to offer conciliatory terms. During the cease-fire the French reopened the waterline at Reinschdorf to give the citizens pure drinking water again. They also sent medicine from their stores to Kosel's hospital. In all, 263 persons in the city died from illness during June.[46] The Prussians ratified an agreement on June 18 to deliver the fortress to the French as long as no relief force arrives before July 18. This ended the siege of Kosel. Resisting for 123 days, the garrison had lost 1,314 men from combat, desertion and disease.[47]

Friedrich Wilhelm expressed satisfaction with the defense. He promoted officers and decorated soldiers and civilians who had distinguished themselves during the siege. The king promoted the deceased Neumann to major general and erected a cast iron statue of him inside the Oder bastion. The sovereign also pledged to provide funding to rebuild Kosel once peace is restored. Contending with bombardments, the besiegers' attempts to starve the population out, mutiny, desertion and a debilitating illness, David von Neumann had conducted an uncompromising and genuinely heroic defense of the fortress. It held out much longer than more formidable strongholds. One can only imagine how differently Bonaparte's autumn and winter campaigns might have developed had Gneisenau and Neumann, instead of being assigned comparatively small garrisons, been in command at Magdeburg and Hameln.

During the fighting at Kosel, the French also had to deal with Danzig, Graudenz, Kolberg and Neisse. The resistance offered by all five fortresses required the invaders to shift divisions and artillery from one objective to another. This prolonged investments and drained enemy resources. The battle for Danzig prevented the enemy from conducting an effective operation against Graudenz immediately to the south. Napoleon spent seven months trying to neutralize the smaller Russian army commanded by General Bennigsen, who crossed lances with the *Grande Armée* at Pultusk in December 1806, Eylau in February 1807 and Friedland in June. "The winter campaigns of 1806 and 1807… demonstrate that a field commander of mediocre talent was sufficient to spoil Napoleon's continuous and often militarily baffling series of easy victories."[48] A study of the French warlord's campaigns illustrates the importance he assigned to concentrating his forces; yet Prussian strongholds in Pomerania and Silesia compelled him to transfer away formations that he wanted to use against Bennigsen.

The defense of Neisse, which earned praise from the French general directing the siege, contributed to the winter hardships confronting the invaders. Beside the river of the same name west of where it joins the Oder, Neisse was considered by the Prussian command the most important Silesian fortress next to Schweidnitz. Despite this, Lindener implemented half measures to upgrade it. On October 28 he ordered only the main wall, the Kardinal and Kapuziner redoubts and Fort Preussen armed. Works already equipped with cannons were to be disarmed. Lindener did not plan to open dams and flood the surrounding countryside. The garrison consisted of two battalions of the Pelchrzim Infantry Regiment and a motley rifle battalion drawn from different service branches including pensioned veterans from the Müffling Regiment. Lindener dismissed new recruits mustered to augment the garrison. The population provided four to five thousand workers daily. They continued working even at night to repair

Armed with a saber, the 26-year-old Rosalie von Bonin secures the
treasury of a Silesian town to prevent its seizure by the French. With
a small escort, she carried money to pay Götzen's troops operating
in Glatz, often riding behind enemy lines.

fortifications. Local farmers gathered stores of gunpowder from nearby depots
and delivered them to Neisse.

Prince Anhalt-Pletz came on December 13 and countermanded Lindener's
instructions. Major Harroy, the *Ingénieur de la place* (resident engineer), recommended that the Enveloppe, the outer wall, be armed together with the main
wall. Pletz concurred and cannons were distributed there. Local woodsmen provided lumber from the timber-rich region for construction of palisades, barracks
and watch towers for gun crews. All but two bridges were dismantled and the
pair remaining barricaded. Moats were cleared of obstructions and refilled. With
the energetic support of the population, Neisse was rapidly converted to a formidable bastion. The prince transferred troops to reinforce the garrison, activated
retired officers and promoted corporals and sergeants to positions of command.
Recruits for the artillery received four to five hours of training per day. The
garrison swelled to 6,124 men and 280 civilian laborers.[49] Pletz instructed the
townspeople to gather enough food to sustain every household for six months.
Meal, grain and fodder flowed into Neisse as did oxen, pigs and sheep.

On January 30, 1807, the fortress was fully prepared. One shortcoming was the inability to flood the approaches. Two dams had been demolished in 1798 and 1799 to prevent inundating arable land. Without them it was now only possible to partially submerge the area. The defenders were at least able to create muddy conditions for the besiegers. Neisse had 267 cannons, 29 howitzers and 48 mortars in position with the heaviest concentration of guns on the northern front. The store of powder and shot was immense. The rural community and residents of Neisse were committed to the struggle. According to Höpfner, "The spirit of the burghers, like everywhere in Silesia, was loyal and devoted; the people were ready to relinquish whatever they possessed without complaint if it contributes to defense of the fortress."[50] Neisse's commandant was Hans von Weger, who was 68 years old. The governor was Georg von Steensen, a Danish-born officer aged 73.

Prussian patrols spotted the enemy on February 22. A Württemberg division under General Freiherr von Seckendorff arrived directly from Schweidnitz, which had capitulated on February 07. The division tallied 7,100 men at full strength. During much of the battle for Neisse only about half that number was available. Troops taking part in sorties from the garrison burned down various buildings beyond the walls. Neisse experienced its first alarm on February 25. Seckendorff's sappers dug parallels to site their siege guns close enough to the town to begin the bombardment. Fortress artillery shelled their positions on the morning of March 02. They inflicted casualties and disrupted the dig. That night the *Rheinbund* troops opened fire on the Kaninchen and Friedrichstadt redoubts with a howitzer battery but the guns on the walls soon put it to silence. A strong snowstorm obscured visibility. This enabled 72 members of the garrison to desert. Despite their superior firepower, the Prussian artillerymen were consistently tormented by the accurate marksmanship of a company of *Jäger*, Württemberg sharpshooters, whom defenders on the walls attempted in turn to pin down with harassing fire.

On February 25, Napoleon wrote Jérôme in Silesia that the *Grande Armée* suffered heavy losses in the battle of Eylau. The emperor instructed him to determine whether the Württemberg division will suffice to control Glogau and Breslau and hold Prince Pletz in check. The sieges of Kosel and Neisse were no longer a priority and 6,000 Bavarian troops under General Deroy were to proceed to Warsaw. Jérôme placed Vandamme in charge of the Württembergers and rerouted the siege corps headed for Neisse to Glogau, where a depot was established. Two battalions of *Jäger* and two of light infantry as well as the Schröder Regiment, 3,100 men in all, rose from the trenches surrounding Neisse and departed for Glogau on March 05. This left 3,300 riflemen and two cavalry regiments to blockade Neisse. The Prussian garrison sent 100 hussars under command of Ferdinand von Schmiedeberg to reconnoiter the enemy position. They found the trenches abandoned due to standing water. The patrol became embroiled in a firefight but eluded encirclement and returned to the fortress with a loss of three men killed.

The defenders now focused on the Württemberg sharpshooters at Schilde who were perpetually harassing the Prussians at the Kaninchen redoubt. Schmiedeberg stealthily led out 300 horsemen and 95 infantry volunteers with a pair of cannons from the fortress before dawn on March 08. The wheels of the cannons were wrapped in straw to muffle the sound. Their objective was to eliminate the position of the troublesome enemy marksmen. A head-on surprise attack was repulsed, but the Prussian cavalry circumvented Schilde and captured 130 members of the Württemberg 1st *Fussjäger* Battalion, three *Chevaux-legers* and two officers including Captain Freiherr von Brusselli who was seriously wounded. The Prussians had a dozen casualties and the Württemberg *Jäger* over 20 men killed. The troops under Schmiedeberg's command reentered the fortress with the prisoners grouped in the center of the column. A throng of onlookers were on hand to welcome the volunteers. A citizen of Neisse described the scene:

"A crowd of people gathered to greet the homecoming victors and aroused the envy of their brothers in arms who had not taken part in the sortie. A large group encircled the victors and joyfully greeted them with shouts of 'bravo!' The captured *Jäger* stood cowering beside the Church of Jerusalem. Huddled in overcoats threadbare from the ravages of time, they appeared deeply distressed by the burden of their fate; especially when the rucksacks strapped to their backs were taken from them and emptied before their eyes. They yielded an immeasurable booty of money, watches and so forth. The soldiers thoroughly searched the prisoners' pockets and took their scarves that had money concealed in them. The stunning quantity of valuables captivated everyone's spirits and within half an hour transformed the lifeless Friedrichstadt into an outdoor market. Here silver spoons, golden and silver watches, silver-plated cabinet fittings and silver garlands were auctioned off to the highest bidders, for the most part to Hebrew merchants. Soon all the shops were filled and reverberated from the rejoicing of the merry warriors. Within the city, everyone was delighted over the successful sortie. People came from all sides to see the prisoners and could talk of nothing else but the events of the day... Everyone praised the glorious feat of arms of the soldiers."[51]

Steensen learned on March 14 that members of the Württemberg division attempted to extort a clergyman at the parsonage at Schilde for 1,500 thaler by threatening to hang his family. The governor protested to Vandamme. At the same time, Count Götzen wrote to General Lefebvre about the marauding of *Rheinbund* troops blockading Neisse. The conduct of the Brüssel and Neubronn Battalions and the *Jägerregiment zu Pferde* (mounted rifle regiment) was particularly reprehensible; there were cases of soldiers murdering civilians in the quest for loot.[52] Jérôme advised Napoleon that the mood in Silesia has become so resentful that the population is only waiting for the right moment to stage an uprising and that the Württemberg division cannot control the province without reinforcements. He cautioned the emperor that it would be a serious mistake to leave Vandamme in charge of Silesia, given the odium associated with his name.[53]

After a week at French headquarters in Breslau, Vandamme returned to Neisse on March 12. The day before his arrival a Prussian raiding party captured 217 horses that Württemberg troops had taken from locals for the army. The sorties were risky since the element of surprise was often lost. A predawn raid on March 17 conducted by over a thousand Prussians against a detachment of *Chevaux-legers* in Stephansdorf blundered into an ambush because a deserter forewarned the enemy. Vandamme had siege guns at Schweidnitz transferred to bombard Neisse. Six batteries opened fire on April 16. One round struck an ammunition wagon in the fortress. The explosion detonated a powder magazine and caused dozens of casualties. The next day, the garrison shifted 30 howitzers and mortars from non-threatened positions to the southern wall where the enemy concentrated his firepower. Fortress artillery destroyed six of the besiegers' cannons in a short time and inflicted heavy losses on the gunners. Bombs from Vandamme's 70-pound mortars wreaked havoc within the city; rounds striking three-story buildings penetrated down to the cellar.

Vandamme, whom Silesians nicknamed *Verdammt* (damned), sent couriers to the surrounding villages warning locals not to take food to the garrison under pain of death. A farmer's wife caught trying to smuggle butter into Neisse was shot on his order.[54] The rural population depended on sales of their products at the town market for their livelihood and continued to infiltrate enemy lines at night to peddle foodstuffs inside the fortress. Butchers from Niemerzheide, a town a mile from Neisse, slipped past *Rheinbund* sentries to buy cattle from area farmers. They planned to sneak the animals into Neisse. Upon learning of their purpose, the mayor of Niemerzheide had the butchers arrested and placed in irons. He intended to hand them over to the French. This would mean certain death since they were violating Vandamme's decree. The men escaped arrest and made their way to Neisse. They reported to Steensen's staff what had happened.

The following night, Captain Schmiedeberg and 100 hussars eluded enemy pickets and made their way to Niemerzheide. The white coats of the riders resembled those worn by enemy cavalry. The squadron's bugler, born in Ansbach and speaking the Württemberg dialect, tricked the watch at the town gate into raising the barrier and obligingly leading Schmiedeberg's disguised raiders to the mayor's residence. Under the pretext that they are under orders to take the mayor to General Vandamme, the Prussians mounted him on the extra horse they had brought and rode out of town to the well wishes of the sentries. Only when the column turned toward the fortress instead of toward French headquarters did the mayor realize he has fallen into Prussian hands. The captain turned the treacherous politician over to the commandant.[55] Vandamme's force was not numerous enough to contain the garrison, so harassing sorties against French lines were a steady torment. The warm spring sunshine thawed the snow. This flooded enemy trenches and battery positions and created further misery for his troops.

The heavy mortars the French had brought from Schweidnitz—formerly Prussian guns, therefore—caused such devastation to the city that a delegation of

Serving as Prince Anhalt-Pletz's adjutant, Count Götzen waged a guerrilla war ambushing French replacements and supply convoys. With 7,000 men under his command, he prevented the enemy from taking control of the mountainous Glatz region of Silesia.

citizens visited the commandant on April 18 to ask him to surrender the fortress. The same day, a direct hit destroyed the apothecary and the entire supply of medicine. This had catastrophic consequences for the sick and injured. Steensen declined the delegation's request and turned away a French envoy two days later. The artillery duel resumed with unrelenting fury. Both sides suffered mounting losses. On April 25, a round from the fortress struck an enemy powder magazine and blew it sky high. Without medications, disease spread in Neisse during the latter half of April. Enemy barrages and illness caused 32 Prussian deaths in a nine-day period.[56] Steensen committed a tactical error in agreeing to a prisoner exchange. In return for a group of Prussian officers and rankers, most of whom were wounded, he traded over a hundred of the Württemberg *Fussjäger* taken prisoner at Schilde; the marksmen who had sniped at Prussian gun crews during winter. The *Jäger* resumed their previous occupation. This aroused the ire of garrison artillerymen toward their commandant for placing them at the mercy of the deadly sharpshooters for a second time.

Late at night on May 04, a dragoon named Klösel slipped out of Neisse and rode to Glatz to update Count Götzen on conditions within the fortress. Upon hearing his report, the count dispatched Lieutenant Karl von Rottenburg to return with Klösel to Neisse. Rottenburg brought 10,000 thaler worth of redeemable bonds to pay tradesmen repairing damaged fortifications. He was empowered by the king to attend war councils and prolong the defense. The lieutenant described his impressions upon inspecting the fortress: "After assigning 800 men to help with the artillery, the loss of 700 men sick and 500 through death or desertion, there were still 4,000 men in service of whom only half were fit for duty. Three eights of them were poorly armed and one eighth consisted of pensioned soldiers. The cavalry still had 400 riders with 300 horses. A number of guns were scattered about the walls with shot-up carriages and burned-out priming vents. To repair one piece required pirating components from three others. There were still nearly 5,500 hundredweights of powder and an abundance of cannonballs in the fortress.

"The fortifications have already suffered damage in various places. The necessary repairs cannot be made by a garrison that has become exhausted from inordinately strenuous duty. There are no trusses on the outer wall so the line can be infiltrated. Only with difficulty can the sentries be kept at their post. Some of the locks have already been damaged, especially Lock Number One. Except for butter and meat there is no shortage of groceries. There is a complete lack of money, in that expenses can only be covered until May 15; the budget requires 30,000 thaler monthly. There is no medication to properly care for the sick and the wounded. Morale of the soldiers is dispirited, apathetic and sullen, inclined toward desertion. There is scarcely a house left that is undamaged and the Customs Street quarter may be considered demolished. There are alarming privations among the poorer classes."[57]

On May 29, two French envoys were admitted into Neisse to arrange a meeting between Vandamme and the governor. Steensen requested a 24-hour cease-fire. He convened a session of the war council consisting of Generals Heinrich von der Lahr and Weger, all of the staff officers and Lieutenant Rottenburg. At the meeting, Colonel Wernitz and Major Harroy described the condition of the fortress: "The fortifications and their weaponry are no longer capable of resisting an assault with certainty. The ammunition will only allow for 16 more days of defense if it is expended to the utmost as has been the case so far. The palisades along the entire front that is under attack from the enemy… are shot up and cannot be repaired. The lack of fascines is significant. The main locks, especially Lock Number One, are in poor condition… so that there is a danger that we will lose the outer flooding completely. It therefore appears that the fortress can only be held for certain in the coming month through a cease-fire."[58] Opinions were divided, but the council approved entering into talks with the enemy.

The meeting between the French general and Steensen, Weger, Lahr, Rottenburg and a few Prussian staff officers took place the next morning in a tent in the village of Heidersdorf. The governor and commandant agreed to surrender Neisse and Fort Preussen if no relief column arrives by June 16. With the sanction of Rottenburg, the king's representative, the capitulation was ratified on June 03. During the 16-day cease-fire, Vandamme provided Neisse's hospital with medicine and wine from French stores. Early on June 16, Württemberg *Jäger* ceremoniously took over guard duty in the fortress. Prussian soldiers destroyed the cannons and rolled bombs and grenades into the moat. They smashed their rifles and sabers or pitched them into the water as well. At seven o'clock in the morning the procession of over 4,000 men, led by the marching band and with flags flying, defiled out of Neisse through the Jerusalem Gate. By the terms arranged with Vandamme, most members of the garrison were paroled to return to their homes.

Neisse endured 123 bombardments during the siege. Only five of the town's 508 private homes were undamaged. During some periods, typhus claimed as many as 30 lives a week. The 98-day investment cost the garrison 200 killed in action, 450 wounded, 600 sick, 300 taken prisoner and 550 deserters; a third of the original force.[59] Throughout the siege, Prussian assault troops had repeatedly attacked enemy positions in bold sorties. They made life for the besiegers as risky as it was for the beleaguered. During the ceremony on June 16, Vandamme said to Steensen and Weger, "Because of the way that you defended the fortress, we have the greatest regard for you and for your garrison. For this reason, you, Herr Governor and you, Herr Commandant, are free from captivity. You may also choose four officers who like you, may leave at once to remain in the service of the king."[60] This was an extraordinary gesture of respect, as officers taken prisoner were customarily granted personal freedom only on condition that they abstain from military service for a specified period or until exchanged.

Prince Jérôme moved against the last Silesian fortresses, Glatz and Silberberg, right after the fall of Neisse. Vandamme met Götzen and members of his staff on June 19 to try and persuade them to surrender Glatz. With hat under his arm, Vandamme expressed how supposedly privileged he feels to be authorized to negotiate with the outstanding commander of such valiant troops and to propose an agreement as honorable as the man he is offering it to. He pledged to allow all Prussian troops in Silesia to march unmolested with their weapons including artillery to rejoin the main army if the remaining fortresses surrender. Götzen thanked him for the honorable terms but retorted that he cannot accept without permission from the king. Vandamme dropped the flattery and announced that there are 20,000 men and 300 siege guns at his disposal to reduce Glatz to rubble. The count was unmoved. The Frenchman lost patience and declared to Prussian officers present, "It is atrocious that so many brave officers who have done more than their duty must suffer because of the stubbornness of one individual. Under the circumstances, disobedience is completely justifiable. There is no longer a king of Prussia and the Russian-Prussian army has just been totally vanquished. The king is probably dead on the battlefield, since he has been missing since the battle."[61]

The taunt angered the Prussian officers and Götzen had to restrain Major Görtz, who had drawn his saber, from hacking Vandamme on the spot. The French general threatened to leave "no stone atop another" on Götzen's private estate, to deliver the count's relatives to the mercy of his marauding soldiers and hang commandants of fortresses still resisting. Götzen patiently concluded the dialog by stating that he will refrain from an appropriate response out of customary respect for an official envoy.[62] The attack on Glatz, conducted by Deroy and Vandamme with French and *Rheinbund* contingents, proved as merciless as predicted. A French surprise attack with vastly superior numbers overwhelmed a fortified camp of the defenders at night. A Prussian report described how "the bitterness of the enemy, and these were Bavarians and Württembergers, was so great there that they cut down Prussian officers who had already surrendered and clubbed the wounded to death with their rifle butts."[63]

Since Glatz was poorly prepared to defy a siege and insufficiently stocked with munitions, Götzen spared the town the distress of bombardment. He rode to Wartha to meet personally with Prince Jérôme and negotiate the surrender of the fortress on June 25. It was to be relinquished to the French on July 26 unless a relief force comes to its aid. The invaders had less success investing the final Silesian fortress, Silberberg. Friedrich the Great had ordered construction of the complex because during the Seven Years' War, the Austrian army had crossed the undefended Silberberg pass to raid the Glatz district. The four-phase building project began in 1765 and continued for twelve years. During 1768, over 4,000 artisans and laborers were involved. Although the garrison in 1807 consisted of just two understrength battalions, a *Jäger* company and 40 cavalrymen, the modern, well-designed fortress was anchored in bedrock and virtually impervious to siege.

The investment began on June 26. Deroy with a force of Bavarian and Württemberg troops attacked Fort Spitzberg and a row of palisades outside the village of Silberberg, but were driven back with heavy losses by accurate fire from the fortress artillery. He then bombarded the town for 48 hours. The barrage destroyed 150 houses and the church. His men entered the village and looted private homes. On June 29, Deroy proposed negotiations. The fortress commandant, the 61-year-old Colonel Schwerin, replied that "a hail of bombs, grenades and rocks will be hurled back at you. We await your attack."[64] The next day the French resumed the shelling with three howitzers and three mortars. Combat operations abruptly came to an end with news of a cease-fire concluded between Napoleon and Friedrich Wilhelm III. Under terms of the subsequent treaty, fortresses still holding out or last to surrender were to remain under Prussian control and not be dismantled. As a result, the fortress of Silberberg is largely intact to this day. It remains an imposing monument to the era of the great Friedrich and to Prussian defiance during the country's darkest hour.

Chapter 11

Behind the Scenes

Bumbling or Treason?

Historians generally attribute the betrayal of the Prussian fortresses by "dishonorable rogues" like Benekendorff, Kleist, Lecoq, Romberg and Ingersleben to defeatism caused by the lost battles of Saalfeld, Jena and Auerstedt and Hohenlohe's surrender at Prenzlau. Other factors are cited, especially German sympathy for ideals propagated by the French Revolution. Many Germans initially felt conflicted about their rulers' animosity toward the new France. It became fashionable in Berlin for women of affluent families to decorate apparel with tricolor ribbons. On July 14, 1790, citizens in Hamburg and other cities celebrated the first anniversary of the storming of the Bastille in Paris by staging a "brotherhood festival" and erecting a "liberty tree."[1] Under the Bourbons, the French aristocracy and clergy had controlled much of the land. When the revolutionary regime disenfranchised the church, it lifted an enormous tax burden from the people's shoulders. The average income of the French farmer increased and the entire working population likewise experienced previously unknown prosperity.[2]

Admiration for social reform in France supposedly compromised the will of many Germans to fight against Napoleon after he became emperor. Prussians were disillusioned with the Hohenzollerns' protection of the aristocracy's ancestral privileges and preeminence in the army. "Every small step forward, even the slightest improvement in affairs of state regarding public welfare had to be wrested from the landowners through endless strife," observed one historian.[3] John Rocca, the Swiss cavalryman who had served with Napoleon's army in Spain, made this observation: "For more than a century, the primary endeavor of various princes belonging to the German Reich has been to perfect the military establishment that keeps them in power and serves their personal ambition. The fact that in so doing they have accustomed their subjects to the strictest, pettiest submission has weakened the people's national character. The sense of belonging to a nation is the only insurmountable bulwark that nations have to set against foreign invasions."[4]

Freiherr vom Stein wrote Friedrich Wilhelm III that the people's "feelings of citizenship and community spirit have been destroyed by barring them from any participation in administration of the affairs of state. Every impulse to make sacrifices for the benefit of all has been lost."[5] In offering such generalizations, Rocca and Stein may have been promoting a political agenda influenced by an aversion of absolutism and the conviction that a modern state form must replace it. Many historians have shared this view. The Englishman Petre summarized that the king of Prussia was "haunted by the dread of what he considered the worst of evils, the political power of his own people, was out of touch with them, and… dreaded popular movements almost as much as he feared Napoleon."[6] Höhn concluded, "The shameful surrender of the Prussian fortresses after the defeat of 1806 and the sympathy of the middle class with the French can only be fundamentally understood when it becomes clear that the French were the active representatives of ideals that German burghers largely agreed with."[7]

A 19th-Century chronicle of the 1806 campaign maintains that "there were some sincere and warm friends of the fatherland, but there was no universal enthusiasm. The war of 1806 was something less than popular. Very few from among the nation understood what it was about and why their sons should let themselves get shot dead… The pro-fatherland attitude only developed later, when people knew Napoleon and his French better and after putting up with their arrogance for years, learned to abysmally hate them."[8] In northern German states, "most of the population regarded the collapse of Prussia and Napoleon's triumph with indifference."[9] Outside of Prussia, the situation in many parts of Germany was indeed similar to that of France before the revolution; despotic, colorless rulers and empty treasuries. Practically the entire German intelligentsia, according to a 20th-Century German historian, welcomed the Revolution.[10]

There is compelling evidence to suggest that such sweeping statements, at least with respect to Prussia, are exaggerated. Many of the political "ideals of '89" advocated by the Revolution had already become law in Prussia or were close to implementation. The population enjoyed freedom of worship and the press a measure of latitude. In the evangelist north, the church was subordinate to state authority and its property classified as secular. The 19th-Century historian Heinrich von Treitschke pointed out that the "rural, provincial administration was civic-minded and imposed strict limitations on the nobility's previously inherent rights. What remained of the old social order could be revised through the will of the reformers peacefully. Only the smaller German states… mirrored the transgressions of the previous French aristocratic regimen. In the Reich's cities the slothfulness and corruption of age-old nepotism held sway and in the territories of the princes, dukes and knights, the despotism of petty tyrants. The very existence of this rotten, inflexible state form made a mockery of the ideals of the century."[11]

The Prussian administration was more progressive than that of neighboring German states. The country "had overcome the aging, class-dominated state without utterly destroying its form."[12] The people were understandably indignant about being excluded from a say in government. However, an objective examination of the events of 1806 offers countless examples of patriotism and allegiance to the sovereign manifest among large segments of the population. When invaded by an opposing army, almost any nation will relegate resentment about infringements of civil liberty to the back burners. As the Russian people demonstrated during World War II, a population will fight for an indigenous tyrant before submitting to foreign yoke regardless of the politics involved. Further, the canton system inducted lads into the army from Prussia, Pomerania and Silesia. It takes a leap of faith to presume that most citizens of the kingdom were rooting for Napoleon when he was fighting against regiments that their fellow countrymen, including relatives, serve in.

The fall of the Prussian fortresses betrayed the shortcomings of a scant minority of overaged commandants. Many had been bold officers in their youth, but their sense of duty sprang more from pride of their class than love of country. In most cases neither the junior officers nor townspeople supported their craven submission to the invaders. Notable exceptions were some public officials and merchants who were influenced by personal or commercial considerations and tried to dissuade wavering commandants from offering resistance. In Berlin, the citizenry reacted to Napoleon's theatrical entry with aloofness. Women held handkerchiefs to their faces to conceal their weeping. In Breslau, which the French began bombarding on November 19, the population was equally defiant. The merciless cannonade escalated on December 10 when the enemy deployed heavy siege guns. Five weeks into the carnage, a delegation of citizens appeared before the governor to declare that the people are "prepared to sacrifice everything for king and country and support the garrison as much as possible with everything it needs."[13]

The people of Danzig also supported the war effort. During 76 days of bombardment, Kalckreuth quickly became popular among the city's inhabitants "and throughout the siege always understood how to motivate them to self-sacrificial devotion" in defense of the fortress.[14] A citizen wrote in his journal that "anyone who talks of surrender is endangering his own safety."[15] The French corps surrounding Danzig hurled nearly 20,000 bombs and cannonballs over the walls in eleven weeks. At the end there were 1,544 sick and wounded in the fortress hospital. On May 11, Kalckreuth publicly posted a cabinet letter in the *Fritzischen Garten* (Fritz's Garden) expressing Friedrich Wilhelm's praise for the "uncommonly honorable deportment" of Danzig residents.[16] Wine merchants supplied the troops from their cellars without charge. Neisse, a fortress just south of Breslau, received orders to prepare for defense on October 23. "The work was carried on with élan, whereby the population energetically participated. Four to five thousand workers were on the job daily and when the moonlight allowed, the work continued at night as well."[17]

The patriotism of Prussian civilians during a war their army was losing runs contrary to the historical contention that the population either sympathized with France or at least felt detached from the fate of the country. People scorned the *Federbüsche*, a derisive nickname for generals that refers to the feathers adorning their headgear, for military defeats and surrender of the fortresses. Also disliked was the officer corps, due to its social aloofness and arrogance. One historian

During the French siege of Danzig, townspeople brought food and drink
to soldiers on the walls and cared for those who were sick, injured or too
exhausted to remain on duty. The population never wavered in its support
of the commandant and the garrison.

wrote, "In the garrison towns the authority of the military was often difficult
to endure, with the burden of quartering troops in the many places that lacked
barracks, the army's demand that it should pay less for groceries, the haughtiness
of aristocratic officers and the demeaning position of the mayor in Prussian rural
communities compared to that of the garrison commander, from whom the
mayor was not safe from abuse. All this emphasizes how deeply the social worth
of the citizenry had diminished in the age of the aristocratic court."[18] Historian
Lehmann described conditions in garrison towns as follows: "Senior and junior
officers insulted, thrashed and locked up burghers they found troublesome. The
(military) governor of Breslau threatened the privy council with a cane…

"One day the military governor came to the consecrated ground where a community buried its dead. The place seemed perfect to him for building a training
center for a regiment quartered nearby. Without regard for the burial mounds
and crosses he ordered construction to begin. A cry of outrage came from the
community affected by this arbitrary act, but none of the objections mattered;
the barbarian answered that the dead will rest just as peacefully. In another
village the arrogance of the worthy representatives of the military led to the most

unpleasant disputes, even to rioting and bloodshed. No wonder that a wealth of acid criticism, especially across the border, was in circulation… One gibed that Prussia is not a country that has an army but an army that has a country."[19] A Danzig citizen wrote to a friend, "I always found it upsetting how most Prussian generals and commanders regard burghers as though they are dogs and treat them like they're just there to serve them."[20] When billeted at the *Gasthof zum Mohren* inn in Gotha, Gneisenau became so disgusted with the swagger and pretense of officers in his battalion that he stopped dining with them and took his meals with the landlord's family instead.[21]

The overbearing behavior of aristocratic officers unavoidably influenced the attitude of locals once war broke out. In some cases, this became detrimental to military operations. When the army was marching along the Saale to block the French invasion, bakers in Halle refused to provide bread for the troops until forced to do so.[22] When Napoleon moved his artillery to the summit of the Landgrafenberg on the night of October 13/14, as Marwitz recalled, "not one person (from Jena) crept the half mile to our camp to tell us what was happening in front of us."[23] The rearguard of the main army falling back after the defeat at Auerstedt set fire to the Elbe bridge at Wittenberg to delay pursuit by Davout's corps. The townspeople, relying on the span for local trade, extinguished the blaze enabling the French to cross the river. Blücher, who had no intention of surrendering his corps as Hohenlohe had done, found his escape from French forces compromised when local peasants informed Bernadotte of the direction of his retreat.

Information provided to Murat's cavalry by townspeople in Erfurt and Weimar put it on the trail of Prussian formations withdrawing into the Harz mountains.[24] When Napoleon demanded that state ministers and civil servants of Prussia swear allegiance to him, not one refused to take the oath. The patriotic Pomeranian writer Ernst Moritz Arndt compared the conduct of the Germans to that of the Russian peasantry during Napoleon's 1812 invasion of their country: "As the Russian army fell back, most residents of the cities, country towns and villages followed. They left the French only empty spaces, burned-down villages and scorched fields. Some cities even went up in flames. Such was the proud spirit that burned within this nation! Most harmful to the enemy was that during the retreat, public administration everywhere simply dissolved. Napoleon found it quite different within the indulgent Germany."[25]

Some politicians provided the enemy with direct military assistance. When Napoleon invaded Poland, he ordered Davout to establish a supply depot at Warsaw. Even though the city was still occupied by Prussian troops, on November 13 the president of the Prussian chamber of deputies there ordered the finance office to comply with Davout's demands.[26] Random acts of civilian collaboration with the invader created hardships for the Prussian army, but the marked similarity of circumstances surrounding the capitulation of the fortresses and poorly executed military operations suggests that clandestine forces may

When Napoleon was in Berlin, city officials pledged fealty to him. This set the tone for collaboration with the enemy. On the left of Bonaparte is the bald Davout. The peacock Murat, with golden tassels dangling from his boots, is at right.

have also been at work to systematically undermine resistance. Some bastions, to be sure, were fiercely defended. These include Danzig, Graudenz, Kolberg, Kosel and Neisse. The question of whether organized treachery was involved in the fall of others is nevertheless worth examining, since rarely has a nation as historically renowned for military prowess as Prussia been so thoroughly vanquished.

A case in point is the surrender of Hameln, which otherwise defies explanation and left at least one historian dumbfounded: "How was it possible that such a fine fortress, in completely renovated condition with an oversize garrison, sufficiently equipped with guns, ammunition and foodstuffs, and which the emperor of France declared to be one of the best in Germany, could be handed over on the most unfavorable terms imaginable to a siege corps no stronger than the garrison? (The French) had no siege equipment, set up no batteries, unhitched not a single gun and had still had not fired any cannonballs into the fortress."[27] No less suspicious was the betrayal of Prince Anhalt-Pletz's relief attacks to relieve Breslau. The plans for both were leaked in advance to Vandamme. The evening before the second operation of December 30, an unnamed Württemberg officer supposedly infiltrated the Prussian camp, eavesdropped on the staff's situation conference and snuck out undetected to report the details to the French general.[28] Even had an intruder eluded the sentries, which is unlikely, one must question how he would have known where in camp the nocturnal conference was taking place and how he could have hidden close enough to monitor it.

General Lindener, who had remained at Breslau against orders, was so mistrusted that after the fortress fell that he was believed to have accompanied the French to Schweidnitz to advise them where to position their batteries for an effective bombardment.[29] There were cases of suspicious actions by senior officers that suggest, as Marwitz contended, that "because of their political views they should be regarded as being in league with the enemy."[30] Before the battle of Saalfeld Captain Gneisenau wrote that a deep mistrust of his commander in chief the Duke of Brunswick has begun to infect the army.[31] Prince Louis Ferdinand wrote Scharnhorst that the Duke of Brunswick, Haugwitz, Lombard and Lucchesini "have betrayed us."[32]

Even before the campaign began, 34,000 reservists in Silesia, Prussia and Warsaw were never mobilized: "The reason for such a significant number of troops to be left behind has never been established with certainty," concluded Höpfner.[33] Councilman Lombard fled Berlin out of fear of public backlash due to his sympathy for France. Within the capital, a rumor spread that Lombard clandestinely delayed sending certain dispatches to Petersburg for twelve days, so that the Russian auxiliary troops would not reach the war zone in time. The queen, who had always mistrusted this man, knew of the accusations and ordered him arrested.[4]

While Napoleon was in Gera on the morning of October 13, he received intelligence that the Prussian army intends to withdraw to Magdeburg: "How Napoleon gained this information so soon has never been determined."[35] Blücher testified about being shelled by a Prussian battery during the battle of Auerstedt: "I confronted Captain von Meerkatz right on the spot about his carelessly firing at me during the attack." He replied that he had been following orders of a staff officer who said the cavalrymen are French.[36] During the engagement at Auerstedt, Blücher's horsemen abruptly about faced and rode away from the enemy. He attempted to rally them for another charge. An officer approached and told him that during the attack someone ordered retreat to be sounded. Blücher tried but was unable to discover who was responsible.[37]

Toward noon the Prussians began to fall back at Auerstedt. The right flank withdrew first under pressure from Morand's division. The Prussian left wing later followed suit to avoid being outflanked by an enemy column moving toward Poppel. It had forced back the Rheinbaben Grenadier Battalion. Scharnhorst recalled, "After our infantry, two-and-a-half divisions strong, had driven the enemy back on both flanks and fought on without support, the right wing began to retire. The left continued to hold, even though outflanked. On the right stood the greater part of our cavalry, so it could not be circumvented. It was then on this wing that something happened that was *not normal for the circumstances*, and… led to the loss of the battle."[38] Scharnhorst was referring to the retreat that he felt was unnecessary. He believed that Morand's division was too weak to push the Prussians back. This invites speculation on whether or not the retreat was *ordered*, as had been the case when Blücher's cavalry charge was aborted.

After the battle, the intact part of the Prussian army divided and went in different directions. The larger part, believing the retreat to Magdeburg cut off, withdrew northwest into the nearly impassable Harz mountains. The stop at Sömmerda, Kalckreuth's negotiations at Weissensee and tarrying at Greussen wasted so much time that the army had to make two consecutive nocturnal marches to escape the pursuing enemy. As a result, many formations simply dissolved. The lopsided defeats at Jena and Auerstedt aroused public suspicion regarding the motive of the supreme command. On November 04, the Berlin newspaper *Spenerschen Zeitung* published an open letter bluntly accusing the Duke of Brunswick of treason. He supposedly "only concentrated the army on the Saale to protect the duchy of Brunswick." A flood of bitter criticism and libel followed: "The duke was faulted for his haughty contempt for the most elemental rules of warfare and his proud refusal to accept good advice, but also for despair, panic, cowardice and recklessness."[39] Gneisenau wrote after the campaign, "There has been a lot of talk about treason."[40]

On October 15, the Supreme War Council ordered that Spandau be arranged for defense. Berlin sent 24 cannons there four days later, but with the wrong ammunition.[41] False intelligence led to the capitulation of Blücher's corps at Ratekau. Pursued by a French army four times the size of his corps, he made a stand at Lübeck on November 07. Bernadotte, the French commander, wrote that "every square, every street was a battlefield. Blücher personally led several cavalry charges in the streets."[42] Without enough time to prepare Lübeck for defense before the enemy's arrival, the general withdrew to Ratekau after heavy fighting. He had intended to proceed from Ratekau to Travemünde, but received secondhand information, supposedly stemming from an artillery officer who just came from there, that the city has fallen to the French. Blücher thereupon surrendered to Murat, Soult and Bernadotte at Ratekau. He learned afterward that Travemünde was not already captured.[43]

During Prussia's struggle against Polish insurgents, General Dombrowski moved his Polish division against Dirschau on the morning of February 23, 1807. He was "fully informed of the disposition of the Prussians due to treachery and captured the town," wrote Höpfner.[44] "The dragoons claimed it was treason," recalled an eyewitness.[45] North of Dirschau, in Danzig, the casemate at Fort Hagelsberg where the governor issued orders to his officers was hit by a pinpoint bombardment on April 30 at the precise hour that a situation conference was scheduled. Kalckreuth had unexpectedly left the room prematurely to speak with Major Horn and narrowly missed being killed by a bomb than penetrated

The city council of Lübeck did not want to resist the French and allowed Blücher's corps into the fortress when he pledged not to make a stand there. Once he was inside the walls, Blücher announced that "circumstances have changed" and defended the town.

the roof. It claimed the life of General Laurens and a lieutenant and seriously wounded another officer. The timing of the surprise barrage "was more than likely the work of a traitor."[46]

Another singular occurrence at Danzig was the virtually effortless capture by the French of the Holm, the fortified island crucial to defense of the fortress. Officers regulated the issue of brandy to the troops to prevent excessive drinking. Yet the Holm garrison, comprised almost exclusively of Russians, was intoxicated the night of the French raid. One citizen lamented, "When a critical analysis of all of the mistakes is prepared by investigators, the loss of the Nehrung and of the Holm will probably be described as the greatest blunders. The cause of this loss simply defies human comprehension. There was no longer any point to bring up supplies or reinforcements via navigable waters and the mouth of the river. Not one boat could get through, not one man could reach the city by these routes, since the watchfulness of the besiegers surpassed everything imaginable... One was already so used to treason or bribery that these elements were blamed for everything that went wrong."[47]

In May, the garrison of Kosel conducted sorties to destroy enemy battery positions or herd cattle into the fortress. Most of these operations were betrayed to the enemy in advance by lantern signals from inside the walls. They enabled the French to prepare for the raids and forced the Prussians to abort them. The defenders were never able to discover who in Kosel was forewarning the enemy.[48] A survivor of the siege of Kolberg, a small coastal fortress in Pomerania that the French were unable to conquer, wrote this about Joachim Nettelbeck. He was a brewer who mobilized the town's residents to combat fires and assist the garrison: "With great reluctance, he wrote in his memoirs about the malignant distrust, the treason, the covert arrangements, enemy messages and liaisons and the crooked fortress commanders at Magdeburg, Küstrin and Stettin. He arranged for a committee to be selected from the citizenry whose members would position themselves in pairs by day and by night at all three city gates. They were to keep a sharp eye on everyone who passed in and out."[49]

Some of the mistakes cited above may have been unintentional and are not uncommon in warfare. The consistent number of bad decisions based on faulty intelligence or pure speculation about the enemy's disposition, misdirected troop movements and readiness of seasoned commanders to lay down arms however, suggests a pattern. "The pacifist cult spread like an insidious poison" in Prussia, including within the officer corps.[50] Möllendorff toasted Napoleon on his birthday in August 1806 when visiting the French embassy, and after the campaign dined with the emperor when he came to Berlin.[51] Massenbach, whose advice to Hohenlohe at Jena and at Prenzlau contributed to the defeat, was "an admirer of Napoleon and could imagine nothing better and more glorious for Prussia than to place the fate of the state in the hands of the French ruler."[52] Petre added, "there were not lacking men who openly accused Massenbach of treachery."[53]

Some Prussian officers attributed the disaster of 1806 to the prolonged period of peace and prosperity following the Seven Years' War. Friedrich the Great himself opined that "excessive wealth is the doom of nations."[54] Colmar von der Goltz, the military historian who became a general of infantry in the Prussian army, shared this perspective. His views on the subject, expressed in a study published in 1907, reflect the Spartan, anti-democratic disposition manifest among senior aristocratic officers: "A long period of peace and a pampered attitude toward life that labels passion as unrefined and risk-taking as foolish confounded our traditional Prussian heroism… The men of Magdeburg, Prenzlau and Stettin came from the same stock as we ourselves. In their early years they had been valiant and bold like our younger generation is today. They succumbed to a protracted, insidious threat that gradually enveloped them in its net and completely overwhelmed their defenses in the hour of doom…

"The philosophy of the times preaches free development of the personality. Everything standing in its way should be should be swept aside and the people should tolerate as few limitations imposed by the state as possible. The power of the authorities and of one's superiors is becoming ever more restricted. On one hand this makes organizing and directing the masses more difficult and on the other, makes people more sensitive to every action taken from above... The 'poor guy' who shouldn't have to bear a burden on his weak shoulders... whose wages increase while his hours decrease and who always hears about what he's entitled to from the state and society and knows nothing about his obligation to either, will become less and less suited to give his all for the fatherland in the great hour of need."[55] What Goltz overlooks is that mass participation in national defense during the 1807 campaign was impossible, regardless of whether enlightened burghers were prepared to take up arms for their country or not. Fearing an armed citizenry, the king and his staff blocked initiatives to actively involve the public in the fighting. Lettow-Vorbeck concluded that "the unfortunate course of this campaign is purely the result of bad leadership."[56]

The Secret Societies under Napoleon

General Ludendorff, who after World War I became a historian, published tracts about how secret societies manipulate European politics. He offered a perspective of Prussia's defeat in 1806 seldom addressed by 19th-Century historians but shared by some of the statesmen and soldiers of the time. Ludendorff contended that Napoleon "waged his early wars as an ally of Freemasons on the continent who were to some extent influenced by France, and won such easy victories that a military explanation for them is lacking."[57] German lodges interpreted Paris's *Declaration of the Rights of Man* as a victory for liberty over despotism. This brought them into conflict with their governments. Shortly after becoming Holy Roman Emperor, Franz II banned public officials from becoming Freemasons. Duke Max IV of Bavaria, subsequently King Max I, was himself a mason but due to suspected subversion by the Illuminati forbade civil servants to belong to a lodge. In October 1798, Friedrich Wilhelm III outlawed "secret societies potentially detrimental to universal security... that conceal their purpose or pretend it is something else, or employ covert means to achieve a declared objective, or secretly utilize mystical, hieroglyphic rituals."[58]

German princes suspected an affiliation between Freemasonry and France. They regarded masonic lodges as a potential fifth column in wartime. Watched by the police in their own countries, it was unavoidable that some German Freemasons would hope for a French victory over the coalitions. In 1790 for example, the former Illuminati Rudolf Becker in Saxony told his brothers in the *zum Rautenkranz* (Of the Diamond Laurel) lodge in Gotha that "a Freemason during these times must not remain indifferent but must choose a side." He left little doubt as to his own sympathies and urged members of the military who were present to "observe a wise neutrality if the people require your help during an uprising."[59] This so angered some lodge members that they reported him to the authorities; proof that patriotic Germans also belonged to the sect. Lodges for army officers were established, including the *Minerva* lodge in Potsdam founded in 1768. Prussian officers joined the *Parfait Union* (Perfect Union) in Magdeburg and *Zu den Drei Degen* (Of the Three Swords) in Halle.[60]

There is a similarity between the treachery of Eickemeyer, the former Illuminati who sabotaged the defense of Mainz in 1793, and the actions of Massenbach and Hüser at Prenzlau. Hüser, who lied to Hohenlohe that the artillery is low on ammunition, was a member of the Grand Lodge of Freemasonry in Prussia.[61] Massenbach was responsible for convincing his commander in chief to surrender and Eickemeyer persuaded Mainz's General Gymnisch to do so. Affiliated with Freemasonry, Massenbach opposed Prussia's pact with the czar, whose father had outlawed lodges in Russia. He told Hohenlohe, "The alliance with Russia is our certain doom and whoever wants to sincerely serve the state should try to prevent the king from pursuing it. The state can only be rescued by an alliance with the French… The moment we become allied with Russia, I prefer to leave Prussian service and enter that of France."[62] Bülow told Hohenlohe that Massenbach should be arrested and later testified to the general staff, "Various witnesses to the situation then, especially Major Count Loucey and Major von Marwitz, assert that Colonel von Massenbach's actions were intentional and it was his plan to arrange everything so that the corps could not be rescued, because he has been led astray by wrong political views."[63]

At the Congress of Verona in 1822, Count Haugwitz submitted a lengthy memorandum for assembled monarchs urging them to abolish Freemasonry in their respective kingdoms. Excerpts quoted below offer insight into his impression of the sect's agenda before and during the coalition wars: "In 1777, I took charge of a branch of the lodges in the Prussian state and was also involved with our brothers in Poland and Russia. Had I not seen it for myself, it would have seemed unbelievable to me now how carelessly governments can allow mischief of this sort to go on without notice. The grand masters did not just constantly correspond using code, but attended to matters personally through envoys. The objective was to exercise a dominant influence over throne and altar, just as it had been with the Knights Templar… The deeper I delved into the meaning of this singular, mysterious tapestry, the more convinced I became that something of an entirely different nature is going on behind the scenes… All the threads were woven into a fabric, cloaked in religious mysticism, to mesmerize the layman and prepare him for a genuinely deceptive purpose.

"At this time, I realized that what began in 1788 and soon erupted into the French Revolution, the king's murder with all its attendant cruelty, had not been decided upon right then. Instead, it had been ushered in through liaisons, conspiracies and so forth and God knows how long it had already been at work. My first concern was to convey all of my discoveries to Friedrich Wilhelm III. We had the impression that regarding every connection among masons, from the humblest member to the those of the loftiest grades with whom I was acquainted, the overt religious sentiments are right in step with criminal plans of every nature and the former serve as a façade for the latter. This opinion, which Friedrich Wilhelm shared completely, led me to decide to cease participating. The prince considered it advisable for me not to sever ties with the masons. He saw having honest men in the lodges as a means to turn them away from treacherous influences and convert them into harmless societies… It is no figment of the imagination that this secret sect that has existed for centuries threatens humanity more today than ever before."[64]

Hans von Kottwitz, a philanthropist from the Silesian aristocracy who devoted himself to the welfare of the working class and the unemployed, had joined a lodge at age thirteen. Later in life he wrote Friedrich Wilhelm, "All of the revolutionary upheavals that have occurred for a long number of years stem from Freemason chapters and from secret societies of various denominations that stand for the same principles. The strife, deceit, abominations and progressive chaos of all kinds that we witness before our eyes can primarily be attributed to Freemasonry… For 50 years since the day I enrolled, in every avenue of the Freemason order I heard only the voice of deception. From this toxic well of misfortune springs a torrent of malice, as well as disdain of authority, order and morality to this day."[65] The similarity can be seen between the warnings of Kottwitz and the writings of French Revolutionaries. Jean-Paul Rebaut, a politician in the National Convention, said, "To make the people happy, their ideas must be reconstructed, laws must be changed, morals must be changed, men must be changed, things must be changed, everything, yes *everything must be destroyed*, since everything must be remade."[66]

During a public speech at Ayesbury on September 20, 1876, the prominent English statesman Benjamin Disraeli warned of Freemasonry's allegedly insidious grip on European affairs. Even though over half a century had passed since Haugwitz and Kottwitz expressed their views about the sect, the striking similarity of Disraeli's observation is worth comparison: "The governments of the present day have to deal not merely with other governments, with emperors, kings and ministers, but also with the secret societies which have everywhere their unscrupulous agents and can at the last moment upset all the governments' plans… The secret societies… have reckless agents which countenance assassination and which, if necessary, could produce a massacre."[67] The question relevant to the events of 1806/07 is the extent to which the goals of Freemasonry were made to conform to Napoleon's political objectives. The lodges, like so many others, met their match in the architect of "the proudest, cleverest, best-organized despotism in recent history."[68]

Nothing was sacred to Bonaparte; neither nations and their customs, nor religion, nor marriage, nor human life. They existed to serve his personal ambition to dominate Europe and establish a dynasty to govern future generations. When courting the Vatican, he privately told an aide, "Considering my position of power in Italy it can be assumed that sooner or later I'll be able to force the pope to my will."[69] He signed a concordat with Rome in 1801 restoring Catholicism as the religion of France, albeit without returning church lands confiscated by the previous revolutionary government. At that time, Napoleon promised the pope to make all of Germany Catholic again.[70] The emperor subsequently dealt the

Vatican a serious blow by establishing the *Rheinbund*, because it caused Franz II to dissolve the Holy Roman Empire in August 1806. The empire had been the "sword of the church" and mainstay of the Catholic faith in Europe for centuries. The former Holy Roman Emperor Franz II became Franz I of Austria. In France, Napoleon reserved the authority to appoint bishops and oversee church revenues.

Bonaparte sought to control the masons as well. Monarchs saw secret societies, international in character and espousing French values, as a threat to their power. The Illuminati for example, preached that "love of country and loyalty to a prince are like the love of a jackass for its stall."[71] Napoleon did not ban lodges as was the case in Russia but held them on a tight leash. During a discussion about the penal code at a council meeting on August 26, 1809, Count Honoré Muraire of the prosecutor's office asked to exempt lodges from the statute forbidding public meetings of more than 20 persons. Napoleon, who attended the session, objected. He told the council, "There is nothing to be feared in patronizing Freemasonry, but if granted authority it will become dangerous. As it is today, it is dependent on me. But I don't intend to become dependent on it!"[72] He said on another occasion, "The army is an order of Freemasons. There is a certain arrangement among them (those in the army) that they all recognize, seek and understand; and I am the grand master of their lodges."[73] The French police kept them under surveillance.

Despite describing himself as "grand master," there is no documentary evidence that Napoleon ever joined a lodge. When Bonaparte was first consul of France, Marshals Kellermann and André Masséna and the jurist Jean-Jacques Cambacéres warned him that suppressing Freemasonry will alienate many of his sympathizers in France. Napoleon opted instead to align the sect's interests with his own as much as possible. The first step was to consolidate the *Grande Loge de France* and the *Grande Orient de France* into a single order in 1799. The introduction in 1804 of the 33-degree system by the *Grande Loge Ecossaise* (Grand Lodge of Scotland) divided the membership. Masséna, a former smuggler who had risen through the ranks in the revolutionary army and belonged to the *Grande Orient*, and Kellermann of the *Grande Loge Ecossaise* reunified the members on December 03 of that year. The *Grande Orient* became the umbrella order for French members. Napoleon's brother Joseph, who had never been a Freemason, assumed the office of grand master of the lodge.

The emperor's brother-in-law Murat became substitute grand master of the *Grande Orient*.[74] Brother Louis Bonaparte served as grand master of the newly founded *Grande Loge Ecossaise de France* which then merged with the *Grande Orient*. Jérôme, the fourth brother, also tenanted a lofty position in the order.[75] Joseph Bonaparte and Murat belonged to the lodges in name only, since their official duties kept them away from Paris most of the time. Circumstances were much the same for Marshal Lefebvre, who had besieged Danzig. He was the grand master of the lodge *Ordre du Christ* in Paris.[76] These appointments were not made at the behest of Napoleon. In August 1803, the *Grande Orient* had already decided to confer "honorary" titles of rank on members of his entourage, with Napoleon's permission, to strengthen its ties to the regime.[77] Cambacéres, who practically ran the government during Bonaparte's campaigns, said in December 1806, "In my eyes, all masons will become children of one and the same family; I will protect all of their rites and teachings."[78]

With the rise of Napoleon, French masons who had not fallen victim to Paris mobs or the Reign of Terror emerged from the woodwork to assume a greater role in public affairs. "Whoever wanted to become favored at court joined a lodge. All classes up to those right next to the throne hastened to the temples and took the honorary offices generously bestowed on them."[79] The integration of the political-military establishment with Freemasonry made the *Grande Orient* a "first-class instrument of power" for the emperor.[80] Bonaparte envisioned the role of the order in his continental ambitions as an intelligence service. Its military officers were capable of using their affiliation with members in opposing armies to gather information to help him assess enemy strength and intentions when waging war.[81] An ex-member of the Illuminati wrote that "Napoleon was the idol of the Jacobins in France and of the Illuminati in Bavaria. They were his most loyal, avid supporters, his hirelings, his good companions."[82]

French Freemasons may have naively assumed that Bonaparte will transform European states into a league of republics liberated from absolutism. In fact, the *Rheinbund* included small duchies whose populations were no better off than before the coalition wars began.[83] Napoleon did not infringe upon the ancestral regional authority of despots who in exchange provided soldiers to fuel his military campaigns. The arrangement was so blatant that some Prussian landowners saw the French imperator as a potential ally to protect their own privileged position: "The policy of these super-rich aristocrats was aimed at making any abrogation of their sovereignty over the land impossible, with Napoleon's help if necessary, and declaw the Prussian reformers."[84] Among the titled individuals in question was Prussian state minister Count Karl Freiherr vom Altenstein and Count Friedrich zu Dohna, "rich noblemen… who could scarcely be surpassed in narrow-mindedness and cowardice."[85] It was indeed ironic that Napoleon, the self-proclaimed "lawgiver of nations," led the people of France, who "consider themselves to be the messiahs of freedom," into perpetual wars that blocked social reform in lands they conquered.[86]

The Peace of Lunéville signed between France and the Holy Roman Empire in February 1801 reaffirmed French dominion over German territory west of the Rhine. In order to extend his control over the population, Napoleon allowed the establishment of *Grande Orient* lodges in major cities. French Freemasons founded *La Grande Famille* in Speyer in 1802 and *De l'Union Philantropique* in the fortress of Landau the following year. The *La Constance*, *La Concorde* and two *Grande Orient* lodges opened in Aachen and the *Rose Mystérieuse* and *Les Amis Réunis* in Mainz.[87] The *Grande Orient* permitted a Jewish chapter to establish the *L'Aurore Naissante* in Frankfurt am Main in 1808. Trier dedicated

La Réunion des Amis de l'Humanité in 1804 and *La Persévérance* followed in 1805 in Lauterburg. From 1806 to 1809 Bonn, Koblenz, Worms and Neustadt am Hardt became homes to new lodges. There were two in Cologne. After Napoleon created the *Rheinbund* in July 1806, French Freemasons spread their order to cities east of the Rhine. Düsseldorf founded the *St. Joachim* lodge within a month, named in honor of Murat. After the conquest of Prussia, French lodges were established in Darmstadt, Fulda, Hamburg, Lübeck, Berlin and Warsaw.

These lodges expanded the influence of the *Grande Orient* beyond France and her dependencies into formerly enemy territory. Accepting nonFrench Freemasons as members, chapters revered Napoleon or at least propagated the liberal ideals of liberty, brotherhood and equality he supposedly promoted. "The overall political significance of these lodges was that the brotherly unification of French and nonFrench members was supposed to facilitate Napoleonic rule, in that it helped to inwardly strengthen and secure it," according to one analysis.[88] The *publicly* expressed mission, as the mason Ludwig Börne claimed in a speech in Frankfurt in 1809, sounded more altruistic: "The efforts of Freemasons correspond to the loftiest purpose of humanity, in that they seek to remove all elements that keep the human race divided such as dissimilarity of states, diverse religions, customs and languages, and make them uniform."[89] A substantial number of German military officers, including Prussians, belonged to lodges. Twenty-four percent of the membership of the Westphalian lodge *Hieronymus Napoleon zur Treue* consisted of army officers.[90]

Throughout Germany, "The mutual hatred among various classes thwarted every attempt to bring political order to the abundance of creative energy of the people," as Treitschke observed, so that a program to eliminate inveterate social barriers seemed progressive.[91] Freemasonry promised "to create a new people comprising those of every nation bound together by science, morality and virtue... to strive for the welfare of all to make the entire human race a family of brothers united by affection, wisdom and labor."[92] The French "were supposed to educate and perfect humanity while the king of Prussia had closed ranks with the most sinister powers of the reaction."[93] In addition to political indoctrination conducted by the lodges, the interface of French and German officers and the exchange of ideas provided Napoleon's agents with valuable information about attitudes and developments in armies of occupied or vassal states. The fact that his marshals were grand masters further suggests a military purpose intended for Freemasonry as an intelligence-gathering branch.

Writing in the second person as Caesar had done, Napoleon stated that "One of the emperor's greatest ideas was the concentration and geographic grouping of those peoples of Europe who have been divided or fragmented by policy." The unification of Germany would allegedly "require more time."[94] In the perception of Bavarian Freemasons, European nations were "to work their way out of the dungeon of their nationalities" to restore the "pure and basic form of human nature."[95] Börne proclaimed that "the barriers will fall asunder, then all

mankind will embrace one another as brothers and the entire earth will be-
come a universal lodge for a loving family."[96] The reality was quite the contrary.
Napoleon habitually employed troops from German states to combat other
Germans; as already shown, regiments from Bavaria and Württemberg besieged
Prussian fortresses.

Napoleon's unprecedented victory over Prussia in 1806 may have involved
coordinated sabotage by masons within her officer corps and civil service. It is
also likely however, that those who committed treason acted out of personal
conviction rather than as part of a conspiracy orchestrated by Freemasonry.
Blücher, Scharnhorst and Hohenlohe belonged to masonic lodges but did not
betray their king. Ludendorff acknowledged that "Freemason historians are right
when they state that many of the men who worked for Prussia's resurrection
were Freemasons."[97] Further, Napoleon himself did not promote the goals of
Freemasonry. Inside France, he dropped the principles of the Revolution and
established the administrative system of an absolute state. It was veiled in the
trappings of Revolutionary ideals but in substance had not the slightest thing
in common with them. Regarding foreign policy, he used the impetus of the
Revolution in his battle against kingdoms that stood in the way of his imperialistic ambition.

Freemasonry preached that all European nations must shake off nationalism,
but Napoleon appealed to French nationalism. The origin of the term "chauvin-
ism" stems from one of his soldiers. European Freemasons must have realized
that the ideals of liberty, equality, international brotherhood and freedom of the
press were illusory in French-dominated Europe. Lodges were manipulated by
the emperor to serve as an instrument of policy. Educated Freemasons prominent in society and public service could not fail to see the order being misused to
advance Napoleon's agenda. "The fatal weakness of his course was that he did not
in reality unite Europe but only oppressed her; that he did not awaken the dynamic elements in her nations but trampled them," maintained a German historian.[98] His uncompromising attitude toward control of the church, Freemasonry
and the continent itself would eventually turn all against him and ultimately the
population of France as well. His advisors warned him about this, but Bonaparte
was a solitary, guarded man disinclined to heed the counsel of others.

Chapter 12

The Dead of Jena Rise

A Lesson in Leadership

A man serving in the war against France remarked, "at this time, the enemy became accustomed to a method of capturing our fortresses that expended more words than it did gunpowder."[1] Even in this dark hour however, examples of heroism and defiance helped revitalize the spirit of Prussia and inspire the people not to lose heart. Among them were the battle of Eylau on February 08, 1807, and the defense of the fortress of Kolberg. The latter, an obscure Baltic seaport at the estuary of the Persante River between Stettin and Danzig, held off the Napoleonic juggernaut for four months. It was the confrontation of a Prussian David against the French Goliath; the garrison of a diminutive fortress dwarfed in size and strength by Magdeburg, Hameln, Breslau and Danzig outfought a well-organized siege corps of a victorious, seemingly invincible army. The struggle also revealed, perhaps as much as any wartime episode, the decisive influence of capable leadership.

Kolberg's defenses were decrepit until the king ordered them upgraded on October 23. There were so few serviceable cannons that the commandant removed those on the outer bastions to reposition on the main wall; even then there were not enough to defend the inner perimeter. Gun carriages needed an overhaul and there was but one wheelwright in the town. The overaged artillery company consisted of 86 gunners to man 72 weapons. Nettelbeck, the former seaman who organized the population to prepare for siege, wrote, "as good as nothing had been done to maintain the fortress. The wall and trenches had fallen in and there was no trace left of the palisade. Just three cannons in the Pommern bastion were mounted on carriages. They were only there to fire an alarm shot if sorties from the garrison are being pursued. All the rest of the guns were lying on the ground overgrown with grass and their carriages were rotting in sheds." He also cited "the inadequate number of defenders and their nonmilitant attitude, since the more proficient among them had joined the field army. There was general despondency nurtured by the stream of refugees and hourly reports of bad news."[2]

Defense capabilities largely depended on the region's topography. Kolberg is on high ground and was shielded from attack on its western side by the river. The marshy lowland south of town could be flooded to a depth of several feet. Two canals drawing water from the Persante fed man-made ditches to serve as water barriers. The harbor area was formed by two dams protected by breastworks. The main wall had six bastions and there were several outer forts guarding remaining access points. The most geographically feasible location to launch an attack was from across the Binnenfeld. Fort Wolfsberg was on a hill over 25 feet above sea level and dominated the approach. The supply of food and ammunition was not an issue, since reinforcements and supplies could land by sea. Control of the harbor area was crucial. The French had to simultaneously besiege Danzig, splitting their forces. In January 1807 Britain and Sweden made peace with Prussia to unite against the common enemy. As long as the Prussians held Kolberg, an allied landing corps could disembark there to harass Napoleon during his winter campaign in Poland.

The elderly commandant, Colonel Ludwig von Lucadou, had served in the army during the Seven Years' War. Upon learning of the Prussian defeat at Jena, he began arming the fortress. When the French vanguard crossed the Oder River, the Stettin chamber of deputies instructed civil servants in Pomerania to swear allegiance to Napoleon. Lucadou told local provincial councils to ignore the order. He directed them to send revenue they collected to Kolberg instead of to Stettin and used it to finance fortress upgrades. On November 08, Lucadou turned away a French colonel who demanded the town surrender. The commandant sent a letter to Stettin's board of governors advising them that their subservience to the enemy is treason. Lucadou did not requisition cattle, produce and grain from neighboring villages. He regarded this as a transgression against laws protecting private property, with the result that the foodstuffs would soon fall to the French.

Characteristic of old school Prussian officers, Lucadou regarded the war as an affair of the army and disdained civilian involvement. Before war clouds began to gather in 1805, Kolberg maintained five companies of militia to guard the walls and gates. Major Feilke, a town merchant, formed them into the Burgher Grenadier Battalion.[3] While the town was preparing to meet the French invasion, the men paraded in the town square and Nettelbeck told Lucadou, "We're resolved to share the same burdens and dangers as the military in these uncertain times. We're about to organize a battalion of 700 to 800 citizens who will be fully equipped and ask permission to present ourselves to you… We are of good will and want to do our duty." After a long silence the commandant retorted in his French accent, "Put an end to this game like good boys! For heaven's sake go home! What good does it do me to have you here?"[4] The men dispersed after Nettlebeck told them what the colonel had said, deeply offended by the underserved belittlement.

A nationalist spirit nonetheless prevailed among citizen and soldier. The townspeople contributed money to care for the wounded.[5] At the request of *Jäger* Captain Otto, a Kolberg shoemaker named Gaulke arranged for the town rifleman's guild to donate 50 long-barreled hunting rifles, called *Wallbüchsen*, capable of outranging military small arms. In the hands of *Jäger* marksmen, these weapons accounted for many an enemy soldier during the siege.[6] Recruits streamed in from the countryside to join the garrison. The lack of uniforms and equipment made it impossible to properly outfit them. As a result, many transferred by sea or along coastal roads to Danzig or to the field army. By the beginning of March, the well-provisioned, fully repaired fortress had a garrison of 3,700 infantry and *Jäger*, 200 cavalry and over 600 artillerymen with 106 guns. In addition, a volunteer corps consisting of 960 infantry, 450 riders and 50 artillerymen with eleven light guns operated independently outside of the fortress. Its audacious and unorthodox commander, Ferdinand von Schill, supported the garrison with harassing attacks and raids against French supply columns.

While the renovation was under way, the commandant maintained his haughty contempt for civilian participation. Nettelbeck visited Lucadou and reminded him of the extensive work still required to get the fortifications ready to defy a siege. The militia had volunteered to dig out old water channels, restore palisades and remount cannons to assist the garrison. The commandant scoffed in reply, "The burghers! Always the burghers! I don't want them and I don't need them!"[7] Nettelbeck, who as a young man had taken part in the defense of Kolberg during the Seven Years' War, called attention to the importance of repairing trenches and breastworks beyond the walls to control the approaches to the town. He asked Lucadou for permission to proceed with the work. "What happens outside the city," the colonel gruffly answered, "doesn't concern me. I'll know how to defend the fortress from within. For all I care you can dig outside when and where you want. It has nothing to do with me."[8]

Lucadou's ideas about how to defend the fortress included ordering dung heaped onto rooftops to blunt the detonation of mortar rounds that cause fires, and that the pavement be lifted from the streets to prevent injury from fragmentation produced by exploding bombs. Nettelbeck informed him that the rooves are too steep to prevent the dung from sliding off and that many buildings cannot not support the additional weight. He also said that removing cobblestones from the streets will hamper the passage of mobile firefighting equipment and ambulances, and that in three previous sieges no one ever considered it necessary to tear up the pavement. The commandant ultimately became so annoyed with Nettelbeck that he ordered him arrested. Lucadou announced his intention to have him court-martialed and shot. The regional counsellor warned Lucadou of the negative impact this will have on morale. Upon learning of the colonel's intent, a large crowd gathered outside of his residence in protest. Lucadou released Nettelbeck.

In January, Napoleon established a supply route from Stettin to Danzig via the cities of Gollnow, Köslin and Stolp. The troops marching east to invest Danzig had orders to take Kolberg along the way. The task initially fell to General Pietro Teulié, an Italian in the emperor's service. His corps comprised one French and two Italian regiments, 280 riders and an artillery company with ten guns.[9] It loosely surrounded Kolberg on March 08. The corps could do little more than try to contain the garrison and protect the supply line. Less than a week later, Schill's scouts slipped 42 Prussian recruits past French pickets and into the fortress. The blockade of Kolberg began on March 14. Napoleon assigned the one-armed Louis Loison to assume command of the operation eleven days later. A general of mediocre talent, Loison had once been disciplined for sacking an abbey in Luxemburg but was reinstated.

The military situation compelled Lucadou to reconsider using civilian volunteers. "The patriotic burghers," Nettelbeck recalled, "once again offered the commandant their services inside the fortress, to assume primary guard duty and man the necessary posts along the inner wall as well as at the gates. This time, dictated by necessity, the men's good will was acknowledged and the offer gratefully accepted. They therefore assumed these responsibilities beginning on March 25."[10] According to another account, "The burgher battalion increasingly conducted itself like a troop of the regular army and without interruption occupied the main guard posts and the main wall."[11] Marshal Mortier came on April 05. He negotiated a temporary truce with the Swedes, whereby they agreed to stop sending aid to the fortress. He then proceeded to Danzig. He left Loison with 4,215 troops to maintain the blockade. Schill took advantage of the enemy's vulnerability and attacked enemy forces deployed on the western side of the Persante on April 12. The operation could have rolled up Loison's entire corps, but was only partially successful due to lack of coordinated support from Lucadou; he disliked Schill for his free-spirited disregard for Prussian discipline.[12]

The French retired to the eastern bank of the river. The population, angry with Lucadou for his cavalier attitude and for ordering houses outside the walls torched, blamed him for the failure of Schill's operation. "The low opinion of our commandant gradually transformed into hatred and hostility," wrote Nettelbeck, "and all the more since there were some good officers in the garrison whose hearts were in the right place and who possessed clear insight, but had to keep their thoughts to themselves."[13] Nettelbeck had written the king before the French arrived describing Lucadou's unfitness to command and requesting a replacement for him. In April the king contemplated who to substitute. His advisor Karl von Beyme remarked, "Your majesty, on the day that the letter from the Kolberger Nettelbeck was delivered, I encountered a young officer on the staircase. Upon seeing him it occurred to me that he would be the right commandant for a beleaguered fortress. It's just too bad that he's so young."[14] Friedrich Wilhelm told him, "Beyme, get the personnel file of Major von Gneisenau." Upon perusal, Beyme was surprised to read that the officer was 47 years old. "We'll give him a try," the king decided.

Gneisenau was at Danzig. He had transferred there with one Neumark and two Pomeranian reserve battalions on April 04. He then received the order to travel by sea to Kolberg to assume command. He soon boarded ship and set sail. Making west, the vessel approached the harbor and the outline of Kolberg gradually took shape on the horizon. First to come into view was the tower of the *Marienkirche* (Church of Mary) projecting above the walls and bastions. Gentle hills rose beyond the sandy coastline, dunes to the left and a small forest on the

Neidhardt von Gneisenau, the defender of Kolberg who became chief of staff of Blücher's Army of Silesia in 1813. The following spring, Gneisenau led his troops into Paris ahead of England's Duke of Wellington and was promoted to field marshal in 1825.

right. Houses and granaries became visible. All presented a tranquil, pastoral appearance. Only as the boat conveying the major prepared to land did the damage wrought by nearly two months of siege become apparent. The vice-commandant Karl von Waldenfels, a comrade of Gneisenau from Jena, greeted him at the dock. The new commander told him, "We pulled in our tails like dogs but now we'll show them our teeth again!"[15] It was April 29, 1807. Gneisenau had never defended a fortress, but as a young officer had served in America in 1782/83 and learned techniques of wooden fortification construction unknown to European armies.[16]

Höpfner described Gneisenau in these words: "In his mid-forties and of an imposing yet engaging presence, energetic by nature, sound in military training and perceptiveness, always denying himself and keeping the main purpose before his eyes, unshaken by misfortune, he was just the man to quickly lift the spirits of the garrison and gain the complete confidence of the soldiers and citizens."[17] As a major replacing a colonel in command, Gneisenau tried to mollify his predecessor's mortification by allowing him to remain in the primary residence. Lucadou lived in Kolberg throughout the siege but as a recluse. Waldenfels introduced Gneisenau to Nettelbeck. He conducted him on a tour of the fortifications. The next day the commandant visited the bastion Preussen and introduced himself to its officers and men. He addressed a throng of residents in the town square in a forceful yet paternal way, explaining his principles of defense, intentions and what he expects of the people. His words of encouragement evoked a thunderous ovation.

An eyewitness offered a narrative of Gneisenau's first meeting with public officials: "When we burgher representatives were introduced to him the day after his arrival, his rousing speech moved us to tears. Our spirits were reanimated. We swore to live or die beside him and not ask him to surrender the fortress even if everything goes up in flames. A senior military person also said of him that he understands how to shore up the lax discipline… and how to get the most out of the various means of defense available. His wisdom and his energy were good harbingers of a glorious and successful defense. Just like the Duke of Württemberg during the third Russian siege of Kolberg in 1761, his method was to keep the enemy away from the fortress as long as possible by digging field trenches and embroiling him in constant skirmishes."[18] Since the terrain prevented Loison from completely surrounding the town, Gneisenau dispatched junior officers to visit villages and enlist recruits for the garrison.

On April 26, the 2nd Pomeranian Reserve Battalion consisting of 14 officers and 540 rankers under Captain Karl von Steinmetz disembarked from ships that had sailed from Memel three days earlier. The week witnessed the arrival of additional contingents to support the French as well. These included a Polish regiment and one sent by the Duke of Saxony comprising battalions from Weimar and Gotha, Altenburg and Meiningen, plus two Württemberg regiments and a battalion from Italy. Loison was dissatisfied with these units; the Italians performed badly in nocturnal engagements and his German troops sympathized with the Prussians. A third of those from Thuringia and 20 percent of the men from Württemberg deserted before reaching Kolberg.[19] The French general encamped his German auxiliaries furthest from the fortress, but this facilitated their escape. "Deserters from the enemy complained a lot about privations in their camp," recalled a resident of the town.[20] Those defecting to Kolberg said more would have come, but the French told the men that Prussians ship their prisoners to Siberia. Gneisenau snuck scouts into the *Rheinbund* encampment at night to advise the soldiers of the untruthfulness of the claim. A Kolberg citizen observed, "It is very depressing when, as so often happens, one German is fighting against another as is the case here."[21]

Napoleon formed an observation corps on May 03 to prevent British landings along the Baltic coast. The following day he ordered a formal investment of Kolberg. Loison had 8,100 troops. On the 13th, he received a battery of heavy guns. To besiege the fortress, the French first had to capture Wolfsberg. The fort was about 900 yards beyond Kolberg's outer wall. General Teulié, who remained with the siege corps after Loison replaced him in command, led an assault on the night of May 18. Some 1,600 Italian, Polish and Württemberg troops, followed by 600 workers with trenching tools, overwhelmed the 160-man garrison in fierce hand-to-hand combat. The laborers began to demolish Wolfsberg's fortifications. Gneisenau wasted no time gathering his forces for a counterattack. They dislodged the enemy from the fort after hours of heavy fighting during which little quarter was given. By dawn the next morning, Wolfsberg was again in Prussian hands. They had suffered 250 casualties and the French considerably more.[22] Gneisenau's concept of conducting a mobile defense outside of the fortress, supported by artillery fire from blockhouses and trenches beyond the walls, proved its value. Loison then tried to eliminate Wolfsberg by digging parallels and bombarding it.

Enemy reinforcements poured in. Gneisenau kept pace thanks to support from allied ships. A Royal Navy corvette and a Swedish frigate shelled French parallels on May 26. Two British transport ships brought 10,000 rifles with corresponding ammunition, 6,000 sabers, 30 cannons and ten howitzers with 300 rounds per gun to the fortress. Captain Petersdorf, a Prussian officer who had landed in England on April 11, had persuaded his hosts to send military aid. While the shipment was being prepared, he learned from the newspapers of a cease-fire between the British and Napoleon. Petersdorf visited the foreign secretary, George Canning, to inquire about the status of the delivery. Even though the new treaty required the crown to stop supplying arms to Prussia, Canning reassured his visitor, "An Englishman does not break his word once given; You will get the weapons promised, even when it is not impossible that these same may be used by the Prussians against us."[23] The new guns were particularly welcome; some of Kolberg's iron cannons were in such poor condition that barrels occasionally burst after firing just ten rounds. Gneisenau later told his adjutant Major Brandt that he lost more gunners to such mishaps than to enemy action.[24]

On June 04, a ship brought news of Danzig's surrender. Gneisenau feared that the French will transfer the siege corps deployed there to Kolberg to take the fortress. Loison received eleven heavy guns from Danzig. He placed 20 guns in redoubts bordering the Binnenfeld and bombarded Wolfsberg for several hours on June 11. He offered a cease-fire if the Prussians evacuate the fort and return to Kolberg together with their transportable artillery. The defenders accepted. French workers entered Wolfsberg and began renovations to mount their cannons there. Gneisenau considered this a violation of the truce and opened fire on the laborers. Teulié was killed in the barrage. A few days later, Prussian grenadiers assaulted Wolfsberg to prevent the enemy from bringing his guns to within range of the harbor. At anchor were three British vessels laden with supplies. The grenadiers recaptured the fort; Gneisenau estimated enemy losses at nearly a thousand men. The Italians who fell into Prussian hands were massacred in retaliation for their recent abuse of civilians in Naugardt.[25] During the battle Gneisenau lost his friend and vice-commandant Waldenfels. He was killed leading his troops over the barricades.

After three consecutive counterattacks the French recaptured Wolfsberg. Gneisenau launched another assault to retake the fort on the 19th, but his troops were repulsed with heavy losses. A truce followed for both sides to collect and bury the dead. Nettelbeck was among the volunteers who searched for survivors: "I can scarcely describe what a lamentable scene this was. Try to imagine for yourself what a place must look like that is barely 200 feet across and covered with four to five hundred bodies piled next to and atop one another, some of them so frightfully mutilated and torn apart that quite often, friends could not recognize their friends among the bloody and smashed figures. Not even the most insensitive soul could turn from this mass of broken, in some cases still writhing bodies without a sense of horror."[26] From Wolfsberg, the French dug parallels closer to the fortress to move up their artillery. The season favored the defenders. The enemy could only dig redoubts for the guns under cover of darkness and the short June nights limited the time available for the labor.

A Swedish frigate brought four heavy mortars and a large quantity of ammunition and powder to Kolberg on June 29th. Loison also received reinforcements. A Dutch regiment of over 1,600 infantry and more heavy guns joined the siege corps on June 21. By the close of the month, it had swollen to 14,000 men including 275 engineers and over 60 guns. After the fall of Wolfsberg, the French prepared to assault Kolberg. Allied ships still delivered food and ammunition, but incessant fighting, round-the-clock duty manning the walls, often under enemy fire, and daily repair of damage was taking a toll on the troops and the militia. The town's finances were exhausted and Gneisenau printed paper money to pay the soldiers and purchase necessities. Upon assuming command, he had threatened to break the saber and rip the epaulettes from the uniform of any officer who fails to do his duty, and told the townspeople that he will hang "from the nearest strong tree" anyone who publicly disparages the soldiers or writes the king to complain about them.[27] He authorized women and children to leave the fortress beginning June 12, but refused permission for men to seek safety beyond its walls.

As Loison prepared an all-out attack, the defenders "were not lacking in spirit," wrote Höpfner. "The example of the selfless commandant inspired everyone. Officers and soldiers fought with the greatest devotion. The officers were the first into action. This proved a great advantage in the battles that occurred here such as assailing trenches and the like, even though some found an honorable death thrashing the enemy. The 4th Italian Line Regiment was practically annihilated and no less were the Poles, who were most hated of all. Since the day that the fighting began up until June 27, Major Gneisenau had sent nearly 500 prisoners by sea to Prussia."[28] The onslaught began on July 01 at 3:00 a.m. A battery of six mortars and four howitzers along the Körlin Dam opened fire on the city and outer fortifications. Massive infantry attacks against every position followed. Two thousand Italian and Dutch troops advanced along the beach in two columns against the machine house where the Prussians controlled the flooding. Tirailleurs set the building ablaze. The bushes were too damp for the flames to spread, but smoke drove the defenders out.

On the right bank of the Persante, the attackers forced Schill's infantry from

Kolberg is bombarded by French artillery. The Persante River is to the left of the fortress. The Binnenfeld to the right of town is larger than depicted in the illustration. Fort Wolfsberg rests atop the hillock in the middle of the Binnenfeld. The French encampment is at far right. A Swedish frigate lurks offshore.

its fortified position at the Maikuhle. This enabled the French to capture the harbor. Constricted by flood zones, the French had to advance on a narrow front and were unable to fully deploy. "The enemy appeared to have disregarded any notion of sparing his own troops, so as to capture the fortress no matter what the cost."[29] On the eastern side of the river, the Prussians abandoned the first line of trenches. Although nowhere was Kolberg's outer wall breached, the fortress was separated from its port facility; only along the beach could the garrison now access the sea. Loison ceased fire at ten o'clock in the morning and sent an envoy to offer Gneisenau the opportunity for an "honorable capitulation." The envoy warned that refusal will result in complete destruction of Kolberg. He added hypocritically that the blood of the garrison will be on Gneisenau's hands. The major refused and the bombardment resumed. Loison adjusted the barrage to concentrate on the town. Prussian guns returned fire but could not prevent the avalanche of destruction that followed.

The only respites from the shelling were occasional pauses for gun barrels to cool. Every hour an average of 193 rounds struck the city.[30] Citizens battled to control fires fanned by high winds. A corn granary and the courthouse were set ablaze. Nearly 20 rounds landed on the *Marienkirche*, killing some of the 800 wounded within. A pastor mounted the pulpit to console the distressed refugees and the injured with an impromptu sermon. Totally unhinged, a man interrupted, "None of this is true!" and with fists clenched charged the pulpit.[31] Direct hits on the jail enabled prisoners of war to escape. They looted abandoned houses. Other captives were released to assist in combating the flames. "With scarcely diminished fury" recalled Nettelbeck, "the bombardment continued throughout July 01 and wreaked destruction. Our firefighting system was effective enough to contain the fires that started here and there. Only late in the evening did the administration building catch fire. Since it was filled with flammable material the structure burned to the ground... The enemy guns combined for a renewed effort. Their ruinous effect, the continuous noise of buildings caving in, falling shingles and shattering windows were so deafening that they often drowned out the thunder of the guns."[32]

During the barrage, Loison fired an estimated 6,000 rounds into Kolberg. A soldier of the garrison offered this account: "As always, Kolberg's citizens displayed supreme spirit and tenacity. They demonstrated that they can bear the hour of greatest misery and deepest distress with enduring steadfastness. One saw this night the bombs exploding in the air high above the unfortunate town, raining their devastating fire on the houses below. One could hear the most solid buildings collapse with a fearful din. Here and there bombs and grenades ignited fires that raged wildly, greedily consuming the already damaged dwellings. It genuinely seemed as though we were all destined to perish in Kolberg. Some whose composure allowed them to still think clearly must have been reminded by this of Sodom and Gomorrah. But the spirit of the Kolbergers paid no heed. They instead scorned every attack and every hazard so cruelly directed against our poor city. We were greatly inspired by the response of our unshakable commandant to three enemy demands for surrender during the 36-hour bombardment. The responses were no different than had just a single round been hurled at us. The fearlessness of the garrison did not wane and the spirit of the citizens did not falter, even though they saw with anguish how their houses collapsed and went up in flames."[33]

Unknown to the Prussians, Friedrich Wilhelm had agreed to a cease-fire on June 25. Furnished with a French pass, Lieutenant Holleben left Königsberg on June 28 to bring news of the truce to Kolberg. When he arrived at Loison's headquarters in the village of Tramm, the French general stalled arranging an escort for him to proceed to the fortress. Loison hoped to crush Kolberg under the bombardment and force its surrender before hostilities ended. Napoleon had promised to name him Duke of Kolberg. The continued barrage "had no success beyond reducing more houses in the town to ashes and shedding more blood."[34] Eventually resigned to the fact that Gneisenau will not give in, Loison assigned a general to accompany Holleben into Kolberg. "Suddenly the guns of the enemy batteries fell silent," recalled Nettelbeck. "A long, empty stillness took the place of all the shell bursts and thundering of the final judgment."[35] The men on the walls watched with anticipation as an enemy general and an unidentified officer approached under a flag of truce.

Nettelbeck continued, "As the outline of the figure became more defined, we recognized to our amazement that he is a Prussian officer. Keener eyes assured us that he bears the countenance of their friend Lieutenant von Holleben of the 3rd Neumark Reserve Battalion. A few weeks ago, he had left by sea for Memel escorting a group of enemy prisoners. It seemed impossible, but it was so! The first words he uttered, almost breathlessly, when he plunged into his circle of acquaintances was, 'Peace! Kolberg is saved!'"[36] There were 1,567 infantrymen and 100 cannoneers left in the fortress, two "invalid" companies of soldiers barely fit for duty and a few cuirassiers. The garrison had lost 55 officers, 213 NCOs and 2,593 men killed, wounded and missing including desertions. There were but six remaining out of 50 fusiliers under Lieutenant Briesen's command. Schill's mobile corps forfeited 682 infantry and 40 artillerymen. Twenty-seven civilians perished and 42 were injured, mostly during the July bombardment. The Prussians estimated enemy casualties at over 6,000. This included a thousand men squandered in fruitless assaults during the final two days. The French grossly understated their losses. Loison reported that his artillery fired 25,940 rounds during the four-month battle.[37]

Major Gneisenau had employed aggressive tactics the French were unaccustomed to. Instead of sitting with the garrison inside of the fortress and awaiting attacks, he constructed fortifications beyond the walls. From these his men launched frequent sorties to keep the enemy at bay and prevent him from breaching the outer wall. A soldier of the garrison wrote this of the commandant: "He allowed the previously closed spiritual services to resume, remarking that the consolation of religion should at very least not be taken from the people in times of distress and danger. He was active and robust in body and soul, as much a valiant warrior as a connoisseur of human nature. He was circumspect in the art of how to properly treat those around him and how to gain the respect, trust and love of the civilian class as well. His cheerful attitude was especially important for coordinating a defense as difficult as was Kolberg's. Together with honesty and steadfastness of character, he combined an animated spirit and experience in armed service and possessed the necessary caution and presence of mind to be truly talented in the art of war."[38] The king promoted Gneisenau to lieutenant colonel and awarded him the *Pour le Mérite*.

On July 31, Friedrich Wilhelm wrote into the cabinet order praising Kolberg's commandant, "Your vigorous and sound endeavors as well as the honorable conduct of the garrison and its faithful burghers will add an eternal, unforgettable page to the annals of the fatherland's history of these perilous times."[39] Regarding the civilian population, even after 36 hours of steady bombardment, "no one thought about surrendering."[40] Some 20th-Century historians disparage Kolberg's stalwart defense as pointless, because Napoleon and the king of Prussia were about to reach an understanding and the town could have been spared destruction had it capitulated. This typically academic, modern disdain of heroism overlooks the inspiration that the outcome of the siege gave the people of Prussia. After a string of abject defeats, here was a comparatively insignificant bastion that defied France, restored faith in the army and offered hope for the future. The bearing of the townspeople and tenacity of the garrison scarcely supports the opinion of chroniclers like Goltz and Höhn, that Prussia was supposedly defeated because the people were infected with liberal values of the Enlightenment and had grown soft from a long period of peace and prosperity.

The Battle of Eylau

A military campaign can lose impetus as it progresses. Forced marches, casualties, desertion, combat-related stress, steadily extending supply lines, prolonged separation from home, disease and continuous exposure to the elements take their toll on man and horse and gradually diminish the striking power of an army. Conducting operations in foreign countries places a strain on the populations compelled to provide foodstuffs and tribute. It can make enemies of the occupation among the increasingly restless inhabitants. None of these factors dissuaded Napoleon from rousing his soldiers for a winter offensive. In November 1806, Friedrich Wilhelm refused to accept the emperor's peace offer because it stipulated that he abandon the alliance with Russia. Only by destroying the Russian and Prussian armies in Poland could Bonaparte conclude the war on his terms. Political considerations overshadowed the disadvantages of conducting military operations in cold weather. Napoleon felt the timing favorable since the czar was also in conflict with Turkey and shifted 80,000 troops from Europe to the Black Sea.

Hearing the emperor's proclamation of December 02, 1806, French troops were not happy about the operation. They longed for a respite. Those who had marched from Berlin that autumn were acquainted with Poland's inhospitable climate. General Rapp wrote, "Our soldiers were less satisfied. They showed a lively repugnance to cross the Vistula. Misery, the winter, the bad weather, had infused them with an extreme aversion of this country."[41] Proceeding with his corps up the Vistula River from Bromberg, Augereau wrote the emperor, "We're crossing a desolate land without means of subsistence. The soldiers bivouac but many of them have no overcoats. The roads are hideous and the season is harsh." Marching east from Schneidemühl to Bromberg, Lannes described the muddy road as "practically impassable. It leads over ground where horses sink to their bellies."[42] Rapp wrote that "the country was clayed and cut up by marshes; the roads were frightful. The cavalry, infantry, and artillery were lost in the deep mud. None could get out of it save by untold labor."[43]

Napoleon presumed his adversaries were in retreat. General Bennigsen was withdrawing to join up with an army of 37,000 men on its way from Russia under General Friedrich von Buxhöwden. The emperor ordered Lannes to cross the Narew River in pursuit. The Russian general, like Yorck after Jena, knew that an army can lose more personnel falling back than fighting a battle. Bennigsen therefore made a stand on the southern periphery of Pultusk. The town is just north of Warsaw on a narrow front marked by forests and sloping terrain. Napoleon had written Lannes that his corps faces "comparatively insignificant forces that will give ground," and that cavalry patrols confirm the assessment.[44] Lannes had misgivings about the disadvantageous lie of the land. In compliance with the unconditional obedience the emperor demanded, he attacked at 11:00 a.m. on December 26. His corps numbered 20,000 men. Lannes wrote that "the rain and the hail overwhelmed our soldiers" and that "the field on which we were about to do battle had been converted to a sea of mud."[45]

The French advanced confidently, having bested the Russians at Austerlitz a year ago. The enemy they faced, they did not realize, outnumbered them by two to one. Lannes's corps was deficient in artillery since the mire prevented crews from bringing many batteries forward. Bennigsen enjoyed vast superiority in this arm. The French were exposed to devasting cannonades, especially against their center. Through skillful deployment of his reserves and timely counterattacks, Bennigsen held Lannes in check as the battle raged past nightfall. Davout sent a division under Joseph de Fournier, the Marquis d'Aultanne, in support. This enabled the French to withdraw to their assembly areas after hours of fruitless assaults. With the manpower at his disposal, the Russian commander could have routed Lannes's corps had he taken the offensive before d'Aultanne arrived. He overestimated the strength of the force opposite him and held his position. Regarding casualties, Petre wrote that those of Lannes "had been very heavy in the savage hand-to-hand fighting… His and d'Aultanne's losses are greatly understated by the French. On the whole, it is probable that they were not less than 7,000 in killed, wounded, and prisoners."[46]

The French themselves published the casualty figures of between six and 700 dead and 1,500 wounded including three generals and Marshal Lannes. Höpfner maintains, "It is certain that the losses of the French were significantly greater than those of the Russians, since throughout the entire battle they were exposed to their enemy's violent artillery fire. They themselves could only counter with a small number of guns. Also, all of their attacks failed."[47] The French found themselves grappling with an opponent who proved alarmingly tougher and more tenacious than anticipated. Serving on Bennigsen's staff at Pultusk, Major Knesebeck assessed the qualities of the Russian fighting man: "These people are steady, indifferent to suffering, valiant and can endure fatigue and hardship to an unbelievable degree. When properly led much can be done with them. This is indisputably the only nation that can hold its own against the French."[48]

After the battle d'Aultanne, who was chief of staff of Davout's corps, wrote him, "Some very distressing things have happened here. It was not possible to take the Pultusk position. The troops of Marshal Lannes were unable to do it. My division had to hold its position until eight o'clock in the evening to protect his corps from getting into difficulties and then it fell back… I have many wounded. The troops fought the whole day in knee-deep mud and I therefore find it necessary to rest here for the moment. The worst of it is that the ammunition is exhausted and it appears almost impossible to bring up the ammunition carts. I'll do my utmost to get the division to Skaszewo tomorrow morning, but will unfortunately have to leave 23 captured cannons behind. Perhaps it would be good to support my retreat with another division."[49] This report bears little resemblance to the exuberant dispatches French commanders sent up the chain of command when they were pursuing the vanquished Prussian army in October.

The same day, Murat's corps fought a smaller but equally disappointing engagement at Golymin twelve miles northwest of Pultusk. The Russian 4th Division of General Dmitry Gallitzin had paused there to rest after a nightlong retreat toward Makow. When Murat's advance guard appeared, the soldiers were too fatigued to resume the march. Gallitzin thereupon deployed them in front of Golymin and spent the rest of the day beating off uncoordinated French attacks. His division, together with a few regiments from the 5th Division, numbered around 17,000 men and occupied defensible ground. The French had nearly 38,000 troops on hand. Due to the mud, they could not bring the artillery forward. The Russians positioned 28 cannons grouped into two batteries behind their main battle line. The crews bombarded the enemy virtually unmolested, since the attackers had nothing of sufficient range to fire back with. The divisions of Augereau and Davout advanced in marshy terrain. The troops were lashed alternately by rain and snow squalls. Despite their numbers they made little headway. This allowed Gallitzin to retreat toward Makow that night. Murat confessed to Napoleon, "We thought the enemy had 50,000 men."[50] Such was the impression the dogged Russian resistance made on the invaders.

Rebuffs at Pultusk and at Golymin and negative reports from his marshals persuaded Napoleon to suspend the campaign. Poland was not rich in resources like Germany; Murat wrote him, "The want of foodstuffs broke nearly all bonds of obedience and suppressed every feeling of humanity... Sire, it is painful for me to describe to you the heartrending scene that every marshal has surely already formed of his own situation. We not only find nothing in the villages for man and horse, but the places are abandoned; all of the inhabitants have fled."[51] The *Grande Armée* would have to rely on logistical support from home. The supply line was vulnerable to raids from Prussian cavalry. On January 01, the emperor ordered his formations billeted for the cold season. The poverty of the countryside and limited opportunities to forage made it necessary to disperse the locations where various corps took quarters. Most troops remained in the vicinity of Warsaw. Bonaparte saw no danger in decentralizing the army, since he presumed that the enemy is also in need of a rest and will remain inactive. In this he was in error.

Ney disregarded Napoleon's order to take shelter and advanced instead. He intended to take Königsberg, which at that time is where Friedrich Wilhelm resided. This rash maneuver exposed not only Ney's own force, but endangered Bernadotte's corps as well. Had the allies shown more initiative, they could have attacked and inflicted a serious defeat on either. Ney's corps was strung out over 50 miles. The marshal did not yet realize that the Russians are on the move; nor was he aware of the proximity of the Prussian corps under Anton von L'Estocq. Ney finally complied with the emperor's orders and withdrew south on January 20. He reached Neidenburg without being drawn into battle. Ney narrowly escaped disaster thanks to the sluggish progress of L'Estocq and Bennigsen. Bernadotte extricated his troops from the danger zone after clashing with the Russians advancing under General Yevgeni Markov at Mohrungen on January 25. The inconclusive engagement cost both sides about 2,000 casualties. Russian cavalry captured a French baggage column, including Bernadotte's personal luggage containing 12,500 ducats and valuables he had looted from palaces in German duchies.[52]

Bennigsen momentarily contented himself with screening Königsberg and maintaining communication with Danzig, but was under orders to drive the French back across the Vistula. He and Buxhöwden had held a war council on January 02 and resolved to strike against the enemy's left wing. After forcing Ney and Bernadotte back later that month, Bennigsen halted his army for a three-day rest near Deutsch-Eylau. The Prussians proceeded west toward Marienwerder and Graudenz. At the end of January, L'Estocq reached Freystadt, a town just east of the two fortresses on the Vistula. On the 24th, Bernadotte sent a message to the emperor stating that according to allied deserters, Bennigsen is massing a force of 80,000 troops near Preussisch-Eylau. Having also received a report from Davout of increasing Russian activity, Napoleon finally realized that the enemy is not in hibernation as originally presumed. He resolved to muster the *Grande Armée* and draw the Russians into a battle of annihilation.

With the allies moving toward the Vistula, Bonaparte assembled his forces to their southeast to proceed north toward Allenstein and sever their supply line to Russia. He planned the operation too quickly to make sufficient arrangements to provision his troops during its execution. He did surpass what Bennigsen achieved for his own soldiers in this field.[53] The counteroffensive was scheduled to begin on February 01. The French chief of staff, Louis-Alexandre Berthier, assigned an ensign fresh baked from the military academy to carry a dispatch to Bernadotte containing the complete operational plan. Unfamiliar with the country, he was intercepted on route by a Cossack patrol sent out by Prince Pyotr Bagration. Since Berthier had dispatched only this one courier, Bernadotte did not receive his marching orders. What was worse for Napoleon was that after Bagration read it, he forwarded the captured document to Bennigsen's headquarters. Now alerted to the trap Napoleon was setting, the general retreated before it could be sprung.

Soult's IV corps was first to reach Allenstein on February 03. The town is on the Alle River, which the French had to cross to catch Bennigsen. The Russian

14th Division under General Nikolai Kamenskoi and three Prussian batteries defended a defile further north at Bergfried, where a bridge spans the Alle. The main Russian army deployed on the western side of the river at Jonkendorf. Bonaparte drew up his force opposite this mass. He hoped to root it to the spot while Soult, supported by Davout's III Corps, forced the crossing at Bergfried and outflanked Bennigsen. A seesaw battle for the bridge and the town followed. The French captured both but were unable to cross in strength and stop the Russian retreat after dark. "Bergfried was certainly not the decided success that Napoleon represented it to be," observed Petre. "Even accepting the account most favorable to the French, they had done no more than get across the river and could not risk occupying the farther bank in force at night."[54] The emperor understated the number of casualties he took in the battle. Nearby, cavalry squadrons sent forward by Ney and Murat skirmished with 1,500 Prussians from the Auer Dragoon and Wagenfeld Cuirassier Regiments without serious losses on either side. The French thought they faced 6,000 Prussian cavalrymen.[55]

Bennigsen continued his retreat north with the *Grande Armée* in pursuit. He about faced at Preussisch-Eylau 20 miles south of Königsberg to make a stand. Together with Murat's cavalry, Soult was again first on the scene. His corps went into action at 2:00 p.m. on February 07 against the Russian rearguard. Commanded by Prince Bagration, the rearguard defended a plateau a mile in front of Eylau. The prince was one of the ablest of the czar's generals. He stalled the advance of an overwhelmingly superior French force long enough for Bennigsen to move his heavy artillery into position. Bagration then conducted an orderly withdrawal under French pressure and rejoined the main army. Höpfner lists Russian strength at 58,000 men, grouped into 126 infantry battalions and 145 cavalry squadrons. Considering losses from recent combat and forced marches, this is probably a good estimate.[56] Bennigsen also had 400 cannons. This was nearly a third more than what was available to the French and the Russian army was fully concentrated at Eylau. Napoleon began the battle with 54,000 troops.[57] The corps of Davout and Ney were still en route to the combat zone. Bernadotte had no orders and missed the engagement completely.

Fighting on the first day focused on control of Preussisch-Eylau. It continued until Bennigsen ordered his units to relinquish the town at ten at night. Both armies bivouacked outdoors without nourishment. Although Napoleon had tried to arrange delivery of provisions, wagons laden with bread and brandy could not get to the front because of the poor condition of the roads, bad weather and baggage columns crowding the way. The next morning opened with an artillery duel and some minor skirmishes. Once the first elements of Davout's III Corps appeared on Bennigsen's left, Napoleon staged a frontal attack against the left and center of the Russian battle line with Saint Hilaire's division and Augereau's VII Corps. The emperor hoped to keep his enemy busy repelling this headlong advance until Davout outflanked him. Augereau and Saint Hilaire however, marched straight into a blizzard. Snow squalls impaired visibility;

French and allied troops clash at Preussisch-Eylau. French war artists mainly illustrated battles of the *Grande Armée* in which Napoleon was personally in command. His image is a prominent feature of almost every such canvas, indulging his self-idolatry and projecting the aura of an infallible leader.

the VII Corps lost direction and drifted away from Saint Hilaire's division. Accidently bombarded by their own artillery, the French soldiers plodded forward until the blizzard suddenly lifted. To their horror, they found themselves squarely in front of the Russian artillery position in the center of the line.

Augereau's troops reeled before the unexpected and destructive fire of 70 cannons and soon fell back. Bennigsen seized the moment and launched a counterattack with cavalry and infantry. The French corps was smashed and the survivors driven back. Saint Hilaire's division on its right made no headway. Davout, whose III Corps numbered 15,000 troops, was gradually driving the Russian left flank inward but Napoleon's center was in shambles. French losses in the battle were enormous. Marshal Augereau and General Heudelet were wounded. Generals Desjardins and Jean-Joseph Hautpoult were killed. Desjardins' division was wiped out. General Cornineau and Colonel Dahlman of the Guard Chasseurs also lay dead on the battlefield. Many staff and other officers shared their fate. Only cadres remained of Augereau's corps and the cavalry that went into action with it. All officers in both battalions of the 14th Line Infantry Regiment died in action. Only five officers of the third battalion of the 24th Regiment were still alive. According to its own report, by just past 10:00 a.m., Augereau had already lost 929 men killed and 4,271 wounded.[58]

To salvage a critical situation, the emperor ordered Murat, waiting in the wings with the reserve cavalry, to attack the Russian line with the entire mounted force. Perhaps under the influence of embellished French accounts and fanciful illustrations by Napoleonic-era painters, historians tout this as one of the most spectacular charges of all time. Murat supposedly led 11,000 horsemen across the battlefield wreaking havoc on the Russian infantry, cavalry and artillery in repeated attacks. In reality, such a rapid charge in a snow-covered field was impossible. In areas where the snow had been trampled underfoot by rifle regiments, it was compact and icy; too slippery for man and horse to negotiate at a gallop. Considering the weight of a fully-equipped cuirassier and the lamentable condition of the starved, fatigued and shivering mount he rode, the gait of the animals participating in Murat's attack was likely slow and unsteady. As Goltz pointed out, "On the day of the battle deep snow covered the ground and made all movement difficult. The cavalry was especially affected."[59] Further, bad visibility caused by the driving snowstorm would have impeded the orientation of the squadrons.

The accepted figure of 11,000 horsemen is also doubtful. It describes the mounted divisions at full strength. Malnourishment, poor roads, hooves improperly shod for winter and losses from illness or combat during the previous week would have thinned the number of horses fit for duty: The reserve cavalry fought every day during the advance to Eylau. It probably lost at least 2,500 horsemen.[60] Also, difficulties in moving artillery and supply wagons forward on Poland's wretched trails required detailing cavalry horses to assist the teams. Murat arranged his squadrons in a long, tightly grouped column that stomped across the battlefield and neither destroyed nor dispersed the Russian line. Bennigsen's infantry did not even form battle squares, the usual defense to repel a cavalry charge. The maneuver cost the French 1,500 riders but provided some respite for the harassed formations of Augereau and Saint Hilaire. Napoleon did not deploy his last reserve, the Imperial Guard, to administer the coup de grâce. Had Murat's action been as successful as popularly believed, the emperor would probably have exploited it by committing the guard. Until he could account for the whereabouts of L'Estocq's corps that might appear on the battlefield at any moment, he opted to keep a strong reserve on hand.

The Prussians meanwhile, fended off Ney during their forced march to Eylau and arrived on the Russian flank. Though L'Estocq was in charge, operations were actually directed by Scharnhorst as chief of staff. From the high ground at Althoff, Scharnhorst could see the danger that Davout posed to the Russian left wing. In his endeavor to outflank Bennigsen, the French marshal had extended his own right wing ahead of the rest of his corps to the village of Kutschitten. Here Scharnhorst saw the weak spot in Davout's deployment and decided to attack. He grouped his soldiers into three infantry and two cavalry columns. All

Prussian infantry charges Davout's troops among the birch trees near Kutschitten, turning the tide at the battle of Eylau in February 1807. The victory helped restore confidence in the Prussian army and unsettled Napoleon.

were to advance on Kutschitten simultaneously. Scharnhorst's Russian regiment was in the center. To its right was the Schöning Regiment and to the left the Rüchel and Towarczys Regiments. The Fabecky Grenadier Battalion and the rest of the cavalry followed. With trumpets blaring and drums beating, the Prussians marched behind the Russian battle line and parallel to it to the opposite side of the field. Officers called upon Russian stragglers to join the march without success. The only reinforcements were 200 Cossack horsemen.

The Prussians wrested Kutschitten just northeast of Eylau from the enemy's 51st Regiment and four companies of the 108th. Scharnhorst's men captured one of the regimental eagle standards. It was given to Queen Luise on her birthday the following month. The Prussians then wheeled right from Kutschitten onto the Domnau road. They fell upon the flank of Davout's III Corps, whose soldiers were defending a birch forest south of the road. Scharnhorst brought up the artillery and bombarded the position. His infantry formed a line and resumed the advance, again to the accompaniment of horn marches. The French withdrew after suffering heavy losses, were chased with the bayonet and ejected from the woods. Davout tried to rally his men with the admonishment, "The valiant will find a glorious death here, and only cowards will become acquainted with the desolation of Siberia!"[61] He was unable to regroup his formations for a counter-attack in the chaos and ensuing darkness.

Ney reached the combat zone at half past seven in the evening. His corps attacked the right wing of Bennigsen's army and fought several indecisive skirmishes. The fighting died down at ten o'clock. Both armies bivouacked in snow-covered terrain. Scharnhorst and some Russian generals urged Bennigsen to reopen the battle after sunrise. He chose to fall back. A vexed Scharnhorst wrote the king's adjutant in Königsberg on February 09, "It is a great misfortune that the battle did not resume the next morning. The troops were indeed fatigued to the utmost, but the enemy was in the same situation."[62] Knesebeck was also irked by Bennigsen's tendency to retreat after a successful defense, gibing that another three victories and the Russian army will be at the gates of Petersburg. The *Grande Armée* suffered nearly 30,000 casualties at Preussisch-Eylau.[63] Many wounded subsequently died from their injuries as preparations to care for them had been hasty and improvised. The Russians lost around 18,000 men though estimates vary.[64] Prussian casualties amounted to less than 900. Losses were low because the troops advanced toward Davout's flank on lower ground than that where the enemy stood and the French musketry aimed to high; most rounds sailed over the soldiers' heads.

Bennigsen's general retreat north to Königsberg was poor strategy as it could sever the army's line of communication to Russia. Scharnhorst ignored instructions to form a Prussian rearguard and took his troops east along the Domnau road instead. The villages were deserted and no one could be located to serve as a guide in the desolate, snow-covered terrain. Officers found two grenadiers indigenous to the region whom they perched on a gun carriage to lead the column. The troops reached Domnau and Friedland the next day. This secured the supply route to the czar's empire. Scharnhorst's decision probably saved the Russian army from annihilation. He was decorated for his service at Eylau, but the Prussian monument to Preussisch-Eylau bears the image of L'Estocq. The old general had been a "completely passive spectator at the battle" and did not issue a single order that contributed to the success of the corps.[65] When Scharnhorst decided to march east in defiance of Bennigsen's directive, he did not even wake L'Estocq, who had retired to bed, to tell him.

Napoleon's *Bulletin de l'armée* listed French casualties at 1,900 dead and 5,700 wounded. It stated that the Russians lost 7,000 killed and 12,000 to 15,000 wounded, and "a great number of prisoners" were taken.[66] According to Höpfner's analysis, "The losses of the French must have been greater than the Russians since they were the attackers and most of their attacks were unsuccessful. This is proven by hospital records discovered later, the destruction of Augereau's corps and the body count made of the dead still on the battlefield eleven days after the engagement who were buried by the Prussians. Nearly 10,000 corpses were found here. The greater measure of these were Frenchmen, even though the French had already buried some of their dead after the battle. They were only prevented from continuing because the ground was frozen."[67] Augereau's corps had 3,000 men left out of 15,000.[68] The emperor contributed to the verity of the popular expression, "to lie like a bulletin" by describing Preussisch-Eylau as a glorious triumph for the *Grande Armée*. He remained there eight more days, unnecessarily prolonging the men's exposure to the elements. He feared that immediately retiring to a hospitable region might give the impression that he had been defeated.[69] This is the man who wrote, "It would be better to fight the bloodiest of battles than to place the troops in an unhealthy locality."[70]

From Eylau to Tilsit

Napoleon must have been disquieted by the fact that his army fought three successive engagements in February without a victory. The grand sweep north to trap the Russian army was thwarted at Pultusk, Golymin and Preussisch-Eylau. French casualties outnumbered those of the allies. Soult's corps was mauled and survivors of Augereau's were distributed to replace losses in other divisions. The army lost five eagle standards and seven flags at Eylau. During this battle, "The big cavalry attack of the French was a matter of desperation brought on by earlier mistakes," concluded Höpfner. "The heavy losses of the cavalry must have been all the more distressing to Napoleon because he was already at a numerical disadvantage in this service branch."[71] Davout and Saint Hilaire lost two thirds of their personnel at Eylau.[72] When Napoleon rode past his troops after the battle, some responded with angry shouts of "long live peace" intermingled with the customary acclaim, *"vive l'empereur!* The truth about the real outcome at Preussisch-Eylau gradually trickled into Paris. The commodities exchange experienced a drastic drop in share values as a result.[73] Eylau was "a severe blow on the reputation for invincibility of Napoleon."[74]

What may have particularly surprised Bonaparte was the unexpected toughness, obstinacy and resilience of his opponents. The Russians were accustomed to privation and harsh climatic conditions. They coped with the season's miserable weather better than the French did. The Prussian soldier he faced at Eylau remained steadfast and courageous, but unlike at Jena, properly led. Scharnhorst handled the formations deftly; this was a novelty for the French warlord who was accustomed to matching wits with mediocre commanders like Bennigsen or bunglers like the Duke of Brunswick and Prince Hohenlohe. Just as the Russian troops had surpassed their performance at Austerlitz in 1805, the Prussian achievement at Eylau was a striking contrast to the dismal failure of the previous October. The Prussian army now demonstrated that it is by no means out of the game. Its odyssey to Preussisch-Eylau, hence before it even reached the battlefield, was in itself a superior tactical achievement.

The Prussian corps covered nearly 90 miles in five days on narrow, winding roads cut with deep, jagged furrows caused by wagon wheels churning the mud.

The ruts were frozen solid in many places and toilsome to traverse. Sometimes the cavalrymen dismounted and led the horses on foot. On the night of February 07/08, Lieutenant Carl von Kurssel brought orders from Bennigsen's headquarters for L'Estocq. They directed him to march his corps to Althoff. The village was next to the right wing of the Russian army at Preussisch-Eylau. The troops set off at 7:30 the next morning. They followed a route that skirts the northern periphery of the Eylau forest. Scharnhorst struck camp without waiting for the Plötz Division to catch up. It was made up of less reliable soldiers from southern Prussia and some new East Prussian regiments, and "every quarter-hour was precious. What he had with him were predominantly old Prussian troop contingents firmly bound to the state by language, custom and beliefs, which they were ready today to bleed for once again."[75] In Goltz's words, "It was probably clear to every officer, or at least to the greater majority of them, that the affair would determine the future of Prussia."[76]

The vanguard consisted of ten squadrons of the Auer Dragoon Regiment and the Bredow Battery. Among the grenadiers, line infantry, fusiliers, hussars, dragoons and artillerymen to follow was the Russian Wyburg Infantry Regiment. Since the corps had moved off without gathering all of the formations from their dispersed encampments, it consisted of half of the infantry, most of the cavalry and only the mounted artillery which represented about a fourth of L'Estocq's guns. Throughout the trek, Ney's VI Corps maintained constant pressure on the column. The French moved to occupy Schlautienen, the next village on the road to the Eylau, to block Scharnhorst's progress. The Prussians beat them to the town by minutes. "To reach the destination of the march," wrote Lehmann, "required a combination of sound judgment, ruthlessness and resolve that only one man in the entire army possessed."[77]

Scharnhorst sent half of the advance guard cavalry against Ney. He drove the other half, reinforced by the ten squadrons of the Towarczys Cavalry Regiment and the furthermost horse battery, rapidly through Schlautienen to seize the high ground opposite the town. This he defended with two Prussian and three Russian companies. He directed the bulk of the column not to follow the advance guard through Schlautienen, but to turn north toward Pompicken and march along the parallel road from there to Althoff. This decision decided the outcome of the battle of Eylau. The units engaged at Schlautienen held off Ney's corps long enough for the main column to reach Pompicken without incident. A second enemy contingent took the village of Wackern. It cut off the Prussian rearguard under General Moritz von Prittwitz that was fighting to delay the French pursuit. Two companies of his fusiliers drove the French from the town in a bayonet charge. The commander of one of the fusilier companies was Captain Wilhelm von Krauseneck. He would become chief of the Prussian general staff in 1829. The action at Wackern occupied the enemy long enough for the units holding Schlautienen to disengage and rejoin the main column.

Under Scharnhorst's direction, the corps repeatedly sidestepped pitched battles with Ney. It engaged in sporadic artillery duels and cavalry skirmishes and sent fusiliers forward to prevent the French from disrupting the march. The column detoured from the main route while Prittwitz's horsemen and fusiliers kept the enemy busy. Ney lost sight of the column in the contours of hills and overgrown marshlands that the road winds through. Visibility was further obscured by a snowstorm. He did not realize that Prittwitz's cavalry and riflemen were the rearguard. Some of Ney's units marched parallel to the column, separated from it by a bog. They tried to cross several times but Scharnhorst detached units to repulse them. Five infantry companies from the Schoening and Viborg Regiments rejoined the main force after repelling French attacks. The Pabecky Grenadier Battalion held the road through Pompicken open until the rest of the column passed though the village.

According to Goltz summarized, "More and more, the rearguard attracted the enemy's attention… General (Franz) von Plötz, coming over from Bomben, joined with Prittwitz. They fought side by side with their inferior forces so skillfully throughout the day that Ney mistook them for L'Estocq's entire corps and pursued them to Kreuzburg."[78] Plötz had been with the reserve at Bomben and hastened to Schlauthienen, where Prittwitz was engaged, upon hearing the din of battle. Höpfner wrote, "Both generals understood just how to hold back the enemy long enough for General L'Estocq to escape his interference. They fought for most of the day without giving away their weakness." The Prussians "knew how to fundamentally exploit the terrain, avoid a major battle and not for a moment lose sight of the objective to link up with Bennigsen… a model of how to conduct a flank march against a very near and powerful enemy."[79] Scharnhorst detached several battalions to check the French but still brought 5,584 combatants to Althoff by 1:00 p.m. The force comprised eight infantry battalions, 29 cavalry squadrons and 16 guns. The small rearguard delayed Ney's 14,000 soldiers until they arrived too late.

According to Goltz, "Napoleon saw his hopes for the outcome of the big battle on the 8th bitterly disappointed. (The Prussian) bearing in combat was flawless. There had been no hesitation, no wavering and no indecision. The failure to act that was repeatedly responsible for the misfortunes on the Saale and during retreats to the Oder was nowhere apparent. Everyone was where he was supposed to be and did his duty promptly and energetically. When moving through Wackern and withdrawing from Schlauthienen and Pompicken, no officer and no soldier lacked presence of mind and determination. During the battle for Kutschitten as well as in the attack on the birch forest, all the battalions acquitted themselves in a manner worthy of the infantry of Friedrich the Great." After the battle Napoleon rhetorically asked if the Prussian dead at Jena have risen from the grave. At Eylau, "operations were now imbued with a fresh spirit, and this spirit was that of Scharnhorst. Despite the ambiguous nature of his authority and contrary influences, he knew how to give credence to his views about how best to fight the war right up to the decisive day. There can be no doubt that the idea to carry out the renowned flank march to the right in the face of Ney's interference was his. No one else in L'Estocq's entourage had up till then demonstrated enough insight to be credited with such a plan."[80]

Within the French army, the requisition system proved inadequate for procuring enough food in the worsening climate. Deliveries from France were insufficient. By late October, shortages of food, boots and warm apparel had led to looting and even grave robbing. Ney wrote the emperor that the breakdown of discipline "has reached such a point that the lives of officers are no longer safe."[81] Soult reported, "The trail of the corps is marked by arson, destruction and loathsome, scarcely conceivable offences. The voice of those in command is scarcely heeded. The lives of officers are often in peril. To complete the misfortune, the resources of the country are destroyed upon the approach of French troops."[82] During the battle of Eylau, marauding French soldiers stole the horses and personal belongings of their chief surgeon and members of the medical staff while they were administering to the wounded.

Strained by the winter campaign and shocked over unexpected Russian resistance, the French began to despair of winning the war. Napoleon established military hospitals at Posen, Thorn, Bromberg and Gnesen. He arranged for the evacuation of the sick and injured and drew the *Grande Armée* into winter quarters near the Vistula. He sent Bertrand to Friedrich Wilhelm with conciliatory terms only days after the battle at Preussisch-Eylau. Bertrand pledged that all territories Prussia possessed before the war will be restored and that French troops will leave the country. Her alliance with Russia he insisted be terminated. The king could not honorably void the compact with the czar and rejected the proposals. Hardenberg commented, "Napoleon only wants to separate the king from Russia to rob Prussia of respect, tear her completely away from Czar Alexander and from England and make her the slave of France. Petersburg and London must be informed immediately and a declaration issued that the king will remain firmly and faithfully committed to the common cause."[83]

Fighting resumed as Bennigsen and L'Estocq advanced into areas evacuated by the French. There were a few skirmishes, but by late March the armies on both sides were settled into winter encampments. Bonaparte used the period of tranquility to besiege Danzig and replenish manpower. The troops did not begin receiving adequate supply deliveries at regular intervals until April. By the time Danzig capitulated in May, French divisions were almost at full roster. Bennigsen, his divisions also replenished, resume operations on June 05. The main weight of his offensive was directed against Ney's VI Corps. Facing superior enemy forces, Ney concentrated his units at Guttstadt. He conducted an adroit fighting withdrawal, deftly maneuvering and counterattacking with Tirailleurs. He held up the Russians long enough for the VI Corps to retreat in good order to Ankendorf.

Terrain here favored the defender; Bennigsen renewed the offensive the next day without success. Ney's formations escaped across the Passarge River.

His corps could have been surrounded and possibly destroyed, but for the poor execution of the Russian plan. Bennigsen blamed Prince Fabian von der Osten-Sacken, a subordinate general who had served at Pultusk. The Russians retreated and Napoleon counterattacked on June 08. The warlord advanced with 50,000 men against what he at first presumed to be Bennigsen's rearguard at Heilsberg on the Alle River. Davout and Mortier were to simultaneously march their corps around the Russian right to cut the defenders off from Königsberg. Unfortunately for Bonaparte, his adversary had recently fortified the position where the entire Russian army now awaited an attack. Russian engineers had constructed a series of redoubts and other obstacles there which, together with the marshy terrain on the flanks, made the defenses virtually insurmountable.

The *Grande Armée* attacked on June 10 with the corps of Soult and Murat and one of Lannes's divisions. They were repulsed with heavy losses. Considering Napoleon's reputation as a tactician, it is surprising that he opted for a frontal assault against an entrenched enemy defending redoubts flanked by marshes. Soult's corps alone lost 8,286 men. The French listed their casualties as 1,398 dead and 10,059 wounded with 864 men taken prisoner. The chief of staff of the guard was killed in action. Most of the Russian cavalry and two infantry divisions did not even take part in the fighting. Bennigsen's losses amounted to between six and eight thousand men. "Of the tactics of the French in this terrible combat," judged Petre, "there is not much that is favorable to be said. Napoleon attacked a very strong position with very inferior forces, for it was not till too late in the day to save the situation that Lannes's corps, Ney and the guard could reach the battlefield."[84] The circumstances were embarrassing enough for some French accounts to omit mention of Napoleon's presence at Heilsberg. This was perhaps to give the impression that he bore no responsibility for the defeat. He in fact was on the field by 10:00 a.m.

The next day Napoleon drew a lesson from 18th-Century cabinet warfare, when generals outmaneuvered the enemy instead of locking horns in battles of attrition. By shifting formations to circumvent the Russian line, he compelled Bennigsen to abandon Heilsberg and fall back. This was much to the protest of Prussian staff officers attached to his command. Bennigsen was in poor health that spring. This perhaps contributed to his increasingly bad judgment regarding tactical decisions. Less than a week later, on June 14, he imprudently moved his army across the Alle at Friedland to attack Lannes's corps deployed on the western side of the river. While Lannes kept the Russians busy, Napoleon brought up the rest of the *Grande Armée* and overwhelmed them with a force of 80,000 men. The Russians fought with their backs to the water and were unable to conduct an orderly withdrawal. Some divisions lost 40 percent of their roster. Many soldiers drowned as they attempted to swim to the opposite bank of the Alle. Bennigsen's casualties amounted to around 16,000 men.

Worth mentioning is that when Bennigsen first established the position near Königsberg, Scharnhorst pointed out to him that if he loses the battle, the

During the battle of Heilsberg on June 10, two squadrons of Prittwitz Hussars ride down the French 55th Line Regiment to block its attempt to outflank the right wing of Bennigsen's position. One of the Prussian hussars captures the enemy's eagle standard during the charge.

Russian army will have the sea at its back. The only alternatives, Scharnhorst cautioned, will then be to punch its way through the enemy or to surrender. Bennigsen replied, "I don't need a retreat route. I won't be beaten. If I'm not victorious I want to be destroyed and don't care about the place where this happens!"[85] After Bennigsen was defeated and his army trapped, he asked Napoleon for a cease-fire. The French did not pursue his retreating formations as they had done with surviving Prussian units after Jena. This is because Napoleon hoped to make peace with the czar and thought it impolitic to unnecessarily offend him or his troops. The French victory at Friedland induced Alexander to request an armistice with France.

Bennigsen wrote his sovereign that the defeat at Friedland has not diminished the army's spirit or courage. He considers it his duty to inform the czar of this so that he will not cave in to "Bonaparte's arrogant demands." Bennigsen drafted a plan to continue operations against France. The czar was disappointed in what he regarded as token support from England and opted for a cease-fire instead. The truce was ratified on June 21. Napoleon concluded a separate armistice with Prussia a few days later. Alexander I and Bonaparte met on July 07 on a raft constructed by French engineers and moored in the middle of the Neman River at Tilsit. At the meeting, during which no one else was present, the French ruler expressed his ambition to dissolve Prussia. In the interest of Russian national security, the czar wanted this independent buffer state between his empire and France's *Rheinbund* vassals preserved. He made no secret of his disapproval when Napoleon proposed ceding East Prussia and Silesia from the Hohenzollern kingdom.

Napoleon gave in; he required peace with Russia more than the czar needed it with France. Further, the frightful number of casualties taken by the *Grande Armée* unsettled the French populace. No one at home had expected the troops to suffer such bloodletting only months after the victories over Prussia. Between the time the army had departed the camp at Boulogne and the battle of Friedland in June, France had 35,000 men killed in action and 150,000 wounded. Half in the latter category were medically discharged from active service.[86] Bonaparte was anxious to end hostilities with Russia to plan a heavy blow against rebellious Spain without disruption. He threw his ally Turkey overboard by pledging to aid Alexander in his war against her in exchange for the Franco-Russian treaty. "Only out of consideration for the czar did Napoleon relinquish his firm resolve to destroy Prussia. He reduced her by half instead," wrote Treitschke.[87]

Höpfner maintained, "There is no doubt that Napoleon wished to drive the king from the land of his father. Mobilization of the Prussian army in 1805 would have robbed him of all his earlier victories had it led immediately to war; and this, together with rejection of the peace offer after the battle of Preussisch-Eylau, must have fueled the inextinguishable hatred of a man like Napoleon far more than any gratitude he may have felt for the king's support in earlier times... But since he couldn't destroy Prussia, he could now at least do everything possible to humiliate her."[88] Czar Alexander was also anxious to end hostilities so that he could devote his resources to waging war against Turkey. The result of Napoleon's compact with the czar, Petre observed, was "aggrandizement of the power of Napoleon to an enormous, of Russia to a small extent, at the expense of Prussia."[89]

Bonaparte met Friedrich Wilhelm on the Nemen River on July 09 and dictated peace terms. Prussia forfeited her Polish territory. Bialystok went to the czar and the rest became the Grand Duchy of Warsaw under the administration of Saxony. Prussia's provinces west of the Elbe River were taken from her as well. The Prussian city of Cottbus went to Saxony. Other western territories were incorporated into the new Kingdom of Westphalia totaling 1,100 square miles under Napoleon's brother Jérôme. Prussia shrunk from its prewar size of 124,868 square miles to 61,339. The kingdom now had 4,938,000 inhabitants compared to 9,743,000 before Tilsit.[90] These were the combined populations of Brandenburg, Pomerania, East and West Prussia and Silesia. The country was scarcely larger than she had been in 1740 and was geographically indefensible. Napoleon levied crippling reparations totaling 154 million francs, reduced the following year to 119 million. He fixed this exorbitant amount for an excuse to maintain military occupation for noncompliance. Treitschke called the conditions "the cruelest of all French peace treaties, unheard of in form and content."[91]

Napoleon's settlement was a complete departure from that of an 18th-Century cabinet war. Bonaparte was the antithesis of a king who conquers his enemy's army to obtain a favorable basis for negotiations and annex a strip of land, but then continues to acknowledge the sovereignty of the vanquished state. The emperor's elimination of Prussia as a Great Power was a step toward his goal of transforming Europe into a conglomerate empire under French hegemony or more specifically, under that of his family. Until this realm was established there could be no peace for Napoleon. The treaty concluded with Prussia, in which he reduced her to a diminutive kingdom superficially recognized as a peer in continental affairs, bore no resemblance to the mutual respect of cabinet war politics. For Bonaparte, peace meant the complete and ultimate subordination of Europe to France. Only countries that accept this arrangement could hope to maintain cordial relations with the "heartless despot" and his *Grande Armée*. Napoleonic peace meant the complete destruction of the previous oligarchic order. Gneisenau concluded, "This upstart wants to overthrow every ancient throne that still exists."[92]

After dismembering a state built by over 150 years of prudent leadership, sacrifice and courage, Napoleon boasted in a letter to the sultan of Turkey, "Prussia has disappeared." Even the journalist Gentz, scorned by Bonaparte as a "wretched scribe," lamented, "It would be beyond ridiculous to even think about the resurrection of Prussia."[93] A statesman who unlike the emperor did not allow impressive military victories to cloud his judgment was French foreign minister Talleyrand. He advised Napoleon to moderation when dealing with Friedrich Wilhelm III at Tilsit. Talleyrand possessed enough experience in international affairs to realize that a race as stalwart as the Prussians, when confronted with the alternative of subjugation to rebellion, will in time fight back. The lesson of how France's policy in Spain provoked an uprising was not lost on him. Other French officials shared this view, among them Louis de Bignon. He served as commissioner of finance and domain in occupied Prussia. As for Napoleon himself, the victory at Friedland restored his confidence in his infallibility. He told General Yorck, "I don't fear Prussia. From now on she can no longer hurt me. For this reason, I have no reason to spare her."[94]

Visiting Danzig on June 01, 1807, Bonaparte demonstrated what this attitude portends. After inspecting the battered fortifications, he ordered them repaired at the town's expense. Despite the devastation caused by months of siege, he imposed a "war tax" on the distressed population of 20 million francs. He responded to pleas for mitigation with disparaging observations about the loyalty of the citizens to the Prussian regime. He mocked them for their support of the garrison during the fighting. As soon as Napoleon left Danzig, Lefebvre raised the "contribution" by another 400,000 francs. The French removed the city's famous painting of the last judgment from the *Marienkirche* and shipped it to the Louvre in Paris. On three previous occasions, European monarchs had offered to purchase the painting for extravagant sums but the city had refused to sell.[95] Such was the treatment Prussia suffered under the *Grande Nation.* The philosopher Charles de Villers, exiled from France after the Revolution and witness to the sacking of Lübeck in November 1806, predicted, "The French armies have beaten the German armies because they are stronger. For the same reason, the German spirit will ultimately conquer the French spirit. I believe myself to have already seen signs of this outcome. Providence will take its course."[96]

Chapter 13

Tribute and Tribulation

Asleep on the Laurels

Friedrich Wilhelm III met with Bonaparte at Tilsit without bargaining chips; the army was beaten, most fortresses lost and his ally the czar made peace with France. "Often in this campaign," wrote Goltz, "Napoleon's intense personal hatred toward Prussia, now prostrate before him, had been apparent. His later remarks give the impression that he sensed that even in this stricken state, the country of the great Friedrich will become his bitterest, most dangerous enemy in the future."[1] For the king, little remained but to accept the terms dictated by the "little corporal." Friedrich Wilhelm's servile foreign policy accommodating Napoleon before the war and the army's defeats in 1806 did little to enhance the crown's esteem among the population. At this time, an act of courage and humility by a German woman virtually saved the Prussian monarchy and restored its prestige. This was Queen Luise's meeting with Bonaparte on July 06, just before his sessions with the czar and her husband. After the cease-fire, Napoleon and Friedrich Wilhelm had already met before Tilsit and the king knew what was in store for his country.

The queen of Prussia bore little similarity to the aristocratic ladies of the court who submitted to Napoleon's licentious advances during his stay in Berlin. The incarnation of feminine virtue and dignity, she had urged her husband to take a firm stand against France. She had a better understanding of military matters than he did and encouraged him to have more self-confidence.[2] Luise's patriotism was an inspiration to the soldiers: "She it was who had been the spirit of the war," observed Petre.[3] Rarely adorned in the ornately embroidered, elegant finery worn by royals during the age, the queen often dressed in ungarnished apparel. Borcke offers this recollection: "Among the most memorable experiences from this time was a trip to Pyrmont and Nenndorf that I undertook in the company of some friends. This summer of 1806, during which our unforgettable Queen Luise was also at Pyrmont, was certainly one of the most wonderful seasons the place ever had and the last happy time that this adored woman knew. The presence of the queen had attracted a large number of outsiders, among them many officers of the army... All paid homage to the queen who, free from the constraint of court etiquette, mingled with guests of the resort and the common people in an informal and unpretentious way. Wherever she appeared she won the love, respect and admiration of all."[4]

Sick with typhus, Queen Luise left Königsberg for Memel in January 1807. Waiting with her physician Dr. Hufeland, she sits bundled in a carriage while the escort prepares a walkway for her to enter a ramshackle farmhouse for the night.

During the Saale campaign, Luise had accompanied the Queen's Dragoons in the uniform of an officer. Napoleon mocked her "amazon" attire. She left the war zone right before Jena to return to Berlin. She went from there to Königsberg to join her children and await the king. Typhus broke out, especially among refugees, infected Luise and compelled her to leave the city. "Never will I forget the night of December 22," recalled her physician Christoph Hufeland. "She lay in mortal danger. I watched over her while a storm raged with such fury that it tore away a gable of the old manor house where she rested... On January 05, we transported her 20 miles in a cart in bitter cold amid a terrible storm and snow squalls across the Kurische Nehrung to Memel. We spent three days and three nights travelling. The days were tormented by the sea's rushing waves that we sometimes had to hurry to avoid. The nights we spent in miserable quarters. On the first night the queen lay in a room with a broken window and the snow was blowing onto her bed. There was no food or refreshment. No queen had ever suffered such distress! I was in constant anxiety that an apoplexy will strike her. Yet her spirit did not wane. She maintained her faith in God and touched every one of us."[5]

Once in Memel and having recovered, Luise entertained officers returning from frontline service. Among them was Heinrich von Hellwig, who after Jena had freed 8,000 Prussian soldiers from French captivity with 40 hussars. The king awarded Hellwig the *Pour le Mérite*. The queen hung the decoration around his neck and told him, "Had everyone done his duty as you did, we wouldn't be here!"[6] When she agreed to meet with Napoleon, whom Luise referred to as "the monster," it was to try to persuade him to mollify his peace terms. Hardenberg and the king relied on her natural, unforced charm and keen insight into the relevant issues for the success of her mission. The prospect of conversing with Bonaparte can hardly have intrigued the queen; he had unchivalrously maligned her in his bulletins for months. One he composed in Weimar described Luise as "a woman with a pretty face but not much of a brain." A bulletin he issued from Potsdam implied that she is unfaithful in her marriage.[7]

That this vulgar insinuation would come from a man who was scarcely a model of fidelity is beyond hypocrisy; it rivals the accusation that he, of all people, made that Luise is a "war monger." Just before the meeting she wrote in her diary, "What I have to overcome, what this is costing me, only my God knows! Since even though I don't actually hate the man, I still see him as the one who has brought such misfortune to the king and his country. I marvel at his talent but his character, obviously so deceitful and phony, I cannot love. It will be difficult for me to be polite and nice to him. Once again, the hardest trial is demanded of me, but I'm used to making sacrifices."[8] Before the session, Hardenberg counseled her on how to present Prussia's case. Countess Lisinka Tauentzien described Luise's appearance on the day of the meeting: "The queen wore a white crepe gown with silver embroidery, her pearl necklace and with a pearl diadem in her hair. She was fraught with anxiety, yet despite the emotional atmosphere of the time I can scarcely remember when she looked more beautiful than during these days that were such a burden on her."[9]

Visiting the royal lodgings in Tilsit, Napoleon scaled the narrow staircase to Luise's chamber to begin the dialog. After pleasantries were exchanged, the emperor challenged her with the question, "How could you start a war against me?" Retaining her composure, the queen answered in French that it is the fame of Friedrich the Great that allows the Prussians to overestimate themselves. Napoleon changed the subject, but throughout the conversation Luise tactfully but persistently returned to the matter of her country's fate. She warned Bonaparte that this "intolerable" peace treaty will not endure. He promised to consider her supplication, but told his entourage afterward, "I'm not going to disrupt my plans to please a woman."[10] He offered the queen a rose after hosting her and the king at dinner the following evening and fancied himself the gallant. Libel of Luise published in the French and *Rheinbund* press however, ceased immediately. Only the emperor could have ordered such an abrupt reversal of editorial policy. He said in exile years later, "I had the greatest admiration for her. She was elegant, full of spirit and engaging in the most captivating way."[11]

Though her mission was not successful, the queen restored faith in the royal house. The population marveled at the pluck of the defenseless woman who stood alone, fighting for her country in her own way, against the warlord who had maliciously tried to destroy her reputation. Until her premature death three years later, Luise would influence the king in favor of political and military reform and actively support Stein and Scharnhorst. Despondent over the Tilsit treaty and French occupation, she never fully recovered her emotional poise. A letter to her father reveals an astute grasp of the age, her faith in a supreme justice and how inseparably bound her fate was to that of Prussia: "It's over for us, if not forever at least for now. For myself I have no more hopes for this life. It is becoming ever clearer to me that everything that has happened had to happen. Divine providence has unmistakably introduced to the world a new state of affairs. There will be a new order of things since the old has outlived itself and collapsed on its own. We have fallen asleep on the laurels of Friedrich the Great, who as master of his century created a new age. We have not progressed since then and for this reason the times have passed us by…

"We can learn a lot from our enemy. What he did and what he caused is not lost on us. It would be blasphemous to say that God is with him; but he is no doubt a tool in the hand of the Almighty; an instrument to bury what has become lifeless but remains outwardly fixed. I believe firmly in God, therefore in a moral order of things in the world. I do not see this as the rule of force. Because of this I believe that a better age will follow these times… It may be good for our children that they learn about the serious side of life while still young. If they were to grow up in affluence and comfort, they would think that it will always be so. That things may turn out differently, they will now realize in the serious countenance of their father and in the sadness and tears of their mother."[12] Napoleon privately described Luise as "the only man in Prussia" and later confessed that she was "mistress of the conversation" by preventing him from diverting their discussion from matters of state. On Luise's birthday in 1813, the king instituted the Iron Cross medal in two classes to be awarded for valor in wartime; Germany's first combat decoration that all ranks were eligible for. It is fitting that its introduction commemorates the birth of a woman who disapproved of social barriers in Prussia, the "queen of another era" as Talleyrand described her.

As she left Tilsit in her carriage, Luise leaned her head against the cushion and wept over what was in store for the country. The military defeats, excesses of the *Grande Armée* on Prussian soil and humiliating treaty were but a prelude to the period of abject subjugation to follow. One of the most detrimental influences was the Continental System. On November 21, 1806, Napoleon issued the Berlin Decree: All exchange of wares and mail, and indeed connection between Europe and England were outlawed. French customs agents confiscated goods of English manufacture and English property in mainland ports. Merchant vessels caught running the blockade were seized. Europe relied on overseas trade for economic stability. Curtailing trade with the British maritime empire had a ruinous impact on commerce. Every country allied to or dependent on Napoleon was affected. The emperor was either oblivious to the extent of suffering caused by the embargo or smugly unconcerned. He ignored the counsel of his ministers toward moderation. Persuaded of his infallibility, he contemplated even more grandiose enterprises, among them an expedition against the British in India.[13]

The Continental System contributed to Prussia's woes. Abandoned by the czar, who exchanged the alliance with his friend Friedrich Wilhelm for the table scraps Napoleon tossed him, the Prussian monarch could not even return to Berlin. He resided with the royal family on the periphery of his truncated kingdom. "The people's anger over French administration rose slowly at first," one account maintained. "Only when prices for sugar, coffee, tobacco and spices climbed drastically and there seemed no end to the stifling taxation to meet reparation payments did it become clear to the common man what Napoleonic rule means. By then every housewife had become hostile to the foreign oppressor."[14] In addition to the over 100 million francs demanded by France in war reparations, the Prussians were required to pay an additional 216 million to finance the military occupation of their country. This together with the embargo brought the state close to bankruptcy. Many people lost everything they owned and stood practically on the brink of oblivion.

Napoleon appointed the former chief commissary of the *Grande Armée*, Pierre Daru, to manage the French administration. "Bloodsucker" Daru had helped craft the Tilsit treaty and ruthlessly exploited Prussia during his tenure in office. By the close of 1807, the loss to the country in currency, foodstuffs and material resources exceeded a billion francs.[15] French soldiers drove villagers from their homes and demolished the cottages to provide straw and wood for constructing barracks.[16] The French garrison east of the Elbe River, with the exception of East Prussia, tallied 160,000 men. Only by drastically reducing spending in public administration, auctioning some royal palaces and monarchial possessions and relinquishing more fortresses to the French did the country manage to pay Napoleon so that his troops will leave. The evacuation agreement was signed in Paris on September 08, 1808.

The people of Prussia endured frightful privations during the period of "liberation" from absolutism by the grace of France. Conditions scarcely differed from the misery of the Thirty Years' War. In East Prussia, only 3.5 percent of the cattle were still alive in 1807. There was therefore no milk for the children, little meat and few plow animals for cultivating the fields. Out of 5,845 babies born in Berlin, 4,500 died in infancy. Parents refused small pox vaccinations for their children with the explanation that it will be better for them if they perish.[17] To meet the financial burden of maintaining its French garrison, the city of Königsberg introduced a progressive tax for all citizens that increased to 20 percent of their income. According to a Breslau newspaper report of June 21, 1808, "Silesian authorities travel from village to village instructing residents as to what wild plants are edible to consume as food when nothing else is available."[18] As though in mockery of their suffering, the people of the plundered country had to prepare banquets for the officers of French garrisons.

Treitschke summarized, "Countless assets were destroyed. The entire wealth of the Prussian aristocracy was gone as well. The arbitrary territorial revisions wrecked the customary traffic in trade of entire regions. Thousands of faithful civil servants lost their jobs in the mutilated state… Bitterness grew and grew. The longer that any decisive action was postponed, the mightier and more passionate was the belief that the day-to-day existence under foreign domination cannot and must not continue; that this ruin of everything in German life transgresses against God and history and is the fantasy of a deranged criminal mind."[19] The Prussian dramatist Heinrich von Kleist wrote, "By and by, it came to a point that when the church bell rang to herald a death, no one asked who it was for anymore. The misfortune of the last hour had become a routine occurence."[20]

German states allied with Napoleon also fared badly. When the Saxon army surrendered after Jena, the emperor ordered Bernadotte to confiscate Saxon horses for his dragoons that lack mounts. The mortified soldiers also had to turn over their weapons. A Frenchman wrote, "The impression that these measures made on the cavalry regiments was frightful. It was unavoidable that great disorder and the most serious excesses occurred during the transfer. General von Zezschwitz's order to gather the firearms and lead the dismounted personnel away proved superfluous, since the men smashed their weapons along the roadside."[21] Many soldiers gave their horses to local farmers instead of handing them over to the enemy. French troops occupied Saxony as though in an enemy country. Napoleon levied a war tax of 25,425,000 francs on Dresden. French officials confiscated English wares in Leipzig, the city renowned for international trade fairs. Petre summarized, "Saxony became… the vassal of Napoleon, sacrificing, for the furtherance of his insatiable ambition, her wealth, her prosperity, and the flower of her population, without any return beyond the empty distinction of being raised to the dignity of a kingdom."[22]

When in November 1806 French and *Rheinbund* troops drove Blücher's corps from Lübeck, which was in Hanover, the invaders plundered vast stores of wine in the cellars and unleashed a drunken rampage that included raping female patients of the lunatic asylum.[23] Among the witnesses to the spree was a seven-year-old boy who was at home when the French looted his parents' townhouse. It was Helmuth von Moltke, who would later become a Prussian field marshal and chief of the general staff. Just south of Hanover was Jérôme's new kingdom of Westphalia. The state adopted two official languages, French and German, with the former having priority in civil administration. Napoleon announced that Westphalia will become a paragon of democratic government, abolishing serfdom and ancestral privileges of the nobility, introducing France's codified justice system including public trial by jury, equal rights before the law and religious tolerance. He wrote to Jérôme, "What nation would want to return to arbitrary Prussian rule after it has enjoyed the benefits of a wise and liberal administration? The peoples of Germany, France, Italy and Spain demand civil equality and liberal ideas."[24]

The reality did not correspond to such idealistic rhetoric. Hessen-Kassel for example, was to be incorporated into Jérôme's Westphalian kingdom. Hessen-Kassel's small army had fought on the side of Prussia in 1806 and mutinied against the French. Many among the rural population joined the revolt, which the emperor's troops suppressed in two weeks. Napoleon ordered all villages in the area where the insurrection took place burned down. He instructed his field commanders there "to shoot a large number of individuals" as well.[25] The emperor's imperialistic ambitions were incompatible with granting freedom to his subjects. The tyrannical pettiness of his military governors was so unbridled that in Berlin, French commandant Hulin arrested the theater director August Iffland for staging a celebration in honor of Queen Luise. The French destroyed all the foundries in Berlin to render the capital incapable of manufacturing firearms.

The population of Westphalia was subordinate to the dictates of French foreign policy. Tax collectors levied a heavy burden on the country to help finance military adventures. Recruitment officers inducted more soldiers per capita from Westphalia than from anywhere else in Europe. Most of these men would subsequently perish serving in the *Grande Armée* in Russia in 1812. Avaricious local politicians took ownership of properties confiscated by the state from private citizens. No dissent was tolerated. Freedom of expression gave way to censorship of the press. From throughout the *Rheinbund*, Spain and Italy, financial "contributions" to the war effort flowed into France. By 1812, Westphalia became insolvent. In 1811 Napoleon told members of the French chamber of commerce, "Since the Peace of Tilsit I have collected over a billion francs in reparations. Austria is bankrupt and England and Russia will soon follow. I alone have money! I raise 900 million in taxes annually. I lay 300 million aside and store it in the cellar of the Tuileries Palace. The bank of France is full of silver, the Bank of England has none!"[26]

Germans residing on the western side of the Rhine "saw the true face of French policy," one study maintained. "They have been duped by the illusion that slogans about 'freedom' and 'equality' promote the perfection and harmonization of all humanity. They see instead with indignation that they have become victims of an extremely nationalistic agenda... Despite the cosmopolitan catch phrases, the French are pursuing the policies of Louis XIV."[27] The Prussian reformer Stein observed, "Throughout Germany a deep feeling of dissatisfaction held sway over the unsavory oppression of the nation by a marauding, unjust conqueror. The hope to break his demeaning chains is universal."[28] Princes of *Rheinbund* states did not share this attitude, since Napoleon protected their elite status in exchange for fealty. The despots governing Germany's minor kingdoms, dutchies and principalities rejoiced over the degradation of Prussia. As Treitschke related, "Their officers liked to brag about how valiantly they themselves have helped

German families forced to quarter French soldiers endured theft, intimidation and often brutality at the hands of the conquerors. The conduct of his army unmasked Napoleon's swindle about supposedly liberating the peoples of Europe from despotism.

topple the northern Germans' arrogance and couldn't say enough about Prussian stupidity. According to the official press in Munich and Stuttgart, the clash at Jena is the only memorable battle in Prussian history."[29]

A popular caricature reproduced from a London newspaper made its rounds in *Rheinbund* courts. It depicts a diminutive "Bony" (England's nickname for Bonaparte) at Tilsit embracing the czar with such vehemence as to shake the barge moored on the Nemen, in turn causing Friedrich Wilhelm to lose his balance and tumble into the river. Common people, whether in Prussia or in *Rheinbund* lands, began to regard Prussia as the only state capable of rallying Germany to defy Napoleon. Stein told the czarina that the German people are loyal and virtuous and only the wretchedness of their princes is to blame for the country's demise.[30] Inside Prussia, hostility to the French gradually united all strata of the population. Goltz wrote, "Only in widespread misfortune did the people of Prussia come together again, love their fatherland, hate the enemy and join the common cause without regard for personal welfare. Genuine camaraderie returned to the officer corps as well."[31] The seeds of resistance took root; one night, farmers stole a cannon from the wall of the Westphalian fortress of

Magdeburg and smuggled it to the Prussian garrison at Spandau. Locals spied on French military movements and reported them to Prussian officers. Critical thinkers asked themselves, "Why are the Germans as individuals so accomplished, but as a nation nothing?"[32]

Seeds of the Downfall

Historians who lived at the twilight of the Roman Empire fix its decline as starting right after the victory in the Third Punic War over Carthage. Built on the Mediterranean coast in what is now Tunisia, Carthage was a seafaring commercial rival of Rome. She fought three successive wars against the Romans and ultimately succumbed in 146 B.C. Having eliminated the only serious trade competitor, Rome gradually augmented her economic and military influence to become the dominate power on the continent. It therefore seems incongruous to fix the beginning of the end of Roman greatness to the time of a successful campaign that took place over a century before the city-state became an empire and 500 years before this empire bowed from the stage of world affairs.

Rome, the ancient historians argued, lost too much of her robust agrarian manhood in the Punic Wars to regenerate such valuable human resources. The state relied more and more on foreign volunteers and conscripts to fill the legions. The army ceased being a microcosm of Roman society fused together by common ancestry. With the fall of Carthage there was no longer a significant external threat to unify the Romans in a spirit of self-sacrifice and stand as one to ensure the welfare of all. Material wealth, patronage and social status supplanted the martial virtues of honor, courage and obedience in the Patrician caste. Rome continued to conquer and administer other peoples and produce great generals, but the substance was gone. Society fragmented and the qualities that originally made the Romans capable of their legendary achievements gradually eroded.

Napoleonic France was another empire crumbling from within. As she waged one war after another, the flower of French manhood fell on the battlefields of Italy, Spain, Poland and Germany. The replacements consisted of young French draftees or soldiers whose countries had been conquered by France. The ideals of the Revolution vanished; the cries of "liberty, equality and fraternity" on the lips of men fighting to transform the world in the first coalition wars were replaced by *vive le empereur!* and homage to a warlord whose personal ambition would ultimately cost over two million Europeans their lives. Napoleon's troops continuously displayed extraordinary valor in combat. At the same time however, allegiance shifted from France and her people to a single individual. Indeed, the army was bound to a man whose military fortunes were at high tide; yet his adversaries were nations that had lost their independence and were being forced into a "fight or die" situation. Germans and Spaniards are spirited peoples and were unwilling in the long run to accept such a fate. They were motivated by a desire for freedom morally superior to anything Bonaparte could offer his legions.

Telltale signs of disarray in the French army were already apparent during the 1806/1807 campaign. Discipline became markedly looser. Looting, arson and desertion were commonplace; soldiers filled their knapsacks with stolen goods instead of with military necessities or personal belongings. This at one point caused Marshal Soult to order the troops' packs and supply wagons searched every four days.[33] Marauders left camp to raid villages and rob the inhabitants. Officers who intervened were threatened. Napoleon did not pay the troops on a regular basis because, he explained, he prefers they spend their wages in France instead of abroad. "The war will nourish the warrior," but having the men exist on the resources of conquered territories is in itself an invitation to pillage. In 1807, the situation was serious enough for the emperor to consider withdrawing across the western bank of the Vistula. After the supply situation improved in April, he ordered the army to resume training to shore up discipline and keep the men occupied.

Direction of the French army was on shaky ground. Napoleon defined unity of command as "the first necessity in war" and had the advantage of being supreme head of state as well as leader of the army. He was not answerable to government ministers for his decisions. He once remarked, "I made this campaign without consulting anyone."[34] In the long run, the absolute authority he exercised proved disadvantageous. In 18th-Century armies, the quartermaster general and his subordinates were responsible for arranging supply deliveries, determining the best route for troop movements, reconnoitering terrain, where to site encampments and conveying orders to regimental and battalion commanders. During the Napoleonic era, quartermaster staffs gradually became involved in planning offensives, individual attacks and strategic withdrawals. This was necessary because armies had become too large for one man to manage, plus they were organized into divisions combining infantry, cavalry, artillery, engineer companies and support personnel. Theaters of operations expanded. This required more attention to logistics.

"A general staff," as defined by historian Trevor Dupuy, "is a highly trained, carefully selected group of military generalists whose function in peace or war is to assist the nation's military leadership—or a general commanding a field force of combined arms elements—in planning, controlling, directing, coordinating, and supervising the activities of all military subordinate elements in the most effective possible, mutually supporting efforts."[35] The function of Napoleon's general staff, by contrast, was limited to simply carrying out his orders. His obsession with personal control pervaded practically every element of his military and civil leadership.[36] Colonel Jean-Baptiste Vachée recalled, "The staff in no way participated in the emperor's intellectual work; it was never taken into his confidence; it had but to obey scrupulously... The emperor himself said that the general staff is the least necessary part of the grand headquarters." Napoleon told his chief of staff Berthier, "Keep strictly to the orders I give you; I alone know what I must do." Berthier himself wrote, "I am nothing in the army. I receive in the emperor's name the reports of the marshals, and I sign these orders for him, but I am personally null."[37]

Napoleon's aide-de-camp, Marquis Armand-Augustin de Caulaincourt, who was an officer of the *Grande Orient* lodge of France, later stated, "The staff foresaw nothing, but on the other hand, as the emperor wanted to do everything himself, and give every order, no one, not even the general staff, dared to assume the responsibility of giving the most trifling order."[38] Caulaincourt recalled on another occasion, "The emperor needed lots of sleep, but he could sleep when he wanted to, during the day or at night. The emperor always rose at eleven o'clock at night, sometimes at midnight. This was because that was when the first reports from the corps came in. He worked for two or three hours, though often longer, to compare the reports, check the troop movements on the map and issue his orders. He dictated all of them to the chief of the general staff or to a clerk and the Prince of Neufchâteau then transcribed them. Sometimes he wrote personally to the leader of an army corps if it was an important matter, to call his attention to something in particular…

"Napoleon was concerned with the most minute details. He wanted everything subject to the force of his genius. He had me come every day to give orders for the headquarters, the ordnance officer, the officers of his staff, or regarding correspondence, couriers, the mail and so on. The officers of the guard, the army commanders, the medical doctor, the commendable Larrey, were given orders at least once a day. Nothing escaped (Napoleon's) attention, no detail appeared to him unworthy of notice."[39] Denigrating the staff to purely an instrument of his mental prowess, Bonaparte demanded blind obedience from field commanders. At the battle of Pultusk for example, Lannes could clearly discern the insurmountable difficulties attendant on assailing the strong Russian position that Napoleon, based on faulty intelligence, had ordered his corps to attack. He expected no reinforcements in the bid to seize the Narew bridge. But French marshals were too accustomed to precisely carry out orders for Lannes to do otherwise. Ney shrugged, "I'm like a loaded rifle. The emperor gives the order and the shot is fired."[40]

In the Englishman Fuller's opinion, "Napoleon's marshals had not been brought up to command, solely to obey, they were followers and not leaders, vassal princes, many of whom had been raised in rank for dynastic, political and personal reasons."[41] The emperor's practice of discouraging independent initiative on the part of yes-men he promoted would eventually have fatal consequences for the *Grande Armée*, especially during the battles of Leipzig and Waterloo. Huge armies covering expansive combat zones cannot be properly directed by a single individual, even one of Napoleon's superior abilities. The disdain he demonstrated for talent in subordinates and their secondary role extended to *publicity* about French feats of arms as well. Commanders received approbation for success in battle, but only in the context that they carried out the emperor's orders bravely and efficiently. The *Bulletin de l'armée* and newspaper articles attributed victories to Bonaparte alone, as for example the short shrift accorded Davout in the press for his outstanding personal leadership at Auerstedt. This awkward association between Napoleon and his senior commanders had an underlying negative influence on the war effort.

The official version of the battle of Marengo on June 14, 1800, is a typical example of Napoleon failing to fairly acknowledge the contribution of a general. After taking part in a coup in November 1799 and becoming first consul of France, Bonaparte led his poorly equipped troops over the Alpine pass of Grand Saint Bernard in May 1800 into Italy to cut off an Austrian army under Michael von Mélas. Napoleon transferred large formations from his main force to block the Austrians' possible routes of withdrawal. He sent General Louis Desaix north with 6,000 men and Jean Cornu de la Poype with 3,500 to the south. Mélas did not retreat however, but launched a surprise attack against the French center. By the time Bonaparte realized what is happening and reached the battlefield his divisions were giving ground, though in order. He sent the Consular Guard infantry and artillery forward to stabilize the line but the units were annihilated by an Austrian cavalry charge. Desaix saved the day by disobeying orders; he turned his division around and marched back to Marengo on his own. Kellermann attacked the Austrian flank with his cavalry and helped turn the tide. Before these counterattacks France's first consul had given the battle up for lost.

The army bulletin of June 15 on Marengo drafted by Napoleon was "a tissue of lies and half-thruths."[42] He claimed that the French center had fallen back to draw the Austrians into a trap. As part of this tactical maneuver, Desaix supposedly about faced his division and returned to the main army on Bonaparte's orders. This was not the case.[43] Since he was killed in action, Desaix could not contradict the fabrication. Napoleon lauded the Consular Guard, which was under his personal command during the battle, for allegedly smashing the Austrian line instead of crediting the success to Kellermann's decisive intervention. Murat in fact wrote Berthier, "I especially have to tell you about Kellermann; through a powerful charge he managed to tilt the balance in our favor."[44] Parisians therefore read of Napoleon's alleged tactical genius at Marengo, when in fact he was outwitted by Mélas. The first consul would have lost the engagement but for the independent judgment, skill and elan of Generals Jean Boudet, Jean-Charles Monnier, Kellermann and Desaix. None of them received the recognition they deserve. Their names were scarcely mentioned, if at all, in the newspapers.[45] The French initially calculated having suffered 7,000 casualties, but Napoleon reduced the number for publication to 700.[46]

Bonaparte also arranged for the press to marginalize Moreau's victory in December over a numerically superior Austrian army at Hohenlinden. The battle ended the War of the Second Coalition and gave France control of Italy and the Netherlands. The seeds of resentment were sown, leading to a precarious situation for Napoleon. The generals, wrote one historian, "were greatly angered over the subjective battlefield accounts and victory reports of their supreme commander. He smugly claimed all laurels for himself regarding operations in the Italian theater of war and attributed the success to his outstanding genius as a warlord. He knew how to bribe Paris newspapers to magnify even the smallest engagements into huge, staggering battles… It evolved into a genuine conspiracy of the mortified Marengo generals against their overbearing commander in chief."[47] The ringleader of the conspiracy, which included among others Augereau, Bernadotte, Claude Lecourbe, Masséna, Moreau and Monnier, was Napoleon's boyhood friend Joséphe Arena. Arrested for high treason, Arena was guillotined on January 20, 1802 following a trial that was a judicial farce. "I am now free of a dangerous enemy," Bonaparte said. "Since the Italian army I've feared nothing so much as the audacity of this Arena."[48]

The execution discouraged some generals from further intrigue, but not Moreau, Lecourbe and Monnier. They joined forces with the royalist Georges Cadoudal in Brittany and General Charles Pichégru, both of whom hoped to restore the Bourbon Dynasty. Not all conspirators were monarchists; many republicans opposed the first consul for concessions he made to reactionary opponents of the Revolution. "From April to June 1802, no fewer than four military conspiracies were uncovered aimed either at assassinating the first consul or at overthrowing him," wrote Napoleon's biographer Roger Dufraisse. "Intrigues, plots and attempted assassinations would accompany Bonaparte throughout the years of power. Rarely has a chief of state exercised his functions in such dangerous conditions."[49] Jacobins resented the new ruler for undoing the work of the Revolution. For example, the National Convention had abolished slavery in French colonies in 1794 but Napoleon restored it in 1802. This led to a revolt in Santo Domingo.

The first consul muzzled the French press. On January 17, 1800, the police banned 60 out of 73 newspapers in Paris and forbade new publications. That December, Napoleon escaped injury when an assassin's bomb exploded as his carriage passed the rue Saint-Nicaise, claiming 26 lives. Even though royalists were known to be responsible, Bonaparte blamed the Jacobins in order to rid himself of individuals whose revolution he had betrayed. Some were guillotined and 130 more exiled from France.[50] General Moreau was jailed for treason in February 1804. Napoleon demanded the death penalty. The court considered such a sentence "lynch justice" and condemned Moreau to exile instead. He subsequently migrated to the United States. When Napoleon was crowned emperor in 1804, there were still Frenchmen plotting to oust him. They included a well-organized group under Colonel Jacques Oudet. Royalists and republicans naturally did not work well together, but Bonaparte nevertheless had many enemies in the officer corps. When the pastor's son Friedrich Staps was apprehended trying to assassinate him in Vienna in October 1809, Napoleon asked him if he is "an Illuminato," indicating his suspicion that secret societies are involved.[51]

There were too many officers dissatisfied with him—estimates run in the thousands—for the despot to eliminate them, so he resorted to bribery. Those with principles who could not be bought he assigned dangerous missions in combat. Before the battle of Aspern in 1809, the minister of police Joseph Fouché wrote Oudet, "If you have just twelve determined men, strangle Napoleon in his bed, throw him into the Danube in a sack and then everything will be fine!"[52] On the night after the battle of Wagram in July 1809, the emperor had 22 army officers suspected of plotting against him secretly shot and listed as killed in action.[53] He did this over the objection of General Savary. Oudet himself was eventually tried and spent several years under fortress arrest. The emperor expelled General Claude de Mallet, a passionate disciple of France's republican ideals, from the army in 1807 and temporarily imprisoned him in a fortress in Mantua. He staged an unsuccessful coup in Paris against Bonaparte in October 1812 when the *Grande Armée* was in Russia.

The "lawgiver of nations" had his hands full abroad as well. In October 1807, a French army of 24,000 invaded Portugal. This was because the Portuguese opened their ports to English merchant shipping in defiance of the continental blockade. The emperor sent Murat into Spain with over 60,000 men the following March. They occupied Madrid on the 24th. Spain was ostensibly France's ally, but it soon became obvious that Napoleon wants control of the country's merchant fleet and overseas possessions.[54] In April 1808 he left Paris for Bayonne. He forced the weak Spanish king Charles IV to abdicate in favor of his son Ferdinand, who became Ferdinand VII. An uprising against the French garrison in Madrid took place on May 02. Murat's troops defeated the insurgents in street fighting. After the French regained control of the city, Murat ordered anyone found with a weapon arrested and shot. People with tools of their trade such as scissors, knives and even sewing needles were executed. The French killed hundreds in this bloody reprisal. It incited the population to greater resistance. Province after province repudiated Ferdinand as king and declared war on the oppressor. Local authorities who opposed the uprising were murdered. Joined by the meagre remnants of their army, Spanish farmers and townspeople drove Napoleon's garrison across Ebro.

A French army was beaten at Valencia on June 28 followed by another at Saragossa on July 02. Later in July 17,000 French soldiers surrendered at Bailén. Ferdinand abandoned Madrid with Napoleon's permission. The emperor personally intervened in November. He defeated the Spanish and placed his brother Joseph Bonaparte on the throne in August. As a foreigner and no friend of the Vatican, he was unpopular in Spain. Partisan warfare continued. England sent two military expeditions to support the insurrection. Fighting on the Iberian Peninsula tied down as many as 300,000 French troops over the next six years. Grolman, who had left Prussia to serve in the Spanish forces, wrote Gneisenau in June 1810, "It's remarkable how in 1807 and 1808 all of Spain had been enthusiastic for Napoleon and that Murat and his army were welcomed everywhere as friends and saviors. In contrast, the scenes in Bayonne and on May 02 in Madrid have with one blow exercised such a bad effect on the nation that from this moment on, the bitterest hatred has resulted... Napoleon is unable to comprehend the greatness of the national character here, since it is so foreign in nature to his own base soul."[55]

Napoleon censored coverage of the Spanish rebellion. Neither French nor German newspapers reported it. He could not control information brought to the continent by English smugglers however, and this lanced the press blackout. His order recalling the corps of Ney, Mortier and Claude Victor stationed in eastern Germany confirmed the veracity of what the English said about the uprising in Spain. The rebellion and especially the unprecedented Spanish victory over a French corps of 24,000 men at Bailén encouraged Austria to contemplate another war against France. A wave of nationalism swept the country. The people were concerned that following the example in Spain, Napoleon will depose the Hapsburg monarch and replace him with a member of the Bonaparte family. France had exploited the war against Portugal as a pretext to march her army into Spanish territory and there were apprehensions among Austrians that Napoleon will use their country as a springboard to launch an expedition against Turkey.

War broke out anew between France and Austria in April 1809. The Austrian army was better organized and more modern than the force it had fielded in 1805 and numbered 200,000 men. Napoleon's army suffered a defeat at Aspern just east of Vienna in May. A cannonball killed Saint-Hilaire and another severed Lannes's leg. He died a few days later. Duke Friedrich Wilhelm of Brunswick, son of the bumbling field marshal who had commanded the Prussian army at Auerstedt, took up arms against France when Austria went to war. His lands had been absorbed into the newly created Kingdom of Westphalia where Jérôme Bonaparte sat on the throne. The duke wanted not only to recover his duchy, but to see the French driven from Germany. With financial support from Austria, he raised a volunteer corps of infantry and cavalry initially tallying 2,300 men who fought as partisans. Known for the color of their uniform as the Black Brunswickers, his troops inspired dread among the French for the ruthless guerrilla war they waged.

In Tyrol, the innkeeper Andreas Hofer revolted against oppressive Bavarian rule imposed by France. Fighting broke out in Innsbruck in April 1809 and continued on and off against French and Bavarian troops for months. When Bonaparte defeated the Austrians at Wagram in July, the treaty of Schönbrunn signed by the Hapsburg emperor restored Tyrol to Bavarian sovereignty. Hofer went into hiding but was betrayed to the enemy by one of his countrymen for a reward. The French viceroy of Italy, Eugène de Beauharnais, wanted to pardon the popular freedom fighter. The court-martial board debated his fate but received Napoleon's order, "Give him a fair trial and then shoot him."[56] Bonaparte's imperialism also alienated Italy. Her people had initially welcomed the French, hoping for a better life than under Papal rule. Their expectations proved illusory; during the campaign of 1800, Napoleon confiscated an immense quantity of Italian silver and gold and shipped it to France.[57] Dufraisse described how

Tirolean freedom fighters clash with French and Bavarian troops in the Oberau region during Andreas Hofer's revolt. Hofer was captured in January 1810 and shot by a firing squad on Napoleon's secret order. Bonaparte told Metternich that the execution was carried out against his wishes.

Napoleon "aimed at skimming monies from (Italian states') treasuries and financial establishments. The Mont-de-Piété bank in Milan had to pay annual fees of 1,200,000 francs to a list of soldiers of all grades chosen by Napoleon. These states also had to furnish troops, warships, and even workers." Bonaparte was inclined "to consider the states of Europe as so many colonies of the French Empire."[58]

French fortunes were on the decline, as summarized by the Scharnhorst biographer Lehmann: "In 1798 everyone thought that England would be beaten. Now the English army is on the mainland and actually a threat to that of France. In 1794 and 1796 a handful of (French) troops conquered the Spanish and Portuguese armies. In 1808 the universal opinion was that Spain will be subjugated, that it is madness to resist the might of Napoleon. And yet in three years, France has accomplished nothing against Spain. Austria has waged war against France for 18 years and is still intact. Russia only mustered an auxiliary corps in 1805 and 1806. She waged war in 1807 purely to protect herself and wasn't even prepared. Now she is fully prepared. Everywhere France is held in check by the superior might of England; everywhere Napoleon has aroused feelings of hatred against himself. He even has to muster troops against bands of his own subjects who perpetually meander across France. English, Portuguese and Spanish armies are pressuring him in the south. He has never been in a situation like this."[59]

Secret societies across Europe conspired against France. They supported Hofer's insurrection in Tyrol. In Italy, the Society of Radiance in Bologna and Milan advocated cooperation among all lodges intriguing against the French. Madame Anne Louise la Baronne de Staël, who had been exiled by Bonaparte from France, helped arrange an understanding between Bernadotte and Czar Alexander. This would lead to the marshal leaving French service and joining the coalition in 1813. Napoleon's foreign policy made peace impossible. Abandoning the tenets of the Revolution, replacing France's deposed monarchy with that of his family, his insufferable vanity and the police state he forced on Europe generated increasing hostility. The continental embargo of English wares obstructed international commerce. Superficially at the zenith of power after the victory at Wagram, Napoleon's star was fading. Parts of his empire were in revolt. In only a few years the emperor's hair was thinner, his face and body more corpulent. Military victories had made him overconfident. He could not have imagined after defeating the Austrians in 1809 that his army has fought its last successful campaign.

Chapter 14

Rearmament

The Military Reorganization Commission

After returning from service in Canada during the American Revolution, Gneisenau applied for a commission in the Prussian army. Friedrich the Great, near the end of his life, granted the young lieutenant an audience to determine his qualifications. Throughout the interview the penetrating gaze of the sovereign remained fixed on his guest, revealing an alertness beyond what might be expected of one so infirm. "Old Fritz" opined that "discipline is what holds the army together." Gneisenau parried that an officer's primary duty is to cultivate patriotism in the men, so that they will "know of nothing loftier than honor and the flag," and devotion to their country "creates an army from among the people that cannot be overcome."[1] The king allayed such aspirations with the admonishment, "Don't forget running the gauntlet, lieutenant!" The *Spiessrutenlaufen* (lash run), also called the *Gassenlaufen* (lane run), was army punishment for mutiny, desertion or theft. An officer conducted the offender between two rows of rankers who struck his backside with knotted ropes or leather straps as he passes. To this Gneisenau replied, "On the contrary your majesty, the Prussian soldier would rather follow the call of honor than that of fear." Friedrich answered wearily, "You don't know the race."

Five days before his death, Friedrich commissioned the applicant as a first lieutenant. Although meeting with the king had a positive outcome, Gneisenau would find himself fighting against the *legacy* of the revered monarch in the years to come. After Prussia's conquest by Napoleon, Gneisenau came to believe that only a national army consisting of nobleman, burgher and peasant fighting side by side can liberate the country. This contradicted the perception of senior military commanders he had to persuade. When they were young officers, they had served under the great Friedrich. He had opposed marriage between the aristocracy and "common people or burghers" and so mistrusted his own population that he banned private ownership of firearms for farmers, villagers and most townspeople in March 1786.[2] Only citizens performing municipal guard duty were entitled to bear arms. The old generals wished to preserve the army as an exclusive caste beyond the reach of political reform. Together with his friend Scharnhorst, Gneisenau, like men of vision throughout history, fought a battle against ingrained prejudices on the home front that ran parallel to the struggle against foreign oppression.

By 1807, the standing army was all but destroyed; of 60 infantry regiments of the line that existed in 1806, some with a 200-year tradition, 51 had capitulated and disbanded after the defeat.[3] Without allies, Prussia stood alone against a hostile power that dwarfed her in size. It was clear to any perceptive soldier that the uneven struggle can only be resumed by harnessing the resources of the entire country. Right after Tilsit, Blücher told Scharnhorst to "create a national army. No one should be exempt and it must become a disgrace for anyone who doesn't serve."[4] This meant incorporating burghers into armed service; what reformers called the "alliance between state and nation." The government could not simply merge burghers into the existing military establishment and expand its radius of operation. For the experiment to succeed, the administration had to revamp the army's structure. Public participation depended on the state bringing the spirit and purpose of the war into harmony with the political will of the burghers, to in this way lay the groundwork to make citizens enthusiastic to fight.

Members of the middle class were not excited about military service. They did however, acknowledge the need to transform the army from an instrument of royal despotism filled with rowdies, unskilled labor and misfits into a national fighting force with a progressive attitude toward the relationship between the government and the people. The Immediate Organization Commission had failed to mobilize the human resources of the country prior to the war of 1806 thanks to opposition from the *Stände*, the military hierarchy and the monarchy. The king promoted Scharnhorst to major general on July 17, 1807. Eight days later, Friedrich Wilhelm established the Military Reorganization Commission to revitalize the army. He appointed Scharnhorst chairman. The committee included Gneisenau and Grolman among others. "All reforms were guided by the principle that from now on the army must become a nation under arms; a national army that every man capable of service belongs to," wrote Treitschke.[5]

One prerequisite for making the military acceptable to the middle class was to restore the army's reputation. There were articles galore by German journalists disparaging Prussia's dismal military performance in 1806 and analyzing mistakes. Some expressed the hope that Hulin, the French governor of Berlin, will remain indefinitely. On October 14 a Berlin newspaper, the *Telegraph*, celebrated the anniversary of Napoleon's victory at Jena and declared that all Europe should rejoice in Prussia's humiliation.[6] Scharnhorst wrote Clausewitz, "The base criticism by our journalists demonstrates in the most acute way our egoism, our vanity and the lowly sentiments and perceptions that govern us. I'll never engage in rebuttals or associate with this rabble of the educated class."[7]

He made an exception with his article published in *Minerva* in 1808. It called attention to the sacrifices made during the Saale campaign. Prince Louis Ferdinand had been killed in action and Princes Wilhelm, Heinrich and August wounded. The king's horse had been shot from under him at Auerstedt as he prepared to lead a cavalry regiment forward: "Enemy princes had the advantage of wartime experience over the Prussian, but certainly not of valor, unless death and wounds are no longer proof of being involved in continuous close combat."[8] Brunswick, Hohenlohe and Rüchel had been wounded together with a number of generals, some fatally. The *Minerva* article praised the fighting spirit of the rankers as well; at Danzig for example, a third of the garrison troops were killed or wounded.

Regiments in action at Jena and Auerstedt lost nearly half their officers. During the defense of Kolberg 52 were casualties, most of them in outer fortifications. Scharnhorst concluded, "No one can accuse the Prussian army of a lack of willingness to make sacrifices. It may have made all sorts of mistakes against an enemy who has gained experience and instruction from 14 years of war. Our contemporaries should always offer their reproachful criticism in a spirit of hope that the bloodshed will in the future be reconciled by coming generations."[9] Having set the record straight regarding the army's sense of duty, the next step was "to make the soldier's craft acceptable to the nation and purge it of what makes the craft offensive," as Scharnhorst wrote Stein in July 1808: "Every decree must conform to this overall purpose and revive the martial spirit."[10] Bearing arms was to become "the most honorable of all occupations," Gneisenau proclaimed. Only by giving the common soldier honor could burghers with their political ambition, ethics and sense of self-worth be incorporated into the army.

Shouldering a rifle was to become as prestigious as wearing an officer's sword. Pride of regiment with its esprit de corps no longer mattered, but personal honor based on the privilege of serving one's country. Scharnhorst's maxim, "Every resident of the state is born to defend it," supplanted the previous perception that honor belongs to the officer corps alone.[11] Henceforth, soldiers were not to be regarded as "dutiful prisoners of the Prussian army" in Berenhorst's definition.[12] The endeavor to establish a positive attitude among burghers toward the army demanded that the articles of war and table of punishments be revised. Scharnhorst told the king, "If the nation is to be regarded as defender of the fatherland, it must not in this capacity be threatened with the most degrading punishments."[13] He wrote Stein, "We've opposed cudgel beatings because in the eyes of the public they make the soldier's circumstances the most unfortunate throughout all of society…No civilian is flogged who has not committed the most infamous offense. This has become a national issue. No soldier is so mercilessly whipped as the Prussian and no army has achieved less."[14]

Scharnhorst set his sights on "the inner bond between the army and the nation."[15] The reorganization commission's *Regulations Regarding Military Punishment* of 1808 state, "Universal military conscription will result in placing young people of good education and a refined sense of ethics under the flag as common soldiers. It is to be confidently expected that they will not only willingly obey their superiors and smoothly apply themselves to learning their military duties, but also that they will set an example to their comrades from less educated strata to practical obedience and effective application of their strengths and capabilities. This will contribute to their training and make it possible to maintain order and discipline in the army with moderate treatment."[16] The cudgel beating as a form of punishment was replaced with three grades of arrest and confinement. The *Gassenlaufen*, running the gauntlet, was abolished. Only in cases of a repeated serious offense was a beating authorized, and then "never to be publicized or carried out before the eyes of the public."[17]

Moderate punishment was absolutely necessary were the burghers to willingly commit to military service, but so was abolishing exemptions. The conscription committee published an analysis of the advantages of creating a national army: "Our army that faced the enemy in 1806, with respect to the mechanical function of both the individual and the whole, was superior to the enemy. It fragmented nonetheless, because the bond that joins the majority of individuals in the army to the fatherland is woefully inadequate. The overall purpose of conscription is not to simply place a greater mass of manpower at the state's disposal. It is also to spread the educated class's more correct perception, especially with respect to the principle of honor, to the ranks and give the army an intelligent majority." The report cautioned that it is impractical to expect that "at the outbreak of a war the upper classes will flock to the colors if enticed by the honor to fight for the fatherland."[18] Abolishing exemptions that free the burgher from military service was the only way to dispel the view that the army is "a burden of the lower classes."

The revised penal code provoked the ire of "cudgel officers." They gibed that if thrust into a pitched battle, Scharnhorst would content himself with giving a lecture. Shocked by the mollified punishments, the present Duke of Brunswick charged that they "do not aim to maintain order, but are more likely to transform military authority into a philanthropic swindle."[19] Gneisenau was vexed by this misunderstanding of the new directives. He countered, "It is the custom of troop commanders to busy themselves with trifling matters. Neglecting what actually prepares the troops for war often prevents the officers from distinguishing what is important from what isn't... Many military men understand discipline as merely being handy with a club. The self-discipline generated by animating the soldier's warlike spirit is unknown to them."[20] The king demanded full compliance from the officer corps. He acknowledged that "the transition from a customary practice to a new way of handling things" is difficult. The regulations are nonetheless "to be followed to the letter... without regard for previous proportions."[21]

In July 1809, Gneisenau advised Friedrich Wilhelm of the "recalcitrant attitude of the greater percentage of senior officers," stemming from "their resentment toward new arrangements, especially the abolition of cudgel beatings and removing company commanders from the contracting out of smaller uniform articles." Instead of receiving an allowance to purchase supplies, which officers could skim from by buying inferior quality products, they were paid a fixed salary and no longer controlled procurement.[22] Gneisenau submitted a memo to the sovereign warning of the consequences in case the proposed reforms are neglected: "Sooner or later we can expect to be eliminated from the roster of independent nations… Our military forces in the present sense of the word will secure but one advantage from us, that being the opportunity to perish with honor without anticipating the possibility of a good success. But there is still an element of resistance that the government has either neglected or feared, that we may yet regard as offering us a high probability of a favorable outcome to the struggle. This is arming the people."[23]

A better quality of soldier required an improved type of officer. The surrender of defensible Prussian fortresses had tarnished the aristocratic officer corps. The investigation committee tried their commanders for dereliction of duty and cowardice. Before the proceedings they were confined to house arrest. During this time, they suffered the double mortification of being guarded by deputized civilians. The committee dishonorably discharged 17 generals, 50 staff and 141 subaltern officers. Seven fortress commanders received death sentences though none were executed. Another 85 generals, 584 staff officers and 3,924 subalterns were relieved of duty without dishonor. The majority of subalterns were reinstated in 1813, but almost none of the staff officers and not a single general.[24] The officer corps did not object to the hearings. Its members understood the purge as necessary to restore public confidence in the military. Sentences were not publicized in the press out of consideration for relatives of those on trial. These were often men who had the same surname as the defendant and were good soldiers.

The overhaul of the officer corps did not stop here; Scharnhorst flatly opposed preference for the nobility in positions of command. In Friedrich the Great's army, underaged sons of aristocrats were accepted into regiments and made officers after a rudimentary training course. Scharnhorst argued that reserving these posts for an exclusive caste deprives the army of the talent and knowledge that the rest of the population has to offer. The old system was deeply rooted in military tradition. The periodical *Bellona* cautioned, "There are some classes designated to govern and others to obey. If we try to reverse this arrangement, nothing but confusion will result."[25] Gneisenau wrote sarcastically in a newspaper about how reassuring it must be for aristocratic parents to know that while still children, their sons will become Junkers leading the king's soldiers. One publication described it as a grievous error "to entrust this crucial office, the perfection of the fighting forces that safeguard the welfare and security of the state, to those who are both mentally and physically still children or to equally unsuitable, unworthy men."[26]

An *Immediatbericht* (Ready Report) of the Military Reorganization Commission dated September 25, 1807, decreed that the army is to become a reservoir of the population incorporating the finest qualities of the people. Officers must therefore be drawn from the "elite of the entire nation." The report explained, "Since this preference was previously reserved for a single class, all the talent and expertise of the nation was lost for the army. And this privileged class in no way saw itself compelled by a need to cultivate its military prowess, since its birthright and a long life alone were bound to elevate it to the loftiest

The Military Reorganization Commission convenes in Königsberg. From left to right are Major Boyen, the king, Lieutenant Colonel Gneisenau, General Scharnhorst, Freiherr vom Stein and Major Grolman.

military posts. Herein lies the reason why officers were so far behind other classes in their education. For the same reason the army was regarded as a state within a state, hated by the other classes and to some extent despised, since it was supposed to represent a combination of all moral and physical strengths of the citizens of this state."[27]

Guidelines published on August 06, 1808, state that "From now on, granting officer's rank shall be based only on knowledge and education in peacetime and on outstanding courage and insight during war. All individuals throughout the entire nation who possess these qualities may lay claim to the loftiest positions of honor in the military. The previous preference for a single stratum is completely abolished in the military. Everyone regardless of origins has the same responsibilities and the same rights."[28] For his part, Gneisenau did not want to destroy the character of the old officer corps. There was much worth preserving, for example the custom of Friedrich Wilhelm I of allowing officers to disobey an order they consider dishonorable. Gneisenau advocated not necessarily replacing aristocrats whose families have served for generations, but basing their eligibility to command on talent instead of on birthright. This would include both tactical training and awareness of "their venerable task of functioning as instructor and leader of a respected segment of the population," as the June 08, 1808 regulations for military punishment state.[29]

Modern military academies were necessary to upgrade the quality of leadership. Scharnhorst wrote that "many staff officers know no more about war in the field than a corporal with combat experience."[30] When a general gives orders for an operation or makes decisions in combat, the members of his staff often "don't know what they are supposed to do" to properly implement them. The *Kriegsschule für Offiziere* (War Academy for Officers), founded in Berlin in 1810, provided classes to thoroughly instruct officers in responsibilities of command. In place of recruiting teenage Junkers from the nobility, Scharnhorst established the *Kriegsschule für die Portepéefähnriche* (War Academy for Ensigns) with facilities in Königsberg, Breslau and Berlin. *Portepéefähnrich* was a transitional noncommissioned officer rank for trainees at the academies. The ensigns tied a leather strap wrapped in silver braid with a decorative knot to their sword as a symbol of their status as officer candidates. They had to be at least 17 years of age, have served a minimum of three months as a common soldier and satisfy preliminary educational requirements.

The examination commission defined objectives of the training program: "Not just practical and scientific knowledge are requirements that define a capable officer. The primary qualities that every officer must possess are presence of mind, rapid comprehension, precision, orderliness in his duties and respectable conduct."[31] Scharnhorst demanded advancement based on merit instead of on length of service. In a memo drafted in the summer of 1809, he asked rhetorically, "Should age alone lead one to higher rank? Then active, energetic and ambitious men whose spirit half consumes their body will be held back and lazy, phlegmatic fools, with few exceptions, will stand at the head."[32] The curriculum of the war colleges comprised chemistry, German and French language studies, fortification design and construction, combat tactics for artillery and infantry, campaign strategy and general staff duties. Scharnhorst personally conducted some of the classes. In one exercise, he assigned students an historical European battle to study. The ensign personally inspected the site, drew sketches of the battlefield, marked the movements of the respective armies on a map, described the militarily relevant aspects of the terrain, wrote an account of the operations of both sides and offered his analysis.

Scharnhorst focused training on "learning to assess situations, guidance and independent thinking" and "putting the ideas to the test on actual terrain."[33] From leading patrols to managing an entire corps, he advocated field exercises to supplement classroom instruction. He advised other instructors, "It seems to me that the fundamental principle should be to offer advice to the officer, but impose as few limitations on him as possible. I consider it less of a disadvantage to let him make a mistake than it would be to restrict his independent initiative."[34] Special courses for staff officers trained them to reconnoiter the best routes for an advance, locate suitable bivouacs or housing for the troops during encampment, assign foraging parties, maintain supply deliveries and advise the commanding general. He advocated creation of an office to oversee and coordinate the activity of all four academies. This was to ensure uniform training and cooperation among the various service branches and army corps in the field. War colleges produced highly qualified officers who would gain influence during the course of operations.

Merit promotion made enemies for Scharnhorst. The most prominent critics were the "old villain" Kalckreuth, Count Carl von Lottum and the cantankerous Yorck. They spoke for a clique of malcontents comprising company commanders who profit from contracting supplies, proponents of the linear advance who consider Tirailleur tactics an affront to military discipline, titled gentry whose unqualified offspring tenant patronage positions on the staff, Junkers whose sons henceforth can only qualify for war college through the mortification of competing with commoners on the entrance exam, mulish generals convinced that conscription will destroy the soldier caste and ultraconservative aristocrats fearing the militia will rise against the monarchy. The king privately identified with the anti-reform clique. He established cadet institutes to prepare young noblemen for the admission test free of charge and dumbed down the exam itself to make it easy enough for them to pass.[35] He watered down practically every initiative to achieve a more modern and adaptable state form.

The king tried to hamstring the reorganization commission by appointing adjutants Karl Ludwig von Oppeln-Bronikowski and Ludwig von Borstell to the commission. Friedrich Wilhelm added Lottum as well. He justified the appointment to Stein with the explanation that this officer "has a better comprehension of the existing military system," despite the fact that it is precisely *this system* that the commission sought to replace.[36] A concerned Stein wrote Hardenberg in December 1807, "The spirit of this cabal has again surfaced in the military and I much fear that it will gain the upper hand. Then the old abuses will all be restored." Gneisenau and Scharnhorst submitted their resignations. They felt they will be unable to accomplish anything with half the commission consisting of the opposition. The king, in part influenced by a surprisingly conciliatory letter from Kalckreuth praising Scharnhorst, relented and replaced Bronikowski and Borstell with Boyen and Götzen. Scharnhorst and Gneisenau stayed at their posts. They could at last work with officers equally committed to overhauling Prussia's outdated military structure.

"Give the People a Fatherland!"

The absolute state had long perceived the burghers as a nonpolitical element of society functioning to provide the country with an economic foundation and source of revenue for the regime to conduct its affairs. The cabinet war concept was an expression of this association: The king and standing army took the field while the middle class conducted business as usual. Commercial enterprises were detached from the clash of arms. France's military occupation after the disastrous campaign of 1806 forced the monarchy, if it was to survive, to involve the educated classes in public administration. This represented a tremendous upheaval. In June 1807, Hardenberg wrote the king that Prussia must introduce "democratic principles to a monarchist regime." He warned, "The might of these principles is so great, so universally acknowledged and so widespread that the state that doesn't adopt them can only expect to either perish or be *forced* to accept them."[37]

During the summer of 1807, Friedrich Wilhelm resided in Memel, a Baltic port in the northeastern corner of the kingdom. While Berlin youngsters sang the derisive rhyme, *Unser Dämel sitzt in Memel* (Our Moron Sits in Memel), he contemplated who to assign the task of transforming the Prussian state into a representative government and revive its finances. Hardenberg, his first choice, Napoleon vetoed. The king protested that there is no other suitable candidate to modernize the government. The French emperor proposed Freiherr vom Stein. He accepted the post of chief minister and arrived in Memel on September 30, 1807. His job was to create a system that "no longer limits the freedom and equality of the citizens and satisfies expectations commensurate with our level of civilization to ensure the well-being of the state."[38] When recommending Stein, Bonaparte was unaware of his anti-French sentiments. Stein was an avowed enemy of the "quick-tempered, swaggering, fickle, sinister, immoral character of the French people, whose behavior becomes savage and criminal as soon as the abysmal weakness of the king is apparent."[39]

Like Gneisenau and Scharnhorst, Stein privately planned for an insurrection against the French occupational forces. He reported to the king in August 1808, "What an armed nation in conjunction with the troops on active duty are capable of if both, nation and soldier, are animated by a common spirit, can be seen in Spain and was already seen in the Vendée."[40] In order to win the people for the enterprise, there had to be a war aim extending beyond rescue of the Hohenzollern Dynasty. This meant civil reform; molding Prussia into a state worth fighting for. The fatherland concept was to be the watchword for a new social and political order that holds open the door to advancement for aristocracy, educated and agrarian strata equally. As Gneisenau proclaimed, "It is both proper and sensible for the state to *give* the people a fatherland if they are to energetically *defend* a fatherland."[41] Stein was a confident, industrious man with ample experience in public affairs. During his short tenure in office, he managed some success in revamping government but historically receives more credit for constructive reform than deserved.

The new chief minister opposed the liberalistic formula of merging the people into a collective mass of sovereign individuals. Each stratum would retain its intrinsic character, but the state should assign to it duties according to how it is best suited to contribute to national welfare. In this sense Stein combated the Revolution with its own weapons. He proposed liberating the people from absolutism but not destroying the monarchy or disenfranchising the nobility.

Decentralizing government, he entrusted landowners with political responsibilities for the benefit of their respective provinces. The landowners forfeited neither influence nor regard as they transitioned from self-service to community service. Stein placed great emphasis on German history. He esteemed bearing arms as the "venerable right of every free man," and called upon the population to emulate the strict sense of duty that guided old Prussia. This corresponded to the tenet of Gneisenau, who declared, "Make humanity enthusiastic for its duty first, then for its rights!"[42]

It was advantageous for Stein that he began his work in East Prussia. The province possessed a non-aristocratic landowner class and progressive civil service. Affluent burghers who had purchased estates from impoverished nobles dwelled there. The population was receptive to new ideas about government and regarded the feudal system as untenable. Here was fertile ground for Stein "to replace the arbitrary and irresponsible rule of royal cronies with orderly and reliable ministerial government."[43] In charge of East Prussia's civil service was Friedrich von Schrötter, who energetically supported reform. Based on a study prepared by Heinrich von Schön and Friedrich Staegemann, Stein introduced the *Allgemeines Landrecht* (Universal Right to Land) edict on October 09, 1807, with the king's authority. It abolished the lingering vestige of serfdom and allowed free use of the land. Some 47,000 rural families found the opportunity to acquire farms. Stein considered a robust and free agrarian stratum the foundation for a healthy state and source of good soldiers for the army. He also undertook measures to protect financially distressed noblemen from having to auction their estates.

Stein introduced legislation to "remove everything that has up till now prevented the individual from attaining the level of prosperity he is capable of according to his abilities."[44] His endeavors however, fell short of the intended outcome. Though technically liberated from servitude, peasants were required to compensate landowners for the loss of their traditional rights. Small farms competed on the market with large plantations. New laws allowed only landowners to vote. Stein wanted governmental posts restricted to tenanted burghers, thereby hoping to gain the support of the affluent. Adopting the mindset of the English peerage that the country is "overpopulated," Stein scorned the "ruinous propagation of the homeless class that has no property." He recommended that they migrate to America. He regarded those among his countrymen too poor to own land and yet inconsiderate enough to continue living as "an accumulation of immoral, vicious rabble."[45] A contemporary historian summarized that Stein "energetically accomplished long overdue reform in Prussia, abolished absolutism and introduced communal self-government and a ministerial regime. In the realm of *economic* policy that determines the success or failure of every administration, the reformers made mistake after mistake and negated the greater part of the new programs on their own."[46]

Gneisenau was at odds with Stein over fair distribution of land. The defender of Kolberg advocated seizing estates of noblemen not firmly committed to the nationalist cause. It was clear to Gneisenau that the land question is paramount for liberating the farming community from ancestral bondage. Are soldiers of Prussia, the greater percentage of whom are of rural background, to fight for wealthy landowners and capitalists or for a better life for themselves and their families? Gneisenau even had to overcome resistance from Stein regarding abolishment of cudgel beatings in the army. The state minister considered them "perfectly suitable punishment." Summarizing Stein's land reforms, historian James Sheehan concluded, "Only a few former serfs were able to consolidate their holdings and become independent farmers; many more were legally free, but still economically and socially dependent."[47] Despite shortcomings, Stein's reforms contributed to the rising tide of patriotism in the country. The educated class applauded the liberation of the agrarian population. Many were unaware of how little these measures actually improved its standard of living. They saw them as a sign that Prussia is becoming a modern state worth fighting for.

Legislation to abolish serfdom did not deprive the tenanted aristocracy of its property, yet still generated bitterness among landowners toward the "Jacobin Stein," whom they accused of "robbing our sacred rights."[48] In Brandenburg, Marwitz and fellow opponents of reform objected to the "republican principles" the new laws promote, which were worded in the tenor of French statutes. Marwitz described the *Allgemeines Landrecht* as a "legal expression of the revolution." He claimed that agrarian reforms are "the revolutionary transformation of the fatherland… the war of the impoverished against the propertied, industry against agriculture, mobility against stability, crass materialism against divinely instituted order."[49] Stein created five ministries to discharge the business of government: Interior, Finance, Foreign Affairs, War and Justice. This increased the efficiency of the administration and greatly reduced patronage.

Members of the landed aristocracy, some old school army officers and sycophants at court grumbled that the "insolent foreigner" Stein—he hailed from a Franconian noble family—and his reform clique are "snake breeders" destroying the grand traditions of ancient Prussia. Even Gneisenau was at times taken aback at the vigor with which Stein proceeded. In a Berlin casino, the former minister of justice Baron Eberhard von der Reck exclaimed, "Better to lose three battles like Jena and Auerstedt than have this October edict!"[50] Reluctantly committed to supporting Stein, the king rejected the protests, some of which were justified, submitted by estate holders. New laws also abolished the patrimonial courts of justice conducted by landowners and transferred jurisdiction to the state police. Prussia could not be liberated without a national army. This army could not be created without the support of the burghers and they could only be won for the patriotic cause through social and political reform.

Within the standing army, scions of old military families had relied on birthright for obtaining a commission and on length of service for promotion for so long that their education had fallen woefully behind that of the industrious burghers, who were accustomed to competition to realize career objectives.

Allowing non-nobles of superior learning to seek the officer's career at last threatened to unseat the aristocracy from its position of veneration and leadership in the military. The reform movement defied this customarily exclusive sphere of the noblesse right along with abolishing ancestral estate privileges and servitude. This polarized conservative nobles and reformers and alarmed Prussians who knew that the country needs unity to rid itself of the French. In November 1807 General Grawert, a man not entirely sympathetic to reform, submitted a memo in Breslau warning, "It is impossible for a realm to prosper whose members nurture such hostility toward one another, as is the case with a great part of the nobility and the burghers."[51]

Stein is praised by German historians for his vision of a united Germany. An improved Prussian government was to serve as the nucleus for a national state. To this end, he maintained contact with dukes and princes in other parts of Germany to coordinate resistance against Bonaparte. Stein was in office less than a year when in August 1808, he sent a nonencrypted letter to Prince Ludwig Adolf Peter zu Sayn-Wittgenstein, who resided in French-controlled territory. Stein expressed the hope that Germany will soon rise against the French as the Spanish have done. It was clear from the text that Stein was in contact with patriotic circles in Hesse and Westphalia. The messenger carrying the incriminating letter turned it over to the French police. Napoleon ordered Stein's property in Westphalia seized and pressured Friedrich Wilhelm to dismiss him from office. He declared that Stein, "who seeks to provoke unrest in Germany," is an enemy of France.[52] It is characteristic of Napoleon's tunnel vision that he would not see himself as the real cause of unrest. Stein immigrated to Austria to avoid arrest and probable execution by the French.

On October 24, 1808, Stein drafted a farewell testament summarizing the accomplishments of his year in office: "The last vestige of slavery, inherent submission, is destroyed and the unshakable pillar of the throne, the will of free persons, has been established… In some areas there is still a *Gesindeordnung* (system of servitude) that is paralyzing the people's freedom. As the most recent report from the civic commissioner of the province of Silesia shows, attempts have also been made to resurrect some elements of the previous system through a new order of servitude… Only a few estate owners are making them who are not from among the people… There is no chance that these individuals will gain anything from this at the cost of countless others."[53]

The king was not sorry to be rid of the boorish Stein. His brusque, self-assertive manner scarcely conformed to the decorum observed at court, making his departure somewhat of a relief. Politically, this was a setback for reform. Adherents of the old system rejoiced. Yorck wrote Oppen, "A senseless mind has been trampled down and the other snake breeders will dissolve in their own poison."[54] The dismissal encouraged the reactionary generals to redouble resistance to Scharnhorst's parallel military improvements. The king divided Stein's duties between Count Dohna, minister of the interior, and finance minister Altenstein.

Ultra-conservative, super-rich aristocrats, the pair did nothing to continue Stein's reforms. They also proved incompetent to manage affairs of state and were unable to maintain contributions to France fixed by treaty. On January 08, 1810, an impatient Napoleon confronted General Friedrich Wilhelm von Krusemarck, the German representative at the French court, about the financial shortfall.

The emperor suggested that to reduce spending to release funds for reparations, the king limit the size of the army to a 6,000-man guard: "The savings resulting from this reduction in force will be substantial," Napoleon opined. "This is no longer the time for playing soldier in Prussia. Why an army of 40,000 men? It unsettles France and arouses mistrust among her neighbors." He then threatened to annex more Prussian territory in retaliation or to dissolve the state entirely. "No matter what," he ranted, "I'll be paid!"[55] Just weeks before, he announced the transfer of 30,000 soldiers to Magdeburg. This was to intimidate the Prussians for devoting their fiscal resources to recovery instead of to enriching France. In his Ready Report of January 28, Scharnhorst didn't bother to mention the proposal to disband the Prussian army. He stressed instead the need to expand troop strength and requested 600,000 thaler for rearmament. Dohna and Altenstein cowered before Napoleon and sought ways to appease him. Altenstein was a traitor. He was prepared to offer the imperator Silesia to compensate for the delayed tribute.[56]

The trump card of the reform movement, and indeed of Prussia, was Queen Luise. The extent of her influence over the king will never be known since no written record of their private conversations exists. She had urged him to appoint Stein to state minister in 1807, telling him that Stein has "a great heart, an encompassing mind, perhaps he knows the remedies that are hidden from us."[57] She always supported the reform party against recalcitrant elements in the old aristocracy. After Stein left Prussia, Luise conspired with Hardenberg to oust Dohna and Altenstein. She enlisted the aid of Austria's new foreign minister Metternich to make Napoleon receptive to the idea. Exasperated over Prussia's fiscal mismanagement depriving him of revenue, the Corsican dropped his objection to reinstate Hardenberg as chancellor. His bumbling predecessors were sacked. Hardenberg took office on June 04, 1810. "A virtuoso in the art of dealing with people," he compelled the king to dispense with personal advisors Beyme and the conservative Karl von Nagler.

With Hardenberg at the helm, the reform movement regained impetus. Unlike Stein, he advocated a laissez-faire policy regarding commerce. He believed that the free play of forces, unfettering the economy from government supervision, "will rescue the state and see it flourish again. This, the only means, should therefore not be neglected... We should not recoil from what the number-one principle demands; the most freedom and equality possible."[58] Another departure from Stein's system was Hardenberg's skepticism regarding Prussian Junkers, bitter enemies of social reform, taking over provincial administration of public affairs. He addressed the shortcomings of Stein's land policy which protected the nobility from forfeiture of property. Only through Hardenberg's *Regulierungsedikt* (Regulating Edict) of 1811 were farmers unfettered from residual feudal obligations. The *Landeskulturedikt* (Progressive Land Edict) allowed for fair sale and distribution of country estates. Farmers were required however, to return a portion of their land to the big plantation owners. That same year Hardenberg convened the Rural Delegates Assembly. It fostered political representation for the agrarian community. The chancellor repealed laws that exempted the aristocracy from certain taxes. In March 1812 he granted citizenship to Jews who serve in the military.

A worldly, courtly aristocrat, Hardenberg gained so much influence that critics described his administration as the "state chancellor's dictatorship." His fiscal management was not as successful as the land reform. He auctioned off some royal estates and steadily raised taxes. The latter measure hit the poor the hardest. Prussia remained behind on timely contributions to France, but the chancellor devoted some of the increased revenue to finance secret war preparations. He was just as unpopular with conservative aristocrats as Stein had been, but had the king's support and they did not risk openly defying him. As Stein had pointed out, those resisting modernization were too few in number to stop its progress. The emerging ideal was the fatherland concept. It became popular through the promise of lawfully protected freedoms and universal equality: "Men came together, for the first time in many years, who recognized that the key to the future of the state rests not in the welfare of the church, the princes or the government, but in the well-being of all."[59] The psychological basis for a patriotic uprising against foreign domination was established. This cleared the decks for Scharnhorst to implement his program to create a national army.

The Krümper System

The standing army that had defined European warfare for 150 years obstructed creating a national fighting force. Gneisenau stated in a memorandum that the standing army "divides the interests of the government from those of the people," since its duty is to serve the crown instead of the country. Nothing contributes more to weakening a nation, because the standing army extinguishes the "warlike spirit and sense of community" of the inhabitants when their monarch entrusts defense of their realm to foreign hirelings and professional soldiers. Were this army destroyed in battle, Gneisenau asked, who would be left to preserve the independence of the state? It was time for a conscripted army of the people. "To mold an entire nation into soldiers," wrote Gneisenau, "they must be imbued with a martial spirit right in peacetime."[60] Conditions in Prussia were not exactly the same as peacetime. In violation of the 1808 treaty, whereby Napoleon pledged to withdraw his legions from the entire country, they only evacuated territories east of the Vistula. The population was responsible for nourishing French troops in the provinces between the Elbe and Vistula Rivers. These troops often conducted themselves as though the war was still on.

While Stein and Hardenberg animated the fatherland concept through social and political reforms, Scharnhorst and the reorganization commission explored ways to involve the population in national defense. The program had to be carried out in secret, since the Paris Convention of September 1808 forbade Prussia from expanding the military beyond 42,000 men or forming a militia for ten years. Raising a territorial reserve, the *Landwehr*, in addition to the standing army would arouse Napoleon's ire. When he first learned of the plan, the emperor responded in character with high-handed threats; no violation of the Paris compact by Prussia would be tolerated, even though he himself disregarded its articles whenever expedient. Scharnhorst had submitted a blueprint for creating a national fighting force in April 1806, which the Immediate Organization Commission had rejected as a "fantasy."[61] The draft provided a basis for the new program. He finalized the details in July 1807. The Military Reorganization Commission endorsed the document on September 25 and forwarded it to Friedrich Wilhelm for approval.

Scharnhorst proposed that each regiment send a designated number of experienced soldiers on leave and replace them with conscripted recruits. They would receive basic training and be discharged afterward to return to their civilian occupations. A fresh batch of recruits would take their place. In this way, the army could gradually build a reserve to replace losses from combat and provide the manpower to create new formations. The number of soldiers on active duty was usually around 42,000, but trained reservists could be called up were war declared to rapidly expand the size of the army. On August 06, 1808, the Supreme War Council (OKK) issued instructions for the process: "His majesty has assigned the OKK to arrange that infantry regiments and the foot artillery discharge three to five men per company, or more according to the company's requirements, and induct just as many recruits, train them for a month and at the conclusion of this period release them to go home again. In their place, the same number of additional recruits are to be called up for training. This method is to continue until enough men have been trained to satisfy what is needed to expand the units."[62]

The name of this plan, the *Krümper* System, borrowed a term employed in the textile industry. It refers to the amount of additional fabric merchants include with bolts of material to compensate buyers for *Krümper*—shrinkage. The word became generic for any extra quantity. In the army, soldiers not on active duty for whatever reason were known as *Krümper*. The term could therefore be used in correspondence about military training without arousing the suspicion of the French police. Companies enrolled at least three times as many recruits as recommended by the OKK and extended the specified drill period well beyond one month per group. In 1811, regiments started sending elder soldiers on indefinite leave at their own request. This greatly increased the number of recruits called up to learn the warrior's craft in their place. The army established *Exizierdepots* (Training Units) to intensify *Krümper* instruction. In 1808, the OKK detailed

1810

Ausbildung der Krümper.

Krümper recruits during training. Those in the *Landwehr* wore black, grey or blue tunics with collars color-coded to designate the unit's province; white for Pomerania, black for West Prussia, Yellow for Silesia, red with white buttons for East Prussia and red with yellow buttons for Kurmark and Neumark. Every third man was issued a spade or an axe.

officers and NCOs to various districts to discreetly conduct refresher courses and combat drills for reservists living there. The locations were not at military bases and hence beyond the scrutiny of French inspectors.[63]

Prussian army leaders employed stratagems to disguise the army's augmenting manpower from the French. They shifted regiments from place to place without their replacement battalions, which in turn absorbed the *Krümper* recruits. The regiments then drew from their own reserves to fill the gaps in manpower depleted by the absence of the replacement battalions. The new *Krümper* inductees trained with the replacement units while the French watched the regiments. When ordered to fortresses for garrison duty and further military instruction, recruits were often classified as construction workers. Officers, their orderlies and tradesmen were not included on the official rosters. Companies always conducted exercises with the fixed number of soldiers, even though the formations had additional personnel who rotate in and out for drills. Units were formed, disbanded and reformed again and regiments understated the number of men under arms in official tallies. Every manner of trickery was utilized to confuse the emperor's commissioners.[64]

The *Krümper* system underwent repeated modifications as time progressed and administrators gained experience. In addition to the regular army and rising number of trained recruits, there were thousands of troops in the country who had been discharged to reduce the active-duty roster to 42,000. After the Tilsit treaty, France released Prussian soldiers taken prisoner during the 1806/07 campaign. These men increased the manpower on hand were war to break out anew. Some regiments had over a thousand troops from disbanded formations quartered in their district. The *Leib-Regiment* had nearly 6,000. Scharnhorst wanted every field battalion to have a full-strength reserve battalion available for replacements. Cavalry regiments were only to have one squadron in reserve due to the shortage of horses. Hardenberg continued to fund the clandestine expansion of the army. He paid France less than obligated by treaty but enough to keep Napoleon from taking action. Prussia owed much to his adroit diplomacy during the period of rearmament.

The reorganization commission abolished the practice of recruiting foreigners to serve in the ranks. The cabinet order of November 20, 1807 stated that henceforth, "the army will consist almost entirely of *Einländer* (indigenous persons).[65] Regiments would draw replacements exclusively from their cantons. In the absolutist military establishment, as much as 50 percent of a regimental roster was comprised of men recruited from outside of Prussia or who were shanghaied into service. Grawert had already pointed out that enlisting foreigners "enlarges the army on paper, but correspondingly diminishes its inner strength."[66] The *Krümper* system eliminated the need to seek personnel from across the frontier. A March 1808 memo maintained, "A state that wages war with its resources and its army according to the old custom cannot hold its own against an equally large state whose resources encompass those of the entire nation and whose army is the nation itself."[67]

The Military Reorganization Commission soon relaxed restrictions barring induction of foreigners. Promoted by Stein, the fatherland concept spread across the frontier and came to stand for all of Germany. Memoirs of German soldiers who served in the Napoleonic wars, whether for or against France, often express regret over having to shoot at men of their own nationality. The war department issued a decree on March 18, 1809, stating that foreigners of German ethnicity are permitted to join the Prussian army. Many enrolled in special *Freikorps* (volunteer corps). Some patriots denounced Germans who did *not* enlist as rogues. Marwitz sent draft notices to non-Prussians living in his district. "From the spirit of this national war," the order read, "flows the principle that no German dwelling here is a foreigner."[68] Residents who did not respond to the induction notice Marwitz expelled from the district. The difference between the reformers' recruitment of non-Prussians into the army differed from the absolutist practice in that the men did not enlist as soldiers for hire, but in a spirit of national unity to liberate Germany.

On August 31, 1807, the reorganization commission presented Scharnhorst's "Preliminary Proposal for the Formation of the Reserve Army" to the king. It called for abolishing the table of deferments currently exempting hundreds of thousands from military service. So many burghers were excused from active duty that Prussia had an army of poor farmers and aristocratic officers. The canton system of 1733 and the updated 1792 regulations drew recruits from rural districts and spared the cities. Deferred burghers were forbidden to migrate out of Prussia. Scharnhorst strove for equal representation in the ranks. Requiring members of the educated classes to enroll in armed service was not to enlarge the size of the fighting forces or to fill vacancies with more qualified applicants. Military duty was to be an expression of personal commitment to one's country; to affirm the inseparable bond between state and nation. As one historian summarized, the reforms "were not of a technically military nature. In a very idealistic sense, they aimed at reconciling the army with a nation still developing, to overcome the intellectual schism and to create a truly national army in harmony with the crown, noblesse and burghers."[69]

In the same spirit, Scharnhorst proposed rescinding the accepted custom of *Stellvertretung* (representation), whereby a draftee is permitted to hire another citizen to enlist in his stead and free him from military obligation. The reformers considered it an affront to the honorable soldier that a citizen would refuse to enroll and pay someone to take his place. It was also unfair to poorer families among the nobility who lack the fiscal resources to follow suit, and must instead look on while "the wealthy, uneducated farmer, innkeeper, tenant, baker, brewer, shopkeeper or usurer sends a *Stellvertreter* of the meanest background to stand next to their colleagues, their sons or their siblings" in the ranks, as Scharnhorst put it. The Conscription Commission asked in a Ready Report of February 05, 1810, "how can (the military) caste earn respect if the wealthy and educated are ashamed to be a part of it and substitute the poorest flunky or a beggar instead?"[70]

Friedrich Wilhelm approved the proposals but allowed exceptions two weeks later. Civil servants and owners of large plantations or factories received deferments. Each was required to fully equip a *Landwehr* recruit at his own expense in return. Despite objections from Scharnhorst and Yorck, *Stellvertretung* remained permissible in East Prussia though banned in the rest of the kingdom. This was probably due to Count Dohna, whose political perception had not progressed beyond the 17th Century.[71] Despite these compromises, Scharnhorst finally had his provincial militia. The state solicited participation of burghers whom it had previously hoped to exclude. The compact between government and nation was one of reason. The state urgently needed the total commitment of the burgher, his devotion to the struggle for liberation and his enthusiasm. The political objective of the burgher was participation in government. The reformers guaranteed this and hoped, as they had repeatedly declared, to in this way win the burghers for the fight.

But for the exemptions cited above, all Prussians capable of bearing arms who were not already in the regular army or *Jäger* battalions were eligible for enrollment in the army, the *Landwehr* or the provincial troops regardless of education or affluence. The reorganization commission's Ready Report of March 15, 1808, decreed that "fighting men from the poorer classes" were to serve in the standing army and burghers in the militia.[72] Scharnhorst chose this course out of consideration for the middle class's aversion of harsh discipline and its ingrained perception of the army as a collection of uneducated, unwilling louts under the lash of insensitive officers. The *Landwehr* was designated a *defensive* force; the king could not exercise supreme authority over its deployment as was the case with the standing army. He could not force it, for example, to wage a cabinet war to conquer territory of a neighboring state. This arrangement corresponded to the cognizance of the burgher as a defender of his country unfettered by absolutism. Scharnhorst stressed the importance of declaring that "the state emphatically acknowledges his independence."

Every *Landwehr* battalion was charged with the defense of the province it was raised in, though could also be detailed to fight alongside regular troops. The population of the province elected its officers up to the rank of company chief. The king's General Commission appointed battalion, brigade and divisional commanders. Recruits received two months of basic training from officers of the regular army. At the end of this period, "the schooled (*Landwehr*) officers, non-commissioned officers and men of the provincial troops will receive no further instruction from officers of the standing army," as 1808 regulations state.[73] After completing recruit training, students "who have pursued science and liberal art studies" at a university were "to be transferred to garrisons in cities where they will find the opportunity to continue their education."[74] Treitschke observed, "Most of the volunteers were students. They brought the youthful spirit of academic cheerfulness to the encampments, though they still conformed to strict military discipline… The young volunteers were truly the best soldiers as Scharnhorst had predicted. The bearing of entire formations became less restrained and more ethical through contact with these educated young men."[75]

Scharnhorst admonished army officers detailed to train recruits to exercise moderation: "Treatment of the young men should take into account their previous education and future military specialty. Care should be taken that their service in no way demeans them. At the same time, nothing should be omitted that deeply and inextinguishably anchors them in the indispensable spirit of martial discipline in today's army. No behavior contrary to regulations should be acceptable, no pointless lack of restraint on their part allowed. In this matter they are to be treated just as strictly as in the rest of the military. At the same time however, mistakes resulting from ignorance or awkwardness must always be corrected in a kind and paternal way. We should not expect them to fix everything wrong caused by their understandable unfamiliarity with the nature and details of their duties all at once. Some mistakes they make at the beginning should be overlooked and what they need to learn taught to them step by step in the right order."[76]

Finding officers possessing the patience and tact required to instruct this novel type of soldier, who in many cases was better educated than his instructor, was no easy task. Henceforth, the traditional perception that an officer and nobleman is of greater worth than the non-aristocrat, that military tradition and gentle birth guarantee one's fitness to command, was incompatible with the concept of a national army in which everyone is equal in honor and shares opportunity for advancement. As the *Landwehr* expanded along with the standing army, the political influence of the monarchy diminished. Casualties among aristocratic officers would mount during the war of liberation and open vacancies for positions of command. Many burghers assumed these posts. Noblemen gravitated toward leadership roles in more fashionable cavalry and guard regiments. In this way they demonstrated the desire to maintain a cliquish, social aloofness within the military.

Some German historians set the number of soldiers trained through the *Krümper* system over a three-year period at 150,000 men.[77] The actual number is much less. The introduction of compulsory armed service did not provide enough trained reserves to sufficiently reinforce the army. It was more *symbolic* of the transition of Prussia's military establishment from an exclusive instrument of the monarchy to a conglomerate of various social strata. It provided the political, administrative and *psychological* foundation for the national uprising in 1813. Universal conscription was a programmatic declaration of the future political line of the army in the Prussian state. The internal opponents, reactionary generals who resisted reform and urged the king to delay its progress, were largely overcome. The challenge now was to develop a workable system that could mold the recruits into an efficient fighting force.

What could the soldiers of the regular army, standing side by side in combat with hastily trained *Krümper* hailing from nonmilitary backgrounds, expect of these novices? Many officers understandably harbored reservations about the steadfastness of *Landwehr* battalions when required to maneuver and maintain discipline under fire. Without warfare's transition from the linear advance of the old army to elastic, loose-formation fighting, the *Krümper* system would have been unworkable. There was not enough time to subject the new recruits to the repetitive drill required for echelon attacks, which Rüchel once lauded as "the recognized model for Europe."[78] Nor could free thinking, educated citizens be forcibly stamped into automatons. The Tirailleur system with its emphasis on mobility and personal initiative in combat was easier to learn and perfectly suited for the Prussian national soldier. The *Krümper* was born for the light infantry.

Knesebeck, a leading voice in reform, opined that a burgher's reluctance to enroll in the fatherland reserve is less an aversion of the soldier's craft than it is resistance to "the great amount of compulsion, precision handling of the rifle so unnecessary for wartime service and movements that in his capacity as a soldier, rob the freethinking person of his self-reliance." He advocated a training program "removed from everything pedantic, superfluous and trifling, especially embellishment and appearances." Instruction should "serve but one purpose, that being protection of the fatherland; everything related to the reality of war and nothing of peacetime ornamentation."[79] Aware that many officers stubbornly cling to the old system, Scharnhorst expressed concern that the army could lapse back into the Jena formula in which "mechanical maneuvering kills independent thinking and no one knows what to do in unexpected situations... If we do not work against this spirit with all our energy, the mechanical mentality will triumph once again over brains and vigor."[80]

With the exception of the *Nationalkavallerie* Regiment established by Yorck, the *Landwehr* initially consisted almost exclusively of infantry. Eventually more national cavalry regiments were formed. Developing a practical program to train *Krümper* as foot soldiers and determine how best to deploy them was therefore of paramount importance. Bülow wanted the whole army to adopt Tirailleur tactics, but Scharnhorst promoted "mutual support between dispersed combatants and those in closed formation; in broken terrain fighting individually and spread out, on open ground fighting in mass and in formation." The third rank of an infantry line was to comprise fusiliers schooled in Tirailleur tactics. Prussian light infantry training, as defined in March 1809 guidelines, was to focus on the soldier "shooting, aiming, hitting the target and loading his rifle, exploiting the terrain for his own protection and skillfully moving in conjunction with maneuvers of the battalion."[81]

Scharnhorst valued Tirailleur tactics as a progressive component of maneuvers utilizing both closed-formation mass assaults or dispersed deployment based on what is feasible given the topography, the enemy's disposition and the ebb and flow of combat. The *Landwehr* militia, Scharnhorst instructed, must "use indirect routes, occupy the forward woods and shrubbery and fall upon the enemy in the flank. It must always be where it is more a matter of skillfully exploiting the circumstances, and where it's better to rely on dispersed instead of on conventional fighting... It must never act on its own, but instead always in cooperation with the field troops, occupying uneven territory, reinforcing units of the field troops designated to launch attacks, harass the enemy and defend certain posts."[82] The light infantry was also trained to fight in closed formation to reinforce army regiments when a mass attack offers a better prospect of success than loose deployment. To preserve the militia character of *Krümper* battalions, a cabinet order stipulated, "When assigning men to platoons and companies, those living in a particular village or next to one another must remain together as much as possible."[83]

Jäger formations were a compromise between the line army and provincial militia. They belonged to the regular army but incorporated educated burghers who would show that "the jovial spirit of these freethinking military men is capable of demonstrating obedience," as war minister Karl Albrecht von Hake said.[84] Officers' guidelines for their training read, "*Jäger* detachments consist for the most part of very young men who are not yet accustomed to hardship.

This should be kept in mind as much as possible during marches and in canton quarters, especially in the beginning. Their physical constitution should be conditioned to the hardships of war gradually. In the same sense, when these *Jäger* detachments face the enemy, see that they are not separated from their regiments and battalions, detailed to dangerous posts and exposed to the danger of being suddenly wiped out in such detached positions. The commanding officer must himself take heed that these young men are not seized by an untimely overzealousness that will place them in greater peril than the battalion or regiment itself."[85]

Gneisenau was pleased to see the army become the catalyst for overcoming social barriers in Prussian society: "Sons of princes and children of the richest families flock to join and perform their duty as ordinary soldiers. Men in office leave lucrative posts and do the same. It is stirring to see all the offspring of noblemen and from the loftiest classes of burghers of the finest schooling enroll as riflemen in the countless *Jäger* companies where they provide for their own uniforms, weapons and pay. A majestic enthusiasm prevails."[86] He described in a letter to a friend what a joy it is to observe how young men of "noble and lofty castes forget their previous relationship and attentively heed the orders of their officers… What good fortune to have lived long enough to see the dawn of this historical epoch."[87] Scharnhorst wrote his daughter, "Nearly 3,000 of these educated, intelligent young men have not only revived the spirit of the military, but are already prepared to lead the rawest elements in the course of the war and elevate the military to a higher station."[88]

The actual number of troops under arms in Prussia fluctuated drastically during this period. The regime temporarily reduced the size of the standing army to just 20,000 men in 1810 to cut costs and maintain tribute payments to France. Early the following year, mounting tension between Napoleon and Russia moved the Prussians to implement a massive rearmament phase. The army raised the roster to 75,000. Under French pressure it dropped to 54,000 that autumn. The *official* tally never exceeded 42,000.[89] *Landwehr* training continued, first enrolling volunteers and then inducting men chosen by lottery. The selection generally prioritized single men over family fathers. After the period of basic training, recruits drilled twice a week. The linear tactic was abolished. Scharnhorst replaced it with the *Angriffs-Colonne* (attack column). A battalion divided into blocs of 45 men wide and eight to twelve men deep. This formation remained in use throughout the war of liberation, and indeed for another 50 years until the army was fully equipped with the Dreyse breech-loading rifle.

The Prussian army of 1813 received more modern muzzle-loaders, but maintained the same caliber as weapons in Russian, French and Austrian service. Arming the *Landwehr* was problematic. The Prussian armaments industry was not large enough to produce sufficient quantities of firearms and powder for both the standing army and auxiliary formations. In March of 1813, just 55,000 rifles were available to the *Landwehr*. Russia delivered 15,000 from a captured

French depot to the Prussian army, of which 12,447 were issued to *Landwehr* contingents. The Prussians collected another 4,000 French rifles abandoned by the *Grande Armée* during its retreat through Germany after the 1812 campaign. These were refurbished in a repair facility in Königsberg and also made available. The Pomeranian and Silesian *Landwehr* received English and Austrian rifles. In July 1813, the Royal Navy delivered 39,860 rifles with bayonets to Kolberg, of which 6,368 went to the *Landwehr*. All of its formations would not be properly armed with the *Kuhfuss* (crowbar), as muzzle-loaders were nicknamed, until the autumn campaign of 1813.[90]

Landwehr officers received the same rank and privileges as those of the regular army. The king reserved the right to appoint battalion, brigade and divisional commanders. In the East Prussian *Landwehr*, 24 out of 25 battalion commanders he chose had served in the Prussian army of 1806, at least as company chiefs. Of these, 21 belonged to the aristocracy. In the West Prussian *Landwehr*, nine out the ten battalion commanders had been majors in 1806 and one a lieutenant. All eight cavalry captains and three regimental commanders had also served in the old army. Every one of them hailed from the nobility. They often failed to recognize the character of the soldiers they led. In an engagement in August for example, the second battalion of the 1st Kurmark *Landwehr* Regiment suffered disproportionately high casualties during a bayonet charge because the commanding officer did not deploy a company of riflemen in loose order to open the attack. He considered it pointless due to his negative assessment of the *Landwehr*'s marksmanship.[91]

Very few *Landwehr* formations saw combat during the 1813 spring campaign. After a cease-fire from early June to mid-August expired, they were in the thick of the fighting. Military leaders did not field the *Landwehr* as independent divisions as once contemplated. The troops had insufficient combat experience to face seasoned units of Napoleon's army. It therefore proved better to integrate *Landwehr* battalions into various divisions of the standing army. In this way, the *Landwehr* would fight alongside professional soldiers to compensate for its lack of firsthand knowledge of what to expect in battle. As for the morale of Prussia's auxiliary formations, the impression made by the *Freiwillige Jäger* (Free-Will, in other words *Voluntary* Rifles) on the line regiments they joined soon dispelled the misgivings of army officers as to their value. The *Jäger* and regular army troops quickly bonded: "After a few weeks in the field had passed, battalion and regimental commanders could not have enough volunteer *Jäger*. No one wanted to give them up."[92]

Prerequisites were in place for Prussia to rise against the French as a unified nation. Gneisenau advocated a new nobility, consisting of "those who act with great valor, give excellent counsel, suffer serious wounds and make sacrifices for national defense in this sacred war for the fatherland."[93] Friedrich Wilhelm sensed the danger to his authority posed by the citizens' army. Boyen, who served as Bülow's chief of staff during the 1813 campaign, recalled, "The king set continuous obstacles to block the rearmament proposals of this man (Scharnhorst). This internal discord is the sole reason why at the outbreak of hostilities, Prussia was not at least 30,000 men stronger when she stepped onto the battlefield at Görschen."[94]

Chapter 15

The Wrong Side of the River

Allied with the Enemy

"The French had certainly displayed energy and spirit and had a great and talented warlord at their head," wrote one historian, "but what share of their success is due to the disunity of other nations and the mediocrity and poor judgment of enemy field commanders?" In the words of Stein, none of the statesmen of opposing Great Powers "possess the presence of mind to prop up the sinking structure of the European order or lead their peoples in a tenacious struggle for independence by endeavoring to satisfy the fair and equitable desires of each nation and remedy the lack of a constitution."[1] Napoleon proved adroit at understanding the peculiar interests of continental monarchs and at playing them off against one another. He was able to strike at them individually or in pairs while placating neighboring rulers to remain neutral during his campaigns. Some among the European intelligentsia still revered him as a champion of the rights of man because he superficially restructured the Kingdom of Westphalia to appear an enlightened state.

The reform movement in Prussia threatened to rob France of her political monopoly on "liberty and equality" so sorely lacking in absolute monarchies. Reformers grasped the necessary correlation between casting off the foreign yoke and imposing limitations on the ancestral power of their princes to win the people for the cause. Progressive forces in Germany not only strove to recover national independence but also to develop a citizens' society and found a national state in Germany. The goals set forth by the reformers for the liberation movement gave the uprising of 1813 its substance and moral superiority over the superficial concept of civic progress presented by Napoleon, which was linked to conquering other nations. In one of the ironies of history, the French despot found unlikely allies among the conservative aristocracy of German states. In February 1813 for example, patriotic officers planned to extend the rising tide of anti-French sentiment in northern Germany to the Rhine region and incite a revolt. Influential reactionaries in the coalition stifled the initiative because they did not want a populist uprising there; insurgents could prove difficult for the dynasties to manage.[2]

Preparing Prussia for a war to drive the French out was a persistent battle to overcome opposition by Friedrich Wilhelm III. Historian Frank Bauer summarized, "The historical service of the Prussian army reformers was that they forced their king and his reactionary court toadies, who feared an armed citizenry more than they did a foreign domination that was oppressive and degrading, to go to war against Napoleon, and that they created the decisive prerequisites for the successful prosecution of this struggle."[3] The king prioritized conserving the old order and appeasing Bonaparte. The reformers were at loggerheads with him not only regarding political amendment, but in advocating a foreign policy corresponding to the will of the people and their interests. Hoping to hold onto what was left of his kingdom, Friedrich Wilhelm saw salvation in winning the emperor's good will.

The king failed to realize that concessions to Napoleon guaranteed neither Prussia's survival nor the evacuation of French occupational forces. In January 1808, France's foreign minister Jean-Baptiste Champagny sent the French embassy in Petersburg a memo reading, "The emperor is satisfied with the present situation and nothing is pressuring him to alter it… The question of whether or not to evacuate Prussia does not depend just on her paying France the contributions she owes. It would be easy to reach an understanding on this point. It depends on the difficulties attendant on evacuating this country before everything between France and Russia is settled and on peace with England. The war at sea forces the emperor to remain master of the continent and he can only do this by keeping his army in Prussia."[4] Napoleon based policy toward Prussia on what serves his continental strategy.

Encouraged by the revolt in Spain, Scharnhorst, Gneisenau and Stein urged Friedrich Wilhelm to join France's enemies. Scharnhorst told the king, "Our predecessors gave the Prussian state sovereignty and the nation glory by sacrificing rivers of blood. We will be unworthy descendants if we give up without a fight everything that has been won."[5] Spain was an expansive land whose people waged a guerrilla war the French could not control and set an example for German patriots. The king was unmoved; he sent Prince Wilhelm to Paris to sign a new convention with France in September. In exchange for reducing the French military presence in Prussia, Wilhelm pledged to increase contributions to Napoleon's war chest. He allowed the French to garrison the Oder fortresses Glogau, Küstrin and Stettin with 10,000 men until full payment. No Prussian troops were to come within a day's march of the forts. He agreed to construct roads connecting the fortresses to the nearest *Rheinbund* army camps. The Prussian government recognized Bonaparte's brother as king of Spain. The treaty committed Prussia to providing France with an auxiliary corps of 12,000 men in case of a Franco-Austrian war in 1809 and with 16,000 the following year.[6]

As the Hapsburgs prepared to wage war against France once more, Stein negotiated with Austria regarding a possible secret alliance with Prussia. After Napoleon demanded Stein's dismissal, the king kept him in office for another three months until November 1808. Stein left for Vienna when the French ambassador in Berlin, the Marquis de Saint-Marsan, warned him to flee the country. Prior to departure, Stein advised Friedrich Wilhelm not to trust Napoleon.

He said, "To have faith in a man of whom it is so truthfully said that he has the devil in his heart and chaos in his head is more like blindness than faith."[7] The king however, considered entering a war on Austria's side too risky. He believed that only a coalition including his country, Austria, England and Russia can defy the French. On October 14, 1808, the second anniversary of the battle of Jena, Gneisenau, Grolman and five other leaders of the patriotic party signed a petition for the chief minister stating that they will refuse to allow the Paris convention to be ratified. They were informed that the king approved it several days ago without notifying them.

Only two days before, Napoleon concluded a two-week reception for Czar Alexander in Erfurt. The town was festively decorated on the emperor's order. The agenda included lavish dinner parties, balls, parades and theatrical performances staged by Parisian entertainers. Bonaparte invited all 34 *Rheinbund* princes (attendance was mandatory). The display of pomp was to impress the czar with Napoleon's grandness and alleged desire for friendship. Just before arriving in Erfurt on September 27, Alexander wrote his sister Katharina, "Bonaparte thinks I'm stupid. But whoever laughs last, laughs best."[8] Napoleon wanted a Russian alliance to protect his flank in the war against Austria. He conducted dialogs with the czar and brought along Talleyrand to help persuade him. During a private conversation with the Russian monarch however, Talleyrand said, "Your majesty, why have you come here? You must save Europe and will only succeed if you defy Napoleon. The people of France are civilized, the French ruler is not. The Russian ruler is civilized but the Russian people are not. Therefore, the Russian emperor should be the ally of the people of France."[9]

During the sessions with Napoleon, the czar proved a tough negotiator. Amid escalating outbursts of anger from the French warlord, Alexander wrested approval to occupy Finland and the Danube principalities Moldau and Walachei, the present-day Romania. Bonaparte agreed to withdraw his troops from the Grand Duchy of Warsaw (They were needed in Spain anyway). In return for these concessions, the czar allowed France a free hand to deal with the Spanish uprising and pledged to send troops to assist her in the looming war against Austria. The latter promise was worthless; after leaving Erfurt, Alexander wrote Vienna that in case of war, Austria has nothing to fear from Russia. During the following years, Talleyrand sold the Russians every state secret that he learned of via his friend Fouché, the French minister of police.[10] Napoleon in fact had already relieved Talleyrand of his post as foreign minister because of his suspected involvement in a plot to replace him with Murat. The imperator made Talleyrand accompany him to Erfurt because he prized his skill at diplomacy.

Napoleon's efforts to gain the czar's favor contrast sharply with his imperious attitude toward Prussia; he bluntly dictated terms to Prince Wilhelm at the convention in Paris. Friedrich Wilhelm could have placed France in an embarrassing position had he been less compliant while Napoleon was trying to appease Russia and simultaneously address Spanish and Austrian belligerency. On February 20,

1809, Scharnhorst drafted a memo calculating that with English financial aid, Prussia could field 100,000 troops against France in a coalition war on Austria's side. This would also deprive the French of the auxiliary corps Prussia was obligated by the Paris convention to provide. Scharnhorst reasoned that the Spanish rebellion will siphon significant French reserves and prevent Napoleon from throwing the full weight of his armed forces against the Hapsburgs. Prussian control of the Silesian fortresses would be another obstacle to the French.

Friedrich Wilhelm could not commit. He considered the leadership of the Austrian army inept, having suffered so many defeats in the past. Also, the king was skeptical of promised support from England, since she had provided financial assistance too late in the 1806/07 war to influence the outcome. When the czar refused to entertain the Prussian proposal for a military alliance with Austria and Prussia, this more or less settled the matter for Friedrich Wilhelm. He agreed to reconsider were the Russians to remain neutral and the Austrians to surprise Europe with early victories such as conquering the duchy of Warsaw, but this was no different than fence-sitting. The spineless policy not to offend Napoleon provoked discontent among civil servants and patriots. For example, on May 05 and May 13, the district councils of the province of Prussia repudiated their sovereign's demands that they issue dominion bonds to help cover contributions to France.

Austria declared war on France on April 09, 1809. This prompted German activists to rise against the French without the king's authority. On the 28th the Saxon-born Major Schill, who had fought at Auerstedt and at Kolberg, arbitrarily led his hussar regiment out of Berlin. The purpose was ostensibly to conduct maneuvers. He rode instead to Westphalia to instigate a revolt against the government of Jérôme Bonaparte. Aware of what Schill was contemplating, Scharnhorst had already written him the previous January, "You're at a good post and the time is near when we can count on energetic action… It would be good if you could then try to take Magdeburg and start an insurrection in central Germany. You would not be wanting of the participation of the people there. But wait for the signs and undertake nothing prematurely."[11] Schill did not heed this sage advice and jumped the gun.

Although Westphalian deserters joined Schill's force, the operation did not gain populist support and his troop retreated to Stralsund. There he was overpowered by Napoleon's Dutch and Danish auxiliaries and fell in battle on May 31. He became a martyr for the German independence movement. Schill had started the operation after receiving reports exaggerating the success of Colonel Wilhelm von Dörnberg, a veteran of Blücher's defense of Lübeck who persuaded Jérôme's guard in Kassel to revolt. His mission also failed. Most Westphalians remained loyal to Jérôme, known in the kingdom as *König Lüstig* (the Pleasure King). Despite public acclaim for Schill and Dörnberg throughout Prussia, Friedrich Wilhelm was furious over the "unparalleled insubordination" of the two officers. In a letter to minister Goltz, he described people who laud them as

Verkündigung des Todesurteiles,
an die 11 Schill'schen Offiziere.

After Schill's death, Napoleon ordered eleven of his captured officers shot. Following a sham trial, they listen to the sentence read by a French officer. They were executed in Wesel on September 16, 1809. Some officers Napoleon condemned to become galley slaves.

"rabble and fools."[12] The Prussian monarch discharged L'Estocq and Tauentzien from their Berlin posts and arrested Major Chasot for not notifying the crown when Schill's regiment left the capital in April. He later ordered officers returning from Schill's expedition court-martialed.

When news of Napoleon's defeat by the Austrians at Aspern reached Prussia, Blücher asked Friedrich Wilhelm to provide 30,000 men for him to drive the French from the country. The general wrote, "If this isn't ordered, then I will go and devote what energy I still have to my distressed German fatherland as best I can. Whoever wants to can wear chains, but I won't!"[13] Gneisenau and Scharnhorst signed a joint letter to their sovereign urging military support for Austria: "If your majesty continues to defer a decision demanded by the necessity, security and honor of your crown any longer… Austria will either conquer or perish."[14] The king persuaded himself that Archduke Karl's failure to capitalize on his victory and pursue the retreating French after Aspern is evidence of poor leadership. He took no action. A frustrated Stein wrote, "Prussia will perish without regret or lasting glory. It will be considered a blessing when a power that had once rocked all of Europe with its ambition and after that becomes unsettled by its own fumbling, that has fulfilled its duty neither to itself nor to the European states, ceases to exist."[15]

Napoleon defeated Archduke Karl at Wagram in July and concluded a cease-fire. Prussian patriots still advocated taking up arms. Hardenberg was among those who believed that "only an alliance of the (Prussian) monarchy with Austria… can smash the French empire."[16] Beyme reacted to the king's do-nothing attitude during the war as follows: "We've ruined our relations with everyone thanks to our vacillating policies. Everything, even the glory we gained from our stalwartness during the misfortunes of 1806 and 1807 is lost again." Count Dohna wrote, "The crushing news we've received of the cease-fire makes decisive resolve to intervene more urgent now than ever."[17] The king saw the French victory at Wagram as proof that he was right not to have become involved; disregarding of course, the influence that over 100,000 Prussian troops fighting on Austria's side would have exercised on the battle. In 1809 he outlawed the *Tugendbund* (League of Virtue), a quasi-Masonic association of proactive German patriots including Scharnhorst, Gneisenau and Schill.

Napoleon's victory had a negative consequence for Prussia. This was the dismissal of Austria's foreign minister Count Johann Philipp von Stadion, a leading proponent of social reform. Austria had declared war on France in 1809 on his initiative. Franz I replaced Stadion with Metternich. A political chameleon like Talleyrand, the new minister conducted a clandestine pro-French policy to keep Napoleon in office as a counterweight to Russia and England. Metternich therefore supported the *Rheinbund* as France's ally and opposed mass participation of its German population in a war of liberation. France required the allegiance of the *Rheinbund* princes to maintain control over central Europe. In Saxony for example, there was consequently no reform. "Diplomatic and military necessities required that Napoleon placate the princes and their aristocracies," wrote Dufraisse, which "meant that he could not export the principles of 1789… He had to accept that the constitution of the Confederation of the Rhine expressly guarantees the seigneurial and feudal rights of the annexed princes, a stipulation that set sharp limits to the abolition of feudalism elsewhere."[18]

This circumstance pitted Napoleon squarely against social and political reform. Inside of France, the last important public officials who were affiliated with the previous revolutionary government were replaced, most of them by aristocrats of the former *Ancien Régime* (the pre-1789 order). "In June of 1810, the dismissal of Fouché represented the final break with personnel inherited from the Revolution… Administrative authority came to take precedence over elective, to the benefit of the nobility, large property holders and high-level bureaucrats."[19] The resurrection of Germany was unthinkable without dethroning Napoleon. She could not wrest her freedom from France without breaking the preeminence of the German princes in league with him. Metternich crafted an Austrian foreign policy that indirectly supported Napoleon by promoting the old order. It completely disregarded the future social and economic welfare of European populations. He became "the most important defender of dynastic-reactionary interests" on the continent.[20]

French forces in action at Wagram. Napoleon's army suffered almost as many casualties as the Austrians and was too weak to pursue them when they retreated. Of nearly 300,000 men engaged on both sides, 74,000 were killed or wounded.

Austria under Metternich's influence would never fully commit to a war against Napoleon, which was becoming tantamount to a war against absolutism, even though Bonaparte's heavy-handed diplomacy would eventually force Vienna to side with Prussia. With the Hapsburg state temporarily sidelined after Wagram, the Germans looked to the east for salvation as Franco-Russian relations deteriorated. Galled by the token support the czar provided for his war against Austria, Napoleon augmented the duchy of Warsaw. Ethnic Poles saw this as a foundation to reestablish their old empire. Alexander demanded that he pledge not to restore the kingdom of Poland, but Bonaparte refused. Inside Russia, the alliance imposed at Tilsit was unpopular. The people resented their country reduced to a junior partner in European affairs. The tenanted aristocracy opposed strict compliance with the Continental System because it interfered with the export of Russian grain to England. The czar permitted the English to trade with his country as long as their ships do not fly the British ensign. He also imposed a tariff on French wares imported into Russia.

One country Napoleon exempted from the continental blockade; *France.* He introduced a licensing system for French seafarers. It allowed them to ferry flour, grain and alcoholic beverages to England and return with cotton and colonial wares. All other countries affiliated with France were restricted by the embargo. This was greatly resented in Russia. Despite loose observance of the blockade, her overseas trade had declined by 53 percent from 1806 to 1808.[21] On December 30, 1810, the czar publicly lifted restrictions on nautical commerce with the British Empire. Bonaparte discreetly began preparations for a campaign against Russia. During the final days of 1810, Scharnhorst advised Hardenberg that 30,000 French troops are marching across Hanover, destination unknown. In January 1811, Scharnhorst warned the Russian ambassador that Napoleon plans to invade Russia. Heeding the warning, the czar wrote Friedrich Wilhelm in March that although he will not give Napoleon a pretext to attack, war with France is probable. He proposed an alliance with Prussia and promised to compensate her for damages sustained in the conflict.

Early in 1810, Napoleon suffered another affront from Alexander. The French emperor needed an heir to perpetuate his bloodline and stifle family intrigues. He annulled his childless, faithless marriage to the elegant Josephine that year, much to the resentment of the army. During the search for a suitable replacement, Bonaparte was mortified that the czar refused him the hand of a Russian princess. Seeking to dismantle the Franco-Russian alliance, Metternich, with his sovereign's approval, offered Bonaparte the 19-year-old Archduchess Marie-Louise of Hapsburg. Anxious to marry into European royalty, Napoleon consented but cynically remarked, "It is a womb I am marrying."[22] Since Napoleon's new bride, who privately referred to him as the "Corsican ogre," was the great niece of Marie Antoinette, French republicans regarded the marriage as another slap in the face to the principles of the Revolution. The affair further weakened Napoleon's alliance with Alexander and set the stage for Metternich to support France in the approaching clash of arms.

Situated between two empires about to fight one another, Prussia could not remain neutral. Hardenberg and Scharnhorst escalated the tempo of armaments production and mass conscription. They concealed the scale of rearmament from Napoleon as much as possible. The measures could not entirely escape the attention of French investigators. A welcome pretext was enforcement of the continental blockade. Berlin told the French ambassador that raising troop strength is necessary to garrison North Sea ports like Danzig, Kolberg and Pillau to prevent British smugglers from landing there. On March 14, 1811, the war department announced that the entire coast must be patrolled. Twelve days later, Yorck toured seaside towns in Pomerania and Prussia to determine how many soldiers will be required. The Prussians of course harbored no animosity toward the British. Scharnhorst remarked that "England is the only state that cannot be dominated by Napoleon and will defy him, and can and will stay true to her commitments."[23]

In mid-April, Metternich announced that Austria will remain neutral if France and Russia go to war. He voiced his government's objection to "Russian expansionist plans" (naturally overlooking those of Napoleon). Hardenberg wrote in his diary, "We have to pick a definite side and not make the same old mistakes."[24] He concluded that in view of Metternich's position, an alliance with France instead of with the czar is his country's better option. Were Prussia to fight on the Russian side, Napoleon would destroy her after his victory. Moreover, should the czar opt for waging a defensive war in his own domain, the Prussian state would be indefensible. Scharnhorst protested that the only reason Prussia survived after the 1806/07 campaign is because Alexander refused to allow her to be dismembered by France at Tilsit. Were the king to reject the czar's present offer for an alliance, then he will forfeit Russia's good will. Were an isolated Russia subsequently vanquished by the French, there will be no one to help protect Prussia from Napoleon, whose hostility toward her has been demonstrated time and again.

Hardenberg retorted that the czar's support at Tilsit was predicated on Russian national interest and not on friendship. He predicted that Napoleon will reward Prussia for her loyalty in the coming war by mollifying the terms he has imposed and restore some of her confiscated territory. Hardenberg denied Scharnhorst's accusation that he "has always hoped for an affiliation with France." He stated instead that "I will always regard it as a necessary evil."[25] On July 08, 1811, a memo from Prince Hatzfeld, the man who had welcomed Napoleon to Berlin in 1806, abruptly put Hardenberg's delusional faith in Napoleon to rest. He described his recent conversations with Hugues-Bernard Maret, the new French foreign minister, and Bonaparte himself. Hatzfeld sensed the duplicity of their assurances and concluded that Prussia's security is not on the agenda. Upon reading the memo, Hardenberg displayed that quality so admirable in politicians, an unabashed reversal in policy and principles. He now accepted Scharnhorst's view that Napoleon plans to annihilate Prussia. The king wrote the czar and promised to side with him in the event of war.

Prussian patriots continued military preparations. On August 26, Hardenberg told French ambassador Saint-Marsan that Prussian rearmament is to support France in case she offers Friedrich Wilhelm an alliance against Russia; the opposite of the assurances he made to the czar. From Paris, Maret wrote Marsan in Berlin that Prussian rearmament makes a bad impression on the emperor and he suspects that its purpose is to incite Russia to war. Saint-Marsan relayed this to Hardenberg. He sugar-coated it by claiming that Maret communicated Napoleon's disapproval "in confidence and in a very friendly and delicate way."[26] Anxious not to offend the imperator, Friedrich Wilhelm rescinded the order to establish another 40 reserve and eleven depot battalions and increase the number of men per infantry company. On September 21, Marsan returned with Napoleon's insistence that Prussia agree within three days to disarm. Upon learning of this outrageous demand, Gneisenau urged doubling the pace of rearmament.

At this time, Hardenberg received another assurance from Alexander that he will regard a French invasion of Prussia as an attack on Russia herself and that in case of war, he will not conclude peace with Napoleon unless Prussian sovereignty is guaranteed. Scharnhorst expressed confidence in these pledges in an official report. He wrote, "All of the czar's statements display the utmost frankness and sincerity. He conceals none of his intentions that could be disadvantageous to us. He makes no promises he is unwilling to keep."[27] Meanwhile, there was no end to Napoleon's bullying; on October 07, Marsan insisted on partial demobilization of Prussian troop strength in Pomerania, Prussia and Mark County. His complaint about Blücher led to his being relieved as military commander in Pomerania. Tauentzien took charge in his stead. The secretary of the French legation, Lefebvre, received authorization to tour the provinces to personally monitor the progress of disarmament. The king meekly accepted. Gneisenau said that the terms "are regarded by all upright Prussians as a disgrace that is being forced on them."[28]

Months had passed since Friedrich Wilhelm had requested an alliance with France in May. The only response was a series of one-sided demands from Paris. Perhaps encouraged by the king's continuous acquiescence, Napoleon tightened the thumbscrews on October 29, 1811. He instructed Marsan to inform Berlin that ratification is contingent on Prussia joining the *Rheinbund*. This would be no different than her becoming a vassal of France and relinquishing independence. The *Rheinbund* press maintained a total blackout of news about Prussian civic reform and ridiculed Scharnhorst and Stein as *hirnverbrannt* (crazy).[29] At this time, Schöler reported that thanks to Scharnhorst's negotiations in Petersburg, the czar is prepared to "regard the seizure of any lands belonging to the king and any attack on his state, even in the form of a significant concentration of troops on the Vistula for example, as a declaration of war and will advance with the entire Russian army as soon as the king requires."[30] Hardenberg implored his sovereign to conclude an alliance with Alexander.

Friedrich Wilhelm remained inclined to side with France. He was so in awe of Napoleon that he considered resistance pointless. Another factor influenced his decision: Gneisenau had developed a comprehensive plan to organize a national insurrection patterned after the partisan war in Spain. It envisioned creation of a third fighting force in addition to the regular army and the *Landwehr*. This was the *Landsturm*, local militia resembling American Minutemen. Its members would wear no uniform and employ guerrilla warfare techniques. They would ambush not only French garrison troops and supply convoys but kill collaborators as well. Gneisenau himself wrote, "The enemy may imagine that he is introducing order. For the purpose of hurting him we will organize disorder. He will find it difficult to enlist officials for his administration and will have to bring in either ignorant foreigners or those from the dregs of our society. The severe means they will be forced to adopt to attain their goals will provoke the anger of the population even more."[31]

Plans for a violent national uprising against oppression is the last thing that an absolute monarch like Friedrich Wilhelm wanted to read about. He scribbled in the margin of Gneisenau's proposal, "Who will be able to direct this mess and who wants to?"[32] The king no longer heeded the counsel of Hardenberg and the patriots. To their anger and dismay, he listened instead to members of his entourage who prioritized the integrity of the absolute system. Among the most prominent was Pastor Friedrich Ancillon, a professor at the military academy and the crown prince's tutor. He encouraged the king to favor the French alliance as the better option for safeguarding the monarchy. Of like mind was Christian Friedrich Scharnweber. He drafted an insulting table of punishments for possible offenses committed by *Landsturm* militiamen beyond their military purpose such as "resistance to authority, intimidation, rebellion or mayhem, theft, highway robbery, assault and so forth."[33] This decree clearly reveals what proponents of the absolute state genuinely thought of the common people who were arming to save the throne.

On November 03, 1811, the king opted for the French alliance. He wrote Hardenberg, "Waging any war against the genius and superior power of Napoleon has always appeared questionable to me and without favorable prospects. Such a risky enterprise could still be worth attempting had Russia reached an understanding with Austria and both were willing to devote all of their resources to it. Prussia could then join them and risk her salvation through war one more time. But as long as these two principal powers do not want to make common cause with one another, any war between Russia and France, if Prussia fights on the Russian side, will unavoidably result in her destruction."[34] Friedrich Wilhelm therefore chose a path more likely to safeguard his throne than win freedom for his country. Napoleon marched troops into Brandenburg and Pomerania without notice in February. This was to strongarm the king into accepting harsher terms. In Paris, General Krusemarck signed the compact with France on February 24, 1812. The king ratified it on March 05.

The treaty required Prussia to provide Napoleon with an auxiliary corps of 20,000 men and 60 cannons for the invasion of Russia. The other half of the army was to remain in fortresses. No Prussian troop movements could take place without French permission. French commandants were to assume command of Graudenz and Kolberg. This may have been a personal issue for Napoleon, since these fortresses enjoyed renown for successfully defying his siege corps in 1807. The treaty obligated Prussia to provide the *Grande Armée*, which in name had ceased to exist in October 1808 but was reformed for the approaching campaign, with war materiel. This included 100 tons of rye, 200 tons of wheat, 325 tons of hay, six million bushels of oats, 44,000 oxen, 15,000 horses, two million bottles of beer, 300 tons of gunpower and 150 tons of lead. The Prussians were to make 3,600 horse-drawn carts available to haul supplies between Magdeburg and the Russian border.[35] The French had the right to march troops across Prussia and police the routes themselves.

Every French officer reserved the right to requisition foodstuffs and supplies at his discretion without objection from local magistrates or the population. It is impossible to imagine Friederich the Great ever signing such a compact. That same month Napoleon violated the agreement by occupying Spandau and Pillau. In the spring of 1812, his army entered East Prussia. The province had already suffered during the campaign of 1807 and could scarcely support hundreds of thousands of French troops. On May 02, the governor of Marienwerder, Ludwig Wissmann, wrote the finance ministry in Berlin, "The cattle are dying from starvation and the roads are covered with dead farm horses. There is no time for sowing and no more corn. The winter seed, so promising for a good harvest, must now be used for grazing."[36] Two weeks before Wissmann wrote Berlin, a Düsseldorf newspaper reported that Napoleon is still in Paris, "enjoying the many fruits of the arduous campaigns he has so gloriously led for the welfare of humanity and to reform the world."[37] For his part, the king of Prussia disallowed an initiative by Prussian Field Marshal Wilhelm de Courbière to reinforce and defend the garrison of Graudenz on his own.

The Death of an Army

After the Tilsit treaty, Napoleon continuously interfered in Prussian internal affairs. In 1810, the French ambassador told Hardenberg the emperor "disapproves" of Scharnhorst and wants him removed as chief of the *Allgemeines Kriegsdepartement* (Universal War Department). On June 06, the king complied. Newspaper reports the next day cited the cause as poor health. The reformer remained officially in charge of the general staff and the engineer corps. He signed an agreement on June 30 with his replacement as chief of the war department, General Hake, for Hake to make all reports available to him so that he can formulate the appropriate measures. Scharnhorst then forwarded his proposals to the king. Hake implemented them upon the sovereign's approval. In this way, Scharnhorst's role remained concealed from the French. Only Hardenberg, Boyen, Hake and Friedrich Wilhelm were aware of the covert arrangement. Scharnhorst also oversaw all inventions improving the artillery, engineer corps and infantry armament. That summer he inspected the Silesian fortresses and accompanied his sovereign to review the Silesian brigade.

By 1812, Gneisenau and Blücher were also out of office at Napoleon's behest. Blücher's fault was digging fortifications in Pomerania. These officers were particularly frustrated with critics in the army and royal entourage who welcomed their dismissals. Kalckreuth once tried without success to persuade the king that Scharnhorst is planning a coup. Scharnhorst complained to friends that "our grand seniors know nothing of chivalry and just want to enjoy life. The sentiments and spirit of the upper classes appear more like those of slaves than free, highborn Germans." Reacting to the February 1812 compact, Gneisenau wrote a colleague, "Thanks to cowardice we have signed a treaty of submission that soils us with shame, relinquishes the blood and the property of the people to foreign caprice and exposes the royal family to noticeable danger. The king has given in to his bitterest enemy with hands and feet bound, who will surely topple his throne if Russia is conquered… Never before was a ruler overthrown so

Napoleon's troops parade through a German town on their way east to invade Russia in the summer of 1812. During the years of occupation, not a single French general or military governor was assassinated by the Germans.

voluntarily."[38] Thirty Prussian officers, including Clausewitz and Boyen, were so disgusted that they left the army to fight for the czar. Friedrich Wilhelm threatened some with seizure of property and assets, forfeiture of military decorations and titles and even execution.[39]

After four months of rearmament during 1811, Prussia had a trained force of 124,000 soldiers. She could have mustered 300,000 men had arrangements been made for timely delivery of English ordnance. Also, the Russians deployed 182,000 men on their western frontier. Had Friedrich Wilhelm concluded an alliance with the czar, the combined force could have negated French preparations for a Russian campaign or at very least crushed France's allies Poland and Saxony. This would have forced Metternich to reconsider supporting the French. Instead, Austria provided 30,000 men to guard the right flank of the *Grande Armée* during the invasion of Russia. In December 1811, Scharnhorst had tried to persuade Metternich to join the coalition against France. The passive attitude of Friedrich Wilhelm allowed Napoleon to amass a fighting force in East Prussia of nearly half a million men. "Except in the guard regiments, only one-tenth of the French units were tested veterans," observed Dufraisse.[40]

During the final months of peace, the czar did not make the mistakes Prussia did in 1806 when mobilizing for war. He conducted a skillful foreign policy to rob the enemy of potential allies and adopted a military strategy suited to the geographic characteristics of his empire. In April 1812, he lured Sweden from Napoleon's camp by giving her the green light to annex Norway. He sidelined Turkey, another power the French had hoped to turn against Russia, by offering territorial concessions and concluding a treaty in May. The sultan was already acquainted with Bonaparte's duplicity; at Tilsit, Napoleon had offered to support Russia in violation of France's alliance with Turkey. Alexander made peace with England in July. In the military sphere, he told the Prussian ambassador of the plan "to draw out the war as long as possible, engage in no major battles without the probability of a good outcome, only attack the enemy when it can be done with a vastly superior force, draw him further away from his sources of supply and await him in positions favored by natural surroundings."[41]

On June 24, 1812, the *Grande Armée* crossed the Nemen River into czarist territory. Napoleon presumed that Russia's serfs, inspired by the French Revolution, would rebel against their masters and welcome the invader. He of course had no interest in their emancipation, since this would compromise reconciliation with the czar. The French fielded approximately 450,000 troops. The Prussian corps helped cover the left flank of the army. The Russian commander was Michael Barclay de Tolly, a general of Scottish ancestry who had done much to modernize the army. He frustrated the French strategy by steadily withdrawing his outnumbered force. The Russians burned villages and granaries, evacuated foodstuffs and left little for the enemy to subsist on. Russian rearguards inflicted casualties on Napoleon's advance guard. Patrols and bands of partisans raided French supply columns and depots.

The barren countryside lacked grazing land for the French horses and oxen. Supply trains could not haul enough fodder for the animals. The summer heat and inadequate sources of water caused many of them to perish. This diminished the transportation capacity of Napoleon's army and resulted in shortages. The French exhausted themselves chasing an elusive enemy. The rigors of campaigning in monotonous, uncultivated land and insufficient delivery of provisions contributed to the outbreak of dysentery and other disorders. By mid-August, sickness and desertion had thinned the ranks of the *Grande Armée* by 150,000 men.[42] Another 90,000 were gradually detached to garrison towns and depots and protect rearward communications. By the time Napoleon fought a major engagement at Smolensk from August 16 to 18, he commanded a force of 185,000 men.

Barclay's strategy was working, but relinquishing territory without giving battle looked bad in the press. Caving in to criticism from Prince Bagration and other commanders over the perpetual withdrawal, Alexander ordered Barclay to make a stand at Smolensk. This formidable fortress of 12,600 inhabitants was 230 miles west of Moscow. Eager to come to grips with his adversary, Napoleon planned an enveloping attack to cut off the Russian line of retreat. After fierce fighting however, Barclay escaped with his army intact. He eluded the trap in part due to the dogged resistance of Bagration's infantry defending Smolensk and the poor judgment of Ney who, like in 1807, proved unable to successfully direct large formations in offensive operations. Smolensk was virtually destroyed by bombardment in the battle. Napoleon listed his losses at 700 dead and 3,100 wounded. The actual figure was closer to 10,000. Georges Mouton's corps alone lost 6,000 men.[43] Russian casualties were somewhat higher.

All Napoleon gained from the bloodletting was capturing a burned-out fortress. After contemplating whether or not to abandon the entire enterprise, he resumed the march east. Considering Barclay's retreat tactic demoralizing, the czar appointed General Michail Kutusov the new commander in chief with Barclay in charge of a corps. Even though Kutusov approved of his predecessor's strategy, he was under orders to give battle. The Russians turned to fight again at Borodino. This is a town about 75 miles west of Moscow. The terrain lacked natural defenses but was selected because it blocks the road from Smolensk to the capital. Napoleon had 126,000 soldiers under his command. He faced a Russian army of 155,000. The attack plan he conceived does little credit to his reputation as a general. He ignored Davout's advice to outflank the Russians. Instead, he attempted to punch directly through their line, which Kutusov reinforced with redoubts and trenches.

Fought on September 07, 1812, the battle of Borodino was one of the bloodiest of the Napoleonic wars. The French eventually wore down the Russians and compelled them to retreat. Bonaparte could have routed his adversaries had he committed the Imperial Guard as his generals urged him to do. He felt it important to preserve this superb corps, the trump card of his army, and did not order it forward. This saved the Russian army from destruction. Kutusov withdrew his troops in good order. The French counted approximately 34,000 casualties and the Russians around 44,000, though estimates vary.[44] Murat's corps entered Moscow on September 14. The city was almost deserted. Soon fires broke out in various quarters. The flames transformed the capital with its many wooden structures into a conflagration. Russian incendiaries are believed to have torched the city to deprive the invaders of shelter and provisions. Upon the advice of Freiherr vom Stein and Prussian officers in Russian service, the czar left Napoleon's surrender demands unanswered.

The *Grande Armée* languished in Moscow for over a month. Kutusov's army the French had failed to destroy at Borodino threatened their supply lines. Napoleon led his famished troops from the capital on October 19 and began the odyssey west. Five days later, Kutusov blocked his attempt to use a parallel road to the south of the Smolensk-Moscow highway. This forced the French to march back along the route that they had taken east during early autumn. It was badly furrowed from the earlier passage and the surrounding countryside had already been picked clean of anything to sustain the army. Caulaincourt recalled, "Our junior officers had become accustomed to rapid success after the campaigns in Italy and Germany with the wealth of resources these countries have to offer. In

Survivors of the *Grande Armée's* Russian campaign trudge westward.
They subsequently crossed Germany unmolested. Prussians rejoiced in
the verse, *Mit Mann und Ross und Wagen, so hat sie Gott geschlagen*
(With man, steed and chariot, God has struck them down)!

Russia, we paid dearly for this custom of always expecting victory. The glorious
practice of always marching forward made us just like schoolboys in the art of
retreat."[45] Anticipating a short campaign, Napoleon had ordered neither warm
apparel for the soldiers nor spiked shoes for the horses to afford traction on ice.
As temperatures dropped, men and animals, their resistance to the harsh climate
weakened by hunger, succumbed to the elements. Raids by Cossacks and harassing attacks by the Russian army further thinned the ranks.

Toward the end of November, Marshal Victor's IX Corps fought a desperate
rearguard action while the rest of Napoleon's army traversed the Berezina River
on two overcrowded bridges constructed by French engineers. Nearly 30,000
troops were lost here in combat, drowning trying to swim the icy waters or cut
off on the eastern bank. During the next two weeks, thousands of survivors
who had escaped to the western side were rounded up by pursuing Cossacks.
On December 14, the last of the *Grande Armée* trudged over the Neman River
bridge back into the duchy of Warsaw. Out of 612,000 troops including reinforcements that had participated in the campaign, about 18,000 crossed. Only
half of them were fit for duty.[46] Loison's division lost seven-tenths of its complement in three days. The artillery forfeited 1,200 cannons. All the field equipment
and most of the horses were gone. Out of 50,000 members of the Imperial Guard

that had marched into Russia, just 500 were effective on December 21 and 800 were sick or injured. The II, III and IV Corps, 125,000 men at full roster, had 6,400 men left.[47]

Napoleon left the troops on December 05 to travel to Paris with a mounted escort. At Grodno, he reached the Nemen River nine days ahead of the army. His sledge glided onto a ferry. Napoleon asked the boatman, "Have many French deserters already come across?" The boatman answered, "No sir, you're the first."[48] The emperor tried to prevent details of the fiasco in Russia from reaching central Europe, but the Berlin press reported on November 12 that his army has abandoned Moscow and on the 21st that Napoleon is in Smolensk. The Berezina disaster made coverage on December 10. Four days later, newspapers in Breslau announced that the imperator has passed Glogau. He was travelling via secondary roads with a small escort to avoid attention. "Since mid-November," as Lehmann described, "reports about the huge catastrophe in Russia began reaching Berlin. One from the army that arrived on November 18 emphasized that it is in a sorry state and considered wiped out; that according to statements of every soldier and every Jew coming from the army, faith in the invincibility of the French has been extinguished."[49]

There was more comprehensive press coverage after Berezina. One account described the *Grande Armée*'s circumstances as follows: "Anyone who can escape is fleeing. All order in the army is gone. No corps, no regiment is intact anymore. Only the Imperial Guard can still boast otherwise. No description can accurately portray the horrible conditions facing the army as it rushes to at least reach Vilnius, relentlessly pursued by the merciless Cossacks, ten of whom can chase down 200 Frenchmen at a time with impunity."[50] Prussian officers like Clausewitz, Boyen and Scharnhorst's son-in-law Count Karl von Dohna-Schlobitten, who served in the czar's army during the 1812 campaign, laid the foundation for a Russo-Prussian alliance to defeat Bonaparte. Stein persuaded Alexander to carry the war onto German soil after driving the French from the east. Scharnhorst wrote Hardenberg, "No one in Russia is talking about peace, but also nothing is being said about conquering foreign territory. Their only thought is to destroy the French."[51]

Never before was Napoleon so weak as in this hour. In some formations there were more surviving officers than men. Remaining operational units included Charles Grandjean's division of 12,000 men on the northern wing and two Saxon divisions with a combined strength of 10,000 troops from Prince Karl zu Schwarzenberg's corps in the south. Together with the remnants of Loison's division, the Durette and Heudelet Divisions and Jacques Cavaignac's cavalry brigade, all Napoleon could muster was 41,200 men. A portion of this force had to be detailed to fortress garrisons. Widespread illness depleted the rosters. Napoleon attempted a mass recruitment in the duchy of Warsaw, but not even death threats for noncompliance induced the Poles to respond to the call to arms. On December 14, Bonaparte had the cheek to demand that Friedrich

Wilhelm raise the Prussian contingent of the *Grande Armée* to 30,000 men without offering anything in return. Instead of responding with a declaration of war, which would likely have prevented any French soldiers from reaching the Rhine, the king debated with his advisors. Hardenberg asked in his diary, "Why not destroy the French during their retreat?"

The cabinet urged Friedrich Wilhelm on December 17 to order the *Grande Armée*'s Prussian auxiliary corps to turn on the French. The next day, Hake stated that the enemy will be unable to defend the Vistula and the Russians will cut off Marshal Etienne Macdonald's corps, which Yorck's contingent belongs to, from the rest of the French army. Hardenberg, Knesebeck and Ancillon agreed that public attitude in Prussia is so volatile that if the government does not act soon, a national uprising will break out on its own. In Marwitz's assessment, "The king of Prussia, if he does not hesitate, has a great head start over Napoleon. (Napoleon) has to reassemble his dispersed, weaponless army, put to rest misgivings in France and organize a new army. The king has his army in Silesia ready for action and can gain control for himself of all the resources of northern Germany that both sides are counting on. It's a matter of whether the king of Prussia wants to retake the throne of his forefathers or not. His great ancestor would not have been in doubt for an instant about what to do."[52]

To add to French woes, Kutusov rallied the Russian army to march into German territory. He drafted a proclamation for the troops reading, "Fruitful provinces have become wastelands and transformed into Steppes. Flourishing cities lie in ashes, leveled. The manufacturing industry has disintegrated and the prosperity of many good, peaceful citizens has been undermined. The blood of many a valiant warrior has been shed… This haughty enemy crossed our frontier with grandeur, assuming the right to usurp what is ours. Nothing seemed more certain to him than enslaving us. And what could prevent him? He was dealing with barbarians who in his opinion are a hundred years behind him in enlightenment. His arrival was supposed to herald a new era… true enlightenment is not about a hypocritical countenance, smooth talk, convention or the cut of one's clothes."[53] Most of Kutusov's officers wanted to end the war now that the *Grande Armée* had been driven from the motherland. Alexander resolved to carry the fight into Germany to rid Europe of Napoleon for good. He also planned to annex the duchy of Warsaw.

Even though the czar had repeatedly assured Schöler, the Prussian envoy in Petersburg, he intends to restore Prussia's prewar frontiers, none of Friedrich Wilhelm's advisors endorsed a compact with Russia. In yet another reversal, Hardenberg hoped that were Prussia to remain true to the French alliance, Napoleon will reward her with a slice of Poland to augment the kingdom. Knesebeck and Hardenberg feared that Cossacks will overrun their country. The king was concerned about Metternich's hostility toward Russia; were Prussia to conclude an alliance with her, it might cause Austria to side with France. Friedrich Wilhelm and Hardenberg therefore maintained a "wait and see" policy that was unsuitable for the time and made no use of the advantages their country temporarily enjoyed over France. As Georg Kausch described, "Instead of building on the strength of the nation to conquer or perish with it, they desperately sought foreign alliances at any price. They begged Austria for help, but Emperor Franz and Metternich let them stew. The more victorious Napoleon was, the more Hapsburg could extort from them."[54]

The deliberations took place during a crucial window of opportunity when Napoleon was practically prostrate. "The French army still had neither artillery nor cavalry," wrote Lehmann. "The panic and terror of the catastrophe that had befallen it yet lingered. The rivers were still frozen over and therefore not a protective barrier for the French who were now forced onto the defensive."[55] Bonaparte's troops in Prussia were demoralized. At the beginning of February 1813, 42 Cossacks scattered 1,500 soldiers of Davout's corps. Men of a *Rheinbund* infantry battalion threw away their rifles when charged by a party of these fearsome horsemen. On February 20, a few hundred Cossacks circumvented French lines and ventured into Berlin. Throngs of people enthusiastically cheered them in greeting. A French formation of 5,600 men did nothing to dislodge them; its commanding officer shrugged that his troops are in disorder. Concerned over provoking a confrontation, French artillerymen loaded the few remaining cannons posted at intersections with powder only. At the Hohenzollern castle, the French remained passive while the crowd seized an ammunition cart and pushed it into the river.

"We saw them pass before our battalion," a French gunner recalled, "without weapons or officers. They shouted for joy and cast menacing looks at our soldiers."[56] In some areas of Prussia, people assaulted French soldiers on the street. On New Year's Day 1813, several hundred *Krümper* recruits formed up at Königsberg Castle for review. None made an opening for a French gendarme attempting to push through the formation. Angered at this perceived impertinence, the Frenchman kicked a recruit so violently that he collapsed in pain. His comrades fell upon the gendarme and inflicted a fatal beating. Two French officers attempting to restrain the incensed *Krümper* drew their blades but were themselves assaulted. The recruits broke their swords, tore the epaulettes and headgear from their uniforms and put them to flight. Murat, who witnessed the scene from a window in the castle, sent out the guard with orders not to fire on the gathering crowd that was becoming unruly. The guardsmen arrested the Prussian corporal believed to have provoked the gendarme. The angry townspeople wrested him free on the spot.[57] The French evacuated Berlin on March 04.

Prussian army officers and civil delegations showered Friedrich Wilhelm with pleas to take up arms against refugees of the *Grande Armée*. Yorck wrote Bülow, "What are they thinking in Berlin? Have they sunk so low that they won't risk breaking the chains of slavery that we've had to wear in degradation for the last five years?"[58] At a cabinet meeting at the end of December, an exasperated Bülow asked, "Why negotiate? Why this petty protocol? Just say to Napoleon, you've dishonored us, deceived us and trampled us underfoot. You've used force on us and conducted all sorts of shameful acts in our country. That's why we want a life-or-death struggle against you to destroy you if we can." What kept the Prussian sword in its sheath was "the king's aversion of heroic plans," as Hardenberg described in a letter to Gneisenau.[59] Friedrich Wilhelm parried demands to take action with the formula response, "Napoleon is a great genius and will always find the means" to thwart his adversaries.[60] When news of Napoleon fleeing through Glogau encouraged the Prussians, the monarch wrote Hardenberg, "Embarrassing incidents from every corner will undoubtedly begin again and our situation will become even more awkward. God only knows where all this will end!"[61]

Under Ancillon's influence, the king considered his number-one priority preventing an upsurge of nationalism in Prussia. Ancillon congratulated his sovereign for imprisoning the president of Breslau, Lüttwitz, for an unauthorized call to arms. Cabinet orders of December 19 and 20 had a pronounced anti-*Russian* tenor. They proposed defensive measures such as evacuating military hardware and mustering the militia in case Kutusov's army enters Prussian territory. While Napoleon caught his breath after the escape from Russia, Friedrich Wilhelm contemplated various scenarios that hinged on the actions of Metternich, the czar and Bonaparte. Scharnhorst wrote Hardenberg on February 01, "Napoleon appears to depend on our indecisiveness. Whether in good times or in misfortune, he treats Prussia with mistrust and contempt."[62] "What madness it was," wrote Lehmann, "to hope that Napoleon can be rendered harmless in any way other than by his total destruction."[63] The king perpetually vacillated, ostensibly awaiting a favorable opportunity to take decisive action. But to wait for the right moment to take a bold step negates the very definition of boldness.

Chapter 16

Prelude to Leipzig

The Call to Arms

On June 18, 1815, the pastoral Belgian countryside was host to the battle of Waterloo, popularly fixed as the end of the Napoleonic era. Indeed, this epic confrontation between France and a multi-national army led by the Duke of Wellington, joined by Blücher's Prussians, rid Europe of a pariah who had wreaked havoc on the continent since the turn of the century. Yet the clash of arms that really broke Bonaparte was fought in October 1813, more than a year and a half earlier. As consequence of his decisive defeat at Leipzig, the battle of nations, Napoleon lost control of Poland, Italy and Holland, the *Rheinbund* was dissolved and the vassal states Bavaria, Württemburg and Saxony joined his enemies. His continental embargo on trade with England was formally abolished, even though enforcement was negligible after his defeat in Russia. The warlord whose military strategy rested in attack was gradually forced onto the defensive. The generals he faced made better use of tactics he himself had developed than he did, and troops arrayed against him fought for freedom and independence; the very ideals that had once inspired the French soldier. In a metaphoric sense, the battle of Leipzig was Napoleon's Waterloo. He survived in office for a few more months due to his skill at defensive campaigning and discord in the coalition camp.

Napoleon's centralization of command was an advantage that helped him in diplomacy as well as on the battlefield. The respective coalition states, once they became allies in June 1813, had diverse war aims. Sweden preferred a nominal commitment to harvest some territorial gains. Her crown prince preserved the army from attrition. Austria was more concerned about Russian postwar expansion than ousting Napoleon. The czar wanted Bonaparte gone but was potentially open to compromise once his empire absorbed Poland. England strove for a balance of power on the mainland to capture overseas markets without competition and pursue colonial expansion. German princes hoped to retain sovereignty over their individual fiefdoms regardless of what happened to the rest of Europe and its people. Only for Prussia was the war against Napoleon a life-and-death struggle.

Friedrich WIlhelm tried to stifle populist sentiment in Prussia instead of directing it. The celebrated dissent of Yorck at Tauroggen was an unheard-of breach of royal authority. This general had assumed command of the Prussian contingent of the *Grande Armée* in 1812 after Grawert was relieved due to illness. It was designated the 27th Division of Macdonald's corps and deployed in Courland, a region in western Latvia. Its mission was to protect the left flank of Napoleon's invasion force. Like the Austrian corps in the south, the Prussian troops were therefore spared the disastrous retreat from Moscow. Yorck had a frosty relationship with Macdonald. The Russians had been urging the Prussian corps commander to turn on Napoleon since August, but the staunch royalist would not disobey his king's wishes. He did however, hate the French occupation enough to read correspondence forwarded to him by a Russian general, Count Filippo Paulucci, on December 26. It was a letter from the czar expressing his intention to restore Prussia to her pre-1806 borders.

Yorck met with the 28-year-old Russian General Johann von Diebitsch. He was the son of a Prussian officer who had migrated to the czar's empire in 1798. Diebitsch had shadowed Yorck's corps during its retreat. He brought Clausewitz and Count Dohna-Schobitten to the parley. Wilhelm Henckel von Donnersmarck, an officer present, described the session: "The meeting of the two generals took place on a field between both armies. General von Diebitsch, who was friendly to the utmost, opened by telling the general that the Prussian column is surrounded and the French army is totally destroyed. It is therefore the general's responsibility to the king not to hesitate a moment to dissolve the unnatural pact with the French. The French, General von Diebitsch continued, are now our common enemy. He said that General von Yorck can perform a great service to the Prussian state and make his name renowned for all eternity as the first to contribute to the liberation of the Prussian state. The czar will not rest, he added, until all its territories are returned to it.

"General von Yorck remained outwardly cold and deliberate. He answered that he cannot reconcile his perception of duty to king and country with acting without orders from the king. He said that he will not hesitate for a moment to attack the general and fight his way out of the encirclement, since he sees no infantry with Diebitsch so his position must in any case be weak. While he spoke these words, one could see Yorck's inward struggle between duty and his personal feelings. General von Diebitsch repeated his arguments more emphatically. The negotiations went back and forth for a while until it was agreed that General von Yorck will march around the right with his army and lead it to Tauroggen. He will then remain neutral until orders from the king arrive. Yorck insisted that the entire affair must remain secret for the time being. Only later, on December 30, was the convention concluded at the mill at Poscherun… With this act began the immense work of our liberation from the chains of tyranny. It was General von Yorck who took this step and risked his own head in doing so."[1] Napoleon himself remarked that Yorck's action could alter the politics of Europe.

On the evening of December 29, Yorck told Clausewitz, "You have me. Tell General Diebitsch that I am firmly resolved to break with the French and their cause."[2] Yorck had sent word to Berlin, but received no instructions from the king. Friedrich Wilhelm procrastinated again, unable to reach an independent decision. Transactions at Tauroggen made him "frightened and morose."[3] Boyen recalled that Yorck's decision "upset the king beyond all measure."[4] The monarch sent Major Oldwig von Natzmer to arrest Yorck, but Russian troops would not allow him through their lines. Yorck presumed that the king, in Potsdam with 1,200 Prussian soldiers while 12,000 French troops are in Berlin and Spandau, is not free to act. He marched his corps west and halted behind Russian lines. He met with Stein and Scharnhorst in Königsberg, which the Russians had entered on January 05, 1813, to prepare the insurrection against Napoleon. Stein took over administration of East Prussia on the 22nd without bothering to ask Friedrich Wilhelm's permission. The Brandenburg dramatist Heinrich von Kleist proclaimed, "What Prussia has lost in physical strength must now be replaced with the power of her spirit."[5]

With Hardenberg again inclined toward a Russian alliance, Prussian patriots resumed war preparations on an unprecedented scale. The king was little more than a rubber stamp for more forceful personalities surrounding him and soon there would be no holding back Scharnhorst, Gneisenau, Blücher and Boyen. On January 09, Scharnhorst stressed to General Ludwig Thile, an adjutant in Hardenberg's cabinet, "I believe we need to make up for what we have neglected. Since we are on our own, we must augment our armed forces quickly and secure our fortresses." In a second letter to Thile five days later he wrote, "I cannot calmly accept that we are doing nothing to expand our armed forces. The Prussian state will become a theater of war. If the king makes use of its fighting potential and resources, this will contribute to respect for the king both within Prussia and beyond our borders. It will restore national honor and elevate our self-confidence. Smaller states can survive with a cautious posture because they do not arouse the concern and jealously of their neighbors. Greater states that do not assert themselves perish."[6]

Friedrich Wilhelm left Berlin with a military escort on January 21. Among those accompanying him was the Austrian ambassador and Ludwig von Ompteda as agent of the British government. French ambassador Marsan followed soon afterward. Before departing, the king instructed city officials to "maintain friendly cooperation with the imperial French military."[7] The king reached Breslau on the 25th. Three days later, couriers delivered the czar's letters requesting an alliance and the next day ambassador Krusemarck's report from Paris. The correspondence, together with pressure from Scharnhorst and Boyen, persuaded Hardenberg and his sovereign to pact with Russia. The alliance would be formally concluded in Kalisch on February 28. Prussia pledged to raise a *milice nationale* (national militia) of 80,000 troops for the war. A cabinet order established a commission of Scharnhorst, Hardenberg and Hake to "expand the fighting forces as rapidly and as much as possible."[8]

On February 03, Friedrich Wilhelm ordered formation of *Volontärjäger* (volunteer rifle) units; rather misnamed, since "volunteers" aged 17 to 24 with-

Volunteer *Jäger* and *Landwehr* men bid farewell to friends and family
as they prepare to join their regiments and march to the front.

out prior service were required to report for duty within eight days. The king
was pessimistic as usual. He predicted, "Calling for volunteers is really a good
idea, but no one will come!"[9] The proclamation read, "The precarious situation
confronting the state necessitates a rapid increase in the number of troops on
hand… Love of country and devotion to the king has forever possessed the
inhabitants of the Prussian monarchy and has always been most apparent in
times of danger. It requires only an historic event to channel these sentiments
and thirst for deeds that possesses so many worthy young men to reinforce the
ranks of the older defenders of the fatherland and compete to be first to fulfill
the duties demanded of us."[10] Volunteers were to finance their own uniforms
and equipment. Community-sponsored fund-raisers and merchants contributed
to the cost. Of the 24,841 men who volunteered for national regiments, *Jäger*
detachments and *Freikorps* (Volunteer Corps) and the 24,531 who enlisted in the
regular army and the *Landwehr*, 19,567 were self-equipped.[11]

Stein and his cabinet met in Yorck's house on February 05. Upon Yorck's suggestion, it formed a committee to oversee formation of an East and West Prussian
Landwehr of 20,000 men with another 13,000 in reserve. The call-up became
law on February 08. Men of 18 to 45 years of age were eligible. The war party did
not control foreign policy and in this realm Ancillon still opposed activism. He

considered arousing his countrymen "almost revolutionary."[12] For the patriots, allying with Russia was prerequisite for liberation; Ancillon advocated common cause with France. Many aristocrats shared his view. Karl Friccius, a battalion commander in the *Landwehr*, described their attitude: "A large party has formed in Breslau that even now still considers resistance to Napoleon futile. It prefers to negotiate peace with him rather than risk war. These men hope to maintain their ignominious existence through subservience, cunning and some concessions to have tranquility. They believe that creating a militia or any arming of the people will lead to the greatest misfortune imaginable, because it will jeopardize their estates and the privileges they have. Preserving these things is more important to them than the honor and salvation of the fatherland."[13]

Hardenberg rejected Ancillon's proposals. He at last accepted that compromise with Napoleon is impossible. In other German states, anti-French sentiment was also widespread though not so much among the tenanted aristocracy. In February, there was a revolt in the German Hanseatic cities, which Davout suppressed with customary brutality. When the *Freikorps* was established on February 18, the majority of those flocking to enlist were not Prussians but hailed from northwestern and central Germany.[14] Two Mecklenburg duchies and all four principalities of Anhalt later seceded from the *Rheinbund* to fight against France.[15] Resentment toward the French had spread well beyond Prussia. Napoleon's Russian adventure had cost the lives of 80,000 *Rheinbund* Germans.[16] Once back in Paris, he told a government minister, "Just what do the Parisians want? Of the 600,000 men that I lost in Russia, only 30,000 were Frenchmen. The rest were Italians, Dalmatians, Poles and (he added with a wry smile) mostly Germans."[17] Fixing French dead at 30,000 was a gross understatement; historians estimate that about half the troops in the *Grande Armée* who took part in the Moscow campaign were French.

By the time that Prussia's alliance with the czar was announced in March, some two thirds of the Prussian army had slipped from Friedrich Wilhelm's grasp. Yorck's corps left its encampment at Elding and crossed the Vistula on February 19. Three days later, he and Bülow met with Russian commander Prince Wittgenstein at Konitz and arranged to march to the Oder River. Yorck took this step on his own initiative without instructions from the king. "We live in a time of action, not of asking," he wrote Major Krauseneck.[18] Despite the poverty of population, Prussians from all classes donated 6.5 million thaler to equip the *Landwehr* and care for the wounded. Ompteda reported on February 20, "If the king refuses to make use of the resources his subordinates have placed at his disposal according to the universal will of the nation, or if he simply hesitates to support the efforts Russia is taking on to restore the Prussian monarchy, I consider the revolution unavoidable."[19]

Metternich, distraught over "Prussian Jacobinism," received an anxious letter from his ambassador in Breslau five days later: "It is difficult to describe how inflamed spirits are here. General Scharnhorst has unlimited influence. The military and heads of the sects have taken complete control of the government under the guise of patriotism. The chancellor is being swept along with the current."[20] The Austrian ambassador described Scharnhorst as "well informed and capable, but narrow-minded, petty and hated by the entire army. Slow and indecisive, nothing moves forward with him. He is also one of the leaders of this dangerous sect that surrounds the king."[21] A catechism for the troops prepared by the historian Arndt extolled the uprising for "fatherland, freedom and honor" with almost no mention of loyalty to the sovereign. Allegiance to the royal house was not included in the text of the *Fahnenschwur*, the oath to the flag taken by soldiers of the *Freikorps* upon induction. Recruits swore fealty to the fatherland. The patriotic poet and soldier Theodor Körner declared, "This is not a war that the crown understands. It is a crusade, a holy war!" The philosopher and propagandist Friedrich Schlegel called for a "total war of destruction" against the "depraved" French nation.[22]

Arndt wrote in his catechism, "The *Landsturm* and the *Landwehr* are ancient and respected traditions of the grand and mighty German people that have existed for centuries. This was so until more and more, powerful standing armies were introduced and most governments believed that they don't need militias anymore because nations are secure enough with a standing army. As result of this, the farmer and the citizen came to believe that he should from now on be a defenseless man shunning armed service and have nothing to do with the war beyond being harassed by the enemy in unlucky cases. Thanks to both this arrangement of the states and to public opinion, the skill at arms that made our ancestors such prized and feared men has been forgotten. Only in the last few years has the old belief resurfaced that an entire nation must be armed and practiced in the use of weapons if it does not want to forfeit liberty, honor, fortune, property and spirit…

"In all provinces and districts the German people must rise… Such a national war is now for all Germans: Only through a universal insurrection against the enemy, only through a brotherly and sincere unification of all elements in Germany can Europe and the fatherland be rescued and the horrible power that threatens the freedom and prosperity of the world be torn asunder."[23] A memo Gneisenau submitted to the king in April 1813 stated, "The war we envision is not a war in the usual sense. We're not fighting for a province but for the security of the throne, the independence of the nation, the most sacred values in life, and liberation from a hideous yoke that is destroying the nation's prosperity. This yoke demands our blood to help enslave other peoples who themselves have noble civilizations and reduce them to the level of a primitive culture… to entrust the safety of the throne and national independence to the standing army alone is always dangerous, especially against an enemy who sets everything against us, who risks everything to win."[24]

Gneisenau's vision of a national army in which, as he proposed, "it will be possible for the poorest day laborer to rise to the highest level" of command of course unsettled Friedrich Wilhelm, but his reluctance to lead the populist uprising cost him the right to influence its development. Once war broke out the *Landwehr* did not just fight parallel to the field army as originally planned. It also functioned as a manpower pool for replacements. A directive allowed for entire battalions of *Landwehr* to be incorporated into "the line," as the standing army was then called. The transferred unit was then reformed with new recruits. Military authorities lacked enough uniforms to fully equip the contingents, so soldiers dyed their civilian clothes black to achieve a certain harmony of dress. Black was the only dye that could cover all other fabric colors. This conformed to the tunic color of Lützow's volunteer *Jäger*, the *Lützowsches Freikorps*. The black uniform had red trim and yellow buttons; the color combination later adopted for the German national flag.

Weeks passed before the *Landwehr* law, although ratified, was publicly announced. When Marsan protested that Prussian rearmament violates treaty obligations, Hardenberg parried that the troop buildup is necessary because the Russians are in East Prussia and the king is concerned that the czar may invade. Napoleon was skeptical of this lame explanation, but powerless to prevent rearmament at this stage. The Prussian cabinet introduced new proposals to France on February 15. A month later, there was still no response from Paris. On March

Under the motto "gold for iron," patriotic citizens contribute gold wedding rings, silver tableware and other valuables to the war effort. The *Volksopfer* (people's sacrifice) assisted the financially distressed Prussian state by helping subsidize rearmament in 1813.

17, Hardenberg therefore notified Marsan that the Franco-Prussian alliance of February 1812 is void. That day, Yorck marched his corps into Berlin to the acclaim of the population. His actions at Tauroggen underscored the will of the people to take up arms against Napoleon with or without the sanction of the king. Friedrich Wilhelm issued two proclamations; *An mein Volk* (To my people) and *An mein Kriegesheer* (To my army) from Breslau.

An mein Volk, ghost written by councilman Theodor von Hippel, included the passage, "We are overpowered by France. The peace that tore half my subjects from me brought us no blessings. It inflicted deeper wounds on us than the war itself. The Mark County of our land is sucked dry, the main fortresses are occupied by the enemy, our cultivated fields are stifled as is the productivity of our cities. Free trade is constricted and with it the sources of acquisition and prosperity… The emperor's treaties are just like his wars and will lead us to ruin."[25] Prussia's declaration of war on March 27 was a formality. Marsan pleaded that Napoleon is prepared to make concessions to avoid war. The emperor was too late; the die was cast. When the Prussian ambassador informed Bonaparte, he retorted, "I'd rather have a declared enemy than a friend who is always poised to abandon ship and leave me. This is my punishment for the mistake I made in Tilsit, putting the House of Hohenzollern back on the throne and dignifying it with my alliance. It's not the first time that generosity (!) has proven a bad counselor in politics."[26]

The Spring Campaign

Controlling a country as large as France, Napoleon had the resources to rapidly build a new army. He began with a cadre of 20,000 surviving officers and NCOs. He added naval artillery battalions, harbor garrisons, reserve companies and police detachments. Together with some 40,000 veterans of the peninsula wars, he soon gathered 100,000 trained soldiers to form the nucleus. To this came another 78,000 young men of the national guard and thousands of draftees. The combined force, together with German, Polish and Danish auxiliaries, eventually tallied over half a million troops and outnumbered what Russia and Prussia could initially field. The quality of the French formations did not rival that of earlier campaigns. A large segment of the French population longed for peace. During the 1813 call-up, the police had to arrest many draftees and haul them to induction centers, often in chains.[27] Thousands fled to escape service. By August, two-thirds of Napoleon's soldiers were under the age of 20. They required more nutrition than elder veterans. Ninety thousand were on sick call that August.[28] "Even the marshals began to tire of endless war-waging and wanted peace to enjoy the treasures they had amassed."[29]

The French army was deficient in material resources. There were few horses to equip mounted regiments or train replacements. At the battle of Katzbach on August 26, two-thirds of the rifles issued to some regiments failed to fire. Factories used uncured wood to construct carriages for the cannons, which often cracked under stress.[30] Thanks to the insufficient quantity of weapons in depots, some units went to Germany whose soldiers had never fired a musket.[31] Heavy losses in combat and perpetual warfare diminished morale. The lack of enthusiasm among many conscripts, hasty training and the rapid expansion of the army altered its internal structure. Troops were not as dependable and were inexperienced in coordination of arms. Maneuvers by infantry of the line or dispersed deployment required precision and reliability on the part of the rankers, especially with regard to training and motivation. These qualities were no longer manifest. The French officer corps was good, but not large enough to direct so many units comprised of untested recruits.

Many conscripts went to war with two weeks' basic training.[32] Once assigned to field units, they received practical instruction from the veterans. Makeshift arrangements forced Napoleon to hold the army together as closely as possible when directing a battle. This imposed limitations on the use of dispersed deployment and the line. Behind skirmishers followed columns of the first wave. At Aspern, the deep columns were held in check by Austrian cannon fire. The lines could neither fan out nor be held in column formation because the men lacked the necessary discipline and training. The hallmark of Napoleon's subsequent battlefield maneuvers consisted of deep thrusts with a compact mass at the right moment with strong artillery support. The concentration of cannons at the point of attack somewhat compensated for the inferior quality of individual formations. The French recipe for assault went from the Tirailleur and column advance more and more to a column and battering-ram tactic. The emperor stressed drilling the infantry to form battle squares. This was because of the allied superiority in cavalry.

Prussia's standing army tallied 46,000 soldiers when war broke out in March 1813. The *Krümper* system would in time provide another 95,000 recruits. Together with over 10,000 *Freiwillige Jäger* and 120,000 in the *Landwehr*, the country was able to field 271,000 men by August.[33] Their morale was superior to that of the French, as was that of the population. When Friedrich Wilhelm's national proclamations of February 03 and of March 17 were published in Prussian newspapers and read aloud in churches, the spontaneous public reaction surpassed expectations. Civilians donated valuables to the war economy and in the older provinces it was considered disgraceful for a family to still possess a silver service. "It was the proudest moment of Scharnhorst's life," wrote Treitschke, "when in Breslau he led the king to a window and showed him the rejoicing ranks of volunteers, this colorful array on foot, on horseback and in wagons, an endless procession sweeping past the old gabled edifices of the Ring Street."[34] Scharnhorst graciously nominated Blücher to be Prussian commander in chief and accepted a subordinate role as his first general quartermaster.

To provide the public a gazette with nationalist tenor as an alternative to what Scharnhorst scorned as "the unheard-of wretchedness of Berlin newspapers," the patriot party founded the *Preussischer Korrespondent*, also in Berlin. Hardenberg consented only reluctantly to its publication, reflecting the aristocracy's typical apprehensions about "Prussian Jacobinism." He approved circulation "for the duration of present circumstances" and subject to censorship of the foreign ministry. The first issue hit the newsstands on April 02. Its lead article sought to "awaken the instinct for salvation throughout the entire nation."[35] Professor Henrik Steffens stepped from the lectern after delivering a passionate speech to Breslau students and led the entire male audience to a recruitment office. The student body of Halle enlisted en masse, as did young men from East Frisia and Mark County who were enrolled at Göttingen University. Hundreds of Berlin teenagers joined. Those rejected as physically unfit for duty applied with other regiments in the hope of being inducted.

The *Krümper* recruits and volunteers integrated well into the army. This led Boyen to later write, "I consider it the best infantry I have ever encountered. It is well schooled and without all the petty nonsense. It gained confidence and experience in the battles it fought in; its proud sense of honor was unmistakable."[36] Napoleon sarcastically marginalized the *Landwehr* as a nonmilitant *armée bourgeoise*. Through its wartime service however, its soldiers, who had uniforms and received combat training from the army, helped loosen social barriers in Prussia. Even Marwitz, a long-time opponent of a national fighting force, willingly took command of a *Landwehr* brigade of farm lads from Mark County and praised their courage in action. The highest percentage of recruits again hailed from the agrarian stratum. Within regiments, soldiers from diverse backgrounds never fully cultivated a sense of camaraderie in the field due to lingering class consciousness, but all were united by a desire to liberate their country.

As chief of the general staff, Scharnhorst developed the strategic concept for the army and the *Landwehr*. Considering Bonaparte his teacher, he recognized the value of the enemy's practice of concentrating forces at a decisive point and deploying most of the artillery there to achieve a breakthrough. He did not however, rely entirely on this deployment. Scharnhorst believed that were the French to mass at one place, then dividing one's own force will compel the enemy to do the same. Were this achieved, attacks can be carried out at several points simultaneously; the key element is the personal initiative and superior skill of the general in command. As the campaign developed, the allies would time and again force Napoleon to detach entire corps to defend against enemy armies approaching from various directions. Most of his marshals would prove unable to effectively direct these formations on their own. This was a consequence of the emperor's custom of promoting automatons to corps commanders instead of leaders. Scharnhorst emphasized feint attacks to confound the enemy's detached legions. He felt that this tactic can prove "very effective against a mediocre general, but against a Bonaparte ineffectual and therefore risky."[37]

Scharnhorst advocated Tirailleur tactics in conjunction with operations of the standing army. Though its soldiers received combat training, the *Landwehr* was not subject to the pedantic, rigid discipline of the line infantry and this enhanced its suitability for loose deployment in battle. The Prussians usurped this tactic from Napoleon, who could not always rely on many of the inexperienced conscripts in his regiments to employ them as Tirailleurs. The concepts of *Landwehr* and *Landsturm*, the whole nation participating in the war, unsettled French soldiers. Those who had fought against Spanish partisans in the peninsula campaign remembered all too well the fate of comrades unlucky enough to fall into the hands of insurgents. The specter of such gruesome atrocities being encountered in a populist uprising in Germany haunted Napoleon's troops. As Treitschke in fact recorded, "When it came to hand-to-hand fighting, the long-suppressed rage of the farmers exploded into a fearful bloodlust."[38] Apart from the king's aversion of guerrilla warfare because it provokes reprisals against civilians, Yorck opposed the concept in part out of geographical considerations: "How would something like this be possible in our flat countryside?"[39] Prussia lacks mountainous regions where partisans could camp or seek refuge.

The French did not take a back seat with regard to brutality, as the conduct of Davout and Vandamme demonstrated. General François Roguet, who commanded a division of the Imperial Guard during the 1813 campaign, would later warn his men at Waterloo that he will shoot anyone who brings in a Prussian prisoner.[40] During the first phase of the campaign, most of the coalition soldiers would fight Germans in French service. Blücher issued an order of the day to his troops on March 23 as they prepared to invade Saxony: "Prussians! We're crossing the border of our country and entering a foreign one not as an enemy, but as a liberator. Off to fight for our independence, we do not wish to oppress neighboring people who speak the same language that we do, confess to the same religion and whose troops have often fought victoriously at our side. They feel the same hatred of foreign domination as we, but for now are prevented from turning their weapons against the hatchet men of a foreign tyranny. Be mild and humane toward these people and regard the Saxons as friends in the sacred cause of German independence that we have taken up arms for. See them as future allies."[41]

Scharnhorst pressed for an aggressive campaign strategy. He advocated a march on Magdeburg to destroy the viceroy of Italy's divisions before Napoleon's army coming from France can link up with them. The Prussians attacked and defeated Beauharnais's force of 45,000 men at Möckern on April 05. They inflicted 699 casualties on the French, of whom 235 were fatalities, and pushed them back to Magdeburg. The main Russian army dragged its feet, reaching Dresden on April 24. The new commander was Prince Wittgenstein, who had replaced Kutusov. The belated Russian advance allowed Viceroy Beauharnais to join Napoleon at Naumburg. The emperor now had 180,000 troops at his disposal in Germany not counting fortress garrisons. He wanted to strike quickly, cut the allied army off from Prussia and force it toward the Bohemian frontier. French columns crossed the fateful Saale River at the end of April and proceeded toward Leipzig. At this early stage the coalition could field

Johanna Stegen distributes cartridges to Pomeranian *Jäger* fighting
Napoleon's troops in Lüneville on April 02. She collected rounds from an
overturned ammunition cart, gathered them in her apron and carried them
to the frontline. She found bullet holes in her dress afterward. During their
subsequent occupation, the French put a bounty on Johanna but no one
in town revealed where she was hiding.

just 98,000 troops against him, but had substantially more cavalry; 24,100 riders
compared to 7,600 French.[42]

A major engagement took place at Gross-Görschen on May 02. Wittgenstein
decided to attack the right flank of Napoleon's army near Lützen. The emperor
doubted that the allies will strike while he is still west of the Elster River. He
nevertheless ordered Ney to conduct a "strong reconnaissance" of the area and
move his five divisions to a forward position at Kaja. This is a village nearly three
miles east of Lützen that forms a quadrilateral together with Klein-Görschen,
Gross-Görschen and Rahna. Three of his divisions Ney did not even move up
and he neglected to send out enough scouts. Thanks to insufficient recon, Ney
had no idea what was coming. He reported that beyond the usual patrols, there
is no sign of the enemy. When Napoleon began issuing orders once Wittgenstein
attacked, he based them in part on the erroneous assumption that Ney's entire
III Corps is at Kaja. Bertrand wasn't much help either. He sat with his corps for
two hours awaiting orders even though he could clearly hear the din of battle less
than four miles away.[43]

Wittgenstein conducted the operation poorly. Scharnhorst, who was not
involved in the planning, objected to the site because the jagged terrain is

unsuitable for cavalry. There were still good prospects for success had the Russian general maximized the surprise by rapidly executing the attack. "The battle plan was good," wrote Gneisenau, "but the deployment bad." In Scharnhorst's view, "The affair would have been a superb victory had Wittgenstein operated differently."[44] Against Gneisenau's advice, the commander in chief left 12,000 men and 120 cannons under Count Mikhail Miloradovich behind at Zeitz to unnecessarily guard the army's left flank. The Russian guard corps was not sent forward until nearly nightfall. Diebitsch, assigned by Wittgenstein to arrange the troops, maneuvered them so clumsily that the corps of Blücher and Yorck intersected. He ordered an obsolete linear advance, with the right wing initially holding back. The czar and king of Prussia paraded their troops before they went into action. Gneisenau described how "the formalities and troop deployment continued too long instead of charging at the surprised enemy."[45]

Blücher, Gneisenau, Clausewitz and Scharnhorst with his sons all fought at Gross-Görschen. Encountering Gneisenau on the field, Clausewitz said, "We have no influence on directing the battle, so there's nothing left for us but to fight with saber in hand!"[46] Clausewitz functioned as Russian liaison officer on Blücher's staff. Though the king had begrudgingly approved his request to join the czar in 1812, he was still angry and would not let Clausewitz back into the army. Blücher was wounded and Yorck assumed command. The Prussians wrested three of the four villages from Ney in two hours of heavy fighting. Napoleon had been touring Lützen's battlefield from the Thirty Years' War when he heard the guns and hastened to the combat zone. He was on the scene by two o'clock and sent reinforcements to Ney while the Russians came up to support Yorck. By evening, Napoleon had sufficient numerical superiority for a counterattack that forced the allies back. They retired in order, having held their own against superior enemy forces with the emperor on the field. It was fortunate for them that Ney failed to carry out his orders. Also, he tactically demoted himself from field marshal to frontline officer and personally led infantry assaults instead of maintaining overall direction of the III Corps.

For his part, Wittgenstein wasted his infantry in charges against the four villages near Lützen defended by a larger French force. He failed to fully exploit his advantage in cavalry. The czar's adjutant Count Ludwig von Wolzogen wrote, "In the midst of this, no one was actually in charge or better put, everyone was: The emperor, d'Auvray (Wittgenstein's chief of staff), Diebitsch, Blücher, Scharnhorst, indeed even the adjutant general of Emperor Franz but least of all Wittgenstein, who didn't even know where the brigades and regiments were."[47] That evening, the czar visited Friedrich Wilhelm who had retired to bed. He advised him that the army will retreat in the morning to avoid being outflanked by Ney. With characteristic pessimism, the king exclaimed, "Just like at Auerstedt!"[48] There was however, no comparison. At Gross-Görschen the allies had been outnumbered two to one. They nevertheless inflicted 22,000 casualties on the French. The Prussians lost 8,500 men and the Russians 3,500.[49]

1813

Die Verwundeten von Groß-Görschen

Prussian wounded are evacuated after the battle of Gross-Görschen, also known as Lützen, on May 02. Even though outnumbered, the allies considered it necessary to engage Napoleon at this early stage of the war rather than allow him to march on Leipzig unopposed.

That evening, Blücher, Müffling and Gneisenau discussed resuming the battle in the morning. Lieutenant Leopold Gerlach informed them that "Wittgenstein has given the order to retreat. The superiority of the enemy is too great and the Russians are low on ammunition."[50] The troops' morale was unshaken. In the words of Treitschke, they "had captured a number of trophies and not one had fallen into the hands of the foe. Whenever they had encountered the enemy in equal numbers, they had proven themselves superior... In the Prussian army the troops were proud in the awareness that even though they had fought under foreign and incompetent leaders, they had restored the honor of the flag."[51] According to another account, "This time it was different than at Jena. The troops felt unbeaten. The brigades were of course in disarray, but there was no anxiety or fear of death. Instead, calm self-confidence prevailed. No one sang, as every man had lost a comrade. But all knew that those who had fallen had done so in the firm conviction that this is the beginning of a new dawn for their country."[52] Napoleon had too little cavalry to pursue the retreating coalition forces. He gained nothing but a few nonstrategic villages. He confessed to Berthier, "These animals have learned something."

The animals fell back to the Spree River at Bautzen. Here they turned to confront the French. Napoleon followed with 190,000 men. He was able to increase the French cavalry to 19,500 riders, though the quality of these squadrons was inferior to that of the Prussians and Cossacks. The allies deployed 96,000 troops in an extended position along the eastern bank of the river. The corps of Miloradovich, which had been the rearguard at Gross-Görschen, occupied Bautzen. Kleist's Prussian corps stood to its east. Blücher and Yorck defended the center with Russian divisions under Barclay de Tolly to their right and Andrei Gorchakov on the left. Napoleon attacked on May 20. He hoped to surround and destroy the allied army after its withdrawal from Gross-Görschen. By evening the French had taken Bautzen. The next day he sent Bertrand's IV Corps against Blücher to root him to the spot while Ney's III Corps struck at the junction of Barclay de Tolly's and Blücher's formations. Auguste de Marmont, one of the emperor's few capable marshals, hit the Prussian left wing with the VI Corps and the Imperial Guard.

Despite merciless bombardment and repeated assaults, Blücher held his ground until ordered to retreat. The czar took command of the army at four in the afternoon. Ney's orders were ambiguously worded and he fumbled the attempt to surround the allies. He wheeled his corps south at the wrong place and left a gap for the Prussians to slip through. They withdrew in order. This did not prevent Napoleon from claiming in his bulletin that the retreat "soon turned to flight."[53] The emperor had forced the Prussians from the Spree, but at a cost of 25,000 French dead, wounded and missing against just over half as many on the coalition side. He exclaimed in frustration, "How can there be no results after such a slaughter? No prisoners, no flags! These people didn't leave a nail behind for me!"[54] The Prussian rearguard inflicted heavy losses on the pursuers. Placed in command of the northern part of the army, Blücher ambushed Nicolas Maison's advance guard on May 26 as it emerged from Haynau. The French lost 1,350 men including two colonels and five cannons. The Prussians lost 226 soldiers.[55] After this Napoleon reformed the advance guard to march on in battle order, which all but ended the pursuit. Allied forces reunited and encamped at Schweidnitz. Napoleon dispatched Oudinot's corps to capture Berlin, but it was repulsed in fierce fighting at Luckau by troops under the command of Adolf von Oppen and Bülow.

In two successive engagements, Bonaparte had failed to destroy the coalition army and suffered disproportionately heavy casualties. Many younger soldiers were sick. He realized the need to reorganize his army, especially the cavalry, and welcomed an Austrian proposal to conclude a temporary armistice. Napoleon wrote to both the czar and Franz I expressing his willingness. Friedrich Wilhelm agreed as well. This led to a ceasefire to continue till July 27. The guns fell silent on June 01 while the accord was ratified to formally begin three days later. The French agreed to evacuate Breslau, which they had just occupied. A neutral zone of 15 to 25 miles between the troops of both sides was agreed upon.

The allies pledged to supply food for the French garrisons of Danzig, Modlin, Glogau, Küstrin and Stettin. The ceasefire was eventually extended to August 17. Gneisenau wrote the king on June 05, "The seven-week ceasefire is unnecessary and harmful in military, financial, political and psychological aspects… All reports we receive confirm that the enemy needs the ceasefire far more than we do. He is approaching a state of dissolution. Thanks to the ceasefire we have given him the time and means to recover and bring in reinforcements."[56]

Metternich had proposed the armistice to grant Napoleon a respite. The French warlord's infant son was the grandson of the Emperor of Austria Franz I. The Bonaparte family was bound by marriage to the Hapsburgs and therein lay the seed of a future alliance. For his part, Friedrich Wilhelm approved the cease fire because the lull allowed time for negotiations to expand the coalition. Great Britain joined on June 14/15, Sweden on June 22 and Austria on June 27. England's contribution would be financial, but Austria and Sweden pledged to field troops. The Prussian king and his advisors hoped that the resources made available by these states will negate the necessity of implementing the hated *Volksbewaffnung* (arming the people) of Prussia. In August, Gneisenau wrote Prussia's future minister of culture Johann Albrecht von Eichhorn, "For 20 years the allied powers opposing France have pulled off a lot of stupid ploys. This present cease-fire is the dumbest of them all."[57] During the cease-fire, French troops violated the neutral zone and even fortified it in some areas.

The last act of the spring campaign was a characteristic act of savagery that so marked the Napoleonic era. At the end of February, insurgents in Hamburg rose against French rule. They forced French troops under Laurent Saint-Cyr from the city on March 12. Colonel Friedrich von Tettenborn entered four days later with 1,300 Russian cavalrymen including Cossacks, to the acclaim of the population. His horsemen raided French supply columns in the weeks to follow. When the allies retreated from Bautzen, Tettenborn abandoned Hamburg. On May 30, 38,000 French soldiers under Davout occupied the city. Citizens accused of supporting the insurgency were shot. Surrounding villages from where French soldiers had allegedly been fired on were torched. Davout forced townspeople to build fortifications for the city to withstand a lengthy siege. He converted the churches to stables for the cavalry. Over 20,000 residents too poor to stockpile six months of provisions were driven from their homes to fend for themselves in the countryside. Many subsequently perished in the winter cold.[58]

Respite

Contrary to Gneisenau's misgivings, the cease-fire proved beneficial to the allies. Both sides reinforced their armies, but the addition of Sweden, Austria and England tipped the scales in favor of the coalition. Napoleon simultaneously wore out his welcome in Thuringia and Saxony. When fighting resumed in August, the Prussians would wage it without Scharnhorst, the man who had created prerequisites for eventual victory. At Gross-Görschen, during which two

Scharnhorst sits patiently while an army physician attends to his injured foot at Gross-Gorschen. When the great reformer died from complications caused by the wound, the king lamented, "I'll never be able to replace him!"

horses were shot from under him and a musket ball perforated his shako, he suffered a bullet wound to the foot. Scharnhorst concluded that largely due to Wittgenstein, his country and Russia cannot defeat Napoleon without outside help. He wrote his daughter, "I had a sad day; bad leadership of the army by Count Wittgenstein, lack of comprehension of our particular circumstances and in the battle itself no overall direction. Was anything grand to be expected?"[59] Scharnhorst left after the battle to try to persuade the Austrians to formally join the coalition.

The surgeon who removed the bullet from Scharnhorst's foot promised a full recovery contingent on four weeks' bed rest. Impatient to negotiate with Metternich, Scharnhorst solicited the opinion of General Staff Surgeon Wiebel. He said it is safe for him to go to Vienna if he limits daily travel time. "My wound," Scharnhorst wrote his cherished ward the young Friederike Hensel, "is not dangerous. My heart and the rest of my body are healthy. It's going slowly but certainly improving."[60] Scharnhorst broke his journey when he relapsed with a high fever. After mild recovery, he was back on the road and reached Gabel on May 11. Eight days later he received a letter from Metternich. The foreign minister asked him to go to Prague instead of Vienna to meet with Prince Schwarzenberg, commander of the Austrian observation corps, and his chief of staff Count Joseph Radetzky von Radetz. Scharnhorst wrote Metternich describing the state of the allied fighting forces. He stressed that "the Russian-Prussian army needs help right now."[61]

Scharnhorst may have suspected that Metternich diverted him from Vienna to avoid the influence he might exercise on Franz I to enter the war. He had to comply and proceeded to Prague. After arriving, although bedridden, Scharnhorst pleaded his case to Schwarzenberg and Radetzky. From there he wrote his daughter, "I'd give all seven of my medals and indeed my life to be in command for just one day!" Ravaged by fever, he succumbed to infection from the foot wound on June 28. Gneisenau, who served as second general quartermaster in Blücher's army, took his place as chief of staff. Gneisenau said of his deceased friend, "I am a pygmy compared to this giant, whose deep insight I can only marvel at but can never equal."[62] Stein wrote on July 17, "Scharnhorst's death is a great misfortune. Clarity of comprehension, self-possession, thoroughly knowledgeable, devotion to what is right to the point of self-denial and self-sacrifice, these were the dominant qualities that formed his splendid character."[63]

Despite defusing Scharnhorst's mission, Metternich faced a difficult task trying to preserve Europe's old political order. Prussia had mobilized her national resources by involving the common people in the war effort. Napoleon had dispensed with the republican values of the Revolution and reverted to despotism. France was the logical ally for the conservative Austrian and German noblesse. The Austrian aristocracy's attitude toward a patriotic war with public participation is demonstrated by General Marschall, who led Hapsburg's troops against the French in 1809. He once complained of having to dine at the same table with the innkeeper Hofer, leader of the populist uprising in Tyrol. When Tyrolean rebels brought Bavarian prisoners to the town of Mühlbach to hand over to the Austrians, Marschall announced that it is unworthy of the military to make common cause with peasants and that the Bavarians were captured contrary to the rules of war. He ordered them released on the spot.[64]

The Prussian reformer Theodor von Schön offered this analysis of the political climate in the Hapsburg empire: "Austria is ready to go to war. The people want to fight for independence. The nobility does not want war because it fears that the enthusiasm of the population will lead to overthrow of the aristocracy. Emperor Franz is weaker than a regent… But the army wants revenge, it wants war and has managed to draw the emperor away from his aristocratic entourage to the army at Gitschin. This gives us hope. The Austrian aristocrats have become very worried about the democratic strides that Prussia has made, such as voluntary enlistment and promises to the people."[65] Schön's claim that the people of Austria want war was overly optimistic, but his assessment of the noblesse was accurate.[66] Arndt saw how "Germany's chains have been ever more strongly forged by the German princes. Without a German fatherland and without love and loyalty to Germany, they serve a foreign tyrant with their small, greedy hearts and call him emperor of Europe and the liberator and protector of Germany."[67]

For Metternich, the ideal political constellation was a weakened Napoleon on the throne of France, perpetuation of the *Rheinbund* and Prussia restored to her pre-1806 might. This would balance the Great Powers in Europe and diminish Russian influence over Poland and Turkey. Were Austria to remain neutral and the coalition to defeat Napoleon, Metternich would have no say in a postwar settlement. The Austrian army would react negatively to a policy of nonbelligerency were an opportunity to vanquish Napoleon to present itself. The foreign minister therefore met with the czar in June to lay the groundwork for a military compact. The shrewd Metternich realized that the better chance of achieving his goals rests with joining the coalition and manipulating its statesmen. Stein described him as "superficial, immoral and duplicitous, his actions are like that of a traitor."[68] Napoleon learned of the session. Married to the daughter of the Austrian emperor, he doubted his father-in-law will side against him. He nevertheless invited Metternich to Dresden to discuss Franco-Austrian relations.

Napoleon and Metternich met on June 26 at the Brühl-Marcolini Palace. The foreign minister insisted that the territory taken from Friedrich Wilhelm at Tilsit must return to Prussian sovereignty and the Grand Duchy of Warsaw be divided between Russia, Austria and Prussia. Illyria (Dalmatia) on the Adriatic coast must be restored to Austria, which Napoleon had landlocked after his victory in 1809. The French were to evacuate Prussian fortresses and return Danzig to Prussia. Were these conditions satisfied, Metternich assured his host, Austria will remain neutral and mediate peace between France and the coalition. Friedrich Wilhelm and Czar Alexander considered Austria's conditions too moderate. They wanted the *Rheinbund* dissolved and the French out of Germany. They sanctioned Metternich's proposals because they were certain that Napoleon will categorically reject them.

Bonaparte did in fact refuse the terms. Metternich pleaded in response that French soldiers now are scarcely older than children. He asked how France can fight on once these replacements are burned up. Napoleon blustered in response, "You aren't a soldier and don't know what moves the soul of a soldier. I grew up in the field and to a man like me the lives of a million people mean shit!"[69] The Emperor of the French then angrily pitched his hat to the floor, his habit when negotiations didn't go his way. The next day Austria concluded a convention with the allies stating that if Bonaparte formally refuses Metternich's terms, Austria will declare war on France. Prussia meanwhile, was also active on the diplomatic front.

Berlin concluded a treaty with Britain in Reichenbach two weeks after the ceasefire went into effect. The British pledged to contribute 3.3 million thaler to the war effort. This enabled Prussia to significantly upgrade the ordnance of her army. She was already receiving English weapons shipped to Kolberg, so that by May 16 there were 271,000 men under arms.[70] The political atmosphere was vola-

Ambushed by the French at Kitzen during the cease-fire, the wounded Major Lützow slashes his way out of encirclement with surviving raiders of his *Freikorps*. He reorganized the unit and resumed operations. Lützow commanded an uhlan regiment at the battle of Ligny in June 1815.

tile to the utmost: Operating behind enemy lines, Lützow's *Freikorps* did not learn of the ceasefire agreement until June 11. The raiders were guaranteed safe passage across the demarcation line. On June 17, a force of French and Württemberg troops under François Fournier ambushed them at the village of Kitzen east of Gross-Görschen. Thirty of Lützow's men were killed and 327 taken prisoner. Napoleon personally ordered Fournier's attack. The allies responded by suspending delivery of foodstuffs to French garrisons in the besieged fortresses. On May 22, Scharnhorst had told Gneisenau, "The nation is extraordinarily incensed against the French. Within the army, the hatred of the French is beyond belief."[71]

Hostility toward France intensified in German satellites as well. During the ceasefire, Napoleon concentrated most of his troops in Saxony. The population bore the burden of their maintenance. A poor harvest the previous year made it difficult to meet requirements. According to one account, "In place of the predominantly pro-French attitude at the beginning, disappointment in the great ally and hatred of foreign oppression held sway. The significant financial obligation, the economic downturn caused by the continental blockade, French trade policy as well as 20,000 dead in the campaign of 1812 were not without effect on the thinking of the majority of the people of Saxony."[72] In Württemberg, out of 16,000 soldiers who had marched into Russia with the *Grande Armée*, just 500 returned home.[73] In January 1813, Napoleon ordered the Thuringian capital of Erfurt to furnish 1,000 recruits for the French army. Riots broke out on July 19, the day they were to be mustered. The French garrison resorted to arms to scatter protesters and 20 people were arrested. A French tribunal condemned the wood finisher Johann Günscher and the day laborer Johann Schnabel to death for "inciting insurrection."[74]

On July 10, Friedrich Wilhelm, Alexander and Bernadotte, the former French marshal who switched sides and became Crown Prince Karl Johann of Sweden, met at Trachenberg castle near Breslau to discuss the impending campaign. They approved a strategy proposed by Gneisenau and Russian General Karl von Toll. The coalition divided its force into three components; the Silesian Army led by Blücher, the Northern Army under Bernadotte and the Bohemian Army, also called the main army, commanded by Schwarzenberg. Blücher's contingent, of which 38,500 were Prussians, was initially to remain on the defensive. This army had 76,000 infantry, 24,000 cavalry including 10,000 Cossacks and 339 cannons. The large number of horsemen ensured good reconnaissance. The Russian and Prussian troops, of whom 17,400 belonged to the *Landwehr*, were well trained and morale was high. Upon learning of Scharnhorst's death, Blücher had written Gneisenau, "Better to have lost a battle, just not Scharnhorst!", but worked just as well with the new chief of staff.[75]

Gneisenau himself capitalized on the cease-fire to raise more *Landwehr* battalions for when operations resume. The men lacked uniforms and weapons. As governor general of Silesia, he used his authority to contract communities to manufacture shoes for the troops. He imported blacksmiths from Neisse to produce 20,000 canteens and cooking utensils, drawing on the sheet iron supplies stored at the royal foundries. He prevailed upon soldiers' wives and daughters to sew uniforms. By the time the truce expired Gneisenau had equipped 24 out of the 68 *Landwehr* battalions. "Where would we be," he wrote, "without these *Landwehr* men? It's through them that the state will be rescued."[76] He ordered the Silesian fortresses upgraded, strengthening fortifications and increasing the artillery. Twenty days' rations for the *Landwehr* were stockpiled under his direction. All guns were equipped with horse-drawn carriages.

The *Freiwillige Jäger*, *Freikorps* and *Landwehr* men were a new type of soldier indeed. Their conduct at times contrasted sharply from that of soldiers during the time of Friedrich the Great, as the following episode demonstrates: "On July 11, the commander of the regiment received orders that the *Jäger* squadron is to post sentries just like the other units at the entrance to the village (Lichtenberg in the Grottkau region). Plain sentry duty and providing an honor guard was considered a violation of the king's terms of service. The *Jäger* who had been ordered to stand watch refused and the others followed suit. The incident was reported to the staff. The commanding officer was sent to Ziedel under arrest. The entire squadron had to quickly saddle, ride out and as punishment, occupy an encampment outside of the village. They remained there until the 16th. The horses suffered the most.

"The *Jäger* were cheerful and expressed their merriment by singing joyful

Landwehr recruits receive a church blessing. The Prussian articles of war stated, "Every soldier must lead a Christian and virtuous life, conscientiously fulfill the primary duties of his religion and refrain from any such conduct that dishonors his faith."

songs. There was even a suggestion to invite a tightrope walker and a puppet theater from the neighboring town. Major von Zastrow came riding into the bivouac and said, 'This is supposed to be a punishment camp but looks more like a pleasure camp.' The men finally wanted to return to the village and agreed to perform guard duty. They made a straw hut, placed a stool inside and also procured a novel for the sentry to read. Regimental officers lodged complaints without success that the sentry does not stand to attention and present arms as they ride past, either out of intentional neglect or forgetfulness. The officers eventually wearied of issuing commands without results and left this merry company in peace."[77]

Prussian *Freiwillige Jäger* and *Landwehr* were distributed to all three allied armies. The Bohemian Army was the largest. It tallied 254,500 soldiers and 692 guns. This included 45,000 Prussians of whom 12,500 served in the *Landwehr*. Bernadotte's Northern Army in Brandenburg comprised 122,000 men with 290 guns. There were 74,100 Prussians under his command, the *Landwehr* comprising 40,000 of them. Another 27,000 soldiers stood in Mecklenburg. They belonged to Ludwig von Wallmoden-Gimborn's motley corps of Russians, Swedes, Englishmen, Lützow's 4,000-man *Freikorps* and the Russo-German Legion. This force consisted of Germans in the *Grande Armée* who had been taken prisoner in Russia and volunteered to fight Napoleon. Radetzky modified the Trachenberg plan. In its final form, it demanded a high level of coordination among the three allied armies. Whichever one Napoleon, known to take the offensive, moved against was to fall back and avoid engagement. The other two armies would then attack and overwhelm enemy formations detailed to guard flanks and communications. They would cautiously shadow the main French host by marching parallel to or following it.

Radetzky himself defined the strategy as follows: "In everything, in every possible change of circumstances given the present condition of the army, first and foremost to observe is that no army individually or in any way goes against a superior force and overlooks the joint operation that is to deliver the main blow securely. The goal is to drive the emperor Napoleon away from his strongpoints on the Elbe, group our armies together as closely as possible, avoid any partial defeats and in the end destroy in a decisive battle what starvation and sickness, what hardships in general have left of his army." Radetzky's strategy was to wear the enemy down, "to inflict as heavy losses on emperor Napoleon as possible and continuously deny him the opportunity to employ his physical forces and mental energy at a single point; and to completely rob him of all means to reinforce his army by disrupting his communications with France."[78]

Were Bonaparte to turn against the Bohemian Army for example, Blücher and Bernadotte were to link up and strike at detached units commanded by his marshals. The strategy was always to hit the enemy where he is most vulnerable and deny Napoleon the decisive battle he customarily seeks. The coalition powers would therefore wrest the initiative and dictate the strategy of the campaign. This ambitious plan could only succeed if allied generals rapidly judged Napoleon's intentions and countered quickly with their own maneuvers. It required flexibility, cooperation and above all, strict adherence to the overall concept. French fortress garrisons were to be contained but not besieged. The campaign was planned without the participation of Austrian generals, though coalition leaders correctly calculated that Metternich is under too much pressure to remain neutral let alone join France. He continued to postpone a decision.

Stein observed in July, "Austria is still wavering and uncertain about participation in the war. All negotiations since November have produced no definitive result. Her policy makes a mockery of the dictates of human reason."[79] The Austrian minister attempted to bring Napoleon to the conference table once more. He invited him to Prague for peace talks in July. The emperor sent Caulaincourt instead on the 28th with instructions to stall for time. Metternich issued an ultimatum demanding to know whether the terms he offered a month before are acceptable or not. Caulaincourt, per Napoleon's directive, had to officially reject them. Austria declared war on France on August 12 and joined the coalition. Metternich henceforth pursued the duplicitous tactic of waging war while privately hoping for a draw, contrary to the Prussians and the czar who fought for Napoleon's overthrow. The ceasefire expired on August 17. The stage was set for the final showdown.

Chapter 17

The Battle of Nations

The Summer Campaign

When in exile, Napoleon called it a mistake to agree to the summer ceasefire in 1813. His army had outnumbered the allies during the spring. When hostilities resumed, he no longer enjoyed this advantage. The emperor could muster 427,000 troops in August, 50,000 of whom were *Rheinbund* Germans. Bavaria pledged to send 25,000 men who were not yet available. Tens of thousands of French soldiers were garrisoning fortresses in Germany. Since the occupation had denuded Saxony of resources, Bonaparte established a system of depots to supply the army. This required detailing units to guard them. His main army had 174,000 troops and 560 guns. Ney was initially in charge of the Bober Army comprising 130,000 men with 388 guns. Oudinot was assigned the *Armée de Berlin* of 68,000 combatants with 216 guns. A corps of 15,000 men under Jean-Baptiste Girard was at Magdeburg.[1] Napoleon calculated that if he could destroy one of the three enemy armies, he could persuade the coalition to accept peace on his terms. He anticipated that Bernadotte will march the Northern Army to the combat zone at the velocity of a tired turtle. Napoleon surmised that attacking Schwarzenberg's army might provoke a stronger Austrian commitment to the war.[2]

Blücher was another story. He had fiercely defended Lübeck in November 1806 and although overmatched, had offered battle in May at Gross-Görschen and at Bautzen. Napoleon considered him the most dangerous opponent and overestimated his troop strength. He took personal command of the Bober Army and sent Oudinot, with support from Girard, north to take Berlin. His orders to Oudinot read, "With an army like yours, you will quickly throw the enemy back, take Berlin, disarm the residents and scatter the *Landwehr* and entire mass of poor troops. If Berlin resists, set the city ablaze and try to reduce the city wall to rubble with heavy field guns."[3] The emperor had grossly underestimated the size of the Northern Army; it was almost twice as large as Oudinot's *Armée de Berlin*. The latter consisted largely of Italians and Saxons with inadequately trained cavalry. Girard's two divisions, one of which was made up of raw recruits, had not caught up to Oudinot. Davout received orders to march from Hamburg in support. Napoleon based the decision to take Berlin "on his underestimate of the value of the Prussian levies."[4] He referred to the *Landwehr* as *canaille* (rabble).

Napoleon arranged his divisions on the southern front for defense. He presumed that it will take Schwarzenberg a week to prepare his troops for action. Bonaparte's endeavor to personally lead the Bober Army to annihilate Blücher came to naught. The "old fox," as Bonaparte called him, adhered to the Trachenberg plan and pulled the Silesian Army back. Blücher's men fought costly rearguard actions but eluded a major engagement. In the south, Schwarzenberg marched on Dresden. This was the main French depot. Since the *Grande Armée* had emptied Saxony of food and fodder during the occupation, the stockpile in Dresden was its lifeline. Saint-Cyr was defending the city with 20,000 men. He sent warning to Napoleon, who left Macdonald in charge of the Bober Army and scurried to the Saxon capital to safeguard its stores. The day after Bonaparte received Saint-Cyr's message, Oudinot crossed lances with the Northern Army. His force consisted of the IV, VII and XII Corps together with Jean-Toussaint Arrighi's III Cavalry Corps.

Bernadotte sent a message to Blücher on the afternoon of August 22 to advise him that his outposts were attacked yesterday by Oudinot. Bülow's corps plodded for hours in driving rain to reach Grossbeeren, a village on the southern periphery of Berlin, ahead of the enemy. The first serious battle since the truce expired took place there the next day. It was the baptism of fire for the *Landwehr* of the Northern Army. The engagement began at 9:00 a.m. at Blankenfelde. Bertrand led the IV Corps of 20,000 troops and 66 guns against the *Landwehr* division commanded by Leopold von Dobschütz. The Prussians tallied 13,000 men with less than half the artillery available to Bertrand, but drove him back by 2:00 p.m. The main battle was at Grossbeeren. The Saxon division of Karl Sahrer von Sahr of Jean Reynier's VII Corps captured the village in the afternoon. Reynier assumed the battle is over and ordered the men to make camp. It wasn't: Bülow's Prussian corps of 38,000 men counterattacked at six in the evening.

A rainstorm enabled Bülow to approach undetected. A one-and-a-half-hour artillery duel opened the fighting. As fire from the outnumbered French guns diminished, Prussian formations under Borstell, Louis von Hesse-Homberg and Karl von Krafft launched the attack. The rain prevented muskets from firing, so the bayonet and rifle butt decided the outcome. The Saxons recoiled from the unexpected onslaught and relinquished Grossbeeren. Reynier's troops were in a critical situation, but a counterattack in the Prussian flank by Pierre Durette's division facilitated their retreat. The French lost 3,000 men and thirteen guns. The Prussians had 1,000 casualties. Bernadotte withheld the Swedish corps of Curt von Stedingk, who had served under the Marquis de Lafayette in the American Revolution, and the Russian corps of Ferdinand von Wintzingerode, a Thuringian nobleman in the czar's service. Neither took part in the battle. As Treitschke observed, "Reynier owed the fact that his corps was not completely wiped out to the crown prince of Sweden. Deaf to every plea from Bülow, he allowed only a single Swedish battery and a few Russian guns to take part in the fighting instead of attacking Reynier's left wing to finish the defeated enemy off."[5]

Bülow's infantry storms the French and Saxon camp at Grossbeeren. The commander of France's 19,000-man VII Corps, General Reynier, thought the heavy rain made it safe from a surprise attack. The onset of darkness prevented the Prussians from routing the enemy.

There were some indecisive cavalry skirmishes after nightfall. Oudinot abandoned the enterprise and withdrew to Wittenberg. Bernadotte followed at a safe distance. Upon learning of Oudinot's defeat, Davout returned with his corps to Hamburg. The threat to Berlin was averted. Many Berliners visited the battlefield at Grossbeeren to greet the soldiers of Bülow's corps. They brought wagons laden with bedding for the wounded and wine and pastries for the exhausted survivors. Families roamed among the soldiers, seeking relatives who had fought. The public sense of participation in the war effort was a striking contrast to that of 1806, when the people watched the army's demise with resignation and did not resist French occupation. Only days later, the Northern Army would crown its first success by inflicting yet another setback on the French. This time it was a surprise attack by the *Landwehr* division of General Carl von Hirschfeld fighting its first action.

Girard was marching east from Magdeburg with 10,000 men when the battle of Grossbeeren took place. He did not learn of the *Armée de Berlin*'s defeat until several days later, and then from a Saxon straggler. Cossacks had intercepted Oudinot's couriers. Girard withdrew his corps to a site halfway between Magdeburg and Berlin. He established headquarters in Belzig while the troops encamped on higher ground at Hagelberg, a village slightly further west. Girard positioned scouts facing due east, anticipating a possible raid by General Alexander Chernychov's Cossacks. Approaching from the north, where the French did not expect an attack, were Hirschfeld's 11,400 Prussians. They traversed the Steindorf forest, led by three infantry battalions followed by the bulk of the cavalry. The vanguard struck the French in their left flank. Twelve of Hirschfeld's 15 battalions consisted of Kurmark *Landwehr*, "mature men, indigenous burghers, landowning farmers and skilled craftsmen who knew how to wield hammers and scythes better than muskets," according to a period account.[6]

The *Landwehr* captured Lübnitz, but was driven back by accurate fire from Tirailleurs. The French rallied and began to advance when a column of horsemen appeared in the distance. The Prussians presumed it to be enemy cavalry. The riders were in fact Chernychov's Cossacks. He had observed the battle for hours from beyond Belzig. Now was the moment to attack; he charged with 600 riders into the French rear at Klein Glien. Outflanked, Girard withdrew to a defensive position at Hagelberg. Encouraged by the French retreat, the *Landwehr* regrouped and charged two enemy battalions north of the village. They surrendered without serious resistance. Hirschfeld hesitated to order the general attack to resume. A Kurmark battalion broke from the line and marched on Hagelberg on its own and the others followed. A cloudburst prevented the French from firing and the Prussians took the position with the bayonet. Marwitz, commander of a *Landwehr* battalion, stated, "None received quarter. None escaped. All of them were clubbed to death with the rifle butt."[7] Girard's corps was practically annihilated. Only 3,000 men, mostly without weapons, escaped to Magdeburg. Girard himself was seriously wounded. Prussian losses tallied 37 officers and 1,722 from the ranks.

In the south, Schwarzenberg was on Dresden's doorstep with 80,000 troops by August 25. Saint-Cyr defended a five-mile perimeter hopelessly outnumbered. The allies were poised to deprive Napoleon of his main supply base, but the Bohemian Army halted. The coalition partners convened a war council. Schwarzenberg, the commander in chief of the army, was hamstrung by the czar and king of Prussia. They delayed operations with debates, interfered with his decisions and compromised his authority. The monarchs compensated for their ignorance of military matters by soliciting opinions from advisors. Alexander relied on Diebitsch, Toll, former Napoleonic generals Antoine de Jomini and Moreau, the latter of whom had returned from America, and artillery general Count Alexsey Arakcheyev. A notorious yes-man, Arakcheyev once remarked, "I am the friend of the czar and complaints about me can be made only to God."[8] Friedrich Wilhelm depended on Knesebeck. Only after the czar approved could Russian divisional commanders carry out Schwarzenberg's orders. The exasperated marshal wrote his wife on September 05, "What I have to put up with is unbearable; surrounded by weaklings, dandies of every sort, eccentrics with their big ideas, intrigants, blockheads, blabbermouths and habitual critics. I often feel like just giving up!"[9]

A skirmish in the churchyard for control of a village was the baptism of fire for these men of a *Landwehr* battalion that went into action after the cease-fire expired in August.

Napoleon arrived at Dresden early on August 26 with 70,000 fresh troops. The Bohemian Army launched a poorly coordinated attack on the city. It advanced in several columns without bridging equipment to cross ditches or ladders to scale walls. The operation offered Bonaparte the head-on confrontation he sought. Prussian troops under Kleist and Wittgenstein made modest gains on the right wing, but French reinforcements poured in. With units being burned up in fruitless assaults, allied staff officers realized that it is time to withdraw. Friedrich Wilhelm badgered Schwarzenberg and the czar into maintaining the offensive. Napoleon committed his reserves in a counterattack and sent Vandamme's I Corps of 35,000 men across the Elbe River at Königstein to circumvent the attackers. It was held in check by tenacious opposition from Duke Eugene of Württemberg's two infantry divisions. The assault on Dresden had failed and Vandamme threatened to cut off the Bohemian Army, but the allies renewed the attack the next day.

On the morning of August 27, 154,000 coalition troops faced a French force of 147,000. Overnight rains transformed the field into a sea of mud. Napoleon concentrated on smashing the two wings of the allied army. He gradually pushed it back and Vandamme began slowly moving again. Somehow, the Bohemian Army's unworkable command structure reached the consensus that it is time to retreat. Counterattacks by Prussian cavalry, stubborn resistance delaying Vandamme and the saturated ground saved Schwarzenberg's army from annihilation. Some 10,000 of its troops had been killed or wounded and the French bagged nearly 15,000 prisoners.[10] Most of those captured were Austrians trapped in the mud and unable to fire their muskets due to the rain. After surrendering, they bivouacked outside Dresden. Townspeople provided them food and wine. Most of the captives would be freed by General Johann von Thielmann during the battle of Leipzig. Napoleon mendaciously claimed in the *Bulletin de l'armée* to have taken 50,000 prisoners at Dresden.[11]

At the opening of hostilities, Napoleon had dismissed the *Landwehr* as a "more ridiculous than dangerous assortment of commoners."[12] Yet the warlord faced a Prussia very different from the country he had conquered in 1806. Nearly twelve percent of her male population stood under arms.[13] After the first engagements, hundreds of *Freiwillige Jäger* who displayed leadership qualities were awarded battlefield commissions. Troops of the line army, the *Landwehr* and the *Jäger* battalions combined the martial spirit of Friedrich the Great and that of a nationalist Germany. The Bohemian Army escaped destruction at Dresden and regrouped. It therefore fulfilled the task of drawing Napoleon south and diverting him from his plan to destroy Blücher. It denied him a decisive success on either front. The coalition armies maintained the initiative, conducting a campaign of maneuver not unlike cabinet wars of the 18th Century.

When withdrawing in the face of Napoleon's Bober Army before the emperor left for Dresden, Blücher had told his soldiers, "We have the advantage if we avoid a decisive battle. We are falling back to buy time for the Russian, Austrian and Prussian armies moving against the rear of the enemy. Our army does not see itself as being forced to retreat, but as a voluntary maneuver that will lead the enemy to his doom."[14] Despite the chaos at Schwarzenberg's headquarters, Barclay de Tolly, Blücher, Bülow, Dobschütz, Eugen von Württemberg, Gneisenau and Yorck defeated marshals who, thanks to Napoleon's despotic style of leadership, did not take independent action. When he learned that the emperor took the corps of Marmont and Victor to relieve Dresden and left Macdonald in charge of the Bober Army, Blücher took it on. The Silesian Army had been originally designated an observation corps, but the old general wrested permission to take the offensive if the opportunity presents itself. He had three Russian corps and Yorck's Prussian one under his command. Gneisenau wrote his friend Clausewitz, "You can only imagine how difficult my situation is. Blücher always wants to go forward and considers me too cautious. Langeron and Yorck are always pulling me back and think I'm foolhardy and rash."[15]

Macdonald led the III, V, and XI Infantry Corps made of up *Rheinbund* Germans, Italians and French recruits plus Horace Sébastiani's untried II Cavalry Corps. With 67,000 soldiers, he was to contain Blücher on the eastern side of the Bober River in Upper Silesia. Napoleon's orders read, "The principal object of this army is to hold in check the Army of Silesia, and to prevent it from moving on Zittau to interrupt my communication, or on Berlin against the Duke of Reggio" (Oudinot).[16] Instead of remaining on the defensive, Macdonald advanced across the Katzbach and Raging Neisse Rivers. Blücher deployed his formations for battle on the morning of August 26, the day that Napoleon repulsed Schwarzenberg at Dresden. Prussian reconnaissance spotted the enemy advancing between Goldberg and Liegnitz. Blücher sent the 31,000-man Russian corps of Count Louis Alexandre de Langeron, a French royalist who had entered Russian service in 1790, forward on the left to delay the enemy at the heights around Hennersdorf. Yorck took center and General Osten-Sacken, a veteran of Bennigsen's 1807 campaign, deployed on the right wing.

Macdonald ordered Jacques Lauriston's V Corps of 23,000 troops to storm the high ground. He arrayed his formations badly. The divisions of Jacques-Pierre Puthod and François Ledru were in position too far to the right to guard against a largely imaginary threat. Both divisions were consequently unable to influence the outcome. Lauriston pushed back defending pickets by noon. Having watched the French assault patiently, Blücher announced to his officers, "Now I have enough Frenchmen across. Forward!"[17] Since the powder was damp from thunderstorms, the Prussians drove Lauristen's surprised regiments

The Prussian reserve cavalry under Colonel Jürgasz charges into the mass of Macdonald's troops trapped on the river bank during the battle of Katzbach.

back with the bayonet. The onslaught forced the French into the valley again. Their units lost cohesion and were put to flight. Some 10,000 horsemen formed up on the high ground and charged into the retiring mass of Macdonald's army. This added to the confusion. Heavy rainfall flooded the Raging Neisse. The current washed away bridges and prevented many of the French from escaping to the western bank.

Langeron's Russian cavalry attacked the next day and turned the retreat into a catastrophe. The exhausted French infantry, their rifles unable to function in the downpour, were helpless against Russian mounted attacks. On August 29, General Puthod was forced back to the Bober and surrendered with over 4,000 men. By the 31st, the Silesian Army had bagged 18,000 prisoners and 103 guns. When it was over at Katzbach, Macdonald had lost 30,000 soldiers. Prussian casualties amounted to 2,875 men. "Never has a victory been bought with so little blood," Blücher reported to the king. The "old fox" credited the day's success to Langeron's pursuit. He praised a subordinate in a way that would have been unthinkable for Napoleon. As for General Yorck, Blücher described him as "a toxic character. But when he attacks, no one has a bite like he does."[18] The initial rearguard actions against the Bober Army, the clash at Katzbach, desertion and illness among *Landwehr* conscripts caused by forced marches, had cost Blücher 22,000 soldiers. Between August 27 and September 01, his *Landwehr* had just 3,228 men left despite the fact that only a few of its battalions had taken part in the fighting. Morale was good nonetheless. Replacements raised the roster to 8,540 *Landwehr* troops within two weeks.[19]

Bonaparte received word from Macdonald that the Bober army "no longer exists." He also learned of the defeat suffered by Oudinot, but was depending on Vandamme to salvage the situation by cutting off Schwarzenberg's retreat from Dresden. He ordered the pursuit on August 28, when he was sure that the allies had called off their offensive. Vandamme led his corps on the road from Pirna through Peterswalde strung out in a long column that morning. He expected only minor skirmishes with the Russian rearguard. Vandamme paused at Pirna and asked, "What's that building?" An aid replied, "That's a madhouse, your excellency." The general, soaked from rain and on his 14th campaign, replied, "That's good, gentlemen. That's just where we belong, in a madhouse."[20] Vandamme reached Kulm by ten o'clock. His troops went into action at Priesten, defended by 16,000 Russian soldiers under Alexander Ostermann-Tolstoy. The battle raged the entire afternoon and cost each side about 6,000 men. The French made no headway. The wild card was Friedrich von Kleist's Prussian II Army Corps. Saint-Cyr was chasing it but lost the trail after a skirmish at Glashütte. Kleist himself was using a 1721 map that did not mark all of the roads.

Kleist's patrols discovered a trail that follows the crest of the mountain range and was wide enough to accommodate larger formations. Karl von Grolman steered the Prussian column onto this path and, as Kleist had hoped, caught up to the enemy rear at Kulm. He deployed the artillery and at 11:00 a.m. greeted

Vandamme gallops to elude pursuing Russians at Kulm. The czar banished him to Siberia after his capture. Disliked by practically everyone including Napoleon, he went into exile in Philadelphia in 1815. The king of France permitted him to return home four years later.

the French with an unexpected bombardment. At that moment Vandamme's corps was deadlocked in a pitched battle against Ostermann-Tolstoy, who was steadily receiving reinforcements. Vandamme at first rejoiced at the sound of the cannonade behind him. He presumed that it heralds the arrival of Saint-Cyr in support. No one on either side knew the whereabouts of Kleist's corps until his guns opened fire on Vandamme. A mounted officer rode up and reported to him that Prussians, not Saint-Cyr's men, are attacking in the rear.

Supported by Austrian units, Ostermann-Tolstoy sandwiched the French between his troops and the Prussians. Vandamme abandoned his baggage and made a desperate attempt to punch through Grolman's lines. The attack was repulsed; French regiments formed battle squares for a last stand. Vandamme's corps was smashed. The French by highest estimates suffered 8,000 casualties and lost all of their artillery. Some 10,000 men were taken prisoner. Vandamme was captured. The "hangman" would have been beaten by Prussian soldiers but for the intercession of their officers.[21] He was brought before Alexander, who had watched the battle. The czar denounced him for widespread looting his troops were notorious for. Vandamme sarcastically retorted that at least "history will not reproach me for having murdered my own father," a pointed reference to rumors of Alexander's culpability in the assassination of Czar Paul I.[22] Allied losses at Kulm were around 11,000 killed and wounded. Their sacrifice rescued the Bohemian Army from destruction. Napoleon had so far ordered Oudinot, Macdonald and Vandamme forward in independent operations and all three had been decisively defeated only days apart.

Despite the drubbing at Kulm, Napoleon felt Dresden secure enough to make another bid to conquer Berlin. He again underestimated the military value of the Prussian *Landwehr* defending the capital. The emperor had an equally negative opinion of the Russian soldier, who British historian Petre, true to the ethnic profiling of the Victorian era, described as "a fighter of the utmost bravery and obstinacy, without education or much intelligence."[23] Napoleon assigned the operation to Ney, who was skeptical of the plan. The emperor demoted Oudinot to commander of the XII Corps. The latter, beaten at Grossbeeren in part because of Bonapart's flawed assessment of enemy strength, resented being replaced. Issuing instructions to Ney, Napoleon remarked that it would be "really difficult" to find someone with less brains than Oudinot.[24] The French force, 58,000 troops in all, advanced on a single road. Bülow shadowed the French by marching parallel to the north. Hampered by poor reconnaissance, again a consequence of insufficient cavalry, much of Ney's column was on the road when it clashed with the *Landwehr* at Dennewitz on September 06. This was a Brandenburg village 25 miles southwest of Berlin.

Tauentzien positioned the *Landwehr* infantry of his IV Army Corps behind 19 guns on a hill just north of Dennewitz. The French deployed in a wide arc with the right wing directed north toward Tauentzien and the left west against Bülow's III Army Corps. Attacked by Achille Fontanelli's infantry division, Tauentzien's *Landwehr* gradually gave ground. Bülow arrived early in the afternoon to reinforce the hard-pressed militia. Dennewitz was in the middle of the battle line, but the village of Göhlsdorf became the epicenter of the struggle on the left flank between Bülow and Reynier's Saxons. Supported by Borstell's troops and Swedish artillery, Bülow, who directed the allied operation because Bernadotte kept away, wrested Göhlsdorf from Reynier. When Oudinot's XII Corps reached the battlefield at 3:30 p.m., the French recaptured Göhlsdorf. The Prussians wavered under the impetus of the counterattack and were on the point of losing the battle. Oudinot suddenly received orders from Ney to withdraw his corps and transfer it to the right wing. He complied, leaving only a single regiment behind to help Reynier. It must have been obvious to Oudinot what a mistake the order was, but he had no interest in helping Ney win a battle.

The Prussians, and indeed many of Ney's own troops, perceived Oudinot's maneuver as a retreat. Bülow rallied his men and drove the Saxons from Göhlsdorf. To the right of Dennewitz, Bertrand gradually fell back under pressure from the brigades of Hesse-Homberg and Heinrich von Thümen. The French withdrawal became a rout. Ney and Bertrand took refuge in the center of a retiring battle square formed by Württemburg troops. The engagement was decided when Bernadotte brought his Swedish and Russian contingents for-

Bülow salutes his troops at Dennewitz. Impressed by them in combat, his chief of staff Boyen wrote, "In the agrarian stratum, indeed in the poorer classes in general, rests the real buttress of states. The supposedly cultivated leadership caste fails to recognize this fact."

ward to administer the coup de grace. Prussian generals, especially Bülow, were increasingly dissatisfied with Bernadotte. It appeared to them that he conserved Sweden's resources for a stronger hand in eventual peace negotiations. The Prussians' greatest asset at Dennewitz was Ney. When he ordered Oudinot to transfer the XII Corps away from Göhlsdorf, he couldn't even see the whole battlefield. He thought only of relieving pressure on Bertrand who, as he observed, was stalled near the right flank. Smoke of course obscured visibility, compounded by a thunderstorm. The main problem however, was that Ney "joined in the fighting personally."[25]

As usual, Ney spent part of his time as commander in chief of the Berlin Army galloping around the battlefield brandishing his saber. Leading charges and fighting alongside the men, he had no comprehension of the overall tactical situation when he ordered an entire corps out of the line. Ney had previously botched his assignments at Smolensk, Eylau, Gross-Görschen and Bautzen. That Napoleon would nevertheless entrust an offensive operation to such an impulsive, vainglorious officer testifies to the dearth of talented leaders he had in his stable. In exile years later, Bonaparte remarked, "Ney was marvelously brave and tenacious in retreat. He was good leading 10,000 men but with more than

The Prussian *Landwehr* plows into Ney's troops at Dennewitz. When the French marshal ordered a retreat, it was not possible for messengers to notify all of his units. Many formations withdrew in different directions and became widely dispersed.

that really stupid."[26] Napoleon's most capable marshal, Davout, was at Hamburg managing the garrison. A pensioned general could have discharged the task, but Davout had fallen into disfavor with the emperor during the retreat from Moscow in 1812. Had Davout been in command at Dennewitz, the outcome would not have been so one-sided.

France's *Armée de Berlin* lost 22,000 men, 53 guns and 412 wagons at Dennewitz. The Prussians had roughly half as many casualties. Pursuing Prussian and Swedish cavalry captured over 13,000 of Ney's retiring soldiers over the next 24 hours. The failure to take Berlin had political consequences for France. Bavaria contemplated withdrawing from the French alliance and would join the coalition on October 08. Lefebvre had dined with Bavarian officers prior to this and remarked that had he closed his eyes, he would have imagined from the conversation that he was at enemy headquarters. There was an uprising in Tyrol. Bernadotte used the decline of French fortunes to encourage Saxony to defect. When a French marshal, he had led Saxon troops at Wagram in 1809 and was still popular among them. Despite the pro-French sentiment of their king, the people of Saxony were weary of Napoleon's "blessings."

The Saxon pastor Ludwig Schlosser recalled, "After a lost battle and completely unannounced, 600 Württemburg horsemen and 400 French foot soldiers came and made camp in a large, planted field outside of the village. They hauled tables, chairs and benches, saw-tables and planks, doors and window shutters, timber, straw, hay, cooking pots, dishes, bowls, wheelbarrows, oars, buckets and lanterns from the houses. They not only generously foddered their 600 to 700 horses but took an extra 40 bushels of hay with them. The Württemburgers took charge and shoved the generally cowed Frenchmen aside. They gave very little to the French… On October 06, the village had to provide 1,800 pounds of bread, an ox, 800 portions of oats and four wagons loaded with hay. On the seventh, we had to deliver 200 portions of oats and hay and 200 rations of bread, butter, meat, beer and brandy to Lindenau. We thought to be free of this on the eighth, but that night we had to provide another 200 portions of oats and hay and the same amount of meat and bread."[27]

The French alienated the Saxon soldiers as well. In the *Bulletin d'armée*, Napoleon blamed Ney's defeat at Dennewitz on their alleged cowardice.[28] Smarting under the unjust criticism, a battalion of the Saxon *Leib-Regiment* defected to the Prussians. Supported by locals, coalition raiding parties led by Thielmann and Austrian Count Emmanuel von Mensdorf-Pouilly operated between Erfurt and Leipzig. They seized French convoys and attacked replacement units travelling to the main army. The sorties substantially disrupted deliveries of food and ammunition. The situation became so desperate that in September, Napoleon detailed the entire VI Corps and two cavalry corps to escort a single convoy following the Elbe River to Dresden. "The army is not nourished," he wrote. "It would be an illusion to regard matters otherwise."[29] French communications between Magdeburg and Hamburg were severed by raids. Davout sent Geneal Nicolas Pécheux with a brigade of the 50th Infantry Division, six cannons and a cavalry squadron to reopen the route.

Allied scouts intercepted a French courier and learned of the operation in advance. On September 16 at the Göhrde forest near Lüneberg, the French battled the Russo-German Legion under Wallmoden, first cousin of King George III of England, the King's German Legion and Lützow's *Freikorps*. Pécheux was seriously outnumbered and formed a large square to withdraw his troops. During the retreat, the French became acquainted with Britain's new Congreve rockets, which Captain Richard Bogue's battery fired into the closed formation of retiring soldiers. This fearsome weapon would also be employed at Leipzig in October. The French took 600 casualties and 1,200 men were captured. Among allied losses was Eleonore Prochaska, who had disguised herself as a man and enlisted as a volunteer *Jäger* in the first battalion of the Lützow *Freikorps*. She was mortally wounded when her company captured two enemy cannons and later celebrated as a "Prussian Joan of Arc."

Pécheux's defeat left the French with no flank protection for a future expedition against Berlin. Supply lines from France via Hanover to Magdeburg were compromised. This caused shortages for Napoleon's army during the battle of Leipzig. Alexander Czernitchev's detachment of 3,300 Russian cavalry attacked

Lützow leads a charge during the war of liberation. His *Freikorps* also had infantry and Tirolean marksmen. The poet Theodor Körner fought in his unit. Lützow served under Schill in 1809 but escaped capture after Stralsund because villagers hid him from enemy patrols.

Kassel, the capital of the Kingdom of Westphalia, and forced the French garrison to surrender. Jérôme fled and barely escaped capture. Locals provided food, fodder and intelligence for the raiders. This enabled them to operate behind enemy lines. Germany was becoming untenable for Napoleon, but he could not recross the Rhine without imperiling his alliance system. In France, his political survival depended on military victories. Napoleon did not belong to an established dynasty whose kings can lose wars without jeopardizing their throne.

Boxing in the Imperator

When Napoleon ordered Ney north to take Berlin, he himself led the Bober Army in another attempt to draw the Silesian Army into battle. The French encountered Blücher's advance guard of 10,000 men at Hochkirch. The emperor sent Murat with the III Corps, Macdonald with the V and VI and Sebastiani's cavalry forward. Upon learning that Napoleon is personally in command, Blücher fell back. The French pursued him as far as Görlitz. There Bonaparte gave up the chase. Repeated frustration of his plans weighed heavily on his state of mind; he also became agitated over the large number of stragglers from Macdonald's army loitering in Hochkirch after its rout at Katzbach. While he was angrily berating Sebastiani right on the street, Napoleon drew his pistol and fired at a patriotic village dog that charged forward and began barking at him. The weapon misfired, provoking the Emperor of the French to hurl it at the Prussian canine.[30] From Hochkirch, where his soldiers took the food from the orphanage, Napoleon went to Bautzen on September 06.[31] There he contemplated another thrust toward Berlin, but then returned to Dresden upon receiving word that Schwarzenberg is on the move again. The Austrians subsequently postponed the operation.

A lull in the fighting ensued while both sides awaited reinforcements. On September 09, allied leaders concluded the Teplitz treaty. This formally declared their goal to dissolve the *Rheinbund*, eliminate French autonomy east of the Rhine and restore territories to Austria and Prussia forfeited in 1805 and 1807. This would balance Austria's hegemony in southern Europe and Prussia's in the north. The treaty guaranteed the continued sovereignty of German princes over their former *Rheinbund* duchies. Stein had hoped that German states joining the fight against France will regard political unification as the next logical step after the war. Hapsburg emperor Franz I and Metternich did not share this vision of a unified Germany. Once the French were out, they wished to maintain the independence of the myriad of ex-*Rheinbund* states. Austria could then control their princes and dominate continental affairs. Leadership of a Germany forged together by nationalism and a war of liberation would inevitably fall to Prussia.

Napoleon languished in Pirna uncertain about his next step. His troops were too undernourished to conduct a major operation. Schwarzenberg planned another offensive into Saxony. He solicited the approval of the monarchs to transfer Blücher's Silesian Army to Bohemia. Its mission would be to cover the right flank of the main army when it advances. On September 11, Count Liechtenstein brought Blücher the czar's letter directing his army south in accordance with Schwarzenberg's idea. The general had no inclination to comply. His chief of staff Gneisenau formulated a memorandum citing their objections the same day. Blücher signed the document and sent Major Rühle von Lilienstern to deliver it personally to Alexander and Friedrich Wilhelm. Lilienstern defended its premise in an interview with the sovereigns. The memo argued that were Blücher to move south and leave Bernadotte on his own, the Northern Army will "lapse into inactivity."[32] All were aware of Bernadotte's lackluster commitment so this was a persuasive argument.

Blücher proposed crossing the Elbe with the Silesian and Northern Armies to attack the French from the north. He was in contact with Tauentzien and Bülow, the Prussian corps commanders in Bernadotte's army, to coordinate the operation. The combined force would move against Bonaparte while Schwarzenberg simultaneously advances from the south. The offensive required that all three armies concentrate on the left bank of the Elbe and so far, only Schwarzenberg's was on that side of the river. The czar and the king approved the plan. They ordered Bennigsen's Russian reserve army, also called the Polish Army, to Bohemia to fulfill the role of flank protection originally intended for Blücher. The Prussian general transferred to Bautzen on September 15. He spent a week there resting and preparing his troops. He wrote his wife on the 15th, "Farewell and be content, everything will come out alright. Napoleon is in the soup."[33] Blücher launched a feint attack with Osten-Sacken's corps against Meissen on September 27. He led the rest of the army in a forced march along the Elster River and reached Jessen on October 02.

During this time, Blücher emerged as the driving force behind the coalition war effort. Gneisenau wrote Clausewitz on September 26, "At the headquarters of the main army new plans are constantly being proposed that are never carried out. After two victories, the crown prince of Sweden is lollygagging around between the Nuthe and the Elbe. We're going to open the scene and take the lead role since the others don't want to."[34] Gneisenau was the tactician and Blücher the aggressive, independent leader the army needed. They were the antithesis of French marshals like Berthier, Bertrand, Lannes and Oudinot, who followed orders regardless of whether they were sound. Treitschke summarized the reaction to Blücher's bold initiative at headquarters: "People in King Friedrich Wilhelm's entourage were already expressing their anxiety over the dangerous plans of the Silesian hotspur... Only Stein stood uncompromisingly on Blücher's side and endorsed to the czar every proposal of the old hero. All major decisions of the alliance came from the Silesian Army. Gneisenau was completely right when he wrote his daughter Ottilie that generations to come would be astonished were they ever to learn the secret history of this war."[35]

Descending from the Krkonôse mountains near today's Czech-Polish border, the Elbe River flows northwest through Dresden, bends to the west in a wide arc above Leipzig and turns to the northwest again past Torgau, Wittenberg, Magdeburg and Hamburg before emptying into the North Sea. French garrisons held the river fortresses and bridges to prevent the allies' Northern and Silesian Armies from crossing to the western bank. Napoleon assigned Ney to defend the Elbe with the III, IV and VII Corps. After the defeat at Dennewitz, the marshal had taken his army to Torgau to regroup. The emperor began withdrawing the rest of his troops to the left side of the river on September 24. He established bridgeheads at the fortresses and spans. He faced the possibility of having to abandon Germany and recross the Rhine. In the first two weeks of the summer campaign, Napoleon had lost 150,000 men from combat, desertion and sickness.[36] Denied the opportunity to destroy one of the allied armies in battle, he sat in a trap while they converged on him.

Schwarzenberg was in no hurry. He probed toward Dresden, only to hasten back as soon as Napoleon counterpunched. Everything depended on Blücher. As for Bonaparte, the tactical advantage of defending an unbroken perimeter where units can be smoothly shifted from one front to the next would mean little if his army became completely encircled. Petre maintained that the "indecision such as he showed at this time was certainly not characteristic of Napoleon in better days. It looks almost as if, like a tiger surrounded by hunters, he was half bewildered and unable to make up his mind to do more than make short dashes, first on one part, then on another, of the circle which was steadily closing in on him."[37] Saxon officers wavered. A number of them including the prominent intellectual Dietrich von Miltitz considered it a "disgrace" not to fight for their country's liberation.[38] They planned a mutiny against the French.

Prussian commanders assumed a menacing posture toward *Rheinbund* rulers who stubbornly supported the enemy. Treitschke wrote, "Nowhere was the felony of the German princes more sharply condemned, destruction of *Rheinbund* sovereignty and strengthening of Prussian power more passionately advocated than in the entourage of the Prussian general (Blücher). 'Were it up to me,' General (Friedrich von) Hünerbein said to the crown prince of Hesse, 'your father would get less of his lands back than the dirt under my fingernails!'"[39] Stein wanted to deal harshly with Saxony after the campaign. There was considerable resentment over Prussia's former ally joining Napoleon in 1806. Scharnhorst had opposed Stein's position, believing that magnanimous treatment of the Saxons will make a good impression on other *Rheinbund* states. He had argued, "We have to instruct them and treat them in a paternal way, not with bitterness. The way we conduct ourselves regarding Saxony will have great influence on the other peoples of Germany."[40] The Prussian army received orders to fire on Saxon troops only in self-defense.

German and *Rheinbund* populations were more favorable toward the allied cause than their princes were: After the battle of Dresden in August, people in Leipzig demonstrated sympathy for Prussian wounded brought in for care. The reaction of the French fueled discontent. An eyewitness offered this account: "Here sat a young Prussian soldier of unusually good looks, blood streaming down his face, leaning against the wall with his head bowed. He had been shot in the head and was unconscious, already dying. The French saw how some people had gathered to try and comfort him. The French were unwilling to help and seemed to resent that the entire Prussian nation had not been shot dead here. In their boundless hatred of Prussia, they cursed the people aiding him as traitors, rogues and pigs."[41]

Blücher forced the crossing of the Elbe with his Silesian Army on October 03. Lilienstern scouted the river and selected a site near Wartenburg, just south of Magdeburg, to make the jump. The army constructed two bridges, one of pontoons and one supported by wooden pylons. Ney identified this as the probable crossing point, though he expected Bülow, not Blücher. He sent Bertrand's IV Corps with 14,000 troops and 32 guns there. Blücher tried to persuade Bernadotte to simultaneously cross at Aken. His refusal to do so enabled Bertrand to deploy his entire corps against the Silesian Army. At seven in the morning Prince Karl von Mecklenburg, younger brother of the late Queen Luise, led his brigade over the bridges. Prussian batteries pinned the defenders down. The soldiers formed a bridgehead on the opposite bank. Mecklenburg's men advanced through marshy terrain and stalled at the French line along

General Yorck reviews the victorious second battalion of the *Leib-Regiment* (elite, or honor regiment) on October 03, after crossing the Elbe River to open the final stage of the campaign.

the Wartenburg dike. Yorck sent Steinmetz's brigade forward to relieve them. Steinmetz, who had served at Kolberg, held his position under heavy fire for hours. Mecklenburg turned against the French right and attacked the town of Bleddin. The Prussians drove Friedrich von Franquemont's Württemberg division from Bleddin and outflanked Wartenburg.

On the opposite side of the French line, Colonel Horn, Yorck's friend and a veteran of the siege of Danzig in 1807, grappled with Fontanelli's Italian division. After the first assault against the strongly held dike was repulsed, Horn personally led the second battalion of the *Leib-Regiment* across an orchard and a brook in a renewed attack. Horn was among the boldest, most popular commanders in the army and renowned for kindness toward his men. Leading them with musket in hand, he dislodged five enemy battalions. The Prussian cavalry forced some captured Italian gunners to wheel their cannons around and fire on their comrades. Mecklenburg, now with but a few hundred men remaining, hit Wartenburg from the southwest while Horn pressed the attack from the southeast. Morand's infantry, charged with defense of the village, fell back in disorder. The capture of Wartenburg made further defense untenable and Bertrand withdrew his corps.

Yorck lost 1,548 rankers and 67 officers out of 12,000 men. French casualties amounted to 900 with another thousand taken prisoner. The Prussians captured eleven cannons. The rest of Blücher's army was over the Elbe the next day. Bernadotte's Northern Army crossed at Aken, Barby and Rosslau on October 04 and 05. General Yorck was subsequently honored with the title, Count Yorck of Wartenburg to acknowledge his role in the victory. To Prussian soldiers who fought there, Wartenburg was the "battle of the plums." The troops passed through a plum orchard when marching into the combat zone. They greedily plucked fruit from the trees and many among them gobbled plums even as they charged into battle. Silesian *Landwehr* took part in the fighting at Wartenburg.

On October 07, Gneisenau wrote Hardenberg, "The *Landwehr* played an excellent role here, namely the Sommerfeld Battalion from the Hirschberg district, which consists for the most part of linen weavers… Horn said to them, 'Look! The battalion of the guard infantry regiment is moving against the enemy; they think they're better than you!' The *Landwehr* men answered, 'No! We're just as good as they are,' and together with the others surged toward the foe. Your excellency should see these valiant, unfortunate men who have only the most basic accoutrements and suffer from illness and fatigue. It would rend your heart."[42] The Silesian Army numbered 64,000 men and that of Bernadotte 76,000. Seriously outnumbered, Ney retreated toward Delitzsch just north of Leipzig. Blücher marched his army to Bad Düben, a village slightly east of Delitzsch. He urged Bernadotte to join him and take the battle to Bonaparte. When the Swedish crown prince declined, Blücher exclaimed, "The hell with him if he doesn't want to!"[43]

Napoleon transferred the last French formations across the Elbe. He instructed their commanders, "Before the troops leave the right bank of the Elba, take all of the inhabitants' cattle along, burn down the forests, chop down the fruit trees and destroy all other food sources to denude this region of every means of sustenance and transform it into a desert."[44] This was Saxony's reward for siding with France. Bonaparte took another stab at Blücher, gathering 140,000 troops. He left Murat with 44,000 men to delay Schwarzenberg while he himself marched to confront the Silesian and Northern Armies. Napoleon believed that with Bernadotte and Blücher now on the left bank of the Elbe, he can draw them into battle. Ney arrived at Bad Düben on October 09 and the emperor came the next day. He tarried at Düben castle until the morning on the 14th because he was unable to learn the Silesian Army's precise location. His Saxon adjutant, Freiherr von Odeleben, recalled that "the three days that Napoleon spent here in this small castle surrounded by a moat were perhaps among the most tedious he ever experienced in many a campaign."[45] His secretary Baron Fain wrote that the emperor "remains almost completely shut up in his room, to which his bed and his maps have been moved."[46]

Exchanging correspondence, Bernadotte and Blücher agreed to elude a confrontation with Napoleon until Schwarzenberg hits the French from the south. Blücher crossed the Saale with his army and proceeded to Halle. He was in the city by October 11. News of this reached Napoleon on the 13th. Denied engagement, he briefly considered marching on Berlin but opted for Leipzig instead. Most of the provisions stockpiled at Dresden had been used up, but he could not bring himself to withdraw his forces from the Saxon capital. The decision was more political than military, as Yorck pointed out: "Not so much the mistake of a general as the obstinacy of a ruler who will not admit that he can be compelled to relinquish anything, and… is alarmed for the continuance of his rule, based only on force, as soon as he gives any indication that this force has diminished."[47] Napoleon left Saint-Cyr in Dresden with 35,000 men, intending to return there after defeating the allies. Bennigsen surrounded the city with Count Pyotr Tolstoy's militia corps. These troops were not trained for a major field engagement. Saint-Cyr's large body of troops was therefore contained at almost no cost to the allies.

The defection of France's German satellites dealt an unexpected blow to Napoleon. Jean-Baptiste de Marbot, commander of a French cavalry regiment, wrote of his emperor's dilema: "The enemy's iron ring about to envelop Leipzig was not fully closed when the king of Württemberg, a man of good character, considered it his duty to notify Napoleon that under pressure from England, the *Rheinbund* will soon break away and the emperor will barely have time to fall back with his French troops behind Mainz. He himself, the king, must bow to the will of his people who, together with the rest of Germany, want to join the ranks of his enemies. The emperor was deeply shaken by this announcement from the most loyal of his allies. He contemplated taking a position in the mountains of Thuringia and Hesse to wait for the enemy to attack in this woodland with its narrow defiles so advantageous for defense… (this) "would give the world the impression that he will no longer risk a field engagement. This was too much for the self-esteem of the great general and this attitude became his doom. He failed to see that the plains around Leipzig are expansive enough to enable the overwhelming number of men in the enemy army to fully deploy… His confidence in himself and in the valor of his army won the upper hand over other reflections."[48]

Napoleon left Bad Düben on the morning of October 14 and reached Leipzig by noon. His soldiers drove the faculty and student body from the schools to arrange quarters for themselves. They ejected sick and injured patients from hospitals to make room for their wounded. The destitute, including villagers made homeless by the war, were forced from the poor houses. Ferdinand Grautoff recalled, "We in Leipzig were not well informed of the actual situation… The approach of the allies from various directions and the proximity of the entire French army could naturally not be concealed from us. Beyond that we had no definite information. Living in the dark as we did, the approaching storm seemed more frightening. Shortages in the houses worsened. All deliveries were curtailed and soon even the most elemental foodstuffs were lacking… Disease began to break out and the hospital fever took many a citizen. The Wüttembergers who were transferred to our hospitals after the battle of Wartenburg brought a sickness like dysentery with them. It caused as much anxiety as it did harm. Some of the affluent wanted to leave the city but could no longer do so. Where would they go? Every road was blocked."[49]

On the day Bonaparte arrived in Leipzig, Murat fought an indecisive engagement with the Bohemian Army at Liebertwolkwitz. Schwarzenberg was not advancing with particular haste; he shared command with a Russian ruler who insisted on partial autonomy over his troops, a Hapsburg emperor who did not want a decisive victory and a Prussian king whose dread of Napoleon was only rivaled by fear of his own subjects. It took the army 17 days to march 70 miles.[50] The battle involved all three service arms on both sides, but became famous for spectacular cavalry duels. Murat's squadrons charged in columns while the allies repeatedly struck their flanks and broke them up. The French horse therefore employed structured tactics previously typical of their enemies while coalition forces displayed the flexibility and innovation associated with Bonaparte. A young officer in a Russian hussar regiment, Eduard von Lowenstern, described the experience: "Near the village of Güldengossa and the town of Liebertwolkwitz we fell upon Marshal Augereau, who was leading 10,000 dragoons from Spain. All were fine-looking, strong men riding splendid Andalusian horses. This fearsome mass, with its shiny helmets and broadswords, charged us.

"Markov greeted them with steady cannon fire. The French deployed 50 paces from us and surged upon us. Pikes, sabers and broadswords clanged against one another; many horsemen were thrown from their mounts and trampled right upon the initial impact. Soon we pressed forward with a loud hurrah. Then the same hurrah became a shout of desperation as we fell back. We threw caution to the wind and charged again, once more thrown back. To the right, left, from behind and ahead of us, we saw our riders and the enemy's chopping each other without either side gaining any real advantage. The Prussians recalled that today is the anniversary of Jena and fought like lions to erase this shameful stain."[51] Murat's orders were to delay the enemy and avoid a major battle. Instead, he poured reserves into the confrontation and lost many veteran cavalrymen who would have been of use over the next few days. The Spanish dragoons alone lost a third of their personnel and another 500 were taken captive.[52] Murat, "easily recognized by the extravagance of his costume," was nearly captured twice leading charges.[53]

Two days later, Napoleon had enough troops south of Leipzig to attack the Bohemian Army. There were 138,600 men and 488 guns on hand for the operation. Reynier's 14,000 soldiers were still on the march and would arrive the following day. The emperor held another 49,400 troops and 186 guns under Ney just north of Leipzig. The force was close enough to serve as a tactical reserve. In the ranks of the French army were 11,000 Poles plus 20,000 Germans from

Austrian infantry goes into action at Liebertwolkwitz on October 14. Control of the village would offer the Austrians the opportunity to reconnoiter Napoleon's position. The French remained in possession of the village at the close of the day.

Saxony, Baden, Westphalia and Hesse-Darmstadt. The French cavalry numbered 30,000. Thanks to inadequate reconnaissance conducted by Morand, Napoleon presumed Blücher to be still at Halle; too far away to intervene. Bonaparte expected that true to form Bernadotte would stay out of the action. Time was on the side of the coalition; significant allied reinforcements were on the way. The battle on October 16 was the emperor's only chance to win the campaign. The plan was to destroy the Bohemian Army before it can conduct a joint operation with the other two allied armies and then deal with them in turn.

Based on a draft by Baron Friedrich von Langenau, Schwarzenberg prepared to advance on Leipzig. His initial plan was to confront Napoleon frontally with Prince Wittgenstein's Russian, Kleist's Prussian and Count Johann von Klenau's Austrian corps; 72,000 men in all. Count Maximilian von Merveldt was to lead the Austrian 2nd Army of 52,000 men north between the Elster and Pleisse Rivers to strike at the French right flank. This was marshy, broken terrain that cannot be rapidly negotiated. Blücher and the Austrian Count Ignac Gyulai were to march with 73,000 men on Leipzig. Langenau was a Saxon general who had only entered Austrian service in the spring and wanted to impress Emperor Franz I by assigning the major thrust to Austrian troops. He hated Prussia and relegated Blücher to a secondary role.[54]

Langenau's plan would initially pit Napoleon's 138,000-man army against an allied force half its size. Russian staff officers protested to the czar. Alexander thereupon persuaded Schwarzenberg to shift some of the units originally detailed to attack the French right wing to the main army in the center, but this only raised its tally to 100,000 men. In addition to this, the Austrian marshal directed the Russian and Prussian imperial guard divisions totaling 24,000 troops to Rötha. The village was several hours' march from the battlefield. The Bohemian Army was therefore divided into separate contingents. It was the sort of ill-advised dispersal of forces that had doomed the Prussians at Jena in 1806.

The Battle on October 16

One of Germany's oldest cities, Speyer began as a Celtic settlement on the left bank of the Rhine River. The Roman army established a camp there before the time of Christ. Subsequently populated by Germans, the town built a surrounding wall and a cathedral in the 11th Century. Beneath the imposing spiritual edifice is the arched Speyer crypt. It is the largest medieval example of its kind in Europe. Entombed within are the remains of eight Holy Roman Emperors and German kings together with four queens. The people of the Palatinate tell of a legend associated with this sandstone mausoleum. On the night before the great clash at Leipzig, the eight sovereigns rose from the crypt, crossed the Rhine before dawn and took part in the battle. After Napoleon's defeat they silently returned to their place of rest. While the ancient rulers did not physically fight for Germany at Leipzig on that fateful October 16, the spirit they embodied in life infused those who did. More and more Germans began to feel a sense of kinship with one another, including those still on the side of France, as the mammoth confrontation loomed.

Merveldt later described how "Countless deserters, almost exclusively Germans, especially Saxons and Bavarians, rarely Italians and Poles and almost never Frenchmen, came to us from the enemy army… All the German deserters assured us that among every one of their units the greatest reluctance to serve Napoleon's cause prevails. They said that the next day whole regiments will cross over to us."[55] The largest percentage of deserters were from Württemburg regiments. This was the sense of nationalism encouraged by Stein, Arndt, Blücher and Gneisenau and dreaded by Hapsburg Emperor Franz I, Metternich and Friedrich Wilhelm III. It was an irresistible force that swept all before it and essential for defeating Bonaparte. The coalition's leaders would have to accept it for the time being and begin undermining this inconvenient ardor after the war. At Leipzig, where the greatest land battle to date in European history would be fought, not even Napoleon could withstand its impetus. Even though his army outnumbered that of Schwarzenberg on the southern front and the allied battle plan was weak, he would be denied victory.

The French deployed in a wide arc south of Leipzig. The morning of October 16 was cold and damp. Monotonous rainfall and thick fog accentuated the dreariness. The artillery duel began early and powder smoke further obscured visibility. Wittgenstein delayed the allied attack until eight o'clock when a west wind began to dissipate the mist. He deployed his formations in four columns. The first was Count Klenau's IV Austrian Corps and the Prussian brigade of Count Wieprecht von Ziethen, who had served at Auerstedt. It advanced to the left center of the French battle line and moved toward Liebertwolkwitz. The second column was Prince Gortchakov's corps consisting of the Russian Mesenzov Division and Georg von Pirch's Prussian brigade. Its job was to support Klenau. Wachau, a village to the right center of the French line and not far from Liebertwolkwitz, was the objective of the third column. It was under the command of Duke Eugen of Württemberg and comprised of Joseph von Klüx's Prussian brigade and the II Russian Infantry Corps. Kleist led the fourth column including the Prussian Prince August Brigade, the Russian Levachov Cuirassier Brigade, the Lubny Hussar Regiment and the Russian Helffreich Division into the area between Wachau and Markkleeberg, the next village along the enemy front. Merveldt's troops stumbled through soggy, uneven terrain to fall upon the French right wing at Connewitz.

Württemberg and Kleist began their attacks at eight, Gortchakov at nine and Klenau at ten in the morning. The operation took the French by surprise. They had not expected the Bohemian Army to strike first. There were only weak covering units at Wachau and Markkleeberg. The Russian and Prussian troops took the villages by storm. Napoleon was not on the battlefield until shortly after nine o'clock. He was briefed by Murat on Galgenberg hill. After surveying the area with a telescope, the emperor positioned the artillery of the Young Guard behind Wachau. A hundred guns kept the attackers under steady fire that prevented further advance. Fierce fighting raged in Wachau, which the French recaptured by 11:00 a.m. Württemberg's men clung doggedly to the southern periphery of the village area and continued firing. The French still could not dislodge Kleist's troops from Markkleeberg. Alexander and Friedrich Wilhelm came onto the scene at about the same time that Napoleon did. The czar's adjutant Wolzogen recognized immediately that the allies face a much stronger enemy force and urged him to bring up the Russian Rayevski Grenadier Corps, which was in reserve, and the Russo-Prussian guard corps.

At this time, Merveldt made little headway advancing up the Pleisse. The czar sent Wolzogen to Schwarzenberg to demand that he transfer the men of Crown Prince Hesse-Homberg to the right bank of the Pleisse. He reached his headquarters at 10:30 a.m. Radetzky endorsed the idea and Schwarzenberg committed these troops as well. A Prussian officer described the scene: "Cannon fire thundered along the whole battleline. The mist cleared and the rain clouds dispersed. The cannon flashes from the Connewitz area could easily be seen. A thousand muzzle flashes ceaselessly hurled death into masses of men on the opposite side. *Jäger* and musket fire rattled from all around and soon we heard salvos being fired from entire battalions and regiments… Every line was shrouded in clouds of smoke, through which flashed bursts of flame like fiery tongues. Individual cannon shots could no longer be discerned; every moment there were a hundred, merging into a perpetual, thunderous roar."[56] Wittgenstein's attack stalled by eleven o'clock. Wachau had changed hands three times but ended in possession of the French. The allied assault nevertheless forced Napoleon onto the defensive and disrupted his timetable. He had to direct reserves earmarked for his offensive to threatened areas to stabilize the line.

Marbot described his experience during the battle: "General Sebastiani stood with his three cavalry divisions between Wachau and Liebertwolkwitz and had assigned each one a place where it is to form up. The Exelman Division was to take a position in rolling terrain where hills and ravines intermix with one another. The enemy cavalry was so far away that a surprise attack was not to be feared. For this reason, I took advantage of the cover provided by hills and ravines in our brigade's sector to protect my squadrons from enemy cannon fire. Thanks to this measure, while we were in position here, which was for a long time, I did not lose a single man. The other regiments suffered appreciable losses. One would have imagined that this circumstance would reap the praise of the divisional commander, but the result was the opposite. General (René) Exelman came and ordered me, over the objections of the brigade commander, to advance

Russian artillery fires into Murat's 8,000-man cavalry charge to thwart Napoleon's bid to break the Bohemian Army's line on October 16. The Russians repulsed the attack and the French withdrew closer to Leipzig overnight.

another 100 paces: Every regiment must do its part in sharing the danger. I of course obeyed, but in a short time lost a captain and nearly 20 men killed and wounded. This completely unnecessary loss greatly upset me."[57]

At 2:00 p.m., Napoleon ordered the corps of Macdonald, Augereau and Lauriston forward. They forced the allies back to their original positions. Only Kleist held out against Augereau at Markkleeberg. The emperor assembled the Young and Old Guards, Victor's corps, the reserve artillery and the cavalry for a major thrust to break Schwarzenberg's position. Napoleon was so confident of victory that he ordered that the church bells in Leipzig be rung. As a Leipzig resident recalled, "An overjoyed adjutant of Napoleon came riding to the king of Saxony. Even from afar he was waving a kerchief and shouting 'victory!' as he rode along Grimmaisch Lane... The French boasted about the total destruction of the enemy and scornfully told how Prince Heinrich of Prussia has been captured with 10,000 men. It never occurred to these liars that there was no Prince Heinrich with the Prussian army."[58] Napoleon's message to his vassal King Friedrich August of Saxony was, "The world still revolves around us!"[59]

Attempting to pierce the allied line, the Bordesoulle Division of the French I Cavalry Corps charged Güldengossa. This is where the prince of Württemberg's corps had assembled for the advance that morning. The French horsemen crashed through the infantry and captured 26 guns. They overran the Russian Schewitsch Guard Cavalry Division and rode to within a few hundred yards of Wachtberg hill where the allied monarchs were observing developments. A ditch in front of Wachtberg confounded the riders. They came under Russian artillery fire and were attacked in the flanks by Cossacks, a Russian cuirassier regiment and ten squadrons of Prussian cavalry. Murat's troopers retreated back to their own lines. The French infantry marched on, but it was soon apparent that the attack was losing momentum. Lauriston's corps advanced against Gortchakov. Marshal Victor pushed Kleist out of Markkleeberg and captured the Auenhain sheep farm. Klenau's Austrians made a stand against Macdonald at Seifertshain. This was a pivotal position on the right side of the allied line.

Counterattacks by Nostitz's cavalry, Count Nikolaus von Weissenwolf's grenadier division and Friedrich Bianchi's infantry, all fresh Austrian formations, hit the enemy flanks and retook Markkleeberg and Auenhain. The French position at Wachau was outflanked as a result. Napoleon's right wing was in jeopardy of collapsing. It compelled the emperor to dispatch Joseph Souham's III Corps and some battalions of the Old Guard to stabilize the line. By four o'clock, the French counteroffensive had dissipated. Napoleon's attempt to punch through the allied line floundered on the resistance of the Russian, Austrian and Prussian soldiers. Prince Eugen von Württemberg's troops played an especially important role. They stubbornly contested Wachau in the face of a continuous, murderous bombardment. Of the 9,000 men the prince went into action with at eight that morning, just 1,200 were still under arms by evening.[60]

Neither army was victorious in the battle south of Leipzig on October 16.

Austrian troops emerge from marshy terrain to dislodge the enemy from Auenhain farm. The French army's insufficient reserves, Schwarzenberg's preemptive attack and the pressure exerted by Blücher and Yorck to the north thwarted Napoleon's battle plan on the first day.

The fighting north of the city, where coalition forces defeated the French, contributed to the failure of Napoleon's counteroffensive. Count Gyulai and Blücher prevented two French corps from transferring to the southern front to reinforce Bonaparte's attack. Without these formations, Napoleon was too weak to destroy the main allied army. Gyulai fixed his objective as Lindenau. It was a heavily fortified village northwest of Leipzig on a retreat route for the French army. He mustered his troops early, but delayed the march until hearing the thunder of battle to the south. Gyulai brought forward his artillery and opened fire. Austrian infantry of the Hesse-Homberg Division penetrated the town in two successive assaults but was driven out again. Meanwhile Bertrand's IV Corps was proceeding to the southern front per Ney's orders when General Arrighi, beleaguered at Lindenau, sent a messenger requesting reinforcements. Mindful of the importance of the Lindenau Road, Bertrand marched his entire corps to Arrighi's aid. It pushed back Hesse-Homberg's division, but was then repulsed trying to drive the Austrians away. Gyulai tied Bertrand down for the whole day.

Perhaps the most important engagement on October 16 was fought by Blücher at Möckern. Like Gyulai, Blücher derailed a French formation earmarked to reinforce the southern front. In this case it was Marshal Marmont's VI Corps, considered among the best in the army. Unlike most French units in 1813, it had many soldiers with long service records who were yet to be defeated in the 1813 campaign. Four regiments of French marines formed the backbone of this elite corps, which had 19,500 men on the roster. The night before the battle, Marmont was atop the church tower in Lindenthal gazing at distant campfires to the north. He sent a message to Napoleon advising him of the proximity of the Silesian Army. At 7:00 a.m., Marmont received orders from the emperor to march his troops to Liebertwolkwitz on the southern front. Bertrand's corps was to replace them and guard the western and northwestern approaches to Leipzig, "if the enemy attacks seriously on that side, which seems to me absurd to suppose."[61] Bonaparte believed that Blücher's Silesian Army is at Weissenfels southwest of Leipzig. He did however, authorize Marmont to use his own judgment if the Prussians attack.

Considering Blücher's track record, it is surprising that Napoleon underestimated his resolve to join the fray. Blücher was himself in good spirits and anxious to come to grips with the enemy. The day before the battle, a visiting officer gave this account: "I rode to Blücher's headquarters to announce myself to Colonel Gneisenau. He was unusually friendly to me and outstretched his hand in a good-natured way, spoke of our acquaintance in Kolberg and was hopeful that the great decision will fall in the next few days. There was a heartwarming friendliness and simplicity about Gneisenau's manner that compared to the malcontent Yorck is most refreshing. In the afternoon of the same day, I also managed to personally visit Blücher... It scarcely seemed to bother him that a decisive, bloody battle will be fought by his corps the very next day. He chatted and laughed in a relaxed way, as though we were going to a peacetime maneuver and not to a life-and-death struggle against the greatest field commander of the age.

"Clouds of smoke puffed incessantly from his pipe and he sipped frequently from a glass of Bordeaux taken from the commissary cart of a French general. He joked with officers and soldiers among the Prussian troops defiling past. He didn't seem in the least worried about the strategic plan for the campaign. I kept hearing him say, 'Gneisenau will have already taken care of that,' or 'the ladies' man knows all about that,' or 'we'll have to ask Gneisenau. He'll know best how to do it, since he's the smartest out of our whole gang here.'"[62] At six o'clock the following morning, Blücher dispatched cavalry patrols to scout the French defenses. Charles Vane, the British military commissioner on Bernadotte's staff, delivered a letter from the crown prince two hours later: The Northern Army will not take part in the action that day. The only catalyst Blücher needed however, was the rumble of cannon fire from the direction of Lindenau and Wachau; he ordered his soldiers to attack at 10:00 a.m. The staff had no reliable information about the strength of French forces opposing them. The goal was to tie down as many enemy troops as possible who were needed elsewhere.

The Prussians were confident: Gneisenau said, "Wherever it strikes, our army under Blücher proves its worth by the rapidness and daring of its marches, its exertions and its valor."[63] Langeron's Russian corps deployed to the left and early in the afternoon, attacked Gross-Wiederitzsch and Klein-Wiederitzsch defended by 3,800 Polish soldiers. Blücher, who remained with Langeron on the left flank, sent Yorck's Prussians to take on Marmont's VI Corps between Lindenthal and Möckern. Russian divisions of Generals Osten-Sacken and Guillaume Emmanuel Saint Priest, a French royalist, followed Yorck. A Prussian officer accompanying Saint Priest's advance described how "the Polish division of General (Jan) Dąbrowski had occupied a village and the Russian troops soon became embroiled in a very heated battle with the Poles. It was the most bitter struggle that I ever saw in my life. One could soon see what a deep national hatred there is between Poles and Russians.

"The Russian infantry advanced with courage and determination, but the individual soldiers did not know how to operate independently and with prowess in gardens, streets and houses. The Poles had many older soldiers, some of whom had just come from Spain. Despite significantly fewer numbers, they managed to stubbornly defend the village for a long time. The Russian general seemed to be personally a very brave man. He rode at the front of his assault parties and urged his soldiers on. His general's cap made him easy to spot, so Polish Tirailleurs preferred to shoot at him. I myself saw how his coat was riddled with bullet holes without this having disturbed him in the least… The battle lasted nearly two hours with scarcely an interruption. Then the enemy withdrew from the shot-up, half-burned village and we could gradually advance again."[64]

Marmont abandoned any notion of complying with Napoleon's order to transfer the VI Corps to Liebertwolkwitz. He deployed his troops with Möckern, sited on the bank of the Elster River, on the left and extended his line east toward Eutritzsch. This village was behind Gross-Wiederitzsch where the Poles were fighting the Russians. Marmont, an experienced artillery officer, positioned 84 cannons on elevated ground and another twelve covering the flank at Möckern. Surveying the field, Yorck decided to attack at Möckern. He reasoned that shifting the operation further east of the river will expose his left flank to the Poles at Gross-Wiederitzsch. The operation began at 2:00 p.m. and coincided with the Russian attack. The Prussian I Corps was a battle-hardened formation of 20,800 men. It included regular army troops and Silesian *Landwehr*. Yorck detailed Mecklenburg's brigade to screen the left wing. Marmont stationed the 2nd Marine Regiment in Möckern itself and distributed the mass of his infantry along the line east of town. The Elster River prevented the Prussians from circumventing the village; it could only be taken by frontal assault.

Yorck placed the 8th Brigade of his corps on the left wing of the line. Near the village of Lindenthal just north of Möckern, the fusilier battalion under Major Heinrich von Krosigk charged French battle squares in position there. Among the attacking Brandenburgers was Johann Hechel. He had volunteered for the *Landwehr* and after training been assigned to Krosigk's battalion in September.

His account of the assault is among the most graphic of the period: "Now the order came to advance more quickly. A mounted adjutant beside us asked a hussar who rode toward us, 'Where are the French?' The hussar answered, 'They should be just ahead of us here.' The adjutant said to him, '*Should* be? Sir, you have to ride until the French shoot at you. Then turn back and say, 'Here they are!' The hussar rode off again. Soon they were firing at him and he wheeled his horse around. This time he brought precise information. It had to be at nearly nine in the morning. Three shots from heavy guns heralded the beginning of the battle…

"Toward evening generals and adjutants suddenly came up to us, waved their caps and shouted, '*Alles mit Sturm!*' (All attack!)… The French saw us coming and began to shoot. I thought that everyone of us would fall. The salvoes rang out and our people dropped as if mowed down, but I wasn't yet in the path of the case-shot. I sensed the man on my right no longer and when I looked, in an instant everyone beside me was shattered and sprawled on the ground. Then I heard the sergeant say to me, 'Hechel, keep moving!' I did so and others who were still standing followed. I was so splattered with the blood and brains of those who had been hit that I could scarcely see. I wiped my face and saw the man next to me suddenly staring at me. His mouth was open and his right cheek was shot away. He fell. The charge continued. Now our gunners were also firing case-shot. The major rode up to the enemy cannon, drove the artillerymen back and we captured the whole battery. We rushed upon the *Karree* (battle square) behind it. Our major charged well ahead of us, hacking with his saber to the right and left. Before we could get to him, he fell from his horse, pierced with bayonet thrusts and bullets.

"We saw him fall and we surged forward. The square had again closed when we got to it, but the enemy was shuddering from head to foot. I had pressed forward and stood right before their bayonets, but had to first stop to catch my breath. Then Corporal Böttcher and I inverted our rifles, first struck the bayonets aside and then clubbed the French in the face. Our comrades followed our example. To this day I still don't understand why the enemy stood so closely bunched together and didn't fight back. They let themselves be beaten without resisting or crawled under the dead. We then clubbed their backsides even though they begged, '*pardon, Kamerad*!' Our harsh answer was '*Nix Pardon!*' until the entire *Karree* had been clubbed to death. Only then did we go to our Major von Krosigk who had so bravely led us. He lay on the ground, pale and bleeding, still clutching the saber in his fist. Some of the men wanted to carry him from the battlefield, but he said, 'fusiliers, leave me lie, it's over for me. Go and do your duty!' He commended himself to God and died…

"Blücher sent an adjutant to ask what regiment we are. We answered, the second Brandenburg. 'Ah, the brave Brandenburgers,' said the adjutant, 'Blücher says to tell you he's sending cavalry.' We fought on with renewed courage but then, what a shock! From the side two large battle squares were coming at what was left of us with enemy cavalry behind them. Facing certain death, we formed

The Prussian infantry storms Möckern, which Marmont, one of Napoleon's better marshals, had fortified in advance and defended with elite marines.

into a square to sell our lives as dearly as possible. We put the three French flags we had captured in the middle. We defended ourselves by shooting and I was almost deafened by the thunderous fire. General Yorck saw our distress and sent Brandenburg and Lithuanian dragoons to help us. They hacked into the enemy squares and drove off the French riders. Then the general rode up and called cheerfully to us, 'Your *Karree* belongs with the stars in the sky!' In the distance was another French battle square. It sent an officer to us waving a white handkerchief. It was a savage day. We gave no quarter. We took no notice of the white flag and answered with bullets. The officer fell dead and the men in his square ran off. Many escaped into the nearby woods but we spared the life of none of those we could reach.

"The night finally came… On the morning of October 16, our eleventh company numbered 210 men. That evening there were eight of us left. The next day a few who had been scattered rejoined us, which brought us up to 15 men… Almost all of my good, faithful comrades were gone. I had to go off to the side and weep."[65] To assault the village of Möckern itself, Yorck committed first four, then nine battalions of grenadiers, *Jäger*, fusiliers and *Landwehr* infantry. The Prussians fought their way through the streets with the bayonet. They took heavy losses and were stopped at the far side by French artillery fire. Marmont continually fed reinforcements into the battle and drove the attackers out again. Möckern changed hands six times. Marmont's 2nd and 4th Marine Regiments and the 37th Line Regiment were almost wiped out but the French held the town. Yorck sent in the 2nd Brigade with the same result.

The Prussians had resorted to mass attacks so far, but changed their tactic. Grouped into assault parties of 30 to 40 men each, they targeted individual farmsteads and houses to smoke the French out. Marmont's men fired at them from rooftops and windows. Mecklenburg's soldiers clambered over stone walls of the larger farms and smashed in doors. They took the structures floor by floor in hand-to-hand combat. They were thrown back in a counterattack by Jean Dominique Compans's infantry division. The Prussian 7th and 8th Brigades contested the French line east of Möckern. Before committing Steinmetz's brigade, his last reserve, Yorck arrayed 88 cannons to pulverize the town. He positioned them just 700 yards from the enemy line. They included a Russian battery of 32 heavy guns. Blücher had transferred them from Saint Priest, who had just captured Gross-Wiederitzsch and driven the Poles back to Eutritzsch.

A Prussian artillery major led the Russian reserve battery to Möckern and recorded the experience: "I directed the (Russian) general to a small hillock that seemed to me the most suitable place to deploy the battery. And soon began such powerful detonations that even I, a long-service artilleryman, thought would burst my eardrums. Opposite us Marmont had also brought up a large battery and showered us with a veritable rain of cannonballs. Fortunately, most of them flew past too high over our heads. Yorck's guns thundered next to us, and only when the 32 twelve-pounders we had deployed opened fire was this infernal concert in full swing. I myself had now dismounted from my horse and watched the spectacular panorama, explosions and flashes all around, on foot."[66] Toward five o'clock, Yorck sent in the 1st Brigade. Its remaining three battalions managed to retake Möckern in bitter house-to-house fighting. The Prussians took many casualties in the assault including almost all of the officers. Marmont sent a large column of fresh infantry forward to destroy the brigade. The situation confronting Yorck's corps, worn down from attrition and hours of combat, was critical.

The French VI Corps had fought perhaps the most renowned formation in the Prussian army to a standstill. Though the adversaries were practically equal in numbers, Marmont enjoyed the advantage of a defensible position. But Yorck was not the man to accept defeat. Risking the destruction of his entire corps, he committed his last reserve in a final bid to overcome the enemy. He ordered Major Friedrich von Sohr with three squadrons of Brandenburg hussars to charge the approaching French infantry before it reaches Möckern. Sohr bypassed the village a few hundred yards to the east and formed his squadrons for attack. The haze of powder smoke and clamor of battle concealed the maneuver from the French column. Unaware of what was coming, the infantry did not form battle squares to repel the cavalry. Marching in column, they were practically defenseless when the Prussian hussars surged out of the smoke and surprised them. Sohr's horsemen rode down two infantry battalions and then turned on the enemy artillery. The major himself was wounded but remained in command.

"It was a wild tumult," wrote an eyewitness. "The roar of cannon, musket

Prussian cavalry attacks Marmont's reserve infantry marching to reinforce Möckern. The risky charge decided the battle in Yorck's favor. Marmont would surrender his corps after the allies captured Paris in 1814 rather than sacrifice more lives to keep Napoleon on the throne.

salvos, the beating of drums and blare of trumpets, the stomping of horse hooves interspersed with shouts of every possible command. Unfortunately, there were also repeated cries of pain from hundreds of wounded who lay helpless on the ground and were mercilessly trampled by horses belonging to the charging mass of riders. Men of the splendid Mecklenburg-Strelitz Hussar Regiment rode past me and straight into the enemy, waving their sabers. Right behind them were volunteers of the East Prussian National Cavalry Regiment, in which I had so many friends."[67] Eight squadrons of Württemberg hussars in French service were also scattered in the melee. They had refused an order to attack Steinmetz's brigade in Möckern. Marmont attributed their conduct to treachery. The rest of Yorck's cavalry came forward and drove off the enemy horsemen. All four Prussian brigades renewed the infantry attack. The French broke and turned to flee. Blücher's bold thrust had ravaged one of Napoleon's most formidable corps and prevented it from intervening at Liebertwolkwitz, where it could have tipped the scales in Bonaparte's favor. Marmont listed VI Corps' casualties as between six and 7,000 men. Over 2,000 of his soldiers were captured.

Estimates of Prussian losses at Möckern vary; between 5,600 and 7,969 were killed or wounded.[68] Langeron lost nearly 1,500 men in action against the Poles and French. The Prussians took 40 guns and the Russians thirteen. Though not as well equipped as the regular army, the *Landwehr* fought with valor and tenacity. The Austrians also acquitted themselves well, although their 2ⁿᵈ Army detachment under Merveldt on the Pleisse failed to take its objective. Had the general succeeded in capturing Connewitz, a village southwest of Leipzig, the allies would have captured a bridge the French could use to retreat from Leipzig. Conditions were too muddy for Merveldt to bring up his artillery. Troops commanded by Augereau and Polish Prince Jozef Poniatowski held the crossing throughout the day. The Austrians managed to take Dölitz, a river town just south of Connewitz. Their engineers built a footbridge over the Pleisse there. Merveldt rode across and presumed soldiers wearing white tunics on the opposite side to be Austrians. Not realizing that they were actually Saxon grenadiers in the French army, he fumbled with his saber and ordered them to follow him. They shot his horse from under him and took the nearsighted Merveldt prisoner. Poniatowski had him brought to Napoleon. The count would spend one day in French captivity.

The Battle on the 18th

The first day of battle was frustrating for Napoleon. He had outnumbered the coalition on the southern front but could not achieve a decisive breakthrough. French units that defended the northern and western approaches to Leipzig were substantially weakened. Holding Connewitz had cost Poniatowski a third of his men. The strength of Augereau's corps was reduced by half. Bertrand and Marmont were scarcely better off after fighting Gyulai and Yorck. Allied losses were heavier than the French, but they could afford to lose more men than Bonaparte could. He drew his army into a tighter perimeter around Leipzig. Reynier's corps was the only reinforcement expected. Schwarzenberg and Blücher would be joined by the Northern Army with Bülow's Prussian corps and 30,000 Swedes. The Austrian corps of Count Hieronymus von Colloredo reached the allied camp shortly before 10:00 a.m. on October 17. This added another 21,000 men to the roster. His soldiers were too exhausted from forced marches to be fit for action that day. Bennigsen arrived with 34,000 Russian reserves in the afternoon, as did the Austrian light division of Count Ferdinand von Bubna with another 7,000 troops. The coalition had 295,000 men on the field with 1,360 guns (Petre states 1,466) versus Napoleon's 160,000 with 630 guns.[69]

Napoleon faced a dilemma. He could assemble his forces at Leipzig and retreat across the Elster toward the Rhine. This would save the entire army before the allies could stop him. It would be tantamount to admitting defeat and encourage *Rheinbund* princes to defect to the coalition. The 140,000 French troops garrisoning fortresses in Germany would be lost. There was also the risk that if Napoleon abandons Leipzig, thousands of reluctant conscripts in the ranks will desert on the march and the army could lose cohesion. If he decided to remain in position around Leipzig, there was less chance of a successful outcome than on October 16. The most he could hope for on the 18th was to fight the combined allied armies to a standstill defending Leipzig itself. The emperor first requested an armistice. He summoned Merveldt to his headquarters and asked him to negotiate a truce with the allies on his behalf. Napoleon proposed that he pull his troops behind the Saale, the Russians and Prussians retire behind the Elbe and the Austrians withdraw into Bohemia.

Marbot described the situation: "Napoleon regretted that he had so brusquely rejected the peace proposals offered him two months ago. Now he was compelled to introduce some himself… The allies were too conscious of their numerical superiority not to reasonably hope that even though the decision did not fall in their favor the day before, the next day would bring them the victory. They became even more secure of this in the expectation that German regiments that are still with us will switch to their side during the battle. The leaders of these formations in fact used the respite on the 17th to discuss just how they want to carry out this betrayal. Napoleon's letter delivered by Count Merveldt was not even dignified with an answer."[70] Napoleon had been beaten to the draw on the morning of the 16th when the Austrians attacked first. He did not want a repeat of that occurrence. He sent his soldiers to their forward positions early on the 17th in pouring rain. The allied war counsel convened that morning and decided to rest the troops and postpone the attack until tomorrow.

The French standing ready for battle in the dawn hours of October 17 already had a bad night behind them. A Hessian soldier in Jean Marchand's division of Macdonald's XI Corps wrote this account: "It was the worst bivouac that we experienced in this campaign. The weather was raw and damp. Neither food, water nor wood were on hand. Broken wheels, musket stocks and saddles served as firewood. The rain water, standing in puddles that men and horses had bled into, had to be used for cooking. A large number of patrols were sent out and many pickets posted, so that half the men had to take turns standing under arms."[71] The French army was low on food, fodder, wood and ammunition. The coalition was closing the ring. Napoleon contemplated retreat throughout the 17th. At seven in the evening, he ordered Bertrand to march the IV Corps west to occupy the Saale and Unstrut River crossings in preparation for a general withdrawal. He directed Mortier to hold Lindenau open with two divisions of the Young Guard.

The only combat that day was initiated, not surprisingly, by Blücher. He spent the previous night around a campfire with his staff. Orders that all military operations are postponed until the following day did not reach him in time. He attacked French positions at 10:00 a.m. The corps of Langeron and Osten-Sacken wrested the villages of Gohlis and Eutritzsch from the enemy. Yorck's sorely tried corps remained in reserve. Blücher fought another battle in the evening, but not against the French. The Northern Army had reached the combat zone. Bernadotte resisted commitment. English commissioner Vane reminded him that his government has pledged £1,000,000 to Sweden in war aid. He warned that England will cancel payment if the Northern Army does not fight the next day.[72] During the morning, Blücher sent the *Landwehr* lieutenant Professor Henrik Steffens to ask Bernadotte to speed up mustering his troops. Steffens found the crown prince of Sweden still in bed.

That evening Blücher met with Bernadotte. The prince asserted that the French will try to burst the allied cordon by striking due north and that he, Bernadotte, must bear the brunt of battle. He asked Blücher for 30,000 of his troops to support him. The Prussian replied without hesitation, "It will be an honor for me to personally lead Langeron's corps to your royal majesty."[73] Blücher shifted the point of concentration to the northeast to strike directly at Leipzig, but retained command of his formations. This virtually locked Bernadotte into participating in the operation. Blücher of course did not believe that the French will march north, nor the lie that the czar has placed him under Bernadotte's command. He saw through the former French marshal's ulterior political motive. In his opinion, "In order to remain in good graces with both Paris and Stockholm, the crown prince doesn't want to sacrifice any Swedes or do anything to hurt the French."[74] Regardless of Bernadotte's reluctance, Napoleon could not ignore a force as large and well-rested as the Northern Army and had to deploy troops to guard against a potential attack.

At two in the morning, Bonaparte began arranging his divisions in a half circle to the east and south of Leipzig. He relinquished Liebertwolkwitz and Wachau. This time the French army would be on the defensive, limited to counterattacking in threatened areas. Schönfeld, due east of Leipzig, anchored the left wing of the battleline. The zone from Schönfeld to Paunsdorf, the next village south, was the responsibility of Ney. Under his command were the corps of Reynier, Marmont and Souham, the Defrance and Fournier Cavalry Divisions and the 2nd Saxon Division. The notorious Durette Division, consisting of soldiers under punishment and paroled convicts, was also assigned to Ney. Were Schönfeld lost, the retreat route through Lindenau would be jeopardized. Macdonald defended the central section of the line with the XI Corps, Lauriston's corps, Sebastiani's cavalry and the Nansouty and Walther Guard Cavalry Divisions. Probstheida was at the juncture between the central and right sectors. Defense of the village was entrusted to the French right, which extended to Connewitz. The corps of Augereau, Poniatowski and Victor guarded this line along with the Doumerc, Kellermann and Milhaud Cavalry Corps. Murat was in command.

Napoleon held the Old Guard in reserve behind this section. Jan Dombrowski's Polish division deployed at Leipzig and along the Pleisse River toward Gohlis, a village almost due north of the city. The two most important bastions of the defensive belt were Schönfeld and Probstheida. When the allied armies advanced at 7:00 a.m., the French soldiers had been getting into position for five hours. Schwarzenberg did not mass his troops for a central thrust, but assailed Napoleon's forces all along the line. He divided the coalition armies into six columns. The first column, led by Crown Prince Hesse-Homberg, was made up of the 1st and 2nd Army Detachments, the Bianchi and Weissenwolf Divisions and the Nostiz Cavalry Division. All were Austrian units and totaled 50,000 men. Their first objective was Markkleeburg on the road to Connewitz. Setting off at eight in the morning, they captured the villages of Dösen, Dölitz

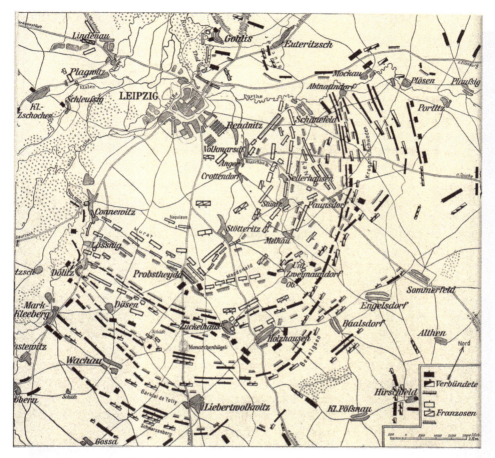

The array of French divisions grouped around Leipzig and surrounding allied units on October 18 saw Napoleon on the defensive.

and Lössnig. Napoleon parried with a division of the Young Guard and another formation. They recaptured the villages and stopped the Austrians. The crown prince was seriously wounded.

The second allied column was also 50,000 men strong and comprised of Kleist's Prussian army corps, Gortchakov's and Eugen von Württemberg's Russian corps and Paul Pahlen's cavalry corps. Barclay de Tolly was in command and assigned to take Probstheida. The town was surrounded with a massive clay wall and heavily defended by infantry, cavalry and artillery. The terrain was flat and without cover. Barclay delayed the attack to bring up cannons in a fruitless attempt to blast holes in the wall. The czar impatiently ordered Probstheida attacked at 2:00 p.m. Bennigsen was in support and sent forward the Prussian brigades of Hans von Zieten and Prince August. They took the village in bitter fighting but were driven out again. The firsthand account of a soldier in a *Landwehr* regiment gives insight into the nature of the fighting: "First to greet the riflemen of the light infantry I belonged to was cannon fire coming from the flank. Not much more and our troop would have been scattered. But we hastily reformed and rushed down to a low path running close to the village's garden wall. This wall was about as tall as a man and equipped with loopholes.

"We waited until the French had fired a mighty salvo at the rest of our men still coming up, then quickly jumped from our trench and surged forward all the way to the middle of the village. The surprised Frenchmen took to their heels and even left a battery of ten guns behind in the center of town. We were overjoyed to take possession of this valuable find when someone behind us shouted, 'French riders have bypassed the village and are falling on us from behind!' We had to abandon those wonderful cannons and take a position behind the buildings to be safe from the heralded horsemen. But these riders didn't come; the Russians had spotted them in time and driven them off again. This was a very unfortunate mistake for us; not only had we not taken the cannons, but when the French saw us clear out, they were suddenly back with their battery and sent a hail of case-shot howling after us. Grimly determined after having been so badly deceived, we wanted to charge the battery again and take back the village. But the French were more attentive now and came at us with such superior numbers that we felt lucky to get away from the village in one piece.

"Now we ran nimbly through the garden and clambered over the clay wall. The French followed closely behind us and picked off some of those climbing over the walls. On the outside we pressed against the wall between loopholes and waited until the French had fired their rifles. Then we left our perilous spot as quickly as we could to find a safer place further away. We had lost too many men to try anything more and from then on took no further part in the battle. Our regiment had taken the field with 2,500 men. At the close of the battle at Leipzig there were just 300 men still fit for duty and 18 officers alone had been killed… One of our bravest officers who had done more than most during the assault on Probstheida was a 17-year-old country nobleman. No less worthy of note is that our battalion drummer, an Israelite not 20 years old, earned the Iron Cross. During the assault on Probstheida he threw the drum on his back, equipped himself with the rifle and ammunition of a fallen soldier and was one of the first to push into the village."[75] After the Prussians were repulsed at Probstheida, Bennigsen sent the Prince of Württemberg's Russians in. Napoleon's fire brigade, a division of the Old Guard, drove them back. Schwarzenberg suspended attacks on Probstheida at four o'clock.

Bennigsen led the third column. It deployed just east of Barclay and tallied 65,000 soldiers. It included the Russian reserve army, the Austrian Army Detachment Klenau, Bubna's Austrian division, Zieten's Prussians and Matvei Platov's Cossacks. The column captured a couple of villages but then Bennigsen halted to await Bernadotte's Northern Army. During Bennigsen's assault on

A Russian corps and a *Landwehr* regiment assault Probstheida on October 18. Napoleon, whose troops are at left, directed the defense from the Quandt tobacco mill northwest of town. Schwarzenberg employed costly frontal assaults instead of bypassing the French and cutting their line of retreat.

Paunsdorf it became clear that Napoleon could no longer rely on his German contingents. Marbot described how "Marschal Ney ordered the Saxons to support a French regiment that is defending Paunsdorf. They marched steadily forward for a while until they were incited by their perfidious leader, General (Gustav von) Ryssel, to run over to the enemy lines. Some of our officers who never would have imagined such treachery were amazed at how fast they ran. General (François) Gressot, the chief of Reynier's staff, rode after them to bridle their mad insolence, but encountered nothing but hostility."[76] Contrary to legend, the Saxons did not turn and fire on the French while deserting.

August Kummer was among the 3,000 Saxon soldiers who defected to the coalition. He wrote that "resentment toward French administration that the men have so often witnessed made them inclined to side with the allies for some time now. We firmly believed that were we to join the ranks of the allies, we could in so doing not just rescue Saxony's integrity but our king as well."[77] Late in the afternoon, the troops learned that Napoleon sent a corps to Weissenfels to cover his retreat to the Saale. Ryssel formed his brigade into a column to cross to the allied lines. He was overruled by General Wilhelm von Zeschau, ordered by King Friedrich August to continue fighting on France's side. Kummer offers this account of the confrontation: "Major General von Ryssel commanded, 'shoulder

rifles, forward march!' He gave this order when he saw that our artillery is crossing over and he received news that our cavalry has already done so. Our brigade
had scarcely advanced a hundred paces when Lieutenant General von Zeschau
rode up and shouted, 'Halt! Order arms!' He turned to General von Ryssel and
said, 'Do me the courtesy of not advancing again until I order it!'

"As soon as the lieutenant general was gone however, General von Ryssel
again commanded, 'Shoulder arms! Quick march forward march!' We had gone
some 300 paces further when General von Zeschau again road up and cried,
'Who dares to have the brigade advance without my having ordered it?' 'Major
General von Ryssel did,' answered Major (Innocenz) von Holleufer of the guard,
who was the interim chief of Battalion Anton. Then General von Zeschau said,
'Major General von Ryssel is relieved of command and you, Herr Major, as the
oldest staff officer of the brigade, are to take command. For this honor, do not
allow the brigade to go forward or back without my orders.' He then turned
to General Ryssel and said, 'You, Herr General, are to ride to General Reynier
and report to him what you did!' Without answering, General Ryssel spurred
his horse and rode over to the allies instead, waving to us with his white handkerchief. At this critical moment the men of our brigade saw the entire Brause
Brigade going over to the allies and without awaiting orders followed its example. When the French saw this, they sent a hail of cannonballs and case-shot after
us. To prevent them from pursuing us, the English flaming rocket battery fired
rockets at the French."[78]

Not all French troops observing the Saxons reacted like the artillerymen
who opened fire. French horsemen of the Defrance Cavalry Division cheered
crews of a Saxon battery of twelve-pounders and two infantry brigades as they
marched off to join the allies, in the mistaken belief that they are about to
attack the Prussians. Zeschau persuaded over 600 Saxon soldiers to remain with
Bonaparte's army. A brigade of Württemberg cavalry, 550 men strong, defected
to the allies at around ten that morning. Bennigsen's third column was not the
only one to benefit from *Rheinbund* contingents switching sides. Bavarians,
Württembergers and Saxons detailed to block the Northern Army from crossing
the Parthe River that flows northeast out of Leipzig also deserted the French.
Together with Langeron's corps loaned to him by Blücher, Bernadotte had 95,000
men under his command. This force was the fourth column of the coalition
army and was to march due south toward Schönfeld and Paunsdorf.

The crown prince planned to force the Parthe with Bülow's corps at Taucha,
a village six miles northeast of Leipzig. Once again, Bernadotte held back.
Instead of ordering it to attack, he assigned Langeron's Russian corps to occupy the ground between Mockau and Plösen to supposedly secure the right
flank of the Northern Army. During the battle, Petre pointed out, "There was
no sign of Bernadotte. The roar of artillery fire was heard on the entire circle
around Leipzig, except in the gap between Bennigsen's right and Langeron's left,
where Bernadotte should have been."[79] The commander of the 1st East Prussian

Landwehr Battalion from Königsberg, Major Friccius, expressed the Prussians' attitude: "The hope that the Swedish infantry that has still not taken part in any of the campaign's battles will finish the grand work here as its crowning achievement was bitterly disappointed. Everywhere there spread a very different opinion of the Swedes."[80]

Blücher was in command of the fifth column of the allied force. It consisted of Yorck's Prussian and Osten-Sacken's Russian corps. Together they tallied 25,000 men. The column's objective was the Leipzig suburb of Halle. Blücher had no patience for the crown prince of Sweden's dilatory tactics. He issued orders to his own formations and to those of the Northern Army as well. Once the roar of cannon fire in the south became audible, Blücher redirected Saint Priest and Langeron, who were waiting in vain for Bernadotte's instructions, to cross the Parthe at Mockau instead of at Taucha. This was to prevent the Northern Army from straying too far away from his own. Otherwise, he would be offering the crown prince another opportunity to lag behind. He assigned the Russians to drive the French back toward Schönfeld. Langeron was not available—which in itself was not detrimental to operations—but his generals obeyed Blücher without hesitation. The corps was in action by nine o'clock.

Blücher ordered Bülow, whose troops also belonged to the Northern Army, to follow. He dispatched his adjutant to advise Bernadotte of the circumstances. At ten, Blücher sent Osten-Sacken's corps against the fortified village of Pfaffendorf. The advance to the Halle suburb floundered on the determined resistance of the Poles. A French guard division reinforced them. Bülow's troops assaulted Paunsdorf toward 4:00 p.m. When the French counterattacked, Bogue's English rocket battery attached to the Northern Army went into action. The Congreve rockets, mounted on two-wheeled carts, were a fearsome weapon; the howling of the projectiles as they hurled toward the target and the smoke trailing across the sky spread panic among the French soldiers. The detonations caused frightful burns on their victims. The Northern Army was finally across the Parthe. Langeron received belated orders from Bernadotte to take Schönfeld, defended by Joseph Lagrange's division. Twice the Russians broke into the town and were ejected. After an artillery bombardment by 60 Russian and 20 Swedish guns, Saint Priest's men captured Schönfeld in the third assault. Ney withdrew his battered formations to Reudnitz.

The coalition army's sixth column, that of General Gyulai, had just 22,000 men. On its roster were the Austrian 3rd Army Detachment and two smaller Austrian and Russian cavalry units led by Mensdorff and Thielmann. Gyulai aimed for Lindenau, just like on October 16. During the first day of battle, he had performed an appreciable service by tying down Bertrand's division so that Napoleon could not employ it on the southern front. On the 18th, the goal was to deprive the French army of its northwestern line of retreat. Guylai's force was too small to defeat Dombrowski's Polish division and elements of the Young Guard defending Lindenau. The day ended with the allies having made modest gains.

None of their thrusts precipitated a collapse of the French front. Napoleon still held Probstheida, although the position was severely constricted by the allies. The other key position on the perimeter, Schönfeld, was in the hands of the coalition. The crucial retreat route via Lindenau was still open.

Given the fact that the governments of Austria and Sweden did not want Napoleon decisively defeated, the conduct of Schwarzenberg and Bernadotte is suspicious. The absence of the Northern Army on October 16 compelled Blücher to keep his entire force intact for the advance on Möckern. His original intention had been to detach a corps to send west to sever the French line of retreat. There were initially just 3,000 French troops defending the Lindenau Road.[81] Bernadotte prevented him from doing so by not supporting his advance from the north. "The real blame for the failure to make an end of Napoleon there and then lies chiefly at Bernadotte's door," maintained Petre. "For days past he had been hanging back; even on the 18th he might easily have been up three or four hours before he was. Then there would have been an overwhelming force against Napoleon's left on the Parthe… The Swedes did practically nothing."[82] Gneisenau wrote Marie von Clausewitz on October 23, "Disregarding all his promises, the crown prince of Sweden always stayed behind us, and to be sure by several miles, without taking part in the fighting. His fine army was of no use to us."[83]

No less dubious is Schwarzenberg disregarding the strategic importance of Lindenau. He had an enormous armed force at his disposal, yet assigned far too few troops to Gyulai to accomplish his mission. When Gyulai's sixth column went up against the Poles and Bertrand's French troops defending the village, instead of sending reinforcements, Schwarzenberg ordered it to pull back. The new directive was for Gyulai to support the first column. This column was not in serious danger of being routed, especially given Napoleon's economy of reserves. Schwarzenberg therefore assigned priority to capturing Connewitz over Lindenau. He countermanded his own order to Gyulai after his column had disengaged from the front at Lindenau and was marching to the Pleisse River. As a result, the Austrian 3rd Army Detachment saw no more action that day.[84] Petre summarized, "It seems strange that when Bertrand drove Gyulai across the Elster, the Austrian was not reinforced, instead being at first told to withdraw farther… When Bertrand issued from Lindenau, Gyulai was actually recalled across the Pleisse… There has always been a suspicion that the allies in this intended to leave open a road for retreat to the French."[85]

A Leipzig resident who witnessed the battle made this observation: "From Lindenau, where the battle had raged yesterday (on October 16), not a shot was heard. The allies had actually pulled back from the place. This was at least some consolation for the people of the city, since it meant that the French still have an escape route out of Leipzig. But why they were left this opportunity, even after the explanations offered in subsequent army bulletins, remains a mystery. The Austrians had considerable forces backing them and could not have been forced out of their strong position. Leipzig was spared as a result, but more so were

Schwarzenberg declares victory to Friedrich Wilhelm, Alexander and Franz I on October 18. Paintings like this exaggerate their military contribution. Schwarzenberg said privately, "We have to carry three monarchs on our backs" at headquarters. When the trio rode into Leipzig, surviving French soldiers stood to attention and presented arms as they passed.

the French themselves."[86] The possibility cannot be overlooked that Hapsburg emperor Franz I, under the influence of Metternich, told Schwarzenberg to keep Napoleon's line of retreat open. The Austrian monarch was at field headquarters when the allies formulated their plan. "The success of the allies is all the more disappointing," Fesser opined, "when one considers that their leadership—especially Schwarzenberg himself—made several bad decisions and 100,000 of his soldiers (the guard and a large part of the Northern Army) didn't even take part in the battle."[87]

The historian Georg Kausch bluntly stated, "In all of the major battles, Leipzig being the most conspicuous, they left the backdoor open for Napoleon. In this way if defeated, he could escape and regroup anew."[88] The French army withdrew from the field virtually unmolested: "Schwarzenberg refused to send the completely intact Russian and Prussian guards in pursuit," wrote Treitschke.[89] He noted that many Prussians were angry over the decision and suspected treachery. Schwarzenberg's explanation is patently absurd: "We didn't have enough troops to strongly occupy all of the exits. Also, it isn't always advisable to drive an enemy to desperation who still has his forces intact."[90] Napoleon's adjutant Odeleben said of the retreat, "Had the enemy broken through here, not a single man would have escaped."[91]

Historian Bauer provided this summary: "Once again there had been downright incomprehensible omissions and mistakes in the direction of the battle on the side of the allies because of shortcomings in their military leadership. These included beginning attacks by the individual columns at different times and with forces that were much too weak, the lack of full use of the superior artillery and cavalry, not committing over 100,000 reserve troops, the delayed advance of the Northern Army and leaving a retreat route open for Napoleon's troops... Why Prince Schwarzenberg left the troops embroiled in such severe fighting on their own remains a mystery. Behind the heights called the monarch's hill on October 18, strong and still fresh Prussian and Russian guard formations had to stand and watch while their comrades in front of Probstheida bled. Because of this the French, who also fought valiantly but even so had to commit their last reserves, were able to hold this village that was their key position."[92]

Chapter 18

The End of an Empire

The Fall of Leipzig

During a counterattack on October 18, Johann Röhrig, a Rhinelander in the French army, observed Napoleon on the battlefield. "We were again in control of the village; but its capture was bought with many human lives. Here I saw the emperor and how he stood in the middle of a hail of enemy case-shot. His face was pale and as cold as marble. At times it betrayed a flicker of vexation. He saw that everything is lost. We were only fighting now for the retreat."[1] Toward 8:00 p.m., the warlord returned to his headquarters in Leipzig, ironically an inn named the *Hotel de Prusse* (Hotel of Prussia). Here he organized the retreat with Berthier. At 2:00 a.m. on October 19, French troops abandoned Probstheida, Connewitz and Stötteritz. Men stayed behind to tend campfires to camouflage the withdrawal. Regiments funneled into Leipzig via its four eastern gates. Since there was but one on the western side of the city, traffic jams were unavoidable. No one thought to illuminate the streets. As a result, some of the wounded resting along the route were trampled by carts. The 1st, 3rd and 5th Cavalry Corps were already on the road to Lindenau. The order of retreat was the Old Guard, two divisions of the Young Guard, the 4th Cavalry Corps, Augereau and Victor's corps and Sebastiani's 2nd Cavalry Corps.

Saint-Cyr was instructed to break out of Dresden with his garrison and head west. It proved a hopeless endeavor. At Leipzig, very few of the 30,000 soldiers assigned to the rearguard were Frenchmen. To the Polish divisions of Dombrowski and Poniatowski, Italians, Westphalians, Hessians and a few other *Rheinbund* units fell the honor of sacrificing themselves so that Napoleon could escape with French elite formations. He left Marmont, Poniatowski and Macdonald in charge of the rearguard. Mist shrouded the early morning hours of October 19. The allies discovered that Probstheida and other strongpoints were evacuated overnight and mustered their troops at 7:00 a.m. The empty villages confirmed the obvious; the French were in retreat. By 8:30 a.m., the sun broke through the haze. Schwarzenberg only committed a portion of the combined allied armies for the concentric assault on Leipzig. By prioritizing the capture of Leipzig instead of bypassing it, Schwarzenberg bought Napoleon another 24 hours to safely withdraw his army.

North of the city, Blücher's Russian corps of Osten-Sacken and Langeron arrayed to attack. Bülow's Prussians were to advance from the east. The brigades of Borstell and Hesse-Homberg covered their flanks. Colloredo and Barclay struck from south of Leipzig and Bennigsen's Russian reserve army from the southeast. Schwarzenberg kept most of the Austrian army out of the fighting.[2] His orders drafted on the evening of October 18 directed Colloredo to send three cavalry brigades under Nostitz to Pegau, a village southwest of Leipzig, to march due north from there and invest the city from the western side. The divisions of Ignaz Ludwig von Lederer, Alois Lichtenstein and Count Bubna were to take part in the operation. There were 40,000 men to block Napoleon's escape. Schwarzenberg countermanded the order at midnight and aborted the maneuver. "It is not clear why Schwarzenberg gave this counter order," wrote Petre. Napoleon was "relieved to learn that the allies were making no serious attempt to cut off his retreat by the left bank of the Elster."[3] One must marvel at how Petre does not grasp the correlation between Schwarzenberg's militarily senseless decisions and the design of Austrian foreign policy to keep Napoleon in office.

The French rearguard gave ground as the allies attacked with massive artillery support. It fell back to the immediate suburbs of Leipzig. Bülow forced the French out of Reudnitz, the last village east of the wall. With his troops about to defend the city gates, Napoleon employed a stratagem to delay the allies while his army defiled west out of Leipzig. August Wichmann, his Saxon adjutant, rode to the coalition camp to negotiate the city's surrender. This he spun as a humanitarian mission to spare townspeople the hazards of bombardment and street fighting. The result was a temporary ceasefire. A citizens' delegation sent by the magistrate begged that the city be spared an assault. The czar informed Bennigsen that surrender talks with the French have broken down. When Bernadotte expressed the desire to parley, Bennigsen replied that he will negotiate with his battery of 60 twelve-pounders.[4] The respite did buy the French time to get more troops out of the city. Bonaparte himself left Leipzig on horseback after calling on King Friedrich August. He and his staff became snarled in the traffic jam at the Ranstädt Gate and this slowed their departure.

When the battle resumed, the Prussians and Russians prepared to storm the Grimmaisch Gate at Leipzig's wall. Major Friccius provided a detailed postwar account: "Ours was the only *Landwehr* battalion not just in Bülow's corps but in all armies of the allies at Leipzig that went into action on October 19… There was a brief cease-fire upon Bennigsen's arrival and when delegates from Leipzig came to the crown prince of Sweden to negotiate the surrender of the city. Since it soon became apparent that the enemy is only trying to buy time, the cannonade began. When the crown prince of Sweden saw Bennigsen's troops advancing toward the wall, he ordered Prince Hesse-Homberg to quickly storm the outer Grimmaisch Gate with his nearest battalion. This was the most formidable position on the eastern side of the city because the French were better prepared for an assault here. Three battalions of the left wing were assigned to carry out the attack…. The troops who advanced to the gate came under heavy fire at close range from the front and from both sides without being able to inflict harm on the enemy behind his bulwark.

"Nothing had been done to prepare for the assault. We had no ladders, no axes, no planks or other equipment on hand; no carpenters, no engineers were at our side. There were no guns nearby to blast open the gate. We were increasingly fired on from every window and rooftop and even from the tower of the Johannis Church. Every minute a round found its mark. A bullet struck my horse in the jaw and it could not be bandaged; I had to abandon him. The strong, beautiful animal writhed in pain and was held for a while by a *Landwehr* man until it pulled loose from the bridle and wildly stampeded off. I then had to perform my duties on foot. It isn't of much use to a staff officer to be on horseback in street fighting anyway, since it just exposes him to more danger. Perhaps I have the loss of my horse to thank for my survival. It wasn't possible to move forward and staying where we were would be certain doom. Our objective was so close that every man preferred death to retreat. The danger increased with every moment. Finally, Gäsebeck discovered a weak spot in the wall between the pillars of the gate and the poor house.

"I seized the weapon of the nearest *Landwehr* man and punched through the thin wall with the rifle butt. It quickly collapsed, since several strong *Landwehr* men helped me batter it down. When the opening was large enough, I jumped through the breach and shouted to my men, 'You won't abandon me!'... Delighted over how quickly we had pushed our way in, the prince said, 'Truly, the *Landwehr* will gain great glory this day, surpassing many line troops!' He saw riflemen of a line regiment who were still standing against the wall without joining us or following our example... The area inside the wall was stuffed with carts, gun carriages and palisades to obstruct our advance. A few men with rifle butts and bayonets could have held us at the small opening for a long time. Instead, the enemy withdrew 30 or 40 paces and turned to face us again. They wanted to avoid hand-to-hand combat and shot at us from a distance. They fired ceaselessly at us and at the breach; many were hit and others had to clamber over the body of a comrade to get through to us. Since retreat was impossible, we gathered closely together and charged the enemy with fixed bayonets. He quickly turned to flee and we, scarcely 50 men strong, put hundreds to flight.

"We were still taking fire from several buildings, so some of our troops pushed inside and the most fearful struggle developed. Some of the Frenchmen were hurled out of upper-story windows. The enemy had obviously not expected us to break into the city so soon and had hoped to hold the gate longer... We linked up with the other *Landwehr* men of our battalion who had since entered through the opening in the gate and reassembled there. At the same time the enemy rushed us with far more men and wanted to drive us into a blind alley, where we would have been finished. Here a horrible melee took place, genuine butchery. Whoever had a rifle made good use of it, driving the bayonet into the nearest Frenchman and then smashing the skull of another next to him

After his *Landwehr* battalion forced the Halle gate, Major Friccius leads the men in bloody street fighting against Napoleon's foreign auxiliaries still defending Leipzig on October 19.

a moment later. In the narrow confines of this space there were piles of dead literally five to six bodies high. Afterward I asked one of our strongest and most fearsome fighters, a chimney sweep named Johann Tiedtke, how many he had cut down here. Twelve, he answered... The surrounded *Landwehr* man Schwartz of the second company struck furiously about and finished off all seven of his opponents...

"Our continuous violent assaults spread such dread among the enemy troops that they finally stood as though frozen and no longer resisted... Later we discovered a gruesome, dishonorable act of cruelty that the French had committed against one of our men. He had been thrown into a sewer head first and drowned. He was found upside down with his legs extended upward."[5] Friccius also mentioned that before the Prussian advance against the Grimmaisch Gate, Bernadotte had assured brigade commander Prince Hesse-Homberg, "The enemy is in full retreat. You will only find wounded. Nothing should prevent you from forming up for a parade." The soldiers cleaned their uniforms and polished their rifles in anticipation of a ceremonial entry. As for Benadotte's own troops, "There were only two battalions near the gate and from among these only one, at most two companies followed us into the town. The Swedes sent into the city fell back as soon as a few bullets flew past them. General (Karl) Adlerkreutz spurned them forward with angry words; but as soon has he turned away from them, they again sought to return to the gate."[6]

Enemy soldiers, among them a Hessian contingent at the Grimmaisch Gate, had fought fiercely to defend Leipzig. As they were forced back further into the city, their thoughts turned to escape. Penetrating Leipzig via the northern Halle Gate, Blücher's regiments joined with Bülow's *Landwehr* coming from the east to trap Polish formations under Dombrowski. Once again, the struggle between Russian and Pole betrayed a passion and mercilessness that rivaled the most savage fighting of the campaign. Major Friccius recalled, "In every garden, house, farm and street the battle was waged with the utmost bitterness. Field Marshal Blücher, who wanted the renown of being the first with his corps to occupy the city, was personally at the head of an assault column formed from the Jekatarinenburg, Rylsk, Polozk, Alt-Ingermanland and Archangelsk Regiments and his beloved 'forward, you valiant Russians, give them your best!' rang out. It was an uncommonly violent struggle here and just as bloody as with the Silesian Army at Möckern… The enemy fought on and there was no talk of surrender. Few prisoners were taken since our embittered soldiers struck down everyone they could get to without mercy.

"There were repeated scenes of the most intense fighting. I remember how a large house on Gerber Street was strongly occupied by Polish soldiers who maintained steady fire on our troops… General von Sacken sent me into this house to prevent another murder scene and in his name, order the Russian soldiers to pardon the enemy if he is willing to lay down his arms. It took much effort to get to the entrance, since the lower level of the house was filled with Russian soldiers fighting while the Poles had fled to the next floor and blocked the staircase with furniture. I climbed the stairs waving a white cloth and called to the Polish officer in command, an older major, that he can accept pardon in the name of General von Sacken. 'I'll never surrender to a Russian! Get out or I'll shoot at you!' he shouted to me in an angry tone. Scarcely had I jumped back a few steps when the Poles opened fire; a bullet tore my cap from my head and several Russians were hit. Now the fight could no longer be prevented. The enraged Russians stormed the stairs, forced their way into the upper floor and after a desperate defense by the Poles, stabbed all of the enemy soldiers to death with the bayonet… In this house alone, 35 of the enemy were killed while eleven Russian soldiers were shot dead and 17 wounded."[7]

Langeron's Russians wrested the Parthe River bridge from Durette's division in close combat. Napoleon's men still in Leipzig congregated at the Ranstädt Gate. It was the only egress available. Those who made it out crowded onto the Elster River bridge on the Lindenau Road. French sappers had placed an enormous explosive charge on a raft secured under the bridge. This was to blow it after the last French soldiers were over and delay pursuit. According to the official French version, the officer assigned the task, Colonel Montfort, rode to Lindenau and ask Berthier what units will be the last to cross. He left Corporal Lafontaine at the bridge with instructions to light the fuse if the span comes in danger of being captured by the enemy. Light infantry belonging to Osten-Sacken's corps

Demolition of the Elster bridge forced surviving defenders to either ford the river or surrender. Macdonald crossed on horseback and reported to Napoleon drenched. He urged the emperor to retreat to France, provoking a brusque dismissal from the warlord.

advanced to within proximity of the Elster, occupied some adjacent buildings and opened fire on the retreating French column from windows. The musketry panicked Lafontaine. He set his torch to the fuse even though the bridge was jammed with French soldiers, horses and carts. The detonation was so deafening that it supposedly woke Napoleon while he was resting at the Lindenau mill and despite the incessant roar of cannons had been sound asleep.[8]

The Leipzig resident Grautoff was on the street when Napoleon left the city. At one point, he was close enough to him to hear him barking orders to his aids. According to Grautoff, "The emperor himself blocked the only escape route. As soon as he had crossed and was in the open, he ordered the bridge at the outer Ranstädt Gate blown up and sacrificed many to certain death. But he himself was rescued! Ridiculously enough, the French bulletin blamed a corporal, who in reality probably never existed, for doing prematurely what was most certainly ordered long in advance… The detonation was scarcely noticed in the city. I was at that moment at a building close to the Ranstädt Gate and not three minutes' walk from the bridge. So great was the tumult among those fleeing and the report of the cannons of friend and foe that I did not even hear the explosion."[9] Regarding the disaster itself, "The detonation was very great," wrote Friccius. "Stones, timber and shredded fragments of horses and human body parts flew into the air. A large, burning beam landing close by would certainly have killed me had my frightened horse not bolted at the same moment. Two Russian *Jäger* standing beside me were crushed. The pandemonium among the refugees crowding together to reach the bridge was indescribable. Russian *Jäger* fired into them ever more eagerly until all had thrown down their weapons. We took many thousands prisoner."[10]

Friccius was on hand to supervise the collection of sabers surrendered by captured French officers. "Since I could not return them, I had the Cossacks snap the blades off against a French carriage wheel… An older French colonel, a genuine warrior type so often found among soldiers who had long served under Napoleon, had tears in his eyes when his fine saber that had an inscription on the blade was broken by the Cossacks. 'I received it from Napoleon in Egypt and carried it with honor for 16 years,' he said to me. I could sense what was in the heart of this old veteran. I picked up the ornately wrought hilt and returned it to the colonel with the words, 'Now at least you have the hilt for remembrance. Keep it in your pocket during captivity, so that it won't be taken from you."[11] Some historians estimate that ten to 15,000 French soldiers who otherwise would have escaped were cut off by the bridge demolition.[12]

Thanks to heavy rainfall, the Elster was deeper and the current stronger than usual. Hundreds of retreating soldiers attempting to swim across or ford the river on horseback were either swept away and drowned or turned back to surrender. Poniatowski was among those who perished in the water. He had been promoted to marshal of France just three days before. Marshal Macdonald, who successfully crossed the river on his mount, described the reaction when the men heard that the bridge was blown: "This fearful news was downright paralyzing. On every face one could read frustration, rage and desperation; I myself no less. I smoldered with anger. It is inconceivable, but nevertheless historical fact, that neither before, during nor after the battle any measures were taken to enable us to cross the Elster at any other point than at the bridge to Lindenau. It would have been easy to bridge this narrow river."[13]

The fighting in Leipzig was almost over by one in the afternoon. French soldiers who escaped faced a difficult trek thanks to inadequate preparations. "The characteristics of the terrain in the territory we occupied caused the greatest difficulties when conducting the retreat," recalled Marbot. "Marshy grasslands, ditches filled with water and three small rivers crisscrossed the land, forming a number of narrow passages, and all had to be negotiated under the eyes of the enemy… Everything could have been overcome had the meadows, ditches, smaller waterways and the Pleisse, Parthe and especially the Elster been bridged in time… Material to construct these indispensable passages was available in abundance in Leipzig with its suburbs and adjacent villages. Time and sufficient labor were not lacking. Even on the 17th, much could have been accomplished. Despite all of this, it is inconceivable that absolutely nothing was done in this direction… Marshal Berthier gave a stereotype answer to practically all the corps commanders, especially in the final two days, who repeatedly asked about

Napoleon rides past weary French troops trudging westward after the defeat at Leipzig. Regarding the enemy he had smoothly vanquished seven years ago at Jena, he confessed, "This is no longer the Prussia of 1806."

constructing the necessary bridges in case of a retreat: 'The emperor has issued no orders for this.' It was notorious how one couldn't get anywhere with him…

"Berthier was a very capable man, energetic and reliable in his work. He nevertheless suffered so often from Napoleon's temper tantrums that he had developed a fear and aversion of the emperor's moods. As a result, he preferred to accept everything thrown at him, never taking the initiative or asking questions, and just obeying orders that he receives in writing. This maintained good relations between servant and master but was highly detrimental to the interests of the army. As great as the genius and industry of the emperor was, it was simply impossible for him to see everything and expedite every detail himself. As a result, when the emperor gave the order to retreat to the Saale on the road to Weissenfels, there was no way to cross the many water barriers in the countryside except on the few existing bridges."[14] Marbot stated that after the war, General Jean-Jacques Pelet and Baron Fain claimed that Napoleon had ordered construction of additional bridges. Marbot himself doubted "how much faith history will have in these belated assertions," especially by Pelet who idolized Bonaparte. Macdonald recalled, "Aware of the urgent necessity to provide crossings, a staff officer of the engineer corps had already asked whether or not he should construct them. He was told he must wait until the emperor gives the order."[15]

The withdrawal west of Leipzig was miserable, as Marbot recorded: "During the march, the emperor, coming from Leipzig, rode at a gallop past the long column. This time he didn't hear the usual cheers that accompany him wherever he shows himself. The troops were angry about the total neglect of measures to make it easier for them to march from the battlefield... Arriving at Markranstädt, a small town two hours from Leipzig, we stopped for a few hours to rest. During the break we heard a faint detonation and concluded that the Elster bridge was just blown. No one had the remotest notion that it was a premature detonation. On the contrary, we were all pleased that the last of our troops must have passed the bridge and the enemy cannot follow us for the time being."[16] Isadore Lehmann, who took part in the march, wrote, "One couldn't even count 20 soldiers in a regiment who still had rifles. This huge army made a comical impression during its retreat. Here a cuirassier with half a sheep wrapped in his overcoat and a pot with cooked fruit in hand, there a dragoon with two geese hanging around his neck, a cavalryman without a shako, another without boots and a third barefoot and most without weapons. The infantrymen were loaded like pack animals and few had rifles… There was a high level of insubordination."[17]

The three allied monarchs entered Leipzig at 1:00 p.m., even though there was still sporadic fighting after the Elster bridge exploded. After forcing their way in via the Halle Gate, Blücher's men did not tarry there. They turned toward

General Blücher enters Leipzig on October 19 after his troops had broken through the Durette Division at the Halle gate. He sent Yorck on an eleven-hour march with his corps to try and block the French retreat to the Saale.

Lützen to pursue the French army. Blücher road into the inner city and met with Friedrich Wilhelm, Franz I and Czar Alexander. The king thanked him with tears in his eyes. Blücher was in a bad mood because Napoleon had escaped. He grumbled, "He saved himself but hasn't gotten away yet."[18] Blücher took his Russian corps to Weissenfels on October 21, the day after the French had evacuated the town. Prince Wilhelm wrote him in the sovereign's name, "You perform services to the state faster than I can keep up with in expressing my gratitude. You may regard the latest proof of this as your promotion to field marshal." The king heaped honors and decorations on the old warrior. This led him to remark, "I'm overloaded like an old carriage horse, but knowing that I degraded that tyrant makes up for everything."[19] Blücher's Russian soldiers christened him "Marshal Forward," a nickname posterity associates with his memory to this day.

Leipzig was not seriously damaged, since allied leaders spared it from bombardment during the battle. Circumstances confronting the population were dire nevertheless; thousands of sick and wounded soldiers jammed the 56 provisional hospitals established in the city. The region had been denuded of foodstuffs to nourish the excessive number of soldiers present during the months of French occupation and more recently when opposing armies were massed there. It was not possible to properly feed the prisoners and patients. Tens of thousands of dead littered the streets and surrounding countryside or actually formed human dams in the rivers. Some 60 local villages were battered from combat operations and several totally destroyed. A typhus epidemic claimed the lives of 10,000 wounded soldiers and over 3,000 of Leipzig's residents. According to eyewitness Grautoff, "The poor injured French lay helpless for four or five days on the damp battlefield while the advancing victors protected and cared for their own wounded behind their front… Hundreds of them died horribly from starvation…

"More than 20 witnesses confirm how French soldiers crawled up to dead horses that were already decomposing and bored into the hind quarters with their weak hands or using some dull knife, then ripped out the flesh and consumed the carrion!… With a bayonet or even their teeth, they gnawed flesh from the bones of the animals and ate it raw. They frequently glanced anxiously about to see if a comrade might risk driving them away from their spot. Often six or eight unfortunates lay around a fallen steed, all digging away with hands and teeth beneath the animal's thick hide to bite the last of the flesh from bone… Close to the Grimmaisch Gate I found a Frenchman lying with a leg wound… The next day I brought him some bread and wine. When he saw them, tears welled up in his eyes."[20] Many seriously wounded soldiers who were evacuated to hospitals subsequently died from their injuries due to the inadequate supply of medicine. Most lightly wounded men survived.

Leipzig residents sought to relieve the suffering of the sick and injured survivors. Parallel to acts of mercy were examples of inhuman barbarism. Marbot described how when the Elster bridge was destroyed, "a countless number of our men, mostly undressed and almost all wounded, were trying to escape by

French soldiers rounded up after their defeat at Leipzig languish under the watch of Russian Kalmuck and Bashkir horsemen.

jumping into the river and swimming to our side. Their pursuers showered them with a fearsome hail of bullets… Those who had managed to swim to this side had discarded their weapons and therefore had no way of defending themselves. They ran across fields in fear of falling into the hands of 400 to 500 Prussians, Saxons and Badeners. Not satisfied with the slaughter in the city, they made a footbridge with planks across the foundation of the demolished bridge and crossed over to kill as many refugees as possible… My pen cannot describe the rage that seized the men of my two regiments and me when we heard the sounds of this uneven struggle. We seethed with anger and thirsted for revenge."[21]

Recent research fixes French losses, including *Rheinbund* auxiliaries, Italians and Poles, at 73,000. Some estimates are as high as 110,000. The allies captured 325 cannons and 900 ammunition carts. The aggregate of Russian, Austrian, Prussian and Swedish losses is 53,600 dead and wounded. These include 16,000 Prussians, 14,800 Austrians, 22,600 Russians and 200 Swedes.[22] Many of the sick and injured on both sides perished during the days and weeks to follow. Grautoff estimated the number of wounded in Leipzig during the battle at nearly 45,000, of whom 600 to 800 died every day.[23] The 140,000 French soldiers trapped in fortress garrisons in Germany eventually surrendered. These gloomy statistics did not prevent Napoleon from claiming in his *Bulletin de l'armée* that "the armies clashed on the battlefield of Leipzig on October 16. The French army was victorious. The Austrians were beaten and thrown out of all of their positions."[24] This was the day that even though he had more men on the field than Schwarzenberg, Napoleon's attack was repulsed and Marmont lost Möckern. The emperor purported that on the 18th as well, "victory belonged to the French." Their perimeter was pushed further inward toward Leipzig and Ney was unable to hold the pivotal Schönberg.

According to the bulletin, "Along the entire line, the enemy fell back and bivouacked behind the battlefield that remained in control of the French. The French army maneuvered in the night to reform behind the Elster and make direct contact with Erfurt, where it awaited delivery of needed ammunition." Napoleon wrote that "the army, although always victorious, suffered exceptional losses" due to the premature demolition of the Elster bridge and the betrayal of Saxon and *Rheinbund* troops. There is no substance to his claim that the Saxons turned their 60 cannons on the former French ally. Only about 5,000 Germans in Bonaparte's army switched sides and over a thousand Saxons did not.[25] Considering the number of soldiers engaged at Leipzig, their defection could not have exercised as much influence as Napoleon claimed. Petre concluded, "It would be an exaggeration to say that the desertion of this handful of Saxons at this late stage of the conflict had any significant effect on the outcome of the battle."[26]

The Great Betrayal

Schwarzenberg's decision not to assault Leipzig from the west, allowing Napoleon to escape with his army, subjected Europeans to nearly six more months of war. Civilians paid the price for Austria's duplicitous foreign policy as the French army fell back toward the Rhine. While in Germany in 1813, Lady Priscilla Burghersh, a youthful Englishwoman, described the circumstances in her letters: "No language can describe the horrible devastation these French have left behind them, and without seeing it one could form no idea of the country through which such a retreat as theirs has been made. Every bridge blown up, every village burnt or pulled down, fields completely devastated, orchards all turned up, and we traced their *bivouaques* all along by every horror you can conceive. None of the country people will bury them or their horses, so there they remain, lying all over the fields and roads, with millions of crows feasting… They told us the French soldiers were in such a state of starvation they took the earrings from their ears and implored for bits of bread, which none of the inhabitants would give them."[27]

Blücher was the only allied commander anxious to chase the French. The coalition did nothing to prevent Bertrand from taking the Saale crossings at Naumburg, Kösen and Freiburg. It made no attempt to destroy the bridges before Napoleon's troops arrive. "It seems more might have been done," maintained Petre. "With the great superiority of the allies in the east, they might apparently have reinforced Blücher, so as to enable him to interfere with the retreat by way of Schkeuditz (a suburb northwest of Leipzig). There was a quantity of cavalry which had done very little on the 18th, and might have been sent… against the line of retreat."[28] The French crossed the Saale at Weissenfels on October 20. Napoleon was in Erfurt three days later. His rearguard beat off an attack by Yorck at Freyburg while it was traversing the Unstrut River. The emperor brushed aside a Bavarian army of 30,000 men under Count Karl Philipp von Wrede attempting to block his progress at Hanau. Blücher was unable to reach the combat zone in time to help and was furious with Schwarzenberg's tardiness. When Napoleon crossed the Rhine on November 02, "Marshal Forward" growled, "He shouldn't have gotten through. God forgive those who dragged their feet on this."[29]

Russia and Prussia pressed forward while Austria and England were hesitant. Metternich arranged for peace talks in Frankfurt. On November 09, the Austrian minister offered to end the war if France will revert to her frontier of 1792. Napoleon did not reply. Metternich thereupon voiced no objection to Stein's insistence that the war be carried onto French soil. Coalition forces freed Denmark and the Netherlands from French control. Blücher and Gneisenau wanted to march on Paris. The Austrian general staff set Langres, far east of the capital, as the objective instead. The main army crossed the Rhine on December 21 and proceeded slowly through Baden, Alsace and Switzerland toward Langres.

Blücher's Silesian army crosses the Rhine at Kaub on January 01, 1814, to carry the war into France. In the river stands the picturesque Pfalzgrafenstein castle. Built early in the 14th Century, the edifice was used to reinforce toll collection on the Rhine.

Napoleon marched out to meet it with a new force of 70,000 men. Although Schwarzenberg had 190,000 troops, Bonaparte had shorter supply lines and an army small enough for him to retain personal control of operations. Blücher got his 21,500 Prussians and 62,300 Russians over the Rhine on January 01 and handed the emperor his first defeat inside France a month later at La Rothière. Schwarzenberg then directed Blücher to continue west along the Marne River while the Austrians maintained a slower pace on the Aube further south.

During the advance, the Prussian field marshal addressed French citizens in Lorraine. He reassured them that the coalition forces do not come as enemies of the people and promised that the first order of business once peace is restored will be to release all prisoners of war. In Nancy, he told the city council, "All the peoples of Europe have become enemies of this once so prosperous France. And why? Because of the destructive ambition of one individual. God has judged him severely and destroyed 600,000 Frenchmen in two campaigns. They are victims of the limitless aspirations of a ruler who squanders the blood of a nation that he is foreign to. An entire generation wiped out! I am sorry to be unable to spare you the burden that war brings with it. Whatever I can do to ease it will be done. We wage war only against those who wish to perpetuate it. I have rescinded the unpopular contributions." The speech was translated and printed on flyers distributed in the thousands. He told his soldiers, "I have promised the inhabitants on the left side of the Rhine protection and security. I do this in your name, so you must hold to it!"[30]

Napoleon marched his small host north to fight the Silesian Army and defeated Blücher in four successive engagements in six days. The combined Prussian-Russian force successfully withdrew after each battle. The setbacks were too much for the timorous Schwarzenberg; he decided to turn back. Blücher followed the Marne north and amalgamated Bülow's corps coming from Belgium into his army. Napoleon expected the Prussians to retreat to Germany after their defeats in the first half of February, but the Silesian Army continued toward Paris instead. Bonaparte gave chase but was soundly defeated by Blücher and Gneisenau at Laon on March 09 and 10. Losing 6,500 men in the battle, Napoleon withdrew to Soissons. The victory encouraged Schwarzenberg to about face and resume the march on Paris. Metternich again negotiated with the French, this time at Châtillon. He broke off talks on March 19 because Napoleon was still recalcitrant. The emperor attacked Schwarzenberg at Arcis-sur-Aube on March 20. He did not realize that he was facing the entire Austrian army. After two days of battle his troops retreated with heavy losses.

Instead of pursuing the enemy, Schwarzenberg convened a war council and the French escaped. The Austrians defeated Mortier and Marmont on the 25th. Napoleon planned to maneuver his army behind the coalition forces to cut their supply lines. On the advice of Talleyrand, who had ridden from Paris to meet the czar, Schwarzenberg and Blücher continued west. They took Paris after heavy fighting on March 31. The population welcomed them. To finance

Landwehr troops sight Paris in March 1814. The invasion of France would have been unnecessary had Schwarzenberg not allowed Napoleon to escape Leipzig. "The leaders of the Austrian army were indifferent to the greater losses anticipated from prolonging the war," historian Bauer concluded.

a hopeless campaign, Napoleon had doubled property taxes and rescinded civil service pensions. The administration had drafted 120,000 men in October and another 300,000 men in November.[31] His marshals refused to continue the struggle; Marmont surrendered his entire corps over the objections of his officers. Army commanders forced Napoleon to abdicate at Fontainebleau. In disguise and using a false name, he made his way to the coast to begin exile on the Mediterranean isle of Elba. When people recognized him during the journey through France, they pelted his carriage with stones and threatened to lynch him.[32] Thus ended the war of the sixth coalition. Prussian and Russian soldiers bivouacking in Paris heard an order of the day from Gneisenau reading, "I expect the army not to dishonor itself by behaving arrogantly, but as victor to conduct itself humanely and with humility."[33]

When it was over Gneisenau wrote Princess Luise Radziwell, "We've taken our revenge in a way that knows no parallel in history. We've become poor, but rich in martial glory and proud of taking back our independence."[34] War had indeed impoverished the Prussians. "And how this people had suffered!", observed Treitschke: "Only a few months ago the capital heard the clamor of battle close to its walls, the farmers' fields were wasted, rooms stripped and without décor and scarcely was there a home that did not mourn the loss of a son or a brother."[35] Diplomats from Russia, England, Prussia, Austria, France and Sweden convened in November 1814 in Vienna to determine the future continental order. Interspersed with balls, banquets, concerts, parades and boar hunts, the Congress of Vienna was as much a celebration of aristocratic pomp as it was a diplomatic session. Metternich, who chaired the conference, considered his primary task "to devote myself to propping up rotten buildings," in other words to restore the oligarchy of Great Powers and reestablish absolutism as the dominant political system.[36]

The French cabinet invited Louis XVIII, brother of the beheaded Bourbon king, to assume the throne of France. He belonged to an established dynasty and was a friend of the coalition, so England, Russia and Austria advocated conciliatory peace terms. Talleyrand participated in the talks. The congress reaffirmed conditions of the Paris peace treaty signed in May 1814, by which France retained her borders of 1790. No reparations were initially imposed. This created a hardship for Prussia, whose war debt was 200 million thaler. Prussia did however, augment her territory; the congress restored lands taken from her by Napoleon at Tilsit except for most of her former Polish territory. She received two-fifths of Saxony with 850,000 inhabitants. Prussia gained Swedish Pomerania, portions of both Westphalia and the Rhineland and Danzig with its surrounding territory. Beyond the Victoria statue and chariot dismounted from atop the Brandenburg Gate and Friedrich the Great's sword and medals, the French were required to return to Prussia scarcely any art treasures stolen by Napoleon and hauled to the Louvre. Berlin's representatives at the congress, Hardenberg and Stein, demanded the fortresses of Strasbourg and Landau, but did not energetically promote their country's interests.

After Napoleon returned for his "hundred days" terminated by the battle of Waterloo in June 1815, France was required to pay 700 million francs in reparations. A fifth of this amount was remitted to Prussia. Metternich ensured that princes of the former *Rheinbund* duchies remain in control of their respective kingdoms. The diplomats in Vienna divided Germany into 39 autonomous states, the *Deutscher Bund* (German Confederation), with a parliament. Three of Napoleon's minions in Europe—Murat in Naples, Jérôme in Westphalia and Karl von Dalberg in Frankfurt—were dethroned. Within Germany, the petty tyrants received amnesty for their previous support of Napoleon and were accepted into the coalition six weeks after the allied victory at Leipzig. These former *Rheinbund* princes "displayed not the remotest patriotic spirit" for Germany, which is probably why Metternich wanted them in power.[37] Shortly after the battle of nations, he destroyed the influence of the central administrative system Stein had introduced to promote cooperation and reform among western German states.

At the behest of the czar, who was himself under the influence of spiritual mystics, the trio of despots ruling Russia, Austria and Prussia concluded the "Holy Alliance" in September 1815. The purpose was to return Europe by the grace of God to the absolutist system of the 18th Century. In the minds of these

After the battle of Waterloo, Gneisenau rallies Prussian cavalrymen to chase down retreating elements of French army. He therefore prevented Napoleon from reforming his divisions as had been the case after Leipzig.

sage monarchs the woefully underdeveloped political intuition of their subjects made it necessary to govern them by divine right. By joining this pretentious alliance, Friedrich Wilhelm III reneged on the commitment he made to his people to provide a constitution and involve them in government. When he issued his *Aufruf an mein Volk* proclamation from Breslau on March 17, 1813, "this was tantamount to a repudiation of absolutism," maintained Lehmann: "By allowing the nation to form a militia, he officially acknowledged that salvation of the common good is no longer possible by means of the old monarchy."[38] When Napoleon escaped from Elba and returned to Paris on March 20, 1815, this compelled the king of Prussia to tell the population that a third war must be waged against France. He pledged to provide a constitution and institute parliament in his "Decree for Implementing Representation of the People" two months later.

Friedrich Wilhelm promised to draft a constitution in 1810, 1812, 1813, 1815, 1820 and 1821. Not once did he keep his word.[39] Prussia's constitutional commission met only once and that was in July 1817. Democratic values had already taken root in the public consciousness and the war of liberation greatly strengthened this tendency. Prussia's customary, rigidly defined class structure dividing aristocrat, burgher and farmer had given way to a wartime system wherein all strata fulfill their duty toward a common political goal. Whoever performed honorable wartime service became respected for life regardless of

social background. In assessing the value of the Silesian militia, Gneisenau had
informed the king, "One cannot fail to see in the establishment of the *Landwehr*
the good spirit that animates the nation... Regarding the men themselves, all in
all they demonstrate a martial spirit and much good will."[40] The sacrifices of his
countrymen made little impression on the sovereign and his entourage, as Boyen
pointed out: "Almost all of them feel themselves called upon to preserve the surviving institutions and individual class interests. In so doing they offer sad proof
that among this circle there isn't a single one who understands the times we live
in and its requirements."[41]

Friedrich Wilhelm revealed his attitude toward the Silesian militia when Paris
capitulated. In preparation for the victory parade, the troops repaired their worn
uniforms and cleaned their accoutrements as best they could. After months of
campaigning, tunics and trousers were singed from campfires and stained from
mud, blood and powder smoke. Tears were patched with nonmatching material.
The men's hair was not trimmed nor were many clean shaven. The battalions
formed up for inspection and wildly cheered the king when he arrived. "They
look bad," he growled disapprovingly. "Filthy people!"[42] He forbade the Silesian
Landwehr to parade into the city. These troops had often borne the brunt of
battle. At Wachau for example, a single *Landwehr* regiment lost three quarters
of its personnel repelling French attacks. The day before the debacle at Leipzig,
men of the 3rd Kurmark *Landwehr* Cavalry Regiment sent a delegation to their
commanding officer asking to go into action the next morning to wipe clean the
shame of Jena.[43] While inspecting another of Blücher's formations before the
parade, the king again expressed dissatisfaction with the soldiers' scruffy appearance. He asked General Yorck, "Have you seen my guardsmen?" Yorck replied,
"Majesty, these *are* your guardsmen!"[44]

The war with France was over, but Prussia faced a renewed internal struggle between the old aristocracy and big estate holders against the politically
energized citizenry. The titled class sought to reassert ancestral privilege; the
common people, many of whom had previously worked the estates as sharecrop-
pers, now had the affront to demand a voice in government and a constitution.
Conservative nobles wished to return to the Prussia of Friedrich the Great while
the rest of the population expected to advance into the modern age. The reform
party's progress before the war is largely due to Queen Luise's influence on her
weak-minded husband. She, like Scharnhorst and Gneisenau, believed that
freedom-loving people fight harder to overthrow foreign tyranny than vassals
do. She was the nemesis of royal advisors who promoted the absolute state. The
queen's cause of death at age 34 was not conclusively established. One postmor-
tem report stated pneumonia, another typhus. Considering what the aristocracy
had to gain by her demise, the contradiction invites suspicion that this spirited
young woman in the prime of life may have been poisoned.[45]

Once the deeply mourned Luise was gone, the king was gradually dominated by a reactionary camarilla including the theologian Ancillon and Prince

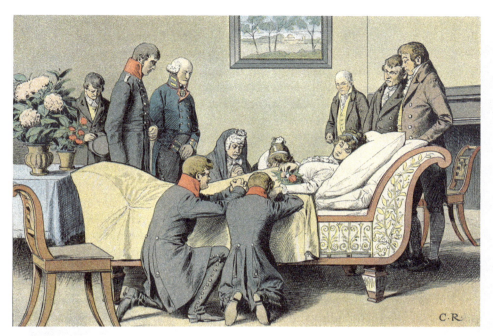

Queen Luise on her death bed on July 19, 1810. Her two eldest sons kneel beside her, while the king and Chancellor Hardenberg stand in silent grief to the left.

Wilhelm Ludwig zu Sayn-Wittgenstein. The latter became chief of political police in 1812 and Prussian police minister in 1814. Both men were lackeys of Metternich and Sayn-Wittgenstein maintained frequent contact with him.[46] Ultraconservative members of the royal entourage presented the king with a copy of a brochure by Theodor Schmalz, a Berlin University law professor, pointing out the allegedly foreign nature of Prussia's reform movement: "Are we Germans or Frenchmen? This accursed hatching of constitutions has been a characteristically French vice for 26 years. Napoleon created them by the dozen, like decrees; our political scribblers create them by the dozen, like newspaper articles."[47] Traditionalist nobles argued that since the military danger from France is over, there is no need for reform. They also opposed German unification.

Friedrich Jahn for example, was a Brandenburg-Prussian educator who founded gymnastics programs in 1810 to promote physical fitness in the young. The purpose was also patriotic, in that participants felt themselves an elite of the nation preparing to overthrow the French yoke. Jahn assisted in establishing the Lützow *Freikorps* and was a battalion commander during the war of liberation. After the victory over Napoleon, Jahn helped form the *Burschenschaften* (student fraternities) in Jena. The town was in a duchy known to champion liberal values.

Burschenschaft members were young adults in the universities who fostered liberalism and nationalist ideals. Eight of the eleven men founding the fraternities had belonged to the Lützow *Freikorps*. Jahn was an outspoken critic of the betrayal of the common man in Prussia. His involvement in the *Burschenschaft* put him squarely in Sayn-Wittgenstein's crosshairs. Jahn was arrested in 1819 and imprisoned for over five years without trial. The *Turnvereine* (gymnastics clubs) he sponsored were eventually shut down.

In 1818, representatives of the governments of England, Russia, Austria, France and Prussia convened the Congress of Aachen to prevent the spread of democratic ideals in Europe. Metternich sent two memorandums to Friedrich Wilhelm persuading him that drafting a constitution to allow the people a say in government will lead to a Parisian-style overthrow of the monarchy as in 1789. The memos warned of a potential "dissolution of Prussia... because such an innovation cannot be introduced into a great state without a revolution or without leading to a revolution."[48] Metternich somehow convinced the king that political reform will also weaken Prussia's defense capabilities, despite the fact that the war of liberation demonstrated the opposite. Friedrich Wilhelm's reversal on reform caused patriotic Prussians to organize protests. This led the absolutist clique surrounding the king to institute a police state as oppressive as Napoleon's. Nationalist professors, among them Arndt, were dismissed from German universities and patriotic students blacklisted.[49] Dissidents immigrated to the United States.

The aristocracy's efforts to block reform received a boost in March 1819. Carl Ludwig Sand, a member of a radical fringe of the *Burschenschaften*, stabbed to death August Kotzebue, a diplomat in Russian service. Kotzebue published an anti-liberal periodical in Mannheim that ridiculed the German unification movement. Metternich welcomed the assassination. He boasted to his publicist Gentz that "at the cost of poor Kotzebue," the "wonderful Sands" has provided the pretext to take action against the student societies.[50] Metternich gathered representatives of the German states at Karlsbad in August to draft a resolution to combat alleged subversion and terrorism associated with constitutional circles. More professors lost their jobs and students on watch lists were barred from civil service. Hundreds of students were imprisoned or exiled and some were condemned to death. Gentz, instrumental in composing the text of the Karlsbad Resolution, wrote in his diary that its ratification is "a victory more important than the battle of Leipzig."[51] Gentz played a major role in suppressing academic freedom throughout the German states. The *Untersuchungsgesetz* (Investigation Law) established an international bureau to ferret out "revolutionary agitation" throughout the *Deutscher Bund*.[52]

Just before proceeding to Karlsbad, Metternich visited Friedrich Wilhelm at a resort in Teplitz on August 01. Exaggerating the influence of the small clique Sands had been associated with, the Austrian diplomat induced the king to order a reluctant Hardenberg to draft a communique declaring that "universal representation of the people" is "incompatible with the territorial and political structure of the realm."[53] Friedrich Wilhelm enforced the oppressive Karlsbad decrees inside Prussia. The *Burschenschaften* were outlawed and the press completely muzzled. Prussians were henceforth at the mercy of the Central Investigative Commission. It was established to eradicate "revolutionary activity and liaison with demagogues."[54] Officers of the commission determined what constitutes "revolutionary activity" and were accorded broad interpretation. The Prussian state minister Wilhelm von Humboldt drafted a proposal denouncing the Karlsbad Resolution. Justice minister Beyme, war minister Boyen and army chief of staff Grolman endorsed Humboldt's proposal. All four were dismissed by the king as consequence.

This was the end of the reform movement during the reign of Friedrich Wilhelm III. In one historian's verdict, "he was not the only king to cast doubt on the concept and value of hereditary monarchy. He was however one of the worst, because in a historically decisive, progressive age he was an utter failure."[55] Perpetuating aristocratic privilege was not Metternich's only purpose in combating a constitution for Prussia. It served Austrian foreign policy as well. Gneisenau himself provided the explanation: "If a new constitution is drafted soon for the revived and expanded Prussian monarchy and granted to the people by the king, that will be the strongest bond binding the new acquisitions to the old provinces; the other German states will compare our condition with theirs. In this way, the desire will be awakened to be united with us and the way will be clear for new acquisitions, made not by force of arms but by liberality of principles."[56] The constitution, in Gneisenau's view, would encourage the common people and younger, enlightened nobles throughout Germany to fall in with Prussia; Austria could never assert herself over a conglomerate of German states unified by Berlin.

Even without Metternich's influence, Friedrich Wilhelm was ill-disposed toward the "demagogue general" as his reactionary entourage called Gneisenau. When the allies captured Leipzig, the sovereigns spoke with military commanders in the city. Gneisenau wrote Clausewitz that evening to describe his experience: "When everyone had gathered in the marketplace in Leipzig, the king offered some friendly words about his contentment with our army. Nothing to me personally. I still haven't heard a single word of praise about our crossing the Elbe and the following combat occurrences. Czar Alexander by contrast, said the nicest things as did Emperor Franz and Prince Schwarzenberg. But you can see how deeply rooted the king's repugnance is toward anyone who does not share his political views."[57] During the victorious campaign, Blücher had followed his chief of staff's lead; the orders, operational plans and battlefield deployments of the Silesian Army always came from Gneisenau. Being snubbed by an ungrateful king in the town square was nothing more than a petty, studied insult to the general responsible for getting him there in the first place.

Both Blücher and Gneisenau protested to the king about his meek acceptance of the peace settlement in Vienna. Friedrich Wilhelm had actually tarried in the Austrian capital during part of the conference without intervening. Prussian patriots had expected their country to annex all of Saxony and were dissatisfied with the final division of territory. Vienna's creation of the *Deutscher Bund* was to sustain former *Rheinbund* princes who had served Napoleon and prevent Prussia from uniting Germany. Blücher even weighed the possibility of deploying the Silesian Army to force revision of the settlement. In the letter of resignation he submitted, "Marshal Forward" threatened to take the matter to the public for a decision. He and Gneisenau only deepened the rift between the reform movement and the king, who considered their criticism insubordination.[58] The monarch complained to British officer Sir Robert Wilson that Gneisenau, the hero of Kolberg, is a "wicked, insolent fellow" who has to be "watched constantly."[59] In 1818, Gneisenau demanded a Prussian constitution guaranteeing public trials, freedom of the press, abolishing both the secret police and postal inspection, and those in power being accountable for their actions.

Despite the king's suspicions, neither Blücher nor Gneisenau were revolutionaries even remotely approaching the Jacobin example. The old marshal had studied the French Revolution and regarded the men who had guillotined both the king and the French noblesse as murderous opportunists without morals.[60] He saw how republican corruption and mismanagement had brought France to the brink of anarchy. This had paved the way for the people to accept a new despot, as long as he could restore order, who made himself emperor and subjected the country to a state of almost perpetual warfare until deposed. Blücher considered the Prussian monarchy preferable to a revolution and reign of terror like in France. Gneisenau had never been disloyal to the king, yet censors opened his mail and his enemies at court continually undermined him. Even before defeating Napoleon, Gneisenau felt so insecure about his position in the army that he once asked Hardenberg if he would appoint him postmaster general after the war.[61] Boyen was watched by the secret police on suspicion of high treason.[62] This was the thanks of the Hohenzollern king to those who liberated Prussia from foreign oppression and saved his crown.

Conclusion

After the liberation, Prussian patriots asked Caspar David Friedrich, a Pomeranian painter renowned for the romantic, dreamlike quality of his landscapes, about erecting a statue of Scharnhorst. The artist was skeptical that the monarchy will honor the fallen soldier who had reformed the Prussian army and displayed such talent for getting factions with rival views and interests to work together. "So long as we remain the menials of princes," Friedrich replied, "nothing great of this kind will be seen. Where the people have no voice, the people will not be allowed to be self-aware and honor themselves."[63] Like many disillusioned subjects, the painter left Prussia for a country with a more liberal regime, in his case the kingdom of Saxony. Within the Hohenzollern realm, once the danger from France was eliminated, the king and his advisors concerned themselves with extinguishing the revolutionary spirit that had accompanied the dreaded *Volksbewaffnung* (arming the people). For over six years, Friedrich Wilhelm had faced the tortuous dilemma of either accepting Napoleonic domination or weaponizing a population that was becoming increasingly cognizant of its human rights.

For the first time in the history of the Hohenzollerns, Prussia had an army that was not at the personal disposal of the king but represented the entire nation. This was the offspring of an armed force historically born out a comparatively small kingdom's necessity to defend itself against powerful neighboring states. Over a period of nearly 200 years, it was gradually expanded and upgraded by a series of prudent monarchs, honed in combat and capable of adapting in defeat. The Thirty Years' War ended the age of mercenaries and created the prerequisites for the standing army. Drawing on lessons from Spain, the Netherlands and France, Prussia's became the best on the continent. It compensated for the country's diminutive size and lack of natural frontiers by the superior quality of the troops. During the reign of Friedrich II, Prussia acquired a legendary reputation for prowess in action in the Seven Years' War. The great Friedrich added a hitherto unknown element to military convention of the age; this was the camaraderie he shared with ordinary rankers, taking his place with them on the battlefield, warming himself beside them at the campfire, sharing rations and pitching his tent in their midst.

Friedrich the Great reestablished the military's social barrier between highborn and peasant after peace was restored. This did not discourage officers like Gneisenau, whom he commissioned as a lieutenant. To them, the novel bond between superior and subordinate, noble and common, conformed to the burgeoning spirit of the Enlightenment. Blücher, described as the "soul of the Prussian army," angrily led his staff from the table where a banquet was prepared in his honor when the host smugly confided that only regimental officers of noble birth are invited. Six years after the death of Friedrich II, the coalition wars against the French Republic began. France demonstrated the advantages of a progressive system of government willing to nurture energetic and talented elements from all of society and elevate them to positions of command. Prussia's defeat by Napoleon was among the most one-sided in history. It was an inevitable consequence of the stubborn refusal to adopt political ideals overtaking the absolutist system. The thoroughness of the collapse left no doubt that a new approach to national defense must be found. It is the mark of a great nation that in a time of crisis it can produce men to assume positions of leadership, after a prolonged internal struggle against conservative elements in power, who are capable of resurrecting the state and restoring the country's freedom and honor.

The war of 1806 and 1807 overcame the concept that national defense belongs to the standing army alone, just as the Thirty Years' War closed the chapter on mercenary armies. In its place came the national army patterned after the French

Volunteers in Breslau present themselves to the king after his March 1813 proclamation calling for a national army. He never grasped that the Prussian revolution was loyal to the crown, unlike the Jacobin uprising in France in 1789.

example. Generals who had served under Friedrich the Great decades before still held that noble blood is prerequisite to be an officer. To this Scharnhorst retorted, "If only aristocratic children, despite their lack of knowledge and tender age, have the right to be commissioned and men with experience and spirit are subordinate to them with no prospect for promotion, it will help titled families but be bad for the army. This will never earn the respect of the nation and remain a joke to the educated strata."[64] The reformer parried misgivings that an armed citizenry will rise against the ruling class by explaining, "It need not be feared that such a militia is dangerous, as long as it consists of rankers from the middle class... Only a militia from the lower classes can be a cause for concern."[65]

The king and his military advisors never fully accepted this argument, but were simply swept along by the forceful personalities of Scharnhorst, Gneisenau, Blücher, Boyen and Grolman. The dynasties of Europe became so fearful of the Prussian example that the czar told his generals in September 1815, "Gentlemen, it is very possible that we will one day have to come to the aid of the king of Prussia against his own army."[66] What could better demonstrate that the wealthy and privileged of the world often feel a stronger kinship with those of similar fortune in other countries than they do with the common people of their own? Friedrich Gentz's remark that the Karlsbad Resolution reaffirming the preeminence of European dynasties is a greater victory than the battle of Leipzig is another example of this cosmopolitan mindset, which is based on entitlement and materialism instead of on patriotic convictions.

The war of liberation, despite the destruction it wrought in Germany and the universal bloodletting, led to a positive development for the country. This was the rise of the German unification movement. Before Bonaparte was drawn into battle for the last time, men of vision like Stein, Arndt and Jahn grasped that division of the Teutonic states is, in the tradition of Richelieu during the 17th Century, a product of the foreign policy of rival powers. Napoleon and Metternich both promoted this disunity; Bonaparte with the *Rheinbund* and Metternich with the *Deutscher Bund*. The professed objective was ostensibly to keep peace on the continent, but was actually to prevent Germany from ever asserting herself as the largest single nation in central Europe. The war of liberation pitted German against German; during the first phase of the conflict, over half of the troops crossing lances with Prussia hailed from German states allied with Napoleon.[67] This sickened many soldiers on both sides of the fratricidal struggle.

Karl August Jordan, who fought at Möckern and Leipzig in the East Prussian National Cavalry Regiment, wrote after the battle, "May there never again be a time when Germans fight against Germans and German troops treat another German land as an enemy! Our swords and lances were spotted with German blood before we could liberate our great fatherland.... The first attack of our regiment at Leipzig was unfortunately against German formations."[68] At the battle of nations, Saxons, Westphalians, Hessians and Bavarians serving under the French banner, whose lands had been occupied and ruthlessly exploited by France, placed more value on nationality than on the politics of their respective princes and joined the coalition. Frontline officers like Blücher and Gneisenau could scarcely concern themselves about common ethnic ties while waging a military campaign, especially since so many of the regiments opposing them were German. After Napoleon's exile however, they too saw unification in the country's future.

As Lehmann pointed out in a lecture to university students in 1913, "None of the creators of the army and in fact of the new Prussia were born Prussians. Stein was Rhenish-Franconian, Scharnhorst from Hanover, Gneisenau half Frankish and half Swabian... Blücher hailed from Mecklenburg and State Chancellor Hardenberg was also a Hanoverian."[69] Humboldt stated, "It will never be possible to stop Germany from wanting to be one state and one nation; the inclination, if not toward unity at least toward some kind of association remains... in every heart and mind."[70] The patriot Heinrich von Gagern said of the *Burschenschaften*, "We want more communal spirit among the individual German states, greater unity in their policies and values, the closest federal cooperation rather than independent policies of each state and above all, we desire that Germany as a land and the German people as a nation be esteemed."[71]

The wars Prussia doggedly waged from the 17th to the early 19th Century were milestones in the development of the army and the nation. Destruction of life and property, depleted public resources, indebtedness and mourning accompanied every struggle. During periods of recovery, Prussian military leaders tried to improve the army in preparation for future confrontations. Before Napoleon's invasion, they safeguarded the country's independence and protected the monarchy. The population was subject to a regime "that in its form was absolutely militaristic," as a French hussar officer who served in the campaign of 1806 wrote. "When a German province was conquered by the French and its people received no more orders from their prince, the lower classes who were unaccustomed to acting on their own free will didn't know what to do without a directive from their government or from their aristocratic masters."[72] Napoleon expressed surprise at the lack of aggressive resistance from the population he encountered invading Germany.[73] This was a marked contrast to the Spaniards and Russians, and indeed to the passionate disposition of the French in 1789.

This rigidly structured system so serviceable to the highborn collapsed more because of resistance to modernization, especially the failure to adopt the lessons of the French Revolution, than due to Napoleon's genius. The only option for Prussia to regain her freedom was to embrace an entirely novel concept of national defense; that of arming the people. While the nobility stagnated because positions of authority were guaranteed by birth regardless of ability or performance, the population was enlightened, restless and motivated. When the government recruited the Prussian middle class, the burghers, into the officer corps and the *Landwehr*, it incorporated a social stratum that surpassed the aristocracy in education, talent, free will and initiative. Pride of tradition, loyalty and courage were indeed inherent virtues of the leaders of the old army. In the long run they were not in themselves sufficient to command progressive, prosperous and self-reliant individuals, unrestrained by martial convention, who were successful in private enterprise by virtue of superior schooling, imagination and enlightened values. Advances in military technology alone required soldiers of superior intellect and personal development.

Prussian patriots drew the middle class to the colors by promising political reform. The notion that the public will become involved in government and transform the country into a beacon of the Enlightenment, thus putting it ahead of other German states in this realm, evoked a pride in the nation that is the true genesis of patriotism. They also appealed to the population's customary allegiance to the monarchy, whose cherished Queen Luise had so affectionately bonded to the people. Friedrich Wilhelm III served as the poster boy for the liberation movement. He provided the image of authority and legitimacy. Many non-Prussians joined the *Landwehr*, offering evidence of a German nationalist sentiment beyond the Hohenzollern kingdom. Austria, Russia and *Rheinbund* states maintained conventional standing armies while their leaders stood aghast at the success of Prussia's social and military revolution. Prussia was the driving force behind the defeat and pursuit of Napoleon across Europe. Without Blücher and Gneisenau, he would have plunged the continent into war again within a few years. That Metternich believed he could contain Bonaparte in a weakened France attests to his failure to comprehend the ambitious nature of the resourceful and duplicitous Corsican.

Once Napoleon was in exile, Friedrich Wilhelm betrayed his people and sandbagged reform. To safeguard his reign, he felt it necessary to return the army to its ancient role of royal instrument instead of maintaining it as a national fighting force. In 1806, out of 8,000 officers in the Prussian army, only 695 were burghers, most of whom served in the artillery.[74] By 1818, slightly more than half the commissioned officers were aristocrats. The following year, the *Landwehr* became subordinate to the line army and lost its independent character. Scions of titled families assumed positions of command once more. They gradually regained authority over regiments and administration. By 1860, just 14 percent of colonels and generals in the Prussian army were non-nobles.[75] Now that the external danger had passed, Friedrich Wilhelm no longer needed the population as an ally in foreign affairs. He secured the legitimacy of his throne through the Holy Alliance with Austria and Russia. He destroyed the inner foundation of his pact with the public by withdrawing the pledge to share political power. He could not however, eradicate the vitality and spirit of the people of Prussia. The concepts of fatherland and constitution remained their ideals, just no longer attainable by working *with* the absolute state but from then on, *against* it.

After the war of liberation, Friedrich Wilhelm reduced taxes for large estate holders and rescinded assessments that Hardenberg had imposed on them in 1811. Common people assumed the fiscal burden to cover the shortfall. The revised tax structure and new land laws favored the affluent for decades to come: Between 1834 and 1858, hundreds of thousands of German planters lost their farms to big landowners.[76] When a wave of revolutions shook Europe in March 1848, Prussia was not spared. The Metternich system established at the Congress of Vienna, designed to perpetuate absolutism and hold the peasantry in bondage, was rocked to its foundation. Workers across the continent rose in protest against meager wages and political oppression. The Germans participated and also demanded unification. Metternich was forced from office and migrated to England. The Karlsbad decrees were abrogated. The uprising in Berlin claimed 254 lives but this was less than the number of casualties in some capitals. The new Prussian king, Friedrich Wilhelm IV, withdrew the army to avoid escalation of the bloodbath and made concessions. They fell short of what was initially promised the rioters to restore order. Prussia became a constitutional monarchy. This was a long overdue step toward granting people human rights they are entitled to and toward the unification of Germany.

Prussia's odyssey from martial, absolute state to constitutionally governed monarchy that eventually welded the Germans together has elements that are witnessed time and again throughout history. Visionaries who seek to bring government into conformity with the will of the people struggle against those in authority who oppose change. The clique in power, tenanting privileged positions thanks to political or social connections, shifts priority from contributing to the community to consolidating and maintaining control over it. To this end it harnesses the resources of the state. Without competition at the top, the passion for creative endeavor in those belonging to this exclusive minority wanes. Complacency trumps the ambition to realize full potential in life and stagnation supplants ingenuity. Instead of helping the nation grow and embrace progress, they intuitively regard anyone promoting novel trends that benefit humanity as a menace to their lofty station in society. In the long run, such a caste cannot hope to lead a vibrant nation. Only by disarming, weakening or oppressing the population can it retain control. In virtually every field of endeavor—among them public administration, finance, education, commerce, national defense and industry—such reactionary, ruthless creatures are forever present, prolonging the status quo by confounding wholesome values, obstructing reform and tormenting men and women who conceive and promote it. The history of Prussia at war is a lesson in both the greatness and the tragedy of mankind.

Bibliography

Bainville, Jacques, Geschichte zweier Völker, Hamburg 1939/41

Bathe, Rolf, Männer am Feind, Oldenburg/Berlin 1940

Bauer, Frank, Die Völkerschlacht bei Leipzig, Berlin 1988

Berenhorst, Georg Heinrich, Betrachtungen über die Kriegskunst, Leipzig 1798/99

Bohn, Eduard, Vierzehnheiligen in Thüringen, Apolda 1858

Borcke, Johann Friedrich Ernst von, Kriegerleben des Johann von Borcke, Berlin 1888

Börner, Karl-Heinz, Vor Leipzig 1813, Berlin 1988

Böttiger, Karl Wilhelm, Geschichte des Kurstaates und Königreiches Sachsen, Gotha 1870

Burghersh, Priscilla, The Letters of Lady Burghersh, Edinburgh Review Jan. 1894-April 1894, London 1894

Clausewitz, Carl von, Notes on Prussia in her Grand Catastrophe of 1806, Leavenworth 1922

Cochenhausen, Friedrich von, Die Verteidigung Mitteleuropas, Jena 1940

Connelly, Owen, Blundering to Glory, Maryland 2006

Decker, Carl von, Die Schlachten und Hauptgefechte des siebenjährigen Krieges, Berlin 1837

Deutsche Wehrzeitung (periodical), Coburg 1864

Die Schlacht von Jena oder Auerstädt geliefert den 14. Oktober 1806, Leipzig 1806

Dittrich, Adolf, Erinnerungen an Mainz, Wien 1858

Dorn, Günter and Joachim Engelmann, Die Schlachten Friedrichs des Grossen, Augsburg 1996

Duffy, Christopher, Friedrich der Grosse und seine Armee, Stuttgart 1983

Dufraisse, Roger, Napoleon, New York 1992

Dumont, Daniel, Die Belagerung der Stadt Mainz durch die Franzosen im Jahre 1792 und ihre
	Wiedereroberung durch die teutschen Truppen im Jahr 1793, Mainz 1793

Dupuy, Trevor, A Genius for War. The German Army and General Staff 1807-1945, London 1977

Eckert, G., Von Valmy bis Leipzig, Hannover und Frankfurt/Main 1955

Engelmann, Joachim, Feldmarschall Blücher, Friedberg 1982

Fesser, Gerd, 1806 Die Doppelschlacht bei Jena und Auerstedt, Jena-Quedlinburg, 2006

Fesser, Gerd, 1813 Die Völkerschlacht bei Leipzig, Jena-Quedlinburg, 2013

Fevers, Kurt, Vernichtungskrieg, Düsseldorf 1941

Fichtel, Konrad, Roms Kreuzzüge gegen Germanien, Tübingen 2004

Fontane, Theodor, Preussische Generäle, Bad Langensalza/Thüringen 2018

Friccius, Carl, Geschichte der Befestigung und Belagerung Danzigs, Berlin 1854

Friccius, Carl, Zur Geschichte der Errichtung der Landwehr in Ost und West Preussen und in Lithauen
	im Jahre 1813, Berlin 1838

Fuller, J.F.C., The Conduct of War, New Brunswick 1961

Gagern, Hans Freiherr von, Mein Anteil an der Politik Band 1: Unter Napoleons Herrschaft, Stuttgart
	und Tübbingen 1823

Gaupp, J., Belaerungsgeschichte der Festung Glogau, Glogau 1807

Gerber, Paul, Die Schlacht bei Leuthen, Berlin 1901

Geschichte des Feldzuges vom Jahre 1806, Darmstadt 1852

Gieren, Gerhard, Der freimaurerische Kriegsverrat von 1806, München 1939

Goltz, Colmar Freiherr von der, Von Jena bis Pr. Eylau, Berlin 1907

Goltz, Colmar Freiherr von der, Von Rossbach bis Jena und Auerstedt, Berlin 1906

Graf, Gerhard, …des Krieges Elend Die Schlacht bei Möckern, Leipzig 2012

Grautoff, Ferdinand, In Leipzig während der Völkerschlacht, Leipzig 1913

Grollmann, Hauptmann von, Einige Briefe geschrieben vor und nach der Schlacht bei Jena und
	Auerstädt, 1807

Gronau, W., Christian Wilhelm Dohm nach seinem Wollen und Handeln, Lemgo 1824

Grosser Generalstab, Das Preussische Offizierkorps und die Untersuchung der Kriegsereignisse, Berlin 1906

Gudzent, Christa, Neidhardt von Gneisenau, Berlin 1987

Günther, Gerhard, Deutsches Kriegertum im Wandel der Geschichte, 1934

Gürtler, Heinz, Deutsche Freimaurer im Dienste napoleonischer Politik, Berlin 1942

Hallmark, James, The Prussian-Saxon Army and the Battles of Jena and Auerstadt, Denton 1995

Heigel, Karl, Deutsche Geschichte vom Tode Friedrichs des Großen bis zur Auflösung des alten Reiches, Stuttgart und Berlin 1899

Heine, Gerhard, Gneisenau ein grosses Leben, Oldenburg 1938

Heise, Karl, Entente Freimaurerei und Weltkrieg, Basel 1920

Herbst, Wilhelm, Encyklopädie der Neueren Geschichte, Gotha 1884

Herre, Franz, "1813 Die Lorbeeren von Leipzig," in Damals (periodical) Heft 9/1981, Giessen

Höcker, Gustav, Jena und Auerstädt ein geschichtlicher Rückblick auf Preußens Unglückstage, Leipzig 1907

Hoffmann, Anton, Darstellung der Mainzer Revolution, Frankfurt und Leipzig 1793

Hofschröer, Peter, Leipzig the Battle of the Nations, Oxford 1993

Hofschröer, Peter, Prussian Cavalry of the Napoleonic Wars (1), New York 1985

Höhn, Reinhard, Frankreichs demokratische Mission in Europa und Ihr Ende, Darmstadt 1940

Höhn, Reinhard, Revolution Heer Kriegsbild, Darmstadt 1944

Höhn, Reinhard, Scharnhorst Soldat Staatsmann Erzieher, München 1981

Höpfner, Eduard von, Der Krieg von 1806 und 1807, Berlin 1850

Hornung, Klaus, Scharnhorst Soldat Reformer Staatsmann, Esslingen-München 1997

Jolles, Mathys, Das deutsche Nationalbewusstsein im Zeitalter Napoleons, Frankfurt 1936

Jordan, Karl August, Zur Geschichte des ehemaligen ostpreussischen Nation-Kavallerie-Regiments in den Feldzügen von 1813 und 1814, Leipzig 1846

Kausch, Georg, Die unbequeme Nation, Deutscher Freiwirtschaftsbund Selbstverlag, 2012

Klein, Johannes, Aus der Belagerung von Neisse 1807, Neisse 1865

Klein, Karl, Geschichte von Mainz während der ersten französischen Occupation 1792-1793, Mainz 1861

Klopfleisch, Dr. Ch., Die Schlacht bei Jena nach den besten Quellen und Schriften, Jena 1862

Kloss, Georg Franz, Geschichte der Freimaurerei in Frankreich, Darmstadt 1852

Kluge, Christine, Die geplante Vernichtung, Wahlsburg 2012

Knötel, Richard, Die eiserne Zeit, Kattowitz Breslau Berlin Leipzig 1913

Korthaus, Eberhard, Heldinnen der Befreiungskriege gegen Napoleon, Berlin 2020

Krippendorf, Johann Adam, Schilderungen der merkwürdigsten Kriegsbegebenheiten bey Auerstädt, Naumburg 1808

Kugler, Franz, Geschichte Friedrichs des Grossen, Leipzig 1930

Kutzen, Joseph, Friedrich der Grosse und sein Heer in den Tagen der Schlacht bei Leuthen, Breslau 1851

Leers, Johannes von, Odal, Struckum 1991

Lehmann, Max, Aus dem Leben Knesebecks, Preußische Jahrbücher Band 34, Berlin 1874

Lehmann, Max, Die Erhebung von 1813, Göttingen 1913

Lehmann, Max, Scharnhorst, Leipzig 1886, 1887

Leidolph, Eduard, Die Schlacht bei Jena, Jena 1926

Lettow-Vorbeck, Oscar, Der Krieg von 1806 und 1807 Erster Band, Berlin 1891

Lettow-Vorbeck, Oscar, Der Krieg von 1806 und 1807 Zweiter Band, Berlin 1892

Lezius, Martin, Die Entwicklung des deutschen Heeres, Berlin 1936

Lezius, Martin, Fridericus Rex Unser König und Herr, Reutlingen 1936

Luden, Heinrich and Johanna Schopenhauer, Die Schlacht von Jena und die Plünderung Weimars im Oktober 1806, Heidelberg 2006

Ludendorff, Erich, Kriegshetze und Völkermord, München 1928

Lützeler, Felix Franz Egon, Hinter den Kulissen der Weltgeschichte, Leipzig 1937

Maack, Berthold, Preussen Jedem das Seine, Tübingen 1980

Maass, Dr., Die Belagerung Colbergs im Jahre 1807, Colberg 1857

Malmesbury, James Harris, Diaries and Correspondence of James Harris, First Earl of Malsbury Vol. 3, London 1845

Marwitz, Friedrich August Ludwig von der, Jena 1806, Berlin 1937

Meister, Werner, 200 Jahre Schlacht bei Auerstedt, Apolda 2005

Menzel, Karl Adolf, Geschichte der Belagerung von Breslau, Breslau 1808

Müffling, Friedrich Karl Ferdinand von, see Weiss

Nettelbeck, Joachim, Die Beagerung Kolbergs, Reutlingen 1940
Otto, Karl-Heinz, Die Langen Kerls, Wittenberg 2003
Petre, F. Loraine, Napoleon's Campaign in Poland 1806-1807, 2009
Petre, F. Loraine, Napoleon's Conquest of Prussia, London & New York 1907
Petre, F. Loraine, Napoleon's Last Campaign in Germany 1813, 2011
Pflugk-Harttung, I. von, 1813-1815 Illustrierte Geschichte der Befreiungskriege, Stuttgart/Leipzig 1913
Pickert, Johann Christoph, Lebens-Geschichte des Unterofficier Pickert, Göttingen 2006
Ranke, Leopold von, Denkwürdigkeiten des Staatskanzlers Fürsten von Hardenberg bis zum Jahre 1806, Leipzig 1877
Rehtwisch, Theodor, Die grosse Zeit, Leipzig 1913
Rehtwisch, Theodor, Leuthen Blätter der Erinnerungen, Leipzig 1907
Reuter, Claus, Das Schicksal der Preussischen Festungen im Feldzug Napoleons 1806/07, Cospeda 2011
Reuter, Claus, Thüringen Seine Geschichte, Die Schlacht bei Jena und Auerstedt 1806, Scarborough 2011
Riegelmann, Hans, Die europäischen Dynastien und ihrem Verhältnis zur Freimauerei, Berlin 1943
Rossberg, Adolf, Freimaurerei und Politik im Zeitalter der französischen Revolution, Berlin 1942
Rotenhan, Siegmund Johann von, Freimüthig-patriotische Beobachtungen und Bemerkungen über die gegenwärtigen öffentlichen Angelegenheiten in Teutschland, Leipzig 1818
Scherr, Johannes, Blücher, seine Zeit und sein Leben, Leipzig 1863
Schlosser, Ludwig, Aus den Kriegsjahren 1806/1807, Cöln am Rhein, 1911
Schmidt, Adolph, Danzig, während der Belagerung im Jahr 1807 in Briefen von einem Augenzeugen, Hamburg 1807
Schmidt, Dorothea, Die preussische Landwehr 1813, Berlin 1986
Schreckenbach, Paul, Der Zusammenbruch Preussens im Jahre 1807, Jena 1906
Schreiber, Ernst, Französische Ausweisungspolitik am Rhein und die Nordfrankenlegion, Berlin 1929
Schulze-Wegener, Guntram, Illustrierte deutsche Kriegsgeschichte, Graz 2010
Seyfart, Johann Friedrich, Geschichte des seit 1756 in Deutschland und dessen angränzenden Ländern geführten Krieges, Sechster Band, Frankfurt und Leipzig 1765
Sheehan, James, German History 1770-1866, Oxford New York 1989
Sichelschmidt, Gustav, Die Herrschaft der Internationalisten, Berg 1994
Sneedorf, Frederik, Briefe eines reisenden Dänen, Züllichau 1793
Somary, Felix, Krise und Zukunft der Demokratie, München 1952
Sommermeyer, Julius, Preussen und die Campagne von 1794 gegen Frankreich, Berlin 1905
Sorel, Albert, L'Europe et la Révolution Francaise, Paris 1892
Stein, Freiherr vom, Briefwechsel, Denkschriften und Auszeichnungen, Berlin 1932
Stieve, Friedrich, Wendepunkte europäischer Geschichte, Leipzig 1940
Tacitus, Cornelius, The Agricola and the Germania, London 1948
Thiel, Rudolf, Preussische Soldaten, Berlin 1940
Thiele, Ralph, Jena und Auerstedt 1806, Frankfurt am Main/Bonn 1996
Titze, Jörg, Die Berichte der sächsischen Truppen aus dem Feldzug 1806 (II), Norderstedt 2019
Treitschke, Heinrich von, Deutsche Geschichte im neunzehnten Jahrhundert, Leipzig 1927
Uhle-Wettler, Franz, Der Krieg, Hamburg Berlin Bonn 2001
Uhle-Wettler, Franz, Höhe und Wendepunkte deutscher Militärgeschichte, Graz 2006
Uhle-Wettler, Franz, Kreta und Arnheim, Graz 2004
Uhle-Wettler, Franz, Rührt Euch!, Graz 2006
Unger, Wolfgang von, Blücher, Berlin 1907
Usczeck, Hansjürgen, Gerhard von Scharnhorst, Berlin 1988
Valentini, Georg Wilhelm von, Erinnerungen eines alten preussischen Offiziers, Glogau und Leipzig 1833
Vonolfen, Wilhelm, Erich Piel, Dr. Peter Seifert, Der Weg zum Reich, Dortmund 1944
Wahl, Hans, Prinz Louis Ferdinand von Preussen, Dachau bei München, 1940 (reprint of 1917 edition)
Walter, Dierk, Preussische Heeresreformen 1807-1870, Paderborn 2003
Webster, Nesta, The French Revolution, Costa Mesa 1988
Weddigen, Otto, Festschrift zur hundertjährigen Wiederkehr der Befreiungskriege, Leipzig 1912
Weiss (genannt Müffling), Friedrich Karl Ferdinand von, Operationsplan der Preussisch-Sächsischen Armee im Jahr 1806, Weimar 1807
Whitman, Sidney, Imperial Germany, New York 1897

CPSIA information can be obtained
at www.ICGtesting.com
Printed in the USA
BVHW012341190622
640069BV00009BA/142